THE RESTAURANT GUIDE 2020

AA

Published by AA Publishing, a trading name of
AA Media Limited, whose registered office is
Grove House, Lutyens Close, Lychpit, Basingstoke
RG24 8AG. Registered number 06112600.

27th edition published 2019

Ⓟ AA Media Limited 2019

The contents of this book are believed correct at
the time of printing. Nevertheless, the Publisher
cannot be held responsible for any errors or
omissions, or for changes in the details given in
this guide, or for the consequences of any reliance
on the information provided by the same. This
does not affect your statutory rights.

Assessments of AA-inspected establishments
are based on the experience of the Hotel and
Restaurant inspectors on the occasion(s) of their
visit(s) and therefore descriptions given in this
guide necessarily dictate an element of subjective
opinion which may not reflect or dictate a reader's
own opinion on another occasion. See pages 6–7 for
a clear explanation of how, based on our Inspectors'
inspection experiences, establishments are graded.
If the meal or meals experienced by an inspector
or inspectors during an inspection fall between
award levels the restaurant concerned may be
awarded the lower of any award levels considered
applicable. The AA strives to ensure accuracy of
the information in this guide at the time of printing.
Due to the constantly evolving nature of the subject
matter the information is subject to change.

The AA gratefully receives any advice regarding
any necessary updates. Please email:
aa.restaurants@aamediagroup.co.uk

Website addresses are included in some entries
as specified by the respective establishment.
Such websites are not under the control of
AA Media Limited and as such AA Media Limited
will not accept any responsibility or liability in
respect of any and all matters whatsoever relating
to such websites including access, content, material
and functionality. By including the addresses of
third party websites the AA does not intend to
solicit business or offer any security to any person
in any country, directly or indirectly.

Image credits: The Automobile Association
wishes to thank the following photographers and
organisations:

4 (top) and 522: Martin Irvine Photography of dish
is by Chef Alex Greene; 4 (centre, top) courtesy of
Chapter One; 4 (centre, bottom) courtesy The Dower
House; 4 (bottom) courtesy of MO; 5 courtesy of The
Harrow at Little Bedwyn;

Every effort has been made to trace the copyright
holders, and we apologise in advance for any
unintentional omissions or errors. We would be
pleased to apply any corrections in a following
edition of this publication. Photographs in the
preliminary pages and gazetteer are provided by
the establishments.

This book was compiled by the AA Lifestyle Guides
team and Servis Filmsetting Ltd.

Restaurant descriptions were contributed by
Jackie Bates, Phil Bryant, Mike Pedley, David Popey,
Allen Stidwill, Mark Taylor and Stuart Walton.

AA Lifestyle Guides would like to thank Carly
Bristow, Geoff Chapman, Liz Haynes, Lin Hutton,
David Popey and Jacqui Savage for their help in the
preparation of this guide.

Cover and internal page design by Austin Taylor.

Maps prepared by the Mapping Services Department
of AA Publishing.

Maps © AA Media Limited 2019.

Contains Ordnance Survey data © Crown copyright
and database right 2019.

Ireland map contains data available from
openstreetmap.org © under the Open Database
License found at opendatacommons.org

Printed in the UK by Bell & Bain.

ISBN: 978-0-7495-8193-0

A05705

CONTENTS

Welcome to the AA Restaurant Guide 2020

We're often asked, by both members of the public and chefs, 'what does it take to be a Rosette-worthy' place to eat? Well, in one easy sentence – 'it's all about the food'.

New to the guide

There are over 130 new restaurants in the guide this year – most have received either 1 or 2 Rosettes, but a couple have gone straight in at three Rosettes, including Fordwich Arms (page 176) and The Salutation (page 179). We've spotlighted many of the new entrants in a special feature on page 14.

You might also spot a few new faces around the book – so often unseen in the kitchen, we interviewed 10 chefs to ask them about their work and favourite dishes. You'll see the results throughout the guide.

And the winner is...

Our award winners are chosen as best in class by our Hospitality Awards panel. The Restaurants of the Year for each of the home nations and London represent both established and up-and-coming places to eat (see page 18). Likewise, the winner of our Food Service Award (page 22) is a consistent member of the upper echelons of the Rosette ranks and a worthy winner.

The AA Chefs' Chef of the Year has both an international career and a very social set of venues that have taken the dining world by storm – see page 20 for details.

Toasting the best

The AA Wine Awards (see page 24) single out three restaurants that our inspectors feel have shown a real passion for and knowledge of wine. This year's trio were chosen from around 900 wine list submissions. We've also highlighted over 200 notable wine lists throughout the guide – so look out for 🍷 NOTABLE WINE LIST.

Up and coming chefs

It's not just the established and experienced venues that are celebrated by the AA. This year sees the fourth annual AA College Restaurant of the Year award (see page 26), which is designed to mirror the main Rosette award process by highlighting the best catering college teams.

Things can change

The transient nature of the hospitality industry means that chefs move around all the time, and restaurants may change ownership. Unfortunately, some close. As any change at the multi-Rosette level requires a new inspection to verify their award, some of these restaurants appear in the guide with their Rosette level suspended at the time of going to press.

2020 vision

What does the future have in store for our nation's restaurants? It's been a tough trading year for many and it's only with your support that many can keep going. As we stand on the verge of a brand new decade, let's raise a glass (and perhaps order a three-course meal) to the future of excellent cuisine, happy times and a full and healthy life.

Using the guide

A few handy tips to help you get the most out of using the *AA Restaurant Guide*. We send an annual questionnaire to restaurants and the information we provide is based on their responses.

1 ORDER: Restaurants are listed in country and county order, then by town and then alphabetically within the town. There is an index by restaurant name at the back of the guide.

2 AA ROSETTE AWARD: Restaurants can be awarded from 1 to 5 Rosettes (see pages 8–9). 'Rosettes suspended' indicates that an award of 3 Rosettes or above was suspended shortly before going to press.

3 FOOD STYLE: A summary of the main cuisine type(s).

V indicates a vegetarian menu. Restaurants with some vegetarian dishes available are indicated under Notes. The description may provide further information about the food style.

4 NOTABLE WINE LIST: The NOTABLE WINE LIST symbol indicates a wine list chosen as notable by an AA panel (see pages 24–25).

5 MAP REFERENCE: Each town or village is given a map reference – the map page number and a two-figure reference based on the National Grid. For example:

Map 18, SD49

18 refers to the page number of the map section at the back of the guide
SD is the National Grid lettered square (representing 100,000 sq metres) in which the location will be found
4 is the figure reading across the top and bottom of the map page
9 is the figure reading down at each side of the map page. For Central London and Greater London, there is a map section starting on page 208.

6 CHEF: The name of the chef(s) is as up-to-date as possible at the time of going to press, but changes in personnel often occur, and may affect both the style and quality of the restaurant.

7 SEATS: Number of seats in the restaurant and private dining room.

8 OPEN/CLOSED: We note if a restaurant is open all year. Otherwise, we list a period or periods when a venue is closed. Check in advance via the venue's website for daily opening times.

9 PRICES: We list minimum prices for Starter (S), Main (M) and Dessert (D) based on details provided by the restaurant. Service charges are not included here and may vary depending on the size of the party. Most restaurants will have some form of service charge.

10 PARKING: Number of spaces for on-site parking or nearby parking.

11 NOTES: Additional information regarding the availability of vegetarian dishes and their policy towards children. We recommend that you phone in advance to ensure that the establishment you have chosen has appropriate facilities.

Please note, 6–11 are omitted from an entry where a restaurant has not responded to our request to update their information.

Photographs
Many restaurants have chosen to enhance their entry by purchasing photographs.

NOTTINGHAM · *MAP 11, SK53*

World Service

◉◉ MODERN BRITISH 🍷 NOTABLE WINE LIST ·

0115 847 5587 | Newdigate House, Castle Gate, NG1 6AF

www.worldservicerestaurant.com

Renaissance-styled Newdigate House was built in 1675. Its idiosyncratic interior mines a colonial vein, the warm orange and copper hues of the main dining room offset with oriental artefacts: Buddha heads, Indian statuary and objets d'art in vitrines. The cooking has a gentle East-meets-West theme.

Chef James Nicholas **Seats** 80, Private dining 34 **Closed** 26 December and 1–7 January **Prices from** S £6, M £16.95, D £6.50 **Notes** Vegetarian dishes, No children under 12 years at dinner

1

2

3

4

5

6

7

8

9

11

How the AA assesses for Rosettes

First introduced in 1956, the AA's Rosette award scheme was the first nationwide scheme for assessing the quality of food served by restaurants and hotels. It has been a 5-tier system since 1992.

A consistent approach

The Rosette scheme is an award, not a classification, and although there is necessarily an element of subjectivity when it comes to assessing taste, we aim for a consistent approach throughout the UK. Our awards are made solely on the basis of a meal visit or visits by one or more of our hotel and restaurant inspectors, who have an unrivalled breadth and depth of experience in assessing quality. Essentially, it's a snapshot, whereby the entire meal, including ancillary items (when served) are assessed. Of all the restaurants across the UK, approximately 10% are of a standard worthy of 1 Rosette and above.

Rosette worthiness

For AA inspectors, the top and bottom line is the food. The taste of a dish is what counts, and whether it successfully delivers to the diner the promise of the menu. A restaurant is only as good as its worst meal. Although presentation and competent service should be appropriate to the style of the restaurant and the quality of the food, they cannot affect the Rosette assessment as such, either up or down. The summaries opposite indicate what our inspectors look for, but are intended only as guidelines. The AA is constantly reviewing its award criteria, and competition usually results in an all-round improvement in standards, so it becomes increasingly difficult for restaurants to reach an award level.

The next level

Receiving a Rosette is a huge achievement and something not to be underestimated. We are often asked by chefs and proprietors: "What is the difference between 1 and 5 Rosettes and how can I get to the next level?" We answer that it's how well a chef manages to apply advanced technique while retaining maximum flavour, and assuming an appropriate quality of source ingredients.

While we endeavour to work with the industry and promote great cooking across the UK, it is of paramount importance for chefs to always serve their market first. We recommend they don't chase awards, but see them as something to celebrate when they come along. Where, however, the winning of Rosettes is an aspiration, the simple guidelines, shown opposite, may help. Experiencing AA food tastings, enhanced food tastings or signing up to one of the AA Rosette Academies can also give further insight and guidance, but these are separate from the awards process and do not influence any assessments.

Announcements of awards

One and two Rosettes are awarded at the time of inspection. Three and four Rosette awards are announced twice during the year, but never at the time of inspection. Five Rosettes are awarded just once a year and never at the time of inspection.

✿ One Rosette

These restaurants will be achieving standards that stand out in their local area, featuring:

- food prepared with care, understanding and skill
- good quality ingredients
- The same expectations apply to hotel restaurants where guests should be able to eat in with confidence and a sense of anticipation.

✿✿ Two Rosettes

The best local restaurants, which aim for and achieve:

- higher standards
- better consistency
- greater precision apparent in the cooking
- obvious attention to the selection of quality ingredients.

✿✿✿ Three Rosettes

These are outstanding restaurants that achieve standards that demand national recognition well beyond their local area. The cooking will be underpinned by:

- the selection and sympathetic treatment of the highest quality ingredients
- timing, seasoning and the judgment of flavour combinations will be consistently excellent
- these virtues will tend to be supported by other elements such as intuitive service and a well-chosen wine list.

✿✿✿✿ Four Rosettes

Among the top restaurants in the UK where the cooking demands national recognition. These restaurants will exhibit:

- intense ambition
- a passion for excellence
- superb technical skills
- remarkable consistency
- an appreciation of culinary traditions combined with a passionate desire for further exploration and improvement.

✿✿✿✿✿ Five Rosettes

The pinnacle, where the cooking compares with the best in the world. These restaurants will have:

- highly individual voices
- exhibit breathtaking culinary skills and set the standards to which others aspire, yet few achieve.

The Top Restaurants of 2020

Restaurants with 3, 4 or 5 Rosettes represent the best in the UK. They are often internationally recognised and serve cuisine of the highest standard. The restaurants in this year's list all had 3 or more Rosettes at the time of going to press.

@@@@@
ENGLAND
BERKSHIRE
The Fat Duck, Bray
BRISTOL
Casamia Restaurant, Bristol
CAMBRIDGESHIRE
Midsummer House Restaurant, Cambridge
CUMBRIA
L'Enclume, Cartmel
DEVON
Lympstone Manor Hotel, Exmouth
LANCASHIRE
Moor Hall Restaurant with Rooms, Ormskirk
LONDON
Restaurant Story, SE1
Marcus, SW1
Claude Bosi at Bibendum, SW3

Hélène Darroze at The Connaught, W1
Pollen Street Social, W1
Sketch (Lecture Room & Library), W1
Core by Clare Smyth, W11
NOTTINGHAMSHIRE
Restaurant Sat Bains with Rooms, Nottingham
OXFORDSHIRE
Belmond Le Manoir aux Quat'Saisons, Great Milton
CHANNEL ISLANDS
JERSEY
Bohemia Restaurant, St Helier
SCOTLAND
EDINBURGH
The Kitchin, Edinburgh
WALES
CEREDIGION
Ynyshir, Eglwys Fach

@@@@
ENGLAND
BERKSHIRE
Restaurant Coworth Park, Ascot
BUCKINGHAMSHIRE
The Hand & Flowers, Marlow
CHESHIRE
Simon Radley at The Chester Grosvenor, Chester
CORNWALL & ISLES OF SCILLY
Paul Ainsworth at No. 6, Padstow
Restaurant Nathan Outlaw, Port Isaac
CUMBRIA
Forest Side, Grasmere
CUMBRIA
Hrishi at Gilpin Hotel & Lake House, Windermere
COUNTY DURHAM
The Orangery, Darlington
GLOUCESTERSHIRE
Le Champignon Sauvage, Cheltenham
GREATER MANCHESTER
Adam Reid at The French, Manchester
LANCASHIRE
Hipping Hall, Cowan Bridge
Northcote Restaurant, Langho
LINCOLNSHIRE
Winteringham Fields, Winteringham
LONDON
Dinner by Heston Blumenthal, SW1
Seven Park Place by William Drabble, SW1

▲ The Angel at Hetton, Hetton, North Yorkshire

The Five Fields, SW3
Restaurant Gordon Ramsay, SW3
Alain Ducasse at The
    Dorchester, W1
Alyn Williams at The Westbury,
    W1
The Greenhouse, W1
Murano, W1
Roganic, W1
Texture Restaurant, W1
The Ledbury, W11

MERSEYSIDE
Fraiche, Oxton

NORFOLK
Morston Hall, Blakeney

OXFORDSHIRE
Orwells, Henley-on-Thames

RUTLAND
Hambleton Hall, Oakham

SHROPSHIRE
Old Downton Lodge, Ludlow

SURREY
Matt Worswick at The Latymer,
    Bagshot
Sorrel, Dorking

SUSSEX, WEST
Gravetye Manor Hotel,
    West Hoathly

TYNE & WEAR
House of Tides, Newcastle upon
    Tyne

WEST MIDLANDS
Hampton Manor, Solihull

WILTSHIRE
The Dining Room, Malmesbury

YORKSHIRE, NORTH
The Burlington Restaurant,
    Bolton Abbey
The Angel at Hetton, Hetton
The Black Swan at Oldstead,
    Oldstead

YORKSHIRE, WEST
The Man Behind The Curtain,
    Leeds

CHANNEL ISLANDS
JERSEY
Tassili, St Helier

SCOTLAND
EDINBURGH
Number One, The Balmoral,
    Edinburgh

Restaurant Martin Wishart,
    Edinburgh
21212, Edinburgh

PERTH & KINROSS
Andrew Fairlie at Gleneagles,
    Auchterarder

WALES
ISLE OF ANGLESEY
Sosban & The Old Butcher's
    Restaurant, Menai Bridge

MONMOUTHSHIRE
The Whitebrook, Whitebrook

VALE OF GLAMORGAN
Restaurant James Sommerin,
    Penarth

REPUBLIC OF IRELAND
DUBLIN
Restaurant Patrick Guilbaud,
    Dublin

COUNTY WATERFORD
The House Restaurant,
    Ardmore

❀❀❀

ENGLAND
BEDFORDSHIRE
Paris House Restaurant,
    Woburn

BERKSHIRE
The Hind's Head, Bray
The Waterside Inn, Bray
The Crown, Burchett'S Green
The Royal Oak Paley Street,
    Maidenhead
The Vineyard, Newbury
The Woodspeen – Restaurant
    and Cookery School, Newbury
L'Ortolan, Shinfleld

BUCKINGHAMSHIRE
The Artichoke, Amersham
The Coach, Marlow
Humphry's at Stoke Park,
    Stoke Poges
The Cliveden Dining Room,
    Taplow

CHESHIRE
1851 Restaurant at Peckforton
    Castle, Peckforton

**CORNWALL & ISLES OF
    SCILLY**
Hell Bay, Bryher
Merchants Manor, Falmouth

The Seafood Restaurant,
    Padstow
Kota Restaurant with Rooms,
    Porthleven
Hotel Tresanton, St Mawes

CUMBRIA
Lake Road Kitchen, Ambleside
Rothay Manor Hotel, Ambleside
Allium at Askham Hall, Askham
The Cottage in the Wood,
    Braithwaite
Rogan & Co Restaurant,
    Cartmel
Holbeck Ghyll Country House
    Hotel, Windermere

DERBYSHIRE
Fischer's Baslow Hall, Baslow
The Peacock at Rowsley,
    Rowsley

DEVON
The Old Inn, Drewsteignton
The Coach House by Micahel
    Caines, Kentisbury
Great Western,
    Moretonhampstead
Boringdon Hall Hotel, Plymouth
The Elephant Restaurant by
    Simon Hulstone, Torquay

DORSET
Summer Lodge Country House
    Hotel, Restaurant & Spa,
    Evershot

ESSEX
Le Talbooth, Dedham
Haywards Restaurant, Epping

GLOUCESTERSHIRE
Buckland Manor, Buckland
The Greenway Hotel & Spa,
    Cheltenham
Lumière, Cheltenham
Jackrabbit Restaurant,
    Chipping Campden
The Slaughters Manor House,
    Lower Slaughter
Wilder, Nailsworth
The Feathered Nest Country
    Inn, Nether Westcote
Lords of the Manor, Upper
    Slaughter

HAMPSHIRE
The Montagu Arms Hotel, Beaulieu
Cambium, Brockenhurst
36 on the Quay, Emsworth
The Elderflower Restaurant, Lymington
Hartnett Holder & Co, Lyndhurst

HERTFORDSHIRE
THOMPSON St Albans, St Albans

KENT
The West House Restaurant with Rooms, Biddenden
ABode Canterbury, Canterbury
Fordwich Arms, Canterbury
Thackeray's, Tunbridge Wells (Royal)
The Salutation, Sandwich

LANCASHIRE
The Freemasons at Wiswell, Whalley

LEICESTERSHIRE
John's House, Mountsorrel

LONDON
Galvin La Chapelle, E1
Cornerstone by Chef Tom Brown, E9
Anglo, EC1
The Clove Club, EC1
Club Gascon, EC1
City Social, EC2
La Dame de Pic, EC3
The Frog Hoxton, N1
The Gilbert Scott, NW1
Odette's, NW1
Peninsula Restaurant, SE10
Amaya, SW1
Ametsa , SW1
A. Wong, SW1
Céleste at The Lanesborough, SW1
1koyi, SW1
Pétrus, SW1
Roux at Parliament Square, SW1
Elystan Street, SW3
Trinity Restaurant, SW4
Medlar Restaurant, SW10
Chez Bruce, SW17
Corrigan's Mayfair, W1
CUT at 45 Park Lane, W1
Galvin at Windows Restaurant & Bar, W1

Gauthier Soho, W1
Le Gavroche Restaurant, W1
Hakkasan Mayfair, W1
Kitchen Table, W1
Locanda Locatelli, W1
Mere, W1
The Ninth, W1
Orrery, W1
Pied à Terre, W1
Portland, W1
The Ritz Restaurant, W1
Roka Charlotte Street, W1
Roka Mayfair, W1
Sketch (The Gallery), W1
Social Eating House, W1
The Square, W1
Umu, W1
The River Café, W6
Kitchen W8, W8
Launceston Place, W8
Min Jiang, W8
Clos Maggiore, WC2
Frog by Adam Handling, WC2
Kerridge's Bar & Grill, WC2

LONDON, GREATER
Chapter One, Bromley
The Glasshouse, Kew
Bingham Riverhouse, Richmond Upon Thames

MERSEYSIDE
The Lawns Restaurant at Thornton Hall, Thornton Hough

NORFOLK
The Neptune Restaurant with Rooms, Hunstanton
Benedicts, Norwich
Roger Hickman's Restaurant, Norwich
Titchwell Manor Hotel, Titchwell

NORTHAMPTONSHIRE
Rushton Hall Hotel and Spa, Kettering

NOTTINGHAMSHIRE
Alchemilla, Nottingham

OXFORDSHIRE
Shaun Dickens at The Boathouse, Henley-On-Thames
The Wild Rabbit, Kingham
The Oxford Kitchen, Oxford

SHROPSHIRE
Fishmore Hall, Ludlow

SOMERSET
The Bath Priory Hotel, Restaurant & Spa, Bath
Dan Moon at the Gainsborough Restaurant, Bath
The Dower House Restaurant, Bath
The Olive Tree at the Queensberry Hotel, Bath
Castle Bow Restaurant, Taunton
The Mount Somerset Hotel & Spa, Taunton
Little Barwick House, Yeovil

SUFFOLK
The Bildeston Crown, Bildeston
Tuddenham Mill, Newmarket

SURREY
Stovell's, Chobham
The Clock House, Ripley

SUSSEX, EAST
etch. by Steven Edwards, Brighton & Hove
The Little Fish Market, Brighton & Hove

SUSSEX, WEST
Amberley Castle, Amberley
Langshott Manor, Gatwick Airport
Restaurant Tristan, Horsham
The Lickfold Inn, Lickfold
AG's Restaurant at Alexander House Hotel, Turners Hill

WARWICKSHIRE
The Cross at Kenilworth, Kenilworth
The Dining Room at Mallory Court Hotel, Royal Leamington Spa
Salt, Stratford-upon-Avon

WEST MIDLANDS
Adam's, Birmingham
Carters of Moseley, Birmingham
Purnell's, Birmingham
Simpsons, Birmingham
The Wilderness, Birmingham

WILTSHIRE
The Bybrook at The Manor House, an Exclusive Hotel & Golf Club, Castle Combe
Restaurant Hywel Jones by Lucknam Park, Colerne

The Methuen Arms, Corsham
The Harrow at Little Bedwyn,
  Little Bedwyn
Red Lion Freehouse, Pewsey
WORCESTERSHIRE
The Back Garden, Broadway
MO, Broadway
Brockencote Hall Country House
  Hotel, Chaddesley Corbett
Pensons, Tenbury Wells
YORKSHIRE, NORTH
Yorebridge House, Bainbridge
Black Swan Hotel, Helmsley
Forge, Middleton Tyas
The Hare Inn, Scawton
The Park Restaurant, York
YORKSHIRE, SOUTH
Jöro Restaurant, Sheffield
YORKSHIRE, WEST
Box Tree, Ilkley
CHANNEL ISLANDS
JERSEY
Ocean Restaurant at The
  Atlantic Hotel, St Brelade
Restaurant Sirocco@The Royal
  Yacht, St Helier
Samphire, St Helier
Longueville Manor Hotel,
  St Saviour
SARK
Stocks Hotel, Sark
SCOTLAND
ABERDEENSHIRE
Douneside House, Tarland
ANGUS
Gordon's, Inverkeilor
ARGYLL & BUTE
Restaurant at Isle of Eriska,
  Eriska
Airds Hotel and Restaurant,
  Port Appin
Inver Restaurant, Strachur
SOUTH AYRSHIRE
Glenapp Castle, Ballantrae
Lochgreen House Hotel, Troon
DUMFRIES & GALLOWAY
Knockinaam Lodge, Portpatrick
EDINBURGH
Castle Terrace Restaurant,
  Edinburgh

▲ Sketch (Lecture Room & Library), W1

The Pompadour, Edinburgh
Timberyard, Edinburgh
FIFE
The Cellar, Anstruther
The Peat Inn, Peat Inn
Road Hole Restaurant, St Andrews
Rocca Restaurant, St Andrews
GLASGOW
Cail Bruich, Glasgow
The Gannet, Glasgow
HIGHLAND
The Cross, Kingussie
Kilcamb Lodge Hotel, Strontian
The Torridon, Torridon
SOUTH LANARKSHIRE
Crossbasket Castle, Blantyre
PERTH & KINROSS
Fonab Castle Hotel & Spa,
  Pitlochry
STIRLING
Roman Camp Country House
  Hotel, Callander
Cromlix and Chez Roux, Dunblane
SCOTTISH ISLANDS
The Three Chimneys & The
  House Over-By, Colbost
Kinloch Lodge, Isleornsay
Loch Bay Restaurant, Stein

WALES
CONWY
Bodysgallen Hall and Spa,
  Llandudno
GWYNEDD
Palé Hall Hotel & Restaurant,
  Bala
MONMOUTHSHIRE
The Walnut Tree Inn,
  Abergavenny
PEMBROKESHIRE
The Fernery, Narberth
POWYS
Llangoed Hall, Llyswen
SWANSEA
Beach House Restaurant at
  Oxwich Beach, Oxwich
NORTHERN IRELAND
BELFAST
Deanes EIPIC, Belfast
OX, Belfast
COUNTY ANTRIM
Galgorm Resort & Spa,
  Ballymena
COUNTY FERMANAGH
Lough Erne Resort, Enniskillen
REPUBLIC OF IRELAND
COUNTY CLARE
Gregans Castle, Ballyvaughan
COUNTY KILKENNY
The Lady Helen Restaurant,
  Thomastown

The Thrill of the New

With restaurants falling like ninepins over the last year it may seem like the UK's gastronomic gold rush is over. We beg to differ: the AA's inspectors have been thrilled with the quality of the hundreds of new entries plus the brand new 3- and 4-Rosette award winners around the country.

Despite the recent bloodbath in the restaurant scene there's plenty of scope for ambitious chefs to succeed. Our attitudes to dining have changed in line with our awareness and love of foodie culture; armchair chefs inspired by the likes of *MasterChef* and *The Great British Menu* want a taste of the inspirational culinary experiences that are available across the UK, and don't want to have to head for London to find them. Sure, the sheer size and financial muscle of the capital means that many of the UK's culinary high-flyers are clustered in London and the Home Counties, but there's a healthy demand for good food everywhere, and where better to look for it than in

our latest round-up of Rosette-winning restaurants.

West Country winners

Head down to the West Country and you're spoilt for choice with 25 new entries and multi-Rosette winners across Devon, Cornwall, Dorset, Somerset, Gloucestershire and Wiltshire. High-flying destination dining addresses with three Rosettes are always worth a detour: new awards in the 2020 Guide include the Dining Room at Lords of the Manor, where Charles Smith combines French classicism with more contemporary, ingredients-led ideas; the Methuen Arms for Leigh Evans's refined modern British dishes, and Whatley Manor, where Niall Keating's classy contemporary cooking draws inspiration from Asia and France.

Midlands masters

The Midland stars reinforce the message that the new wave of modern British cooking is firmly established in Brum thanks to high-profile chefs such as Glynn Purnell and Adam Stokes; now the 'rock and roll fine dining' from Alex Claridge at The Wilderness has earned its third Rosette for some inspired work.

Worcestershire is having quite a moment too with six newcomers, including MO in Dormy House, and Pensons on the Netherwood estate both achieving three Rosettes. Over the county line in Shropshire, Karl Martin now boasts four Rosettes at Old Downton Lodge for highly individual cooking that places the finest local and home-grown produce at the heart of things

In a reinvented, once-derelict coaching inn in Nottingham, Alex Bond at Alchemilla is helping to ignite the city's interest in foodie culture with of-the-moment cookery that's not remotely vegetarian, but deftly shifts the creative spotlight onto the veggie elements.

Elsewhere, The Cross at Kenilworth and John's House near Loughborough are creating three-Rosette food that's as dynamic and individual as you'll find anywhere in the UK.

Northern delights

Food-wise, things are far from grim up north. If you're in the market for exceptional contemporary country house dining, top of the pile with three Rosette awards are Rothay Manor and Allium at Askham Hall (Cumbria). Yorkshire's dynamic dining scene is boosted further still by the welcome addition of seven newcomers – The George at Easingwold, The Coach House in Middleton, Clark's In Scarborough, Macleod's in Skipton, The Star on the harbour at Whitby. If you're in York and like a bit of historical setting with your food, seek out the Bow Room Restaurant at Grays Court and the Refectory Kitchen in the Principal York Hotel. Buoyed up by the tourist pound and a healthy country house dining scene, Cumbria has never been short of great places to eat, and continues to raise the bar wIth new Guide entries Mizu, for pan-Asian dining by Derwentwater, modern country house cooking in The Lancrigg, contemporary European ideas in Plato's, and the pubby comforts of the Pentonbridge Inn.

◀ (opposite) Restaurant MO

▶ Pensons

The Thrill of the New

Culinary capital

With its global reputation, economic clout and huge population, London and the surrounding counties will always be a magnet for chefs at the cutting edge, notably Oli Marlow who gains four Rosettes at Roganic with highly technical, precisely engineered dishes that bear the Simon Rogan stamp of faultless provenance and freshness. This year we also welcome Tom Brown to the rarefied ranks of three-Rosette winners, sending out dazzling seafood sharing plates in Cornerstone, his first solo venture since moving on from the Nathan Outlaw empire. At Ikyoi, Jeremy Chan is thrilling diners with

▼► Kerridge's Bar & Grill

his exciting take on West African cuisine, while Tom Kerridge's first big-city venture has a super-posh setting in the Corinthia Hotel, and Ben Murphy at Launceston Place creates food full of flair and invention. And let's not forget Stem, the latest venture from Mark Jarvis (of Anglo and Neo Bistro fame) who's serving up bang up-to-date food in a Mayfair townhouse.

In Kent, The Salutation and The Fordwich Arms, and in Essex, Haywards Restaurant

▲ Panorama Bistro & Terrace

▲ etch.

country boltholes such as Arisaig House, Moor of Rannoch Restaurant & Rooms and Glenmorangie House – a pilgrimage destination for malt whisky fans. And if its 300 private acres with all the spa and golf trimmings aren't enough, the Isle of Eriska hotel has consolidated its position as an exclusive retreat with three-Rosette dining in its classy restaurant.

Welsh dragons

The Welsh valleys and mountains aren't merely easy on the eye, they also provide a cornucopia of native produce for some seriously good restaurants, including eight new entries in the 2020 Guide. In Caernarfon, look out for The Gun Room in Plas Dinas, a country house on an intimate scale, and Tŷ Castell for a tapas-style menu with a global accent. In Snowdonia National Park, Padarn Brasserie looks over Llanberis, while Gem 42 in Newport puts a contemporary spin on Italian cuisine in an exuberant setting. Fancy a pub meal? The revamped Lion Inn in the Blaenavon World Heritage site and The Hare and Hounds in Cowbridge will sort you out with hearty and inventive meals based on excellent local materials.

all win three Rosettes for imaginative, high-quality cooking. If you're heading for the Sussex seaside, grab a table at etch. in Hove, where Steven Edwards is firing on all cylinders with his exciting new-generation Brit cooking.

Celtic Tigers

Ireland continues to cement its own culinary identity with 15 new entries, a quartet of which are in County Cork – the Coastal Restaurant in Castletown, along with Greene's, Panorama Bistro & Terrace and The Restaurant at Liss Ard. Four more venues join the ranks of Dublin's top culinary addresses: No 10 Fleet Street, Seasons Restaurant, The Italian Kitchen and Woodlock Brasserie.

Blessed with some of the finest produce in the land, the chefs in Scotland certainly know what to do with it, coming up trumps with 11 new entries. They are an eclectic bunch, ranging from the latest additions to Tom Kitchin's empire – French bistro-style cooking at Southside Scran in Edinburgh, and 'from nature to plate' menus In The Stables at the Bonnie Badger – to the Ship Inn in Elie for its unfussy food and beachside beer garden; Daisy Tasker in Dundee, where you'll find 21st-century cuisine in a former jute mill-turned-hotel, or a trio of

▲ Southside Scran

Restaurants of the Year 2019–20

Potential Restaurants of the Year are nominated by our team of full-time inspectors based on their routine visits. We look for somewhere that is exceptional in its chosen area of the market. While the Rosette awards are based on the quality of the food alone, the Restaurants of the Year awards take into account all aspects of the dining experience.

Scotland winner ▶
SUGAR BOAT, Helensburgh, Argyll & Bute (*see page 445*)

An all-day bistro with real foodie credentials, Sugar Boat is located in the heart of town, with tables out front and back. Hearty modern cooking features big flavours and an essentially simple approach to treating Scottish produce with care and attention.

◀ Wales winner
BRYN WILLIAMS AT PORTH EIRIAS, Colwyn Bay, Conwy (*see page 496*)

Floor-to-ceiling windows offer sweeping views of Colwyn Bay, and exposed steelwork, pendant lights and industrial-chic create the feeling of a hip, big-city eatery. There is clear passion on the plate here with a real sense of keeping it real and local.

◄ **England winner**
FORDWICH ARMS,
Canterbury, Kent
(*see page 176*)

Chef-patron Daniel Smith has worked in some of the country's top restaurants and the seasonal menu focuses on provenance, showcasing the best of local Kentish ingredients. The food is delivered in a relaxed, comfortable and welcoming style, perfect for all year round and every occasion.

London winner ►
CORNERSTONE BY CHEF TOM BROWN,
London E9 (*see page 222*)

Tom Brown, formerly at the Capital and a Nathan Outlaw protégé, launched his debut restaurant back in April 2018 to widespread critical acclaim. The 46-cover restaurant showcases Tom's own style of simple, clean and produce-driven cooking. The dishes are ideal for sharing.

Chefs' Chef of the Year 2019–20

A popular and coveted title, this unique award, introduced in 1996, offers all AA Rosette-awarded chefs the chance to decide which of their peers deserves the ultimate recognition for their performance over the past twelve months.

Jason Atherton An A-lister among the UK's elite chefs who have achieved household-name status, Jason Atherton always wanted to be a chef, leaving his hometown of Skegness to hone his craft in the kitchens of culinary deities including Pierre Koffman, Marco Pierre White, Nico Ladenis and Ferran Adria at El Bulli. After joining the Gordon Ramsay group in 2001, Atherton learned a thing or two about empire building with the Maze restaurants and left to begin building his own brand – The Social Company – in 2010. His flagship Mayfair venue Pollen Street Social launched in 2011 to huge acclaim; in 2017 it joined that rarefied group of UK restaurants with five AA Rosettes. Since then, Atherton has rolled out a global portfolio of restaurants – 18 at the last count – from glossy 3-Rosette winners in London such as Social Eating House, and City Social in the Gherkin skyscraper, to destination dining venues in New York, Dubai, Shanghai and the Philippines.

Frequently seen on TV screens over the last few years on *Saturday Kitchen, Great British Menu* and fronting the BBC2 series *The Chefs' Brigade*, Atherton flies the flag for British culinary talent by taking on Europe's finest restaurants, and clearly has no intention of slowing down. The UK's lucky diners can hopefully look forward to many more years of his endlessly thrilling food.

Previous winners

RAYMOND BLANC, OBE
Belmond Le Manoir aux Quat' Saisons,
  Great Milton, Oxfordshire

HESTON BLUMENTHAL
The Fat Duck, Bray, Berkshire
Hinds Head, Bray, Berkshire
Dinner by Heston Blumenthal,
  London SW1
The Crown at Bray, Berkshire

CLAUDE BOSI
Bibendum, London SW3

MICHAEL CAINES
The Coach House by Michael Caines,
  Kentisbury, Devon

DANIEL CLIFFORD
Midsummer House, Cambridge,
  Cambridgeshire

ANDREW FAIRLIE
Andrew Fairlie at Gleneagles,
  Auchterarder, Perth & Kinross

CHRIS AND JEFF GALVIN
Galvin La Chapelle, London E1

SHAUN HILL
Walnut Tree Inn, Abergavenny,
  Monmouthshire

PHILIP HOWARD
Elystan Street, London SW3

TOM KERRIDGE
The Hand and Flowers, Marlow,
  Buckinghamshire

The Coach, Marlow, Buckinghamshire
Kerridge's Bar & Grill, London WC2

PIERRE KOFFMANN

JEAN-CHRISTOPHE NOVELLI

NATHAN OUTLAW
Restaurant Nathan Outlaw,
  Port Isaac, Cornwall
Outlaw's Fish Kitchen,
  Port Isaac, Cornwall

GORDON RAMSAY
Restaurant Gordon Ramsay,
  London SW3

SIMON ROGAN
L'Enclume, Cartmel, Cumbria

GERMAIN SCHWAB

RICK STEIN
The Seafood Restaurant,
  Padstow, Cornwall
Rick Stein at Sandbanks,
  Sandbanks, Dorset

KEVIN VINER

MARCUS WAREING
Marcus, The Berkeley,
  London SW1

MARCO PIERRE WHITE

JOHN T WILLIAMS
The Ritz Restaurant, London W1

MARTIN WISHART
Restaurant Martin Wishart, Edinburgh

AA Food Service Award 2019–20

Introduced in 2013, this award recognises restaurants that deliver excellent standards of service and hospitality. The teams at these restaurants demonstrate technical service skills, and their food and beverage knowledge is of the highest standard.

The Ritz Restaurant
LONDON, W1
(see page 272)

A champion of haute cuisine, The Ritz Restaurant is one of the most opulent dining rooms in London. Its landmark setting, a beautiful and spacious room with stunning ceiling fresco of sunlit clouds and over 100-year history makes it a truly remarkable venue to experience classic cuisine. Executive chef John Williams is a true master of his craft, producing a range of exquisite dishes from both classic and contemporary folds.

While the setting is both formal and traditional, as you might expect from such a revered Piccadilly institution, guests are made to feel completely at home by the engaging, professional team. Hospitality and service

are delivered so fluently, that the overall experience feels completely seamless.

It is all underpinned by a passionate, professional team that have a well-deserved reputation of being one of the best in the industry. Regular and on-going training and development ensure the highest technical standards combined by excellent product knowledge. It also comes as no surprise that the team always shine and are recognised in industry competitions that honour service excellence.

FINALISTS
Moor Hall Restaurant with Rooms, Ormskirk, Lancashire *(see page 188)*
Adam Reid at the French, Manchester *(see page 150)*

AA Restaurants with Rooms of the Year

Introduced in 2017, this award recognises AA-rated guest accommodation that is also a dining destination. This year the award was presented at the AA B&B Awards, held at St Ermin's Hotel, London.

The Lodge on Loch Goil,
LOCHGOILHEAD, ARGYLL & BUTE
(see page 445)
First impressions of a peaceful retreat in a stunning, sheltered lochside setting will live long in the memory. The Lodge has an Arts and Crafts heritage, featuring hand painted wallpaper, stained glass by Daniel Cottier, parquet floors and oak throughout, individually chosen furnishings.

Restoring the Lodge has been a real labour of love for the current owners over the past fifteen years. Rooms are very individual, and rangefrom a summer house jutting over the water to a superb suite with wrap-around balcony.

Guests can also relax in a loch-side tree house and even arrive by boat or sea plane. A small walled kitchen garden feeds into imaginative cuisine in the evening and superb breakfasts to wake up to. Hospitality is generously given, ensuring the warmest of Scottish welcomes.

FINALISTS
The Greyhound on the Test, Stockbridge, Hampshire *(see page 162)*
Plantation House, Ermington, Devon *(see page 112)*

AA Wine Awards 2019–20

The annual AA Wine Awards, sponsored by Matthew Clark Wines, attracted a huge response from our AA recognised restaurants with over 950 wine lists submitted for judging. Three national winners were chosen.

ENGLAND AND OVERALL WINNER
Hampton Manor, Solihull
(See page 391)

SCOTLAND
Castle Terrace, Edinburgh
(See page 452)

WALES
Penmaenuchauf Hall, Dolgellau
(See page 499)

All the restaurants in this year's guide were invited to submit their wine lists. From these the panel selected a shortlist of over 200 establishments who are highlighted in the guide with the Notable Wine List symbol ▲NOTABLE WINE LIST.

The shortlisted restaurants were asked to choose wines from their list (within a budget of £80 per bottle) to accompany a menu designed by last year's winner, Park House in Cardiff.

The final judging panel included last year's winner Adam Pledger, owner of Park House, Nick Zalinski, Business Director, Matthew Clark Wines (our sponsor) and Simon Numphud, Managing Director, AA Hotel & Hospitality Services. The judges' comments are shown opposite.

What makes a wine list notable?

We are looking for high-quality wines, with diversity across grapes and/or countries and style, and the best individual growers and vintages. The list should be well presented, clear and easy to navigate. To reflect the demand of diners, there should be a good choice of varied wines available by the glass.

Things that disappoint the judges are spelling errors on the lists, wines under incorrect regions or styles, split vintages (which are still far too common), lazy purchasing (all wines from a country from just one grower or negociant) and confusing wine list layouts. Sadly, many restaurants still do not pay much attention to wine, resulting in ill-considered lists.

To reach the final shortlist, we look for a real passion for wine, which should come across to the customer; a fair pricing policy (depending on the style of the restaurant); interesting coverage (not necessarily a large list), which might include areas of specialism, perhaps a particular wine area; and sherries or larger formats such as magnums.

The AA Wine Awards are sponsored by:
Matthew Clark, Whitchurch Lane, Bristol, BS14 0JZ
tel: 01275 891400
email: enquiries@matthewclark.co.uk
web: www.matthewclark.co.uk

Hampton Manor, Solihull – the winning wine selection:

MENU	WINE SELECTION
Canapés – Beetroot macaroon with black pudding mousse, comte gougeres	Aperitif: Sparkling Rose Ancre Hill Non Vintage, Monmouth, Wales
Starter – Veal sweetbread with green apple and Alba white truffle	2017 Wild Air, Sauvignon Blanc, Storm Wines, Henel-en-Aarde, South Africa
Fish course – Cornish turbot, Oscietra caviar, caulifower, buttermilk and pickled fennel	2013 Taurus, Domaine de l'Ecu, Muscadet, France
Meat course – Highland Wagu beef sirloin with parsnip, roscoff onion and black truffle with Wagu shin pie, truffle potato espuma and grated cured heart.	2015 Naoussa, Diamantakos, Naoussa, Greece
Cheese course – Fourme d'Ambert, Crassane pear, walnut, celery ketchup	Sweet organic wine Non Vintage, Georgas Famílt, Sparta, Greece
Pudding course – Apple, white chocolate, muscovado	Digestif: 2017 Late harvest Chenin Blanc, Cullen, Margaret River, Australia

Judges' notes
HAMPTON MANOR

Super impressive list, wonderfully curated. Features include funky producers and difficult to source wines via innovative keg system. Wow, what a list - totally engaging, stylish and really clever. Takes you on a journey, with lots by the glass. The wine list is definitely a feature in its own right and organised in an innovative way, very helpful. A list that pushes the boundaries; such personality.

CASTLE TERRACE

A beautifully laid out list that is really accessible and easy to read. Whilst leaning towards French wines, overall it's nicely balanced with a strong New World selection. Vintage selections are excellent, pricing appropriate and absolutely loved the magnum selections. A list packed full of interest.

PENMAENUCHAUF HALL

A list full of passion and much effort. The hotel clearly know their market and customers, love the tasting notes and the vintage chart is a nice addition and clever little thing. Really good pricing and nice sherry selection. You sense there is a real personality behind the list, and it's very accessible.

Other lists that impressed the judging panel this year included

* Llangoed Hall, Llyswen
* Beach House Restaurant at Oxwich Beach
* Prestonfield, Edinburgh
* Cail Bruich, Glasgow
* THE PIG near Bath, Hunstrete
* Restaurant Tristan, Horsham
* The Rex Whistler, London SW1

AA College Restaurant of the Year 2018–19

Now in its third successful year, the AA College Restaurant of the Year celebrates the very best of future talent. Open exclusively to all People 1st Accredited colleges, each holding an AA college Rosette for culinary excellence, at either the Award or Highly commended levels, many of these colleges are People 1st centres of excellence.

This year's entrants had to produce an advertising video to highlight their college restaurant to prospective guests, a marketing analysis and plans for the future. Judging took place at the Park Plaza County Hall London, where the teams not only faced a panel of industry judges but also benefited from an inspirational talk from AA-award winning chef and restaurateur Angela Hartnett. After a tough judging day and plenty of debate, the three finalists were agreed upon by our panel of industry experts.

WINNER
Academy – Cheshire College South & West

RUNNERS UP
Trevenson Restaurant – Cornwall College (Camborne)
The Brasserie – Milton Keynes College

SUGGESTIONS _Create_

ENGLAND

■ BEDFORDSHIRE

BOLNHURST
MAP 12, TL05

The Plough at Bolnhurst
◉ MODERN BRITISH

01234 376274 | Kimbolton Road, MK44 2EX
www.bolnhurst.com
The Plough is a whitewashed 15th-century country inn and the restaurant is a striking contrast: the airy extension features lofty oak-beamed ceilings while full-length windows flood the room with light. Top-quality produce is transformed into big-flavoured modern dishes on daily-changing menus.

Closed 27 December to 14 January

FLITWICK
MAP 11, TL03

Hallmark Hotel Flitwick Manor
◉◉ MODERN, TRADITIONAL

01525 712242 | Church Road, MK45 1AE
www.hallmarkhotels.co.uk
A Georgian house in its own wooded parkland, classic British dishes with modern European influence are the stock-in-trade at Flitwick. Making a strong impact are a starter of braised pig's cheek scattered with dried grapefruit and crumbled walnuts, alongside silky parsnip purée.

Open All Year

HENLOW
MAP 12, TL13

The Crown
◉ MODERN BRITISH

01462 812433 | 2 High Street, SG16 6BS
www.crownpub.co.uk
The busy pub on the main road through the village functions as a quintessential rural hostelry, full of enthusiastic local custom in both bar and dining room. Despite modernisation it retains its pub ethos, and boasts a young, classically trained chef.

Closed 25-26 December

LUTON
MAP 6, TL02

Adam's Brasserie at Luton Hoo
◉ MODERN BRITISH

01582 734437 | Luton Hoo Hotel, Golf & Spa, The Mansion House, LU1 3TQ
www.lutonhoo.co.uk
The extensive Luton Hoo Estate, with its golf course and magnificent gardens, is home to this spa hotel. Adam's Brasserie is found in the former stables, where high ceilings and large windows give a sense of space, and the menu is a roster of feel-good dishes.

Chef Chris Mouyiassi **Seats** 90, Private dining 280
Open All Year **Prices from** S £6, M £9, D £6 **Parking** 100
Notes Vegetarian dishes, Children welcome

Wernher Restaurant at Luton Hoo Hotel, Golf & Spa
◉◉ MODERN BRITISH *V* ▮ NOTABLE WINE LIST

01582 734437 | The Mansion House, LU1 3TQ
www.lutonhoo.co.uk
When only the full stately-home extravaganza will do – the sort of place where the chaps are required to sport jacket and tie at dinner – the magnificent Wernher in Luton Hoo is hard to top, with its marble panelling, ornate chandeliers and opulent fabrics.

Chef Ruth Hanson **Seats** 80, Private dining 280
Closed 1st 2 weeks in January (Monday to Thursday all day, Friday and Saturday lunch) **Parking** 316
Notes Vegetarian dishes, Children welcome

WOBURN
MAP 11, SP93

Paris House Restaurant
◉◉◉ MODERN BRITISH *V*
See pages 32-33

The Woburn Hotel
◉◉ MODERN BRITISH, FRENCH

01525 290441 | George Street, MK17 9PX
www.thewoburnhotel.co.uk
The cooking at the stylish Olivier's Restaurant is rooted in the great French traditions but it is very much of the present, so roast cod fillet, for instance, is served with brandade and chorizo and bean cassoulet. Combinations in dishes intrigue without seeming wacky.

Chef Olivier Bertho **Seats** 40, Private dining 90
Prices from S £5.80, M £16.50, D £7.50 **Parking** 80
Notes Vegetarian dishes, Children welcome

WYBOSTON
MAP 12, TL15

The Waterfront Restaurant at Wyboston Lakes
◉ TRADITIONAL BRITISH, EUROPEAN

0333 700 7667 | Great North Road, MK44 3BA
www.thewaterfronthotel.co.uk
The Waterfront Restaurant offers a relaxed and modern brasserie-style dining experience with views over the south lake. The breads are home made and served with tapenade as well as oil and balsamic vinegar. For dessert, tuck into tiramisù with Madagascan vanilla cream and biscotti.

Closed 25-26 December

■ BERKSHIRE

ASCOT
MAP 6, SU96

The Barn at Coworth
◉◉ BRITISH
01344 756784 | Blacknest Road, SL5 7SE
www.coworthpark.com

There's a fine-dining restaurant at this lavish country hotel, plus this converted barn where you can tuck into classy brasserie-style food. It looks great with its open-to-view kitchen, unbuttoned vibe and cheerful service team sporting orange polo tops, and there's a fabulous terrace, too.

Chef Tom Hankey **Seats** 75 **Open** All Year
Prices from S £10, M £18, D £12 **Parking** 100
Notes Children welcome

Bluebells Restaurant
◉◉ MODERN EUROPEAN
01344 622722 | London Road, Sunningdale, SL5 0PU
www.bluebells-restaurant.co.uk
After moving from Sunninghill to Virginia Water's western extremity, and completely refurbishing its new premises, Bluebells remains committed to modern British cuisine. That said, international influences are noticeable, as in lamb rump with pea and edamame bean fricassée, and squid ink-cured hake with soba noodles, shimeji mushroom, soy, ginger and chilli broth.

Chef Tamas Baranyai **Seats** 85, Private dining 30
Closed 25–26 December, 1–11 January and bank holidays
Parking 25 **Notes** Vegetarian dishes, Children welcome

Restaurant Coworth Park
◉◉◉◉ MODERN BRITISH 🅅 ◣ NOTABLE WINE LIST
01344 876600 | London Road, SL5 7SE
www.coworthpark.com

A Georgian mansion house built on a scale intended to impress, Coworth Park lords it over its acreages of rural Berkshire in shimmering wedding-cake white. It's surrounded by wildflower meadows and ancient woodland and comes fully loaded with a luxuriant portfolio of amenities, taking in everything from deep tissue massages to polo. It also has an elegant interior of high ceilinged spaces imbued with period splendour that is entirely agreeable and happily relaxed, including a very pretty dining room where guests can admire a copper-hued chandelier of oak leaves and the view over the rose terrace while mulling over menus fizzing with clever contemporary ideas.

Here, Adam Smith's cooking stands out from the crowd with an imaginatively modernised take on country-house cooking; whether you opt for the full-works seven-course taster or Best of British menus supplementing the main carte, you can expect top-class produce handled with light-touch dexterity. A starter of sautéed duck liver is balanced with pink grapefruit and basil, with puffed rice and black olive, and basil and onion brioche adding texture. Main course gives star billing to superb quality Waterford Farm lamb, timed perfectly pink, and served alongside an onion stuffed with braised shoulder, roasted shallot, turnip, onion purée and a killer jus.

Fish is handled with similar creativity, perhaps stuffed Dover sole in the company of morels and risotto and sauced with Jura wine. Well-judged combinations of crystal-clear flavours are again to the fore in a dessert that riffs on a millefeuille theme, layering caramelised puff pastry with white chocolate parfait, vanilla cream, wild strawberries, lime, and strawberry sorbet, or an

Continued on page 34

Paris House Restaurant

@@@ **MODERN BRITISH** *V*
01525 290692 | London Road, Woburn Park, MK17 9QP
www.parishouse.co.uk

Makes a powerful first impression

A well-known TV commercial of yesteryear featured an American entrepreneur who loved his electric razor so much he bought the company that made it. In similar vein, the 9th Duke of Bedford was so taken by the look of this ornate, black-and-white, Tudor-style cottage built for the 1878 International Exhibition in Paris, that he acquired, dismantled, and shipped it back to the UK, where he reassembled it on his Woburn Estate. It's actually through a grand gateway in the 22-acre deer park, a location that puts it in somewhat exalted company in the restaurant pantheon.

Phil and Claire Fanning, who own the place, run it with uncompromising passion and have developed it into one of the region's most compelling dining establishments. But it's not just the building's exterior that fascinates the observer: the interior has bags of style, with modern chandeliers, sleek

> "... a love of Japanese cooking shows in his newly introduced sentaku"

contemporary furniture, and artworks that include a wall of seasonally changing, food-related works that are for sale. This seasonality characterises executive chef Phil's innovative modern British menus, although a love of Japanese cooking shows in hls newly introduced sentaku (carte) that sits alongside his six-, eight- and 10-course tasting menus, with wine flights. Taking the sentaku route could mean beginning with brandade, here herb-crusted sea bass, then roast loin of venison with black pudding, chicory and hazelnut, followed by poached rhubarb with ginger, orange and rum. From the tasting menus might come

Moroccan-spiced skate with wheat berry and harissa; rabbit with ceps, chestnut and tarragon; cured breast of duck with confit gizzard, kohlrabi and – that Japanese influence again – umeboshi mayonnalse. Artisan cheeses wlth garnishes are there for the finish. Vegetarian and six- and eight-course menus are also offered at lunch. Professional service is very much part of the whole proposition.

Chef Phil Fanning
Seats 37, Private dining 12
Closed Christmas
Prices from S £8, M £28, D £8
Parking 24
Notes Vegetarian dishes, Children welcome

...fection involving 62% Valrhona
...e chocolate, hazelnut and tonka bean
...h might catch the eye; otherwise, go for
...ury finish with a perfectly ripened
...eseboard served with home-made breads
...nd marinated figs.

Chef Adam Smith **Seats** 66, Private dining 16 **Open** All
Year **Prices from** S £17, M £45, D £18 **Parking** 100
Notes No children under 8 years
See advertisement opposite

BAGNOR MAP 5, SU46

The Blackbird – Restaurant & Public House
◉◉ CLASSIC EUROPEAN
01635 40005 | RG20 8AQ
www.theblackbird.co.uk
A family-run pub that plays Sixties to Eighties
music all day. Not only that, but the interior
resembles a front room from a bygone age, with
a fretwork-fronted wireless, commemorative
mugs and table doilies. Dishes on the imaginative
menu, however, are bang up to date.

Chef Dominic Robinson **Seats** 38 **Closed** 25–26
December, 1 January and 1st week in January
Prices from S £10, M £24, D £9 **Parking** 15
Notes Vegetarian dishes, Children welcome

BRAY MAP 6, SU97

Caldesi in Campagna
◉◉ TRADITIONAL ITALIAN
01628 788500 | Old Mill Lane, SL6 2BG
www.caldesi.com
Here, in an immaculate house on the edge of
Bray, expect classic Italian stuff made with
(mostly) British ingredients. Among antipasti,
deep-fried courgette flowers are filled with
ricotta and basil, and to finish, traditional
desserts might include Sicilian lemon tart.

Chef Gregorio Piazza **Seats** 50, Private dining 12
Closed Christmas for approximately 5 days
Prices from S £9.50, M £16.50, D £7.95 **Parking** 8
Notes Vegetarian dishes, Children welcome

The Crown at Bray
◉◉ TRADITIONAL BRITISH
01628 621936 | High Street, SL6 2AH
www.thecrownatbray.com
Devotees of the British pub know The Crown is
safe in Heston Blumenthal's hands. His third
address in the village, this 16th-century inn offers
real ales, a well-constructed wine list and a menu
that owes much to pub traditions while
honouring the Blumenthal name.

Chef Matt Larcombe **Seats** 50 **Open** All Year **Parking** 37
Notes Vegetarian dishes, Children welcome

The Fat Duck
◉◉◉◉◉ MODERN BRITISH 𝑽 NOTABLE WINE LIST
01628 580333 | High Street, SL6 2AQ
www.thefatduck.co.uk
Heston Blumenthal's The Fat Duck, and its
telegenic proprietor himself, have entered the
modern pantheon of culinary legend with the
four-hour marathon of idiosyncratic and
inventive eating that is one of those bucket-list
experiences that will stay with you forever. A
foodie pilgrimage here has never come cheap –
the entrance fee is £325 these days – and that's
before you bring jaw-droppingly expensive wine,
sundry drinks and the 12.5% service charge into
the equation – but when you appreciate the work
that goes into each dish – the craft, the passion,
the time – the cost seems easier to justify, and
the stellar staff can cope with eight or so
languages to keep the international punters
informed as they go along. What follows
consumes you as much as you consume it, as a
parade of highly conceptualized dishes unfold,
arriving on sandy beaches accompanied by
gigantic seashells or perched on great white
cushions floating in mid-air. Ice cream is crab
flavoured, and rocket-shaped ice lollies taste of
Waldorf salad – Blumenthal's mission is to mess
with your head and recreate the sense of thrilled
anticipation one had as a child when the family
set out on a summer holiday, and that joy is
tangible in the intensity of the flavours as much
as in the entertaining menu concept that it
generates. A turbot course brings fish of
remarkable quality, alongside smoky torched
cucumber, caviar and a heavenly reduced broth.
Botrytis cinerea is the 'noble rot' that produces
the mouldy grapes destined for legendary
dessert wines such as Sauternes, but chez
Heston it's the name of a dessert designed to
resemble a bunch of grapes, each exploding with
contrasting flavours and textures. That's
ultimately what great cooking is about: when all
the theatrical ingenuity makes sense and has
purpose delivering flavour, emotion and
craftsmanship; something the Fat Duck is
incomparably good at.

Chef Heston Blumenthal **Seats** 42 **Closed** 2 weeks at
Christmas **Notes** Children welcome

COWORTH·PARK

ASCOT

Dorchester *Collection*

STAR OF
THE SHOW

A twist on tradition. A taste of the country.
A feast for the senses. The British ingredients.
The fresh talent. The Michelin star.
Adam Smith, executive chef at Coworth Park.
Perfection just happens.

ASCOT +44 (0)1344 876 600
DORCHESTERCOLLECTION.COM

#DCmoments
f CoworthPark
🐦 CoworthParkUK
📷 CoworthPark

BRAY continued

The Hind's Head

◉◉◉ BRITISH

01628 626151 | High Street, SL6 2AB

www.hindsheadbray.com

The nearby Fat Duck's culinary pyrotechnics aren't for everyone's tastes or budget, so for a glimpse of that Blumenthal wizardry consider what was once Bray's village boozer, where Heston offers true-Brit cooking in tune with the building's 15th-century heritage. The space is split between a clubby lounge bar upstairs with eccentric hunting-lodge touches in its funky decor, while the main ground-floor restaurant offers a carte, a five-course taster or a budget-friendly set-lunch menu, all offering well-crafted versions of robust British dishes. Layers of clear flavours are key to a modern take on Waldorf salad, with caramelised scallops highlighted by celery gel and flowers, pickled and candied walnuts, sea vegetables and dill oil. Technically astute cooking produces a delightful main course of chicken and Alsace bacon with grilled lettuce, broad beans, pea purée and mint oil. Pudding is so simple but so good: zingy lemon tart is helped along by racy raspberry and verbena sorbet.

Chef Peter Gray **Seats** 82, Private dining 18 **Closed** 25 December **Prices from** S £11.50, M £24.50, D £10.50 **Parking** 40 **Notes** Vegetarian dishes, Children welcome

The Waterside Inn

◉◉◉ FRENCH *V*

01628 620691 | Ferry Road, SL6 2AT

www.waterside-inn.co.uk

Accept the valet parking graciously; the little car park is a squeeze. In fact, prepare to do everything with grace. This is The Waterside, which wrote the book on refined dining a couple of generations ago. With its views on to the little jetty and its moored boats, and tree canopies shading these peaceable upper reaches of the Thames, the word 'idyllic' soon flies to most lips, and the cooking plays its part, Alain Roux maintaining the formidable standards of the legendary Michel Roux père. A slice of rich game terrine with a roundel of foie gras at its heart is encased in truffled pastry and comes with a bouquet of saladings and candied walnuts. Main courses are finely calibrated to the rest of the menu, building substance without overfacing, as witness a well-timed tranche of cod topped with apple and parsnip remoulade, accompanied by savoury bread pudding and a cream sauce of cider and black garlic, or the celebrated grilled rabbit on celeriac fondant with glazed chestnuts in Armagnac. A beguiling dessert is the white chocolate mousse with ginger sponge and Campari-laced orange sorbet, but if you choose to skip, there are regiments of exquisite petits fours to compensate.

Chef Michel Roux, Alain Roux **Seats** 75, Private dining 8 **Closed** 26 December to 30 January **Prices from** S £40.50, M £55, D £32 **Parking** 20 **Notes** No children under 9 years

BURCHETT'S GREEN
MAP 5, SU88

The Crown

◉◉◉ BRITISH, FRENCH

01628 824079 | SL6 6QZ

www.thecrownburchettsgreen.com

The 19th-century pub is a cut above your average village watering hole, its original features offset by understated country-chic furnishings, slate floors and bare tables laid with fresh flowers and classy tableware. At the beating heart of the enterprise is chef-patron Simon Bonwick, who clearly has an ongoing love affair with French gastronomical ways and an intuitive grasp of how ingredients work together in each dish. This is sharp, precise cooking with intense flavours that leave a big smile on your face. Menu descriptions seriously underplay what arrives on the plate, as in a multi-layered starter of falafel with harissa-spiced grains atop a wafer-thin croûte, all highlighted by pomegranate, reduced balsamic and parmesan crisp. Main-course turbot Lyonnaise delivers precision-timed fish of exceptional quality served with crisp onions, tiger prawns, celeriac, beetroot, broccoli and spinach, all cooked spot-on, plus silky mashed potato and a punchy jus.

Chef Simon Bonwick **Open** All Year **Notes** No children

CHIEVELEY
MAP 5, SU47

Crab & Boar

◉◉ MODERN EUROPEAN

01635 247550 | Wantage Road, RG20 8UE

www.crabandboar.com

The Crab & Boar has a stylish interior: walls in the interconnecting rooms are decorated in muted tones, with exposed beams, while bare wooden tables are smartly set and chairs are a mixed bag, all presenting a refined ambience.

Open All Year

COOKHAM
MAP 6, SU88

The White Oak
◉◉ MODERN BRITISH

01628 523043 | The Pound, SL6 9QE

www.thewhiteoak.co.uk

The team behind the White Oak reopened it in 2008 as a modern dining pub. Set in Stanley Spencer's beloved Cookham, it has splashy contemporary artwork, bare tables and generous washes of natural light from a skylight and patio doors onto the garden.

Chef Graham Kirk Seats 80, Private dining 12 Closed Christmas Prices from S £6.50, M £13.95, D £6.50 Parking 32 Notes Vegetarian dishes, Children welcome

FRILSHAM
MAP 5, SU57

The Pot Kiln
◉◉ BRITISH, EUROPEAN

01635 201366 | RG18 0XX

www.potkiln.org

This rural red-brick country inn is worth tracking down for its proper pubby vibe and unpretentious approach to modern British cooking. The owners source their produce with care, but what makes The Pot Kiln stand out from the herd is its passion for game.

Closed 25 December

HUNGERFORD
MAP 5, SU36

Blandy's at Inglewood NEW
◉ MODERN, CLASSIC BRITISH

01488 687010 | Templeton Road, Kintbury, RG17 9AA

www.blandysbistro.co.uk

Housed in a handsome Georgian mansion in extensive gardens, Blandy's is the epitome of English elegance, overlaid with a gently contemporary edge. High ceilings, chandeliers, ornate plasterwork and panelling set a grandiose tone in the dining room, where you can expect meticulous plates of seasonal, produce-driven, modern food with sound classical foundations.

Chef Gert Pienaar Seats 66, Private dining 16 Open All Year Prices from S £7.25, M £13.25, D £7 Parking 50 Notes Vegetarian dishes, Children welcome

HURLEY
MAP 5, SU88

Hurley House
◉◉ MODERN BRITISH

01628 568500 | Henley Road, SL6 5LH

hurleyhouse.co.uk

In the village of Hurley and close to Marlow and Henley-on-Thames, the candlelit restaurant at Hurley House has a refined feel with green leather banquettes, tan leather chairs and linen napkins on the unclothed tables. It all adds up to create a mood of informality.

Chef Emanuele Privitera Seats 42, Private dining 28 Open All Year Prices from S £7, M £18, D £7.50 Parking 65 Notes Vegetarian dishes, Children welcome

MAIDENHEAD
MAP 6, SU88

Fredrick's Hotel and Spa
◉◉ MODERN BRITISH

01628 581000 | Shoppenhangers Road, SL6 2PZ

www.fredricks-hotel.co.uk

The kitchen team continue to produce assiduously researched contemporary cooking. Take the starters: home-smoked salmon tian comes with potato galette and dill pickle, and pork is put to good use in rillettes and crackling salad with pickled apple.

Chef Charlie Murray Seats 60, Private dining 120 Open All Year Parking 80 Notes Vegetarian dishes, Children welcome

The Royal Oak Paley Street
◉◉◉ MODERN BRITISH 🍷 NOTABLE WINE LIST

See page 38

NEWBURY
MAP 5, SU46

Donnington Valley Hotel & Spa
◉◉ MODERN BRITISH V

01635 551199 | Old Oxford Road, Donnington, RG14 3AG

www.donningtonvalley.co.uk

A likeable, informal sort of place, not least the Wine Press restaurant: a light-filled, raftered room on two levels. There's much to like on the menu too, with lots of modern takes on conventional British fare, such as a scrumptious Old Spots pig terrine.

Chef Darren Booker-Wilson Seats 150, Private dining 210 Open All Year Prices from S £8, M £12.95, D £6 Parking 200 Notes Children welcome

MAIDENHEAD   *MAP 6, SU88*

The Royal Oak Paley Street

◉◉◉ **MODERN BRITISH** 🍷 NOTABLE WINE LIST

01628 620541 | Paley Street, Littlefield Green, SL6 3JN
www.theroyaloakpaleystreet.com

The Parkinson family have lavished heaps of TLC on the Oak, transforming it into a dining pub of our times. Inside, the low-beamed bar and brick fireplace retain echoes of its 17th-century roots, though, with winged armchairs, sofas and walls lined with posh artwork, it's more about aperitifs than pints at the bar these days. A bright extension, with a beamed ceiling and doors opening onto a splendid modern terrace, adds sunny day appeal. Head chef Leon Smith continues the Oak's kitchen ethos, built around prime seasonal ingredients, simplicity and bold flavour, while looking smart on the plate too. Starters like pig's head and foie gras fritter with wild garlic mayonnaise and pickled vegetables illustrate the bold style. A three-way serving of lamb might follow, the loin, crispy sweetbread and shank ravioli teamed with heritage carrots and navarin sauce, while classy desserts show form to the end.

Chef Leon Smith Seats 80, Private dining 20 Open All Year Prices from S £9, M £18, D £9 Parking 70 Notes Vegetarian dishes, Children welcome

NEWBURY continued

The Vineyard

Rosettes suspended MODERN BRITISH **V** NOTABLE WINE LIST

01635 528770 | Stockcross, RG20 8JU

www.the-vineyard.co.uk

The Rosette award for this establishment has been suspended due to a change of chef and reassessment will take place in due course. Spoiler alert: no wine is made at The Vineyard, but they do have a world-class cellar that runs to a staggering 30,000 bottles by way of compensation. The vinous theme of this opulent, contemporary country house is apparent as soon as you're through the door, with a glass floor above the wine vault. Style-magazine rooms, chic public areas and a glossy spa are what to expect. Expert sommeliers guide the way through that astonishing cellar, starting with around 100 available by the glass.

Chef Tom Scade **Seats** 86, Private dining 140 **Open** All Year **Parking** 100 **Notes** Children welcome

The Woodspeen – Restaurant and Cookery School

MODERN BRITISH

01635 265070 | Lambourn Road, RG20 8BN

www.thewoodspeen.com

A restored late Georgian farmhouse is the setting for a very 21st-century combination of restaurant and aspirational cooking school, a place where picture windows frame the sylvan views and chefs beaver away at an open pass to create colourful dishes that are constructed with a light touch, but that deliver layers of beguiling complexity. That's in evidence in a starter of luxurious mushroom velouté with floating fritters of smoked eel and harissa-spiked peanuts to boot. Mains emphasise thoroughbred meats, to the extent of allowing an oxtail raviolo to inveigle its way into a dish of grilled monkfish and balsamic red onion, while meat dishes themselves might run to gamey pheasant on spiced Puy lentils with parsnip rösti and cavolo nero. A slice of British classicism arrives at dessert stage by way of silky custard tart with nutmeg ice cream and a purée of salt caramel and apple.

Chef John Campbell **Seats** 70, Private dining 12 **Closed** 26 December **Parking** 30 **Notes** Vegetarian dishes, Children welcome

READING

MAP 5, SU77

Caprice Restaurant

MODERN BRITISH, INDIAN

0118 944 0444 | Holiday Inn Reading M4 Jct 10, Wharfedale Road, Winnersh Triangle, RG41 5TS

www.hireadinghotel.com

After driving along the M4 it is with relief that one can walk across the footbridge over the River Loddon into the impressively modern Holiday Inn. The Caprice and its terrace, stunners in their own right, offer a carte plus Indian and vegan menus. Sea bass, corn-fed chicken breast, lamb loin, and various pork cuts feature.

Chef Leon Sharp **Seats** 120, Private dining 40 **Open** All Year **Prices from** S £8, M £19, D £7.50 **Parking** 132 **Notes** Vegetarian dishes, Children welcome

See advertisement on page 40

Chez Mal Brasserie

MODERN EUROPEAN, INTERNATIONAL

0118 956 2300 | Malmaison Reading, Great Western House, 18–20 Station Road, RG1 1JX

www.malmaison.com

By all accounts the world's oldest railway hotel, the early Victorian property is a real charmer. Its historic past is recognised in some decorative touches, but this being a Mal, the overall finish is glamorous and stylish. Settle into the Malbar for a pre-dinner cocktail.

Chef Szabolcs Deli **Seats** 64, Private dining 22 **Open** All Year **Prices from** S £8, M £13.50, D £4 **Notes** Vegetarian dishes, Children welcome

The French Horn

TRADITIONAL FRENCH, BRITISH

0118 969 2204 | Sonning, RG4 6TN

www.thefrenchhorn.co.uk

The riverside setting is a treat, with the dining room opening on to a terrace, at the family-run French Horn, which is full of old-school charm with slick and well-managed service. The menu looks across the Channel for its inspiration, with a classically based repertoire.

Closed 1–4 January

2 AA ROSETTE
Caprice Restaurant

As a stylish two-AA-rosette-awarded establishment, the **Caprice Restaurant & Terrace** is the epitome of fine dining, offering immaculate service and first-rate cuisine. This *tranquil oasis* is located in the exceptional new four Silver Star Holiday Inn Reading M4 Junction 10.

Guests are spoilt for choice as the menu caters for all tastes, with a seasonal à la carte menu featuring the finest local ingredients and a set menu priced from only £25.95. The kitchen brigade even includes pâtissiers who prepare an array of tempting treats that are well worth the extra calories. For something more informal, try the stunning Monty's Lounge Bar, serving authentic Indian specialities. At night, the hotel is transformed, with music from the talented resident pianist.

The hotel offers a range of stunning features including the Esprit Wellness & Spa with 19m Pool, Sauna and Steam Room and Large Gym. The pampering spa treatments will leave you feeling rejuvenated and refreshed. 'The Academy' is the ideal venue for hosting Meetings & Conferences, Weddings and Christmas Parties.

E: fb@hireadinghotel.com T: 0118 944 0444 W: www.hireadinghotel.com
Wharfedale Road, Winnersh Triangle, Reading RG41 5TS

SHINFIELD
MAP 5, SU76

L'Ortolan
◉◉◉ MODERN FRENCH V♪ NOTABLE WINE LIST
0118 988 8500 | Church Lane, RG2 9BY
www.lortolan.com

Synonymous with modern British gastronomy since the 1980s, L'Ortolan is a smart, country-house style restaurant in a beautiful red-brick former vicarage. Chef Tom Clarke produces sophisticated, contemporary cooking, full of precise, thoughtful detail. You'll find plenty to admire in the presentation, too – dishes are attractive and carefully balanced, whichever menu you choose from. A starter of goose liver parfait comes with intriguing flavours of coconut and mango; main courses are just as interesting, maybe halibut with curried lentils and tamarind, or stone bass with clams and preserved lemon. Desserts offer an intriguing interpretation of familiar flavours – the 'toffee apple' with apple, pecan and caramac, for example. The wine list majors on France and Italy, while the rest of Europe and the New World have a voice, but with a softer accent. There's a chef's table in the kitchen, a relaxing bar and private dining rooms alongside fine-dining standards like canapés, pre-desserts and petits fours.

Chef Tom Clarke **Seats** 58, Private dining 22 **Closed** 2 weeks Christmas to New Year **Prices from** S £12.50, M £16, D £11 **Parking** 30 **Notes** No children under 3 years

THATCHAM
MAP 5, SU56

The Bunk Inn
◉◉ MODERN BRITISH, FRENCH
01635 200400 | Curridge, RG18 9DS
www.thebunkinn.co.uk

A short canter from Newbury Racecourse, this convivial inn is still very much the village hub where locals prop up the bar by the open fire with a glass of ale and a packet of crisps, but its confident modern cooking also attracts foodies.

Open All Year

WHITE WALTHAM
MAP 5, SU87

The Beehive
◉◉ BRITISH
01628 822877 | Waltham Road, SL6 3SH
www.thebeehivewhitewaltham.com

With the cricket ground opposite, The Beehive is the epitome of the English village pub. A bar menu, daily-changing lunch and dinner menus, and a specials board reveal season-driven, modern British dishes known for their gimmick-free, 'less is more' simplicity. Start with Dorset snails with garlic butter, gorgonzola and grilled sourdough and follow with calves' liver, crisp bacon, onions and mash.

Chef Dominic Chapman **Seats** 75 **Closed** 25–26 December **Prices from** S £6.95, M £16.95, D £5.95 **Parking** 40 **Notes** Vegetarian dishes, Children welcome

WINDSOR
MAP 6, SU97

The Brasserie at Sir Christopher Wren
◉ MODERN EUROPEAN
01753 442400 | Thames Street, SL4 1PX
www.sirchristopherwren.co.uk

Part of a hotel comprising several buildings clustered around a cobbled street by the River Thames, the menu in the brasserie is appealingly modern. A typical meal might begin with tempura prawns and plum dipping sauce and continue with cumin-roasted rump of lamb, spinach, sweet potato, aubergine caviar and cherry tomatoes.

Chef Darran Kimber **Seats** 120, Private dining 100 **Open** All Year **Parking** 14 **Notes** Vegetarian dishes, Children welcome

Caleys Brasserie *NEW*
◉ MODERN BRITISH
01753 483100 | Macdonald Windsor Hotel,
23 High Street, SL4 1LH
www.macdonaldhotels.co.uk/windsor

Smack on the high street, this relaxed, contemporary brasserie delivers an appealing line in uncomplicated modern dishes. Start with ham hock terrine with wholegrain mustard mayonnaise, followed by baked sea trout with crab cake, cavolo nero and crab bisque sauce. A Josper oven ensures prime steaks and grills arrive at the table seared to perfection.

Chef Daniel Woodhouse **Seats** 75, Private dining 120 **Open** All Year **Prices from** S £7, M £16, D £7 **Parking** 30 **Notes** Vegetarian dishes, Children welcome

The Dining Room Restaurant

◉◉ MODERN BRITISH

01753 609988 | The Oakley Court, Windsor Road, Water Oakley, SL4 5UR

www.oakleycourt.co.uk

With turrets, gables and 37 acres of well-tended grounds, Oakley Court is a prime example of a Victorian Gothic castle. The half-panelled dining room, with its crisply clothed tables and formal service, Is the place to head for creative modern British cooking.

Closed Christmas and New Year

The Greene Oak

◉ MODERN BRITISH

01753 864294 | Oakley Green, SL4 5UW

www.thegreeneoak.co.uk

Very much a dining pub, The Greene Oak is a charming old place with bright, homely decor and cheerful staff who keep it all ticking along nicely. The kitchen makes good use of local seasonal ingredients, focusing on gently contemporary British- and European-inspired ideas.

Open All Year

WOKINGHAM
MAP 5, SU86

Miltons Restaurant

◉◉ EUROPEAN, INTERNATIONAL

0118 989 5100 | Cantley House Hotel, Milton Road, RG40 1JY

www.miltonsrestaurant.co.uk

The Cantley House Hotel is a 17th-century barn, with a split-level dining space done in a rustic-chic manner, and modern brasserie food is the name of the game. Duck and bacon ballotine with seared foie gras and apple rösti is a well-conceived and well-executed starter.

Open All Year

■ BRISTOL

BRISTOL
MAP 4, ST57

Adelina Yard

◉◉ MODERN BRITISH

0117 911 2112 | Queen Quay, Welsh Back, BS1 4SL

www.adelinayard.com

Owner-chef couple Jamie Randall and Olivia Barry have made quite an impact on the local scene since opening this stylish restaurant at the end of 2015. Located on the water's edge in the city's revitalised harbourside area, the open-plan kitchen provides an informal setting.

Chef Jamie Randall, Olivia Barry **Seats** 35 **Closed** 23 December to 8 January, 3 April and 21 July **Prices from** S £8, M £19, D £8 **Notes** Vegetarian dishes, Children welcome

Berwick Lodge

◉◉ MODERN BRITISH

0117 958 1590 | Berwick Drive, Henbury, BS10 7TD

www.berwicklodge.co.uk

The Victorian gent who built this manor house back in the 1890s picked a good spot, surrounded by 18 acres of gardens and woodland. The smart boutique restaurant, Hattua, is the perfect setting for creative modern dishes which look as good as they taste.

Chef Istvan Ullman **Seats** 80, Private dining 16 **Open** All Year **Prices from** S £11, M £23, D £10.50 **Parking** 100 **Notes** Vegetarian dishes, Children welcome

The Bird in Hand

◉ MODERN BRITISH

01275 395222 | Weston Road, Long Ashton, BS41 9LA

www.bird-in-hand.co.uk

The modern British dishes at this unassuming village pub make good use of wild mushrooms and herbs foraged locally by the chefs and staff. International influences are evident too, as in carpaccio of dry-aged rump of beef with tempura wild-garlic flowers, while sea bream, and pulled shoulder of woodland-reared pork are other possibilities.

Chef Felix Rayment **Seats** 30 **Closed** 25 December **Prices from** S £6, M £14.50, D £6 **Notes** Vegetarian dishes, Children welcome

Casamia Restaurant

◉◉◉◉◉ MODERN BRITISH *V* NOTABLE WINE LIST

0117 959 2884 | The General, Lower Guinea Street, BS1 6SY

www.casamiarestaurant.co.uk

Casamia's location, in the redeveloped General Hospital overlooking Bathurst Basin in Bristol's docklands, is very different from the leafy suburb of Westbury-on-Trym, where self-taught chef Peter Sanchez-Iglesias opened it first time round. Possibly uniquely, he has a second restaurant in the same building, so he can nip easily from one to the other to check how things are going. Passing through the monumental stone archway you enter a sleek, subtly monochrome interior with linen-clad tables, a tiled floor, and walls hung with periodically rotating arboreal pictures. In the open kitchen, a battalion of chefs works with calm concentration to produce driven-by-the-seasons tasting menus – a four-course (except Friday and Saturday evenings), and a longer version (Wednesdays to Sundays). Ingenious, novel and well-nigh flawlessly executed, they are undeniably aimed upmarket. The chefs themselves then bring them to the table and talk them through with diners, which is handy because the economically worded menus give little away; even their website reveals only 'what we're cooking at the moment', as in 'beef', 'lamb', 'hake'.

So then, what might Sanchez-Iglesias and his team be cooking today? Well, quite possibly a vinaigretted vegetable salad that comes with sheep's-milk mousse and carrot jam, to be followed by a risotto simmered in beetroot juice, with yogurt sorbet and pickled fennel. Or perhaps it will be concentrated duck broth stocked with oyster mushroom, apple, mooli and a poached quail's egg; perhaps honey-glazed duck accompanied by celeriac, fermented lentils, chia seeds in ponzu, mustard greens with chilli, baby lychee, and pak choi with orange. A dessert of passionfruit and mini-meringues could find itself paired with an intense tarragon mousse. You'd expect the carefully chosen wine pairings to complement the complex detail of each dish – and they do. Casamia, like many top restaurants today, requires payment on booking, with drinks and service added on the day.

Chef Peter Sanchez-Iglesias, Kelvin Potter **Seats** 30 **Closed** Christmas, New Year and bank holidays **Notes** Children welcome

Glass Boat Restaurant

◉◉ MODERN FRENCH

0117 929 0704 | Welsh Back, BS1 4SB

www.glassboat.co.uk

This converted 1920s barge has been moored in the heart of Bristol's Harbourside area since 1986. It's a handsome and appealing restaurant with walnut floors, a beautiful marble bar and lovely river views; the menu offers modern French bistro fare with plenty of imagination.

Chef Jake Platt **Seats** 120, Private dining 40 **Closed** 24-26 December **Prices from** S £6.50, M £14, D £5.50 **Notes** Vegetarian dishes, Children welcome

Hotel du Vin Bristol

◉ FRENCH, BRITISH

0117 925 5577 | The Sugar House, Narrow Lewins Mead, BS1 2NU

www.hotelduvin.com

In a former sugar warehouse close to the waterfront, the casual French-inspired bistro at the Bristol HdV is a buzzy and easy-going venue. Factor in the world-class wine list, and you've got a compelling package. The bilingual menu deals in classic stuff.

Open All Year

The Ivy Clifton Brasserie

◉ BRITISH

0117 203 4555 | 42-44 Caledonia Place, BS8 4DN

www.theivycliftonbrasserie.com

Set in the heart of Clifton, just moments from the famous suspension bridge, this former bank has been tastefully converted into a must-visit restaurant in this area. Taking inspiration from her London big sister, it is a great casual dining all-day concept.

Open All Year

The Ox

◉ MODERN BRITISH

0117 922 1001 | The Basement, 43 Corn Street, BS1 1HT

www.theoxbristol.com

Head down to the basement, a one-time bank vault, and you'll find a restaurant that the old boys of yesteryear would have admired, with its oak panels, ox blood leather seats and murals. They'd have appreciated the red-blooded menu too – steaks are their thing.

Closed Christmas

Paco Tapas

⊛⊛ ANDALUSIAN TAPAS

0117 925 7021 | 3A Lower Guinea Street, BS1 6SY

www.pacotapas.co.uk

Located directly on the docks at Bristol harbourside, this bustling tapas bar offers authentic dishes from the owners' Andalusian home. Much of the produce comes directly from the region while daily specials are added by way of fresh fish and seafood delivered daily from the Cornish coasts.

Chef Peter Sanchez-Iglesias, Kelvin Potter **Seats** 28 **Closed** 24–26 December, 1 January **Prices from** S £3, M £11, D £5 **Notes** Vegetarian dishes, Children welcome

The Pump House

⊛⊛ MODERN BRITISH

0117 927 2229 | Merchants Road, Hotwells, BS8 4PZ

the-pumphouse.com

On Bristol's Floating Harbour, this Victorian former hydraulic pumping station is now a buzzy gastro pub and restaurant with a mezzanine seating area. Food is predominantly British, with charcoal grills and tasty potato and cheddar dumplings; and seafood, such as River Exe mussels, gilthead bream and Skrei cod, delivered daily from West Country fishermen.

Chef Toby Gritten **Seats** 50 **Closed** 25 December **Prices from** S £6, M £15, D £6 **Parking** 20 **Notes** Vegetarian dishes, Children welcome

riverstation

⊛ MODERN EUROPEAN

0117 914 4434 | The Grove, BS1 4RB

www.riverstation.co.uk

This lively venue is glazed from top to bottom to make the most of its harbourside location, both from the ground-floor café-bar and the industrial-chic first-floor restaurant. Inspiration is drawn from far and wide to create bright, up-to-date dishes rooted in good culinary sense.

Closed 24–26 December

Root

⊛ BRITISH, SHARING PLATES

0117 930 0260 | Unit 9, Cargo 1, Gaol Ferry Steps, BS1 6WP

www.eatdrinkbristolfashion.co.uk

Originating at the Queen Square Festival, Root is the restaurant venture of Eat Drink Bristol Fashion, and is stationed on the historic dockside at Wapping Wharf. In a vibrant, chattery atmosphere, with seating around the bar overlooking the kitchen, a menu of small sharing plates encompasses globally influenced cooking with plenty of attitude.

Chef Rob Howell **Seats** 32 **Closed** 25–26 December **Notes** Vegetarian dishes, Children welcome

Second Floor Restaurant

⊛⊛ MODERN BRITISH *V*

0117 916 8898 | Harvey Nichols, 27 Philadelphia Street, Quakers Friars, BS1 3BZ

www.harveynichols.com

Overlooking the old Quakers Friars Dominican friary in the heart of Cabot Circus shopping quarter, this gold and beige-hued, second-floor dining room is a supremely relaxing place. The kitchen turns out a menu of lively modern British and European food. There are interesting wines on offer too.

Chef Louise McCrimmon **Seats** 60, Private dining 10 **Closed** 25 December, 1 January and Easter Sunday **Prices from** S £7, M £22, D £6.50 **Notes** Vegetarian dishes, Children welcome

The Spiny Lobster

⊛ MEDITERRANEAN, SEAFOOD

0117 973 7384 | 128 Whiteladies Road, Clifton, BS8 2RS

www.thespinylobster.co.uk

Mitch Tonks' seafood brasserie and fish market maintains a rigorous commitment to freshness and simplicity, using fish and shellfish mostly landed by the Brixham boats. The dining room sports linen-clothed tables, staff are friendly, and top-class materials slapped onto a charcoal-burning Josper grill can't be beaten.

Chef Charlie Hearn **Seats** 45 **Closed** 25 December and 1 January **Prices from** S £6, M £12.50, D £4 **Notes** Vegetarian dishes, Children welcome

Tare Restaurant *NEW*

⊛⊛ MODERN EUROPEAN *V*

0117 929 4328 | Unit 14, Museum Street, Wapping Wharf, BS1 6ZA

tarerestaurant.co.uk

Operating out of a converted shipping container in the up-and-coming Wapping Wharf harbourside development, Tare offers intimate, relaxed and modern dining. The carefully sourced top-quality produce contributes to the regular and seasonal menu updates including a six-course tasting menu. There are some interesting bottles beers and ciders too.

Chef Matt Hampshire **Seats** 24 **Closed** Christmas to New Year **Notes** Children welcome

Wilks Restaurant

◉◉ MODERN BRITISH, CLASSICAL FRENCH
0117 973 7999 | 1–3 Chandos Road, Redland, BS6 6PG
www.wilksrestaurant.co.uk
The sober seaweed-green frontage in the Redland district conceals a bright white interior adorned with the works of local studio and street artists. A versatile culinary output stretches from set menus to tasting menus of five and seven courses, with many memorable highs, including the top-drawer meats.

Open All Year

■ BUCKINGHAMSHIRE

AMERSHAM
MAP 6, SU99

The Artichoke

◉◉◉ MODERN EUROPEAN V NOTABLE WINE LIST
01494 726611 | 9 Market Square, Old Amersham, HP7 0DF
www.artichokerestaurant.co.uk
Amersham's finest continues to set a regional standard for dazzling modern cooking delivered with engaging brio in an atmosphere enlivened by views of the kitchen pass. Laurie Gear offers a sheaf of tasting menus, as well as the standard prix-fixe, a set lunch and vegetarian options. He's the kind of chef unafraid to do the simplest things: a plate of just al dente risotto flavoured with parsley roots and dressed with melted Lancashire Bomb. For fish, there could be skate wing garnished with diced apple, sea beets and triple-cooked chips seasoned with powdered capers and vinegar, in a sauce of mussels and cider. Succulent venison sausage is partnered with a terrine of potato cooked in beef dripping, red cabbage purée and beetroot. To finish, there may be Cambridge burnt cream offset with poached rhubarb, blood orange and aerated white chocolate. Preliminaries include the unmissable Chiltern Black Ale bread with lamb-fat butter.

Chef Laurie Gear, Ben Jenkins **Seats** 48, Private dining 16 **Closed** 2 weeks at Christmas, 1 week April (from Easter Sunday), 2 weeks in August/September **Notes** No children under 8 years at dinner

Gilbey's Restaurant

◉◉ MODERN BRITISH
01494 727242 | 1 Market Square, HP7 0DF
www.gilbeygroup.com
Housed in Old Amersham's 17th-century former grammar school, the fully renovated Gilbey's offers the style and intimacy you'd expect. Open with cream of Jerusalem artichoke soup with hazelnut and spinach pesto, then progress to steamed St Austell Bay mussels in white wine and parsley, or dolce gorgonzola and casarecce pasta with honey-candied walnuts. To finish, consider duo of sorbets.

Chef Adam Whitlock **Seats** 50, Private dining 12 **Closed** 23–28 December **Prices from** S £7.95, M £17.95, D £7.95 **Notes** Vegetarian dishes, Children welcome

Hawkyns by Atul Kochhar

◉◉ MODERN BRITISH, MODERN INDIAN
01494 721541 | The Crown, 16 High Street, HP7 0DH
www.hawkynsrestaurant.co.uk
Set within The Crown, a Tudor-style building in the pretty town of Amersham, Hawkyns is run by the celebrated Indian chef Atul Kochhar. Set against a backdrop of original wooden beams, stripped floorboards and brick fireplaces, the scrubbed farmhouse-style tables and mismatched chairs add an informal pub feel but the food is a combination of the best British and Indian cooking.

Chef Atul Kochhar **Seats** 60, Private dining 40 **Open** All Year **Parking** 35 **Notes** Vegetarian dishes, Children welcome

AYLESBURY
MAP 11, SP81

The Chequers Inn

◉ MODERN BRITISH V
01296 613298 | 35 Church Lane, Weston Turville, HP22 5SJ
www.thechequerswt.co.uk
Dating from the 16th century, The Chequers Inn ticks all the 'quintessential inn' boxes with its open fireplace, venerable beams and polished flagstone and timber floors. The kitchen turns out a strong please-all roster of inventive modern gastro pub dishes.

Chef Jamie Maserati, Dritan Lani **Seats** 60, Private dining 32 **Open** All Year **Prices from** S £7.50, M £17.50, D £6.50 **Parking** 30 **Notes** No children under 6 years

Hartwell House Hotel, Restaurant & Spa

@@ MODERN BRITISH V ⚑ NOTABLE WINE LIST

01296 747444 | Lower Hartwell, HP17 8NR
www.hartwell-house.com
One-time residence of the exiled Louis XVIII, this majestic stately home is set within 90 acres of parkland. Befitting the grand setting, everything looks good on the plate and flavours are nicely handled. Beef carpaccio might be followed by seared fillet of halibut, prawn dumpling, pickled mooli and Thai shellfish broth.

Chef Daniel Richardson Seats 56, Private dining 36
Open All Year Parking 50 Notes No children under 6 years

BEACONSFIELD

MAP 6, SU99

Crazy Bear Beaconsfield

@ BRITISH, INTERNATIONAL

01494 673086 | 75 Wycombe End, Old Town, HP9 1LX
www.crazybeargroup.co.uk
The word 'restraint' was not in the designers' brief when they converted this 15th-century coaching inn into a flamboyant, English-themed restaurant. It's a high-energy place, with a menu covering classics, chargrilled meats and some lively modern global ideas. The set-up has its own farm shop.

Open All Year

The Jolly Cricketers

@ MODERN BRITISH

01494 676308 | 24 Chalfont Road, Seer Green, HP9 2YG
www.thejollycricketers.co.uk

This congenial, cricket-themed pub is the hub of the village. A concise menu lists its modern dishes as Openers, Main Play and Sticky Wickets; batting first could be fried English goats' cheese and candied walnuts; next in might be grilled skate wing, seaweed and sour cream jacket potato; leaving plum and hazelnut crumble as last man at the culinary wicket.

Chef Matt Lyons Seats 36, Private dining 22
Closed 25–26 December Prices from S £6, M £14.50, D £6 Parking 10 Notes Vegetarian dishes, Children welcome

BRILL

MAP 11, SP61

The Pointer

@@ MODERN BRITISH

01844 238339 | 27 Church Street, HP18 9RT
www.thepointerbrill.co.uk
The Pointer's roots extend deep into its local community. As well as being a welcoming pub in the picturesque village of Brill near Aylesbury, it also encompasses a working organic farm and kitchen garden, and an adjacent butcher's shop for take-outs of its pedigree meats.

Closed 1 week January

BUCKINGHAM

MAP 11, SP63

Duke's Restaurant & Bar

@ MODERN BRITISH

01280 822444 | Buckingham Villiers Hotel,
3 Castle Street, MK18 1BS
www.villiers-hotel.co.uk
Overlooking a courtyard, the refurbished restaurant at the Villiers Hotel offers a range of booths and seating options. The kitchen focuses on tried-and-tested dishes, but more ambitious ideas are just as well handled, such as roasted rump of lamb, shepherd's pie, Merguez sausage, peas, samphire, courgette and lamb jus.

Chef Paul Stopps Seats 70, Private dining 150 Open All Year Prices from S £6.50, M £18, D £6.50 Parking 52 Notes Vegetarian dishes, Children welcome

BURNHAM

MAP 6, SU98

Burnham Beeches Hotel

@@ MODERN BRITISH, EUROPEAN

01628 429955 | Grove Road, SL1 8DP
www.corushotels.com/burnham
Close to Windsor, this extended Georgian manor house is set in 10 acres of attractive grounds. The oak-panelled Gray's restaurant is a formal affair with white linen and views of the pretty garden. The gently contemporary dishes are based on classical themes and techniques.

Open All Year

CUBLINGTON
MAP 11, SP82

The Unicorn

◉ MODERN, TRADITIONAL BRITISH

01296 681261 | 12 High Street, LU7 0LQ

www.theunicornpub.co.uk

This 17th-century inn serves the local community well. It has a shop, opens for coffee mornings and afternoon teas on Friday and Saturday and serves bar snacks all day. Menus show interesting ways with seafood and meat is deftly handled too.

Chef Christopher George **Seats** 60, Private dining 30 **Open** All Year **Prices from** S £5, M £11, D £6 **Notes** Vegetarian dishes, Children welcome

GERRARDS CROSS
MAP 6, TQ08

The Three Oaks *NEW*

◉◉ MODERN BRITISH

01753 899016 | Austenwood Lane, Chalfont St Peter, SL9 8NL

Part of the draw at this attractive gastro pub is attentive service from a cheerful young team. There's a lovely garden for those balmy days, while inside, the place has a smartly updated look – a brick fireplace, bare wood tables and easy-on-the-eye colours. Expect to find accomplished contemporary cooking built on top-drawer produce.

Chef Jason Biswell **Seats** 70 **Open** All Year **Prices from** S £5, M £12.50, D £5.90 **Parking** 20 **Notes** Vegetarian dishes, Children welcome

GREAT MISSENDEN
MAP 6, SP80

Nags Head Inn & Restaurant

◉ BRITISH, FRENCH

01494 862200 | London Road, HP16 0DG

www.nagsheadbucks.com

Only a 15-minute stroll from the enchantments of the Roald Dahl Museum in the High Street, the family-run Nags Head is a 15th-century country inn by the River Misbourne. Lightly modernised inside, it makes a relaxed, welcoming setting for creatively fashioned cooking, and dishes with the populist touch.

Closed 25 December

MARLOW
MAP 5, SU88

The Coach

◉◉◉ FRENCH, BRITISH

3 West Street, SL7 2LS

www.thecoachmarlow.co.uk

The Coach is a cosy, pubby sort of venue dominated by the L-shaped bar, with elbow-to-elbow tables, and an open kitchen where chefs are part of the buzzy dynamic, pitching in to help chatty staff whisk dishes out to the tables. Head chef Tom De Keyser turns out tapas-sized plates with the same DNA as the garlanded Hand & Flowers, Tom Kerridge's mothership up the road – deeply satisfying, big on flavour and glowing with technical finesse. Divided between 'meat' and 'no meat' dishes, the menu reads like a roster of big-hearted modern pub fodder – crispy pig's head with celeriac remoulade and spiced date sauce, perhaps. From the 'no meat' side might come potted crab with cucumber chutney and smoked paprika butter. The Coach doesn't take bookings, and with the Kerridge name to draw in the crowds, make sure to turn up nice and early with fingers firmly crossed.

Chef Tom De Keyser, Tom Kerridge **Seats** 40 **Closed** 25-26 December **Prices from** S £7.50, M £11, D £8.50 **Notes** Vegetarian dishes, Children welcome

Danesfield House Hotel & Spa

◉◉ MODERN BRITISH

01628 891010 | Henley Road, SL7 2EY

www.danesfieldhouse.co.uk

Built in 1901, Danesfield House boasts a magnificent setting in 65 acres of beautiful gardens which are overlooked by The Orangery restaurant. The no-frills, Anglo-French cooking is rooted in classic technique. Scallops sauce vierge might be followed by breast of corn-fed chicken, pommes Anna, sweetcorn, bacon jam and red wine jus.

Chef Billy Reid **Seats** 84, Private dining 18 **Open** All Year **Prices from** S £14.95, M £29, D £10 **Parking** 100 **Notes** Vegetarian dishes, Children welcome

Glaze Restaurant

@ MODERN BRITISH, INDIAN

01628 496800 | Crowne Plaza Marlow, Fieldhouse Lane, SL7 1GJ

www.cpmarlow.co.uk/dine

The flagship restaurant of the Crowne Plaza Marlow, Glaze is a light-filled, stylish modern space, with full-drop windows enjoying views over the lake in the grounds from raspberry-coloured banquette seating. Seasonally-changing menus of brasserie cooking and Indian cuisine keep up with the times in every sense.

Chef Robert Quehan **Seats** 150, Private dining 300 **Open** All Year **Prices from** S £6.50, M £19, D £7.50 **Parking** 300 **Notes** Vegetarian dishes, Children welcome

See advertisement opposite

The Hand & Flowers

@@@@ FRENCH. BRITISH *V*

01628 482277 | 126 West Street, SL7 2BP

www.thehandandflowers.co.uk

Tom Kerridge's career speaks not just of a commitment to culinary excellence, though there is that too of course, but of thinking about cooking in ways that are neither excessively precious nor alienating in their technicality. What Kerridge is about, above all, is food that people want to eat, rather than baffling peculiarities they feel they ought to try. The nerve-centre remains the whitewashed country pub with its hanging baskets (plus its private dining space, The Shed, just up the road), where an atmosphere of endearing bonhomie prevails amid the bare tables and half-boarded walls. Marlow regulars doubtless appreciate the fact that the kitchen prides itself as much on producing a matchless roast beef and Yorkshire pudding for Sundays, as it does on working creative transformations on familiar ingredients. Beef toast and dripping comes with mustard butter, English asparagus and salad cream, while at main it's undoubtedly the pedigree meats that the principal emphasis rests. West End Farm pork belly with smoked cheek beignet, black pudding and gherkin ketchup vies for attention with Essex lamb 'bun' with sweetbreads and salsa verde. It's all pretty substantial, but don't even think of resisting the signature chocolate and ale cake with salt caramel muscovado ice cream.

Chef Tom Kerridge **Seats** 54, Private dining 9 **Closed** 24–26 December **Prices from** S £14.50, M £39.50, D £16 **Parking** 20 **Notes** Children welcome

The Riverside Restaurant

@ MODERN BRITISH

01628 484444 | Macdonald Compleat Angler, Marlow Bridge, SL7 1RG

www.macdonaldhotels.co.uk/compleatangler

There's a magnificent view of the Thames from the Riverside's conservatory dining room, while the service team, slick and professional, ensure there's nothing to detract from the occasion, be it a summer lunch or wintertime dinner. Tables on the outdoor terrace are a treat, and in demand, in warm weather.

Chef Etharome Rayappan **Seats** 90, Private dining 100 **Open** All Year **Prices from** S £9, M £22, D £9 **Parking** 100 **Notes** Vegetarian dishes, Children welcome

Sindhu by Atul Kochhar

@@ MODERN INDIAN *V*

01628 405405 | Macdonald Compleat Angler, Marlow Bridge, SL7 1RG

www.sindhurestaurant.co.uk

This is Macdonald Hotels' second restaurant within its Compleat Angler on the River Thames by Marlow Weir. Atul is an acclaimed chef, renowned for his modern Indian cuisine and passion for sustainable fishing. Desserts work well and bhapi doi, rose yogurt cheesecake, is no exception.

Chef Prabhu Ganapati **Seats** 58 **Closed** 25 December **Parking** 100 **Notes** Children welcome

The Vanilla Pod

@@ BRITISH, FRENCH *V* NOTABLE WINE LIST

01628 898101 | 31 West Street, SL7 2LS

www.thevanillapod.co.uk

The culinary bar is set high in this stretch of the Thames Valley stockbroker belt, and The Vanilla Pod delivers a sure-footed take on modern British cooking, its roots clearly in the French classics. The setting is a handsome townhouse where TS Eliot once lived, and today the restaurant has a chic contemporary look in brown and cream.

Chef Michael Macdonald **Seats** 28, Private dining 8 **Closed** 23 December to 10 January, Easter weekend, 28 May to 6 June, 27 August to 5 September **Notes** Children welcome

CROWNE PLAZA
MARLOW

Glaze Restaurant

Experience superb food and fine wine in Crowne Plaza Marlow's stylish Glaze Restaurant, awarded an AA Rosette for culinary excellence.

Glaze Restaurant offers contemporary, eclectic cuisine in a great atmosphere, with floor-to-ceiling windows providing stunning and uninterrupted views over the landscaped grounds and lake.
Choose from the creative seasonal modern British À La Carte menu or the new authentic Indian menu.

The Splendid Afternoon Teas are also highly recommended.
Whether you are looking to enjoy an intimate meal for two or simply meet a few friends for cocktails on the lawns, we've got the perfect environment for you.

To make a reservation please contact: Glaze Restaurant
T: 01628 496 800   E: events1@cpmarlow.co.uk
W: www.cpmarlow.co.uk/dine
Crowne Plaza Marlow, Fieldhouse Lane, Marlow, SL7 1GJ

STOKE POGES

MAP 6, SU98

Humphry's at Stoke Park

◉◉◉ MODERN BRITISH *V*

01753 717171 | Park Road, SL2 4PG

www.stokepark.com

Innovative cooking amid Georgian magnificence

The luxuriant acres of Stoke Park were turned into Britain's first country club in 1908, the domed and pillared mansion house at its centre surveying some of the grandest golf the nation had to offer. Since then, the place has played host to pro-am tournaments and rock concerts, as well as providing locations for British cinema from James Bond to Bridget Jones. The interiors are splendidly preserved, particularly in the magnificent marble-pillared, extravagantly corniced and deep-piled dining room, arrayed in sunny golds and pastel yellow and named in honour of Humphry Repton, who created the gardens.

It's a grand showcase for the cooking of Chris Wheeler, a confident and inspired practitioner whose work stands out from the crowd in innovative dishes that mobilise the full range of contemporary technique, while maintaining respect for the prime materials. That's clear from the

"It's a grand showcase for the cooking of Chris Wheeler"

off in an opener of confit salmon boosted with teriyaki, lime-pickled cucumber and toasted peanuts. The rabbit terrine may seem more mainstream, but its accompaniments of mustard seed-pickled carrots, prune and Armagnac purée and cumin crackers lift it to a higher level. Main courses are built on impeccable prime materials, treated both with respect and with inventive energy. A workout of top-grade pork offers precisely cooked and deeply flavoured loin, belly and cheek, together with home-made black pudding, choucroute, houmous, charred baby gem lettuce and a punchy barbecue sauce to

bring it all to life. If you can be tempted away from the meaty dishes, another winner might be a perfect balancing act of turbot, gently poached in almond milk and teamed with crab risotto and roasted almond beurre blanc. To finish, Valrhona's Dulcey chocolate provides the foundations of a creamy délice matched with salted caramel, caramelised pecans and the acidic lift of yogurt sorbet.

Chef Chris Wheeler
Seats 50, Private dining 146
Closed 24–26 December, 1st week in January
Parking 400
Notes No children under 12 years at dinner

STOKE POGES
MAP 6, SU98

Humphry's at Stoke Park
◉◉◉ MODERN BRITISH **V**
See pages 50-51

TAPLOW
MAP 6, SU98

Berry's Restaurant and Terrace
◉ CLASSIC BRITISH
01628 670056 | Taplow House Hotel, Berry Hill,
SL6 0DA
www.taplowhouse.com
The original Elizabethan manor was destroyed by fire, so today's house is a handsome piece of Georgian architecture instead, with suitably formal public rooms. The elegant Berry's Restaurant looks over the six acres of landscaped grounds, with huge French doors opening onto the terrace.

Chef Kostas Kritikos **Seats** 40, Private dining 86
Open All Year **Prices from** S £9, M £21, D £8 **Parking** 40
Notes Vegetarian dishes, Children welcome

The Cliveden Dining Room
◉◉◉ MODERN BRITISH **V**
01628 668561 | Cliveden Estate, SL6 0JF
www.clivedenhouse.co.uk
Dripping with a history of high society scandal and lording it over a whopping 376-acres of National Trust estate, Cliveden belongs unquestionably in the premier league of England's stately homes. The dining experience is pretty special too, in an impeccably elegant, swagged and chandeliered restaurant with shimmering views over parterre gardens to the Thames. Paul O'Neill's dazzling cooking is more than a match for this luxurious setting. There are vegan and vegetarian menus as well as the standard à la carte, from which you might choose a perfectly-timed autumn truffle risotto, or English asparagus soup, followed by wild garlic gnocchi with peas and broad beans, or a deceptively simple dish of Jurassic Coast rose veal, with sweetbreads, carrot and black garlic. There's nowhere to hide here – so quality ingredients and sound technique are essential. At dessert, a pear soufflé with pear compôte and vanilla bean ice cream is a delightfully presented, elegant dish.

Chef Paul O'Neill **Seats** 78, Private dining 60 **Open** All Year **Prices from** S £15, M £25, D £12 **Parking** 60
Notes Children welcome

WADDESDON
MAP 11, SP71

The Five Arrows
◉◉ MODERN BRITISH
01296 651727 | High Street, HP18 0JE
www.waddesdon.org.uk
Part of the Rothschild Estate, this small Victorian hotel stands at the gates of Waddesdon Manor but has none of the airs and graces of the grand French château-style stately home. The relaxed restaurant sports a smart, contemporary look with wine-related prints on the walls.

Open All Year

WOOBURN
MAP 6, SU98

Chequers Inn
◉◉ BRITISH, FRENCH
01628 529575 | Kiln Lane, Wooburn Common, HP10 0JQ
www.chequers-inn.com
A 17th-century former coaching inn, there's no denying that the Chequers has moved with the times. The Anglo-French cooking in its chic and spacious restaurant delivers compelling flavour combinations. Eating out on the sunny patio in summer is a delight.

Chef Pascal Lemoine **Seats** 60, Private dining 60
Open All Year **Prices from** S £6.95, M £13.95, D £7.45
Parking 50 **Notes** Vegetarian dishes, Children welcome

■ CAMBRIDGESHIRE

BARTLOW
MAP 12, TL54

The Three Hills
◉◉ MODERN BRITISH
01223 890500 | Dean Road, CB21 4PW
www.thethreehills.co.uk
The Three Hills is a charming 17th-century, Grade II listed pub with a lovely garden leading down to a river. A collection of wicker bulls' heads on the oak-beamed orangery's white clapboard-style walls are a sign this is a restaurant that reflects its rural location.

Chef Keith Deeks **Seats** 62, Private dining 34
Prices from S £7, M £14, D £7 **Parking** 25
Notes Vegetarian dishes, Children welcome

CAMBRIDGE
MAP 12, TL45

Hotel du Vin Cambridge
◉ FRENCH BISTRO
01223 227330 | 15-19 Trumpington Street, CB2 1QA
www.hotelduvin.com
Hotel du Vin's Cambridge outpost is all reclaimed wooden floors, banquettes, unclothed wooden

tables, candlelight, an open-to-view kitchen and references to wine all around. The place is normally humming, and well-drilled staff deliver authentic, well-executed bistro staples. Good-quality rustic bread is part of the package.

Open All Year

Midsummer House Restaurant

◉◉◉◉◉ MODERN BRITISH V 🥂 NOTABLE WINE LIST

See pages 54-55

See advertisement on page 56

Quy Mill Hotel & Spa, Cambridge

◉◉ MODERN EUROPEAN, BRITISH, FRENCH

01223 293383 | Church Road, Stow-Cum-Quy, CB25 9AF

www.cambridgequymill.co.uk

Situated in the miller's house, and overlooking the waterwheel and mill race, the Mill House Restaurant makes the most of this feature, while putting on a distinctly contemporary country inn look. By night it's an intimate place with open fires, candlelight and cool jazz.

Chef Gavin Murphy **Seats** 48, Private dining 80 **Closed** 25 December **Prices from** S £8, M £18, D £9 **Parking** 90 **Notes** Vegetarian dishes, Children welcome

Restaurant 22

◉◉ MODERN BRITISH V

01223 351880 | 22 Chesterton Road, CB4 3AX

www.restaurant22.co.uk

The converted Victorian townhouse near Jesus Green conceals a discreetly elegant and comfortable dining room in shades of fawn, brown and beige. The monthly-changing set-price menu consists of three courses and a sorbet, and the cooking is distinguished by a lack of unnecessary frill and flounce.

Chef Sam Carter **Seats** 22, Private dining 12 **Closed** 22 September to 1 October, 22-31 December **Prices from** S £9.50, M £18.50, D £9 **Notes** No children under 12 years

ELY
MAP 12, TL58

The Anchor Inn

◉ MODERN BRITISH V

01353 778537 | Bury Lane, Sutton Gault, Sutton, CB6 2BD

www.anchor-inn-restaurant.co.uk

Right out in the sticks, a few miles from Ely, The Anchor was built more than 360 years ago for workers digging the canals that drained the Fens. The heritage of the building looms large when you get inside, with oak panels, quarry tiles and

hefty beams. Although very much a pub (with real ales), the contemporary British food is the star attraction, with the menu packed with regional ingredients.

Chef Ken Walton Whitelock **Seats** 60 **Open** All Year **Parking** 10 **Notes** Children welcome

The Dining Room

◉ MODERN BRITISH

01353 887777 | Poets House, 40-44 St Mary's Street, CB7 4EY

www.poetshouse.uk.com

The Dining Room restaurant at Poets House in the centre of Ely offers a good selection of seasonal dishes using fresh and locally sourced ingredients. The smart dining space is beautifully decorated in shades of grey right down to the softly padded chairs.

Open All Year

FORDHAM
MAP 12, TL67

The White Pheasant

◉◉ BRITISH, EUROPEAN

01638 720414 | 21 Market Street, CB7 5LQ

www.whitepheasant.com

The White Pheasant is a modern foodie pub with simply decorated interior, log fires and plain wood tables, but chef-proprietor Calvin Holland's cooking sets it a cut above the average. The kitchen sources the very best materials from local producers.

Open All Year

HINXTON
MAP 12, TL44

The Red Lion Inn

◉ CONTEMPORARY BRITISH

01799 530601 | 32 High Street, CB10 1QY

www.redlionhinxton.co.uk

With its timeless rustic cosiness, the timbered Tudor Red Lion's bar is a great spot for classic pub grub, but seekers of contemporary British cuisine head for the airy, oak-raftered restaurant, where there's an eclectic carte pitched just right for the kitchen's ambitions.

Chef Jiri Wolker **Seats** 60 **Open** All Year **Prices from** S £6, M £12, D £6.50 **Parking** 43 **Notes** Vegetarian dishes, Children welcome

Midsummer House Restaurant

⊚⊚⊚⊚⊚ **MODERN BRITISH** ꝟ⬛ NOTABLE WINE LIST
01223 369299 | Midsummer Common, CB4 1HA
www.midsummerhouse.co.uk

Beautiful, confident cooking in an elegant Victorian villa

As Midsummer House forges ahead into its third decade, Daniel Clifford's elegant, sophisticated modern British cooking continues to go from strength to strength. The comfortable Victorian villa stands with its back to the Cam and looks out on the grazing cows of Midsummer Common from the front. The sunny conservatory dining room is the perfect combination of formal and informal, smart in slate and charcoal, with starched white linen and a calm, friendly atmosphere. A window to the kitchen opens onto the cheffy action, where Clifford, along with head chef Mark Abbott and their intensely focused team, are busy constructing precise, thoughtful dishes delivered via an eight-course tasting menu and, from Wednesdays to Saturdays, a lunch menu of a mere three courses.

The somewhat terse menu descriptions belie the complexity of the food, where

> "... where every ingredient has been carefully considered and is beautiful to look at – this is eating elevated to its highest level"

every ingredient has been carefully considered and is beautiful to look at – this is eating elevated to its highest level. Seasonal flavours are spot on, and a meal might begin with Jerusalem artichoke and chicken consommé, enhanced with mushroom, sunflower seeds and winter truffle, before moving on to a palate-priming salad of new season onions with pear, elderberry, and onion sorbet. Things get richer with compositions like confit chicken oysters, cockles, cuttlefish and sea herbs, and you might follow that with suckling pig, the belly crisp, the cheek glazed and matched with carrot and ginger.

Another winner is a perfectly balanced dish starring a superb Scottish scallop, its sweetness contrasted against stuffed leek, potato and truffle.

Next up, a richly satisfying combination of Anjou pigeon, the leg given hoisin treatment, with a salad of salt-baked beetroot, walnut and blue cheese. Lemon posset might follow, teamed with olive oil cake, mint and black olive tuile, then the coriander white chocolate dome with coconut and mango and snowy jasmine rice is a delicate, exotic finale.

Chef Daniel Clifford
Seats 45, Private dining 12
Closed 2 weeks Christmas to New Year

See advertisement on page 56

MIDSUMMER HOUSE

Midsummer House is located in the heart of historic Cambridge. This Victorian Villa encapsulates Daniel Clifford's vision for culinary perfection and is home to some seriously stylish food.

Daniel Clifford's quest for culinary perfection has taken the restaurant to another level over the past 13 years; his cooking has a modern-focus which is underpinned by classical French technique offering seriously sophisticated food with dishes arriving dressed to thrill.

Upstairs there is a private dining room, and a sophisticated bar and terrace for alfresco drinks with river views. Our private dining room is the perfect location for small weddings, lavish birthday celebrations, simple family gatherings or corporate entertaining.

Midsummer Common, Cambridge CB4 1HA

Tel: 01223 369299 • **Fax:** 01223 302672

Website: www.midsummerhouse.co.uk

Email: reservations@midsummerhouse.co.uk

HUNTINGDON
MAP 12, TL27

The Old Bridge Hotel
◉ MODERN BRITISH ⚑ NOTABLE WINE LIST

01480 424300 | 1 High Street, PE29 3TQ

www.huntsbridge.com

An unusual feature of this ivy-clad, 18th-century townhouse is its own wine shop, where you can fix your own tastings. Biased towards British dishes, the restaurant-and-terrace menu suggests dishes such as baked scallops with samphire; steak pie, buttered Savoy cabbage and triple-cooked chips; pickled mackerel with carrot, caper and cress salad; and treacle sponge with vanilla cream.

Chef Jack Woolner **Seats** 80, Private dining 60 **Open** All Year **Prices from** S £6.95, M £14.95, D £5.95 **Parking** 60 **Notes** Vegetarian dishes, Children welcome

KEYSTON
MAP 11, TL07

Pheasant Inn
◉◉ MODERN BRITISH, EUROPEAN ⚑ NOTABLE WINE LIST

01832 710241 | Loop Road, PE28 0RE

www.thepheasant-keyston.co.uk

Every inch the classic thatched village inn, the Pheasant flaunts its centuries-old pedigree, with simple furniture, welcoming open fires and oak beams. For over 50 years the place has been known for fine food – way before anyone added the gastro prefix to pub – and continues to deal in European-influenced cooking that's full of fresh ideas.

Chef Simon Cadge **Seats** 80, Private dining 30 **Closed** 2-15 January **Prices from** S £5.95, M £11.95, D £6.95 **Parking** 40 **Notes** Vegetarian dishes, Children welcome

MELBOURN
MAP 12, TL34

Sheene Mill
◉◉ MODERN, TRADITIONAL BRITISH

01763 261393 | 39 Station Road, SG8 6DX

www.sheenemill.com

The 16th-century mill house no longer works the River Mel, but the waterway and pond are reminders of its former life. Now, there are glorious gardens, a spa and stylish bedrooms, while the restaurant is watched over by an engaging service team.

Open All Year

PETERBOROUGH
MAP 12, TL19

Bull Hotel
◉ MODERN EUROPEAN, BRITISH

01733 561364 | Westgate, PE1 1RB

www.peelhotels.co.uk

From the outside, this 17th-century former coaching inn displays its period credentials but there's a contemporary swagger once you get inside, not least in the brasserie-style restaurant out back. With cream-painted brickwork high-back chairs and darkwood tables, the vibe is informal and cheerful.

Chef Sam Carson **Seats** 80, Private dining 200 **Open** All Year **Prices from** S £5.95, M £15.95, D £5.95 **Parking** 100 **Notes** Vegetarian dishes, Children welcome

ST NEOTS
MAP 12, TL16

The George Hotel & Brasserie
◉◉ MODERN BRITISH

01480 812300 | High Street, Buckden, PE19 5XA

www.thegeorgebuckden.com

The Furbank family brought this old coaching inn back to life in 2003 by creating a cool and contemporary venue and respecting the integrity of the old building. The menu delivers feel-good flavours based on quality ingredients (including some stuff they grow themselves).

Chef Benaissa El Akil **Seats** 60, Private dining 30 **Open** All Year **Prices from** S £6.95, M £11.95, D £6.95 **Parking** 25 **Notes** Vegetarian dishes, Children welcome

STILTON
MAP 12, TL18

Bell Inn Hotel
◉◉ MODERN BRITISH **V**

01733 241066 | Great North Road, PE7 3RA

www.thebellstilton.co.uk

Dating from 1642, this rambling village coaching inn has a contemporary outlook when it comes to cooking. The kitchen turns out bright ideas displaying a good balance of flavours. Open with chicken liver parfait, mango chutney and toasted brioche before Moroccan lamb loin, harissa-spiced couscous, bok choi and red pepper purée.

Chef Morgan de Smidt **Seats** 60, Private dining 20 **Closed** 25 December, bank holidays **Prices from** S £9, M £15.50, D £8 **Parking** 30 **Notes** Children welcome

WHITTLESFORD
MAP 12, TL44

The Red Lion at Whittlesford Bridge
@ MODERN, TRADITIONAL BRITISH

01223 832047 | Station Road, CB22 4NL
www.redlionwhittlesfordbridge.com
Just off the M11 outside Cambridge, The Red Lion can trace its history back to the early Edwards, as is evidenced by its low-slung timbered façade and beamed interiors. Winter warmth radiates from the brick fireplaces, and staff are a model of friendly efficiency.

Open All Year

WISBECH
MAP 12, TF40

Crown Lodge Hotel
@ MODERN, TRADITIONAL

01945 773391 | Downham Road, Outwell, PE14 8SE
www.thecrownlodgehotel.co.uk
A modern hotel kitted out to host conferences and meetings, Crown Lodge is a useful local resource. The flexible approach to dining means you can go for simple things like fish and chips or a burger, but there's also a more ambitious carte.

Closed 25–26 December and 1 January

◼ CHESHIRE

ALDERLEY EDGE
MAP 16, SJ87

Alderley Edge Hotel
@@ MODERN, CLASSIC BRITISH *V*

01625 583033 | Macclesfield Road, SK9 7BJ
www.alderleyedgehotel.com
The wealthy industrialist who built this hilltop Victorian Gothic pile certainly bagged pole position for its views over lush grounds, gardens and the countryside. The kitchen doesn't stint on top-class ingredients and its modern British dishes are well rehearsed and delivered.

Chef Colin Starkey **Seats** 80, Private dining 120 **Open** All Year **Prices from** S £6.50, M £14.50, D £6.50 **Parking** 82 **Notes** Children welcome

ALSAGER
MAP 15, SJ75

Stables *NEW*
@ BRITISH

01270 884000 | Manor House Hotel, Audley Road, ST7 2QQ
www.manorhousealsager.co.uk
Part of the Manor House Hotel close to Crewe and Stoke-on-Trent, this split-level restaurant is packed with original features including oak beams and stone fireplaces. Try the pan-fried sea bass, dill crushed new potatoes, sprouting broccoli and sauce vièrge but leave room for the rhubarb gin trifle.

Chef Andrew Keeling **Seats** Private dining 20 **Open** All Year **Notes** Vegetarian dishes, Children welcome

BROXTON
MAP 15, SJ45

Carden Park Hotel, Golf Resort & Spa
@ MODERN BRITISH *V*

01829 731000 | Carden Park, CH3 9DQ
www.cardenpark.co.uk
A country estate with a Jacobean core, Welsh mountain views and a three-acre vineyard. The cooking style encompasses Asian-style red mullet terrine with wakame seaweed and sesame salad; and pan-roasted chicken breast and leg crépinette with hay-smoked mash and roasted cauliflower. Chocolate mousse, salted caramel and milk ice cream is in there too.

Chef Graham Tinsley MBE **Seats** 300, Private dining 80 **Parking** 500 **Notes** Children welcome

BURWARDSLEY
MAP 15, SJ55

The Pheasant Inn
@ BRITISH, EUROPEAN

01829 770434 | Higher Burwardsley, CH3 9PF
www.thepheasantinn.co.uk
Midway along the Sandstone Trail in rural Cheshire, the far-reaching views from The Pheasant stretch as far as the Welsh hills. Pub classics done well rub shoulders with more contemporary ideas on their crowd-pleasing menu. Steamed Menai mussels followed by Italian-influenced pork saltimbocca then local Cheshire Farm ice cream is one way to go.

Chef Gareth John **Seats** 120 **Open** All Year **Prices from** S £5.95, M £12.50, D £5.50 **Parking** 60 **Notes** Vegetarian dishes, Children welcome

CHESTER
MAP 15, SJ46

Brasserie ABode
🏵️🏵️ MODERN CLASSIC FRENCH *V*
01244 405820 | Grosvenor Road, CH1 2DJ
www.brasserieabode.co.uk/chester
The Cheshire outpost of the ABode hotel group occupies a shiny modern rotunda overlooking Chester racecourse. Its restaurant is on the fifth floor, with stellar views over the castle and lush countryside. There's a contemporary finish, with stylish fixtures and rather glam light fittings.

Chef Sean Sutton **Seats** 90, Private dining 16 **Open** All Year **Prices from** S £7, M £15, D £6.50 **Parking** 36 **Notes** Children welcome

La Brasserie at The Chester Grosvenor & Spa
🏵️🏵️ MODERN EUROPEAN *V*
01244 324024 | Eastgate, CH1 1LT
www.chestergrosvenor.com
La Brasserie offers commendable support to its superstar sibling the Simon Radley restaurant. With all the swagger of an authentique Parisian outfit, it has black-leather banquettes, shimmering brass and a giant hand-painted skylight, plus a menu that builds confidently on classic ideas.

Chef Simon Radley, Gareth Jones **Seats** 80 **Closed** 25 December **Prices from** S £7.95, M £16.95, D £6.75 **Notes** Children welcome

Chef's Table
🏵️🏵️ MODERN BRITISH
01244 403040 | Music Hall Passage, CH1 2EU
www.chefstablechester.co.uk
At the end of a narrow alley between a dress shop and a coffee house, Chef's Table is a quirky, fun and chatty place for some enterprising modern cooking with bold flavours and plenty of veggie dishes in the mix. The setting fits the mood with its minimal good looks, local artworks and views of the kitchen action.

Chef Liam McKay **Seats** 26 **Closed** Christmas and New Year **Prices from** S £5.75, M £14.95, D £6.50 **Notes** Vegetarian dishes, Children welcome

King's Grill Restaurant
🏵️ BRITISH
01244 305000 | Hallmark Hotel Chester The Queen, City Road, CH1 3AH
www.hallmarkhotels.co.uk/hotels/The-Queen-Chester
This Victorian railway hotel was given an eye-popping makeover, with much use of loudly patterned fabrics. There are three restaurants, the principal one being a sleek space with kitchen views. The style is brasserie, with quality ingredients treated with respect in vigorously flavoured dishes.

Open All Year

Palm Court
🏵️ MEDITERRANEAN, EUROPEAN
01244 570560 | Grosvenor Pulford Hotel & Spa, Wrexham Road, Pulford, CH4 9DG
www.grosvenorpulfordhotel.co.uk/gallery/palm-court
The sprawling red-brick hotel has a swish spa, luxe bedrooms, and pretty gardens, but the main dining option Palm Court stands out with lots of palm trees and greenery. Expect modern brasserie food.

Chef Richard Scutt **Seats** 160, Private dining 200 **Open** All Year **Prices from** S £6.25, M £13.95, D £6.50 **Parking** 200 **Notes** Vegetarian dishes, Children welcome

Restaurant 1539
🏵️ MODERN BRITISH
01244 304611 | Chester Race Company Limited, The Racecourse, CH1 2LY
www.restaurant1539.co.uk
Part of the Chester Racecourse complex, 1539 was given a cool half-million's worth of upgrade in 2014. The full-drop windows of the restaurant are still a major feature, and if your heart isn't given to equestrianism, swivel round for an ambient view into the kitchen.

Open All Year

Simon Radley at The Chester Grosvenor

@@@@ MODERN FRENCH 𝐕 NOTABLE WINE LIST

01244 324024 | Eastgate, CH1 1LT
www.chestergrosvenor.com

The hotel has a prime spot within the ancient Roman walls of the city, next to the historic Eastgate Clock, and with its Simon Radley restaurant, The Chester Grosvenor is the undoubted epicentre of the city's culinary activity. The opulent dining room is rich with shades of gold and cream, with plush chairs to sink into, and a smart and well organised team on hand to service your needs. The dress code is smart, but this is the 21st century, and the mood is suitably buoyant. The fixed-price menu and eight-course tasting menus (vegetarians get their own bespoke version) offer up Mr Radley's creative take on contemporary British and European cookery, with superlative ingredients and flavour combinations that are nearly always compelling. Take an idea of beautifully caramelised scallops and tender suckling pig, with wild nettles and gooseberries adding layers of sharp and sweet, or another seafood-meat pairing, with braised turbot and chicken wings, wee dumplings and blackened artichokes. A lobster and fennel roll is the star of a halibut main course (with poached mussels and saffron sauce), while two might share Edge's beef sirloin, smoked on Douglas Fir needles. There's just as much skill and modern pizzazz in desserts such as the en coque – a chocolate and apple ensemble that is something to behold. The wine list is an epic journey into some of the world's best vintages.

Chef Simon Radley, Ray Booker **Seats** 45, Private dining 14 **Closed** 25 December **Notes** No children under 12 years

The Sticky Walnut

@@ MODERN EUROPEAN

01244 400400 | 11 Charles Street, CH2 3AZ
www.stickywalnut.com

The Sticky Walnut is spread over two floors, with chunky wooden tables, blackboards and an open kitchen. With cracking desserts like a deconstructed lime cheesecake with pecan butter biscuits and chocolate sorbet, this is a kitchen that delivers real impact.

Closed 25–26 December

CONGLETON
MAP 16, SJ86

Pecks

🏵 MODERN BRITISH

01260 275161 | Newcastle Road, Moreton, CW12 4SB

www.pecksrest.co.uk

Walls painted purple and grey-green, provide the backdrop in the new mezzanine space for 'Plat du Jour' lunches and 'Dinner at Eight', a seven-course 'theatrical cavalcade of culinary delights'. Dishes to look out for – rabbit tagliatelle, baked goats' cheese, roast loin of lamb, baked plaice fillet and spiced baked aubergine lasagne.

Chef Les Wassall **Seats** 110, Private dining 36 **Closed** 25-30 December **Prices from** S £7.50, M £12.50, D £8 **Parking** 30 **Notes** Vegetarian dishes, Children welcome

See advertisement opposite

CREWE
MAP 15, SJ75

Crewe Hall

🏵 MODERN EUROPEAN

01270 253333 | Weston Road, CW1 6UZ

www.qhotels.co.uk

Jacobean Crewe Hall is reminiscent of a grand stately home with magnificent interiors, but there's nothing stuffy about it, and that especially goes for the Brasserie, housed in a modern wing of the building, with its open-plan layout and buzzy atmosphere.

Chef Dion Jones **Seats** 120 **Open** All Year **Parking** 500 **Notes** Vegetarian dishes, Children welcome

KNUTSFORD
MAP 15, SJ77

Cottons Hotel & Spa

🏵 ITALIAN

01565 650333 | Manchester Road, WA16 0SU

www.cottonshotel.co.uk/food-drink

A large, modern hotel at the edge of town, Cottons' menu is an appealing Mediterranean brasserie-style package. Try the lemon and black pepper queenie scallops with chilli mayonnaise; chicken liver parfait, Armagnac prunes, baby leeks, pickled mushrooms and toasted brioche.

Chef Adrian Sedden **Seats** 80, Private dining 30 **Open** All Year **Prices from** S £4.95, M £14.95, D £4.95 **Parking** 120 **Notes** Vegetarian dishes, Children welcome

Mere Court Hotel & Conference Centre

🏵 MODERN MEDITERRANEAN

01565 831000 | Warrington Road, Mere, WA16 0RW

www.merecourt.co.uk

Mere Court Hotel has bags of appeal. Dating from the turn of the 20th century, this imposing Arts and Crafts house has plenty of period swagger. The oak-panelled Arboretum Restaurant is an elegant spot with lake views, and is the setting for upbeat European-inspired cooking.

Open All Year

The Mere Golf Resort & Spa

🏵🏵 INTERNATIONAL

01565 830155 | Chester Road, Mere, WA16 6LJ

themereresort.co.uk

The Mere is a must for Cheshire's fairways fans, plus it's a good location for accomplished brasserie dining in the open-plan Browns. Linen tablecloths and relatively formal service are slightly at odds with the overall tone, but the food makes some good modern statements.

Chef Mark Fletcher **Seats** 76, Private dining 60 **Open** All Year **Prices from** S £5, M £18.50, D £7 **Parking** 400 **Notes** Vegetarian dishes, Children welcome

LYMM
MAP 15, SJ68

The Church Green British Grill

🏵🏵 MODERN BRITISH

01925 752068 | Higher Lane, WA13 0AP

www.thechurchgreen.co.uk

Chef-patron Aiden Byrne will be a familiar face to *MasterChef* fans, and his focus is on traditional British grill cooking, with excellent prime materials and touches of modern technique. On the menu might be a serving of home-made black pudding with a crisply poached egg (quite a feat) and caper and rocket salad, and comfort-pud finales like Bakewell tart with black cherry and Amaretto ice cream.

Chef Aiden Byrne **Seats** 50 **Closed** 25 December **Parking** 25 **Notes** Vegetarian dishes, Children welcome

MOTTRAM ST ANDREW
MAP 16, SJ87

Mottram Hall

🏵🏵 MODERN BRITISH

01625 828135 | Wilmslow Road, SK10 4QT

www.qhotels.co.uk/mottramhall

A dapper 18th-century pile, Mottram Hall's attractions stretch as far as golf, pampering in the spa, and modern country-house dining in the classy Carrington Grill. The food keeps step with the times and is well prepared from high-quality raw materials.

Open All Year

NANTWICH

Rookery Hall Hotel & Spa

◉◉ MODERN BRITISH

01270 610016 | Main Road, Worleston, CW5 6DQ

www.handpickedhotels.co.uk/rookeryhall

Rookery Hall was built in 1816 by a Jamaican sugar plantation owner whose wealth is evident in the sumptuous interior. Cooking-wise, sound technique and accuracy are hallmarks. Try breast of Yorkshire grouse with creamed potato, bread purée, cabbage and bacon fricassée, watercress cream and wood sorrel.

Chef Mark Walker **Seats** 90, Private dining 160 **Closed** 31 December **Prices from** S £7, M £18, D £7 **Parking** 100 **Notes** Vegetarian dishes, Children welcome

PECKFORTON

1851 Restaurant at Peckforton Castle

◉◉◉ MODERN BRITISH *V*

01829 260930 | Stone House Lane, CW6 9TN

www.peckfortoncastle.co.uk

Peckforton may look like a medieval castle, but the clue to its true vintage lies in the restaurant's name. Conjured from the imagination of a wealthy Victorian gent, this imposing building, with its turrets and crenellations, still does justice to the lofty ambition of its originator. It's 21st-century incarnation as a hotel and wedding venue features pampering treatments, luxe bedrooms and a host of outdoor activities, and the 1851 Restaurant has made it a dining destination, too. The stylish dining room matches the modern thinking in the kitchen. Chef Jason Hodnett has a knack for coaxing out the max from flavours; in an attractively presented starter of duck – confit leg, seared breast, served with Williams pear – or in a visually stunning main course of hake with squid ink linguine. A clean and simple dessert of meringue with refreshing flavours of lemon and passionfruit closes the show.

Chef Jason Hodnett **Seats** 65, Private dining 160 **Open** All Year **Parking** 300 **Notes** No children under 16 years

PUDDINGTON

Macdonald Craxton Wood Hotel

◉ MODERN BRITISH

0151 347 4000 | Parkgate Road, Ledsham, CH66 9PB

www.macdonaldhotels.co.uk/craxtonwood

Set in 27 acres of peaceful woodland, this grand-looking hotel near Chester is stylish and relaxed.

Muted colours and dining chairs in striped fabric add an elegance to the restaurant. It's here that the Josper grill comes into its own for main-course meat dishes.

Open All Year

SANDIWAY

Nunsmere Hall Hotel

◉◉ BRITISH, EUROPEAN

01606 889100 | Tarporley Road, Oakmere, CW8 2ES

www.nunsmere.co.uk

A delightful country house with its own lake. Start with a drink in the Captain's Bar, then glide in state to a berth in the Crystal dining room, where pictures of polo players adorn the walls. The cooking keeps things firmly anchored in European tradition.

Chef Mark Burke **Seats** 60, Private dining 120 **Parking** 120 **Notes** Vegetarian dishes, Children welcome

TARPORLEY

Macdonald Portal Hotel Golf & Spa

◉ MODERN

01829 734100 | Cobblers Cross Lane, CW6 0DJ

www.macdonaldhotels.co.uk/the portal

The Portal's restaurant has panoramic views of its golf courses and the Cheshire countryside beyond. Comfortable leather banquette seating and unclothed tables make for an unfussy look, and the cooking follows suit with classic steaks and grills supporting forays into the modern British style.

Open All Year

WARMINGHAM

The Bear's Paw

◉ MODERN EUROPEAN, BRITISH

01270 526317 | School Lane, CW11 3QN

www.thebearspaw.co.uk

A Victorian pub given a modern makeover inside, with lots of light wood, and library shelves in the dining room. Local farmers supply the kitchen with quality north-western produce, with cheeses and ice creams also sourced from within a tight radius.

Chef Scott Cunningham **Seats** 150 **Open** All Year **Prices from** S £5.95, M £11.95, D £5.25 **Parking** 75 **Notes** Vegetarian dishes, Children welcome

WARRINGTON
MAP 15, SJ68

The Park Royal
◉ MODERN BRITISH

01925 730706 | Stretton Road, Stretton, WA4 4NS
www.qhotels.co.uk

The opulent country hotel at Stretton began life more humbly in late Georgian times as the vicarage for nearby St Matthew's, but has grown in grandeur with the years. Its expansive restaurant, Topiary in the Park, takes its name from the sculpted greenery on view.

Chef Andrew Richards **Seats** 200 **Open** All Year
Prices from S £6.95, M £14, D £7.50 **Parking** 400
Notes Vegetarian dishes, Children welcome

WILMSLOW
MAP 16, SJ88

The Stanneylands
◉ BRITISH

01625 525225 | Stanneylands Road, SK9 4EY
www.stanneylands.co.uk

Despite being over the county border in Cheshire, Wilmslow has long been a gentrified refuge from nearby Manchester and the airport, which makes Stanneylands ideal for those seeking an escape from urban bustle. This stylish country hotel delivers a gently modern repertoire.

Open All Year

■ CORNWALL & ISLES OF SCILLY

BODMIN
MAP 2, SX06

Trehellas House Hotel & Restaurant
◉ TRADITIONAL

01208 72700 | Washaway, PL30 3AD
www.trehellashouse.co.uk

Trehellas House is a modern country hotel, its rooms spread between an inn and coach house. Its beamed, slate-flagged dining room makes a homely setting for bright Cornish cooking mixing innovation and tradition. Proximity to Camel Valley makes that vineyard's benchmark fizz the obvious aperitif.

Open All Year

BOSCASTLE
MAP 2, SX09

The Wellington
◉◉ MODERN BRITISH, FRENCH

01840 250202 | The Harbour, PL35 0AQ
www.wellingtonhotelboscastle.com

There's a traditional bar with real ales and blackboard menus and a charming restaurant with chandeliers at this 16th-century coaching inn with a castellated tower. The kitchen sources its materials from within the county and serves bright, modern ideas with their roots in the classics.

Open All Year

BRYHER (ISLES OF SCILLY)
MAP 2, SV81

Hell Bay
◉◉◉ MODERN BRITISH *V*

01720 422947 | TR23 0PR
www.hellbay.co.uk

Not nearly as alarming as it sounds, Hell Bay is actually an idyllic secluded cove embraced by benign gorse-laden hillocks. Reached by ferry from St Mary's or Tresco, tiny Bryher is small enough to get around on foot, and the unassuming white hotel is the perfect spot to set off from. There is much to love in its Cornish art-filled rooms and sea views, while on the food front Richard Kearsley's assured, confident cooking is a major draw. You're in the right place when it comes to fish and seafood, whether it's treacle-cured salmon with lemongrass and ginger purée, compressed watermelon and toasted sesame, or mains like roasted fillet of wild sea bass with confit fennel, saffron velouté and brown shrimps. There are thoroughbred meats too, with slow-braised blade of local Tresco beef, soft truffle polenta, crispy onion and red wine jus, while for dessert maybe plump for the passionfruit soufflé with coconut sorbet.

Chef Richard Kearsley **Seats** 70, Private dining 12
Closed 14 October to 16 March **Prices from** S £7.50,
M £12, D £7 **Parking** 5 **Notes** Children welcome

CALLINGTON
MAP 3, SX36

Langmans Restaurant
◉◉ MODERN BRITISH

01579 384933 | 3 Church Street, PL17 7RE
www.langmansrestaurant.co.uk

This restaurant offers finely-crafted regional food in an unassuming venue between the moorlands of Bodmin and Dart. A digestive pause will do nicely before Cornish and West Country cheeses appear, prior to two desserts. A chocolate version of the B52 cocktail shot might precede crumble.

Open All Year

Brasserie on the Bay

◉◉ MODERN MEDITERRANEAN, BRITISH

01326 312707 | St Michaels Resort,
Gyllyngvase Beach, Seafront, TR11 4NB
www.stmichaelshotel.co.uk/dine/brasserie-on-
the-bay
There's a stylishly upmarket vibe at this seaside
hotel with its hip-looking bar and nautically
themed restaurant. The panoramic view is
inspiring, jaw dropping even. The kitchen buys
materials solely from local producers, and its
passion for cooking is palpable in well-executed
modern dishes with a hint of the classics.

Open All Year

Falmouth Hotel

◉ BRITISH

01326 312671 | Castle Beach, TR11 4NZ
www.falmouthhotel.com
Nothing becomes a seaside town like a great
white hotel, lording it over the waters from the
headland. The elegant dining room has sweeping
views over the bay and a menu that works its way
round the seasonal calendar in both British and
international modes.

Open All Year

The Greenbank Hotel

◉◉ MODERN BRITISH

01326 312440 | Harbourside, TR11 2SR
www.greenbank-hotel.co.uk
The house that became the Greenbank Hotel has
occupied this spot since 1640, and in 2015 its
restaurant received a top-to-toe facelift. The
head chef delivers a please-all roster of classics
and modern dishes with Cornish produce as a
starting point for his menus.

Chef Nick Hodges **Seats** 90, Private dining 20 **Open** All
Year **Prices from** S £6, M £14, D £7 **Parking** 60
Notes Vegetarian dishes, Children welcome

Merchants Manor

◉◉◉ MODERN BRITISH

01326 312734 | 1 Weston Manor, TR11 4AJ
www.merchantsmanor.com
Built in 1913 for a local brewing family, Merchants
Manor, a white-fronted house on a hill, retains a
pleasingly historic air, with its lofty-ceilinged
interiors preserving much of their Edwardian
splendour. Bright interiors create a cheery

ambience and the Rastella dining room adds to
an all-round feel of well-being with white linen
and vintage candles. Local suppliers buttress the
menus, as does the hard-working wood-fired
oven – affectionately nicknamed Bertha – and
what emerges is a roster of smartly presented,
modern dishes full of precision and inspiration.
To start, there could be confit Newlyn mackerel
with Alexanders and apple, followed by locally
landed monkfish with porcini and potato, or rare
breed pork cheek teamed with marmalade and
brassicas. Steaks from the grill are a good bet
too, served with ale-pickled mushrooms, onion
rings and smoked tomato BBQ sauce. Finish,
perhaps, with Milk and Honey, an assemblage of
milk sorbet, Cornish honey, lemon posset and
caramelised white chocolate.

Chef Hylton Espey **Seats** 64, Private dining 20 **Open** All
Year **Prices from** S £8, M £17, D £8 **Parking** 30
Notes Vegetarian dishes, Children welcome

The Pendennis Restaurant

◉◉ MODERN BRITISH

01326 313042 | The Royal Duchy Hotel, Cliff Road,
TR11 4NX
www.royalduchy.co.uk
With palm trees framing splendid sea views
across the bay from its alfresco terrace, the
Royal Duchy Hotel certainly has that Riviera
touch, and its Pendennis Restaurant makes the
most of that glorious setting. Done out with
traditional elegance, it's a fitting backdrop for
confident, gently contemporary cooking. Simple
intuitive combinations are the style.

Open All Year

See advertisement opposite

Penmorvah Manor

◉ CLASSIC BRITISH

01326 250277 | Budock Water, TR11 5ED
www.penmorvah.co.uk
The stone-built manor house has stood in its six
acres of wooded gardens near Falmouth since
1872. The atmosphere is white-linened gentility,
the culinary style is modern brasserie, with well
turned-out dishes making an impact on both eye
and palate.

Chef Mark Firth **Seats** 60, Private dining 60 **Open** All
Year **Prices from** S £6, M £12, D £4.50 **Parking** 100
Notes Vegetarian dishes, Children welcome

FOWEY
MAP 2, SX15

Fowey Hall
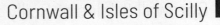 BRITISH *V*

01726 833866 | Hanson Drive, PL23 1ET
www.foweyhallhotel.co.uk

Writer Kenneth Grahame was a regular visitor to this grand Victorian pile overlooking Fowey Estuary – it was the inspiration behind Toad Hall in *The Wind in The Willows*. The wood-panelled restaurant showcases the unpretentious food, made with the best ingredients sourced from the region.

Chef Wesley Pratt **Seats** 36, Private dining 20
Prices from S £8.50, M £21, D £8.50 **Parking** 36
Notes Children welcome

GOLANT
MAP 2, SX15

Cormorant Hotel & Restaurant
 MODERN EUROPEAN

01726 833426 | PL23 1LL
www.cormoranthotel.co.uk

The Cormorant occupies a roost above the estuary, as a seat on the sunny terrace confirms.

A pastel-hued dining room is the setting for Mediterranean-style cooking with Cornish produce in evidence throughout. At dessert, why not go Caribbean with pineapple Tatin and coconut ice cream?

Open All Year

HELSTON
MAP 2, SW62

New Yard Restaurant
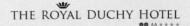 BRITISH

01326 221595 | Trelowarren Estate, Mawgan, TR12 6AF
www.newyardrestaurant.co.uk

On Cornwall's stunning Lizard peninsula, the New Yard Restaurant is at the heart of the historic Trelowarren Estate. Occupying the former stable yard, the distinctive interior sports a chequered floor, arched windows and bare wooden tables, while the open-plan kitchen produces punchy, seasonal cooking.

Chef Jeffery Robinson **Seats** 50, Private dining 20
Closed January **Prices from** S £7, M £13, D £7
Parking 20 **Notes** Vegetarian dishes, Children welcome

HUGH TOWN (THE ISLES OF SCILLY)   *MAP 2, SV91*
Spirit *NEW*
◉ MODERN BRITISH *V*
01720 422316 | St Mary's Hall Hotel, Church Street, TR21 0JR
www.stmaryshallhotel.co.uk
Local sourcing is key at the Spirit restaurant in this handsome townhouse hotel set in charming Mediterranean gardens. Served in a gently updated setting, rare breed meats come from the owners' farm, while fish and seafood are hauled in daily by local boats to form the bedrock of carefully prepared, fuss-free dishes.

Chef Ben Hingston, Phil Fallows **Seats** 70 **Closed** 18 October to 15 March **Notes** Children welcome

LITTLE PETHERICK   *MAP 2, SW97*
Old Mill Bistro *NEW*
◉ MODERN BRITISH
01841 540388 | PL27 7QT
www.oldmillbistro.co.uk
Set in a 16th-century, former corn mill in a postcard-pretty hamlet, this homely family-run bistro comes with a full complement of beamed and stone-floored character. Service is warm and informed, while the cooking is full of panache, with sharply defined flavours and confident combining of impeccably local and seasonal materials.

LIZARD   *MAP 2, SW71*
Fallowfields *NEW*
◉◉ BRITISH, FRENCH *V*
01326 567500 | Housel Bay Hotel & Restaurant, Housel Cove, TR12 7PG
www.houselbay.com
On the spectacular Lizard peninsula, the granite-built Housel Bay Hotel dates back to Victorian times and the light and airy Fallowfields restaurant boasts stunning Atlantic views. As befits the coastal setting, local fish is a strength here, perhaps in a main of sea bass, tiger prawn, bisque, crab ravioli, cavolo nero and curry oil.

Chef Joseph Fallowfield **Seats** 35, Private dining 16 **Closed** 2 January to 10 February **Parking** 32 **Notes** No children under 8 years

LOOE   *MAP 2, SX25*
Trelaske Hotel & Restaurant
◉◉ MODERN BRITISH
01503 262159 | Polperro Road, PL13 2JS
www.trelaske.co.uk
In a rural location between Looe and Polperro, this small hotel is surrounded by four acres of grounds. Dishes are Intelligently composed to allow flavours to sparkle. Perhaps kick things off with the starter of crabmeat with pink grapefruit and rösti.

Chef Ross Lewin **Seats** 40 **Closed** November to March **Parking** 60 **Notes** Vegetarian dishes, No children under 5 years

LOSTWITHIEL   *MAP 2, SX15*
Asquiths Restaurant
◉◉ MODERN BRITISH
01208 871714 | 19 North Street, PL22 0EF
www.asquithsrestaurant.co.uk
Its black and white decor, smartly set tables and elegant staff create positive impressions of this restaurant opposite the church, where food is taken seriously. Confit duck and beetroot pastilla is teamed with pomegranate molasses and couscous, with an alternative perhaps of kedgeree with a Scotch egg and pea cream. Fish gets a decent showing, maybe a well-timed roast hake fillet, curried cauliflower, a courgette bhaji and potato purée.

Chef Graham Cuthbertson **Seats** 28, Private dining 10 **Closed** Christmas and January **Prices from** S £8, M £17, D £8 **Notes** Vegetarian dishes, Children welcome

LOWER TOWN (THE ISLES OF SCILLY)   *MAP 2, SV91*
Cloudesley Shovell Restaurant
◉◉ MODERN, SEASONAL, SEAFOOD *V*
01720 422368 | Karma St Martin's, TR25 0QW
www.karmastmartins.com
The Karma St Martin's hotel restaurant is named after former Admiral of the Fleet who lost 22 ships off the Scilly coast in a 1707 naval disaster. The seasonally changing menu includes several 'true' catches of the day with whole crab and lobster a speciality. Alfresco dining is available in the summer months.

Chef Nicole Benham Corlette, Mark Taylor, Lucian Branzoiu **Seats** 82, Private dining 40 **Closed** 1 November to Easter **Prices from** S £6.50, M £12.95, D £8.95 **Parking** 10 **Notes** Vegetarian dishes, Children welcome

MAWGAN PORTH
MAP 2, SW86

The Scarlet Hotel
◉◉ MODERN EUROPEAN
01637 861800 | Tredragon Road, TR8 4DQ
www.scarlethotel.co.uk
The Scarlet has impeccable eco credentials, but first and foremost it's about hedonistic pleasures – wining, dining and serious pampering. The kitchen team focuses on the West Country. Dessert of white chocolate mousse is surrounded by honeycomb shell, joined by pistachio cake and griottine cherries.

Chef Mike Francis **Seats** 70, Private dining 20
Closed 2–27 January **Parking** 37 **Notes** Vegetarian dishes, No children

MAWNAN SMITH
MAP 2, SW72

Meudon Hotel
◉ CLASSIC 𝑉
01326 250541 | TR11 5HT
www.meudon.co.uk
Bream Cove Restaurant presents an inviting space amid coastal gardens overlooking Falmouth Bay. The order of the day is modern cooking with a nod to classic cuisine, offering a true flavour of Cornwall and a sound helping of local wines.

Chef Iain McKay **Seats** 75 **Closed** 28 December to January **Prices from** S £8, M £17, D £6 **Parking** 40
Notes Children welcome

MEVAGISSEY
MAP 2, SX04

Trevalsa Court Hotel
◉◉ MODERN BRITISH
01726 842460 | School Hill, Polstreth, PL26 6TH
www.trevalsa-hotel.co.uk
Situated on a clifftop, there is a real sub-tropical feel to this handsome granite and slate house. When the sun shines, a table on the terrace with views across Mevagissey Bay is worth its weight in gold, but the view is special from inside, too.

Closed December to January

MULLION
MAP 2, SW61

Mullion Cove Hotel
◉◉ MODERN BRITISH
01326 240328 | TR12 7EP
www.mullion-cove.co.uk
This solidly built white property on the Lizard Peninsula sits on the clifftop, giving uninterrupted sea and coast views. The kitchen is committed to local suppliers, with day boats providing seafood – an international element is evident in some dishes.

Chef Paul Stephens **Seats** 60, Private dining 20 **Open** All Year **Parking** 45 **Notes** Vegetarian dishes, No children under 8 years

The Restaurant at Polurrian on the Lizard
◉◉ MODERN BRITISH, MEDITERRANEAN 𝑉
01326 240421 | TR12 7EN
www.polurrianhotel.com
This one-time Victorian railway hotel has been reworked in smart contemporary style. From its perch on the cliffs of the Lizard Peninsula, the rather grand restaurant presents those wild, far-reaching coastal views as a backdrop to inventive modern cooking based on tip-top ingredients from local producers.

Chef Charlotte Julian **Seats** 60, Private dining 15
Open All Year **Parking** 35 **Notes** Children welcome

NEWQUAY
MAP 2, SW86

The Samphire Restaurant
◉◉ MODERN BRITISH
01637 872211 | The Headland Hotel and Spa, Fistral Beach, TR7 1EW
www.headlandhotel.co.uk

You'll likely find yourself distracted by the incredible views from The Headland's elegant dining room when you should be perusing the menu – you might even spot dolphins out in the bay. Inside, its smart and sharp – expect crisp linens and formal service.

Open All Year

Paul Ainsworth at No. 6

⊛⊛⊛⊛ **MODERN BRITISH** *V* | NOTABLE WINE LIST

01841 532093 | Padstow Townhouse, 6 Middle Street, PL28 8AP

www.paul-ainsworth.co.uk

Flagship restaurant in a Georgian townhouse

In the centre of this famed foodie town is the flagship of Paul Ainsworth's Cornish flotilla, an imaginatively and elegantly converted Georgian townhouse with three little dining rooms on the ground floor and another upstairs. Striking modern artworks, including a Beth Kerridge sculpture, lend distinction to the spaces, and long-serving staff do their bit to bring a sense of occasion to it all. Many of Ainsworth's dishes, which he tweaks according to season, reflect his research into British culinary heritage, albeit via impeccably modern techniques. Making a transcendent opening is pig's head fritter, a sumptuous crumbed parcel of brawn and capers, served alongside textured Cox's apple, sweetly roasted onion and a cut of subtly smoked eel. Equally inspirational is Jacob's ragu alla bolognese with seaweed butter and 36-month parmesan. Fish of the day from local waters could well be

monkfish roasted on its bone in korma spices, ably supported by the regular accompaniments of white crabmeat on leeks royale with a sliver of crisped fish skin. Another possibility is a chicken version of tournedos Rossini, served in roasting juices with steamed king cabbage. Yet again, you might fancy Bodmin Moor-raised hogget, with red garlic ketchup, sweetbreads and celeriac fricassée. Sheer indulgence characterises a dessert of chocolate mousse and pistachio sponge with warm caramel sauce poured on at the table. If you skip the petits fours you'll miss a little almond cake known as a financier, so moreish it would be easy to consume a dozen of the beauties. The ever-evolving wine list offers the chance to try something from Cornwall's Camel Valley, in addition to a well-represented Europe and then beyond, one way to Canada, the other

'Many of Ainsworth's dishes ... reflect his research into British culinary heritage, albeit via impeccably modern techniques'

to New Zealand. Upstairs is Cici's Bar, named after Paul's daughter; there's also been talk of some judicious space remodelling to create a cooking school.

Chef Paul Ainsworth, Chris McClurgs
Seats 46, Private dining 8
Closed 24–26 December, 13 January to 6 February
Prices from S £14, M £35, D £14
Notes No children under 4 years

NEWQUAY continued

Silks Bistro and Champagne Bar

⊛ MEDITERRANEAN, SEAFOOD

01637 839048 | Atlantic Hotel, Dane Road, TR7 1EN

www.atlantichotelnewquay.co.uk

Although it was built in 1892 this is no gloomy Victorian haunt. Silks is bright and modern, with zebra-patterned bar stools and sunburst-styled café chairs at linen-swathed tables. In the evenings, candlelight softens the scene. Save room for feel-good puddings.

Chef Gavin Hill **Seats** 100, Private dining 24 **Open** All Year **Prices from** S £6.50, M £12, D £4.50 **Notes** Vegetarian dishes, Children welcome

The Terrace

⊛ CLASSIC BRITISH

01637 872211 | The Headland Hotel and Spa, TR7 1EW

www.headlandhotel.co.uk

Located just steps from the famous sands of Fistral Beach, The Terrace restaurant has floor to ceiling glass, wooden floors, and a laid-back beach vibe. The short bistro-style menu presents such starters as garlic prawns and harissa dip, or Cornish mussels.

Open All Year

PADSTOW
MAP 2, SW97

Paul Ainsworth at No. 6

⊛⊛⊛⊛ MODERN BRITISH V NOTABLE WINE LIST

See pages 68–69

Rojano's in the Square

⊛⊛ ITALIAN, MEDITERRANEAN

01841 532796 | Padstow Townhouse, 9 Mill Square, PL28 8AE

www.paul-ainsworth.co.uk/rojanos

This vibrant restaurant brings a pleasing Mediterranean warmth to the local foodie scene. A few tables out front and a heated first-floor balcony keep alfresco-dining die-hards happy, while the kitchen takes its cue from Italian cuisine and Cornish ingredients in a crowd-pleasing roster of sourdough pizzas, classic pasta dishes and daily blackboard specials.

Chef Alex Tozer, Jack Clements **Seats** 72 **Closed** 3 weeks in January **Prices from** S £7.50, M £8.50 **Notes** Vegetarian dishes, Children welcome

St Petroc's Bistro

⊛ MEDITERRANEAN, FRENCH

01841 532700 | 4 New Street, PL28 8EA

www.rickstein.com

The bistro is an informal and relaxing sort of place, with simple tables and chairs on worn wooden floorboards, modern paintings on plain white walls, and professional service from attentive staff. There's a cosy bar and a pleasant lounge for pre-dinner drinks.

Closed 25–26 December

The Seafood Restaurant

⊛⊛⊛ INTERNATIONAL SEAFOOD V

01841 532700 | Riverside, PL28 8BY

www.rickstein.com

Padstow may be rather different these days from the little fishing village of Rick Stein's youth, with great places to eat a dime a dozen, but this is still top of everyone's list, so book well ahead for the busy season. There's a sunny conservatory at the front, a roof terrace, views of the harbour, and a bright, friendly, informal air – seaside colours, comfortable seating, and an eclectic selection of modern art. Sit at the bar with a drink and you'll soon be keen to get cracking – literally, if you go for one of the magnificent fruits de mer platters. Otherwise, you could begin with the seared chipirones, beautifully tender squid stuffed with tuna, mackerel, salmon, prawns, ginger and spring onion, before moving on to Indonesian seafood curry, packed with delicious pieces of sea bass and hake, along with prawns and squid. A delicate floating island with salted caramel pistachios and Grand Marnier anglaise is the perfect finale.

Chef Stephane Delourme **Seats** 120 **Closed** 25–26 December **Prices from** S £9.95, M £19.95 **Notes** No children under 3 years

PENZANCE
MAP 2, SW43

The Bay@Hotel Penzance

⊛⊛ MODERN, SEAFOOD

01736 366890 | Britons Hill, TR18 3AE

www.thebaypenzance.co.uk

The Bay's kitchen sources its materials from the West Country, with fresh fish and shellfish hauled in from Cornish ports to appear in mains such as roast cod fillet with squid and vegetable compôte and seaweed salsa. Fans of local meat have plenty to get their teeth into – perhaps pan-fried pigeon breast with figs, chard and Pernod jus.

Chef Ben Reeve **Seats** 60, Private dining 12 **Closed** 1st 2 weeks in January **Prices from** S £7, M £14, D £6.50 **Parking** 11 **Notes** Vegetarian dishes, Children welcome

Ben's Cornish Kitchen
◉◉ MODERN BRITISH
01736 719200 | West End, Marazion, TR17 0EL
www.benscornishkitchen.com
Seagulls wheel about the thriving little village of Marazion, just outside Penzance, in a coastal scene that may strike a chord with followers of *Doc Martin*. Tropical elements add up to an irresistible dessert of coconut pannacotta with dried pineapple, lime-macerated mango, and spiced caramel.

Chef Ben Prior **Seats** 35, Private dining 20 **Open** All Year
Notes Vegetarian dishes, Children welcome

Harris's Restaurant
◉ BRITISH, FRENCH
01736 364408 | 46 New Street, TR18 2LZ
www.harrissrestaurant.co.uk
The Harris family have run their appealing restaurant on a cobbled side street in the town centre for over 30 years, offering professionally prepared and freshly cooked quality produce (local meats, seafood from Newlyn, for instance), with the kitchen taking an unshowy line.

Chef Roger Harris **Seats** 40, Private dining 20 **Closed** 3 weeks winter, 25–26 December, 1 January
Prices from S £8.50, M £19.95, D £8.50
Notes Vegetarian dishes, No children under 5 years

The Shore Restaurant NEW
◉◉ FISH, SEAFOOD V
01736 362444 | 13–14 Alverton Street, TR18 2QP
www.theshorerestaurant.uk
A paradise for seafood lovers, this smart little restaurant goes for a minimalist contemporary look of white walls, nautical art and unclothed tables. Local boats supply the fish each day, and it's handled with skill and precision by a chef who has a clear classical skill set and a sound grasp of how flavours work together.

Chef Bruce Rennie **Seats** 24, Private dining 8 **Closed** 2 weeks January **Notes** Children welcome

The Tolcarne Inn
◉ SEAFOOD
01736 363074 | Newlyn, TR18 5PR
tolcarneinn.co.uk
Only the high sea wall separates The Tolcarne Inn from the crashing waves on the other side, adding considerable charm to this traditional pub next to Newlyn's fish market. Close links with local fishermen mean the day's catch dictates what appears on the chalkboard menu.

Victoria Inn NEW
◉◉ MODERN BRITISH
01736 710309 | Perranuthnoe, TR20 9NP
Smartly restored without sacrificing any of its traditional charm, the Victoria functions admirably as both a convivial country pub serving local ales and ciders, and a relaxed restaurant worth seeking out. The cooking is all about confident technique, sound local sourcing and lively ideas.

POLPERRO
MAP 2, SX25

Talland Bay Hotel
◉◉ MODERN INTERNATIONAL
01503 272667 | Porthallow, PL13 2JB
www.tallandbayhotel.co.uk
Close to the pretty Cornish towns of Looe and Fowey, the dining room offers lovely views over the gardens and across the bay. Arty knick-knacks add an eclectic touch to the boutique charm of the place and there are similar contemporary twists to the classic cookery.

Chef Nick Hawke **Seats** 40, Private dining 24 **Closed** 31 December **Prices from** S £6, M £14, D £8 **Parking** 23
Notes Vegetarian dishes, Children welcome

PORT GAVERNE
MAP 2, SX08

Pilchards
◉ MODERN BRITISH
01208 880244 | Port Gaverne, L29 3SQ
www.portgavernehotel.co.uk
The Port Gaverne is a traditional inn, set in a tiny cove on Cornwall's dramatic north coast, just five minutes' walk from Port Isaac. Pilchards is their café, slap-bang on the beach. It's relaxed and friendly, offering excellent snacky dishes as well as larger plates.

Closed January to Easter

Port Gaverne
◉◉ MODERN BRITISH, SEAFOOD
01208 880244 | PL29 3SQ
www.portgavernehotel.co.uk
Tucked away in a hidden cove, a hilly but short stroll from Port Isaac, this whitewashed village inn with its hanging baskets and outdoor tables is pretty as a picture, the slate-floored bar giving way to a pair of interlinked dining rooms. The traditionally-based cooking is inventive.

Open All Year

See advertisement on page 72

AA ★★★★★ ❀ ❀

PORT GAVERNE

RESTAURANT & HOTEL

Seasonal food, fresh off the boat, straight from the farm, foraged this morning

The 17th-century Port Gaverne Hotel overlooks a secluded cove on North Cornwall's dramatic coast, 5 minutes' walk from Port Isaac. We've picked up multiple awards for our food & rooms and have a stunning beach bar moments from the water: Pilchards Cafe. Open for lunch & dinner, you can snack at the bar, eat modern a la carte in the restaurant or dine al fresco on produce raised & landed right here on our doorstep.

The Port Gaverne Hotel, Port Gaverne, Port Isaac, Cornwall PL29 3SQ
01208 880 244 | www.portgavernehotel.co.uk | eat@portgavernehotel.co.uk

PORTHLEVEN

MAP 2, SW62

Kota Kai

◉ ASIAN FUSION

01326 574411 | Celtic House, The Shipyard, TR13 9JY

www.kotakai.co.uk

On the upper floor of Celtic House, Kota Kai is blessed with unbeatable views over the inner harbour of Porthleven, Britain's southernmost port. The menu, with its Asian bias, also rewards close attention, listing, for example, bao bun with hoisin sauce, kimchi, spring onions and peanuts.

Chef Jude Kereama, Marcus Houghton **Seats** 100, Private dining 30 **Closed** 25 December, 1 January **Prices from** S £2, M £11.95, D £4.50 **Notes** Vegetarian dishes, Children welcome

Kota Restaurant with Rooms

◉◉◉ BRITISH, PACIFIC RIM, SEAFOOD

01326 562407 | Harbour Head, TR13 9JA

www.kotarestaurant.co.uk

Situated on the harbour head by Porthleven's shingle beach and the bay, Kota aims to bring a Pacific Rim seafood ethos to windblown Cornwall. With a pair of guest rooms on hand, it's a streamlined operation, centred on a tiled dining room under an old beamed ceiling. Jude Kereama hails from New Zealand and brings the Asian-influenced approach of the southern hemisphere to bear on his set menu, or the seven-course tasting menu (plus veggie version). This kicks off with Porthilly oysters, either tempura with baby gem and wasabi tartare, or natural with cucumber and rice wine granita. Next up, a choice between duck breast, beef sirloin, or the 'Spring Rockpool' - a vegetable dashi broth with hake, crab raviolo, Cornish mussels, tiger prawn and seaweed. A pre-dessert of blood orange cream with rhubarb is followed by either chocolate mousse with chocolate torte, or blue cheese ice cream with poached pear.

Chef Jude Kereama **Seats** 40 **Closed** January **Notes** Vegetarian dishes, Children welcome

PORT ISAAC

MAP 2, SW98

Outlaw's Fish Kitchen

◉◉ MODERN BRITISH, SEAFOOD

01208 881183 | 1 Middle Street, PL29 3RH

nathan-outlaw.com

Nathan Outlaw is a big fish in Cornwall with a number of restaurants across the county (plus one in London), the pick of which is Restaurant Nathan Outlaw itself. The Fish Kitchen is a rustic little place right on the harbour, with sea views.

Chef Tim Barnes **Seats** 25 **Closed** Christmas and January **Notes** Vegetarian dishes, Children welcome

Restaurant Nathan Outlaw

◉◉◉ MODERN BRITISH, SEAFOOD *V*

01208 880896 | 6 New Road, PL29 3SB

nathan-outlaw.com

Sitting proud at the top end of Port Isaac, Nathan Outlaw's seafood restaurant makes a virtue of its culinary orientation. The clue is in the view. Immaculately fresh and delicately presented, every fine-tuned dish displays this local man's affinity with the Cornish coasts and, although he has gravitated to the bright lights and the big city in recent years, it's here that the centre of gravity undoubtedly remains. Starters are light but precisely seasoned, as for a gentle cure of monkfish offset with soused carrots and smoked almonds, or the subtle chilli note that echoes through a preparation of sea trout with cucumber. For a main course, the mackerel fillet is cooked sous-vide and torched at the last minute, dressed in a savoury sardine ketchup and greened up with stem broccoli and samphire, while lightly seared salt cod gains from its fondant leeks. Nobody quite understands the modern classic pairing of turbot and oxtail like Outlaw, the sea tang and gamey richness gliding together like waltz partners, held together by an earthy cep purée. For dessert, a blackberry and raisin tart manages an exquisite balance of sweet and sharp, with a regionally unarguable cider sorbet to help it along.

Chef Nathan Outlaw **Seats** 30 **Closed** Christmas and January **Notes** No children under 10 years

PORTLOE

MAP 2, SW93

The Lugger

◉◉ MODERN, CLASSIC

01872 501322 | TR2 5RD

www.luggerhotel.com

Dating from the 16th century, now a luxury hotel, The Lugger overlooks the sea and tiny harbour of a picturesque village on the Roseland Peninsula, with a terrace outside the smart, spacious restaurant for summer dining. Local ingredients are the kitchen's linchpin, particularly seafood.

Chef Richard Lipscombe **Seats** 45 **Open** All Year **Parking** 25 **Notes** Vegetarian dishes, Children welcome

PORTSCATHO
MAP 2, SW83

Driftwood
Rosettes suspended MODERN EUROPEAN
See opposite

REDRUTH
MAP 2, SW64

Penventon Park Restaurant
◉ MODERN BRITISH
01209 203000 | West End, TR15 1TE
www.penventon.co.uk
Set within a Georgian mansion and run by the
same family for over 45 years, the restaurant at
Penventon Park juxtaposes original features with
contemporary artwork and lighting. The food is
just as eclectic, with Asian influences and a
wood-charcoal oven.

Open All Year

ST AGNES
MAP 2, SW75

Rose-in-Vale Country House Hotel
◉◉ MODERN BRITISH
01872 552202 | Mithian, TR5 0QD
www.roseinvalehotel.co.uk
The Valley Restaurant at this gorgeous creeper-
clad Georgian manor house on the north Cornish
coast has a clean-lined contemporary look.
Expect local sourcing with a modern British take.
The main courses draw on local fish landed at St
Agnes – for example, crispy-skinned sea bass is
partnered with tiger prawn tortellini, fennel
purée and potato terrine.

Chef Nathan Deacon Seats Private dining 10 Closed 4
January to 1 February Prices from S £7.50, M £15, D £7
Parking 50 Notes Vegetarian dishes, No children
under 12 years (excluding family events)

ST AUSTELL
MAP 2, SX05

Boscundle Manor
◉◉ MODERN BRITISH
01726 813557 | Boscundle, PL25 3RL
www.boscundlemanor.co.uk
Set in five acres of grounds, this 18th-century
manor offers spa treatments and indoor pool.
The smart restaurant is a draw in its own right.
The candlelit dining room is intimate, and
everything is made in-house, from the bread to
the ice cream.

Open All Year

Carlyon Bay Hotel
◉ MODERN, TRADITIONAL BRITISH *V*
01726 812304 | Sea Road, Carlyon Bay, PL25 3RD
www.carlyonbay.com
Perched on a clifftop, this large hotel, spa and
golf course is an imposing presence above the
bay. The huge windows allow maximum exposure
to the rugged Cornish coast views. The kitchen
keeps things simple and relies on the quality and
provenance of its ingredients.

Chef Paul Leaky Open All Year Notes Children welcome

The Cornwall Hotel, Spa & Estate
◉ MODERN BRITISH *V*
01726 874050 | Pentewan Road, Tregorrick, PL26 7AB
www.thecornwall.com
The Cornwall Hotel restaurant in the old White
House part of the hotel is a classy, contemporary
space done out in a fashionably muted palette.
The menu here treads an uncomplicated modern
path, keeping step with the seasons and making
good use of regional ingredients. For more
casual eating, dine in the bar or the Parkland
Terrace, with Pentewan Valley views.

Chef Andrew Dudley Seats 60, Private dining 16 Open All
Year Parking 100 Notes Children welcome

ST IVES
MAP 2, SW54

Carbis Bay Hotel
◉◉ INTERNATIONAL
01736 795311 | Carbis Bay, TR26 2NP
www.carbisbayhotel.co.uk
The family that run the hotel also own the sandy
beach that is only 90 seconds away, and the view
over sand and sea is breathtaking. The Sands
Restaurant with its glorious sea views and
contemporary finish has plenty of seafood on the
menus up for grabs.

Chef Andrew Houghton Seats 150, Private dining 40
Open All Year Prices from S £9.50, M £17.95, D £8.50
Parking 100 Notes Vegetarian dishes, Children welcome

The Garrack
◉ BRITISH, FRENCH
01736 796199 | Burthallan Lane, TR26 3AA
www.thegarrack.co.uk
Overlooking stunning St Ives Bay, this stylish
hotel restaurant has a contemporary look. The
kitchen may have a global approach to cooking,
but the majority of raw materials are proudly
Cornish. Slow-cooked pig's cheeks could lead on
to cod loin, sautéed potato and pancetta salad,
greens and pea purée.

Chef Tom Avery, Mark Forster Seats 52 Closed 26
December Prices from S £5, M £16, D £5 Parking 20
Notes Vegetarian dishes, Children welcome

Driftwood

Rosettes suspended **MODERN EUROPEAN**
01872 580644 | Rosevine, TR2 5EW
www.driftwoodhotel.co.uk

The Rosette award for this establishment has been suspended owing to a change of chef and reassessment will take place in due course. Independently owned, this beach-house-style hotel stands in seven acres on the Roseland Peninsula, an Area of Outstanding Natural Beauty (Roseland, by the way, gets its name not from the flower, but from the Cornish 'ros', meaning a headland). A pretty woodland path hairpins its way down to the South West Coast Path and a private cove on the turquoise waters of Gerrans Bay. The restaurant, with a terrace, is bright and airy and a fitting context for technically innovative and exciting food. Local materials star, with expressive seafood dishes a particular strength, as in the five- and eight-course tasting menus featuring red mullet, rock oysters or line-caught pollock in seaweed, for example. All but one bedroom have sea views and those on the ground floor have decking, much enjoyed by stargazers and sunseekers.

Chef Seats 34 **Closed** early December to early February (subject to change) **Parking** 20 **Notes** Vegetarian dishes, No children in the restaurant after 6pm

ST IVES continued

Porthminster Beach Restaurant

◉◉ INTERNATIONAL, SEAFOOD *V*

01736 795352 | TR26 2EB

www.porthminstercafe.co.uk

Slap bang on stunning Porthminster Beach, this landmark white building occupies an enviable position. Whether you dine in the restaurant or on the terrace, the sea views are breathtaking. Vibrant pan-Asian dishes dominate the menu, which uses the best local seafood available.

Chef Mick Smith **Seats** 120, Private dining 60 **Closed** 25 December **Prices from** S £6.95, M £15.50, D £7.95 **Notes** Children welcome

Porthminster Kitchen

◉ INTERNATIONAL, PACIFIC RIM

01736 799874 | Wharf Road, TR26 1LG

www.porthminster.kitchen

A companion venue to the Porthminster Beach Restaurant just along the bay, the Kitchen also enjoys a bracing seaside location. Slick, stylish decor resists the indignity of seashells, and the menus deal in populist global cuisine with a Cornish accent.

Chef Michael Smith, Paul Olliver **Seats** 50 **Closed** 25 December **Prices from** S £7, M £13, D £7 **Notes** Vegetarian dishes, Children welcome

The Queens

◉ MODERN BRITISH

01736 796468 | 2 High Street, TR26 1RR

www.queenshotelstives.com

Behind the flower-planted frontage of this pub it's all quite trendy and modern while retaining a traditional feel, so all comers are happy, as they are with the appealingly interesting cooking. Ideas for the dishes are plucked from a variety of different sources.

Chef Chris Richards **Seats** 70 **Closed** 25 December **Prices from** S £6, M £10, D £6 **Notes** Vegetarian dishes, Children welcome

ST MAWES

Hotel Tresanton

◉◉◉ MEDITERRANEAN, SEAFOOD

01326 270055 | 27 Lower Castle Road, TR2 5DR

www.tresanton.com

A stunning cliffside location is the setting for this collection of cottages, transformed by Olga Polizzi into a supremely elegant and understated hotel. Superb views of the Cornish coast and laidback nautical chic contribute to an atmosphere of refined luxury. The calm, airy restaurant, with its mosaic tiled floor and shell-like lighting is classy, with simple table settings and engaging, responsive staff. If you're here in daylight it will be hard to drag yourself away from the views, so give yourself plenty of time for a long lunch. The cooking matches the environment with a pleasing simplicity; the uncluttered dishes have a refreshing Mediterranean influence. Kick off with a couple of Porthilly oysters, or salt cod croquettes with sauce vièrge – a very simple, confident dish. Monkfish with piperade and black olives, is a satisfying main course, and you can keep it simple at dessert with strawberries, clotted cream and ice cream sundae.

Chef Paul Wadham **Seats** 60, Private dining 50 **Open** All Year **Prices from** S £8, M £24, D £8 **Parking** 30 **Notes** Vegetarian dishes, No children under 6 years at dinner

ST MELLION

St Mellion International Resort

◉◉ MODERN INTERNATIONAL

01579 351351 | PL12 6SD

www.st-mellion.co.uk

St Mellion's culinary focus is the An Boesti restaurant, a spacious room with a striking colour scheme of black and white. Try the beef Wellington or loin of lamb with rhubarb, garlic confit and potatoes mashed with rosemary, and a selection of Cornish cheeses.

Closed Christmas and New Year

TRESCO (ISLES OF SCILLY)

MAP 2, SV81

New Inn

◉ MODERN, TRADITIONAL

01720 422849 | TR24 0QQ

www.tresco.co.uk

The friendly and welcoming New Inn sits beside the water, right at the heart of this small community, where guests and islanders mix happily. The fine dining here is based around island produce (everything else has to be brought in by sea, don't forget).

Open All Year

Ruin Beach Café

◉◉ MODERN MEDITERRANEAN

01720 424849 | TR24 0PU

www.tresco.co.uk/eating-on-tresco/ruin-cafe

Next to the beach at New Grimsby, this former smugglers' cottage boasts stunning views. A contemporary space with bare wooden tables and cutlery laid out on crisp tea towels, the food has similarly clean lines. Excellent island ingredients and classic cooking techniques makes for strong flavour definitions and the wood-fired oven is used to good effect.

Chef James Jones **Seats** 65 **Closed** Winter **Prices from** S £7, M £14, D £7 **Notes** Vegetarian dishes, Children welcome

TRURO

MAP 2, SW84

The Alverton Hotel

◉◉ MODERN BRITISH, EUROPEAN

01872 276633 | Tregolls Road, TR1 1ZQ

www.thealverton.co.uk

Dating from 1830, The Alverton is an impressive building designed by the same chap as Truro Cathedral. There is plenty of period charm and a contemporary sheen to the upmarket brasserie. The menu takes a modern European path with a good representation of Cornish ingredients.

Chef Simon George **Seats** 72, Private dining 160 **Open** All Year **Prices from** S £7, M £18, D £7 **Parking** 100 **Notes** Vegetarian dishes, Children welcome

Hooked Restaurant & Bar

◉ MODERN BRITISH, SEAFOOD

01872 274700 | Tabernacle Street, TR1 2EJ

www.hookedrestaurantandbar.co.uk

Tucked away down a quiet street just off the city centre, the open kitchen feeds into a lively buzz in this smart modern brasserie, with unclothed tables, exposed brickwork and high ceilings adding to the jaunty seaside feel. Seafood is the leading suit, with full-size and tapas dishes available daytime and evening.

Chef Robert Duncan **Seats** 36, Private dining 24 **Closed** 25-26 December, 1 January **Prices from** S £3.50, M £12.95, D £4.95 **Notes** Vegetarian dishes, Children welcome

Mannings Hotel

◉◉ MODERN, PACIFIC RIM

01872 270345 | Lemon Street, TR1 2QB

www.manningshotels.co.uk

Mannings is a classic-looking, solid-stone building – Grade II listed no less – but within it is all slick modernity and contemporary attitude. The restaurant has its own entrance, and an interior design spec that includes moody black-and-white photos, stainless steel, and trendy lights.

Chef Scott Williams **Seats** 69 **Closed** 25-26 December **Prices from** S £8.75, M £15.50, D £8 **Notes** Vegetarian dishes, Children welcome

Tabb's Restaurant

◉◉ MODERN BRITISH

01872 262110 | 85 Kenwyn Street, TR1 3BZ

www.tabbs.co.uk

The refurbished Tabb's occupies a white corner building that looks for all the world like a private dwelling. The kitchen's a busy place, producing everything in-house. Pigeon breast, soft-boiled egg, black pasta and sun-dried tomato dressing could be followed by tender roast pork belly, couscous, black olives, green lentils, battered courgettes and sauté potatoes.

Chef Nigel Tabb **Seats** 28 **Closed** 25 December, 1 January and 1 week January **Prices from** S £7.25, M £15.75, D £7.50 **Notes** Vegetarian dishes, Children welcome

VERYAN
MAP 2, SW93

The Dining Room Restaurant NEW
⊛ TRADITIONAL *V*
01872 501111 | The Nare, Carne Beach, TR2 5PF
www.narehotel.co.uk
The more traditional fine dining option at The Nare hotel on the beautiful Roseland peninsula, The Dining Room provides diners with magnificent panoramic sea views and local fish to match. Fresh Portloe crab rillettes could precede a grilled fillet of lemon sole, leek purée, capers, samphire, saffron Parmentier potatoes and champagne velouté.

Chef Brett Camborne-Paynter Seats 60 Open All Year Notes No children under 8 years

The Quarterdeck at The Nare
⊛⊛ TRADITIONAL BRITISH
01872 500000 | Carne Beach, TR2 5PF
www.narehotel.co.uk/dining/the-quarterdeck
The Quarterdeck is a shipshape, yachtie-themed setting of polished teak, gingham seats and square rails. The kitchen produces modern dishes bursting with bold flavours and local fish and shellfish are a strong point too; perhaps choose a luxurious duo of pan-fried turbot and lobster medallion.

Chef Nick Lawrie, Brett Camborne-Paynter Seats 60 Closed 25 December Prices from S £7.50, M £17.50, D £8 Parking 60 Notes Vegetarian dishes, Children welcome

WATERGATE BAY
MAP 2, SW86

Fifteen Cornwall
⊛ MODERN ITALIAN
01637 861000 | On The Beach, TR8 4AA
www.fifteencornwall.co.uk
Floor-to-ceiling windows show off the ever-changing sea views from this large, contemporary space, but it's just as smart and welcoming after sunset. Jamie Oliver's guiding principle remains the same – to give young people a solid grounding in skills and experience.

Open All Year

■ CUMBRIA

AMBLESIDE
MAP 18, NY30

Lake Road Kitchen
⊛⊛⊛ NORTHERN EUROPEAN *V*
015394 22012 | Lake Road, LA22 0AD
www.lakeroadkitchen.co.uk
James Cross's restaurant is deeply rooted in the concept of 'the North', and that means an all-embracing passion for Lakeland and Scottish produce, as well as clear Nordic sensibilities, from the stark simplicity of its sauna-like, Scandi-style pine plank walls and bare tables to a fervour for pickling, foraging and fermenting. Daily-changing menus come in five-, eight- and 12-course versions, and the self-styled 'cold climate cooking' brings remarkable combinations of taste and texture. A revelatory spring meal opens with slow-barbecued, smoky veal rib with a celeriac 'taco', yogurt, fermented cabbage, wild garlic and capers. Along the way, pine nut stew with garlic, parsley purée and oil accompany mussels cooked a la plancha, while gold-standard Skrei cod is simply poached and pointed up with parsley sauce. To finish, the richness of baked New York cheesecake is counterpointed by sea buckthorn sorbet. Home-baked sourdough is a superlative version with crunchy dark crust, served with hand-churned whey butter.

Chef James Cross Seats 21 Open All Year Notes No children under 14 years

The Old Stamp House Restaurant
⊛⊛ MODERN BRITISH *V*
015394 32775 | Church Street, LA22 0BU
www.oldstamphouse.com
It's not widely known that William Wordsworth was Cumbria's 'Distributor of Stamps' back in 19th century, and this is where he plied his trade. The organic and foraged ingredients on show make this is a thoroughly modern sort of restaurant. Prices are fair given the craft and creativity, with the fixed-price lunch a veritable bargain. Start with smoked Furness wood pigeon with beetroot, celeriac purée and pickled cherries. Next up, Alston Moor red grouse with Scottish girolles and truffle jus.

Chef Ryan Blackburn Seats 30, Private dining 8 Closed Christmas Prices from S £9, M £19, D £8.50 Notes Children welcome

Rothay Manor Hotel

◉◉◉ MODERN BRITISH *V*

015394 33605 | Rothay Bridge, LA22 0EH

www.rothaymanor.co.uk

Built by a Liverpool shipping merchant in 1823, many of Rothay's Regency features are still much in evidence. The handsome whitewashed pile is a great example of a traditional Lake District country-house hotel, standing in attractive landscaped gardens a short walk from honeypot Ambleside. New owners have raised the bar in recent years, not least in the restaurant, where a gently contemporary look lines up with adventurous modern country house cooking based on splendid local produce. Nicely timed pigeon opens proceedings, balanced with the sharpness of pickled beetroot, as well as liquorice and hazelnuts. Following that, a fine piece of brill has the added punch of chicken wings, mushrooms, cabbage and shaved truffle, while local lamb might appear as loin, rib and sweetbreads alongside root vegetables, sea buckthorn and cime di rapa greens. The final flourish comes in the form of a rhubarb workout – poached, jelly, crisps, crumb – with sheep's milk, hibiscus and malt.

Chef Daniel McGeorge **Seats** 40, Private dining 20 **Closed** 2-20 January **Parking** 25 **Notes** Children welcome

APPLEBY-IN-WESTMORLAND   *MAP 18, NY62*

Appleby Manor Hotel & Garden Spa

◉◉ MODERN BRITISH *V*

017683 51571 | Roman Road, CA16 6JB

www.applebymanor.co.uk

The outlook over Appleby Castle and the Eden Valley is a pastoral treat, and this Victorian sandstone house was put up by someone with an eye for a view. The 1871 Bistro delivers breezy feel-good dishes while the main restaurant takes a more refined approach.

Chef Chris Thompson **Seats** 100, Private dining 20 **Closed** 24-26 December **Parking** 60 **Notes** Children welcome

ASKHAM   *MAP 18, NY52*

Allium at Askham Hall

◉◉◉ CONTEMPORARY BRITISH ♨ NOTABLE WINE LIST

See page 80

BARROW-IN-FURNESS   *MAP 18, SD26*

Abbey House Hotel & Gardens

◉ TRADITIONAL BRITISH, FRENCH

01229 838282 | Abbey Road, LA13 0PA

www.abbeyhousehotel.com

This grand red-brick house in 14 acres of countryside is home to the charming and gently contemporary Oscar's restaurant. There's nothing stuffy about the place, with a relaxed (but professional) approach all round. The kitchen turns out modern dishes based on good regional produce.

Chef Ashley Wood **Seats** 100, Private dining 24 **Open** All Year **Prices from** S £6, M £15.50, D £6.50 **Parking** 200 **Notes** Vegetarian dishes, Children welcome restrictions apply after 9pm in public areas

BASSENTHWAITE   *MAP 18, NY23*

Lake View Restaurant

◉◉ BRITISH, FRENCH *V*

017687 76551 | Armathwaite Hall Hotel and Spa, CA12 4RE

www.armathwaite-hall.com

Standing in 400 acres of grounds bordering Bassenthwaite, Armathwaite Hall has rich fabrics and acres of oak panelling. The Lake View Restaurant is a high-ceilinged room in rich golds and reds with formally-laid tables. The kitchen steers a course to keep both traditionalists and modernists happy.

Chef Kevin Dowling **Seats** 80 **Parking** 100 **Notes** Children welcome

The Pheasant

◉◉ MODERN BRITISH

017687 76234 | CA13 9YE

www.the-pheasant.co.uk

Dating from the 17th century, this long, low-slung building has a charming, atmospheric bar and a beamed bistro as well as the more formal Fell Restaurant. The kitchen relies on local sources for its ingredients and keeps a finger on the contemporary pulse.

Closed 25 December

ASKHAM

Allium at Askham Hall

◉◉◉ **CONTEMPORARY BRITISH** 🍾NOTABLE WINE LIST
01931 712350 | CA10 2PF
www.askhamhall.co.uk

On the fringes of the Lake District in splendid Cumbrian countryside, Askham dates from the 14th century and is intimate enough to style itself a restaurant with rooms. The Allium restaurant takes a fiercely seasonal view of things, working in harmony with materials reared and grown in the kitchen gardens and the farms within the estate. Expect modern food that is home-grown, certainly, but far from home-spun: texture, flavour and visual appeal combine in style in a starter of crab with lovage, blackcurrant and garden herbs accessorised with a wafer-thin sourdough and squid ink lattice, followed by spiced salt-aged Goosnargh duck breast offset with celeriac, beetroot, plum and a duck fat waffle. Dessert is an intriguing confection balancing the sweet and savoury notes of buttermilk pannacota with apple sorrel and blackberries. Punching well above its weight is the remarkable wine list.

Chef Richard Swale **Seats** 40, Private dining 18 **Closed** Christmas, 3 January to mid February (excluding groups) **Notes** Vegetarian dishes, No children under 10 years

BASSENTHWAITE continued
Ravenstone Lodge Country House Hotel
◉ MODERN BRITISH
017687 76629 | CA12 4QG
www.ravenstonelodge.co.uk
Enjoying an enviable position near Bassenthwaite Lake, this country-house hotel has plenty going on, including a bar and bistro in the former stables. The Coach House restaurant is smartly turned out and the team in the kitchen uses quality regional ingredients.

Chef Anthony Wilson **Seats** 26 **Closed** 15-26 December **Prices from** S £6, M £16, D £6 **Parking** 15 **Notes** Vegetarian dishes, No children under 8 years

BORROWDALE
MAP 18, NY21
Borrowdale Gates Hotel
◉ BRITISH, FRENCH 𝑉
017687 77204 | CA12 5UQ
www.borrowdale-gates.com
Revered Lakeland Fells guidebook author Alfred Wainwright especially loved the Borrowdale Valley, where this classic country house turns out skilfully cooked modern dishes. Get going with Coronation chicken terrine and spiced chicken mini-nugget; then on to pan-fried sea bass, tiger prawn curry and coconut basmati rice, and end with rhubarb cheesecake, warm ginger cake and rhubarb sorbet.

Chef Christopher Standhaven **Seats** 50 **Closed** Christmas, New Year and January **Parking** 25 **Notes** Children welcome

Borrowdale Hotel
◉ MODERN BRITISH 𝑉
017687 77224 | CA12 5UY
www.lakedistricthotels.net/borrowdalehotel
This handsome Victorian hotel has been in business since 1866. Gently made over for the modern world, the place marries contemporary good looks with original features, a formula which works equally well in the restaurant – the kitchen walks a path between tradition and uncontroversial modernity.

Chef Robert Weston **Open** All Year **Notes** Children welcome

Hazel Bank Country House
◉◉ BRITISH
017687 77248 | Rosthwaite, CA12 5XB
hazelbankhotel.co.uk
Set amid four acres in the gorgeous Borrowdale Valley, this classic stone-built Lakeland hotel offers a daily-changing set menu, with a cheeseboard as an optional extra. High-end ingredients are given the modern British treatment with occasional Asian influences in dishes like a starter of teriyaki mackerel and roasted watermelon.

Chef Darren Comish **Seats** 20 **Closed** December to January **Parking** 12 **Notes** Vegetarian dishes, No children

The Leathes Head
◉◉ BRITISH 𝑉
017687 77247 | CA12 5UY
www.leatheshead.co.uk
With lovely gardens in the heart of the unspoilt Borrowdale Valley, this is where to find locally grown, reared and foraged food, although the menu ranges wider. Typical are dill-cured Skrei cod; sea bream with sprouting broccoli; rack of Herdwick hogget; roast cauliflower, sheeps' curd and honey- and thyme-braised chicory.

Chef Noel Breaks **Seats** 30, Private dining 16 **Closed** 3-25 January **Prices from** S £10, M £25, D £10 **Parking** 15 **Notes** Children welcome
See advertisement on page 82

Lodore Falls Hotel
◉◉ MODERN BRITISH 𝑉
017687 77285 | CA12 5UX
www.lakedistricthotels.net/lodorefalls
The Lodore Falls Hotel has enjoyed a magnificent setting on the shores of Derwentwater for over 200 years. The aptly named Lake View Restaurant, stylishly done out with modern furnishings and pristine white tablecloths, is the setting for equally stylish and thoughtfully constructed contemporary menus.

Chef Shane Hamilton **Seats** 140, Private dining 30 **Open** All Year **Parking** 90 **Notes** Children welcome

BORROWDALE continued

Mizu *NEW*

◉ PAN-ASIAN

017687 77285 | Lodore Falls Hotel, CA12 5UX
www.lakedistricthotels.net/lodorefalls
A megabucks refurb of this luxe spa hotel
overlooking Derwentwater brought the opening
in 2018 of Mizu, a sleek, contemporary pan-Asian
restaurant done out in cool, cosmopolitan style,
with floor-to-ceiling windows and lake views. The
chefs at work in the open kitchen provide
culinary theatre, and there's also a heated
riverside terrace.

BOWNESS-ON-WINDERMERE   *MAP 18, SD49*

Belsfield Restaurant

◉◉ MODERN, INTERNATIONAL

015394 42448 | Laura Ashley The Belsfield Hotel,
Kendal Road, LA23 3EL
www.lauraashleyhotels.com/thebelsfield
This lovingly restored Windermere hotel is set in
six acres of landscaped gardens. As you might
expect from a hotel owned by the Laura Ashley
brand, it's tastefully furnished, forming an
elegant setting for a menu that fuses British
dishes with inspiration from further afield.

Chef Chris Lee **Seats** 70, Private dining 60 **Open** All Year
Parking 60 **Notes** Vegetarian dishes, Children welcome

The Ryebeck

◉◉ MODERN BRITISH *V*

015394 88195 | Lyth Valley Road, LA23 3JP
www.ryebeck.com
Formerly known as Fayrer Garden, The Ryebeck
is an appealingly isolated country house
overlooking the shining expanse of Lake
Windermere. The informal conservatory dining
room serves up a delicious view and a modern
British menu that shows off the technical skills
of the team in the kitchen.

Chef Nick Edgar **Seats** 52 **Open** All Year
Prices from S £7.50, M £17, D £7 **Parking** 40
Notes Children welcome

BRAITHWAITE   *MAP 18, NY22*

The Cottage in the Wood

◉◉◉ MODERN BRITISH *V*

017687 78409 | Whinlatter Pass, CA12 5TW
www.thecottageinthewood.co.uk
Located at the top of the Whinlatter Pass, deep
in the Lake District National Park, this restaurant
with rooms is in a building that dates partly from
the 17th century and is surrounded by forest;

from the terrace and front half of the dining
room there are wonderful views down the valley.
The bare wood tables with round slate place
mats prove the perfect foil for very pretty dishes,
inspired by Cumbria's wonderful produce. There's
a six-course tasting menu that takes you on a
culinary journey through the woods and along the
coastline of this stunningly beautiful region,
while the well-balanced set-price menu is equally
exhilarating. From the fabulous canapés and
amuse bouches to the confident, joyful dishes on
the menus – a carefully-constructed crab starter
is both a thing of beauty and completely
delicious – there's plenty of evidence here that
the kitchen is really hitting its stride.

Chef Ben Wilkinson **Seats** 40 **Closed** January
Parking 16 **Notes** No children under 10 years at dinner

CARLISLE   *MAP 18, NY35*

Crown Hotel

◉ MODERN BRITISH

01228 561888 | Station Road, Wetheral, CA4 8ES
www.crownhotelwetheral.co.uk
The Georgian hotel is in a picturesque village a
few miles out of Carlisle, close to Hadrian's Wall.
Its Conservatory Restaurant overlooks the
landscaped gardens, and has a striking raftered
ceiling and red quarry floor tiles. The kitchen
favours a largely modern British approach.

Chef Chris Dowding **Seats** 80, Private dining 120
Open All Year **Parking** 70 **Notes** Vegetarian
dishes, Children welcome

CARTMEL   *MAP 18, SD37*

Aynsome Manor Hotel

◉ MODERN, TRADITIONAL BRITISH

015395 36653 | LA11 6HH
www.aynsomemanorhotel.co.uk
A charming, small country-house hotel in the
untouched Vale of Cartmel with views south to
the Norman priory, meadows and woods. The
cooking shows accurate timings, judiciously
considered combinations and clear flavours on
short, daily-changing menus, with seasonal
vegetables served separately.

Chef Gordon Topp **Seats** 28 **Closed** 25–26 December
and 2–28 January **Parking** 20 **Notes** Vegetarian
dishes, No children under 5 years

L'Enclume

◉◉◉◉◉ MODERN BRITISH *V*

See pages 84–85

See advertisement on page 86

L'Enclume

⊚⊚⊚⊚⊚ MODERN BRITISH *V*
015395 36362 | Cavendish Street, LA11 6PZ
www.lenclume.co.uk

State-of-the-art contemporary cooking at the forge

At first sight, L'Enclume looks like the solid 700-year-old blacksmith's forge it once was (the name is French for 'anvil') – but in the hands of Simon Rogan it has morphed into a world-class culinary destination. Inside, things aren't much different: the sparse interior is all whitewashed walls with minimal adornment, polished stone floors and unclothed tables. In keeping with the bucket-list status of the operation, classy bedrooms dotted around the village allow you to stay over and explore their remarkable wine offering. Most kitchens talk about the local larder these days, but few achieve the level of control over the ingredients' provenance that is achieved here: much of what's on your plate will have been picked fresh from Rogan's organic farm nearby, or foraged from the local countryside; the rest is sourced from trusted local suppliers – now that's what you call 'cuisine de terroir'!

> "What you get is state-of-the-art, contemporary cooking"

Staff, fully up to speed with the kitchen's output, guide you through the complex, multi-layered production that constitutes a visit here. What you get is state-of-the-art, contemporary cooking that aims to maximise flavours and deliver dazzling artistry in every perfect miniature dish. The humble spud is elevated to another plane in an opener comprising potato purée, confit and crisp skin boosted with intense onion powder, then rich salt-baked celeriac arrives with an umami slap from sea kelp sauce and caviar. Sea-fresh flavour distinguishes turbot and mussels with kale and creamy buttermilk sauce, while Rogan's herd of Dexters supplies the beef for an astounding composition of sirloin with black garlic, hen of the wood mushrooms and the subtle balancing acidity of pickled turnip, plus a ragout with Jerusalem artichoke foam that produces deep notes of resonant flavour. More sparkling fireworks arrive in the dessert parade, which stars the signature Anvil confection, a gold-sprayed caramel custard with apple and a burst of pine juice.

Chef Simon Rogan, Paul Burgalieres
Seats 45, Private dining 6
Closed 25–26 December
Parking 7
Notes No children under 6 years at lunch, 12 years at dinner

See advertisement on page 86

CARTMEL continued
Rogan & Co Restaurant
◉◉◉ MODERN BRITISH
015395 35917 | The Square, LA11 6QD
www.roganandco.co.uk
The understudy to L'Enclume sits cheek by jowl with its elder sibling in tranquil Cartmel, with a trickle of a river running alongside it. Behind the stone façade, a modern space has been fashioned, with zinc-topped tables under the gnarled old beams and a happy buzz of contented custom. The Rogan signature style of modernist treatments of gold-standard Cumbrian produce, some of it sourced from the proprietor's own farm in the surrounding valley, is capably expressed in menus that showcase a broad range of technique. Start with cured mackerel and an oyster, a bracing dish set alight with the contrasting sharpnesses of pickled vegetables and wasabi, before turning to a main such as the Rogan farm's pork loin in its own broth with spiced cannellini beans. Cauliflower dressed in Red Leicester, or confit new potatoes with garlic and thyme, are certainly a cut above the side-dish norm.

Chef Simon Rogan, Tom Barnes **Seats** 40, Private dining 10 **Closed** 1st week January **Prices from** S £10, M £20, D £9 **Notes** Vegetarian dishes, Children welcome

CLIFTON
MAP 18, NY52
George and Dragon
◉ BRITISH *V*
01768 865381 | CA10 2ER
www.georgeanddragonclifton.co.uk
Comfy sofas and little alcoves all characterise this popular inn, meticulously renovated by owner Charles Lowther, on his historic family estate. His ancestor, Lord Lonsdale helped found the AA, which adopted yellow, his favourite colour, as its trademark. British cooking relies on the estate for pedigree Shorthorn beef, and pork from rare-breed stock, while game and most fish is also pretty local.

Chef Gareth Webster **Seats** 126 **Closed** 26 December **Prices from** S £7.50, M £13.50, D £6.50 **Notes** Vegetarian dishes, Children welcome

COCKERMOUTH
MAP 18, NY13

The Trout Hotel
◉ MODERN, CLASSIC *V*
01900 823591 | Crown Street, CA13 0EJ
www.trouthotel.co.uk
The Trout has benefited from a full refurbishment in recent years, in keeping with its idyllic Lake District location in the lovely market town of Cockermouth. Elegant glass chandeliers and ornate marble fireplaces add a classy touch.

Chef Alex Hartley **Seats** 56, Private dining 56 **Open** All Year **Prices from** S £5.50, M £16, D £6 **Parking** 40 **Notes** Children welcome

CROSTHWAITE
MAP 18, SD49

The Punchbowl Inn at Crosthwaite
◉◉ MODERN BRITISH *V*
015395 68237 | Lyth Valley, LA8 8HR
www.the-punchbowl.co.uk
A small country house in the Lyth Valley, The Punchbowl is one of Lakeland's homelier places, run with great civility by the hands-on team. A slate-topped bar and modern rustic furniture give the place a fresh look, and the menu shows plenty of fashion-conscious technique.

Chef Oliver Mather, Stuart Green **Seats** 50, Private dining 16 **Open** All Year **Parking** 40 **Notes** Children welcome

ELTERWATER
MAP 18, NY30

Stove at Langdale Hotel & Spa
◉ MODERN BRITISH
015394 37302 | The Langdale Estate, LA22 9JD
www.langdale.co.uk
The gastronomic action at this smart Lakeland resort is in Stove dining room, a contemporary space with an open kitchen with a wood-fired oven, and a mezzanine with valley views. The kitchen takes a broad-minded approach, producing good stuff that hits the comfort food brief nicely.

Open All Year

GLENRIDDING
MAP 18, NY31

Inn on the Lake
◉◉ MODERN EUROPEAN *V*
017684 82444 | Lake Ullswater, CA11 0PE
www.lakedistricthotels.net
In 15 acres of grounds surrounding Ullswater, this hotel's main culinary action takes place in its Lake View Restaurant, the elegant dining room decorated with shades of lilac and fawn. The kitchen makes good use of regional ingredients to produce dishes of modernity and creativity.

Chef James Watt **Seats** 100, Private dining 40 **Open** All Year **Parking** 100 **Notes** Children welcome

GRANGE-OVER-SANDS
MAP 18, SD47

Clare House
◉ MODERN BRITISH
015395 33026 | Park Road, LA11 7HQ
www.clarehousehotel.co.uk
The Read family has owned this traditional hotel with secluded gardens overlooking Morecambe Bay since the 1960s, and their passionate care is evident wherever you look. In the two-roomed dining area, well-spaced tables dressed in crisp linen are attended by smartly turned-out, loyally long-serving staff.

Chef Andrew Read, Mark Johnston, Adrian Fenton **Seats** 36 **Closed** mid December to mid January **Parking** 16 **Notes** Vegetarian dishes, Children welcome

GRASMERE
MAP 18, NY30

The Daffodil Hotel & Spa
◉ MODERN BRITISH
015394 63550 | Keswick Road, LA22 9PR
www.daffodilhotel.com
Made of local stone and with a prime spot by Grasmere, The Daffodil enjoys a fine Lakeland vista, and sensibly the restaurant is up on the first floor to make the best of it. The contemporary finish within extends to the smart restaurant.

Open All Year

Forest Side

◉◉◉◉ MODERN BRITISH *V*

015394 35250 | Keswick Road, LA22 9RN

www.theforestside.com

In the 1840s the new-fangled railway reached what was then known as the 'District of the Lakes', much to the exasperation of the Wordsworths, and brought not just excursioners but relocators into the area, prompting a modest building boom. Among its products was this stone building, so named for its position in the shelter of a stretch of wooded hillside, now sensitively reborn as an appealing country hotel. An expansive dining room staffed with smart, knowledgeable personnel looks out on to the Lakeland setting, which takes on vital importance in Kevin Tickle's regionally inspired, exciting culinary style. There are foragings and gatherings aplenty, as well as prime materials such as Cumbrian rare breed pork, which might form the centrepiece of the multi-course taster, accompanied by smoked potato custard, damsons, and what the menu summarises as 'garden shenanigans'. Technique is key to the surprise element in every dish, from chanterelles cooked in bone marrow with corned brisket, anointed in mushroom broth, to the scorched pear with malt, birch sap and a shot of staggeringly intense ginger beer. Those haunting herbal notes lend fragrance to many dishes, including savory-scented lemon sole and dill-fronded cod and oyster, while autumnal fruits are celebrated in a dessert of salted wild plum with apple and sloes. The vegetarian menu is a tour de force in itself, building up to a principal serving of smoked squash with hen of the woods and vitamin C-laden scurvy grass. Accompanying it all is an inspired collection of biodynamic and natural wines.

Chef Kevin Tickle **Seats** 40, Private dining 10 **Open** All Year **Parking** 44 **Notes** No children under 8 years

The Lancrigg NEW

◉ MODERN, CLASSIC

015394 35317 | Easedale Road, LA22 9QN

www.lancrigg.co.uk

Parts of the house have been around since the 17th century, but a programme of refurbishment has given the hotel's restaurant a minimalist modern look, mixing muted hues of grey and

green with unclothed tables and the elemental Lakeland fell views beyond its full-drop windows. Expect gutsy, modern, country-house cooking full of local flavour.

Chef Mark Batty **Seats** 13 **Open** All Year **Prices from** S £7, M £21, D £7 **Parking** 40 **Notes** Vegetarian dishes, Children welcome

Rothay Garden Hotel
@@ MODERN BRITISH
015394 35334 | Broadgate, LA22 9RJ
www.rothaygarden.com
On the edge of Grasmere, this Victorian hotel sits in riverside gardens, with the panoramic sweep of the Lakeland fells as background. Try Lakeland lamb, served as roast rump and shepherd's pie with carrot purée, parsnip and potato rösti, green beans and rosemary jus.

Open All Year

The Wordsworth Hotel & Spa
@ MODERN BRITISH
015394 35592 | Stock Lane, LA22 9SW
www.thewordsworthhotel.co.uk
Set in two acres of riverside gardens with breathtaking Grasmere views, this was once the hunting lodge for the Earl of Cadogan. These days, this plush hotel offers cutting-edge cooking in the Signature Restaurant, with atmospheric lighting and an airy conservatory.

Chef Jaid Smallman **Seats** 65, Private dining 18 **Closed** Christmas, New Year **Parking** 50 **Notes** Vegetarian dishes, No children under 5 years
See advertisement opposite

HAWKSHEAD
MAP 18, SD39

The Queen's Head Inn & Restaurant
@ BRITISH
015394 36271 | Main Street, LA22 0NS
www.queensheadhawkshead.co.uk
The black-and-white timbered façade of this classic Lakeland inn has been well rooted into Hawkshead life since the 17th century. Inside, there's a lively buzz and the timeless charm of head-skimming oak beams, panelled walls and wood and flagstone floors.

Chef Bart Loagocki **Seats** 62 **Closed** 25 December **Notes** Vegetarian dishes, Children welcome

The Sun Inn
@ TRADITIONAL BRITISH
015394 36236 | Main Street, LA22 0NT
www.suninn.co.uk
This listed 17th-century coaching inn, at the heart of the charming village of Hawkshead, is always popular with locals and visitors alike. Inside, low ceilings, open stonework and wooden floors hark back to former times. The kitchen sends out well considered and generous dishes.

Open All Year

KESWICK
MAP 18, NY22

Brossen Steakhouse
@ MODERN BRITISH
017687 73333 | Inn on the Square, Main Street, CA12 5JF
www.innonthesquare.co.uk/brossen
The Inn on the Square is a revamped hotel with a contemporary edge and a restaurant that is all about prime protein cooked over coals. The dining room is a light, bright and casual space, with a view into the kitchen.

Open All Year

KIRKBY LONSDALE
MAP 18, SD67

Pheasant Inn
@ MODERN BRITISH
015242 71230 | Casterton, LA6 2RX
www.pheasantinn.co.uk
An 18th-century coaching inn with a proper bar complete with real ales and snug. Grab a table by the fire in the bar, or head on through to the slightly more refined restaurant - the menu is the same throughout. Expect dishes that reflect the easy-going pub setting but don't lack ambition and flair.

Closed 25-26 December

Plato's *NEW*
@ MODERN EUROPEAN
015242 74180 | 2 Mill Brow, LA6 2AT
www.platoskirkbylonsdale.co.uk
There is a refreshing informality to this buzzy local restaurant with its open kitchen, unclothed tables and vibrant local artwork. The modern European cooking is equally as unfettered, with the kitchen focusing on flavour combinations that just work, like lamb rump, lentils, kale, chestnut mushrooms, carrot purée and lamb-fat potato cake.

Chef Sam Carter **Seats** 80, Private dining 20 **Open** All Year **Prices from** S £5, M £13, D £6.95 **Notes** Vegetarian dishes, Children welcome

Sun Inn Restaurant
◎◎ MODERN BRITISH *V*
015242 71965 | 6 Market Street, LA6 2AU
www.sun-inn.info
Anyone with foodie inclinations should visit the white-painted, 17th-century Sun Inn, a proper pub with beams, log fires and real ales in the convivial bar, and a smart contemporary dining room. Reliable hands in the kitchen conjure up full-flavoured dishes using the best local and seasonal ingredients.

Chef Joe Robinson **Seats** 40 **Open** All Year
Prices from S £6.95, M £14.25, D £7 **Notes** Children welcome

LEVENS
MAP 18, SD48

The Villa Levens
◎◎ MODERN, TRADITIONAL *V*
01539 980980 | Brettargh Holt, LA8 8EA
www.thevillalevens.co.uk
An imposing Victorian family home that spent many years as a convent before being converted into the smart hotel it is now, The Villa Levens occupies a peaceful spot in the South Lakes. The intimate dining room offers plenty of original features and interesting menus.

Chef Bryan Parsons **Seats** 35, Private dining 25 **Open** All Year **Prices from** S £7.95, M £16.95, D £7.95 **Parking** 130 **Notes** Children welcome

See advertisement below

LUPTON
MAP 18, SD58

Plough Inn
◎ MODERN BRITISH
015395 67700 | Cow Brow, LA6 1PJ
www.theploughatlupton.co.uk
The Plough sports a clean-lined contemporary look without sacrificing the best of its pubby character. It's a classy act with leather sofas, and a Brathay slate-topped bar set against the cosiness of wooden floors, beams, real fires and the like. Comforting modern takes on classic dishes prevail.

Chef Chris McDermott **Seats** 120, Private dining 8 **Open** All Year **Parking** 40 **Notes** Vegetarian dishes, Children welcome

NEAR SAWREY
MAP 18, SD39
Ees Wyke Country House
◉ TRADITIONAL BRITISH
015394 36393 | LA22 0JZ
www.eeswyke.co.uk
Beatrix Potter spent her holidays in this white Georgian house. These days, on a scale small enough to unite guests, a four-course dinner menu is served at a single start time. A pair of choices is offered at most stages.

Chef Richard Lee **Seats** 16 **Closed** 20-28 December **Parking** 12 **Notes** Vegetarian dishes, No children under 12 years

NEWBY BRIDGE
MAP 18, SD38
Lakeside Hotel Lake Windermere
◉◉ MODERN BRITISH
015395 30001 | Lakeside, LA12 8AT
www.lakesidehotel.co.uk
The Lakeside sits, as you might expect, on the southern shore of Lake Windermere, surrounded by wooded slopes. It began as a coaching inn, and is now a substantial building, with a lakeside terrace, spa and pool and a brasserie named after John Ruskin.

Closed 23 December to 16 January

PENRITH
MAP 18, NY53
Devonshire Restaurant
◉ CONTEMPORARY BRITISH
01768 862696 | The George Hotel, Devonshire Street, CA11 7SU
www.lakedistricthotels.net/georgehotel
Penrith's 300-year-old George Hotel is a local institution and full of charm and friendly hospitality. The Devonshire Restaurant is the heart of the operation, stylishly brought up to date. The food, too, is contemporary but with a firm basis in traditional techniques.

Open All Year

FYR
◉ MODERN BRITISH
01768 868111 | North Lakes Hotel & Spa, Ullswater Road, CA11 8QT
fyrgrill.co.uk
Next to Wetheriggs Country Park, this Thwaites-owned hotel occupies an enviable position in Penrith at the edge of the Lake District. FYR restaurant features an impressive bespoke open-fire grill at the heart of the restaurant where guests can experience the theatre of their dishes being cooked in front of them.

Seats 94 **Open** All Year **Prices from** S £4, M £15, D £7 **Parking** 100 **Notes** Vegetarian dishes, Children welcome

PENTONBRIDGE
MAP 21, NY47
Pentonbridge Inn NEW
◉◉ BRITISH, INTERNATIONAL
01228 586636 | CA6 5QB
pentonbridgeinn.co.uk
Tucked away in remote border country, the Pentonbridge Inn is quite a surprise with its stylish modern looks allied to the cosy feel of bare brickwork, tartan rugs and wood-burning fires. Using fresh kitchen garden produce from nearby Netherby Hall, the menu delivers pubby comforts, but also entices with some more ambitious contemporary ideas.

Chef Christopher Archer **Seats** 26 **Open** All Year **Prices from** S £7, M £14, D £6 **Parking** 36 **Notes** Vegetarian dishes, No children under 8 years after 8pm

POOLEY BRIDGE
MAP 18, NY42
1863 Bar Bistro Rooms
◉◉ MODERN BRITISH V
017684 86334 | High Street, CA10 2NH
www.1863ullswater.co.uk

Built in 1863 for the village blacksmith, what is now its contemporary dining room lives up to its bistro billing, with prime ingredients from Britain and beyond underpinning the modern British menu. Start with crapaudine beetroot and ragstone cheese, then move on to céviche-topped Cornish mackerel, and finish with Amalfi lemon parfait, ginger and meringue.

Chef Phil Corrie **Seats** 32 **Closed** 25-26 December, 1st 2 weeks January **Prices from** S £7, M £16, D £7 **Parking** 9 **Notes** No children under 10 years at dinner from 7.30pm

RAVENGLASS
MAP 18, SD09

The Pennington Hotel
◉ BRITISH

0845 450 6445 | CA18 1SD

www.penningtonhotels.com

The venerable black and white hotel wears its age on its sleeve, having started out as a coaching inn in the Tudor era. Culinary modernism is the order of the day in the light, relaxing dining room where seafood is imaginatively handled.

Chef Helen Todd **Seats** 36, Private dining 12 **Open** All Year **Parking** 20 **Notes** Vegetarian dishes, Children welcome

MEET THE CHEF

Daniel McGeorge

ROTHAY MANOR

Ambleside, page 79

What inspired you to become a chef?
I had started a degree in law when I decided that that life wasn't for me, and that I wanted to pursue my passion for cooking. There's no better career than the one you love!

What are the vital ingredients for a successful kitchen?
Teamwork! We are like a small family in the kitchen, and look out for and support each other. Without that bond the work would be so much more difficult.

What are your favourite foods/ingredients?
From my *stages* in Scandinavia I found a love for fermenting, and am enjoying experimenting in this.

What's your favourite dish on the current menu and why?
Currently it is scallop ceviche (which is cured in kombu seaweed) with gooseberry, dashi, fennel, frisse.

RAVENSTONEDALE
MAP 18, NY70

The Black Swan
◉◉ MODERN BRITISH V

015396 23204 | CA17 4NG

www.blackswanhotel.com

Ravenstonedale is a pretty conservation village, and this smart Victorian inn has friendly bars and tranquil riverside gardens. There are two handsome restaurants, equally cosy and welcoming, where you can enjoy the seasonally-changing menus of modern dishes and pub classics. The team work closely with many local suppliers.

Chef Scott Fairweather **Seats** 90, Private dining 14 **Open** All Year **Prices from** S £6, M £12, D £7 **Parking** 20 **Notes** Children welcome

ROSTHWAITE
MAP 18, NY21

Scafell Hotel
◉◉ MODERN BRITISH

017687 77208 | CA12 5XB

www.scafell.co.uk

Surrounded by peaks and the lush greenery of the Borrowdale Valley, the Scafell Hotel is ideal for those seeking time in the great outdoors. The Riverside Bar and lounge bar offer informal dining, with the main restaurant a more formal option. Salmon is cured in-house.

Open All Year

TEMPLE SOWERBY
MAP 18, NY62

The Restaurant at Temple Sowerby
◉◉ MODERN BRITISH

01768 361578 | CA10 1RZ

www.templesowerby.com

Temple Sowerby is a smart family-run country hotel where the kitchen specialises in a boldly modern style with plenty of exciting flavours and unusual ingredients. To start, perhaps Cumbrian rabbit loin, confit leg, pickled celery, celery juice and buttermilk dressing, followed by seared Cornish brill, squid ink gnocchi, hung yogurt, spinach, beurre noisette purée and sea vegetables. Finish with the delightfully named 'Flowers & Herbs' – flowering currant granita, angelica ice cream, yogurt mousse, buckweat praline and wood sorrel.

Chef Jack Bradley **Seats** 24, Private dining 24 **Open** All Year **Parking** 20 **Notes** Vegetarian dishes, Children welcome

A TASTE OF LUXURY AT MACDONALD LEEMING HOUSE

Enjoy the best local produce the UK has to offer in the fabulous surroundings of Ullswater and Regency Restaurant. Take delight in enjoying imaginative food and indulge your senses this summer.

THREE COURSE DINNER

in the Award winning Regency Restaurant
£35 per person

Six course full experience
£45 per person

AFTERNOON TEA FOR TWO

Served traditionally on tiered cake stands with savoury finger-sized sandwiches, followed by scones with jam and cream, a selection of cakes and more…
£24.95 per person

To find out more information and to book visit:
www.MacdonaldHotels.co.uk/LeemingHouse

MACDONALD
LEEMING HOUSE

WATERMILLOCK
MAP 18, NY42

Macdonald Leeming House

@ MODERN BRITISH

017684 86674 | CA11 0JJ

www.macdonald-hotels.co.uk

Macdonald Leeming House is an impressive-looking property boasting direct access to Ullswater. For full-on Lakeland dining, head for the elegant Regency Restaurant, where floor-to-ceiling windows give views to the lake and fells and dishes served are well executed and attractively presented.

Open All Year

See advertisement on page 93

WINDERMERE
MAP 18, SD49

Beech Hill Hotel & Spa

@ MODERN BRITISH *V*

015394 42137 | Newby Bridge Road, LA23 3LR

www.beechhillhotel.co.uk

After canapés and pre-dinner drinks you can soak up the dramatic views over Lake Windermere to the fells beyond from Burlington's Restaurant. The menu is altogether more wide-ranging than that usually found in such environments, adding its own spin on dishes with a French grounding.

Chef Lukasz Zebryk **Seats** 130, Private dining 90 **Parking** 60 **Notes** Children welcome

Briery Wood Country House Hotel

@ MODERN, TRADITIONAL *V*

015394 33316 | Ambleside Road, Ecclerigg, LA23 1ES

www.lakedistrictcountryhotels.co.uk

Set in seven acres of grounds, Briery Wood is a charming, white-painted property, dating to the late 19th century. It's a cosy, relaxing place with an informal atmosphere. In the dining room you'll find attentive staff serving modern country-house style cooking.

Chef Jamie Hopkins **Seats** 40, Private dining 10 **Open** All Year **Parking** 25 **Notes** Children welcome

Cedar Manor Hotel & Restaurant

@ MODERN BRITISH

015394 43192 | Ambleside Road, LA23 1AX

www.cedarmanor.co.uk

Built of grey stone in 1854, the manor occupies a peaceful spot in attractive gardens, complete with eponymous cedar, on the outskirts of Windermere. It's a small hotel with an elegant restaurant and well-trained staff. Seasonality leads the kitchen, which turns out modern country-house dishes.

Chef Roger Pergl-Wilson **Seats** 22, Private dining 10 **Closed** Christmas and 2–19 January **Prices from** S £8.50, M £14.95, D £8.50 **Parking** 12 **Notes** Vegetarian dishes, No children

Cragwood Country House Hotel

@@ BRITISH, FRENCH

015394 88177 | Ambleside Road, LA23 1LQ

www.lakedistrictcountryhotels.com

Built in 1910 from stone quarried in its own 21 acres of grounds, Cragwood has views over Lake Windermere and bags of country-house charm. The two dining rooms have lovely views and smart furnishings. Things get rolling with three canapés and five types of bread.

Open All Year

Gilpin Spice

@@ PAN-ASIAN

015394 88818 | Gilpin Hotel & Lake House, Crook Road, LA23 3NE

www.thegilpin.co.uk/eat-and-drink/gilpinspice

Annexed off the main Gilpin Hotel building with its own entrance, this restaurant is a stunner – divided into three sections, each decorated differently in bright colours. There is an open kitchen with high, comfortable bar-stool seating directly facing the chefs at work. The pan-Asian menu is designed to offer lots of taster dishes rather than the traditional starter–main–dessert options; taster menus for two are available too.

Closed 25 December

Holbeck Ghyll Country House Hotel

@@@ MODERN BRITISH *V*

015394 32375 | Holbeck Lane, LA23 1LU

www.holbeckghyll.com

Holbeck Ghyll began life as a Victorian hunting lodge, when its eminent position overlooking Lake Windermere must have suggested itself as a suitable bolthole for country pursuits. Passing through successive stages of private ownership, it embarked on its career as a hotel in the 1970s, gradually acquiring the accretions of contemporary style in luxury suites, hot tub and steam room, and staging the kinds of weddings at which you will surely want to roll up in a vintage car. Dining goes on in an austerely panelled room, where the window seats are literally that, rather than freestanding chairs, for those with their backs to the view. Having your back to the view is not the luckiest option, as the sweeping panorama over the lake, with Coniston Old Man brooding in the background, is one of the magnetic attractions of Holbeck. Additionally, there's a chef's table for up to 10 diners.

Chef William Dimartino **Seats** 60, Private dining 20 **Closed** 1st 2 weeks January **Parking** 50 **Notes** No children under 8 years

Hrishi at Gilpin Hotel & Lake House
◉◉◉◉ MODERN BRITISH, ASIAN INFLUENCES *V*
See pages 96–97

Langdale Chase
◉◉ BRITISH
015394 32201 | Ambleside Road, LA23 1LW
www.langdalechase.co.uk/food-drink
This impressive Victorian building was 'the first residence in Windermere to have electricity installed' and it still boasts a fabulous late 19th-century interior, full of period details. Six acres of grounds lead down to the lake, and the terraces and reception rooms all enjoy wonderful views.

Open All Year

Lindeth Howe Country House Hotel & Restaurant
◉◉ CLASSIC FRENCH
015394 45759 | Lindeth Drive, Longtail Hill, LA23 3JF
www.lindeth-howe.co.uk
Beatrix Potter not only lived in this classic country house on a hillside overlooking Windermere and the mountains, but wrote some of her tales here. The word 'hillside' undersells what are in fact six acres of sweeping gardens, worth exploring before eating.

Open All Year

Macdonald Old England Hotel & Spa
◉ TRADITIONAL BRITISH, EUROPEAN
015394 87890 | 23 Church Street, Bowness, LA23 3DF
www.macdonaldhotels.co.uk
On the shore of England's largest lake, this Windermere hotel offers superb views across the water towards the fells, particularly through the restaurant's floor-to-ceiling windows and terrace. The menu has broad appeal, from steaks cooked on the grill, through to some gently contemporary dishes.

Open All Year

Merewood Country House Hotel
◉◉ MODERN BRITISH *V*
015394 46484 | Ambleside Road, Ecclerigg, LA23 1LH
www.lakedistrictcountryhotels.co.uk/merewood-hotel
Built in 1812 from stone quarried in the hotel's grounds, Merewood is perfectly positioned to make the best of the views over Lake Windermere. There are 20 acres of woodland and gardens, and this Lakeland country house is equally on the money on the inside.

Chef Carl Semple **Seats** 40, Private dining 32 **Closed** exclusive use days **Prices from** S £7.95, M £29.50, D £7.95 **Parking** 60 **Notes** Children welcome

Miller Howe Hotel
◉◉ MODERN BRITISH
015394 42536 | Rayrigg Road, LA23 1EY
www.millerhowe.com
Miller Howe has become the yardstick by which other country-house hotels are judged. 'Modern British with a twist' is the self-described cooking style. Menus are impressive, with home-grown and wild produce in evidence, while presentation is precise and colourful throughout.

Open All Year

Porto
◉ MODERN BRITISH, EUROPEAN
015394 48242 | 3 Ash Street, Bowness, LA23 3EB
www.porto-restaurant.co.uk
Porto is situated in the heart of Bowness, just a short stroll from Lake Windermere itself. Whether it's the comfortable dining room or an alfresco meal on the heated roof terrace or in the garden, the eclectic, invigorating food blends Asian and European influences.

Chef Slav Miskiewicz **Seats** 68, Private dining 50 **Closed** 24–26 December, 2nd week January to 1st week February **Prices from** S £6, M £12, D £7 **Notes** Vegetarian dishes, Children welcome

Hrishi at Gilpin Hotel & Lake House

◉◉◉◉ **MODERN BRITISH, ASIAN INFLUENCES** *V*
015394 88818 | Crook Road, LA23 3NE
www.thegilpin.co.uk

Modern European food with Asian influences in Lakeland tranquillity

Set in 22 acres of heavenly gardens and woodland near Windermere, the Cunliffe family's tranquil Edwardian bolthole is the very essence of an urbane and luxurious retreat, done out in slick contemporary style and not a hint of chintz. Culinary matters are, as ever, a highlight of a stay, whether it's in Gilpin Spice (with two AA Rosettes) or the flagship trio of dining rooms that goes by the nickname of its head chef Hrishikesh Desai.

Mingling ideas from his own Asian heritage with pin-sharp contemporary European cooking, Desai breaks the crusty country-house dining mould at Gilpin, bringing a genuine feeling of individuality and excitement to the menus. Peerless ingredients are given a seriously labour-intensive workout, starting with the crispy soft-shell crab that comes with a sweet and sour zing and a dazzling array of supporting elements – Bombay celeriac,

crushed peanuts, tamarind chutney and mango gel. Main courses, too, are handled with the same mixture of inventiveness and exciting contemporary eclecticism, as typified in a dish that takes marinated Norfolk quail breast as a focal point then adds in a fritter of confit leg meat with seeds, fruit and nuts, along with compressed apple, yogurt and cardamom gel. Luxurious lobster comes butter poached, and in a dumpling of claw meat with cauliflower, saffron potato, slow-poached lemon, garlic tuile and a subtly aromatised Keralan moilee sauce. Sure, there is plenty going on in these dishes, but nothing is done for novelty's sake, and it all delivers vibrant flavour and artful colour in harmonious balance – a meat dish involving beef fillet with a ravioli of braised

"Peerless ingredients are given a seriously labour-intensive workout"

feather blade, shallot Tatin and pan-fried duck liver with a Tamil-inspired Khozambu red wine sauce being a case in point. A pre-dessert black pepper and crème fraîche sorbet clears the palate for dark chocolate délice of awesome intensity, served with pumpkin pannacotta, banana bread, salted caramelised hazelnuts and white chocolate ice cream.

Chef Hrishikesh Desai
Seats 50, Private dining 20
Open All Year
Parking 40
Notes No children under 7 years

WINDERMERE continued

The Samling

Rosettes suspended **MODERN BRITISH** *V* 🟦NOTABLE WINE LIST

015394 31922 | Ambleside Road, LA23 1LR

www.thesamlinghotel.co.uk

The Rosette award for this establishment has been suspended due to a change of chef and reassessment will take place in due course. The country around Windermere is pretty spectacular from whichever angle you look at it, but The Samling has a particularly enviable prospect, its contemporary dining room of Lakeland slate and full-length glass offering dioramic views of the hotel gardens and the mirror-like expanse of water.

Chef Robby Jenks **Seats** 40, Private dining 8 **Open** All Year **Parking** 40 **Notes** No children

Storrs Hall Hotel

◎◎ **MODERN BRITISH** *V*

015394 47111 | Storrs Park, LA23 3LG

www.storrshall.com

Within 17 acres of grounds on the shore of Lake Windermere, this Georgian villa provides a quintessential Lakeland country house setting. Overlooking the lawns and glorious scenery, the elegant restaurant makes for a relaxed backdrop to the modern cooking. The kitchen displays a sound skill-set.

Seats 82, Private dining 40 **Closed** Christmas, New Year **Parking** 50 **Notes** Children welcome

The Wild Boar Inn, Grill & Smokehouse

◎ **TRADITIONAL BRITISH**

015394 45225 | Crook, LA23 3NF

www.englishlakes.co.uk

The white-painted Wild Boar is a classic inn with a host of stylish bedrooms, a smart bar, and a restaurant with an open kitchen at its heart. They even have an on-site microbrewery. The dining area has oak beams and darkwood tables.

Seats 100, Private dining 22 **Prices from** S £6.50, M £15, D £6.50 **Parking** 30 **Notes** Vegetarian dishes, Children welcome

■ DERBYSHIRE

BAKEWELL *MAP 16, SK26*

Piedaniel's

◎ **TRADITIONAL FRENCH, EUROPEAN**

01629 812687 | Bath Street, DE45 1BX

www.piedaniels-restaurant.com

Piedaniel's is run with great personal warmth and charm by a husband-and-wife team who keep the town supplied with reliable bistro cooking. Main courses nail their colours to the mast of hearty prime cuts while fish gets a look-in too.

Closed Christmas and New Year, 2 weeks January, 2 weeks August

BASLOW *MAP 16, SK27*

Cavendish Hotel

◎◎ **MODERN BRITISH** *V*

01246 582311 | Church Lane, DE45 1SP

www.cavendishbaslow.co.uk

Paintings from Chatsworth's Devonshire Collection abound in this fine 18th-century property, including the elegant Gallery Restaurant. Arrive in the right season and expect estate-reared lamb and game, including perhaps mirin jelly partridge breast with confit leg. For dessert, banana toffee soufflé. The conservatory Garden Room is an alternative place to eat.

Chef Adam Harper **Seats** 50, Private dining 18 **Open** All Year **Parking** 40 **Notes** Children welcome

Fischer's Baslow Hall

◎◎◎ **MODERN EUROPEAN** *V*

See pages 100–101

Rowley's Village Pub and Restaurant *NEW*

◎ **MODERN BRITISH**

01246 583880 | Church Lane, DE45 1RY

With its real fire, Peak District-brewed ales and live music, this newy refurbished pub is very much the village hub but the seasonal food draws diners from afar. Local black pudding, crispy hen's egg, pancetta and tomato salsa might lead on to pan-seared rainbow trout, spring greens and wild garlic sauce.

Chef Matt Booth **Seats** 140, Private dining 24 **Closed** 25 December **Prices from** S £5.50, M £11.50, D £4.50 **Parking** 16 **Notes** Vegetarian dishes, Children welcome

BEELEY
MAP 16, SK26

The Devonshire Arms at Beeley

◉ MODERN BRITISH ♦ NOTABLE WINE LIST

01629 733259 | Devonshire Square, DE4 2NR
www.devonshirebeeley.co.uk
A night in one of the guest rooms would allow
you to say you'd stayed at Chatsworth, sort of, as
this stone-built village inn is situated in the heart
of the estate. Expect cask-conditioned ales and
a terrific wine list, and a menu offering
contemporary pub food.

Chef Lewis Thornhill **Seats** 60, Private dining 14 **Open** All
Year **Prices from** S £6, M £17, D £6.50 **Parking** 30
Notes Vegetarian dishes, Children welcome

BRADWELL
MAP 16, SK18

The Samuel Fox Country Inn

◉◉ MODERN BRITISH

01433 621562 | Stretfield Road, S33 9JT
www.samuelfox.co.uk
A stone-built inn near the Pennine Way named
after the Victorian steel magnate who invented
the folding ribbed umbrella. Breads of the day,
variously flavoured with treacle or with
Henderson's relish and onion, make an
encouraging prelude to tasty dishes.

Chef James Duckett **Seats** 40 **Closed** 2-27 January
Parking 15 **Notes** Vegetarian dishes, Children welcome

BUXTON
MAP 16, SK07

Best Western Plus Lee Wood Hotel

◉ BRITISH, EUROPEAN

01298 23002 | The Park, SK17 6TQ
www.leewoodhotel.co.uk
Country house style exudes from every pore of
Lee Wood, a Georgian grey-stone manor house in
the Peak District. Modern brasserie cooking is
served In an expansive conservatory room with
fronds of hanging foliage overhead and
refreshing views of the grounds all about.

Open All Year

CHESTERFIELD
MAP 16, SK37

Casa Hotel

◉◉ MODERN BRITISH, MEDITERRANEAN

01246 245990 | Lockoford Lane, S41 7JB
casahotels.co.uk
Casa's Cocina restaurant is an über-chic space
with darkwood, white chairs and floor-to-ceiling
windows. The menu has a selection of salads and
tapas running from a board of Spanish
charcuterie to a croquette of hake, cheese and
chives with tartare dressing.

Chef Andrew Wilson **Seats** 100, Private dining 200
Closed 1 January, bank holiday Mondays (only breakfast
available) **Prices from** S £6, M £14.50, D £5 **Parking** 200
Notes Vegetarian dishes, Children welcome

Peak Edge Hotel at the Red Lion

◉◉ MODERN BRITISH

01246 566142 | Darley Road, Stone Edge, S45 0LW
www.peakedgehotel.co.uk
A new-build stone edifice on the border of the
Peak District National Park, the family-owned
hotel is handy for Chatsworth and Haddon Hall.
Next door is the Red Lion, a Georgian coaching
inn that is home to the hotel's bar and bistro.

Open All Year

DARLEY ABBEY
MAP 11, SK33

Darleys Restaurant

◉◉ MODERN BRITISH V

01332 364987 | Haslams Lane, DE22 1DZ
www.darleys.com
This converted silk mill by the River Derwent is
the setting for some bright, modern cooking
making really excellent use of regional produce.
The shady terrace makes the most of the
riverside location, a great backdrop for the
thoroughly contemporary menus. Desserts
demonstrate real creativity.

Chef Jonathan Hobson **Seats** 70 **Closed** Bank holidays,
1st 2 weeks January, 7-14 July **Prices from** S £8.25,
M £24.95, D £8.95 **Parking** 9 **Notes** Children welcome

Fischer's Baslow Hall

◉◉◉ MODERN EUROPEAN *V*
01246 583259 | Calver Road, DE45 1RR
www.fischers-baslowhall.co.uk

Modern cooking in a country retreat

Within easy pottering distance of the Chatsworth Estate and the town of Bakewell, famed for its eponymous pudding, Baslow makes a fine food-centric base for doing the Derbyshire Peak District. It's a fine Edwardian house, built to look a few centuries older in the style of a Stuart manor with protruding wings and mullioned windows, reached by a winding driveway lined with mature chestnut trees. Bounded by box and yew hedges, the grounds and formally laid gardens have been beautifully restored, and with foliage creeping over the façade of the house itself, the proper feeling of gracious country living is established. Under the ownership of the Fischers since the 1980s, it has become one of England's destination country retreats. The dining room works a classically elegant country-house look, all plush fabrics, pastel greys and blues, flowery wallpaper and crisp linen, flanked

"... it has become one of England's destination country retreats"

by views into the grounds, where a kitchen garden supplies many of the seasonal goodies that head chef James Payne deploys as the bedrock of his classically-based modern cooking.

Ingredients are treated with the respect they deserve, so if it all feels and looks impeccably modern, the underlying principles are tried and tested. That's true of a refined starter starring hand-dived scallops atop an onion ring stuffed with ham hock, the richness leavened by lentils and apple in various forms. Mains showcase pedigree meats such as the Derbyshire lamb cutlets and crisp-crumbed sweetbreads that come with charred asparagus and grelot onion purée, all fired up with a North African theme of harissa and spicy chickpeas. Fish cookery is sensitive and accurate, perhaps pairing pan-fried John Dory with an aromatic lemon verbena and ginger bisque and hand-rolled macaroni. Dessert could be rhubarb crumble soufflé of bracing intensity, helped along rather nicely by vanilla ice cream and a shot of rhubarb schnapps.

Chef James Payne
Seats 72, Private dining 20
Closed 25–26 December
Parking 25
Notes No children under 8 years in main dining room

ELLASTONE
MAP 10, SK14

The Duncombe Arms
◉◉ MODERN BRITISH
01335 324275 | Main Road, DE6 2GZ
www.duncombearms.co.uk
In the picturesque village of Ellastone, this attractive whitewashed country inn close to Alton Towers makes for an enjoyable pitstop for a pint but the modern food ensures visitors stay for much longer. Polished wooden tables, linen napkins and fresh flowers provide an informal setting and the cooking is creative, with intelligent flavour combinations.

Chef Chris Gallagher Seats 75, Private dining 12 Open All Year Prices from S £6, M £14, D £7 Parking 30 Notes Vegetarian dishes, Children welcome

FROGGATT
MAP 16, SK27

The Chequers Inn
◉◉ MODERN, TRADITIONAL
01433 630231 | S32 3ZJ
www.chequers-froggatt.com
The Tindalls' country inn in the Hope Valley charms, with a warm colour scheme, wooden pub-style furniture and a fireplace creating a relaxing atmosphere. The menu deftly steers between stalwarts and more modern offerings.

Chef Richard Spencer Seats 90 Closed 25 December Prices from S £7, M £14, D £6.50 Parking 50 Notes Vegetarian dishes, Children welcome

HARTINGTON
MAP 16, SK16

Biggin Hall Hotel
◉ MODERN BRITISH
01298 84451 | Biggin-by-Hartington, SK17 0DH
www.bigginhall.co.uk
Seventeenth century, 1,000 feet up in the Peak District National Park – what's not to like? There's more – oak beams, stone walls, flagstones and great views. Always cosy, the restaurant is full of character, with daily changing, modern British menus that acknowledge vegetarian tastes.

Chef Mark Wilton Seats 50 Open All Year Prices from S £6, M £16, D £6 Parking 30 Notes Vegetarian dishes, No children

HATHERSAGE
MAP 16, SK28

The Plough Inn
◉ MODERN EUROPEAN
01433 650319 | Leadmill Bridge, S32 1BA
www.theploughinn-hathersage.co.uk
Set in nine acres of grounds that slope gently to the River Derwent, the stone-built 16th-century Plough is welcoming and friendly. The courtyard's the place to be in summer, and the dining room is always smartly turned out, as is the cooking.

Chef Mark Rowan Seats 40, Private dining 24 Closed 25 December Prices from S £6.50, M £16, D £6.50 Parking 40 Notes Vegetarian dishes, Children welcome

HIGHAM
MAP 16, SK35

Santo's Higham Farm Hotel
◉ MODERN INTERNATIONAL
01773 833812 | Main Road, DE55 6EH
www.santoshighamfarm.co.uk
Santo Cusimano runs a highly individual rural retreat. With the rolling Amber Valley all about, it's in a prime slice of Derbyshire walking country, and has been fashioned from an old farmstead. Menus mobilise plenty of pedigree local produce and Italian influences are never distant.

Chef Raymond Moody Seats 50, Private dining 34 Open All Year Prices from S £5, M £14, D £6.50 Parking 100 Notes Vegetarian dishes, Children welcome

HOPE
MAP 16, SK18

Losehill House Hotel & Spa
◉◉ MODERN BRITISH V
01433 621219 | Lose Hill Lane, Edale Road, S33 6AF
www.losehillhouse.co.uk
The Orangery Restaurant in this secluded spot in the Peak District National Park offers stunning views from a light-filled, comfortable room with a contemporary look. The kitchen has a modern, creative style, adding novel and intriguing elements to many dishes.

Chef Alfred Olinski Seats 50, Private dining 30 Open All Year Parking 25 Notes Children welcome

MATLOCK
MAP 16, SK35

Stones Restaurant
◎◎ MODERN BRITISH *V*

01629 56061 | 1 Dale Road, DE4 3LT

www.stones-restaurant.co.uk

Stones may be an intimate basement venue, but it has the best of both worlds on fine days, thanks to a stylish conservatory and tiled sun terrace perched above the Derwent. The decor is a mix of subtle earthy tones, to match a Mediterranean-inflected menu.

Chef Kevin Stone **Seats** 44, Private dining 16 **Closed** 25 December to 5 January **Notes** Children welcome

MELBOURNE
MAP 11, SK32

Amalfi White
◎◎ MODERN BRITISH, EUROPEAN

01332 694890 | 50 Derby Road, DE73 8FE

www.amalfiwhite.com

With a terraced garden plus a children's play area, this stylish brasserie has all the attributes needed to make a family-friendly venue all year round. Inside, there's a contemporary space in greys and silvers with a mixture of artwork in the softly-lit dining room.

Chef Matthew Clayton **Seats** 64, Private dining 14 **Closed** 25-26 December, 1 January **Prices from** S £5.50, M £11.50, D £6.25 **Notes** Vegetarian dishes, No children under 8 years after 7.30pm

The Bay Tree
◎ MODERN BRITISH, NEW WORLD *V*

01332 863358 | 4 Potter Street, DE73 8HW

baytreerestaurant.com

Set across different levels, the building was once home to several shops but beyond its stone façade is a contemporary restaurant with clean lines, decorated in very sophisticated shades of muted grey and beige. Menus are thoughtfully constructed, and feature complex but elegant dishes based on top-quality ingredients.

Chef Rex Howell **Seats** 60 **Closed** Christmas, 1 January and bank holidays **Notes** Children welcome

Harpur's of Melbourne
◎◎ MODERN FRENCH

01332 862134 | 2 Derby Road, DE73 8FE

www.harpursofmelbourne.co.uk

The inn evolved in the 19th century from a pair of Georgian houses in this lovely market town. These days, it puts on all sort of special occasions, and there's plenty going on in the smart first-floor restaurant. Pub classics are the backbone of their menu choices.

Open All Year

MORLEY
MAP 11, SK34

The Morley Hayes Hotel
◎◎ MODERN BRITISH

01332 780480 | Main Road, DE7 6DG

www.morleyhayes.com

Morley Hayes has been a dynamic hotel since the 1980s, and with its golf complex, conference facilities and popular wedding venue, it has most bases covered. The kitchen offers a roster of unpretentious modern dishes, with influences from around the globe adding vibrancy and colour.

Closed 27 December, 1 January

REPTON
MAP 10, SK32

The Boot Inn
◎◎ MODERN BRITISH

01283 346047 | 12 Boot Hill, DE65 6FT

www.thebootatrepton.co.uk

Five miles from the National Brewery Centre, you would expect beer to be a strong draw, especially in a styllshly-appointed 17th-century coaching inn. A range of evocatively named ales from its microbrewery is a plank of The Boot's huge popularity. There's something on the menus to suit everyone.

Open All Year

ROWSLEY
MAP 16, SK26

The Peacock at Rowsley
◎◎◎ MODERN BRITISH *V*

See pages 104-105

See advertisement on page 106

ROWSLEY   *MAP 16, SK26*

The Peacock at Rowsley

◉◉◉ MODERN BRITISH *V*

01629 733518 | Bakewell Road, DE4 2EB

www.thepeacockatrowsley.com

Technically creative, nimble cooking in an aristocratic manor

The Peacock is a sturdy-looking mansion built in the 17th century of Derbyshire stone in just the right dimensions to make for a country-house hotel on the human scale. The interiors are deeply comfortable – the bar goes for a village-inn look, with its low ceiling, venerable timber columns and stone walls, while things get rather more formal in the dining room, where contemporary country-chic hues of lime-green and plum are accessorised with old oil paintings and chunky, unclothed wooden tables.

After a stint with Tom Aikens in London, head chef Dan Smith produces a technically nimble rendition of creative British cooking, looking to nearby estates for organically reared meats, as well as the Peacock's own kitchen gardens, for the bedrock of his dynamic modern output. Whether you go for the à la carte or multi-course taster, things set off on a hearty

"Dan Smith produces a technically nimble rendition of creative British cooking"

note: a superb terrine of chicken, duck's liver and pistachio is served alongside cep purée, parsley root remoulade and crisps, a posh quail's Scotch egg made with smoked chicken and foie gras, and the balancing sharpness of pickled pear helping things along. Main courses turn up the volume, building layers of flavour and clever textural balancing from pedigree prime materials – venison timed to perfection comes with pickled and poached pumpkin, a Stilton and venison bun, trompette mushrooms and sweet caramelised Roscoff onions. If you're in the mood for fish, there may be flawlessly timed monkfish, supported by a picturesque array of potato terrine, asparagus, sea kale, and the umami slap of oyster and seaweed sauce delivering deep satisfaction. The kitchen's technical dexterity runs all the way through to impressive desserts, when top-grade Casa Luker chocolate provides the bedrock of an immaculate soufflé, with a ball of prune and sherry ice cream of luxuriant creaminess slotted into its top at the table.

Chef Dan Smith
Seats 56, Private dining 14
Open All Year
Prices from S £7.45, M £24, D £7.45
Parking 25
Notes No children under 10 years on Fridays and Saturdays

See advertisement on page 106

THE PEACOCK AT ROWSLEY

The Peacock at Rowsley is a cosy, chic boutique hotel, originally a manor house in the heart of the Peak District National Park and very close to Haddon Hall and Chatsworth House. Perfect for a countryside break with comfortable bedrooms including four posters and one of the best hotel suites in the region. Our award winning restaurant serves a delicious fine dining menu, crafted by Head Chef Dan Smith. Dan worked with notable chefs such as Tom Aikens before joining The Peacock. The atmospheric bar with open fire is a very convivial place to meet for lunch, dinner or just a drink – with its own menu of freshly cooked seasonal food. Treat yourself to a drink from the extensive cocktail menu. Sunday lunch at The Peacock is a local favourite. The hotel is famed for is excellent fly fishing on the Derbyshire Wye and River Derwent.

For further information or to make a booking please call **01629 733518** or email **reception@thepeacockatrowsley.com**. The Peacock at Rowsley, Derbyshire DE4 2EB

SANDIACRE
MAP 11, SK43

La Rock
◉◉ MODERN BRITISH
0115 939 9833 | 4 Bridge Street, NG10 5QT
www.larockrestaurant.co.uk
Hidden away down a side street in Sandiacre, La Rock's sophisticated and contemporary interior has exposed brick walls, wooden floors, solid oak tables with granite centres and sparkling glassware, and there's a glass-roofed lounge area with inviting comfy sofas; soft music plays in the background.

Chef Nick Gillespie **Seats** 40 **Closed** 12–20 March, 4–12 June, 10–18 September, 2 weeks after 23 December **Prices from** S £8.50, M £19, D £8 **Notes** Vegetarian dishes, No children under 10 years

THORPE
MAP 16, SK15

The Izaak Walton Hotel
◉◉ MODERN, TRADITIONAL
01335 350981 | Dovedale, DE6 2AY
www.izaakwaltonhotel.com
This creeper-clad country house has glorious views over the Dovedale Valley and the Derbyshire peaks. Decorated in rich hues of red and gold, the elegant Haddon Restaurant favours a traditional candlelight-and-linen look, in contrast to the up-to-date and creative menu.

Chef Simon Harrison **Seats** 120, Private dining 40 **Open** All Year **Parking** 50 **Notes** Vegetarian dishes, Children welcome

TIDESWELL
MAP 16, SK17

The Merchant's Yard
◉◉ CONTEMPORARY, CLASSIC
01298 872442 | St Joan's Road, SK17 8NY
www.themerchantsyard.com
The Merchant's Yard is in the centre of the Peak District in the village of Tideswell. The restaurant is found tucked away in a traditional stone building. Set on two levels, the atmosphere is one of relaxed dining with local produce given a global treatment.

Open All Year

WOOLLEY MOOR
MAP 16, SK36

The White Horse & The View @ Woolley Moor NEW
◉ MODERN BRITISH
01246 590319 | Badger Lane, DE55 6FG
www.thewhitehorsewoolleymoor.co.uk
In the hamlet of Woolley Moor on the outskirts of Ashover, this stone-built country inn sits on the eastern edge of the Peak District National Park. It's a glorious setting to enjoy modern British dishes like blue cheese and walnut soufflé, followed by crispy belly pork, spring onion mash and smoked bacon sauce.

Chef Jack Cabourn **Seats** 52, Private dining 28 **Closed** 25–26 December, 1st 3 weeks January **Prices from** S £5.50, M £12.95, D £6 **Parking** 50 **Notes** Vegetarian dishes, Children welcome

■ DEVON

ASHBURTON
MAP 3, SK77

The Old Library Restaurant
◉ MODERN BRITISH
01364 652896 | North Street, TQ13 7QH
www.theoldlibraryrestaurant.co.uk
Housed at the back of the Ashburton library, facing the car park, Joe Suttie and Amy Mitchell's place is a valuable local resource. Happy locals crowd the chunky tables, overseen by a busy kitchen counter, for a short, punchy menu that changes every six weeks or so.

Chef Amy Mitchell, Joe Suttie, Lewis Mitchell **Seats** 24 **Closed** 23–29 December **Prices from** S £6, M £16, D £7 **Notes** Vegetarian dishes, Children welcome

AXMINSTER
MAP 4, SY29

Fairwater Head Hotel
◉ MODERN BRITISH, MEDITERRANEAN
01297 678349 | Hawkchurch, EX13 5TX
www.fairwaterheadhotel.co.uk
Just five miles from Axminster, Fairwater Head enjoys panoramic views over the Axe Valley and stands amidst three acres of manicured lawns. The appealing stone building covered in climbing foliage has a relaxed rural ambience. Flawless Devon produce is worked into modern classics.

Chef David Brown **Seats** 60, Private dining 18 **Closed** January **Prices from** S £8.50, M £17, D £7.50 **Parking** 40 **Notes** Vegetarian dishes, Children welcome

Tytherleigh Arms

◉◉ MODERN BRITISH

01460 220214 | Tytherleigh, EX13 7BE
www.tytherleigharms.com

This family-run, 16th-century coaching inn on the borders of Devon, Dorset and Somerset creates a welcoming atmosphere with its beamed ceilings, wooden floors, and a wood-burner ablaze in the winter months. Local produce drives the menus here, and the well-conceived dishes are prepared with sensitivity.

Chef Jack Luby **Seats** 60, Private dining 37
Closed 25–26 December, 2nd and 3rd weeks of January
Prices from S £5.95, M £13.50, D £6.95 **Parking** 36
Notes Vegetarian dishes, No children under 5 years at dinner

BAMPTON
MAP 3, SS92

The Swan

◉◉ MODERN BRITISH

01398 332248 | Station Road, EX16 9NG
www.theswan.co

The Swan is a smart country pub – warm colours, lots of oak, a few sofas, soft lighting – with a convivial atmosphere. The bar is the heart of the operation, but it's easy to see why the whole place can be full of diners.

Chef Paul & Donna Berry **Seats** 60, Private dining 20
Closed 25 December **Prices from** S £5, M £23, D £6.50
Notes Vegetarian dishes, Children welcome until 7pm

BARNSTAPLE
MAP 3, SS53

The Arlington Restaurant NEW

◉ BRITISH 𝑉

01271 345861 | The Imperial Hotel, Taw Vale Parade, EX32 8NB
www.brend-imperial.co.uk

Set in the Edwardian grandeur of the riverside Imperial Hotel, this elegant old-school restaurant offers plenty of period character with its chandeliers, paintings and fancy plasterwork. It's a fitting setting for gently modern, classically-based cooking that achieves satisfying results thanks to skilful technique and quality ingredients rather than outlandish ideas.

Chef Craig Middleton, Shaun Brayley **Seats** 100, Private dining 40 **Open** All Year **Prices from** S £7.50, M £8.50 **Parking** 50 **Notes** Vegetarian dishes, Children welcome

Seasons Brasserie NEW

◉ MODERN BRITISH

01271 372166 | The Park Hotel, Taw Vale, EX32 9AE
www.parkhotel.co.uk

Warm oak, gleaming marble, soft lighting and cheery service all combine to create a soothing ambience in this smart, contemporary restaurant overlooking Rock Park. The buzzy hub of the hotel, Seasons Brasserie fits the bill whether you're here for coffee and cakes, cocktails or a please-all roster of straightforward modern and traditional cooking.

Chef Luke Scourfield **Seats** 120 **Open** All Year
Prices from S £6.25, M £16.50, D £6.50 **Parking** 70
Notes Vegetarian dishes, Children welcome

BEAWORTHY
MAP 3, SK49

The Blackriver Inn NEW

◉ TRADITIONAL

01409 231888 | Broad Street, Black Torrington, EX21 5PT
www.blackriverinn.co.uk

In picturesque Black Torrington, this has been the village inn for 200 years although the latest custodians took it over in 2018. A menu of 'small' and 'big' plates offers plenty of choice. Try the lamb breast, creamed potato and sweetbread fritter before cassoulet of confit duck, Toulouse sausage, white beans and pork belly.

Chef Richard Devine **Seats** 55, Private dining 28
Open All Year **Prices from** S £5, M £12.50, D £6.50
Parking 12 **Notes** Vegetarian dishes, Children welcome

BEESANDS
MAP 3, SX84

The Cricket Inn

◉ MODERN, SEAFOOD

01548 580215 | TQ7 2EN
www.thecricketinn.com

Smack on the seafront overlooking the shingle beach, with stunning views across Start Bay, The Cricket enjoys an unrivalled location and retains every ounce of its identity as a former fisherman's pub. Blackboard menus advertise what has been freshly drawn from the bay.

Closed 25 December, January

Northcote Manor

Northcote Manor
Burrington
Umberleigh
Devon
EX37 9LZ

Tel: 01769 560501

Fax: 01769 560770

E: rest@northcotemanor.co.uk

www.northcotemanor.co.uk

BIDEFORD

MAP 3, SS42

The Pig on the Hill

◉◉ FRENCH, ENGLISH

01237 459222 | Pusehill, EX39 5AH

www.pigonthehillwestwardho.co.uk

Created in a converted cowshed, The Pig on the Hill is a country pub with a modern restaurant that's reminiscent of an American-style diner – black and white chequered floor, bare wooden tables, large windows creating an airy atmosphere and informal yet professional service.

Closed 25 December

BIGBURY-ON-SEA

MAP 3, SX64

The Oyster Shack

◉ SEAFOOD

01548 810876 | Stakes Hill, TQ7 4BE

www.oystershack.co.uk

A warm-hearted place with a casual atmosphere, where a friendly greeting gets everything off on the right foot. Super-fresh seafood is the name of the game, and it's all the better if you sit outside under the sail-like awning. Giant blackboards reveal what's on offer from crabs and lobsters, to fishy plates such as whole roasted gurnard with anchovy butter.

Chef Andy Richardson **Seats** 60 **Closed** 25 December **Prices from** S £3, M £12, D £4.50 **Parking** 25 **Notes** Vegetarian dishes, Children welcome

BRIXHAM

MAP 3, SX95

The Bonaparte Restaurant *NEW*

◉ MODERN BRITISH *V*

01803 853225 | Berry Head Hotel, Berry Head Road, TQ5 9AJ

www.berryheadhotel.com

Views of the bay are very much the feature here at the Berry Head Hotel's formal dining option. The daily-changing menu offers quality ingredients and traditional cookery. The cuisine is enjoyable and clearly popular with the locals.

Chef Tom Kneal, Haydon Johnson, Canon Vazf, Pedro Faria **Seats** 65, Private dining 26 **Open** All Year **Prices from** S £7.50, M £22, D £10.50 **Parking** 65 **Notes** Vegetarian dishes, Children welcome

Quayside Hotel

◉ MODERN BRITISH

01803 855751 | 41–49 King Street, TQ5 9TJ

www.quaysidehotel.co.uk

The restaurant at the Quayside Hotel majors in seafood and what reaches the menu depends on the catch. They know how to treat this prime product with respect. It takes place in a candlelit dining room with harbour views and a refreshing lack of pretence.

Chef Philip Winsor **Seats** 40, Private dining 18 **Open** All Year **Prices from** S £5.60, M £13.50, D £6.25 **Parking** 30 **Notes** Vegetarian dishes, No children under 5 years

BURRINGTON

MAP 3, SS61

Northcote Manor and Spa

◉◉ MODERN BRITISH *V*

01769 560501 | EX37 9LZ

www.northcotemanor.co.uk

Set in 20 acres of lush Devon countryside, the 18th-century stone manor trades these days as a classy country-house hotel with an impressive restaurant. There's a reassuringly traditional feel, and fine West Country ingredients lead the charge on an enticing menu in the modern country-house mould.

Chef Richie Herkes **Seats** 34, Private dining 50 **Open** All Year **Parking** 30 **Notes** Children welcome

See advertisement on page 109

CHAGFORD

MAP 3, SX78

Gidleigh Park

Rosettes suspended MODERN, CLASSIC *V*

01647 432367 | TQ13 8HH

www.gidleigh.co.uk

The Rosette award for this establishment has been suspended due to a change of chef and reassessment will take place in due course. Sitting in lordly isolation on its bluff above the Teign Valley, Gidleigh nonetheless manages not to feel overly grandiloquent. It still feels like the house it was designed as in the 1920s, albeit one accoutred with oak panelling, fine furnishings and bevies of utterly professional staff. Its trio of adjacent dining rooms is now the territory of chef Chris Eden, formerly with Driftwood in Cornwall.

Chef Christopher Eden **Seats** 45, Private dining 22 **Open** All Year **Parking** 45 **Notes** No children under 8 years at lunch and dinner

Mill End Hotel
◉◉ MODERN BRITISH
01647 432282 | Dartmoor National Park, TQ13 8JN
www.millendhotel.com
The River Teign flows past this pretty white-painted hotel, where a Devon cream tea is just the ticket, with a lush pastoral backdrop. There's an air of genteel formality in the restaurant with its linen-clad tables, while the kitchen's output is modern, seasonal, and well-presented.

Chef Darren Knockton **Seats** 50 **Open** All Year
Parking 30 **Notes** Vegetarian dishes, Children welcome

CHITTLEHAMHOLT   *MAP 3, SS62*
Highbullen Hotel, Golf & Country Club
◉◉ MODERN BRITISH
01769 540561 | EX37 9HD
www.highbullen.co.uk
The Devon View Restaurant at the Highbullen Hotel doesn't disappoint when it comes to the promised vista, and that is indeed the rolling Devon countryside you can see through the bank of windows. The restaurant makes this golfing and spa hotel a useful stopover.

Open All Year

CREDITON   *MAP 3, SS80*
The Lamb Inn
◉ MODERN BRITISH
01363 773676 | The Square, Sandford, EX17 4LW
www.lambinnsandford.co.uk
A 16th-century former coaching house with open fires, low ceilings and a pretty, sheltered garden on three levels, this lovely village pub is unpretentious and welcoming. The accomplished cooking makes good use of quality, local produce, the seasonal menu changing daily. Leave room for comforting desserts.

Chef Andy Bennett **Seats** 48, Private dining 15 **Closed** 25 December; January to March Sunday pm to Tuesday (cold food and hot soup available) **Prices from** S £5.95, M £14.95, D £5.95 **Notes** Vegetarian dishes, Children welcome

Paschoe House *NEW*
◉◉ FRENCH, BRITISH, PAN-ASIAN *V*
01363 84244 | Bow, EX17 6JT
paschoehouse.co.uk
Set in a luxury house in a remote valley, the sumptuous evening meals and notable, creative tasting menus at Paschoe House are worth seeking out. The bold decor in the spacious dining area complements the food, which is certainly innovative and on trend, delivering on all cylinders. One to watch.

Chef Craig Davies **Seats** 30 **Open** All Year **Parking** 40
Notes Children welcome

DARTMOUTH   *MAP 3, SX85*
The Angel *NEW*
◉◉ CONTEMPORARY *V*
01803 833488 | South Embankment, TQ6 9BH
www.theangeldartmouth.co.uk
There has been a notable restaurant on this site since 1974 when Joyce Molyneux opened it as the legendary Carved Angel. Elly Wentworth continues the tradition of a female head chef at the stoves with elegant, seasonal dishes such as braised halibut, seaweed and crab raviolo, charred gem, smoked caviar and lettuce cream.

Chef Elly Wentworth **Seats** 43 **Closed** 1st 2 weeks January **Prices from** S £9.50, M £20, D £9
Notes Vegetarian dishes, No children under 7 years, no children's menu

The Dart Marina Hotel
◉ MODERN BRITISH
01803 832580 | Sandquay Road, TQ6 9PH
www.dartmarina.com
The hotel is a contemporary paradise with neutral colour tones, tasteful and trendy furniture and a swish spa, and it's also home to the River Restaurant. Views of the river are guaranteed through floor-to-ceiling windows, while the menu features regional produce.

Chef Peter Alcroft **Seats** 86 **Closed** 23–26 and 30–31 December **Prices from** S £7, M £16, D £8 **Parking** 100
Notes Vegetarian dishes, Children welcome

The Grill Room

◉ CLASSIC, SEAFOOD

01803 833033 | Royal Castle Hotel, 11 The Quay, TQ6 9PS

www.royalcastle.co.uk

With fishing boats in full view, expect unbeatably fresh fish, while for meat-eaters there'll be prime Devon beef and lamb, maybe even a Chateaubriand. For dinner perhaps, lightly battered lemon sole goujons with lime and chilli, followed by saddle and roasted neck of lamb, leek purée and celeriac Anna, then sticky toffee pudding with vanilla ice cream.

Chef Ankur Biswas **Seats** 60, Private dining 70 **Closed** Christmas **Prices from** S £7, M £15, D £7 **Notes** Vegetarian dishes, Children welcome

The Seahorse

◉◉ MEDITERRANEAN, SEAFOOD *V* ▼ NOTABLE WINE LIST

01803 835147 | 5 South Embankment, TQ6 9BH

www.seahorserestaurant.co.uk

Located in the bustling strip along the Dart waterfront, this is an inviting evening venue, while big windows let in the Devon light on summer days. Local seafood, as you might imagine, features widely on the menus, but there's plenty for non-fish fans as well.

Chef Jake Bridgwood **Seats** 40, Private dining 14 **Closed** 25 December, 1 January **Prices from** S £10, M £18, D £5 **Notes** Children welcome

DODDISCOMBSLEIGH

MAP 3, SX88

The Nobody Inn

◉ MODERN BRITISH

01647 252394 | EX6 7PS

www.nobodyinn.co.uk

This characterful 17th-century inn has a good local reputation, built upon its stylish food, excellent local cheeses, hefty wine list and a 240-long list of whiskies. Reached via winding lanes, inside it has blackened beams, mismatched tables, and walls adorned with plenty of visual interest.

Closed 1 January

DREWSTEIGNTON

MAP 3, SX79

The Old Inn

◉◉◉ INTERNATIONAL

01647 281276 | EX6 6QR

www.old-inn.co.uk

Despite the narrow roads that lead into it on either side, Drewsteignton was once a major staging-post on the coach route from Exeter to Okehampton. A slip of a Dartmoor village to the modern eye, it boasts Duncan Walker's white-fronted, 17th-century inn, a contemporary restaurant-with-rooms that has made the place a destination. The ambience Is homely, with striking modern artworks, and the menu of assured, classically based cooking offers a wealth of enticement. European notes could be as inimitably French as grilled sole fillets with morels and Madeira, followed by Dexter beef pot-au-feu, while quality shines forth from a fillet of halibut crusted in lemon and parsley, served with braised celery. Traditionally conceived desserts punch above their weight as in a textbook tarte Tatin, or a billowing apricot soufflé with vanilla ice cream. A compact wine list is impeccably chosen and complements the heartening simplicity of the approach.

Chef Duncan Walker **Seats** 16, Private dining 10 **Closed** 3 weeks in January **Notes** No children

ERMINGTON

MAP 3, SX65

Plantation House

◉◉ MODERN BRITISH *V*

01548 831100 | Totnes Road, PL21 9NS

www.plantationhousehotel.co.uk

A boutique restaurant in a restored Georgian rectory, with great garden views. The dinner deal here is simple – three courses or five. The five-course option maybe starts with an appetiser, then lentil, leek and Yarg cheese terrine; fillet of turbot with mussels; medallion of fillet steak with smoked lardons; and hand-carved Serrano ham with cave-aged cheddar.

Chef Richard Hendey, John Raines **Seats** 28, Private dining 16 **Open** All Year **Parking** 30 **Notes** Children welcome

EXMOUTH

MAP 3, SY08

Lympstone Manor Hotel *NEW*

◉◉◉◉ MODERN BRITISH

01395 269459 | Courtlands Avenue, EX8 3NZ

www.lympstonemanor.co.uk

It's not often that new country house hotels hit the headlines with such a bang, but when a chef of Michael Caines MBE's stature is the driving force behind the operation, the hospitality world sits up and takes notice. While Lympstone Manor is hardly 'new' – it's a creamy-white, Grade II, Georgian manor built by the Baring banking dynasty – it has been transformed by Michael Caines's vision and now stands proud, a gorgeous building with sublime views over the Exe estuary, set in 28 acres of grounds that were planted with a vineyard in 2018 to produce sparkling wine. The place delivers everything you'd hope from a country house given a stylish 21st-century twist: comfort and sheer class are delivered in equal measure throughout the public areas, the styling working a treat thanks to soft-focus hues, hand-painted wallpapers, designer chandeliers and modern artworks, and the mood is intimate and unbuttoned.

Elegant and outstanding cuisine, augmented by a significant 600-bin wine list, underpin the Lympstone experience, served in three exquisite dining rooms, where the service tone is the same throughout, friendly, engaging and completely devoid of reverentially hushed tones. The cooking delivers a seamless blend of classical technique and precision with contemporary riffs on flavour and texture, opening with cannelloni of basil pasta, filled with sweet langoustine and supported by fennel purée and the sharp kiss of sauce vièrge to counter a creamy langoustine bisque.

Following that, salt cod is married with paprika, crab, samphire and chorizo, an explosion of flavours reined in by the acidity of lemon, while butter-poached Brixham turbot with scallop, leek terrine, cep purée and chive and truffle butter sauce is a dish of silky panache and top-flight technical know-how. Things end with a theme on apple – feather-light mousse, jelly, sorbet, crisps, crumble and caramelised apple purée, all highlighted by vanilla foam.

Chefs Michael Caines, Dan Gamble **Seats** 80 **Open** All year

Saveur
◉◉ MODERN EUROPEAN
01395 269459 | 9 Tower Street, EX8 1NT
www.saveursrestaurant.com
Hidden down a quiet pedestrianised street behind the church, this neighbourhood restaurant ticks all the right boxes when it comes to cosiness, informality and fine cooking. Meaning 'flavour', Saveur celebrates local seafood from Lyme Bay and Brixham as well as other, equally local produce.

Chef Nigel Wright **Seats** 30, Private dining 15 **Closed** 3 weeks January/February **Prices from** S £6.50, M £14.50, D £7.20 **Notes** Vegetarian dishes, Children welcome

HAYTOR VALE
MAP 3, SX77
Rock Inn
◉◉ MODERN BRITISH, CLASSIC
01364 661305 | TQ13 9XP
www.rock-inn.co.uk
The rustic Rock Inn's pre-Victorian air provides a welcoming backdrop to the modern European culinary style on show in its candlelit dining room. A crisp-coated duck Scotch egg with chilli jam and salad leaves is listed among the well-executed starters.

Chef Josh Porter, Sophie Collier, Tom Schofield, Louis Bennett **Seats** 75, Private dining 20 **Closed** 25-26 December **Prices from** S £6.25, M £16.50, D £6.95 **Parking** 25 **Notes** Vegetarian dishes, Children welcome

HONITON
MAP 4, ST10
The Holt Bar & Restaurant
◉ MODERN BRITISH
01404 47707 | 178 High Street, EX14 1LA
www.theholt-honiton.com
The Holt's main dining area is upstairs: open-plan, with a wooden floor, simple decor, candlelight, and pleasant, efficient service. Food is a serious commitment here and standards are consistently high, with the menu a happy blend of the traditional and more à la mode.

Closed 25-26 December

THE PIG at Combe
◉◉ SEASONAL BRITISH 🍷 NOTABLE WINE LIST
01404 540400 | Giltisham, EX14 3AD
www.thepighotel.com/at-combe
Set in an Elizabethan mansion of honeyed stone in 3,500 acres, any hint of starchy country-house formality is banished here, so dining is an informal affair in a rustic-chic setting, and the '25 Mile' menu reveals a kitchen that gets serious on sustainability and localism, with an abundant kitchen garden for seasonal supplies and minimal food miles.

Chef Daniel Gavriilidis **Seats** 75, Private dining 22 **Open** All Year **Prices from** S £7.50, M £16, D £8.50 **Parking** 57 **Notes** Vegetarian dishes, Children welcome

ILFRACOMBE
MAP 3, SS54

Sandy Cove Hotel
◉◉ MODERN BRITISH
01271 882243 | Old Coast Road, Combe Martin Bay, Berrynarbor, EX34 9SR
www.sandycove-hotel.co.uk
With stunning views of both the bay and the wild landscape of Exmoor, Sandy Cove Hotel offers the best of both worlds. Positioned to maximise the vista with large windows (and a terrace when the weather allows), the restaurant offers a hypnotic view.

Open All Year

ILSINGTON
MAP 3, SX77

Ilsington Country House Hotel
◉◉ MODERN EUROPEAN
01364 661452 | Ilsington Village, TQ13 9RR
www.ilsington.co.uk
A substantial white property, Ilsington's diverse menu includes some divertingly appealing dishes. Accompaniments complement the main ingredients without swamping them, seen in main courses of roast chicken with maple and mustard gel, pommes Anna, pea purée, mushrooms, confit tomato and smoked beetroot.

Chef Mike O'Donnell **Seats** 75, Private dining 60 **Closed** 2-17 January **Parking** 60 **Notes** Vegetarian dishes, Children welcome

KENTISBURY
MAP 3, SS64

The Coach House by Michael Caines
◉◉◉ MODERN BRITISH *V*
01271 882295 | Kentisbury Grange, EX31 4NL
www.kentisburygrange.com
On the fringes of Exmoor National Park, just a short, pretty drive to the north coast, Kentisbury Grange is a former Victorian manor lovingly morphed into classy boutique hotel. The old manor's coach house was not forgotten in the transition and has been turned into a stunning restaurant, and with its kitchen under the guidance of Michael Caines, it's quite the dining destination. The impressive space is contemporary rustic, with a stylish bar on the first floor and tables outside for when the mercury has risen in north Devon. Regional ingredients get a good outing on menus that show intelligent flavour combinations in the modern British manner. A first-course squab pigeon comes with beetroot tartare and preserved blueberries, while crab ravioli has spikes of lemongrass and ginger, and a full-flavoured crab bisque. Among main courses,

Cornish sea bass stars with hay-roasted Jerusalem artichokes and a hit of truffles, and slow-cooked pork tenderloin arrives with white pudding purée. For dessert, the apple and blackcurrant soufflé with Granny Smith apple sorbet is a fine, fruity finale.

Chef James Mason **Seats** 54, Private dining 16 **Open** All year **Parking** 70 **Notes** Children welcome

KINGSBRIDGE
MAP 3, SX74

Buckland-Tout-Saints Hotel
◉◉ MODERN BRITISH
01548 853055 | Goveton, TQ7 2DS
www.tout-saints.co.uk
Set in four acres of stunning grounds in South Hams, this handsome William and Mary-era manor house provides a classy country-house package. The interior is packed with period details, not least in the Queen Anne Restaurant where seasonal menus aim to please.

Open All Year

KNOWSTONE
MAP 3, SS82

The Masons Arms
◉◉ MODERN BRITISH
01398 341231 | EX36 4RY
www.masonsarmsdevon.co.uk
In the idyllic village of Knowstone, this thatched 13th-century country inn is set deep in the lush countryside on the Devon and Somerset border. Chef-patron Mark Dodson once cooked under Michel Roux at Bray, which might explain the flair and precision evident in the kitchen.

Chef Mark Dodson, Jamie Coleman **Seats** 28 **Closed** 1st week in January, February half term and 1 week August Bank Holiday **Prices from** S £9.50, M £25.50, D £9.25 **Parking** 10 **Notes** Vegetarian dishes, No children under 5 years at dinner

LIFTON
MAP 3, SX38

Arundell Arms
◉◉ MODERN BRITISH *V*
01566 784666 | Fore Street, PL16 0AA
www.arundellarms.com
What looks like a rural pub on the outside is an elevated country hotel within, with lavish traditional furnishings and a large dining room. The kitchen offers a traditionally based Anglo-French repertoire founded on quality materials. There's a gentle richness to the impact of dishes.

Chef Chris Heaver **Seats** 70, Private dining 24 **Parking** 70 **Notes** Children welcome

LYNMOUTH

Rising Sun
◉◉ BRITISH, FRENCH
01598 753223 | Harbourside, EX35 6EG
www.risingsunlynmouth.co.uk
The Rising Sun rocks with good vibrations with its bar plus an atmospheric oak-panelled dining room. The food strikes a balance between hearty generosity and contemporary combinations, with plenty of seafood dishes. Start with seared king scallops with cauliflower cream and pancetta.

Closed Christmas

MORETONHAMPSTEAD

Great Western
◉◉◉ MODERN BRITISH *V*
01647 445000 | Bovey Castle, Dartmoor National Park, North Bovey, TQ13 8RE
www.boveycastle.com
Built in 1890 by stationery supremo WH Smith, Bovey Castle was reinvented as a 'golfing hotel' by the Great Western Railway company back in 1930, an association acknowledged in its top dining venue, the Great Western restaurant. It's a grand old pile, big, bold, and glamorous, with the requisite spa and golf course to keep 21st-century sybarites busy until dinner. The Great Western is an equally plush space, suitably romantic with art deco lines. Local lad Mark Budd leads the kitchen team, and his fondness for regional ingredients from land and sea looms large in good-looking contemporary dishes that reveal well-honed technical skills and sound classical roots – from starters like squab pigeon with almonds, blood orange and sorrel to mains such as Creedy Carver duck with turnip, Roscoff onions and date sauce or roast fillet of Darmoor beef with beef cheek, boulangère potatoes, Grelot onions and celeriac.

Chef Mark Budd **Seats** 120, Private dining 32 **Open** All Year **Parking** 100 **Notes** Children welcome

Smith's Brasserie
◉ BRITISH *V*
01647 445000 | Bovey Castle, Dartmoor National Park, North Bovey, TQ13 8RE
www.boveycastle.com
Set in 275 acres of stunning countryside in the heart of Dartmoor National Park, Bovey Castle boasts a spa and 18-hole championship golf course. Smith's Brasserie is the more informal of the hotel's two restaurants and offers a relaxed dining experience with broad appeal.

Chef Mark Budd **Open** All Year **Prices from** S £8, M £16, D £8 **Parking** 100 **Notes** Children welcome

OKEHAMPTON

Lewtrenchard Manor *NEW*
◉◉ MODERN BRITISH *V*
01566 783222 | Lewdown, EX20 4PN
www.lewtrenchard.co.uk
In a secluded valley beneath Dartmoor, this Jacobean manor dates back to the 17th century, as the wood-panelled restaurant attests with its ornate plasterwork and heavy-framed portraits. An emphasis on local meat and fish, as well as vegetables and fruits from the manor garden, drives the modern, ingredient-led menu.

Chef Tom Browning **Seats** 35, Private dining 65 **Open** All Year **Prices from** S £7.50, M £15, D £7 **Parking** 30 **Notes** No children under 8 years at dinner

PLYMOUTH

Artillery Tower Restaurant
◉ MODERN BRITISH
01752 257610 | Firestone Bay, Durnford Street, PL1 3QR
www.artillerytower.co.uk
A 16th-century circular gunnery tower on Plymouth waterfront – be sure to grip the handrail tight as you climb the spiral staircase. Arched windows that once served as gun emplacements in three-foot walls surround the dining space, where simple, modern bistro food is the drill.

Chef Peter Constable **Seats** 26, Private dining 16 **Closed** Christmas and New Year **Parking** 20 **Notes** Vegetarian dishes, Children welcome

Barbican Kitchen
◉ MODERN, INTERNATIONAL
01752 604448 | Plymouth Gin Distillery, 60 Southside Street, PL1 2LQ
barbicankitchen.com
The Tanner brothers' vibrant restaurant spreads over two floors of the Plymouth Gin Distillery and packs a visual punch with its whitewashed stone walls, exposed rafters, bold colours and cool artworks. The ambience is youthful and casual, and the brasserie-style menu offers a feel-good foray into contemporary tastes with a West Country flavour.

Chef Martyn Compton, Christopher and James Tanner **Seats** 100, Private dining 22 **Closed** 25–26 and 31 December **Prices from** S £5.95, M £12.95, D £5.95 **Notes** Vegetarian dishes, Children welcome

MAP 3, SX45

Boringdon Hall Hotel

◉◉◉ **MODERN FRENCH** *V*
01752 344455 | Boringdon Hill, Plympton, PL7 4DP
www.boringdonhall.co.uk

Energetic modern cooking overlooking the Great Hall

With a pedigree somewhat more ancient than the average country house, Boringdon is dripping with historical flavour. The place was gifted by Henry VIII as a deconsecrated priory to one of his favoured courtiers, the Earl of Southampton, who in turn sold it on to the Grey family that produced England's nine-day queen.

The Tudor manor is beautifully preserved and makes a sumptuous country house hotel these days, run with engaging charm and due formality, and replete with the full-works package of spa, wedding and conference facilities, not to mention some seriously accomplished, bang up-to-date cooking. Its dining room occupies a gallery overlooking the Great Hall with its moulded plaster coat of arms, where Scott Paton is fully up to the task of matching the grand surroundings with his artfully crafted cooking. Bringing seasonal ingredients into

sharp focus with ingenuity and flair, a slew of menus covers all bases, from a keenly-priced two- or three-course lunch deal, through to a dinner carte, and five- and seven-course tasters, plus veggie and vegan versions to keep a finger on the modern dining pulse, with ideas such as fermented mushroom pâté with lapsang souchong jelly, or roasted celeriac with celery tart and truffle showing admirable versatility.

Opting for the middle ground of the five-course performance, lightly aerated Vulscombe goats' cheese with beetroot in various preparations, elderflower and gingerbread gets things off to a flying start, followed by a scallop taco that brings explosions of distinct flavours from coriander, chilli and parmesan crisp. Asian notes come into play once more in a dish deploying curried emulsion, mango, cardamom and lime in support of excellent Brixham crab. Next up, sea-fresh lemon sole turns up in a thoughtfully composed idea with fennel, leek and nori. It all finishes on a climactic note with intense raspberry mousse, jelly and sorbet with pistachio cream.

Chef Scott Paton
Seats 40, Private dining 26
Notes No children

"... seriously accomplished, bang up-to-date cooking. Bringing seasonal ingredients into sharp focus with ingenuity and flair, a slew of menus covers all bases"

PLYMOUTH continued

Best Western Duke of Cornwall Hotel

◉◉ MODERN BRITISH, EUROPEAN

01752 275850 | Millbay Road, PL1 3LG

www.thedukeofcornwall.co.uk

A Plymouth landmark for the past 150 years, you certainly can't miss the Duke of Cornwall hotel with its imposing Gothic exterior and Corinthian-style pillars. The kitchen works a modern European repertoire with a decent showing of West Country ingredients.

Closed 26–31 December

Boringdon Hall Hotel

◉◉◉ MODERN FRENCH **V**

See pages 116–117

The Greedy Goose

◉◉ MODERN BRITISH

01752 252001 | Prysten House, Finewell Street, PL1 2AE

www.thegreedygoose.co.uk

Occupying Plymouth's oldest building, the contemporary cooking at The Greedy Goose is centred around prime West Country produce, including seafood landed at the nearby fish market. A small plate starter of octopus with Indonesian soy sauce, mango, chilli and lime could lead to malt-glazed pork belly, black pudding, apple and braised carrot.

Chef Ben Palmer Seats 50, Private dining 30 Closed 24 December to 1st Tuesday in January Prices from S £6, M £16 Notes Vegetarian dishes, No children under 4 years

Langdon Court Hotel & Restaurant

◉◉ TRADITIONAL BRITISH, FRENCH

01752 862358 | Adams Lane, Down Thomas, PL9 0DY

www.langdoncourt.com

A 16th-century manor house in the beautiful South Hams, Langdon Court has played host to royal personages and their consorts since the days of Henry VIII and Catherine Parr. A country-house hotel since 1960, local farms and Devon fishermen supply the kitchen.

Open All Year

Rock Salt Café and Brasserie

◉◉ MODERN BRITISH **V**

01752 225522 | 31 Stonehouse Street, PL1 3PE

www.rocksaltcafe.co.uk

With its bare tables, pared back decor and cool artworks, this slate-tiled former pub strikes a relaxed pose but there's clearly a safe pair of hands at the stoves. Expect impressive attention to detail in food that's packed with tight, punchy flavours, and you couldn't ask for a fairer deal than the two- or three-course set lunch.

Chef David Jenkins Seats 60, Private dining 25 Closed 24–26 December Prices from S £6, M £14, D £6.50 Notes Children welcome

See advertisement opposite

The Wildflower Restaurant

◉ CLASSIC BRITISH

01822 852245 | Moorland Garden Hotel, Yelverton, PL20 6DA

www.moorlandgardenhotel.co.uk

The Moorland Garden Hotel's colourful and smart restaurant has views over the pristine garden to wild Dartmoor beyond, with floor-to-ceiling windows and its own terrace to ensure the best is made of the setting. The kitchen focuses on British flavours.

Chef Jake Westlake Seats 70 Open All Year Prices from S £5.95, M £12.95, D £5.95 Parking 120 Notes Vegetarian dishes, Children welcome

---

ROCKBEARE MAP 3, SY09

The Jack In The Green Inn

◉◉ MODERN BRITISH **V**

01404 822240 | EX5 2EE

www.jackinthegreen.uk.com

This family-friendly roadside pub has gained a well-deserved reputation for its upmarket modern British food. With its low-beamed rooms, soft brown leather chairs and a wood-burning stove, the smart interior creates a contemporary atmosphere and innovative menus offer smart, thoughtful dishes with punchy flavours.

Chef Matthew Mason Seats 80, Private dining 60 Closed 25 December to 5 January Prices from S £6.50, M £19.50, D £6.50 Parking 120 Notes Children welcome

---

SALCOMBE MAP 3, SX73

The Jetty

◉ MODERN, INTERNATIONAL **V**

01548 844444 | Salcombe Harbour Hotel & Spa, Cliff Road, TQ8 8JH

www.harbourhotels.co.uk/hotels/salcombe

There are fabulous views over the estuary from The Jetty's prime position within the Salcombe Harbour Hotel. The hotel's spa facilities, and even a private cinema, offer many distractions, but time is never better spent than when sitting in the smart, contemporary restaurant.

Chef Jamie Gulliford Seats 100, Private dining 100 Open All Year Prices from S £7, M £13, D £6.50 Parking 10 Notes Children welcome

SALCOMBE continued

Soar Mill Cove Hotel

◉◉ MODERN BRITISH

01548 561566 | Soar Mill Cove, Marlborough, TQ7 3DS

www.soarmillcove.co.uk

With the stunning cove below, this family-run hotel occupies a fabulous position with sweeping sea views. Needless to say, local fish and seafood get a strong showing in a kitchen that combines classical techniques with modern ideas. Thus, monkfish with boulangère potatoes, mussel and clam provençal with basil purée.

Chef Ian Macdonald **Seats** 60 **Closed** January
Prices from S £8, M £18, D £8 **Parking** 25
Notes Vegetarian dishes, Children welcome

SAUNTON   MAP 3, SS43

Saunton Sands Hotel

◉◉ TRADITIONAL, MODERN BRITISH

01271 890212 | EX33 1LQ

www.sauntonsands.com

The location alone is a draw at this long white art deco hotel overlooking a three-mile stretch of unspoiled sandy beach. Watch the sun set from the terrace or soak up the maritime views from the large and stylish restaurant with original 1930s chandeliers.

Chef Mathias Oberg **Seats** 200, Private dining 60
Prices from S £8, M £16, D £8 **Parking** 140
Notes Vegetarian dishes, Children welcome

SIDMOUTH   MAP 3, SY18

Hotel Riviera

◉◉ MODERN BRITISH

01395 515201 | The Esplanade, EX10 8AY

www.hotelriviera.co.uk

The name may suggest Cannes or Las Vegas, but the spotless bow-fronted Riviera is a prime example of Devon's own seaside grandeur. Terrace tables make the most of the summer weather, and a menu of gently modernised British cooking caters for most tastes.

Chef Martin Osedo **Seats** 85, Private dining 65 **Open** All Year **Prices from** S £10.50, M £16, D £6.50 **Parking** 26
Notes Vegetarian dishes, Children welcome

The Salty Monk

◉◉ MODERN BRITISH ⬛NOTABLE WINE LIST

01395 513174 | Church Street, Sidford, EX10 9QP

www.saltymonk.com

The name is not a reference to a seafaring friar, but rather to the building's 16th-century role as a store for the salt that the monks traded at Exeter Cathedral. The Garden Room restaurant makes a smart yet understated backdrop for the unpretentious cooking.

Chef Annette and Andy Witheridge **Seats** 30, Private dining 18 **Closed** 1 week in November, January
Prices from S £6.50, M £18.50, D £6.50 **Parking** 20
Notes Vegetarian dishes, Children welcome

The Victoria Hotel

◉ TRADITIONAL

01395 512651 | The Esplanade, EX10 8RY

www.victoriahotel.co.uk

The setting at the end of the town's impressive esplanade is alluring, with the expansive bay offered up in all its shimmering glory. From the doorman to the pianist, The Victoria oozes old-world charm and what appears on the plate is generally classically minded.

Open All Year

SOUTH ZEAL   MAP 3, SX69

Oxenham Arms

◉ MODERN BRITISH *V*

01837 840244 | EX20 2JT

www.theoxenhamarms.com

Set in deepest Dartmoor country, the historic Oxenham Arms is still the hub of village life. The place began in the 12th century as a monastery but today contemporary touches blend seamlessly with an ambience of gnarled beams, whitewashed stone walls and stone mullioned windows. A comfort-oriented menu of unfussy country inn food scores many hits.

Chef Lyn Powell **Seats** 80, Private dining 32 **Open** All Year **Prices from** S £5.50, M £7.95, D £4.50 **Parking** 7
Notes Vegetarian dishes, Children welcome

STRETE

The Laughing Monk
MODERN BRITISH
01803 770639 | Totnes Road, TQ6 0RN
www.thelaughingmonkdevon.co.uk
The South West Coast Path runs practically outside the front door of this converted school, and Slapton and Blackpool Sands are a mere mile off. Inside is an airy space with an impressive inglenook and cheery atmosphere, and a kitchen making use of Devon's resources.

Closed Christmas and January

TAVISTOCK

Bedford Hotel
BRITISH
01822 613221 | 1 Plymouth Road, PL19 8BB
www.bedford-hotel.co.uk
Despite the castellated walls, this imposing Gothic building has always been about hospitality, and there is no lack of character or charm in the restaurant, with its moulded ceilings and panelled walls. The kitchen takes a more contemporary position, but a reassuringly gentle one.

Chef Mike Palmer Seats 55, Private dining 30
Closed 24–26 December Prices from S £4.50, M £13, D £6.75 Parking 48 Notes Vegetarian dishes, Children welcome

The Horn of Plenty
MODERN BRITISH V
01822 832528 | Gulworthy, PL19 8JD
www.thehornofplenty.co.uk
With stunning views over the Tamar Valley, this charming, mid 19th-century country house hotel once belonged to the Duke of Bedford's mining chief. A team of six chefs creates award-winning cuisine, as in Creedy Carver duck terrine with slow-cooked duck egg and truffle dressing; pan-roasted hake with lobster ravioli, spinach and carrot purée; and treacle sourdough roll.

Chef Ashley Wright Seats 40, Private dining 16 Open All Year Parking 25 Notes Children welcome

THURLESTONE

Thurlestone Hotel
BRITISH V
01548 560382 | TQ7 3NN
www.thurlestone.co.uk
The view across the golf course and sub-tropical gardens to the sea is a cracker, making The Trevilder restaurant a star attraction. The menu, including the daily-changing 'Market Dishes', makes good use of the region's produce in dishes that have classical foundations.

Chef Hugh Miller Seats 150, Private dining 150 Closed 2 weeks January Parking 120 Notes Children welcome

The Village Inn
MODERN BRITISH
01548 563525 | Thurlestone Hotel, TQ7 3NN
www.thurlestone.co.uk
Among the original building materials of the 16th-century Village Inn are timbers from ships of the Spanish Armada wrecked off the Devon coast. It's all been sensitively spruced up, with plenty of light wood, a log burner, and an outdoor dining space by the pool.

Open All Year

TORQUAY

The Abbey Sands Hotel
MODERN BRITISH, EUROPEAN
01803 294373 | Belgrave Road, TQ2 5HG
abbeysandshotel.co.uk
The restaurant at The Abbey Sands Hotel seeks to reflect local flavours. Expect a good choice for fish of the day or instead tuck into the Chef's Burger with handcut chips. Finish perhaps with a brownie or mixed berry compôte.

Open All Year

Cary Arms
BRITISH, SEAFOOD
01803 327110 | Babbacombe Beach, TQ1 3LX
www.caryarms.co.uk
On a glorious summer's day, the terraced gardens leading to the water's edge are an unforgettable place to eat, but the whitewashed Cary Arms does have more than its fair share of good things: a beamed bar with stone walls and dreamy views.

Open All Year

The Elephant Restaurant by Simon Hulstone

◉◉◉ MODERN BRITISH

01803 200044 | 3–4 Beacon Terrace, TQ1 2BH

www.elephantrestaurant.co.uk

Torquay can consider itself very fortunate that Simon Hulstone has opted to build a long-running enterprise here at his very attractive harbourside venue. Inside, it has a breezy brasserie air, with large gilt-edged mirrors reflecting the scene, and staff who keep things informal and friendly. Glimpses into the kitchen pass at the back reveal a small brigade working in productive harmony to construct modern, locally sourced dishes of obvious allure. A pairing of braised pig's cheek and black pudding is sharpened with pickled apple and textured with hazelnuts, after which a main course like perfectly timed halibut with herbed crab tortellini, fennel and carrot in fragrant lemongrass sauce offers flawless balance. Guinea fowl breast with wild mushroom pithivier in truffled jus is a richer option. Dessert brings refreshment in the shape of thin-shelled lemon tart with passionfruit and banana sorbet and a flat disc of lemon verbena meringue.

Chef Simon Hulstone **Seats** 75 **Closed** 1st 2 weeks in January **Prices from** S £8, M £14, D £8 **Notes** Vegetarian dishes, Children welcome

Grand Hotel

◉ MODERN EUROPEAN

01803 296677 | Torbay Road, TQ2 6NT

www.grandtorquay.co.uk

Occupying a prime position on Torquay's seafront, the Grand certainly has presence, built in Victorian times and expanding as the popularity of the English Riviera grew. The main dining option is the 1881 Restaurant, its genteel formality in keeping with its august past (Agatha Christie spent her honeymoon here). The menu sticks to traditional ideas with just enough contemporary thrust to satisfy both schools.

Open All Year

The Imperial Hotel

◉ MODERN BRITISH

01803 294301 | Park Hill Road, TQ1 2DG

www.theimperialtorquay.co.uk

The Imperial's Victorian founders couldn't have chosen a better spot for their hotel, whose clifftop position has wide-ranging views over the bay and Channel. The kitchen chooses its ingredients diligently, making good use of fish and local produce, and turns out well-considered, carefully-timed dishes.

Open All Year

Orestone Manor

◉◉ MODERN, EUROPEAN

01803 328098 | Rockhouse Lane, Maidencombe, TQ1 4SX

www.orestonemanor.com

This handsome Georgian manor house occupies landscaped grounds over Lyme Bay. The main restaurant is a traditional space with wooden floors and linen-swathed tables – a suitable setting for the kitchen's ambitious à la carte menus. Classic French-accented technique delivers refined dishes.

Chef Neil and Catherine D'Allen, Daryll Sharpe **Seats** 55 **Closed** 3–30 January **Prices from** S £6.50, M £19, D £6.50 **Parking** 38 **Notes** Vegetarian dishes, Children welcome

Seasons

◉ MODERN BRITISH

01803 226366 | Belgrave Sands Hotel & Spa, Belgrave Road, TQ2 5HF

www.belgravesands.com

Set in the Belgrave Sands Hotel, just a stone's throw from the seafront, Seasons restaurant is a bright, comfortable space, with unclothed, dark wood tables and live music in the evenings. Contemporary British cooking features on the six-course menu, with particular attention paid to seasonality.

Chef Stephen Sanders **Seats** 90 **Open** All Year **Prices from** S £6.50, M £18, D £6.50 **Parking** 50 **Notes** Vegetarian dishes, Children welcome

TOTNES
MAP 3, SX86

The Riverford Field Kitchen

@ MODERN BRITISH, ORGANIC

01803 762074 | Riverford, TQ11 0JU

www.riverford.co.uk

Wash Farm is the hub of the Riverford brand, delivering organically grown fruit and veg across the land. Hunker down here at communal tables for hearty organic food, a fixed deal of whatever is on-the-money that day – dishes are always teeming with superlative vegetable and frsh salad accompaniments.

Closed 24-26 December and Monday to Tuesday in January and February

TWO BRIDGES
MAP 3, SX67

Two Bridges Hotel

@@ MODERN BRITISH *V*

01822 892300 | PL20 6SW

www.twobridges.co.uk

Deep in the Dartmoor National Park, the Tors restaurant in this character riverside hotel was refurbished in 2019. Local farmers and fishermen supply the kitchen with top notch produce for modern British dishes like Devon crab ravioli, bisque, brown shrimp and crayfish or Creedy Carver duck, red cabbage, pink peppercorn and pistachio praline.

Chef Mike Palmer **Seats** 85, Private dining 20 **Open** All Year **Prices from** S £5.50, M £9.50, D £7 **Parking** 150 **Notes** Children welcome

WOOLACOMBE
MAP 3, SS44

Doyle's Restaurant

@@ MODERN BRITISH

01271 870388 | The Woolacombe Bay Hotel, South Street, EX34 7BN

www.woolacombe-bay-hotel.co.uk

Overlooking Woolacombe Bay, this stylish hotel is set in six acres of landscaped grounds and is a six-minute walk from the beach. No surprise that the menu in the elegant Doyle's restaurant puts such emphasis on local meat and fresh fish from the Devon coast.

Chef Eduard Grecu **Seats** 80, Private dining 40 **Closed** 2 January to mid February, 15-16 November **Prices from** S £6, M £13, D £6.50 **Notes** Vegetarian dishes, Children welcome

Watersmeet Hotel

@@ TRADITIONAL BRITISH, EUROPEAN

01271 870333 | Mortehoe, EX34 7EB

www.watersmeethotel.co.uk

Surfers hang loose in the Atlantic below as diners enjoy the attentive, uniformed service of the hotel's clifftop Pavilion Restaurant. A frequently-changing menu of British cooking might suggest a three-course meal of wild mushroom and egg-yolk ravioli; halibut fillet with oyster emulsion and bacon; and vanilla pannacotta, cherry compôte and meringues.

Chef John Prince **Seats** 56, Private dining 18 **Closed** January **Parking** 40 **Notes** Vegetarian dishes, No children under 8 years

YEALMPTON
MAP 3, SX55

Kitley House Hotel Restaurant *NEW*

@ MODERN BRITISH

01752 881555 | PL8 2NW

www.kitleyhousehotel.com

With five centuries of history and 600 acres to roam in and work up an appetite, Kitley House offers plenty of special-occasion class. The place is run with due country-house, friendly professionalism, and there's something to suit most tastes on an accessible menu of uncomplicated modern British food that doesn't try to reinvent the wheel.

Open All Year

■ DORSET

BEAMINSTER

Brassica Restaurant
◉ MODERN EUROPEAN
01308 538100 | 4 The Square, DT8 3AS
www.brassicarestaurant.co.uk
On the main square, Brassica occupies a Grade II listed property overlooking the hubbub (or what passes for hubbub) of this small market town. Chef-director Cass Titcombe draws on a wealth of experience to deliver a daily-changing menu of local ingredients and broader European ideas.

Chef Cass Titcombe Seats 40 Closed Christmas Prices from S £6, M £13, D £6.50 Notes Vegetarian dishes, Children welcome

BOURNEMOUTH

The Connaught Brasserie
◉◉ MODERN BRITISH
01202 298020 | 30 West Hill Road, West Cliff, BH2 5PH
www.theconnaught.co.uk
With sandy beaches stretching below, the grand old Connaught rules the roost on Bournemouth's West Cliff. The Blakes restaurant overlooks the hotel's gardens, where candlelit outdoor tables are popular on summer evenings. Inside, the lightly formal tone makes an agreeable ambience for traditionally-based British dishes.

Chef Peter Tofis Seats 80, Private dining 16 Open All Year Prices from S £6, M £10.50, D £6.50 Parking 66 Notes Vegetarian dishes, Children welcome

The Crab at Bournemouth
◉◉ MODERN BRITISH
01202 203601 | Park Central Hotel, Exeter Road, BH2 5AJ
www.crabatbournemouth.com
The epitome of a seafront venue, the Crab is part of the white-fronted Park Central Hotel, but functions as a restaurant in its own right, smartly done out in sandy hues. An array of fresh fish and shellfish is on the menu.

Chef Martin Pacholarz Seats 80 Open All Year Prices from S £7.75, M £16.95, D £7.95 Notes Vegetarian dishes, Children welcome

Cumberland Hotel
◉◉ MODERN BRITISH
01202 290722 | 27 East Overcliffe Drive, BH1 3AF
www.cumberlandbournemouth.co.uk
High up on Bournemouth's East Cliff, this art deco hotel boasts all the monochrome touches of that decadent period. Not that the cooking in the hotel's elegant Ventana Grand Café restaurant is stuck in the 1930s - the food is modern British to the core. As befits a hotel with panoramic sea views, fish gets a strong showing.

Chef Yessica Gorin Seats 50 Open All Year Prices from S £5.95, M £16.95, D £6.25 Notes No children

The Green House
◉◉ MODERN BRITISH
01202 498900 | 4 Grove Road, BH1 3AX
www.thegreenhousehotel.co.uk
The Green House is a striking-looking, centrally located property converted and run on sustainable principles. There are beehives on the roof, and the Arbor (Latin for 'tree' to further underline its green credentials) Restaurant deals in only organic, Fairtrade and farm-assured, mostly local produce.

Open All Year

Hermitage Hotel
◉ TRADITIONAL BRITISH
01202 557363 | Exeter Road, BH2 5AH
www.hermitage-hotel.co.uk
Hardy's Restaurant at the Hermitage, opposite the beach, is a large, traditionally styled room. The interesting menus serve local and sustainable ingredients and offer variety aplenty, as they must with residents eating here perhaps every evening.

Chef Iain McBride Seats 120, Private dining 50 Open All Year Prices from S £5, M £14.50, D £4.50 Parking 60 Notes Vegetarian dishes, Children welcome

No 34 at The Orchid Hotel
◉ EUROPEAN
01202 551600 | 34 Gervis Road, BH1 3DH
www.orchidhotel.co.uk
Close to the beach, No 34 is the flagship restaurant at The Orchid, a contemporary and secluded hotel in Bournemouth's lovely Eastcliff area. The kitchen cuts no corners when it comes to sourcing premium ingredients, much of it sourced from the region.

Open All Year

Roots

◎◎ MODERN EUROPEAN *V*

01202 430005 | 141 Belle Vue Road, BH6 3EN

www.restaurantroots.co.uk

The food here is simple, confident and effective. Service is charming, passionate and knowledgeable, and a key part of the experience. Monthly changing tasting menus, either 5- or 7-course, feature well-executed dishes with punchy flavours.

Chef Jan Bretschneider **Seats** 20 **Closed** 23 December to beginning of January **Notes** Children welcome

CHRISTCHURCH
MAP 5, SZ19

Captain's Club Hotel & Spa

◎◎ MODERN EUROPEAN

01202 475111 | Wick Ferry, Wick Lane, BH23 1HU

www.captainsclubhotel.com

A glass-fronted boutique hotel by the River Stour, where the kitchen serves up modern brasserie fare, fully in keeping with the attractive surroundings. Veggie possibilities include an Indian-spiced cauliflower risotto with coconut and coriander, and the desserts include some crowd-pleasing choices.

Chef Andrew Gault **Seats** 100, Private dining 120 **Open** All Year **Prices from** S £7, M £13, D £6 **Parking** 41 **Notes** Vegetarian dishes, Children welcome

The Jetty

◎◎ MODERN BRITISH *V*

01202 400950 | Christchurch Harbour Hotel & Spa, 95 Mudeford, BH23 3NT

www.thejetty.co.uk

A dashing contemporary construction of glass and wood, The Jetty's culinary output is headed up by Alex Aitken. Provenance is everything here. In fine weather, grab a table on the terrace if you can, although floor-to-ceiling windows provide glorious views over Mudeford Quay. The kitchen turns out contemporary dishes taking inspiration from far and wide.

Chef Alex Aitken **Seats** 70 **Open** All Year **Prices from** S £9, M £19.95, D £6 **Parking** 20 **Notes** Children welcome

The Lord Bute & Restaurant

◎◎ BRITISH, MEDITERRANEAN

01425 278884 | 179-181 Lymington Road, Highcliffe-on-Sea, BH23 4JS

www.lordbute.com

In the grounds of 18th-century prime minister Lord Bute's Highcliffe Castle, this hotel has wonderful neighbours – east Dorset's golden beaches. Among highlights on the classical restaurant and orangery menu are fillet of Jurassic Coast beef stuffed with mushrooms; pan-seared halibut, king prawns, garlic and chilli; and roasted vegetables, spinach, asparagus and mozzarella.

Chef Jeremy Lenton **Seats** 95 **Open** All Year **Prices from** S £7.50, M £14.95, D £7.95 **Parking** 50 **Notes** Vegetarian dishes, Children welcome

Upper Deck Bar & Restaurant

◎ MODERN BRITISH

01202 400954 | Christchurch Harbour Hotel & Spa, 95 Mudeford, BH23 3NT

www.christchurch-harbour-hotel.co.uk/upper-deck

Good views over the water are guaranteed, as is a fine showing of regional produce. The Upper Deck is pretty swanky, featuring a sleek, contemporary bar and an upmarket seasidey vibe, plus there's a terrace. The cooking takes a modern British route through contemporary tastes and, given the setting, plenty of locally-landed fish.

Open All Year

CORFE CASTLE
MAP 4, SY98

Mortons House Hotel

◎◎ MODERN BRITISH

01929 480988 | 45 East Street, BH20 5EE

www.mortonshouse.co.uk

An Elizabethan manor with a well-appointed dining room. In his kitchen, the long-standing head chef, inspired by traditional British and international cuisine, focuses on grilled steaks and local seafood. His repertoire includes smoked ham hock terrine with Scotch quail's egg and fresh piccalilli, and fillet of sea bass with crab and galangal sauce.

Chef Ed Firth **Seats** 60, Private dining 20 **Open** All Year **Prices from** S £7, M £15, D £7.50 **Parking** 40 **Notes** Vegetarian dishes, No children under 5 years

EVERSHOT

MAP 4, ST50

The Acorn Inn

⊛ BRITISH

01935 83228 | 28 Fore Street, DT2 0JW

www.acorn-inn.co.uk

Plumb in the middle of Thomas Hardy's favourite stretch of England, the 16th-century coaching inn makes an appearance in *Tess of the d'Urbervilles* as the Sow and Acorn. The country-style restaurant is a friendly spot to linger and enjoy the seasonal dishes.

Open All Year

George Albert Hotel

⊛ MODERN BRITISH

01935 483430 | Wardon Hill, DT2 9PW

www.georgealberthotel.co.uk

The George Albert opened its doors relatively recently, in 2010, but despite its newness, monogrammed carpets and starched table linen bring a traditional feel to Kings Restaurant. On the menu, main courses bring all their components together in well-balanced harmony.

Chef Andy Pike Seats 40, Private dining 200 Parking 200 Notes Vegetarian dishes, Children welcome

Summer Lodge Country House Hotel, Restaurant & Spa

⊛⊛⊛ MODERN BRITISH

01935 482000 | Fore Street, DT2 0JR

www.summerlodgehotel.com

Starting life as a Georgian dower house, Summer Lodge had another layer added in 1893 when its resident Earl commissioned local architect (and sometime novelist) Thomas Hardy to draw up the plans. It stands in a neat four acres next to an extensive deer park, and is decorated throughout in impeccable country-house elegance. A riot of pinks and purples illuminates the dining room, making a suitably dramatic setting for Steven Titman's exploratory modern cooking. The evening carte offers a wealth of inspired choice, and you might begin with Portland crab tortellini, with sweetcorn purée, chilli, coriander and aromatic lemon grass velouté – a very successful combination of flavours – followed by accurately cooked, tender Creedy Carver duck breast with pear and brown butter purée, hazelnut and potato gratin and thyme jus demonstrating reassuring depth of flavour. For the grand finale, there could be coconut cremeaux tart with lemongrass curd and silky-smooth yuzu and sake sorbet, or choices from the selection of no less than 27 artisan cheeses.

Chef Steven Titman Seats 60, Private dining 20 Open All Year Parking 60 Notes Vegetarian dishes, Children welcome

FARNHAM

MAP 4, ST91

The Museum Inn

⊛⊛ MODERN, TRADITIONAL BRITISH

01725 516261 | DT11 8DE

www.museuminn.co.uk

This 17th-century inn occupies a lovely spot in the Cranborne Chase, a designated Area of Outstanding Natural Beauty. Dorset coast fish and local game make regular appearances on the menu which combines finely-tuned British pub classics with European-influenced dishes like gnocchi, celeriac purée, purple sprouting broccoli, Vichy carrots and goats' curd.

Chef Neil Molyneux Seats 69, Private dining 40 Open All Year Prices from S £5.95, M £13.95, D £7 Parking 14 Notes Vegetarian dishes, Children welcome

MAIDEN NEWTON

MAP 4, SY59

Le Petit Canard

⊛ MODERN BRITISH, FRENCH

01300 320536 | Dorchester Road, DT2 0BE

www.le-petit-canard.co.uk

With nearly two decades in this pretty restaurant behind them, Gerry and Cathy Craig's charm and ever-reliable cooking have paid off. Inside are timber beams, exposed stonework and flowers and candles on linen-clothed tables. Roast breast of Barbary duck comes with apple and five-spice sauce; salmon fillet with brown shrimp, herb butter and pea shoots.

Chef Gerry Craig Seats 28 Closed 2 weeks January, 1 week June and September Notes Vegetarian dishes, No children under 12 years

POOLE

MAP 4, SZ09

Hotel du Vin Poole

◉ MODERN BRITISH, FRENCH

01202 785578 | Mansion House, Thames Street, BH15 1JN

www.hotelduvin.com

Hotel du Vin's Poole outpost is a bit of a landmark just off the quayside, a creeper-covered Georgian mansion. As expected, the kitchen deals in crowd-pleasing brasserie staples from over the Channel, all cooked just so. Start perhaps with escargots in garlic and herb butter.

Open All Year

Rick Stein Sandbanks

◉ SEAFOOD *V* NOTABLE WINE LIST

01202 283280 | 10-14 Banks Road, BH13 7QB

www.rickstein.com

The globetrotting Mr Stein needs no introduction and he's picked a promising spot in well-heeled Sandbanks for another outpost of the ever-expanding empire. The food bears the Stein imprint, nothing too elaborate, just light-touch treatment to let the quality of the produce strut its stuff.

Chef Pete Murt Seats 200 Closed 25 December Prices from S £7.95, M £14.95, D £6.95 Notes No children under 3 years at dinner (not permitted in upper restaurant)

SHAFTESBURY

MAP 4, ST82

La Fleur de Lys Restaurant with Rooms

◉◉ MODERN FRENCH

01747 853717 | Bleke Street, SP7 8AW

www.lafleurdelys.co.uk

Smartly linened-up tables are the order in the dining room of this creeper-covered restaurant with rooms. Lemon-yellow and exposed stone walls produce a relaxing atmosphere, and fixed-price menus, built on a core of modern French notions, offer a variety of choices.

Chef D Shepherd, M Preston Seats 45, Private dining 12 Closed 3 weeks in January Parking 10 Notes Vegetarian dishes, Children welcome

SHERBORNE

MAP 4, ST61

The Green

◉◉ MODERN EUROPEAN

01935 813821 | 3 The Green, DT9 3HY

www.greenrestaurant.co.uk

The Green, a charming Grade II listed building in the centre of picturesque Sherborne, sets its sights on locally and ethically-sourced raw materials. Quality ingredients are evident throughout, and menus are thoughtfully constructed, offering contemporary dishes with classic roots, inspired by the seasons.

Chef Alexander and Sasha Matkevich Seats 40, Private dining 24 Closed 25-26 December Prices from S £5, M £16, D £5 Notes Vegetarian dishes, Children welcome

The Kings Arms

◉ MODERN BRITISH

01963 220281 | Charlton Herethorne, DT9 4NL

www.thekingsarms.co.uk

Sarah and Tony Lethbridge have given this stone-built inn, first licensed in the Regency era, a thoroughly modern makeover, though not to the detriment of its original charm. Sarah heads up the kitchen, capitalising on West Country produce, as well as drying and curing meats.

Chef Sarah Lethbridge, Alex Perreira Seats 120, Private dining 70 Closed 25 December Prices from S £6, M £15, D £7.50 Parking 30 Notes Vegetarian dishes, Children welcome

The Rose and Crown Inn, Trent

◉◉ MODERN BRITISH

01935 850776 | Trent, DT9 4SL

www.theroseandcrowntrent.co.uk

Located on the Ernest Cook Trust estate that surrounds Trent, the inn has a lounge with a large, log-surrounded open fire and comfortable leather sofa; the main bar looks out over fields, and from the restaurant you can survey the valley of the Trent Brook.

Open All Year

Seasons Restaurant at The Eastbury Hotel

◉◉ MODERN BRITISH **V**

01935 813131 | Long Street, DT9 3BY

theeastburyhotel.co.uk

This elegantly refurbished town-centre dining venue offers a hint of country-estate living, with much of produce coming from its garden. Despite the Englishness of the surroundings, the menu looks around the globe for inspiration, and dishes like venison loin, salt-baked swede mash and spiced red cabbage are underpinned with accomplished technique.

Chef Matthew Street **Seats** 40, Private dining 40 **Open** All Year **Prices from** S £8, M £18, D £8 **Parking** 20 **Notes** Children welcome

STUDLAND
MAP 5, SZ08

THE PIG on the Beach

◉◉ MODERN BRITISH

01929 450288 | The Manor House, Manor Road, BH19 3AU

www.thepighotel.com

One of a litter of Pig hotels, this particular porker has its own kitchen garden, and raises its own chickens and quails, while fish and seafood are locally landed. A menu grouping dishes as Piggy Bits, Fishy Bits and so on, might feature crispy brawn, crab bake, New Forest celeriac risotto, and rhubarb and custard ice cream.

Chef James Shadbolt **Seats** 70, Private dining 12 **Open** All Year **Prices from** S £6, M £14, D £7.50 **Parking** 30 **Notes** Vegetarian dishes, Children welcome

WEST BEXINGTON
MAP 4, SY58

The Club House

◉ MODERN SEAFOOD

01308 898302 | Beach Road, DT2 9DF

www.theclubhousewestbexington.co.uk

A 1930s bungalow overlooking the Jurassic Coast, The Club House has the air of somewhere you might expect to pay a membership fee to enter. What it offers instead is a seafood-rich menu of energetic modern cooking, changing daily according to the catch.

Chef Charlie Soole **Seats** 60, Private dining 12 **Closed** 25-26 December **Prices from** S £6.95, M £16.50, D £6.95 **Parking** 10 **Notes** Vegetarian dishes, Children welcome

WEYMOUTH
MAP 4, SY67

Moonfleet Manor Hotel

◉ MEDITERRANEAN

01305 786948 | Fleet Road, DT3 4ED

www.moonfleetmanorhotel.co.uk

The village of Fleet played a central role in J. Meade Falkner's smuggling yarn, *Moonfleet* (1898), and the sparkling-white Georgian hotel, which gazes out over Chesil Beach, is the jewel in its crown. Inside is all squashy sofas and crackling fires, with bracing sea views.

WIMBORNE MINSTER
MAP 5, SZ09

Les Bouviers Restaurant with Rooms

◉◉ MEDITERRANEAN, FRENCH **V**

01202 889555 | Arrowsmith Road, Canford Magna, BH21 3BD

www.lesbouviers.co.uk

A modern house in over five acres of land complete with stream and lake is the setting for this restaurant done out in shades of claret and gold, with contemporary artwork on the walls. Cheese soufflé with watercress and horseradish sauce is a signature starter.

Chef James and Kate Coward **Seats** 50, Private dining 120 **Parking** 50 **Notes** Vegetarian dishes, Children welcome

WINTERBORNE KINGSTON
MAP 4, SY89

Abbots Court **NEW**

◉◉ MODERN BRITISH

01929 448638 | East Street, DT11 9BH

www.abbots-court.co.uk

Expect elegant cooking and a true deftness of touch at this relaxed Victorian farmhouse which sources the ingredients for its weekly-changing menus from foraging, the surrounding walled kitchen garden and the pigs reared on-site. There's a great dynamic between the two chefs and their collective input is channelled into well-executed dishes.

WYKE REGIS
MAP 4, SY67

Crab House Café

◉ BRITISH, SEAFOOD

01305 788867 | Ferrymans Way, Portland Road, DT4 9YU

www.crabhousecafe.co.uk

Situated in a spruced up wooden hut overlooking Chesil Beach, the Crab House Café has natural charms aplenty. Simplicity and freshness is the name of the game, with oysters coming from their own beds and everything sourced from within a 40-mile radius. Rustic benches outside are a treat in the warmer months.

Chef Nigel Bloxham, William Smith **Seats** 40 **Closed** mid December to January **Prices from** S £6.90, M £16.90, D £5.50 **Parking** 40 **Notes** Vegetarian dishes, Children welcome

■ COUNTY DURHAM

BARNARD CASTLE
MAP 19, NZ01

The Morritt Country House Hotel & Spa

◉◉ MODERN FRENCH

01833 627232 | Greta Bridge, DL12 9SE

www.themorritt.co.uk

The arrival of transport by mail coach in the 18th century saw this former farm develop into an overnight stop for travellers between London and Carlisle. Charles Dickens probably stayed here in 1839, hence the fine-dining restaurant is named after him.

Open All Year

BILLINGHAM
MAP 19, NZ42

Wynyard Hall Hotel

◉◉ MODERN BRITISH

01740 644811 | Wynyard, TS22 5NF

www.wynyardhall.co.uk

Built to impress, this vast Victorian pile sits in 150 acres of grounds with its own lake. Inside, marble, mahogany and stained-glass combine in a display of jaw-dropping opulence, a style that continues in the Wellington Restaurant, where the menu offers elegant, classically-based, modern dishes.

Chef Michael Penaluna **Seats** 80, Private dining 30 **Open** All Year **Prices from** S £7.50, M £17, D £7.95 **Parking** 200 **Notes** Vegetarian dishes, Children welcome

DARLINGTON
MAP 19, NZ21

The Orangery

◉◉◉◉ MODERN BRITISH V

01325 729999 | Rockliffe Hall, Rockliffe Park, Hurworth-on-Tees, DL2 2DU

www.rockliffehall.com

Guests are spoilt for leisure pursuits at this impressive Georgian country mansion, from indulgence in the luxurious spa to tackling its 18-hole championship golf course, and a trio of restaurants. Cream of the crop is The Orangery, where gilded wrought-iron columns soar upwards to a glass roof in a romantic Gothic-inspired space, and a large wall of windows opens up sweeping views across the gardens and the action on the fairways. It's an exceedingly pleasant place to linger.

Richard Allen's contemporary 10-course tasting menus, in omnivore, veggie, pescatarian versions, are a delight in conception and delivery. The local and seasonal boxes are ticked by produce from polytunnels and the walled garden, plus foraged ingredients from Rockliffe's 365-acre estate, and the workmanship is first class whether in a dish of beetroot and vibrant smoked eel or a smooth, rich goose liver parfait balanced by apple, hay and pine nuts. Main courses might include beautifully cooked salt-aged Yorkshire duck with charred carrots and nasturtium; and Landrace Yorkshire pork with shrimps, green tomato ketchup and sea vegetables – a great combination of flavours and textures. A pear, sheep's curd and lemon balm dessert is a great dish, as is a simple yet clever combination of cherry and chamomile.

Chef Richard Allen **Seats** 60, Private dining 20 **Open** All Year **Parking** 300 **Notes** Children welcome

DURHAM
MAP 19, NZ24

Fusion Restaurant

◉ PAN-ASIAN, THAI

0191 386 5282 | Ramside Hall Hotel Golf & Spa, Carrville, DH1 1TD

www.ramsidehallhotel.co.uk

Surrounded by 350 acres of grounds including two 18-hole championship golf courses at Ramside Hall, the restaurant at the hotel's spa serves south-east Asian-inspired food throughout the day. Overlooking the spa's thermal suite, the Oriental-styled restaurant combines the dishes of Thailand, Japan and China including 'Make Your Own Bento Box'.

Open All Year

The Rib Room
⊛ INTERNATIONAL
0191 386 5282 | Ramside Hall Hotel Golf & Spa,
Carrville, DH1 1TD
www.ramsidehallhotel.co.uk
Sprawling outwards from a largely Victorian
house, is Ramside's glossy spa and health club.
Culinary options run from straightforward
carvery dishes to the menu in the brasserie-style
Rib Room, a temple to slabs of locally-reared
28-day aged beef.

Open All Year

SEAHAM
MAP 19, NZ44

Seaham Hall – The Dining Room
⊛⊛ MODERN BRITISH ▲ NOTABLE WINE LIST
0191 516 1400 | Seaham Hall, Lord Byron's Walk,
SR7 7AG
www.seaham-hall.co.uk
These days a state-of-the-art spa hotel, the late
18th-century Seaham Hall offers a brace of
stimulating eating options. The Dining Room is a
swish contemporary space with a glossy sheen,
delivering a crowd-pleasing menu aiming
unashamedly at the hearts of carnivores,
although well-sourced fish provides meat-free
alternatives.

Chef Damian Broom **Seats** 40, Private dining 100
Closed 31 December **Parking** 120 **Notes** Vegetarian
dishes, Children welcome

 ESSEX

BRAINTREE
MAP 7, TL72

The Chophouse Braintree
⊛ MODERN, CLASSIC BRITISH
01376 345615 | 34 New Street, CM7 1ES
www.thechophousebraintree.co.uk
Previously a home for 'wayward women' and a
haberdashery, this old inn is relaxed and
informal, with a choice of dining areas and
attentive service throughout. Where possible,
ingredients are sourced from within a 30-mile
radius and the modern British food is
underpinned by classic techniques.

Chef Stefan Clyde **Seats** 62, Private dining 12 **Open** All
Year **Prices from** S £6.95, M £14.95, D £6.95
Notes Vegetarian dishes, Children welcome

BRENTWOOD
MAP 6, TO59

Marygreen Manor Hotel
⊛⊛ MODERN EUROPEAN 𝑉
01277 225252 | London Road, CM14 4NR
www.marygreenmanor.co.uk
Although the house is older than the 17th
century, it was then that its owner named it
'Manor of Mary Green', after his young bride. Its
many original features include exposed beams,
carved panelling and the impressive Tudors
Restaurant, where classic and traditional cooking
holds sway, typically pork fillet and belly; and
bouillabaisse.

Chef Majid Bourote **Seats** 80, Private dining 85 **Open** All
Year **Prices from** S £7.50, M £24, D £7.50 **Parking** 100
Notes Children welcome

CHELMSFORD
MAP 6, TL70

Samphire Restaurant
⊛ BRITISH, MEDITERRANEAN
01245 455700 | County Hotel, 29 Rainsford Road,
CM1 2PZ
www.countyhotelchelmsford.co.uk
The County Hotel has a cheery modern style, as
typified in the Samphire Restaurant, where oak
floors and leather seats in summery pastel hues
of mustard, mint and tangerine add colour to the
neutral, contemporary decor. Uncomplicated
modern British and European cooking is the
kitchen's stock-in-trade.

Chef Roy Ortega **Seats** 64, Private dining 135 **Closed** 24
and 26 December **Prices from** S £6, M £9, D £5
Parking 60 **Notes** Vegetarian dishes, Children welcome

COGGESHALL
MAP 7, TL82

Ranfield's Brasserie
⊛⊛ MODERN BRITISH
01376 561453 | 4–6 Stoneham Street, CO6 1TT
www.ranfieldsbrasserie.co.uk
A fixture of the local dining scene for almost 30
years, its setting may be a 16th-century timbered
house but there's nothing old about the
approach. The mood is laid-back and
cosmopolitan, and the decor akin to an eclectic
art gallery with antique linen-clothed tables.

Open All Year

COLCHESTER — MAP 13, TL92

Church Street Tavern

@ @ MODERN BRITISH *V* ⓘ NOTABLE WINE LIST

01206 564325 | 3 Church Street, CO1 1NF

www.churchstreettavern.co.uk

Just off the main shopping mayhem, the handsome Victorian former bank building has been repurposed as a trendy bar and first-floor restaurant full of light and artwork. Bare tables, banquettes and wood floors fit the smart-casual mood, and the seasonal menu is brim full of up-to-date ideas.

Chef Ewan Naylon **Seats** 75, Private dining 18 **Closed** 25-26 December, 1-7 January **Prices from** S £5.75, M £12.50, D £6 **Notes** Children welcome

Cloisters

@ @ MODERN BRITISH

01206 575913 | GreyFriars Hotel, High Street, CO1 1UG

www.greyfriarscolchester.co.uk

Cloisters restaurant is in the 20th-century part of GreyFriars hotel, once a Franciscan monastery. Parquet floored with an art deco feel, it's known for modern European dishes with a British touch. Proving irresistible, perhaps, might be a starter of oysters from Mersea Island nine miles away.

Chef Liam Keating **Seats** 65, Private dining 30 **Open** All Year **Prices from** S £7.25, M £14.50, D £6.25 **Parking** 38 **Notes** Vegetarian dishes, Children welcome

Stoke by Nayland Hotel, Golf & Spa

@ @ MODERN BRITISH

01206 262836 | Keepers Lane, Leavenheath, CO6 4PZ

www.stokebynayland.com

This purpose-built hotel complex comes complete with spa, high-tech gym, two championship-level golf courses and The Lakes Restaurant, a bright and airy room with panoramic views. The enterprising kitchen sends out ambitious dishes. For dessert, try a palate-challenging doughnut stuffed with sticky toffee bacon.

Open All Year

DEDHAM — MAP 13, TM03

milsoms

@ MODERN BRITISH *V*

01206 322795 | Stratford Road, CO7 6HN

www.milsomhotels.com

A contemporary brasserie in a creeper-covered house in a pretty Essex village, the menu at Milsoms offers everything from posh lunchtime sandwiches to grilled steaks. Dressed crab and Melba toast followed by fried buttermilk chicken burger is one way to go. Leave room for the milk chocolate and caramel mousse.

Chef Sarah Norman, Ben Rush **Seats** 80, Private dining 30 **Open** All Year **Prices from** S £6.50, M £13.50, D £7 **Parking** 80 **Notes** Children welcome

The Sun Inn

@ @ MODERN BRITISH, MEDITERRANEAN ⓘ NOTABLE WINE LIST

01206 323351 | High Street, CO7 6DF

www.thesuninndedham.com

The Sun is a 15th-century village inn with open fires, doughty timbers and panelling. Its culinary leanings are distinctly Italian, with the kitchen turning fresh produce and quality Italian ingredients such as cured meats, cheeses and oils into uncomplicated, well-executed dishes.

Chef Jack Levine **Seats** 70 **Closed** 25-26 December, 3-4 January **Prices from** S £6, M £12.75, D £5.75 **Parking** 15 **Notes** Vegetarian dishes, Children welcome

Le Talbooth

@ @ @ MODERN BRITISH *V*

01206 323150 | Stratford Road, CO7 6HN

www.milsomhotels.com/letalbooth

The former toll house by the River Stour dates from Tudor times, and the Milsom family have pretty impressive staying power too, having run this East Anglian stalwart for over half a century. Sitting out on the canopy-shaded terrace overlooking pretty gardens with the river running by, what's not to like? Inside, the look is smartly formal, setting white-linened tables and neutral, contemporary shades against the period character of leaded mullioned windows and bare beams soaring to the roof. The kitchen stays abreast of culinary trends, sending out modern dishes full of precision and inspiration. Coffee caramel and Jerusalem artichoke purée support a duo of pan-seared scallops and pork belly, as a prelude to a veal dish, the sirloin butter-roasted, and sweetbreads served in open ravioli with wild garlic, pommes soufflées and peppercorn sauce. An inventive dessert teams a Black Forest soufflé with Kirsch-soaked chocolate sponge, vanilla Chantilly and black cherry sorbet.

Chef Andrew Hirst, Ian Rhodes **Seats** 80, Private dining 34 **Open** All Year **Prices from** S £13, M £22.50, D £9.50 **Parking** 50 **Notes** Children welcome

EPPING
MAP 6, TL40

Haywards Restaurant NEW
◉◉◉ MODERN EUROPEAN *V*
01992 577350 | 111 Bell Common, CM16 4DZ
www.haywardsrestaurant.co.uk
Occupying a converted coach house on the fringes of Epping Forest, this smart restaurant looks the rustic-chic part with its high vaulted ceiling, polished wooden tables and floors and colourful artworks. Service is attentive, and the focus here is high quality food that is imaginatively composed and isn't afraid to doff its cap to the Continent. The kitchen draws on regional ingredients to deliver a repertoire of sprightly ideas, kicking off with a deft composition of nicely caramelised scallops, black onion seeds, samphire, pearl barley and bok choi, all brought into vibrant focus by umami-laden dashi broth and blobs of oyster emulsion. Next up, venison fillet is supported by radicchio, potato and swede dauphinoise and purée, with blackberries to leaven all that richness. Dishes can be complex, but everything is there for a reason, witness a neat dessert of aerated chocolate and hazelnut mousse encased within a delicate chocolate shell, alongside salted milk ice cream and caramel.

Chef Jahdre Hayward **Seats** 48, Private dining 14 **Closed** 1-21 January **Prices from** S £11.75, M £25.50, D £11.75 **Parking** 24 **Notes** No children under 10 years

GREAT TOTHAM
MAP 7, TL81

The Bull & Willow Room at Great Totham
◉ MODERN, TRADITIONAL BRITISH
01621 893385 | 2 Maldon Road, CM9 8NH
www.thebullatgreattotham.co.uk
This 16th-century village inn has an uncommonly posh eating area, the Willow Room, where the kitchen produces a repertoire of modern dishes. Opt for a pub classic such as Atlantic prawn cocktail or a plate of goats' cheese mousse, blackberry poached pear and endive salad.

Open All Year

GREAT YELDHAM
MAP 13, TL73

The White Hart
◉◉ BRITISH, EUROPEAN
01787 237250 | Poole Street, CO9 4HJ
www.whitehartyeldham.com
Dating back to the Tudor era, this is a classic timbered country inn set in extensive grounds. Crisp white napery and quality tableware confer distinctive class on the dining room, where the menu might offer salt marsh lamb stuffed with haggis with a pink noisette and a kidney.

Chef K White, Wu Zhenjang **Seats** 44, Private dining 200 **Closed** Seasonal closures **Parking** 50 **Notes** Vegetarian dishes, Children welcome

HARWICH
MAP 13, TM23

The Pier at Harwich
◉◉ MODERN BRITISH, SEAFOOD *V*
01255 241212 | The Quay, CO12 3HH
www.milsomhotels.com
Right on the quayside, The Pier provides super-fresh seafood. You can dine in the first-floor brasserie and take the air on the balcony. Chargrilled Dedham Vale steaks are on offer, but Harwich crab and lobsters make for stiff competition.

Chef John Goff, Stephen Robson **Seats** 80, Private dining 24 **Open** All Year **Prices from** S £7, M £15, D £6.50 **Parking** 12 **Notes** Children welcome

HOCKLEY
MAP 7, TQ89

The Anchor Riverside Pub and Restaurant
◉ MODERN BRITISH
01702 230777 | Ferry Road, Hullbridge, SS5 6ND
www.theanchorhullbridge.co.uk
Shortly before the road ends at the River Crouch is this thoroughly modern gastro pub where, if the weather's kind, you can sit outside in the extensive gardens with something light. Otherwise, head for the restaurant, designed for lingering over a decent three-course meal.

Closed 25 December

HOWE STREET
MAP 6, TL61

Galvin Green Man
◉◉ MODERN BRITISH *V*
01245 408820 | Main Road, CM3 1BG
www.galvingreenman.com
Dating back to the 13th century, this rural inn is run by Essex-born chef brothers, Chris and Jeff Galvin. With the River Chelmer running through the beer garden it's a welcoming place for a pint and the glass-roofed dining room pulls in foodies from all over.

Chef Daniel Lee **Seats** 104, Private dining 40 **Open** All Year **Prices from** S £8, M £14, D £5.50 **Parking** 60 **Notes** Vegetarian dishes, Children welcome

The HOOP

21 High Street, Stock, Essex, CM4 9BD   01277 871137
www.thehoop.co.uk
email:thehoopstock@yahoo.co.uk

A traditional 15th-century, oak-beamed free house, located in the pretty village of Stock, offering gastro food and award winning real ales. In addition, our fine dining restaurant offers an à la carte menu and boutique wine list. Enjoy our large beer garden and beer festival held over the Spring Bank Holiday each year.

ORSETT
MAP 6, TQ68

The Garden Brasserie

◉ MODERN BRITISH

01375 891402 | Orsett Hall Hotel, Restaurant & Spa, Prince Charles Avenue, RM16 3HS

www.orsetthall.co.uk

The 17th-century Orsett Hall was rebuilt, phoenix like, following a fire a decade ago. Its floral-inspired Garden Brasserie is beautiful, with super views of the landscaped grounds, or if you just want a snack, Café Sartoria awaits.

Chef Robert Pearce **Open** All Year **Prices from** S £6, M £12, D £6 **Parking** 200 **Notes** Vegetarian dishes, Children welcome

SOUTHEND-ON-SEA
MAP 7, TQ88

Holiday Inn Southend

◉ TRADITIONAL BRITISH

01702 543001 | 77 Eastwoodbury Crescent, SS2 6XG

www.hisouthend.com/dining/1935-rooftop-restaurant-bar

Calling all plane spotting foodies: both of your interests can be indulged in one fell swoop at the fifth-floor 1935 Restaurant overlooking the aviation action at Southend Airport. Naturally enough, soundproofing is of the highest order, and there's a real sense of occasion.

Chef Michael Walker **Seats** 82, Private dining 14 **Parking** 226 **Notes** Vegetarian dishes, Children welcome

The Roslin Beach Hotel

◉◉ BRITISH *V*

01702 586375 | Thorpe Esplanade, Thorpe Bay, SS1 3BG

www.roslinhotel.com

If you do like to be beside the seaside, The Roslin Beach Hotel has a sea-facing terrace, plus indoor space shielded by glass, so it is beach ready whatever the weather. The tables are dressed up in white linen and there's a buzzy ambience.

Chef Simon Webb **Seats** 100, Private dining 50 **Open** All Year **Prices from** S £8, M £20, D £12 **Parking** 60 **Notes** Children welcome

STOCK
MAP 6, TQ69

Ellis's Restaurant

◉ MODERN BRITISH

01277 829990 | Greenwoods Hotel & Spa, Stock Road, CM4 9BE

www.greenwoodshotel.co.uk

An appealing 17th-century, Grade II listed building set in expansive landscaped gardens, Greenwoods Hotel is just a few minutes from Billericay town centre. Named after the manor house's previous owner, the hotel's contemporary Ellis's Restaurant offers a pleasing array of innovative, fuss-free dishes.

Closed 26 December, 1 January

The Hoop

◉ MODERN BRITISH

01277 841137 | High Street, CM4 9BD

www.thehoop.co.uk

Ancient timbers from redundant warships laid up on the Thames in Tilbury support this thriving 15th-century free house. On the menu are handpicked Devon crab, heirloom tomatoes with gazpacho sauce; Dedham Vale fillet steak with mushrooms and béarnaise; Indonesian fish curry; vegetarian dish of the day; and lemon meringue tart with raspberry sorbet.

Chef Phil Utz **Seats** 40 **Closed** Beer festival week and 1st week in January **Prices from** S £6.95, M £12.95, D £2 **Notes** Vegetarian dishes, Children welcome

See advertisement on page 133

THORPE-LE-SOKEN
MAP 7, TM12

Harry's Bar & Restaurant

◉ MODERN BRITISH

01255 860250 | High Street, CO16 0EA

www.harrysbarandrestaurant.co.uk

It may be a long way from the original Harry's Bar in Venice but this Essex village namesake offers a similarly relaxed and stylish brasserie ambience. The seasonally-changing menu combines modern British dishes with more global influences. The wine list cover the world's best regions.

Open All Year

GLOUCESTERSHIRE

ALMONDSBURY
MAP 4, ST68

The Curious Kitchen at Aztec Hotel & Spa
⊕ MODERN BRITISH

01454 201090 | Aztec West, BS32 4TS

www.aztechotelbristol.co.uk/food-drink

Offering a full package of spa activities and business facilities, the Aztec also has a restaurant and bar which is worth a visit. It's a contemporary alpine chalet-style space, with a high-vaulted ceiling, leather seating and a terrace for alfresco dining. The menu takes a broad sweep through comfort-oriented modern ideas.

Chef Marc Payne **Seats** 100, Private dining 30
Prices from S £5, M £13.50, D £4 **Parking** 200
Notes Vegetarian dishes, Children welcome

ARLINGHAM
MAP 4, SO71

The Old Passage Inn
⊕⊕ SEAFOOD, MODERN BRITISH

01452 740547 | Passage Road, GL2 7JR

www.theoldpassage.com

On the bank of the River Severn, The Old Passage is a white-painted restaurant with rooms. The kitchen's focus is on top-quality seafood, with choices like wild turbot fillet counterbalanced by oxtail, served with braised pak choi, celeriac purée and girolles.

Chef Lewis Dixon **Seats** 50, Private dining 12
Closed 25–26 December **Prices from** S £9.50, M £19.50, D £7.95 **Parking** 40 **Notes** Vegetarian dishes, No children under 10 years at dinner

BIBURY
MAP 5, SP10

The Brasserie NEW
⊕ MODERN BRITISH

01285 740695 | Swan Hotel, GL7 5NW

www.cotswold-inns-hotels.co.uk

If you're already liking the sound of a former coaching inn beside the River Coln, then throw in the proposition of welcoming service and British cooking with a European accent, and the brasserie of the Swan Hotel is a shoo-in. Hearty, no-nonsense cooking is the deal; especially hard to resist is local Bibury trout fresh from the river.

Chef Karol Szmigiel **Seats** 75, Private dining 26 **Open** All Year **Prices from** S £7, M £13, D £7 **Parking** 30
Notes Vegetarian dishes, Children welcome

BUCKLAND
MAP 10, SP03

Buckland Manor
⊕⊕⊕ MODERN, CLASSIC BRITISH ⚑ NOTABLE WINE LIST

01386 852626 | WR12 7LY

www.bucklandmanor.co.uk

At some indeterminate point, the village of Buckland melds into the 10-acre corner in which the old manor stands, next to the village church. It's a delightful Cotswold location for a country house that exudes a sense of history from its every pore. White wood-panelled walls interspersed with mullioned windows overlooking the gardens and the hills beyond are the setting for Will Guthrie's finely crafted modern cooking, which is lent extra fragrance by the products of the manor's own herb garden. Dishes are ingenious and attractive, sparkling with creativity. You might begin with roast quail breast with roast nectarine and curry mayonnaise. Main courses are equally thoughtful, witness fillet of turbot with courgette, saffron chickpea sauce and vièrge dressing, or veal rib-eye with shallot cream, trompettes and purple sprouting broccoli. Round things off with a beautifully refreshing lemon meringue parfait with lemon curd, matcha tea meringue and lemon balm.

Chef Will Guthrie **Seats** 40, Private dining 14 **Open** All Year **Parking** 20 **Notes** Vegetarian dishes, No children under 10 years

CHELTENHAM
MAP 10, SO92

Le Champignon Sauvage
⊕⊕⊕⊕ MODERN FRENCH

01242 573449 | 24–28 Suffolk Road, GL50 2AQ

www.lechampignonsauvage.co.uk

Having breasted the billows of restaurant fashion since the 1980s, the Champignon is in its fourth decade of operations, a remarkable testament to the tenacity and dedication of David and Helen Everitt-Matthias. It has remained in the upper echelons of British gastronomy throughout, achieving its longevity without any attention-grabbing culinary stunts. Indeed, the place itself seems to blend discreetly with the row of shops it rubs shoulders with, and the interior prospect of blond wood and dove-grey, with striking artworks and trimly linened table, creates a civilised, discreet feel. David's cooking, for all its modern ingredients and techniques, retains an underlying sense of classical French cuisine. You might begin with fillet of Cornish mackerel, kohlrabi, avocado purée and caviar, or Dexter

Continued on page 136

beef tartare with corned beef, wasabi mayonnaise and pickled shimeji; perhaps followed by Brecon venison with parsnip purée, baby parsnips, black pudding and bitter chocolate, or red legged partridge with turnip choucroute, walnuts and quince. Delightfully creative desserts might include frozen bergamot parfait, orange jelly, liquorice cream, or blueberry cannelloni with wood sorrel cream and yogurt sorbet. A highly distinguished wine list completes the picture.

Chef David Everitt-Matthias **Seats** 40 **Closed** 10 days Christmas, 3 weeks in June **Notes** Children welcome

The Curry Corner Est.1977
◉◉ BANGLADESHI, INDIAN
01242 528449 | 133 Fairview Road, GL52 2EX
thecurrycorner.com
Occupying a white Georgian townhouse on the edge of Cheltenham's main shopping area, the oldest Bangladeshi curry house in the UK has a chic, contemporary look, featuring ruby-red wall coverings as well as furniture designed by the chef and co-owner. Bangladeshi home cooking is the theme, with spices flown in from India, Morocco and Turkey.

Chef Shamsul and Monrusha Krori **Seats** 50 **Closed** 25–26 December **Notes** Vegetarian dishes, Children welcome

The Drawing Room *NEW*
◉ BRITISH, EUROPEAN
01242 515119 | Cotswold Grange Hotel, Pittville Circus Road, GL52 2QH
www.cotswoldgrangehotel.co.uk
Oodles of period character dovetail to stylish effect with huge floor-to-ceiling windows and clean-lined modern looks in the dining room of this handsome Georgian mansion on a peaceful tree-lined avenue. Expect straightforward dishes – farmhouse terrine with home-made pickle and sourdough toast, then venison loin with pommes Anna, parsnip purée, baby carrots and crispy kale, perhaps.

Chef Graham Wood **Open** All Year **Prices from** S £7, M £14, D £7 **Parking** 19 **Notes** Vegetarian dishes, Children welcome

The Greenway Hotel & Spa
◉◉◉ MODERN BRITISH, FRENCH *V*
01242 862352 | Shurdington, GL51 4UG
www.thegreenwayhotelandspa.com
Set in Shurdington, on the verdant outskirts of leafy Cheltenham, the Greenway is an Elizabethan manor house of Cotswold stone, its façade half-hidden in clambering ivy. Up-to-the-minute spa facilities are always a draw, while the Garden Restaurant is named after its soothing view, with a majestic stone fireplace and venerable oak panelling adding lustre. Marcus McGuinness is a model modern-day practitioner, overseeing a thriving kitchen garden, engaging in forays into the countryside to gather wild provender, and sourcing thoroughbred prime materials, before turning it all into elegant, eye-catching dishes of striking character. Start with gratin of Cornish crab and white port, with sea buckthorn and 'piggy cake', before moving on to poached and roast Cornish brill with pumpkin, hazelnuts, mussels and sage, or spiced Goosnargh duck breast with quince, smoked eel and confit beetroot. Soufflés often feature at dessert – witness a fine dark chocolate version with coffee sorbet and whisky custard.

Chef Marcus McGuinness **Seats** 60, Private dining 22 **Open** All Year **Notes** Children welcome

Hotel du Vin Cheltenham
◉ FRENCH, EUROPEAN
01242 588450 | Parabola Road, GL50 3AQ
www.hotelduvin.com
The restaurant at the Cheltenham branch of this popular hotel chain follows the usual bistro look of wooden floor, unclothed tables, banquettes and a wine-related theme of empty bottles, prints and memorabilia. The menu goes along the expected bistro route.

Chef Paul Mottram **Seats** 120, Private dining 32 **Open** All Year **Parking** 23 **Notes** Vegetarian dishes, Children welcome

Lumière
◉◉◉ MODERN BRITISH *V*
See pages 138-139

See pages 138-139

The Restaurant at Ellenborough Park

Rosettes suspended **MODERN BRITISH**
01242 545454 | Southam Road, GL52 3NH
www.ellenboroughpark.com
The Rosette award for this establishment has been suspended due to a change of chef. Reassessment will take place in due course under the new chef. Although the original house had been pottering along unexceptionally since the 1530s, Ellenborough really hit its stride when the first Earl of that ilk, erstwhile governor general of British India, moved himself and his wife into it 300 years later. The place itself is a sumptuous beauty in Cotswold honey, looking a little like an Oxford college, with a high-glitz panelled dining room at the centre of operations.

Seats 60, Private dining 20 **Open** All Year **Parking** 130
Notes Vegetarian dishes, No children under 12 years at dinner

CHIPPING CAMPDEN
MAP 10, SP13

Fig

⊛⊛ **MODERN ITALIAN, MEDITERRANEAN** *V*
01386 840330 | Cotswold House Hotel & Spa, Upper High Street, The Square, GL55 6AN
www.bespokehotels.com/cotswoldhouse
A handsome Regency building in the middle of Chipping Campden, Fig is the more formal of the two dining options at Cotswold House Hotel. The kitchen stays abreast of contemporary trends and prime ingredients are given a global twist.

Chef Pasquale Russo **Seats** 40, Private dining 30
Open All Year **Parking** 28 **Notes** Children welcome

Jackrabbit Restaurant

⊛⊛⊛ **MODERN BRITISH** *V*
01386 840256 | The Kings, The Square, High Street, GL55 6AW
www.kingscampden.co.uk
A classic Georgian townhouse built in honey-hued Cotswold stone right on Chipping Campden's square, The Kings is a glossy boutique bolthole these days. Inside, it's a smartly casual modern operation with unclothed antique tables, a flagged floor, a log fire, artworks and moody lighting in the beamed Jackrabbit Restaurant. The up-to-date approach carries through to what appears on the plate: headed up by Greg Newman, the kitchen cleverly combines flavour, texture and visual appeal in well-judged modern food built on splendid seasonal ingredients. As well as the carte, there's a six-course tasting menu, taking in dishes like a fresh, spring-flavoured soup of Evesham broccoli and wild nettle, and charred asparagus with a crispy egg yolk and Cotswold 'nduja sausage. Pan-roasted Cornish stone bass is a fine fish course, while chicken breast comes with crispy slow-cooked leg and Jersey Royals. Finish up with Ashlynn goats' cheese, before a honey delice with whipped lemon curd and whisky ice cream.

Chef Greg Newman **Seats** 45, Private dining 20 **Open** All Year **Parking** 12 **Notes** Children welcome

The Seagrave Arms

⊛⊛ **MODERN BRITISH**
01386 840192 | Friday Street, GL55 6QH
www.seagravearms.com
Stone-built and four-square, the 400-year-old Seagrave is a Cotswolds inn of considerable character. Strong classic undertones are discernible beneath the modern British cooking style. A good selection of wines by the glass includes a sparkling white from Nyetimber's South Downs vineyard.

Open All Year

MEET THE CHEF

Charles Smith

LORDS OF THE MANOR,

Upper Slaughter, page 148

What inspired you to become a chef?
As far back as I can remember I always took great pleasure in trying new foods or sitting down to eat a meal. At the age of 14 I started work in a kitchen and immediately fell in love with the buzz of kitchen life.

What are the vital ingredients for a successful kitchen?
Teamwork, humility, discipline and hard work. Having fantastic suppliers that support you and enable you to cook well by the quality of the ingredients. Forming a good honest relationship with suppliers is vital.

What are your favourite foods/ingredients?
I'm always excited as the seasons are coming and going. A few of my favourite products are Cumbrian rose veal, red mullet, Herdwick lamb, Evesham asparagus, pheasant eggs and Gariguette strawberries.

Lumière

◉◉◉ MODERN BRITISH **V**

01242 222200 | Clarence Parade, GL50 3PA

www.lumiere.cc

Accomplished technical wizardry near The Promenade

The Howes' elegant venue lies a little way off the leafy promenade for which Cheltenham is famous. The building may be an unassuming terrace, but indoors looks the very image of a modern dining room – it's an understated classy affair done in a soothing combination of cream and aubergine tones, with banquettes, statement mirrors and abstract artworks all adding up to a setting that says this is an operation of serious culinary intent; the capable hand of Helen Howe on the front-of-house tiller makes for a supremely relaxing experience.

Jon Howe's inventive British cooking delivers vibrant modern flavours, deploying plenty of technical wizardry showcased in tasting menus running from five to six, or nine courses; if you're on a tighter budget, come for lunch on Friday or Saturday and grab the three-course deal. Things begin with a volley of snacks such as cep

> "... inventive British cooking delivers vibrant modern flavours, deploying plenty of technical wizardry"

doughnut with bergamot and lemon, kedgeree arancini with egg yolk and coriander, and a cornet of Stinking Bishop with pear and chervil. The palate suitably primed for a cavalcade of visual and aromatic impact, further courses might see diver-caught Orkney scallop matched with the robust accompaniments of celeriac, ox tongue and ceps; that could be followed by Creedy Carver duck parfait with cocoa, shallot, lime and almond.

A mid-meal tequila shot with salt and lime clears the way for the meaty satisfaction of Cotswold venison teamed with the assertive company of beetroot, Stilton, port and chervil root. Dessert creations are equally dazzling – perhaps Valrhona Guanaja dark chocolate and bourbon cheesecake with sesame, pecan, and brown bread ice cream. Vegetarians are well catered for too, with a menu that's no mere afterthought and shows the same level of creativity in dishes such as salt-baked celeriac with prune, sprout and pickled onion, or Vale of Evesham cauliflower with morels, chervil root and beer vinegar.

Chef Jon Howe
Seats 25
Closed 2 weeks in winter and 2 weeks in summer
Notes No children under 8 years

CHIPPING CAMPDEN continued

Three Ways House

◉ MODERN BRITISH

01386 438429 | Chapel Lane, Mickleton, GL55 6SB
www.threewayshousehotel.com
This Cotswold-stone building dates back to 1870, but it was made world-famous in the 1980s with the formation of the Pudding Club (held every Friday). The food is big-hearted British stuff, although the kitchen team isn't afraid to look further afield for inspiration.

Chef James Woodhams **Seats** 80, Private dining 70
Open All Year **Parking** 37 **Notes** Vegetarian dishes, Children welcome

CIRENCESTER
MAP 5, SP00

Barnsley House

◉◉ MODERN EUROPEAN

01285 740000 | GL7 5EE
www.barnsleyhouse.com
The restaurant at 17th-century Barnsley House is named the Potager, after the ornamental and vegetable garden designed in the 1950s by Rosemary Verey, which it overlooks. Typical of the dishes is perfectly cooked lamb sweetbreads in a noteworthy jus served with no more than morels and garden chard.

Open All Year

Jesse's Bistro

◉◉ MODERN BRITISH

01285 641497 | 14 Blackjack Street, GL7 2AA
www.jessesbistro.co.uk
Tucked into a brick-paved back alley in the town centre, the bistro has an old beamed interior and a British menu that makes excursions to the Mediterranean and East Asia. First up might be Serrano ham with salami, figs and pine nuts and then a seafood main of Duart salmon and tiger prawns in soy and ginger broth, with crispy noodles, brown rice and bok choy. Dark chocolate cheesecake with malted-milk Malteser ice cream makes a great finish.

Chef David Witnall **Seats** 55, Private dining 12
Prices from S £7, M £17, D £7.50 **Notes** Vegetarian dishes, Children welcome

CLEARWELL
MAP 4, SO50

Tudor Farmhouse Hotel & Restaurant

◉◉ MODERN BRITISH

01594 833046 | High Street, GL16 8JS
www.tudorfarmhousehotel.co.uk
The charm-laden grey stone building looks the rustic part but, once inside, its stone walls, beams, wood panelling and inglenooks are overlaid with lashings of boutique bolt-hole style. Nor is the kitchen stuck in the past – its 20-mile menus are full of fresh, up-to-date ideas.

Open All Year

See advertisement opposite

COLEFORD
MAP 4, SO51

The Miners Country Inn

◉◉ MODERN BRITISH, TRADITIONAL

01594 836632 | Chepstow Road, Sling, GL16 8LH
www.theminerssling.co.uk
The Miners is a family-run dining pub in a tiny village in the Forest of Dean. Beamed ceilings and stone floors come as standard, while the restaurant is simply but tastefully decorated. A daily-changing menu selects from the best local produce available.

Open All Year

CORSE LAWN
MAP 10, SO83

Corse Lawn House Hotel

◉◉ MODERN BRITISH ❶ NOTABLE WINE LIST

01452 780771 | GL19 4LZ
www.corselawn.com
The red brick house dates from the Queen Anne period and stands on the village green in front of a large pond where coaches and their horses were once scrubbed clean. Today, modern British cuisine is served in the smart principal dining room – everything is made in house.

Chef Chris Monk **Seats** 50, Private dining 28
Closed 26–27 December **Prices from** S £6.95, M £16.95, D £6.95 **Parking** 60 **Notes** Vegetarian dishes, Children welcome

DAYLESFORD
MAP 10, SP22

Daylesford Farm Café

◉ MODERN BRITISH

01608 731700 | GL56 0YG
www.daylesford.com
On the Gloucestershire farmland that spawned a mini-empire, the Daylesford Farmshop and Café

occupies a smartly converted barn with a New England finish and an open-to-view kitchen. The food makes a virtue of simplicity, with quality ingredients allowed to shine.

Closed 25–26 December and 1 January

EBRINGTON
MAP 10, SP14
The Ebrington Arms
◉◉ CLASSIC BRITISH
01386 593223 | GL55 6NH
www.theebringtonarms.co.uk
Still very much a pub in the heart of the village by the green, the Ebrington has served its community for several hundred years, as is evident from its copious oak beams and flagged floors. The menu takes a contemporary line of original modern dishes and has won awards for its organic content.

Chef Corey Draper, Darral Warner **Seats** 70, Private dining 30 **Closed** 25 December **Parking** 13 **Notes** Vegetarian dishes, Children welcome

GLOUCESTER
MAP 10, SO81
Hatherley Manor Hotel & Spa
◉ TRADITIONAL BRITISH
01452 730217 | Down Hatherley Lane, GL2 9QA
www.hatherleymanor.com
A stylish brick and stone-built 17th-century house, Hatherley Manor is popular as a wedding venue. The Dewinton Restaurant is a relaxed setting for contemporary dining, with rich gold drapes and upholstery and linen-clad tables.

Open All Year

Hatton Court
◉ MODERN INTERNATIONAL *V*
01452 617412 | Upton Hill, Upton St Leonards, GL4 8DE
www.hatton-court.co.uk
A country-house hotel not far from the M5, Hatton Court is smothered with climbing foliage, its little windows barely peeping through the green. The formal dining room is kitted out with linen-clad tables, wood panelling and full-drop windows at one end.

Chef Jeff Lewis **Seats** 75, Private dining 50 **Open** All Year **Parking** 100 **Notes** Children welcome

The Wharf House Restaurant with Rooms

◉◉ CONTEMPORARY BRITISH

01452 332900 | Over, GL2 8DB

www.thewharfhouse.co.uk

Herefordshire & Gloucestershire Canal Trust's delightful restaurant and new lounge bar stand where the old lock-keeper's cottage stood. Its three chefs each bring their own influences to bear on dishes such as fillet and tartare of Cornish mackerel, cauliflower and horseradish purée; pan-fried sea bass with chorizo and potato rösti; and winter vegetable risotto.

Chef David Penny, Maisy Smith, Ryan Horton **Seats** 40 **Closed** 24 December to 8 January **Parking** 32 **Notes** Vegetarian dishes, Children welcome

See advertisement opposite

LOWER SLAUGHTER

MAP 10, SP12

The Slaughters Country Inn

◉◉ MODERN BRITISH

01451 822143 | GL54 2HS

www.theslaughtersinn.co.uk

This artfully modernised, 17th-century Cotswold-stone inn makes good use of its riverside terrace in this peaceful village. In the 1920s the building was a crammer school for Eton College, thus it now has Eton's Restaurant. The modern British menu also covers the bar.

Chef Mark Machemsley **Seats** 60, Private dining 30 **Open** All Year **Prices from** S £6.50, M £17, D £7.50 **Parking** 40 **Notes** Vegetarian dishes, Children welcome

The Slaughters Manor House

◉◉◉ MODERN BRITISH **V** 🍷 NOTABLE WINE LIST

01451 820456 | GL54 2HP

www.slaughtersmanor.co.uk

Built from golden Cotswold stone, this comfortable manor house dates from the 17th century, and offers a stylish 21st-century interpretation of country living. Wonderful period features, like the ornate plaster ceiling in the drawing room, and the delightful formal gardens, rub shoulders with modern decorative touches and pale, soothing colours. The elegant dining room, partly set in the house's original chapel, is an airy, light-filled space, with chairs upholstered in silver-grey and nicely spaced, linen-clad tables. Head chef Nik Chappell originally studied fine art, and his dishes are often picture-perfect explorations of flavour and texture. At dinner you can choose between the set menu and an eight-course tasting menu, maybe starting with spiced and barbecued Cornish lobster tail, served with Kent mango and bisque emulsion. A venison main course is accompanied by a single crisp samosa and subtly acidic pickled turnip. Finish with a light, well-textured pear bavarois with liquorice butterscotch and lemon granité.

Chef Nik Chappell **Seats** 48, Private dining 24 **Open** All Year **Parking** 30 **Notes** Children welcome

MORETON-IN-MARSH

MAP 10, SP23

Manor House Hotel

◉◉ MODERN BRITISH **V**

01608 650501 | High Street, GL56 0LJ

www.cotswold-inns-hotels.co.uk/manor

This Cotswold-stone hotel might date from the reign of Henry VIII, but careful renovation and updating have brought it squarely into the 21st century. The Mulberry Restaurant has generously spaced tables, comfortable chairs and on-the-ball staff, while the kitchen produces appealing dishes without over-complicating things.

Chef Nick Orr **Seats** 45, Private dining 120 **Closed** Christmas (residents only) **Parking** 32 **Notes** No children under 8 years

Redesdale Arms

◉ MODERN

01608 650308 | High Street, GL56 0AW

www.redesdalearms.com

Dating from the 17th century, this inn has been sympathetically updated to give a contemporary edge. There are two dining rooms, one in a rear conservatory, the other overlooking the high street. A glance at the menu shows a kitchen seaming the modern British vein.

Open All Year

NAILSWORTH

MAP 4, ST89

Wilder

◉◉◉ MODERN BRITISH **V**

01453 835483 | Market Street, GL6 0BX

www.dinewilder.co.uk

The arty market town of Nailsworth is as quintessentially Cotswolds English as you could ask for, but don't go thinking the stylish sister restaurant of Wild Garlic Restaurant with Rooms (a one-minute walk away) is in any way twee or chintzy. Wilder offers a neutral, decluttered and modern space where diners all settle in at 7.30pm for an imaginative, daily changing, eight-course tasting menu. The kitchen hauls in whatever's best from the local larder as the basis for sharply seasonal cooking that applies careful attention to detail and well-thought-out flavour combinations. Global influences come thick and

Continued on page 144

THE WHARF HOUSE

RESTAURANT WITH ROOMS

9 course Tasting Menu £52

á la carte menu also available

Available Tues-Sat 12-4pm and 5.30 onwards

Afternoon Tea £17.50

drinks and coffees
light bite Terrace Menu

Available Tues-Sat 12-4pm and 5.30 onwards

Mon & Sun 12-2pm

01452 332 900

www.thewharfhouse.co.uk

Over, Gloucester, GL2 8DB

info@thewharfhouse.co.uk

Directions: Turn off the A40
at traffic lights 250 yds west
of Over Roundabout (junction
A40/A417). GR SO 816197

AA ★★★★ Restaurant with Rooms 2019 Gold Award

AA ●● Rosettes 2019 Culinary Excellence

Green Tourism GOLD

All profits from The Wharf House will be used for the promotion and restoration of the Hereford & Gloucester Canal.

NAILSWORTH continued

fast, as in white miso aubergine with baba ganoush, labneh, shimeji mushrooms and a salty-sweet miso and soy dresssing. Another idea sees perfectly pink duck breast and a crispy bonbon matched with roasted and puréed artichoke, caramelised onions and red wine sauce, while sweet courses include chocolate porter cake with chocolate ganache, ale jelly and malted milk ice cream.

Chef Matthew Beardshall **Seats** 22 **Open** All Year **Notes** Children welcome

Wild Garlic Restaurant and Rooms
◎◎ MODERN BRITISH
01453 832615 | 3 Cossack Square, GL6 0DB
www.wild-garlic.co.uk
This stylish restaurant with rooms, named after the seasonal plant that grows in abundance in this corner of the Cotswolds, has a dedication to cooking local produce. Classic chargrilled steaks and moules frites sit alongside a harissa-spiced lamb burger, smoked salmon linguine and roast chicken breast with forestière sauce.

Chef Matthew Beardshall **Seats** 46 **Open** All Year **Prices from** S £4.50, M £14, D £5.50 **Notes** Vegetarian dishes, Children welcome

NETHER WESTCOTE
MAP 10, SP22

The Feathered Nest Country Inn
◎◎◎ MODERN BRITISH
See pages 146–147

PAINSWICK
MAP 4, SO80

The Painswick
◎◎ MODERN EUROPEAN *V*
01452 813688 | Kemps Lane, GL6 6YB
www.thepainswick.co.uk
The swish Calcot Manor group have sprinkled this grand Palladian mansion with a touch of contemporary boutique chic to go with its original Arts and Crafts features, and the result is a covetable bolthole that exudes relaxed luxury. The kitchen comes up with the modern European-accented dishes.

Chef Jamie McCallum **Seats** 60, Private dining 16 **Open** All Year **Prices from** S £6, M £15, D £6 **Parking** 20 **Notes** Vegetarian dishes, Children welcome

SELSLEY
MAP 4, SO80

The Bell Inn
◎◎ MODERN BRITISH
01453 753801 | Bell Lane, GL5 5JY
www.thebellinnselsley.com
This 16th-century village inn is now the hub of picturesque Selsley. Lunch or dinner can be taken in the comfortable bar or you can enjoy pleasant views from the conservatory-style dining area. Top quality local produce features in pub classics.

Chef Mark Payne **Seats** 55, Private dining 14 **Open** All Year **Parking** 12 **Notes** Vegetarian dishes, No children

STOW-ON-THE-WOLD
MAP 10, SP12

The Kings Head Inn
◎ BRITISH
01608 658365 | The Green, Bledington, OX7 6XQ
www.kingsheadinn.net
This mellow stone Cotswolds pub comes with a classic bar with wobbly floors, log fires, and head-skimming beams. It's a textbook example of a switched-on village pub with cooking that's a definite notch or two up.

Closed 25–26 December

Number Four at Stow *NEW*
◎ MODERN BRITISH
01451 830297 | Fosse Way, GL54 1JX
www.hotelnumberfour.com
With its wood-burning stove, exposed brickwork and muted tones, there are hints of country style in this split-level boutique hotel restaurant but also elements of modernity. From the seasonal modern British menu, try the pork belly and tenderloin, rhubarb, potato rösti, spring Savoy cabbage and pork pie sauce.

Chef Michael Bailey **Seats** 50, Private dining 15 **Open** All Year **Prices from** S £7.95, M £14.95, D £6.50 **Parking** 30 **Notes** Vegetarian dishes, Children welcome

Old Stocks Inn

◉◉ MODERN BRITISH

01451 830666 | The Square, GL54 1AP

www.oldstocksinn.com

An appealing package of bright and funky modern decor, a fun ambience, an array of regionally-brewed craft beers and an inventive take on contemporary pub grub makes this revamped 17th-century Cotswolds inn worth checking out.

Chef Ian Percival **Seats** 37, Private dining 18 **Prices from** S £7.50, M £14, D £7.50 **Parking** 8 **Notes** Vegetarian dishes, Children welcome

The Porch House

◉ MODERN BRITISH

01451 870048 | Digbeth Street, GL54 1BN

www.porch-house.co.uk

Claiming to be the oldest inn in England, the original building has been dated to AD 947, although 21st-century decor matches its undoubted period charm. The bar is stocked with real ales, while the restaurant turns out some impressive modern British dishes.

Open All Year

Wyck Hill House Hotel & Spa

◉ MODERN BRITISH

01451 831936 | Burford Road, GL54 1HY

www.wyckhillhousehotel.co.uk

Overlooking the Windrush Valley, Wyck Hill House is surrounded by 50 acres of grounds in the Cotswold Hills. The finely-tuned cooking on the seasonal menus takes provenance seriously. Start perhaps with heritage beetroot salad, goats' cheese and caramelised hazelnuts before oven-roasted Cornish hake, Jerusalem artichokes, salsify and chive cream sauce.

Chef Mark Jane **Seats** 50, Private dining 120 **Open** All Year **Parking** 120 **Notes** Vegetarian dishes, Children welcome

STROUD   MAP 4, SO80

The Bear of Rodborough

◉ BRITISH, INTERNATIONAL

01453 878522 | Rodborough Common, GL5 5DE

www.cotswold-inns-hotels.co.uk

This Cotswold hotel with its own vineyard is a handsome beast, its identity emphasised by two stuffed bears in reception. The dining room enjoys ravishing countryside views and a menu of thoroughgoing British modernism.

Open All Year

Burleigh Court Hotel

◉◉ BRITISH, MEDITERRANEAN

01453 883804 | Burleigh, Minchinhampton, GL5 2PF

www.burleighcourthotel.co.uk

Built of Cotswold stone early in the 19th-century, this imposing, ivy-clad manor house overlooks Golden Valley and the River Frome. Its Georgian-style interior incorporates an oak-panelled lounge and a dining room decorated with scenes of the house's history, where large windows reveal a beautiful garden.

Chef Adrian Jarrad **Seats** 34, **Closed** Christmas **Prices from** S £5.95, M £16.95, D £7.50 **Parking** 28 **Notes** Vegetarian dishes, Children welcome

TETBURY   MAP 4, ST89

Calcot

◉◉ MODERN BRITISH

01666 890391 | Calcot, GL8 8YJ

www.calcot.co

Calcot is a boutique-style hotel of Cotswold stone with a health spa and a light-filled restaurant called The Conservatory. The kitchen works around a repertoire of imaginative modern dishes, and flavours have real punch. Expect modern twists to classic dishes.

Open All Year

The Close Hotel

◉ MODERN BRITISH

01666 502272 | 8 Long Street, GL8 8AQ

www.theclose-hotel.com

The Close Hotel is a handsome 16th-century pile, boasting period details and contemporary elegance. There are two dining options in the form of a brasserie and fine-dining restaurant. The modern British menu strikes the right balance in this setting, with creative combinations proving very tempting.

Open All Year

Hare & Hounds Hotel

◉◉ MODERN BRITISH *V*

01666 881000 | Westonbirt, GL8 8QL

www.cotswold-inns-hotels.co.uk

The Beaufort Restaurant is the culinary heart of this Cotswold-stone hotel just outside Tetbury. There's an excellent selection of home-made breads (including a Guinness soda bread) to accompany the meal, and ice rhubarb parfait may be your choice of dessert.

Chef Dean Low **Seats** 60, Private dining 10 **Open** All Year **Parking** 40 **Notes** Children welcome

The Feathered Nest Country Inn

◉◉◉ MODERN BRITISH *V*

01993 833030 | OX7 6SD

www.thefeatherednestinn.co.uk

An impressively busy kitchen in beautiful surroundings

Creating the perfect country inn is a tricky equation, and many fail in the quest to balance drinking with eating, but Tony and Amanda Timmer at The Feathered Nest have struck gold in this born-again country hostelry, with respect for the drinking traditions matched by a culinary output that is well worth a detour. There's pretty accommodation, too, if you fancy staying the night. The Cotswold-stone building looks good both inside and out, with a contemporary country-chic interior (stone walls, flagged floors and antique furniture), the feelgood factor ramped up by real fires in winter, and bucolic views from the terrace and garden. Kuba Winkowski runs a hard-working kitchen that bakes, ferments, churns, cures, dry-ages and smokes much of what turns up on your plate. The main menu takes a quirky approach, offering a list of dishes, from which you cherry-pick four to six that take your fancy.

Start, perhaps, with an Iberian combo of softly poached octopus ramped up with saffron aïoli and a spicy broth of chorizo and potato, then move into Italian mode with partridge tortellini in game consommé accompanied by warm brioche topped with pheasant heart, truffle and cheese. Seasonal meats receive appropriately robust treatments, as when partridge arrives with potato, a powerful porcini sauce and spinach, or a serving of beautifully tender sika venison is deftly matched with celeriac and a muscular chocolate and elderberry jus.

For dessert, a quenelle of silky-smooth, home-made vanilla ice cream is slotted into a perfectly risen apple pie soufflé. The simpler lunch menu offers a pair of options at each stage, perhaps herring with

> "Tony and Amanda Timmer at The Feathered Nest have struck gold in this born-again country hostelry"

beetroot, wasabi and pumpernickel bread, before hogget with bulgur wheat, asparagus and wild garlic, and then an intriguing finisher of mango, sea buckthorn, meringue and sorrel. Vegetarian and children's menus indicate a diligent willingness to please everybody.

Chef Kuba Winkowski
Seats 60, Private dining 14
Closed 2 weeks February and July, 1 week October, 25 December
Parking 45
Notes Vegetarian dishes, Children welcome

THORNBURY

MAP 4, ST69

Ronnie's of Thornbury

@@ MODERN BRITISH

01454 411137 | 11 St Mary Street, BS35 2AB

www.ronnies-restaurant.co.uk

Ronnie's occupies a 17th-century building done out with a smart contemporary look that seamlessly blends stone walls, beamed ceilings, wooden floors, and neutral hues pointed up by paintings and photos by West Country artists. A menu of satisfyingly unfussy and hearty modern cooking satisfies all comers, with a keenly priced set lunch for bargain hunters.

Chef Ron Faulkner **Seats** 62, Private dining 30
Closed 25–26 December and 1–8 January
Prices from S £11, M £20, D £7 **Notes** Vegetarian dishes, Children welcome

Thornbury Castle

@@ MODERN BRITISH, EUROPEAN

01454 281182 | Castle Street, BS35 1HH

www.thornburycastle.co.uk

Step inside the oak doors and you'll find everything expected of a 500-year-old castle: log fires, panelling, stone staircases, suits of armour, tapestries. The menu in the hexagonal Tower restaurant is in the modern British pastoral style, with invention and heritage running side by side.

Open All Year

UPPER SLAUGHTER

MAP 10, SP12

Lords of the Manor

@@@ MODERN BRITISH NOTABLE WINE LIST

01451 820243 | GL54 2JD

www.lordsofthemanor.com

Standing proud among Upper Slaughter's glorious honey-coloured Cotswold stone buildings, Lords of the Manor is a former rectory dating from the 17th century that backs on to eight acres of green and pleasant grounds. The interior has the best of both worlds: original features and chic contemporary furnishings. Making the most of the garden views, the classy look of the dining room makes a relaxed setting for modern cooking that combines elements of French classicism with more contemporary, ingredients-led ideas. Orkney scallop tartare with Granny Smith apple and fennel-infused crème

fraîche opens with impressive clarity and balance, while precisely timed Anjou pigeon with salt-baked beetroot, chard, and fig and black pudding condiment represents the more robust end of the spectrum. The same balance and purity of flavours is on display again when it comes to dessert, with malted milk tart with stem ginger and orange rising to the occasion.

Chef Charles Smith **Seats** 50, Private dining 30 **Open** All Year **Prices from** S £7.50, M £18, D £7.50 **Parking** 40 **Notes** Vegetarian dishes, No children under 7 years
See advertisement opposite

WINCHCOMBE
MAP 10, SP02

The Lion Inn
◉ BRITISH
01242 603300 | 37 North Street, GL54 5PS
www.thelionwinchcombe.co.uk
A 15th-century coaching inn in the centre of town, The Lion looks the part with its Cotswold-stone façade and abundance of original features. Alongside the period appeal is a contemporary attitude that sees the beams painted in fashionable grey and some well-chosen shabby-chic furniture.

Chef Taylor Jones **Seats** 36, Private dining 20 **Open** All Year **Prices from** S £7, M £14, D £7 **Notes** Vegetarian dishes, Children welcome

■ GREATER MANCHESTER

BURY
MAP 15, SD81

Red Hall Hotel
◉ MODERN BRITISH
01706 822476 | Manchester Road, Walmersley, BL9 5NA
red-hall.co.uk
The hotel's conservatory-style restaurant goes by the name of Oscar's, and looks rather swish with its contemporary silver and grey tones and herringbone parquet floors. The modern British menu begins with an opener of cigar-like rolls of tuna sashimi filled with dressed white crab meat.

Open All Year

DELPH
MAP 16, SD90

The Old Bell Inn
◉ MODERN BRITISH
01457 870130 | 5 Huddersfield Road, OL3 5EG
www.theoldbellinn.co.uk
A traditional 18th-century coaching inn with a thoroughly contemporary attitude to dining, this pub holds a world record for its collection of 1,100 gins, displayed in the Gin Emporium. In the modern restaurant, hearty, innovative food is created using an abundance of local raw materials.

Chef Mark Kelly, Stuart Brown **Seats** 65 **Open** All Year **Prices from** S £5.95, M £10.95, D £5.95 **Parking** 21 **Notes** Vegetarian dishes, Children welcome

The Saddleworth Hotel
◉ MODERN EUROPEAN
01457 871888 | Huddersfield Road, OL3 5LX
www.saddleworthhotel.co.uk
The Saddleworth feels like a real attempt to create a country inn for the modern era. With landscaped gardens, woodland, and sweeping views over the Lancashire moorland, it's not far from Oldham yet feels pleasingly remote from anywhere.

Open All Year

DIDSBURY
MAP 16, SJ89

HISPI
◉◉ CONTEMPORARY BRASSERIE
0161 445 3996 | 1C School Lane, M20 6RD
www.hispi.net
A third crowd-funded venture from the team behind Heswall's Burnt Truffle and Chester's Sticky Walnut, this one is named after the trendiest cabbage variety in British catering. It features stripped-back minimalist decor, an open kitchen, and a menu of inviting contemporary brasserie food.

Adam Reid at The French

🌐🌐🌐🌐 MODERN BRITISH *V* NOTABLE WINE LIST

0161 235 4780 | The Midland, Peter Street, M60 2DS

www.the-french.co.uk

The Midland Hotel looks as grand as a city hall, in a city not short on municipal grandeur. It was constructed in the Edwardian decade to lure discerning travellers to Manchester and has been given fresh impetus in the most recent generation, not least by means of a dining room firing on all culinary cylinders. Adam Reid makes his presence felt with a fully up-to-the-minute operation that embraces small-plate dining while sitting at the kitchen counter, as well as grand tasting processions served in the glitzy French restaurant, a handsome room done in moody blue and grey beneath giant crystal globes. Choose from four, six or nine courses, and expect energetic, precise combinations such as vibrant curried Cornish squid with spinach and potato, served with malted bread and fabulous beef and onion butter. Goosnargh duck with lentils, beetroot and sour cherry is a classy main, the duck meltingly tender, with textural interest coming from praline and sweet cubes of beetroot. An intense dish of forced Yorkshire rhubarb with baked English custard is a real highlight – served with a mint butter described as 'a revelation', the dish as a whole is truly stunning.

Chef Adam Reid **Seats** 48 **Closed** Christmas, 2 weeks in August **Notes** No children under 8 years

Brasserie ABode

🌐🌐 EUROPEAN BRASSERIE

0161 247 7744 | ABode Manchester, 107 Piccadilly, M1 2DB

www.abodemanchester.co.uk

Relaxed, all-day dining with a menu that features plats du jour with a comfortingly, nostalgic nod and time-honoured classics. Generosity and value are at the heart of the Brasserie whether it's Sunday lunch, classic dishes with plentiful sides or cocktails with a side serving of nibbles.

Open All Year

Chez Mal Brasserie

🌐 MODERN BRITISH, INTERNATIONAL

0161 278 1000 | Malmaison Manchester, Piccadilly, M1 3AQ

www.malmaison.com

This prime piece of heritage industrial architecture is plumb in the city centre. The interior is boutiqued to the max, while cocktails and upscale brasserie food draw in the crowds. In The Smoak Bar & Grill, the open-to-view kitchen produces surprising versions of modern comfort food.

Open All Year

El Gato Negro Tapas *NEW*

🌐 SPANISH

0161 694 8585 | 52 King Street, M2 4LY

www.elgatonegrotapas.com

Set over three floors of a stripped-back, industrial-themed building In Manchester's busy city centre, this buzzy tapas bar has a charcuterie station and restaurant with an open kitchen. Chargrilled octopus with capers, shallots and aïoli; and pork belly, celeriac purée, straw potatoes and raisins marinated in PX sherry are among the menu highlights.

Chef Simon Shaw **Seats** 120 **Closed** 25 December, 31 December **Notes** Vegetarian dishes, Children welcome

George's Dining Room & Bar

🌐 MODERN BRITISH

0161 794 5444 | 17–21 Barton Road, Worsley, M28 2PD

www.georgesworsley.co.uk

The name of this gastro pub pays homage to Victorian architect Sir George Gilbert Scott, but this place does not look backwards. The setting is stylish, with tan leather banquettes and neutral creamy hues, and the food is very much what you'd expect of a 21st-century kitchen.

Chef Gabe Lea **Seats** 140, Private dining 14 **Open** All Year **Prices from** S £6.50, M £12.50, D £6.50 **Parking** 17 **Notes** Vegetarian dishes, Children welcome

Greens

🌐 MODERN VEGETARIAN *V*

0161 434 4259 | 43 Lapwing Lane, West Didsbury, M20 2NT

www.greensdidsbury.co.uk

TV chef Simon Rimmer's lively restaurant draws the crowds with exciting vegetarian cooking. Precisely flavoured dishes are the hallmark of the kitchen, with inspiration picked up from around the globe in a menu that bursts with bright and appealing ideas.

Chef Simon Rimmer **Seats** 84 **Closed** 25–26 December and 1 January **Prices from** S £4.50, M £11.95, D £6.50 **Notes** Children welcome

Harvey Nichols Second Floor Bar and Brasserie

◉ MODERN INTERNATIONAL

0161 828 8898 | 21 New Cathedral Street, M1 1AD

www.harveynichols.com/manchester

Overlooking Exchange Square and the hustle and bustle of the city centre's retail therapy heartlands, the slick, contemporary second-floor brasserie provides a rather glamorous respite. An all-day menu increases its allure, so you can pop in for brunch, afternoon tea or cocktails, then dive into the kitchen's brasserie-style roster of modern European ideas.

Chef Ervin Pongracz **Seats** 140 **Closed** 25 December, 1 January and Easter Sunday **Prices from** S £6, M £10, D £6 **Notes** Vegetarian dishes, Children welcome

Hotel Gotham

◉◉ MODERN EUROPEAN

0161 413 0000 | 100 King Street, M2 4WU

www.hotelgotham.co.uk

The sleek art deco lines of a vintage bank building make a good setting for this hip restaurant in a glossy boutique hotel. Parquet floors, metal-topped tables and semi-circular windows all feed into the retro styling, while the menus are all about modern British and European combinations.

Open All Year

The Lowry Hotel

◉◉ CLASSIC, TRADITIONAL

0161 827 4000 | 50 Dearmans Place, Chapel Wharf, Salford, M3 5LH

www.thelowryhotel.com

With floor-to-ceiling windows commanding spectacular views over the canal and the Lowry Bridge, The River Restaurant enjoys plenty of natural light, with glass and leather decor giving it a contemporary feel. The elegant surroundings are juxtaposed with informal, chatty service.

Open All Year

Mr Cooper's

◉◉ INTERNATIONAL

0161 235 4781 | The Midland Hotel, Peter Street, M60 2DS

www.mrcoopers.co.uk

'Food for the flexitarian' is the stock-in-trade at Mr Cooper's, another of the dining options in Manchester's trendsetting Midland Hotel. The all-day cooking is executed with great flair and attention to detail, opening with a small plate section. Grills offer sturdy sustenance for larger appetites.

Closed 25–26 December and 1 January

WOOD – Manchester

◉◉ MODERN BRITISH *V*

0161 236 5211 | Jack Rosenthal Street, First Street, M15 4RA

www.woodmanchester.com

Dine out front by all means, although the main dining space is inside, past the bar and the finishing kitchen. Menu wording is economical: scallops, burnt cauliflower and panch phoran (a sort of five-spice) is an example. The chef here won the BBC's *MasterChef* title in 2015.

Chef Simon Wood **Seats** 88, Private dining 22 **Closed** 25-26 December **Prices from** S £9.50, M £18, D £7.50 **Notes** Children welcome

MANCHESTER AIRPORT

MAP 15, SJ88

Best Western Plus Pinewood on Wilmslow

◉ MODERN, TRADITIONAL

01625 529211 | 180 Wilmslow Road, SK9 3LF

www.pinewood-hotel.co.uk

This good-looking red-brick hotel is home to the thoroughly modern One Eighty restaurant, a sleek-looking space with darkwood tables and fashionably muted tones. The menu maintains the brasserie attitude and reveals keen creativity in the kitchen. Expect honest cookery produced with very good skill levels.

Open All Year

OLDHAM

MAP 16, SD90

The Dining Room at The White Hart Inn

◉◉ MODERN BRITISH

01457 872566 | 51 Stockport Road, Lydgate, OL4 4JJ

www.thewhitehart.co.uk

The Dining Room restaurant is now the gastronomic centre of attention inside this rambling village inn that overlooks Manchester and the Cheshire plains. A seven-course tasting option showcases the kitchen's expertise and the seasonal menu. Lots of style and flair on offer and a good wine list.

Closed 26 December and 1 January

ROCHDALE
MAP 16, SD81

Nutters
⊕ MODERN BRITISH *V* ◊ NOTABLE WINE LIST

01706 650167 | Edenfield Road, Norden, OL12 7TT
www.nuttersrestaurant.co.uk

This grand old house is run as a family affair by the larger-than-life TV chef Andrew Nutter. The menu takes a modern British path, with plenty of flavours from Asia and regional ingredients providing a sense of place. There's a good value 'business lunch' menu with three courses and a six-course surprise menu.

Chef Andrew Nutter **Seats** 167, Private dining 120 **Closed** 1–2 days after both Christmas and New Year **Prices from** S £5.30, M £23.50, D £5.40 **Parking** 100 **Notes** Children welcome

WIGAN
MAP 15, SD50

Riviera
⊕ FRENCH, MEDITERRANEAN

01942 832895 | Haigh Hall Hotel, School Lane, Haigh, WN2 1PF
www.haighhallhotel.co.uk

The period magnificence of this Regency property is overlaid by a touch of contemporary, boutique style. The restaurant fits the old-meets-new bill and has its heart in sunny Mediterranean dishes from France and Italy, taking top-class ingredients as the basis for uncomplicated, soundly executed dishes.

Open All Year

■ HAMPSHIRE

ALRESFORD
MAP 5, SU53

Pulpo Negro
⊕⊕ MODERN SPANISH

01962 732262 | 28 Broad Street, SO24 9AQ
www.pulponegro.co.uk

Alresford – famous for its watercress, steam railway and clear-running chalk streams – has rather improbably added a sunny slice of the Med to its quintessentially English appeal with the arrival of Pulpo Negro. There's a smart-casual, modern feel-good vibe about the place, with its floorboards, café-style chairs, pews and wooden tables. On offer, an appealing tapas menu and well-selected Spanish wines (alongside a good showing of sherry and gin) send all home happy.

Chef Andres Alemany **Seats** 40, Private dining 35 **Closed** 25–26 December, 1 January and bank holidays **Prices from** S £3 **Notes** Vegetarian dishes, No children under 5 years

ALTON
MAP 5, SU73

The Anchor Inn
⊕⊕ MODERN, CLASSIC BRITISH

01420 23261 | Lower Froyle, GU34 4NA
www.anchorinnatlowerfroyle.co.uk

The 16th-century Anchor has all the elements of a traditional country inn down to its low beams, walls full of pictures and double-sided bar. It's a popular spot, attracting not just drinkers, but also takers for a wide-ranging menu displaying high levels of culinary skill.

Chef Josh Revis **Seats** 70, Private dining 24 **Open** All Year **Parking** 30 **Notes** Vegetarian dishes, Children welcome

ANDOVER
MAP 5, SU34

Esseborne Manor
⊕⊕ MODERN BRITISH *V*

01264 736444 | Hurstbourne Tarrant, SP11 0ER
www.esseborne-manor.co.uk

In an Area of Outstanding Natural Beauty, Esseborne is a dignified Victorian country house where chef Dennis Janssen creates modern dishes that sparkle. It's not all whizz-bang, though, as there is evident classical thinking going on, and there's a tasting menu too.

Chef Dennis Janssen **Seats** 35, Private dining 80 **Open** All Year **Prices from** S £7, M £14.50, D £7 **Parking** 40 **Notes** Children welcome

The George and Dragon
⊕⊕ BRITISH

01264 736277 | The Square, Hurstbourne Tarrant, SP11 0AA
www.georgeanddragon.com

A smart 16th-century coaching inn that proves to be a great draw for local and those from further afield. Its light and airy, low-ceilinged spaces, bare tables and fires provide just the right setting for an essentially British menu of pub favourites and more innovative dishes.

Chef Sam May **Seats** 65, Private dining 24 **Open** All Year **Parking** 18 **Notes** Vegetarian dishes, Children welcome
See advertisement opposite

GEORGE & DRAGON

The George and Dragon is a modern coaching inn set in the centre of beautiful Hurstbourne Tarrant. We're passionate about food made from only the freshest seasonal ingredients and our chefs make everything in-house. We add new dishes every week and serve them up in warmly relaxing surroundings, along with a range of local beers, craft spirits and stunning wines.

OPEN FOR BREAKFAST, LUNCH & DINNER
Everyday From 8AM

BRITISH TAPAS LUNCH MENU
Monday - Friday

BED & BREAKFAST
with 9 beautiful double en-suite bedrooms

THE SQUARE, HURSTBOURNE TARRANT ANDOVER, HAMPSHIRE, SP11 0AA

01264 736277 | georgeanddragon.com | info@georgeanddragon.com

BARTON-ON-SEA
MAP 5, SZ29

Pebble Beach
◉ BRITISH, FRENCH, MEDITERRANEAN, SEAFOOD
01425 627777 | Marine Drive, BH25 7DZ
www.pebblebeach-uk.com
A clifftop perch gives this modern bar-brasserie a sweeping vista across Christchurch Bay to the Needles and the Isle of Wight. Inside is a buzzy split-level venue where high stools at the oyster bar allow views of the open-plan kitchen. The alfresco terrace is irresistible.

Chef Karl Wiggins **Seats** 90, Private dining 8 **Open** All Year **Prices from** S £10, M £20, D £8 **Parking** 20 **Notes** Vegetarian dishes, Children welcome

BASINGSTOKE
MAP 5, SU65

Audleys Wood Hotel
◉◉ MODERN BRITISH
01256 817555 | Alton Road, RG25 2JT
www.handpickedhotels.co.uk/thesimondsroom
This striking Victorian property stands in seven acres of grounds and woodland and has all the trappings of a luxury country-house hotel. The Conservatory Restaurant with its high vaulted ceiling and small minstrels' gallery serves a seasonally-changing menu.

Chef Gordon Neale **Seats** 55, Private dining 40 **Open** All Year **Prices from** S £5.50, M £10, D £7 **Parking** 70 **Notes** Vegetarian dishes, Children welcome

Glasshouse Restaurant
◉◉ MODERN INTERNATIONAL *V*
01256 783350 | Oakley Hall Hotel, Rectory Road, Oakley, RG23 7EL
www.oakleyhall-park.com
Jane Austen enthusiasts will find references to Oakley Hall in her work. As a young woman, she was a frequent visitor. The Glasshouse restaurant is the setting for classically based modern British menus that draw their raw materials from the kitchen garden.

Chef Sebastian Smith **Seats** 80, Private dining 300 **Open** All Year **Prices from** S £6.50, M £25.95, D £8.50 **Parking** 100 **Notes** Vegetarian dishes, Children welcome

BAUGHURST
MAP 5, SU56

The Wellington Arms
◉◉ MODERN BRITISH
0118 982 0110 | Baughurst Road, RG26 5LP
www.thewellingtonarms.com
The Wellington Arms is a dining pub with a capital D. A good deal of what you eat will have found its way into the kitchen from the garden, and the rest won't have travelled very far. The old pub itself has scrubbed up nicely.

Chef Jason King, Helen Slater **Seats** 40, Private dining 16 **Open** All Year **Prices from** S £6.50, M £12, D £4 **Parking** 25 **Notes** Vegetarian dishes, Children welcome

BEAULIEU
MAP 5, SU30

The Drift Inn NEW
◉ MODERN BRITISH
023 8029 3344 | Beaulieu Hotel, Beaulieu Road, SO42 7YQ
www.newforesthotels.co.uk
Surrounded by New Forest heathland, The Drift Inn has a welcoming dog- and family-friendly attitude and an upmarket country inn ambience, with open fires adding to the overall sense of well-being. The kitchen stocks its larder with fine local bounty as the bedrock of a nifty menu of sturdy, up-to-date pub dishes.

The Master Builder's at Buckler's Hard
◉ MODERN BRITISH
01590 616253 | Buckler's Hard, SO42 7XB
www.themasterbuilders.co.uk
Named after the man who built ships for Nelson's fleet on the grassy areas running down to the Beaulieu River, the restaurant in this rustic 18th-century hotel offers tranquil river views. The straightforward modern British cooking is underpinned by well-sourced local ingredients. Try the fillet of venison, pommes Anna, romanesco and glazed figs.

Chef Michele Mirabile **Seats** Private dining 40 **Open** All Year **Prices from** S £6, M £14.50, D £6.50 **Parking** 60 **Notes** Vegetarian dishes, Children welcome

The Montagu Arms Hotel
◉◉◉ MODERN EUROPEAN
01590 612324 | Palace Lane, SO42 7ZL
www.montaguarmshotel.co.uk
The Montagu Arms sits in a prime New Forest spot and takes it name from the blue-blooded family who live across the river on the Beaulieu estate. It's the quintessential wisteria-draped, 17th-century country hotel, and the sumptuous comforts within – including a spa – do not disappoint. With its oak panels, linen-swathed tables and French windows opening onto a sun-trap garden, the Terrace Restaurant sets a suitably elegant tone for some fine-tuned and innovative cooking from new-broom head chef Matthew Whitfield, who took the helm in 2019.

Exemplary use of local produce defines a dish of New Forest asparagus with a slow-cooked hen's egg, burnt onion powder and Hampshire rapeseed oil mayo, while main-course duck comes honey glazed and pointed up with Szechuan pepper and ginger, alongside heritage carrots, stuffed cabbage leaf and potato purée. To conclude, top-flight pastry skills add lustre to a caramelised custard and rhubarb tart, deftly flavoured with a hint of lemon balm and matched with zippy rhubarb sorbet.

Chef Matthew Whitfield Seats 60, Private dining 32 Open All Year Prices from S £14, M £22, D £12 Parking 50 Notes Vegetarian dishes, No children under 12 years at dinner

Monty's Inn

◉ TRADITIONAL BRITISH
01590 614986 | The Montagu Arms Hotel, Palace Lane, SO42 7ZL
www.montaguarmshotel.co.uk
Specialising in hearty, unpretentious food that doesn't try to punch above its weight, Monty's Inn goes for a clubby look involving wood-panelled walls, wooden floors and unclothed tables in a posh country pub setting. Kick things off perfectly with a home-made local pork Scotch egg.

Chef Robert McLean Seats 50 Open All Year Prices from S £6.95, M £13.25, D £5.95 Parking 40 Notes Vegetarian dishes, Children welcome

BRANSGORE
MAP 5, SZ19

The Three Tuns

◉ BRITISH, EUROPEAN
01425 672232 | Ringwood Road, BH23 8JH
www.threetunsinn.com
The picture-postcard 17th-century thatched inn deep in the New Forest is a delight in summer, festooned with flowers, and cosy in winter as blazing log fires warm the low beamed bar. The welcoming scene draws foodies and forest visitors for its charm and character.

Closed 25-26 and 31 December

BROCKENHURST
MAP 5, SU30

The Balmer Lawn Hotel

◉◉ MODERN BRITISH
01590 623116 | Lyndhurst Road, SO42 7ZB
www.balmerlawnhotel.com
This imposing pavilion-style Victorian hunting lodge in a charming New Forest setting does good business as a friendly, family-run operation with an excellent spa, sports and conference facilities. Expect modern cooking with a healthy showing of prime-quality, often local, materials.

Chef Chris Wheeldon Seats 80, Private dining 100 Open All Year Prices from S £7, M £16, D £8 Parking 100 Notes Vegetarian dishes, Children welcome

Cambium

◉◉◉ MODERN BRITISH ⬧ NOTABLE WINE LIST
01590 623551 | Careys Manor Hotel & SenSpa, Lyndhurst Road, SO42 7RH
www.careysmanor.com/cambium
The Careys Manor Hotel is to be found in the New Forest, an environment its restaurant celebrates in every particular. Cambium is a technical botanical term for the inner tissue of plants or trees, and you only have to contemplate the decor, which incorporates leafy screens and a central bare-twigged tree with purple flowers stuck on it, to note the homage paid to the sylvan setting. Alastair Craig's cooking plays its part too, with plates that look pretty and deliver convincing natural flavours. Kick off with a light, refreshing starter of picked white crab, served with a custard of the brown meat, avocado, and pink grapefruit granita, followed by beautifully cooked pink duck breast, accompanied by miso glazed parsnips, pickled mooli and cavolo nero. Dessert might take the form of a well-timed chocolate and caramel fondant with whisky ice cream and candied orange.

Chef Alistair Craig Seats 94, Private dining 40 Open All Year Prices from S £8, M £15, D £10 Parking 83 Notes Vegetarian dishes, No children under 8 years

THE PIG

◉◉ BRITISH ⬧ NOTABLE WINE LIST
01590 622354 | Beaulieu Road, SO42 7QL
www.thepighotel.com
This is a restaurant for our times, with cocktails served in jam jars and massages available in the old potting shed. Here, in the wilds of the New Forest, the passion is for home-grown and foraged ingredients. It's a buzzy place with a retro interior.

Chef James Golding Seats 95, Private dining 14 Open All Year Prices from S £6, M £12, D £7 Parking 40 Notes Vegetarian dishes, Children welcome

Rhinefield House Hotel

@ @ CLASSIC, TRADITIONAL BRITISH *V*

01590 622922 | Rhinefield Road, SO42 7QB

www.handpickedhotels.co.uk/rhinefieldhouse

The present house sprang up in the late Victorian era. A Tudor-Gothic hybrid architecturally, the interiors are awash with finely crafted mouldings, copperwork, and beautiful examples of the lavatorialist's art, and a room modelled on the Alhambra.

Chef James Verity **Seats** 58, Private dining 20 **Open** All Year **Parking** 150 **Notes** Children welcome

BROOK
MAP 5, SU21

The Bell Inn

@ @ MODERN BRITISH

023 8081 2214 | SO43 7HE

www.bellinn-newforest.co.uk

In the ownership of the same family since George III was on the throne, The Bell is in a picturesque New Forest village not far from Lyndhurst, and is more than a simple country inn: it has a pair of golf courses and 28 indvidually styled, en suite bedrooms. The interior looks the modernised rustic part, with blackboard menus and log fires in winter, and plenty of gracefully presented local produce on offer. Dogs are welcome here.

Open All Year

BURLEY
MAP 5, SU20

Burley Manor

@ BRITISH, MEDITERRANEAN

01425 403522 | Ringwood Road, BH24 4BS

www.burleymanor.com

Burley Manor was built in 1852 by a magistrate and custodian of the surrounding New Forest. A hotel since the 1930s, this grand former home enjoys fabulous parkland views and a peaceful patio. In the restaurant, the menu has Mediterranean influences.

Open All Year

Moorhill House Hotel

@ MODERN, TRADITIONAL BRITISH

01425 403285 | BH24 4AG

www.newforesthotels.co.uk

Deep in the ancient woodland of the New Forest, near the pretty village of Burley, this hotel sits in handsome gardens and is done out in light, attractive country-house style within, with log fires in winter. In the elegant dining room, straightforward, well-executed dishes are served.

Open All Year

CADNAM
MAP 5, SU21

Bartley Lodge Hotel

@ MODERN BRITISH

023 8081 2248 | Lyndhurst Road, SO40 2NR

www.newforesthotels.co.uk

In eight delightful Hampshire acres, the Grade II listed, 18th-century Bartley Lodge boasts many original features. A 'flexible dining' approach means the menu is available throughout the hotel, including in the Crystal Restaurant, with its elegant centrepiece chandelier and delicate blue and gold colour scheme.

Chef Lee Wheeler **Seats** 60, Private dining 90 **Open** All Year **Prices from** S £5, M £12.95, D £6 **Parking** 90 **Notes** Vegetarian dishes, Children welcome

DOGMERSFIELD
MAP 5, SU75

Wild Carrot at Four Seasons Hotel Hampshire

@ CONTEMPORARY BRITISH *V*

01252 853100 | Dogmersfield Park, Chalky Lane, RG27 8TD

www.wildcarrotrestaurant.co.uk

Set within the expansive acreages of the Dogmersfield Estate, the Four Seasons' dining options include a bistro and café, but the main event is the Wild Carrot restaurant, a light-filled dining space with French windows and an upscale, gently contemporary sheen.

Chef Paolo Belloni **Seats** 100, Private dining 24 **Open** All Year **Prices from** S £11, M £20, D £9 **Parking** 100 **Notes** Children welcome until 7.30pm

EMSWORTH
MAP 5, SU70

Fat Olives

@ @ MODERN BRITISH, MEDITERRANEAN

01243 377914 | 30 South Street, PO10 7EH

www.fatolives.co.uk

A few steps from the quayside of the pretty Emworth harbour, this 17th-century fishermen's cottage provides the setting for Lawrence and Julia Murphy's smart brasserie. The stripped-out interior of cream walls, wooden floors and unclothed tables is as unvarnished and honest as the food. Excellent ingredients do the talking on a menu that's an appetising fusion of modern, well-thought-through ideas.

Chef Lawrence Murphy **Seats** 25 **Closed** 1 week Christmas, 2 weeks in June **Prices from** S £6.95, M £15.95, D £7.25 **Notes** Vegetarian dishes, No children under 8, no age restriction Saturday lunch

36 on the Quay
◉◉◉ MODERN BRITISH, EUROPEAN
01243 375592 | 47 South Street, PO10 7EG
www.36onthequay.co.uk
This well-known and long-running restaurant-with-rooms has a wonderful setting, in a 17th-century building right on the harbour in this lovely little fishing village. It's a great place to watch the sun go down – have a drink outside in the courtyard before heading in to the bright, airy dining room. The menu is quite traditional, with interesting contemporary interpretations of classic dishes and flavour combinations, and tasting menus are available at both lunch and dinner. A neatly presented starter of poached trout comes with cherry, soy, puffed rice, shimeji mushrooms and spring salad, while main courses might take in interesting vegetarian options like barbecued beetroot, celeriac and Mayfield cheese, with courgette, and beetroot emulsion to the rather meatier Welsh Wagyu beef with wild garlic pesto and beef tartare. Pineapple arctic roll with date purée, coconut sorbet, muscovado mousse and coconut crumb is a great dessert, or there's a tasting plate of six British cheeses.

Chef Gary Pearce **Seats** 45, Private dining 12 **Closed** 1st 2/3 weeks January, 1 week May, 1 week October, 25-26 December **Notes** Vegetarian dishes, Children welcome

FAREHAM   *MAP 5, SU50*
Solent Hotel & Spa
◉ MODERN BRITISH, EUROPEAN, INTERNATIONAL
01489 880000 | Rookery Avenue, Whiteley, PO15 7AJ
www.solenthotel.co.uk/food-drink
A modern hotel with spa facilities among woodland, yet close by the M27, The Solent's refurbished Terrace Restaurant is a cheery contemporary space. Separated from the bar by an open fireplace, it offers cosy nooks and booths and an easygoing ambience. The wide-ranging menu aims to please all-comers with a roster of modern dishes.

Open All Year

FARNBOROUGH   *MAP 5, SU85*
Aviator
◉◉ MODERN INTERNATIONAL *V*
01252 555890 | Farnborough Road, GU14 6EL
www.aviatorbytag.com
The TAG timepiece manufacturer's aviation-themed hotel has landed on the Hampshire-Surrey border, in the vicinity of the celebrated air show at Farnborough. The uncomplicated, modern brasserie food has something to please all tastes including a repertoire of classic cuts of steak, done on the charcoal grill.

Chef Mateusz Mitka **Seats** 120, Private dining 8 **Open** All Year **Prices from** S £8, M £17, D £7.50 **Parking** 169 **Notes** Children welcome

HIGHCLERE   *MAP 5, SU45*
The Yew Tree
◉◉ MODERN BRITISH
01635 253360 | Hollington Cross, RG20 9SE
www.theyewtree.co.uk
A classic English country inn in a ravishing setting near Highclere Castle. Traditional English cooking is the order of the day, overlaid with modern flourishes. The menu offers a list of 'The Usual Suspects' that keeps the fish and chips and burger brigade content.

Open All Year

HORDLE   *MAP 5 SZ29*
The Mill at Gordleton *NEW*
◉ MODERN BRITISH
01590 682219 | Silver Street, SO41 6DJ
www.themillatgordleton.co.uk
Whether you settle in the cosseting bar, the contemporary river-view restaurant or the newly-built orangery, this creeper-clad inn serves properly satisfying modern British food. From bread to soups, sauces, ice cream and puddings, it's all made in-house from scratch using local and organic ingredients from producers in the nearby New Forest.

Chef Ian Gibbs **Seats** Private dining 18 **Notes** Vegetarian dishes, Children welcome

HURSLEY *MAP 5, SU42*

The King's Head

◉ CLASSIC BRITISH

01962 775208 | Main Road, SO21 2JW

www.kingsheadhursley.co.uk

An ivy-clad Georgian inn at the heart of a village community near Winchester, The King's Head has a lightly worn touch of refinement, with candlesticks on wooden tables, equestrian prints, a tartan banquette, and a menu of sound, regionally based cooking.

Open All Year

LYMINGTON *MAP 5, SZ39*

The Elderflower Restaurant

◉◉◉ MODERN BRITISH, FRENCH

01590 676908 | 4A Quay Street, SO41 3AS

www.elderflowerrestaurant.co.uk

A Grade II listed building on a cobbled street close to the quayside is home to Andrew and Marjolaine Du Bourg's restaurant, where regional produce gets to stand centre stage. The antiquity of the building is evident through the old beams, but there is a contemporary neutrality to the interior, a confident charm that is matched by the output from Andrew's kitchen. Both the couple have experience in top-end addresses and they created their own in 2014, giving Lymington a restaurant with serious chops. Andrew is from Yorkshire (via South Africa) and Marjolaine hails from western France, and you may well notice evidence of this happy alliance on the menu, alongside a genuine creative streak. Via à la carte and two tasting menu options, expect winning flavour combinations such as crab lasagne with a delicious lobster bisque, or a celebration of Keyhaven lamb, with anchovy and celeriac purée and nori seaweed.

Chef Andrew Du Bourg **Seats** 40 **Open** All Year **Prices from** S £8, M £23, D £8 **Notes** Vegetarian dishes, No children under 12 years at dinner Friday, Saturday and Valentine's Day

The Mayflower

◉ MODERN BRITISH

01590 672160 | King's Saltern Road, SO41 3QD

www.themayflowerlymington.co.uk

The first radio signal was transmitted to the Isle of Wight from the beacon ship after which this coastal pub is named. That nautical history is honoured in the design theming in the present-day restaurant, where seashells and ships' accoutrements abound.

Open All Year

Stanwell House Hotel

◉◉ MODERN BRITISH, EUROPEAN

01590 677123 | 14–15 High Street, SO41 9AA

www.stanwellhouse.com

'Tin' (and other metals) give the Etain restaurant its main theme, as it notches up over a decade of service. The contemporary style and cool pale colours set the scene for a seasonally-changing menu accompanied by a good wine list.

Open All Year

LYNDHURST *MAP 5, SU30*

The Crown Manor House Hotel

◉◉ MODERN BRITISH

023 8028 2922 | High Street, SO43 7NF

www.crownhotel-lyndhurst.co.uk

The fireplace just inside the entrance once provided instant defrosting for travellers who had braved the horse-drawn carriage transfer from the railway station. Such is the Crown's history, which extends from 15th-century beginnings to a late Victorian makeover, its panelled dining room a refreshing space today for contemporary brasserie cooking.

Open All Year

1820 Grill & Brasserie

◉◉ MODERN BRITISH

023 8028 6129 | Forest Lodge Hotel, Pikes Hill, Romsey Road, SO43 7AS

www.newforesthotels.co.uk/forest-lodge-hotel

On the outskirts of Lyndhurst, this hotel's restaurant has a new name and is a hugely stylish environment. The menu covers a lot of ground, from burgers and light bites to a well-conceived starter of quail three ways (poached breast, confit leg and a Scotch egg).

Chef Prince Alexander **Seats** 60, Private dining 10 **Open** All Year **Prices from** S £6, M £13, D £6 **Parking** 60 **Notes** Vegetarian dishes, Children welcome

Hartnett Holder & Co

◉◉◉ ITALIAN **V**

See opposite

Hartnett Holder & Co

@@@ **ITALIAN** *V*

023 8028 7177 | Lime Wood, Beaulieu Road, SO43 7FZ

www.limewood.co.uk

Lime Wood looks out over the peaceable expanses of the New Forest. The kitchen here is in the hands of Luke Holder, and overseen by Italian food superstar Angela Hartnett. The seasonal menus work indeed to an Italian template, with antipasti and primi before the main course, and a wealth of respectfully treated natural ingredients running through them. A serving of Cornish crab with smoked eel, radish and apple is the perfect palate-primer for a pasta dish such as guinea fowl agnolotti with lardo di Colonnata, onion and sage. At main, there could be a copiously crammed fish stew incorporating monkfish, red mullet, langoustines and scallops, or one of the locally reared meats, perhaps Saddleback pork fillet with king cabbage and roasted Cox's apple. Fragrant desserts such as saffron pannacotta with rosewater and pistachios, or chocolate-orange tart with blood orange sorbet, make for memorable closing notes.

Chef Angela Hartnett, Luke Holder **Seats** 70, Private dining 16 **Open** All Year **Prices from** S £12, M £28, D £9.50 **Parking** 90 **Notes** Children welcome

MILFORD ON SEA
MAP 5, SZ29

Verveine Fishmarket Restaurant
◉◉ MODERN, SEAFOOD
01590 642176 | 98 High Street, SO41 0QE
www.verveine.co.uk
Stylish, understated decor and fish-related artworks feed into the sense of a committed operation at this dinky fish restaurant tucked away, appropriately enough, behind a fishmonger's. It's an intimate, elegant dining room, reached via the open kitchen, and the deal is 3 to 10 courses of finely-honed cooking.

Chef David Wykes Seats 32 Closed 25 December to 18 January Notes Vegetarian dishes, No children under 8 years at dinner

NEW MILTON
MAP 5, SZ29

The Dining Room
◉◉ MODERN BRITISH *V*
01425 282212 | Chewton Glen, Christchurch Road, BH25 6QS
www.chewtonglen.com
The cuisine at Chewton Glen is one of its highly regarded features. In the light, subtly hued Dining Room, modern British classics include pressed duck liver with almond, plum sake and toasted brioche; Isle of Gigha halibut with sticky chicken wings, aubergine, miso and lotus root; and Valrhona chocolate and orange mousse.

Chef Simon Addison Seats 164, Private dining 70 Open All Year Prices from S £9, M £22, D £12 Parking 150 Notes No children under 8 years after 8pm
See advertisement opposite

The Kitchen
◉ ITALIAN, AMERICAN
01425 282212 | Chewton Glen, Christchurch Road, BH25 6QS
www.chewtonglen.com/thekitchen
Staff are friendly and service is polished at this modern venue, purpose-built as a restaurant and cookery school. Take a seat in one of the deep burgundy leather chairs or banquettes at copper-topped tables and peruse the menu of crowd-pleasing dishes cooked up by chefs James Martin and Adam Hart.

Chef James Martin, Adam Hart Seats 50, Private dining 12 Open All Year Prices from S £5, M £10, D £7 Parking 40 Notes Vegetarian dishes, Children welcome
See advertisement opposite

NORTHINGTON
MAP 5, SU53

The Woolpack Inn
◉ CLASSIC BRITISH
01962 734184 | Totford, SO24 9TJ
www.thewoolpackinn.co.uk
In a tiny hamlet within the pretty Candover Valley, this Grade I listed flint-and-brick inn has retained its traditional country pub feel with open fires, flagstoned floors and real ales, although the emphasis is on food, a combination of pub grub and European influences.

Open All Year

OTTERBOURNE
MAP 5, SU42

The White Horse
◉ MODERN, TRADITIONAL BRITISH
01962 712830 | Main Road, SO21 2EQ
www.whitehorseotterbourne.co.uk
Descending from a hike along the spine of the South Downs, you couldn't ask for a more fortifying pitstop. This village hostelry looks every inch the modern dining pub with wooden and quarry-tiled floors, bare beams and mismatched tables. The mood is unbuttoned and family-friendly.

Chef Kunal Nadkarni Seats 90 Open All Year Prices from S £6, M £12, D £6.50 Parking 25 Notes Vegetarian dishes, Children welcome

PORTSMOUTH
MAP 5, SU60

Restaurant 27
◉◉ MODERN EUROPEAN *V*
023 9287 6272 | 27a South Parade, PO5 2JF
www.restaurant27.com
Family-run with a heartfelt passion for local materials, chef-proprietor Kevin Bingham's stylish restaurant is a high-ceilinged, modern space dressed up in grey, with unclothed tables, and walls hung with eclectic artworks. Two six-course tasting menus with veggie alternatives showcase the kitchen's modern European sensibilities. Expect ambitious, thoughtfully composed dishes delivering on-trend ingredients and well-defined flavours.

Chef Kevin Bingham, Annie Martin-Smith Seats 34 Closed Christmas and New Year Notes Children welcome

CHEWTON GLEN
HAMPSHIRE

An English Original...

At Chewton Glen we are fortunate enough to have two fantastic dining options, The Dining Room and The Kitchen.

The Dining Room, is a truly cosmopolitan and quintessentially English resturant. Offering a nexus of beautiful conservatories, intimate dining spaces and a stunning open wine room, The Dining Room is as formal or relaxed as the mood takes you. The menu has been carefully created for you to enjoy classic Chewton Glen favourites as well as innovative creations from our culinary team.

The Kitchen, is a purpose-built cookery school and relaxed dining space for enjoying and learning about food. An informal dining experience with an open layout offers you the chance to watch the Chefs at work. The à la carte menu features wood-fired pizzas, gourmet burgers, superfood salads and much more.

Call 01425 282212 or email reservations@chewtonglen.com to book your table...

Chewton Glen | New Forest | Hampshire | BH25 6QS
chewtonglen.com

RELAIS &
CHATEAUX

PRESTON CANDOVER
MAP 5, SU64

The Purefoy NEW
◉◉ BRITISH **V**

01256 389514 | RG25 2EJ

thepurefoyarms.co.uk

A red-brick Victorian village pub close to Basingstoke, The Purefoy benefits from a large garden tailor-made for serious alfresco dining in summer. Otherwise, grab a table near the real fire and enjoy modern British dishes like fillet steak served with celeriac, chestnut crumb, creamed potato, spinach and red wine jus.

Chef Gordon Stott **Seats** 34 **Open** All Year
Prices from S £5.95, M £12.95, D £6.50 **Parking** 14
Notes Children welcome

ROMSEY
MAP 5, SU32

The White Horse Hotel & Brasserie
◉◉ MODERN BRITISH

01794 512431 | 19 Market Place, SO51 8ZJ

www.thewhitehorseromsey.co.uk

Romsey resident and future prime minister Lord Palmerston first mounted his political soapbox here. At its heart is a brasserie-style dining room, where well-executed modern British cooking with some European influences holds sway, typified by local beer-battered fish and chips; seared scallops with crispy oxtail; and marinated lamb rump with sweetbreads.

Chef Nick O'Halloran **Seats** 85, Private dining 100
Prices from S £8, M £18, D £7 **Notes** Vegetarian
dishes, Children welcome

See advertisement opposite

ROTHERWICK
MAP 5, SU75

The Oak Room Restaurant
◉◉ MODERN BRITISH **V**

01256 764881 | Tylney Hall Hotel, Ridge Lane, RG27 9AZ

www.tylneyhall.co.uk

Following a refurbishment, The Oak Room at Tylney Hall remains one of Hampshire's exemplary country-house restaurants. What arrives in front of you will be a gently updated take on a traditional English or European classic, thus pan-seared scallops come with artichoke and miso caramel, and Herefordshire lamb loin with a harissa-spiced lamb cigar and roasted San Marzano tomatoes.

Chef Mike Lloyd **Seats** 80, Private dining 120 **Open** All
Year **Prices from** S £10.50, M £22, D £10 **Parking** 150
Notes Children welcome

ST MARY BOURNE
MAP 5, SU45

Bourne Valley Inn
◉ BRITISH

01264 738361 | SP11 6BT

www.bournevalleyinn.com

Known as BVI to its friends, this village pub has become a magnet for foodies, with its main dining area in a converted barn with beams and a rustic-chic look. The menu presses the comfort button with a mix of pub classics and honest down-to-earth cooking.

Open All Year

SOUTHAMPTON
MAP 5, SU41

The Jetty
◉◉ MODERN

023 8110 3456 | Southampton Harbour Hotel & Spa, 5 Maritime Walk, Ocean Village, SO14 3QT

www.southampton-harbour-hotel.co.uk

The Jetty is part of the rather spectacular Southampton Harbour Hotel and enjoys panoramic views across Ocean Village Marina. There's a terrace for outdoor dining, surrounded by sunshine and yachts. It's chic and elegant, with a bright airy feel and cheery turquoise and yellow highlights.

Chef Alex Aitken **Open** All Year **Notes** No children

STOCKBRIDGE
MAP 5, SU33

The Greyhound on the Test
◉◉ MODERN BRITISH

01264 810833 | 31 High Street, SO20 6EY

www.thegreyhoundonthetest.co.uk

The Greyhound has no shortage of appeal, from upmarket, sumptuous bedrooms to a restaurant with that opened-up, country-chic vibe. The menu is a thoroughly up-to-date affair with regional produce at its heart. You're sure to go home happy after dark chocolate brownie with chocolate mousse.

Chef Chris Heather **Seats** 60, Private dining 16
Closed 25–26 December **Prices from** S £4.95, M £15.25,
D £5.50 **Parking** 20 **Notes** Vegetarian dishes, Children
welcome

The Peat Spade Inn

◉ MODERN BRITISH

01264 810612 | Village Street, Longstock, SO20 6DR
www.peatspadeinn.co.uk
A stolid-looking red-brick country inn where close-set tables add to the dining-room buzz. Rustic cooking with more than a soupçon of French influence proves abidingly popular, seen in the form of fried chicken livers on sourdough toast with charred sweetcorn in peppercorn sauce.

Open All Year

The Three Cups Inn

◉ MODERN & TRADITIONAL BRITISH

01264 810527 | High Street, SO20 6HB
www.the3cups.co.uk
This 16th-century coaching inn is still very much a pub offering local ales, but it's also a dining destination with low-ceilinged dining room and an orangery extension opening up to the garden. The kitchen makes good use of local foodstuffs. There are bedrooms, too.

Closed 25–26 December

WINCHESTER   MAP 5, SU42

Avenue Restaurant at Lainston House Hotel

Rosettes suspended MODERN BRITISH *V*

01962 776088 | Woodman Lane, Sparsholt, SO21 2LT
www.lainstonhouse.com
The Rosette award for this establishment has been suspended due to a change of chef and reassessment will take place in due course. The imposing red-brick manor house is of 17th-century vintage, with an avenue of mature lime trees leading to it. It's that arboreal feature that is referenced in the name of the dignified dining room, where varnished oak panels set with contemporary wall lights, a marble fireplace and simple modern table settings establish the mood. Open-air dining on the terrace will coax the sun-lovers out.

Seats 60, Private dining 120 Closed 25–26 December
Parking 100 Notes Children welcome under 12 years in private room or dine at 6.30pm

WINCHESTER continued

The Black Rat

◉◉ MODERN BRITISH

01962 844465 | 88 Chesil Street, SO23 0HX

www.theblackrat.co.uk

In an inconspicuous white-fronted former pub on the edge of town, The Black Rat sets its sights firmly on culinary modernism. Lots of good technical skills and techniques – good flavours and consistency across all dishes and efficient service to boot.

Chef John Marsden-Jones **Seats** 40, Private dining 16 **Closed** Christmas and New Year **Prices from** S £11, M £22, D £9 **Notes** Vegetarian dishes, No children under 12 years at dinner, children must choose from the regular menu at lunch

The Chesil Rectory

◉◉ MODERN BRITISH

01962 851555 | 1 Chesil Street, SO23 0HU

www.chesilrectory.co.uk

A beautiful half-timbered building dating from 1450, The Chesil Rectory is the oldest house in Winchester. Enter through a low door to be greeted by a brilliantly preserved interior with low beams, charming inglenook fireplaces and exposed brickwork, updated with lime green banquettes and stylish chairs. The kitchen puts a gently modernised spin on classic French dishes.

Chef Damian Brown **Seats** 75, Private dining 12 **Closed** 25 December and 1 January **Prices from** S £6.95, M £13.95, D £7.50 **Notes** Vegetarian dishes, No children under 10 years at dinner

Holiday Inn Winchester

◉ MODERN, TRADITIONAL BRITISH

01962 670700 | Telegraph Way, Morn Hill, SO21 1HZ

www.hiwinchester.co.uk

On the edge of the South Downs National Park, the restaurant at this large purpose-built hotel goes to great lengths to source local produce. The high culinary standards elevate the cooking well above that normally seen in hotel chains and the modern cooking appeals to both leisure and corporate guests.

Chef Chris Keel **Seats** 128, Private dining 200 **Open** All Year **Prices from** S £7, M £14, D £6 **Parking** 170 **Notes** Vegetarian dishes, Children welcome

Marwell Hotel

◉◉ MODERN EUROPEAN *V*

01962 777681 | Thompsons Lane, Colden Common, Marwell, SO21 1JY

www.marwellhotel.co.uk

A pastoral retreat in the manner of an African safari lodge, Marwell Hotel is set in wooded grounds next door to a wildlife park, so the odd screech of a monkey is to be expected. The kitchen applies modern styling to mostly traditional dishes.

Chef Phil Yeomans **Seats** 70, Private dining 120 **Closed** 24–26 December **Prices from** S £7.95, M £19.95, D £7.95 **Parking** 100 **Notes** Children welcome

Running Horse Inn

◉◉ CLASSIC BRITISH

01962 880218 | 88 Main Road, Littleton, SO22 6QS

www.runninghorseinn.co.uk

The Running Horse is a revitalised village inn with a relaxed and informal dining environment: a wood-burning stove in a brick fireplace, some banquette seating, wooden tables and a mixture of artwork adorning the walls. The kitchen delivers stimulating full-flavoured dishes.

Open All Year

WOODLANDS

MAP 5, SU31

Woodlands Lodge Hotel

◉ MODERN BRITISH

023 8029 2257 | Bartley Road, Woodlands, SO40 7GN

www.woodlands-lodge.co.uk

When we say this hotel is 'in the New Forest', we mean it. The ancient woodland can be accessed directly from the Lodge's gardens, making it the perfect spot for a walking break. Hunters restaurant serves capably rendered modern British dishes with plenty of verve.

Chef Darren Appleby **Seats** 30, Private dining 35 **Open** All Year **Prices from** S £5.50, M £13, D £6 **Parking** 80 **Notes** Vegetarian dishes, Children welcome

■ HEREFORDSHIRE

AYMESTREY
MAP 9, SO46

The Riverside at Aymestrey
◉◉ CLASSIC BRITISH *V*
01568 708440 | The Riverside Inn, HR6 9ST
www.riversideaymestrey.co.uk
Close to Ludlow and Hereford on the edge of
Mortimer Forest, this 16th-century black and
white timber-framed inn features a kitchen that
is serious about its food, with produce from their
own garden. The menu changes daily and dishes
are simple and honest.

Chef Andy Link **Seats** 60, Private dining 40 **Open** All
Year **Prices from** S £5.75, M £13, D £6 **Parking** 20
Notes Children welcome

EWYAS HAROLD
MAP 9, SO32

The Temple Bar Inn
◉◉ MODERN BRITISH
01981 240423 | HR2 0EU
www.thetemplebarinn.co.uk
Still a proper pub complete with a pool table,
well-kept real ales, oak beams, flagstones and a
blazing fire, this is an inviting spot with a friendly
atmosphere and accomplished cooking. The
restaurant is in the old stables block and there's
a courtyard for alfresco dining.

Chef Phillippa Jinman, Jo Pewsey **Seats** 30, Private
dining 45 **Closed** 25 December, 1 week January to
February and 1 week in November **Prices from** S £5,
M £12, D £6 **Parking** 12 **Notes** Vegetarian
dishes, Children welcome

LEDBURY
MAP 10, SO73

Feathers
◉ MODERN BRITISH
01531 635266 | High Street, HR8 1DS
www.feathers-ledbury.co.uk
The heavily timbered Feathers is a wonderful
slice of Tudor England, its oak-panelled
venerability thrown into relief by a modern
brasserie named after the hop variety Fuggles,
and an upmarket dining room, Quills. Sirloins and
fillets of local beef are a big draw.

Open All Year

ROSS-ON-WYE
MAP 10, SO52

Conservatory Restaurant
◉ BRITISH
01989 763174 | King's Head Hotel, 8 High Street,
HR9 5HL
www.kingshead.co.uk
Dating from the 14th century, the King's Head is
woven into the historic high street's fabric and
comes with all the fireplaces and oak beams
you'd hope for in an inn of this vintage. The
cooking takes a modern tack, letting prime local
materials do the talking in flavour-led dishes.

Chef Ricky Barlow, Antony Humble, Ashley Kibble
Seats 32 **Closed** 25 December **Prices from** S £5.75,
M £12.95, D £5.95 **Notes** Vegetarian dishes, Children
welcome

Glewstone Court Country House
◉◉ TRADITIONAL BRITISH, EUROPEAN
01989 770367 | Glewstone, HR9 6AW
www.glewstonecourt.com
With pleasant views over the surrounding
countryside, this family-owned Georgian retreat
makes very good use of local and high quality
produce. The Cedar Tree Restaurant offers
seasonal fare with regularly changing tasting
menus also available. The taster menu with wine
flight is a very popular choice here.

Chef Vicky Lyons, Thomas Patchett **Seats** 70, Private
dining 32 **Closed** 24–27 December **Prices from** S £8,
M £18, D £8 **Parking** 28 **Notes** Vegetarian
dishes, Children welcome

Wilton Court Restaurant with Rooms
◉◉ MODERN BRITISH
01989 562569 | Wilton Lane, HR9 6AQ
www.wiltoncourthotel.com
A riverside setting on the Wye makes for much
natural diversion at Wilton Court. The house
itself partly dates back to around 1500 and was
once the local magistrate's court. Today, the
Mulberry Restaurant delivers an intelligent
modern British repertoire.

Chef Laura O'Brign **Seats** 40, Private dining 12
Closed 1st 2 weeks in January **Prices from** S £6.25,
M £14.25, D £7.25 **Parking** 25 **Notes** Vegetarian
dishes, Children welcome

SYMONDS YAT [EAST]
MAP 10, SO51

Saracens Head Inn
@ BRITISH
01600 890435 | HR9 6JL
www.saracensheadinn.co.uk

In a stunning location on the River Wye, the Saracens Head can be reached by its own ferry, operated by hand, just as it has for the past 200 years. There's a relaxed atmosphere throughout this 16th-century inn, from the dining room to two terraces.

Closed 25 December (all day); 24 December and 26 December to 4 January (evenings)

UPPER SAPEY
MAP 10, SO66

The Baiting House
@@ MODERN BRITISH
01886 853201 | Stourport Road, WR6 6XT
www.baitinghouse.co.uk

Just 20 minutes from the M5, The Baiting House is set in the beautiful Teme Valley countryside and a popular stop for walkers. The property still has a traditional country pub feel but it is also thoroughly modern in its approach to food.

Chef Charles Bradley, Scott Harrison, Harry Tyler
Seats 48, Private dining 30 Closed 25 December, 7–20 January Prices from S £6, M £14, D £6 Parking 50
Notes Vegetarian dishes, Children welcome

WHITNEY-ON-WYE
MAP 9, SO24

Rhydspence Inn NEW
@ TRADITIONAL BRITISH
01497 831262 | HR3 6EU
www.rhydspence.com

Dating from the 14th century, the black-and-white timbered Rhydspence Inn is a cosy, time-honoured hostelry – the sort of place to settle into with a newspaper and pint of local brew, or tuck into some proper, no-nonsense British cooking. Expect the likes of tournedos Rossini with Madeira sauce or Pernod-flamed salmon with lemon butter.

Chef Mark Price Seats 42, Private dining 42 Open All Year Prices from S £5.50, M £11, D £5.50 Parking 40
Notes Vegetarian dishes, Children welcome

■ HERTFORDSHIRE

BERKHAMSTED
MAP 6, SP90

The Gatsby
@ MODERN FRENCH
01442 870403 | 97 High Street, HP4 2DG
www.thegatsby.net

In what locals call Berko, the art deco, former Rex cinema is now a modern brasserie providing not just modern European cuisine but also piano accompaniment. Honey-roast ham hock rillettes and celeriac remoulade is one way to start, with pavé of Loch Duart salmon, tiger prawns and squid ink risotto to follow.

Chef Matthew Salt Seats 65 Closed 25–26 December
Prices from S £7.95, M £16.95, D £7.95 Parking 10
Notes Vegetarian dishes, Children welcome

BISHOP'S STORTFORD
MAP 6, TL42

Down Hall Hotel & Spa
@ CONTEMPORARY BRITISH
01279 731441 | Hatfield Heath, CM22 7AS
www.downhall.co.uk

The house originally dates from the 1300s, but its impressively grand Italianate exterior shows the mark of a Victorian makeover. With period details such as ornate cornices and white-painted columns, the dining room has a vibe reminiscent of an upmarket French brasserie.

Closed 24 and 31 December

CHANDLER'S CROSS
MAP 6, TQ09

The Stables Restaurant at The Grove
@ MODERN BRITISH V
01923 807807 | WD3 4TG
www.resdiary.com/restaurant/thestables

The stable block of the Georgian mansion is now an informal eatery with pared-back and sleek decor reaching to the rafters. The open-to-view kitchen is equipped with a wood-fired oven and chargrill, but the menu has more going for it than pizzas and steaks.

Chef Andrew Parkinson Seats 120, Private dining 100
Open All Year Prices from S £7.50, M £15.50, D £6
Parking 300 Notes Children welcome

DATCHWORTH
MAP 6, TL21

The Tilbury
◉◉ MODERN BRITISH | NOTABLE WINE LIST

01438 815550 | Watton Road, SG3 6TB
www.thetilbury.co.uk

A good local watering hole and a place to eat seriously good food, The Tilbury's kitchen is driven by quality, starting with carefully-sourced produce. A pub menu lists the likes of cottage pie or fish and chips with mushy peas and tartare sauce. Alternatively, move up a gear with pan-fried turbot paired with girolles, baby onions, kale and mash.

Chef Thomas Bainbridge **Seats** 80, Private dining 16 **Closed** some bank holidays **Prices from** S £6.50, M £12.50, D £6.50 **Parking** 40 **Notes** Vegetarian dishes, Children welcome

See advertisement on page 167

ELSTREE
MAP 6, TL19

The Cavendish
◉◉ MODERN BRITISH

020 8327 4700 | The Manor Hotel Elstree, Barnet Lane, WD6 3RE
www.themanorelstree.co.uk

This 16th-century manor house has been restyled in plenty of contemporary beige. Setting off the mullioned windows in the Cavendish dining room, it makes for a cheering ambience in which to dine on some well-considered country-house cooking.

Open All Year

FLAUNDEN
MAP 6, TL00

Bricklayers Arms
◉ BRITISH, FRENCH

01442 833322 | Black Robin Lane, Hogpits Bottom, HP3 0PH
www.bricklayersarms.com

The Bricklayers is a cheery Georgian pub with a cosy atmosphere, rustic oak beams, log fire and brick bar, with a garden and terrace. Food is a serious commitment, the kitchen sourcing locally and seasonally, supplementing the main menus with daily fish and vegetarian specials.

Chef Claude Paillet, Miro Schelling **Seats** 95, Private dining 50 **Closed** 25 December **Parking** 40 **Notes** Vegetarian dishes, Children welcome

HATFIELD
MAP 6, TL20

Beales Hotel
◉ MODERN BRITISH

01707 288500 | Comet Way, AL10 9NG
www.bealeshotels.co.uk

The contemporary brasserie-style dining room at Beales Hotel looks surprisingly small for a hotel, but such intimacy creates an aura of exclusivity. Served by well-informed staff, the food being served is a mix of modern British classics and Mediterranean magic.

Open All Year

HEMEL HEMPSTEAD
MAP 6, TL00

Aubrey Park Hotel
◉ MODERN EUROPEAN

01582 792105 | Hemel Hempstead Road, Redbourn, AL3 7AF
www.aubreypark.co.uk

It stands in nine acres of rolling countryside, dates back to 1287 and has an Iron Age hillfort in the grounds. Old in parts indeed, but Aubrey Park's interiors are contemporary, particularly the light, bright Brasserie, where friendly staff serve bistro classics.

Chef Stuart Gauld **Seats** 56 **Open** All Year **Prices from** S £6.50, M £12.50, D £6.50 **Parking** 140 **Notes** Vegetarian dishes, Children welcome

HITCHIN
MAP 12, TL12

Needham House Hotel
◉◉ MODERN BRITISH

01462 417240 | Blakemore End Road, Little Wymondley, SG4 7JJ
www.needhamhouse.co.uk

The hotel's relaxed brasserie – an uncluttered, modern space with unclothed tables, booth seating and an open kitchen – provides the setting for some well-executed contemporary cooking. The menu aims to please with a mix of casual old favourites and more elaborately worked dishes.

Open All Year

CHEZ MUMTAJ

Modern French-Asian Dining

Restaurant & Saffron Lounge Champagne Bar

Centurian House 136-142 London Road,
St Albans, Herts AL1 1PQ

Call 01727 800033

info@chezmumtaj.com   www.chezmumtaj.com

- Modern French-Asian Dining
- Saffron Lounge & Champagne Bar
- Private Dining
- Prix Fixe Menus

- Tasting Menu
- Open Theatre Kitchen
- Canapés Parties
- Corporate Dining

Award Winning Chef Chad Rahman,
Winner of a Gold Medal, Three Silver Medals and
Three Bronze Medals at The Culinary World Cup 2018
at EXPOGAST, Luxembourg

Opening hours for the Saffron Lounge and Restaurant
12noon - 2.30pm & 6 - 11pm Tues to Sun

ST ALBANS
MAP 6, TL10

Chez Mumtaj
◎◎ FRENCH, ASIAN
01727 800033 | Centurian House,
136-142 London Road, AL1 1PQ
www.chezmumtaj.com
Maybe it's the subtle lighting, leather banquettes
and wood panelling, but there's a touch of the
gentlemen's club about this spacious restaurant,
where pan-Asian and French cooking sometimes
get quite neighbourly. Concise lunch, dinner and
Asian tapas menus list Malaysian-style buttered
black tiger prawns; corn-fed tandoori chicken
with curly kale, saffron basmati; and sweet
potato-stuffed beignets.

Chef Chad Rahman **Seats** 100, Private dining 16
Closed 25-26 December **Prices from** S £6.50, M £14.95,
D £5.50 **Notes** Vegetarian dishes, Children welcome
See advertisement on page 169

The Restaurant at Sopwell House
◎◎ MODERN BRITISH
01727 864477 | Cottonmill Lane, Sopwell, AL1 2HQ
www.sopwellhouse.co.uk
A splendid stately hotel, equipped with spa and
wedding facilities, with dining divided among
conservatory, brasserie and restaurant,
depending on your preferred style. The last is a
glamorous, high-ceilinged setting for modern
cooking of great vigour.

Open All Year

St Michael's Manor
◎◎ MODERN BRITISH, EUROPEAN
01727 864444 | Fishpool Street, AL3 4RY
www.stmichaelsmanor.com
St Michael's orangery-style Lake Restaurant is
the setting for food with impeccable provenance.
Choose from an essentially British carte the
interesting starter of seared duck breast and leg,
potato spaghetti, pomegranate and plum sauce.
Pan-roasted cod loin comes with quinoa, prawn
bisque and asparagus; and for vegetarians
there's a dish called celebration of broccoli,
almond and watercress.

Chef Jorge Martinez **Seats** 130, Private dining 22
Prices from S £6.50, M £12.50, D £5.50 **Parking** 80
Notes Vegetarian dishes, Children welcome

THOMPSON St Albans
◎◎◎ MODERN BRITISH *V*
See pages 172-173
See advertisement opposite

TRING
MAP 6, SP91

Pendley Manor Hotel
◎◎ TRADITIONAL BRITISH
01442 891891 | Cow Lane, HP23 5QY
www.pendley-manor.co.uk
The Victorian section at Pendley (there's also a
modern annexe) offers period grandeur in
spades, particularly in the Oak Restaurant where
oak flooring, lofty ceilings, colourful patterned
wallpaper, and swagged-back drapes at vast bay
windows make an imposing setting. The cooking
is totally 21st century.

Open All Year

WELWYN
MAP 6, TL21

Auberge du Lac
◎◎ MODERN BRITISH
01707 368888 | Brocket Hall Estate, Brocket Road,
AL8 7XG
www.aubergedulac.co.uk
The 543-acre estate of Brocket Hall is the setting
for this elegant restaurant in an old hunting
lodge on the edge of a lake. After drinks in the
reception area, dinner is served in the dining
room with its beautiful views of the main house.

Chef Matt Edmonds **Seats** Private dining 18 **Closed** 27
December and some dates in January **Parking** 50
Notes Vegetarian dishes, No children at dinner

The Waggoners
◎ FRENCH
01707 324241 | Brickwall Close, Ayot Green, AL6 9AA
www.thewaggoners.co.uk
With its venerable beams, inglenook fireplace
and convivial ambience, the setting is that of a
rather romantic, quintessentially English
17th-century inn, albeit with a nod to 21st-century
tastes in the restaurant. There are seasonal
influences drawn from the wider European
cuisine.

Open All Year

The Wellington
◎ MODERN BRITISH
01438 714036 | High Street, AL6 9LZ
www.wellingtonatwelwyn.co.uk
The Wellington, on Welwyn's pretty high street, is
an old coaching inn with rustic-chic exposed
brick walls, real fires and a bar stocked with
proper beers. The focus is firmly on the gastro
side of the pub spectrum, with a simple,
unpretentious menu.

Chef John Beardsworth **Seats** 90 **Open** All Year
Parking 40 **Notes** Vegetarian dishes, Children welcome

Mid-Week Dining

Luncheon

2 Course Set Lunch Menu £18.50

3 Course Set Lunch Menu £23.00

Main Course, Side & Beverage £14.50

Ladies That Lunch Package £35.00

Available Wednesday to Saturday

Evening Dining

2 Course Set Evening Menu £21.00

3 Course Set Evening Menu £25.00

Mid-Week Date Night Package £35.00

Available Tuesday to Thursday

Conservatory & Terrace
Dining Availability

f *thompsondining*

🐦 *@thompsondining*

📷 *thompsondining*

www.thompsonstalbans.co.uk

THOMPSON St Albans

◉◉◉ **MODERN BRITISH** *V*
01727 730777 | 2 Hatfield Road, AL1 3RP
www.thompsonstalbans.co.uk

Classy contemporary cooking with interesting combinations

Set in a row of four weatherboarded cottages in the town centre, Phil Thompson's restaurant has put St Albans firmly on the gastronomic map with cooking that goes from strength to strength. Inside, it's a notch or two up from your average eatery, the dining room looking the business in restrained shades of grey, with linen-clad tables, and local artworks adding class to the walls (for sale, if anything catches your eye). Thompson's output is nothing if not inclusive, appealing to the local constituency with veggie versions of the taster and à la carte, plus a kids' menu, a 'Ladies that lunch' formula, a Sunday roast special menu and, if you want a budget way in, mid-week set lunch and dinner deals are an absolute steal.

Whichever tempts you in, it's all underpinned by sound classical technique and is all about sharply judged flavours, vivid combinations of on-trend ingredients

and gorgeous presentation. Inspired starters might showcase smoked pork jowl with baked turnip, turnip and Mont d'Or cheese purée, mushroom and pear. Sure-footed and technically astute cooking is also a hallmark of main courses, bringing on the likes of bitter-roasted sirloin of Dedham Vale beef, say, served with Madeira-braised snails, beef fat-roasted cabbage, Roscoff onions and mustard seeds, while fish-based ideas might see poached Cornish turbot matched with steamed mussels, roast salsify, mussel cream and lavender.

Vegetarians will be delighted to see that meat-free dishes are no mere afterthought: Wye Valley asparagus with radish, kale and Jersey Royal mousse might lead on to buttered new season

> "Phil Thompson's restaurant has put St Albans firmly on the gastronomic map"

morels with creamed leeks, cauliflower and thyme. Desserts show the same feel for astute flavour and texture combinations with a well-conceived composition involving Brillat Savarin and vanilla cheesecake with Yorkshire rhubarb, toasted pistachio and basil ice cream providing an interesting finisher. An intelligently complied wine list delivers a global spread of bottles at sensible prices.

Chef Phil Thompson
Seats 90, Private dining 50
Notes Children welcome

See advertisement on page 171

WELWYN continued

The White Hart

◉ MODERN BRITISH

01438 715353 | 2 Prospect Place, AL6 9EN

whitehartwelwyn.co.uk

Beside the river in the village of Welwyn, this 17th-century coaching inn is owned and run by brothers James and Tom Bainbridge, it's an inn that oozes charm, from the cosy bar to the flagstoned restaurant with its inglenook fireplace. The thoroughly modern brasserie-style menu has something for everyone.

Chef Dan Defusto **Seats** 44, Private dining 40 **Open** All Year **Prices from** S £6, M £12, D £5 **Parking** 20 **Notes** Vegetarian dishes, Children welcome

WELWYN GARDEN CITY
MAP 6, TL21

Tewin Bury Farm Hotel

◉◉ MODERN BRITISH

01438 717793 | Hertford Road (B1000), AL6 0JB

www.tewinbury.co.uk

A complex of barns on a working farm has been skilfully converted into this characterful modern hotel. The restaurant is a handsome room with a beamed ceiling above rafters, mustard-yellow banquettes, and a boarded floor. Many of the kitchen's raw materials are produced on site.

Open All Year

WILLIAN
MAP 12, TL23

The Fox

◉◉ MODERN BRITISH

01462 480233 | SG6 2AE

www.foxatwillian.co.uk

If you lived in a village with just the one pub, you'd hope for it to be a stylish gastro pub such as this, its bar bristling with real ales, an open-plan dining room and 25-seat conservatory, plus a kitchen whose ambition goes beyond pub grub.

Chef Aron Griffiths **Seats** 100, Private dining 25 **Open** All Year **Prices from** S £5.95, M £16.95, D £4.95 **Parking** 40 **Notes** Vegetarian dishes, Children welcome

■ ISLE OF WIGHT

NEWPORT
MAP 5, SZ48

Thompsons

◉◉ MODERN EUROPEAN *V*

01983 526118 | 11 Town Lane, PO30 1JU

www.robertthompson.co.uk

Robert Thompson has long been an ambassador for the island and his eponymous restaurant has a genuine buzz to it. An open-plan kitchen ensures proper engagement with guests in the uncluttered dining room, and shows a serious commitment to island produce. Dishes are eloquently executed.

Chef Robert Thompson **Seats** 50 **Closed** Christmas and 10 days in both November and February to March (check website for exact dates) **Notes** Children welcome

RYDE
MAP 5, SZ59

Three Buoys *NEW*

◉ MODERN EUROPEAN *V*

01983 811212 | Appley Lane, PO33 1ND

www.threebuoys.co.uk

In a lovely location overlooking Appley Beach and the Solent, Three Buoys occupies the first floor of an unassuming building. The seafood menu features daily specials depending on what's available and the resulting dishes are contemporary in style and show off the skill of the small team. Try the balcony either for dinner or cocktails (blankets provided in cold weather).

Chef Matt Egan **Seats** 40 **Closed** 3-14 January **Prices from** S £6.50, M £14.50, D £6 **Notes** Children welcome

SEAVIEW
MAP 5, SZ69

Seaview Hotel

◉◉ MODERN BRITISH

01983 612711 | High Street, PO34 5EX

www.seaviewhotel.co.uk

In the picturesque fishing village of Seaview, on the island's north-east coast, this long-established hotel is just 50 metres from the sea that supplies much of the fish on the menu. The cooking is refined with classic techniques letting tip-top ingredients speak for themselves.

Chef Tom Bull **Seats** 50, Private dining 25 **Closed** Christmas **Parking** 10 **Notes** Vegetarian dishes, Children welcome

VENTNOR

MAP 5, SZ57

The Royal Hotel

◉◉ MODERN BRITISH

01983 852186 | Belgrave Road, PO38 1JJ

www.royalhoteliow.co.uk

The Royal is a handsome slice of Regency grandeur on the Isle of Wight's south-east coast. Inside, is a classic English tableau fully loaded with crystal chandeliers, parquet floors and decorative ironwork. The island's own Gallybagger cheese opens proceedings in a soaring soufflé.

Open All Year

Smoking Lobster NEW

◉ BRITISH, PAN-ASIAN *V*

01983 855938 | Esplanade, PO38 1JT

www.smokinglobster.co.uk

Bleached wooden floorboards, unclothed tables and a minimal white decor jazzed up with monochrome images of fish set a suitably maritime mood in this easygoing eatery. As its name suggests, fish and seafood are king, and the pocket-sized galley kitchen sends out a nice line in Asian-accented dishes to go with the glorious sea views.

Chef Adam Fendyke, Giancarlo Giancovich **Seats** 35 **Closed** January **Notes** Vegetarian dishes, Children welcome

■ KENT

BIDDENDEN

MAP 7, TQ83

The West House Restaurant with Rooms

◉◉◉ MODERN EUROPEAN *V* ⑨ NOTABLE WINE LIST

01580 291341 | 28 High Street, TN27 8AH

www.thewesthouserestaurant.co.uk

This charming, tile-hung, 16th-century weaver's cottage in the picture-perfect village of Biddenden, The West House has all the twisty beams and interesting nooks and crannies you could possibly wish for. This is a family business, with husband and wife team Graham and Jackie Garrett running the kitchen and front-of-house respectively. There's a relaxed, friendly atmosphere in the dining room, with fresh flowers on the unclothed tables and fantastically seasonal dishes on the menu. Graham is a passionate and enthusiastic advocate of using the best possible produce in the most interesting ways, with an emphasis on simplicity and depth of flavour. A beautiful piece of main-course turbot is set on smoothly rich and creamy potato purée with crunchy pickled cucumber running through, along with light horseradish sauce that adds further complexity. Finish with mango cheesecake, accompanied by a divine mango sorbet and a refined and punchy mango salsa with a gentle kick of chilli.

Chef Graham Garrett **Seats** 32 **Closed** 24–26 December, 1 January **Parking** 7 **Notes** Children welcome

CANTERBURY

MAP 7, TR15

ABode Canterbury

◉◉◉ MODERN EUROPEAN *V*

01227 766266 | High Street, CT1 2RX

www.abodecanterbury.co.uk

An ornate arched portico announces the Canterbury branch of the go-ahead gastronomic hotel chain, which offers a champagne bar for that indispensable aperitif, and an expansive dining room with varnished floor, white walls and an appealing modern brasserie feel. There is also a chef's table, where up to a dozen inquisitive types can keep a beady eye on the kitchen flurry. The name of the game is well-balanced, technically accomplished cooking with much use of Kentish produce, and there's a tasting menu if you fancy it. Start with braised pig's cheek with pickled lotus root and crispy shallot, or crab with lime confit, mooli, and peanut chilli caramel. Main courses might include sea bass with Jerusalem artichoke, smoked artichoke and chorizo sauce, or fillet of Kentish beef with salsify, oyster mushrooms and lovage. Dessert could be black sesame brûlée with honey and nutmeg ice cream, or go for the local cheeses with home-made chutney.

Chef Catalin Jauca **Seats** 76, Private dining 12 **Open** All Year **Parking** 40 **Notes** Children welcome

The Corner House NEW

◉◉ BRITISH

01227 780793 | 1 Dover Street, CT1 3HD

www.cornerhouserestaurants.co.uk

A 16th-century former coach house overlooking Canterbury's city walls, this stylish restaurant deals in no-nonsense modern favourites. Mains include chicken supreme, wild garlic, gnocchi, asparagus, leeks and wild mushrooms, or confit pork belly, black pudding, purple sprouting broccoli, mash and cider jus. Leave room for stout cake and coffee ice cream.

Chef Matt Swordor **Seats** 30 **Open** All Year **Prices from** S £6, M £16, D £6 **Notes** Vegetarian dishes, Children welcome

Fordwich Arms *NEW*

◉◉◉ BRITISH V ⬛NOTABLE WINE LIST

01227 710444 | 1647 King Street, Sturry, CT2 ODB
www.fordwicharms.co.uk

The 1930s country boozer with a terrace and garden looking over the River Stour was begging for a makeover, and that's just what it got when high-flying young chef-patron Dan Smith took the helm in 2018 and immediately turned the place into a foodie destination. The updated stripped-back style looks the part without detracting from the period charm of its oak-panelled dining room, cosy open fires and 1930s-vintage bar. Smith's cooking is firmly in the new-wave modern British camp, allying sharp technique with intriguing combinations of first-class materials. Spitfire ale sourdough and rye bread with smoked pork fat and braised onions is a storming start, before poached Whitstable oysters that come pointed up with diced apple, caviar and light creamy sauce. Main-course venison of buttery tenderness is served as fillet and confit with celeriac, damson, smoked bone marrow and a full-throttle jus. For dessert, perhaps, baked St Clements cheesecake with Cointreau granita.

Chef Daniel and Natasha Smith **Seats** 60, Private dining 36 **Closed** 25 December **Prices from** S £13, M £26, D £9.50 **Parking** 12 **Notes** Children welcome until 6pm

The Goods Shed

◉ BRITISH

01227 459153 | Station Road West, CT2 8AN
www.thegoodsshed.co.uk

This restaurant for the farmers' market next to Canterbury West station has chunky wood tables with views through majestic arched windows over the comings and goings below. It uses the market produce to the full, the selections changing with every service.

Closed 25-26 December and 1-2 January

The Compasses Inn

◉◉ MODERN BRITISH

01227 700300 | Sole Street, CT4 7ES
www.thecompassescrundale.co.uk

Run by Rob and Donna Taylor, this inn in a quiet hamlet has become a real destination dining spot, such is the growing reputation for Rob's accomplished cooking. Divided into two sections, the bar and restaurant, this has all the country pub attributes.

Chef Robert Taylor **Seats** 48 **Closed** Bank holidays **Prices from** S £7.95, M £18.95, D £7.50 **Parking** 30 **Notes** Vegetarian dishes, Children welcome

MEET THE CHEF

Shane Hughes

THE SALUTATION

Sandwich, page 179

What inspired you to become a chef?
It was less of an inspiration than a necessity, my mother was a busy single mum and my older sisters weren't interested in cooking. I started cooking snacks, baking and taking charge of Sunday lunch. At the age of 10 I was very comfortable in a kitchen and loved the feeling of achievement that cooking gave me.

What are the vital ingredients for a successful kitchen?
Creativity, passion, hard work and trust, if you can give and receive these things then you're on the road to running a successful kitchen; mind you, it's a tough recipe to crack.

What are your favourite foods/ingredients?
High-quality aged meats and super-fresh fish, all sourced locally and paired with high-quality vegetables; what else do you need?

DARTFORD MAP 6, TQ57

Rowhill Grange Hotel & Utopia Spa

◉◉ MODERN EUROPEAN

01322 615136 | Wilmington, DA2 7QH

www.alexanderhotels.co.uk

A substantial 18th-century manor in acres of grounds that include a pond, Rowhill Grange is now an upmarket boutique hotel. RG's is the serious dining option, where roast hare (a welcome appearance) is served with textures of cauliflower and beer onions, for instance.

Open All Year

DEAL MAP 7, TR35

Dunkerleys Hotel & Restaurant

◉◉ MODERN BRITISH

01304 375016 | 19 Beach Street, CT14 7AH

www.dunkerleys.co.uk

Run with down-to-earth friendliness by Ian and Linda Dunkerley, this relaxed seafront hotel has a jauntily inviting air. Fuss-free dishes bring fresh local materials together in well-balanced combinations, and seafood is the main event. There's meat on the menu too, if fish really isn't your thing.

Chef Ian and Ben Dunkerley Seats 36 Open All Year Prices from S £7.95, M £12.95, D £6.95 Notes Vegetarian dishes, Children welcome

EGERTON MAP 7, TQ94

Frasers

◉◉ MODERN BRITISH

01233 756122 | Coldharbour Farm, TN27 9DD

www.frasersegerton.co.uk

Guest house accommodation and a cookery school are part of the set up here, along with a barn-style dining room with high ceilings and exposed timbers. Proceedings could open with parsnip and apple soup, parsnip crisp and white truffle oil and follow with pot-roasted pheasant.

Chef Kevin Bennett Seats 30, Private dining 70 Open All Year Parking 30 Notes Vegetarian dishes, No children

FAVERSHAM MAP 7, TR06

Read's Restaurant

◉◉ MODERN BRITISH

01795 535344 | Macknade Manor, Canterbury Road, ME13 8XE

www.reads.com

Chef-patron David Pitchford's Georgian manor house has long been a Kentish destination for those in the know. Set in lush and peaceful grounds, it feels like a country retreat, and is run with the friendly, grown-up affability we hope to find in such places.

Chef David Pitchford Seats 50, Private dining 30 Closed Bank holidays Parking 30 Notes Vegetarian dishes, Children welcome

FAWKHAM GREEN MAP 6, TQ56

Brandshatch Place Hotel & Spa

◉◉ MODERN BRITISH

01474 875000 | Brands Hatch Road, DA3 8NQ

www.handpickedhotels.co.uk/brandshatchplace

It might be a handsome Georgian manor house built by an early 19th-century Duke of Norfolk, but the cooking in the Dining Room Restaurant is decidedly 21st-century British. Good examples include Middle Whiteback ham hock terrine starter; Brixham Bay sea bass with fennel potatoes, and wild mushroom and pearl barley risotto mains; and a lemon meringue dome dessert.

Chef Christopher Tomlinson Seats 60, Private dining 110 Open All Year Prices from S £6, M £16, D £9 Parking 100 Notes Vegetarian dishes, Children welcome

FOLKESTONE MAP 7, TR23

Rocksalt Rooms

◉◉ MODERN BRITISH

01303 212070 | 2 Back Street, CT19 6NN

www.rocksaltfolkestone.co.uk

Sitting on the harbour with a curving terrace cantilevered out over the water, a huge sliding glass wall to capitalise on the view and a classy, well-designed interior with oak floors, Rocksalt's menu has seafood at its heart. Save room for baked egg custard tart though.

Open All Year

GRAFTY GREEN MAP 7, TQ84

Who'd A Thought It

◉◉ BRITISH 𝑉

01622 858951 | Headcorn Road, ME17 2AR

www.whodathoughtit.com

A champagne and oyster bar with rooms in a Kentish village not far from the M20 designed with racy opulence. As well as a menu of modern classics, shellfish platters and thermidor will please seafood purists, as will sticky toffee pudding with butterscotch sauce for those with a sweet tooth.

Chef David Kirby Seats 50 Closed 25 December Parking 45 Notes Children welcome

HAWKHURST

The Queen's Inn NEW
◉ MODERN BRITISH

01580 754233 | Rye Road, TN18 4EY

www.thequeensinnhawkhurst.co.uk

Rejuvenated by dynamic new owners, this inviting pub now offers an appealing line in hearty food. Inside, there is rustic-chic charm, pleasingly fuss-free service and a menu of unpretentious cooking that supports local producers. A separate dining room serves charcoal-grilled meat and fish dishes, plus pizzas from a wood-burning oven.

HYTHE

Hythe Imperial
◉ MODERN, TRADITIONAL **V**

01303 267441 | Princes Parade, CT21 6AE

www.hytheimperial.co.uk

This elegant hotel stands looking out across the Channel from its prominent position on the seafront. Dishes are served on the finest tableware, in keeping with the grandeur of the setting, and menus include tried and tested favourites with an eye on seasonal produce.

Chef Ben Daffron **Seats** 80, Private dining 80 **Open** All Year **Prices from** S £6, M £16, D £5 **Parking** 200 **Notes** Children welcome

LENHAM

Chilston Park Hotel
◉◉ MODERN BRITISH

01622 859803 | Sandway, ME17 2BE

www.handpickedhotels.co.uk/chilstonpark

Secluded in 22 acres of sublime landscaped gardens and parkland, Chilston Park brims with enough period authenticity, antiques and oil paintings that you might be inspired to dress as Mr Darcy or Elizabeth Bennet for dinner in the unique, sunken Venetian-style Culpeper's restaurant. The food is right up-to-date though.

Chef Ross Pilcher **Seats** 45, Private dining 20 **Open** All Year **Prices from** S £6, M £15, D £7 **Parking** 100 **Notes** Vegetarian dishes, Children welcome

LEYSDOWN-ON-SEA

The Ferry House Inn
◉ MODERN BRITISH

01795 510214 | Harty Ferry Road, ME12 4BQ

www.theferryhouseinn.co.uk

The Ferry House, a country inn alongside the Swale Estuary, has put the Isle of Sheppey on the culinary map. It's possible to eat in the bar, but the majority of diners book into the raftered Barn Restaurant. The kitchen's style is modern British.

Chef Vitalijs Kaneps **Seats** 40, Private dining 20 **Closed** 24–30 December **Prices from** S £5.25, M £12.95, D £5.50 **Parking** 70 **Notes** Vegetarian dishes, No children under 10 years

MAIDSTONE

Fish on the Green
◉◉ BRITISH, FRENCH

01622 738300 | Church Lane, Bearsted Green, ME14 4EJ

www.fishonthegreen.com

The pretty village green setting can be described as quintessentially English, and Fish on the Green has netted a strong local fan base with its fresh, unpretentious interior, clued-up staff, and excellent fish and seafood from a kitchen that treats super-fresh materials with intelligent simplicity. If you don't fancy fish, there are always appealing meat and veggie dishes in the mix.

Chef Peter Baldwin **Seats** 50 **Closed** Christmas **Prices from** S £7.55, M £18.95, D £6.95 **Parking** 50 **Notes** Vegetarian dishes, Children welcome

MARGATE

The Ambrette
◉ MODERN INDIAN

01843 231504 | 44 King Street, CT9 1QE

www.theambrette.co.uk

Overlooking the sandy bay and the Turner Contemporary gallery, Dev Biswal's cheery eatery combines modern British and Indian flavours into an exciting fusion, amid a bright and neutral contemporary decor that is more Anglo than Asian. The presentation of dishes is also more akin to European mode and there's bags of flavour and plenty of Kentish produce to boot.

Open All Year

Buoy and Oyster – Margate NEW
◉◉ MODERN BRITISH, SEAFOOD **V**

01843 446631 | 44 High Street, CT9 1DS

www.buoyandoyster.com

Overlooking the beach in Margate's up-and-coming Old Town, this inviting fish and seafood-oriented restaurant is looking dapper after a refurb in 2018. Bare brickwork, an open kitchen and local artwork work a maritime look; beach views, outdoor tables, and well-tuned modern British food with an emphasis on fish and seafood seal the deal.

Chef Simon Morriss **Notes** Children welcome

Sands Hotel

◉◉ MODERN EUROPEAN
01843 228228 | 16 Marine Drive, CT9 1DH
www.sandshotelmargate.co.uk
A breath of fresh air on the Margate seafront, Sands Hotel offers a contemporary experience with sweeping sea views. The kitchen team turn out impressive modern food based on first-class regional ingredients. There are classical foundations to many of the dishes, but there's no shortage of creativity either. The terrace is a fair-weather treat.

Open All Year

SANDWICH   MAP 7, TR35

The Lodge at Prince's

◉◉ MODERN BRITISH
01304 611118 | Prince's Drive, Sandwich Bay, CT13 9QB
www.princesgolfclub.co.uk
The Lodge occupies a substantial purpose-built property of white walls and red roofs with a brasserie-style restaurant, a coolly elegant space In shades of pale blue and grey. Fashionable foams feature in some starters. Puddings do the trick, especially the light and delicate vanilla and coconut pannacotta.

Chef Ricky Smith **Seats** 55, Private dining 20 **Open** All Year **Parking** 100 **Notes** Vegetarian dishes, Children welcome

The Salutation NEW

◉◉◉ MODERN EUROPEAN V
01304 619919 | Knightrider Street, CT13 9EW
www.the-salutation.com
Fans of Victoriana will no doubt be intrigued to learn that this handsome country house was once home to the renowned architect Sir Edwin Lutyens. Ensconced in glorious gardens, the interiors are restored to their full glory and the cooking is a perfect fit with the contemporary boutique country house mood. Chef Shane Hughes is well versed in modern culinary trends and applies honed techniques to well-sourced materials in a starter of seared hand-dived scallops with a galette of crispy rabbit and mozzarella pointed up with rabbit jelly, cherry tomato and tarragon and sweet mustard dressing. Main courses deliver neat spins on intuitive combinations, as in a slow-cooked duck

leg and spiced honey-glazed breast with carrot purée, bok choi and ginger cream sauce. For pudding, baked American cheesecake rich enough for its own Swiss bank account comes with bourbon-marinated Kentish cherries, peanut butter ice cream and cherry jelly.

Chef Shane Hughes **Seats** 60, Private dining 36 **Open** All Year **Prices from** S £12, M £25, D £9 **Parking** 17 **Notes** Children welcome

STALISFIELD GREEN   MAP 7, TQ95

The Plough Inn

◉◉ MODERN BRITISH
01795 890256 | ME13 0HY
www.theploughInnstalisfield.co.uk
High up on the North Downs, with far-reaching views, stands this 15th-century, timber-framed, Wealden hall house. Dining takes place in both a cosy pubby area, where an impressive list of past landlords is displayed, and a second space, more restaurant-like, yet still informal.

Chef Richard Baker **Seats** 69 **Closed** 1st week January **Notes** Vegetarian dishes, Children welcome

TENTERDEN   MAP 7, TQ83

The Swan Wine Kitchen

◉◉ EUROPEAN
01580 761616 | Chapel Down Winery, Small Hythe Road, TN30 7NG
www.swanchapeldown.co.uk
This striking, bare timber and galvanised steel building lies in the grounds of Chapel Down Winery, one of England's leading winemakers. Both the bar and terrace offer delightful countryside views, while from the open-plan kitchen comes a short but appealing choice of modern European dishes.

Chef Lloyd Bartlett **Seats** 65, Private dining 18 **Parking** 100 **Notes** Vegetarian dishes, Children welcome

TUNBRIDGE WELLS (ROYAL)   MAP 6, TQ53

Hotel du Vin Tunbridge Wells

◉ BRITISH, FRENCH ⧠ NOTABLE WINE LIST
01892 526455 | Crescent Road, TN1 2LY
www.hotelduvin.com
A Grade II listed Georgian mansion is home to HdV's operation in Tunbridge Wells and the enormous wine lists remain an integral part of the attraction of this hotel chain. The cooking continues on a solid French bistro basis, as well as more Anglo comfort-food.

Open All Year

The Kentish Hare

◉◉ MODERN BRITISH **V**

01892 525709 | 95 Bidborough Ridge, Bidborough, TN3 0XB

www.thekentishhare.com

Brothers Chris and James Tanner transformed a closed-down pub into a dynamic, splendidly appointed contemporary restaurant. Dishes that are squarely in the modern manner might include a starter of seared scallops, wafer-thin cauliflower slices, pine nuts and raisins in curry oil.

Chef C and J Tanner, David Boswell **Seats** 64 **Closed** 1st week in January **Prices from** S £7.95, M £16.95, D £6.95 **Parking** 24 **Notes** Children welcome

The Spa Hotel

◉◉ MODERN, TRADITIONAL BRITISH

01892 520331 | Mount Ephraim, TN4 8XJ

www.spahotel.co.uk

Tunbridge Wells has no shortage of buildings built in the 18th century to capitalise on the spa business. This hotel has a brasserie on site (Zagatos), while the main Chandelier Restaurant provides something rather more refined and worth the visit.

Open All Year

Thackeray's

◉◉◉ MODERN EUROPEAN **V**❶ NOTABLE WINE LIST

01892 511921 | 85 London Road, TN1 1EA

www.thackerays-restaurant.co.uk

Once home to the novelist William Makepeace Thackeray, author of *Vanity Fair*, this lovely, white-weatherboarded old building dates back more than 300 years. Inside, it's full of delightful period details – sloping ceilings, odd little corners, uneven steps – a fine setting, with bags of character. The dining room is a great combination of ancient and modern, with stylishly up-to-date touches and smart table settings. The food, too, is elegantly contemporary and intelligently constructed, with precise presentation and refined, intricate re-workings of classic combinations. Service hits all the right notes of friendliness and professionalism. Begin with maple-glazed roasted veal sweetbreads with orzo pasta and flaked osso bucco, girolles and winter truffles, before moving on to cannon of lamb with roast pear, braised neck fillet, toasted almonds, and potato and thyme terrine. Bring things to a close with roast banana soufflé with white chocolate and lime crème anglaise and kalamansi sorbet.

Chef Pat Hill **Seats** 70, Private dining 16 **Open** All Year **Notes** Children welcome

The Twenty Six

◉◉ MODERN BRITISH

01892 544607 | 15a Church Road, Southborough, TN4 0RX

www.thetwenty-six.co.uk

When it comes to the number of seats there are for diners in this cosy restaurant from Scott Goss, the clue is in the name. To keep things interesting for visitors and staff, the menu changes every day but innovative dishes stick rigidly to the seasons.

Open All Year

WEST MALLING
MAP 6, TQ65

The Swan

◉◉ MODERN BRITISH

01732 521910 | 35 Swan Street, ME19 6JU

www.theswanwestmalling.co.uk

The Swan started life as a coaching inn back in the 15th century and it still draws the crowds. Inside, you'll find brasserie-style menus on offer, showcasing high-quality Kentish farm produce in carefully-constructed dishes inspired by global flavours and techniques.

Chef Lee Edney **Seats** 90, Private dining 30 **Closed** 1 January **Prices from** S £6.50, M £16, D £6 **Notes** Vegetarian dishes, Children welcome

WHITSTABLE
MAP 7, TR16

The Sportsman

◉◉ MODERN BRITISH

01227 273370 | Faversham Road, Seasalter, CT5 4BP

www.thesportsmanseasalter.co.uk

The Sportsman has a distinctly rustic, unpretentious look, with scuffed floorboards and plain walls hung with pictures above half-panelling. Everything is made in-house, including the butter. You might choose to start with an appetiser of super-fresh oyster topped with warm chorizo.

Chef Stephen Harris, Dan Flavell **Seats** 50 **Closed** 25-26 December, 1 January **Prices from** S £9.95, M £21.95, D £8.95 **Parking** 20 **Notes** Vegetarian dishes, Children allowed at lunch only

WINGHAM
MAP 7, TR25

The Dog at Wingham

◉◉ MODERN BRITISH

01227 720339 | Canterbury Road, CT3 1BB

thedog.co.uk

Close to Canterbury, this lovely village pub is set in a former monastery that dates from the 13th century. The airy, wood-panelled restaurant is illuminated by leaded windows and the shabby-chic furniture adds a relaxed and rustic touch. Seasonal British-led ingredients drive the menu.

Chef Sam McClurkin, Roberto Mantegna **Seats** 50, Private dining 20 **Open** All Year **Prices from** S £7.50, M £18, D £7.50 **Parking** 14 **Notes** Vegetarian dishes, Children welcome

WROTHAM
MAP 6, TQ65

The Bull
◉◉ MODERN BRITISH ◢ NOTABLE WINE LIST

01732 789800 | Bull Lane, TN15 7RF

www.thebullhotel.com

Lying just below the North Downs, this 600-year-old inn features Korean fried wings on the bar menu; slow-cooked smoked pork belly rib comes from the smokehouse; while restaurant options include monkfish fillet in pancetta; and Sri Lankan-style butternut-squash curry.

Chef James Hawkes, Rowan Brooks **Seats** 60, Private dining 12 **Closed** 1 January **Prices from** S £6.50, M £11.50, D £7.50 **Parking** 30 **Notes** Vegetarian dishes, Children welcome

WYE
MAP 7, TR04

Wife of Bath
◉◉ MODERN SPANISH

01233 812232 | 4 Upper Bridge Street, TN25 5AF

www.thewifeofbath.com

Part of Mark Sargeant's growing collection of pubs and restaurants, The Wife of Bath has been a restaurant here since the 1960s. The dining room's wood floors and grey wash walls give the place a cool Nordic look but the menus take their inspiration from northern Spain.

Open All Year

■ LANCASHIRE

BLACKBURN
MAP 18, SD62

The Millstone, Mellor
◉ MODERN BRITISH

01254 813333 | Church Lane, Mellor, BB2 7JR

www.millstonehotel.co.uk

Owned by Thwaites Brewery, whose ales are at the pumps, it's not all about beer at this old coaching inn. It also deals in feel-good menus that offer up pub classics, lunchtime sandwiches, locally sourced steaks cooked on the grill, and a few global flavours.

Open All Year

BURNLEY
MAP 18, SD83

Bertram's Restaurant
◉◉ BRITISH

01282 471913 | Crow Wood, Royle Lane, BB12 0RT

www.crowwood.com

Crow Wood, a modern hotel with extensive spa and leisure facilities, is set in 100 acres of woodland. Bertram's Restaurant, a stylish space with unclothed dark wood tables and smartly upholstered chairs, is popular with locals and guests alike. Prosecco cocktails get a meal of wide-ranging options off to a good start.

Chef Spencer Burge, Gary Entwistle **Seats** 80, Private dining 43 **Closed** 26 December, 1-2 January **Prices from** S £5.95, M £11.95, D £6.50 **Parking** 200 **Notes** Vegetarian dishes, No children

White Swan at Fence
◉◉ MODERN BRITISH

01282 611773 | 300 Wheatley Lane Road, Fence, BB12 9QA

www.whiteswanatfence.co.uk

Retaining all that makes the British pub such a national asset, while applying the highest standards in every department, the team at the White Swan create something special. It's a pub all right, but there's home-made damson vodka, and a chef delivering powerful flavours.

Chef Tom Parker **Seats** 40 **Closed** 26 December, 1 January **Prices from** S £6, M £16, D £6 **Parking** 20 **Notes** Vegetarian dishes, Children welcome

CHORLEY
MAP 15, SD51

Brookes Restaurant
🏵 MODERN CLASSIC

01257 455000 | Best Western Park Hall Hotel, Park Hall Road, Charnock Richard, PR7 5LP
www.lavenderhotels.co.uk/park-hall

Brookes Restaurant is the principal dining room at Park Hall Hotel and is a smart venue done in salmon and blue tones, where friendly service is the norm. Modern brasserie cooking comes up trumps with dishes such as seared hake fillet in brown shrimp butter with curried cauliflower and chive mash.

Chef Jamie Kennard Seats 120, Private dining 50 Open All Year Prices from S £6.95, M £16.95, D £6.95 Parking 400 Notes Vegetarian dishes, Children welcome

CLITHEROE
MAP 18, SD74

The Assheton Arms
🏵 CONTEMPORARY, SEAFOOD

01200 441227 | Downham, BB7 4BJ
www.seafoodpubcompany.com/the-assheton-arms

Although decidedly inland, this pub's ownership by Joycelyn Neve's Seafood Pub Company guarantees excellent Fleetwood-landed fish and seafood, although your dining choice extends way beyond what a trawler can net. Malaysian seafood curry and Morecame Bay plaice with mussels both make a showing on the menus.

Open All Year

The Parkers Arms
🏵 MODERN BRITISH

01200 446236 | BB7 3DY
www.parkersarms.co.uk

Once the coach house of next-door Newton Hall, the white-fronted Parkers Arms hides in a Ribble Valley village near the Trough of Bowland. Inside, are stone floors and low ceilings, with a conservatory feel in the dining area. Nearly all produce is sourced within 30 miles.

Chef Stosie Madi Seats 100 Closed 25 December Prices from S £8, M £17, D £8 Parking 30 Notes Children welcome

COWAN BRIDGE
MAP 18, SD67

Hipping Hall
🏵🏵🏵🏵 MODERN BRITISH *V*

015242 71187 | LA6 2JJ
www.hippinghall.com

In case you were wondering, the word 'hipping' is an old term for the stepping-stones that cross the Broken Beck stream running through the hall's delightful gardens. Built in the 17th and 18th centuries, the pocket-sized country house is in a beautiful spot on the borders of Lancashire, Yorkshire and Cumbria, and is done out with a classical elegance, and offers a real draw in its stylish restaurant, where boarded floors, walls done in local pigments, soaring oak beams and a rustic fireplace feel rooted into the area.

Oli Martin's cooking is on a roll, his 21st-century approach teaming prime local produce with of-the-moment techniques in four-, six- and 10-course tasters (with veggie alternatives). An opening dish of butter pie – crisp pastry filled with a harmonious trio of Mrs Kirkham's cheese, truffle and onion – is a modern, northern-inspired classic. Next up, a composition of Mull scallop, kohlrabi and smoked eel is dedicated to delivering the essence of each ingredient, while meaty satisfaction comes in the shape of Shorthorn beef with onion and hay, or tender Goosnargh chicken supported by seaweed and shiitake mushrooms. A crossover dish of Yorkshire rhubarb with buckwheat and sorrel paves the way for an inspired finisher of apple with Douglas fir and honey.

Chef Oli Martin Seats 34, Private dining 14 Parking 20 Notes No children under 12 years

GREAT ECCLESTON
MAP 18, SD44

The Cartford Inn
🏵🏵 MODERN BRITISH

01995 670166 | Cartford Lane, PR3 0YP
www.thecartfordinn.co.uk

On the banks of the River Fylde, this 17th-century coaching inn is enlivened by local artists' work and the owners' eye-catching memorabilia. The menu revels in Lancashire's fine produce, bringing it together in imaginative ideas that aim to comfort rather than challenge.

Closed 25 December

See advertisement opposite

LANCASTER
MAP 18, SD46

Lancaster House
⊛ TRADITIONAL BRITISH
01524 844822 | Green Lane, Ellel, LA1 4GJ
www.englishlakes.co.uk
Practically on the doorstep of the Lake District,
Lancaster House is an events and leisure hotel
on the university campus. Foodworks is the
promising name of its restaurant, and a relaxed,
hang-loose brasserie feel predominates, offering
a seasonal menu of readlly understandable fare.

Open All Year

LANGHO
MAP 18, SD73

Northcote
⊛⊛⊛⊛ MODERN BRITISH 🗸 NOTABLE WINE LIST
See pages 184-185

LOWER BARTLE
MAP 18, SD43

Bartle Hall Hotel
⊛ MODERN BRITISH
01772 690506 | Lea Lane, PR4 0HA
www.bartlehall.co.uk
Between Blackpool and Preston, Bartle Hall is
conveniently positioned for the M6 and the Lake
District. Set within extensive gardens, this
former private residence can be traced back to
the 16th century although these days it's a
comfortable modern hotel and wedding venue.

Open All Year

LYTHAM ST ANNES
MAP 18, SD32

Bedford Hotel
⊛ MODERN BRITISH
01253 724636 | 307-313 Clifton Drive South, FY8 1HN
www.bedford-hotel.com
The Bedford is a welcoming, family-run Victorian
hotel with lots going on. Its Cartland Restaurant
has plenty of period charm, with decorative
plasterwork, warm pastel tones, black-and-white
prints of film stars and neatly laid tables. The
cooking steers sensibly clear of left-field flavours.

Open All Year

Northcote

@@@@ MODERN BRITISH 𝓥 🍷 NOTABLE WINE LIST

01254 240555 | Northcote Road, BB6 8BE

www.northcote.com

Fine dining with refined Lancashire sensibilities

Northcote continues to retain a firm hold on its status as a gem of the North. The Victorian red-brick house in the Ribble Valley, with the Forest of Bowland clustering in the view from the terrace, has been extended and decorated over the decades in tasteful modern style, with an elegant cocktail bar overlooked by portrait photos of Brigitte Bardot and Frank Sinatra, and with contemporary paintings and sculpture adding class throughout.

Before you settle in to eat, take a wander around the kitchen gardens, from where much of the menu's wares emerge, ensuring that the kitchen dances to a seasonal beat through the year. Lisa Goodwin-Allen produces dishes that have a cosmopolitan polish and broad range of reference but, fear not – the Lancashire accent remains firmly rooted here. Menus still take the shape of six-course tasting, four-course gourmet and à la carte,

supplemented by a monthly-changing lunch deal, and the splendid salt-aged sirloin with Yorkshire pudding still a star of the Sunday lunch repertoire.

A winter meal kicks off with refined and tender hand-cut beef tartare with roast and puréed celeriac, smoked marrowbone and beef-fat brioche. Next up, scallop is treated to a welter of textures comprising clam chowder, crisped bacon and chervil, while main course brings knockout red leg partridge helped along by a rich bolognese of leg meat, hen of the woods mushrooms and squash. If you're giving meat a swerve, plant-based dishes could include warm roasted celeriac, with truffle, morels and butter providing powerful bass notes, or charcoal-grilled leek with wild garlic gremolata and Jersey Royals. The end-note

"the kitchen dances to a seasonal beat through the year"

comes with a stunning take on the Eccles cake theme, made with ethereal lightness and turbocharged flavours from Muscat grape, caramelised pastry and iced tea. Accompanying it all is one of the region's outstanding wine lists, its glories dispensed with engaging knowledgeability by a fine sommelier.

Chef Lisa Goodwin-Allen
Seats 70, Private dining 60
Closed Food and Wine Festival
Prices from S £14.50, M £23, D £14.50
Parking 60
Notes Children welcome

LYTHAM ST ANNES continued

Clifton Arms Hotel

 BRITISH

01253 739898 | West Beach, Lytham, FY8 5QJ
www.cliftonarmslytham.com

The present red-brick building dates from early Victorian times and is on the site of what was a small inn. Chic table settings with good napery and floral adornments look the part against the neutral hues of the main dining room, where bay windows give wide sea views. The kitchen delivers contemporary cooking that moves with the seasons.

Chef Paul Howard **Seats** 60, Private dining 140 **Open** All Year **Prices from** S £6, M £15.95, D £5.50 **Parking** 50 **Notes** Vegetarian dishes, Children welcome

Greens Bistro

 MODERN BRITISH

01253 789990 | 3–9 St Andrews Road South, St Annes-on-Sea, FY8 1SX
www.greensbistro.co.uk

For a basement bistro venue Greens looks bright and airy, with ornate high-backed chairs in light wood at smartly clothed tables, and deep green carpeting. The cooking is straightforward bistro fare based on pedigree Lancashire produce, including the county's famous cheese.

Chef Paul Webster **Seats** 38 **Closed** 25 December, bank holidays and 1 week in summer **Prices from** S £5.50, M £14, D £5.95 **Notes** Vegetarian dishes, Children welcome

MORECAMBE

MAP 18, SD46

Best Western Lothersdale Hotel

 MODERN BRITISH

01524 416404 | 320–323 Marine Road, LA4 5AA
www.bfhotels.com

Run by the same family for more than 50 years, this seafront hotel on the promenade in Morecambe has a separate bar and tapas area with an outside terrace area providing wonderful views across the bay to the Lakeland fells.

Closed 22–27 December

The Midland

 MODERN BRITISH

01524 424000 | Marine Road West, LA4 4BU
www.englishlakes.co.uk/hotels/midland

An art deco gem, The Midland was built by the London, Midland and Scottish Railway in 1933 in the 'streamline modern' style. There's a sharp modernity to the restaurant that suits the space, with a contemporary finish and neat white tablecloths. A vegan menu is available at both lunch and dinner.

Closed Christmas and New Year (non-residents)

ORMSKIRK

MAP 15, SD40

The Barn at Moor Hall *NEW*

  BRITISH *V*

01695 572511 | Prescot Road, Aughton, L39 6RT
www.moorhall.com

In five-acre grounds with a lake, and accompanied by one of the UK's top restaurants in a glass-walled modernist extension, this boutique hideaway already has enough going for it. But if you're not up for the full-works, culinary virtuosity of the main attraction, this little sibling is no slouch, serving up sharp contemporary food in a casual, beamed setting.

Chef Mark Birchall, Dom Clarke **Seats** 65 **Closed** 2 weeks in January **Prices from** S £6, M £15, D £8 **Parking** 40 **Notes** Children welcome

See advertisement opposite

Moor Hall Restaurant with Rooms

     MODERN BRITISH *V* NOTABLE WINE LIST

See pages 188–189

See advertisement opposite

MOOR HALL
RESTAURANT WITH ROOMS

scot Road, Aughton, Lancashire L39 6RT • Tel: 01695 572511 • enquiry@moorhall.com • www.moorhall.com

Moor Hall is a stunning grade II* listed building that is steeped in history dating back to the 13th century. Open since March 2017, Moor Hall has already been awarded 2 Michelin Stars, 5 AA Rosettes, ranked #1 restaurant in the UK at the National Restaurant Awards, ranked Number 11 in Good Food Guide UK Top 50 restaurants, named GQ Newcomer of the Year and also winning Restaurant of The Year at the Lancashire Life Food & Drink Awards 2017.

Set in five acres of breathtaking gardens overlooking a beautiful lake, 2 Michelin starred Moor Hall Restaurant with Rooms is in an idyllic setting to enjoy the delicate, produce driven menus inspired by our exceptional natural surroundings and talented chef patron Mark Birchall.

Moor Hall has 7 luxurious guest bedrooms, each one stunningly unique. 5 are located in the main Hall with a further 2 in the gatehouse by the lake. Each of the bedrooms within the Hall has a wonderful view of the lake or gardens.

Following the huge success of Moor Hall, Mark Birchall has also opened a casual dining restaurant The Barn at Moor Hall on the same 5 acre site and it promises great things! Achieving a Michelin Bib Gourmand, 2 AA Rosettes and winning Lancashire Life Newcomer of the Year, The Barn menu ranges from 35 day aged rib eye steaks to a full vegetarian menu, delicious side dishes, children's menu and puddings galore. The Barn has something for everyone including a fantastic selection of hand crafted cocktails, bottled and draught beers.

To make a reservation visit www.moorhall.com or call our reservations team on 01695 572511.

ORMSKIRK

Moor Hall Restaurant with Rooms

◎◎◎◎◎ **MODERN BRITISH** *V* 🍾 NOTABLE WINE LIST

01695 572511 | Prescot Road, Aughton, L39 6RT

www.moorhall.com

Imaginative cooking in a boutique bolthole

The 'restaurant with rooms' concept at Moor Hall is rather more evolved than the usual traditional approach consisting of a few modest rooms bolted onto a notable eatery. The seven rooms here – as plush as anyone could reasonably ask for – form part of a megabucks boutique transformation of a 16th-century manor into a foodie destination. It comprises a chic restaurant and state-of-the-art open kitchen in a modernist extension with a soaring raftered roof and glass walls. With all this investment, the culinary draw has to be a biggie, so rest assured that the showstopping cooking of Mark Birchall, whose time at Simon Rogan's L'Enclume means you will not be disappointed. Expect virtuoso creations built on ingredients that can't be bettered, executed with unsurpassed attention to detail and a highly evolved way of doing things.

The eight-course taster is served at both lunch and dinner, while a four-course lunch option sorts out diners whose time, or perhaps budget, is more limited. Home-grown carrots served in multifarious textures come with ramsons and sea buckthorn cream, all turbocharged with Doddington cheese 'snow'. Next up, crab and turnip broth of remarkable clarity of flavour arrives with anise leaves, hyssop and sunflower seed cream. Elsewhere, the technique is seriously impressive in a combination of turbot, cooked on the bone and pointed up with plump mussels in a light cream sauce, plus sea vegetables and silky artichoke purée, while Holstein Friesian beef is showcased in another complex workout, alongside barbecued celeriac, mustard and shallot.

Desserts, too, are shot through with creativity, among them Worcester

> "Expect virtuoso creations built on ingredients that can't be bettered"

Pearmain apple served as terrine, ice cream and gel in the company of woodruff cream, birch sap and marigold. The wine list is a stunner with a knowledgeable sommelier team to guide the way. There's also a more casual dining venue and bar in a raftered, rustic-chic barn, awarded two AA Rosettes.

Chef Mark Birchall
Seats 50, Private dining 14
Closed 2 weeks in January, 2 weeks in August
Parking 50
Notes No children under 12 years at dinner

See advertisement on page 187

RILEY GREEN
MAP 18, SD62

The Royal Oak
TRADITIONAL BRITISH

01254 201445 | Blackburn Old Road, PR5 0SL
www.royaloak-rileygreen.co.uk
Just a short distance from the Hoghton Tower in
a beautiful part of Lancashire, this roadside inn
has a proper pub atmosphere with traditional
touches of open fires, stone walls and church
pews. The British dishes are straightforward but
cooked with confidence and flair.

Closed 25 December

THORNTON
MAP 18, SD34

Twelve Restaurant and Lounge Bar
MODERN BRITISH *V*

01253 821212 | Marsh Mill Village,
Fleetwood Road North, FY5 4JZ
www.twelve-restaurant.co.uk
Almost under the sails of an expertly restored
18th-century windmill, Twelve's ultra-modern
look comes from its fashionably exposed
ducting, beams and brick, slate floors and sleek
designer furniture. A spring menu offers deep-
fried crispy duck egg, asparagus and broad bean
salad; confit Forest of Bowland lamb shoulder;
and to finish, mango and coconut pannacotta.

Chef Graham Floyd **Seats** 106 **Closed** 1st 2 weeks
January **Prices from** S £6, M £14, D £6 **Parking** 150
Notes Vegetarian dishes, Children welcome
See advertisement opposite

WHALLEY
MAP 18, SD73

Breda Murphy Restaurant
MODERN BRITISH, IRISH *V*

01254 823446 | 41 Station Road, BB7 9RH
www.bredamurphy.co.uk
After a top-to-toe makeover in 2017, this vibrant
enterprise now comprises a contemporary
restaurant, a gin bar and a casual daytime deli/
café. Sitting cheek by jowl with the landmark
Whalley Viaduct, it's ideally placed for friendly
get-togethers accompanied by unfussy bistro
dishes with hearty Irish and British accents.

Chef Adam Jenyon **Seats** 100, Private dining 34
Closed 24–26 December, 31 December to 1 January
Prices from S £5.50, M £12.50, D £5.75 **Parking** 12
Notes Children welcome

The Freemasons at Wiswell
MODERN BRITISH *V*

01254 822218 | 8 Vicarage Fold, Wiswell, BB7 9DF
www.freemasonswiswell.co.uk
A cream-painted inn on a lane in well-heeled
Wiswell, The Freemasons has a pleasantly
bucolic air, with small carpets thrown over the
flagged floor, stressed bare tables and rolled-up
kitchen cloths for napkins. The preference for
rustic flavours such as those that pickling
produces means that pub food meets cutting-
edge gastronomy halfway, and Steven Smith
plays his part with appetisers of Lancashire
cheese tartlets topped with pickled mushrooms,
before a first course like planched foie gras on
toast with smoked eel and Yorkshire rhubarb in
beer vinegar. Fortifying main dishes are the
norm, as in slow-cooked suckling pig with crispy
belly, sticky cheek and black pudding, alongside
silky sweet potato purée in fish-savoury XO
sauce, or cod poached with seaweed, served
with salt cod cannelloni and wild mushrooms in
buttery chicken stock sauce. Finish with Cluizel
dark chocolate mousse, served with pineapple
poached in PX sherry with raisins and razor-
sharp passionfruit sorbet.

Chef Steven Smith, Matthew Smith **Seats** 70, Private
dining 14 **Closed** from 2 January for 2 weeks
Prices from S £9.95, M £20, D £8.95 **Notes** Children
welcome

WREA GREEN
MAP 18, SD33

The Spa Hotel at Ribby Hall Village
MODERN, TRADITIONAL

01772 674484 | Ribby Hall Village, Ribby Road, PR4 2PR
www.ribbyhall.co.uk/the-spa-hotel
As its name makes clear, there are some pretty
swanky spa facilities at this classy adult-only
retreat in 100 acres of Lancashire countryside.
The Brasserie and its Orangery extension are
another string to its bow, done out with orange
and lime leather seats.

Chef Michael Noonan **Seats** 46, Private dining 30
Open All Year **Prices from** S £7, M £16, D £8 **Parking** 100
Notes Vegetarian dishes, No children

TWELVE

AA

RESTAURANT & LOUNGE BAR

for Culinary Excellence
2007–2019

Marsh Mill Village, Fleetwood Road North
Thornton Cleveleys, Lancashire, FY5 4JZ

01253 82 12 12
twelve-restaurant.co.uk
twelveeventmanagement.co.uk

OPENING HOURS:
Tuesday - Saturday for dinner | Sundays 12noon - 8.00pm

- Situated beneath a beautifully restored 18th century windmill
- 5 minute drive from Blackpool
- British cuisine with a modern twist

WREA GREEN continued

The Villa Country House Hotel
◉◉ CLASSIC BRITISH

01772 804040 | Moss Side Lane, PR4 2PE
www.thevilla.co.uk
A 19th-century gentleman's residence, this
gabled mansion stands at the end of a sweeping
drive. Enter, and white-shirted staff in the part-
oak-panelled restaurant will take your dinner
order for, say, crispy duck with asparagus and
confit egg yolk; seared monkfish with chorizo,
white beans, sweetcorn and aubergine; and
caramel chocolate crémeux, pistachio financier
and lime meringue.

Chef Matthew Johnson **Seats** 80, Private dining 20
Open All Year **Prices from** S £4.50, M £13.95, D £6.95
Parking 100 **Notes** Vegetarian dishes, Children welcome
See advertisement below

■ LEICESTERSHIRE

ANSTEY *MAP 11, SK50*
Sapori Restaurant & Bar *NEW*
◉ ITALIAN

0116 236 8900 | 40 Stadon Road, LE7 7AY
www.sapori-restaurant.co.uk
Visitors are drawn to this convivial family-run
Italian in a village on the fringes of Leicester by
its clean-cut contemporary interior of cream and
grey tones, views into the kitchen, and a civilised
ambience. It is also a place for accomplished
cooking that runs the spectrum from Italian
classics to dishes with an imaginative,
contemporary spin.

Chef Andrea Scarpati **Seats** 60 **Closed** 2 weeks from
26 December **Prices from** S £6.25, M £13.50, D £6.50
Notes Vegetarian dishes, Children welcome

LEICESTER

David Ferguson at The Belmont
◉◉ MODERN BRITISH *V*
0116 254 4773 | De Montfort Street, LE1 7GR
www.belmonthotel.co.uk
What started life as a B&B is now a stylish boutique hotel. Located on leafy New Walk, just a few minutes' stroll from Leicester's city centre, guests can enjoy a drink in contemporary Jamie's Bar before a leisurely meal in the sophisticated restaurant.

Chef David Ferguson Seats 60, Private dining 30
Open All Year Prices from S £5.95, M £13.95, D £6.95
Parking 60 Notes Children welcome

LONG WHATTON

The Royal Oak
◉ MODERN BRITISH
01509 843694 | 26 The Green, LE12 5DB
www.theroyaloaklongwhatton.co.uk
The 21st-century incarnation of this thriving gastro pub is seen in a smart interior, some natty bedrooms and a focus on food. That said, real ale is part of the plan, and a few pub classics remain. The kitchen turns out some lively stuff.

Chef James and Charles Upton Seats 45 Open All Year
Prices from S £6, M £12.95, D £6.25 Parking 30
Notes Vegetarian dishes, Children welcome

MARKET HARBOROUGH

Three Swans
◉ MODERN, INTERNATIONAL
01858 466644 | 21 High Street, LE16 7NJ
www.threeswans.co.uk
Dating from the reign of Henry VIII, the Three Swans is on the High Street and has played host to various crowned heads over the generations. A makeover has produced a clean modern look that respects the original features, and smartly attired, tuned-in staff run the dining room with inspiring confidence.

Closed 1 January

MELTON MOWBRAY

Stapleford Park
◉◉ MODERN INTERNATIONAL, BRITISH
01572 787000 | Stapleford, LE14 2EF
www.staplefordpark.com
Stapleford's lineage can be traced back to medieval times, the estate being owned by successive generations of the Earls of Harborough for nearly 500 years. Impeccable staff keep the elevated tone buoyant, and the cooking aims high too.

Chef Tony Fitt Seats 70, Private dining 180
Closed exclusive use days Prices from S £9.50, M £20.50, D £10 Parking 120 Notes Vegetarian dishes, Children welcome

MEET THE CHEF

John Duffin
JOHN'S HOUSE
Mountsorrel, page 194

What inspired you to become a chef?
My father got me a part time job at his friend's restaurant when I was 14. I was blown away with everything do with the restaurant industry and I've been cooking ever since.

What are the vital ingredients for a successful kitchen?
The vital ingredients for our kitchen are the quality produce and of course the team I have working with me every day.

What are your favourite foods/ingredients?
I like most ingredients really, we are lucky to have fantastic meat, vegetables, fruits and such like on the farm where the restaurant is based.

What's your favourite dish on the current menu and why?
I don't have a favourite dish, we go back to some year on year as the seasons change but we use what's best from the farm.

Who are the chefs you admire most? Who has had the most influence on your cooking style?
I admire loads of chefs, Simon Rogan was a big influence, Max Fischer and Rupert Rowley, Sat Bains. Too many to name.

MOUNTSORREL

John's House
◉◉◉ MODERN BRITISH **V**

01509 415569 | 139–141 Loughborough Road, LE12 7AR
www.johnshouse.co.uk

John Duffin has food in his DNA: after working up
an impressive CV in some of London's stellar
kitchens, he returned to his roots by opening his
own restaurant on the family farm where he grew
up. Bare beams and brick walls, wooden floors
and tables all add up to a rustic feel, but think
again if you're expecting food in a similar vein.
Sure, Duffin is committed to a 'farm to plate'
philosophy – much of the produce comes from
his family's land, after all – but the cooking is
ambitious, precise and full of contemporary
verve. Marinated heritage tomatoes bursting with
flavour are nimbly partnered with almond
gazpacho and fresh mint, while main-course
pork belly comes with the balanced flavours of
sweetcorn purée, hen of the woods mushrooms
and gremolata. A clever dessert of meringue
encasing yuzu curd alongside elderflower sorbet
and white chocolate rounds things off nicely.

Chef John Duffin **Seats** 30 **Closed** Christmas and
2 weeks in August **Notes** Children welcome

NORTH KILWORTH

Kilworth House Hotel & Theatre
◉◉ MODERN BRITISH

01858 880058 | Lutterworth Road, LE17 6JE
www.kilworthhouse.co.uk

A top-to-toe restoration overseen by the eagle
eyes of English Heritage means period
authenticity runs seamlessly through this
Italianate 19th-century mansion. The Wordsworth
Restaurant is the fine-dining option: a posh
setting indeed, but the kitchen team certainly
rises to the occasion.

Open All Year

QUORN

The Shires **NEW**
◉ MODERN BRITISH

01509 415050 | Quorn Country Hotel, Charnwood
House, 66 Leicester Road, LE12 8BB
www.quorncountryhotel.info

With manicured gardens and oak-panelled
interiors, the Quorn Country Hotel has a
17th-century house at its heart. The Shires
restaurant begins its modern brasserie path with
seared king scallops, parsnip purée and
pancetta, then continues with guinea fowl
supreme with tarragon, and on to the finish with
egg custard tart and clotted cream.

Chef James Falconer **Seats** 112, Private dining 240
Parking 120 **Notes** Vegetarian dishes, Children welcome

SHAWELL

The White Swan
◉ MODERN EUROPEAN

01788 860357 | LE17 6AG
www.whiteswanshawell.co.uk

Retaining the welcoming ambience of a country
pub, only with comfier sofas, The White Swan is
run by a team that carries a weight of culinary
experience on its young shoulders. A light-filled
dining room with glass-fronted wine store is
the setting.

Closed early January

WYMESWOLD

Hammer & Pincers
◉◉ BRITISH, EUROPEAN **V**

01509 880735 | 5 East Road, LE12 6ST
www.hammerandpincers.co.uk

Having trained at The Savoy, this restaurant's
owners know a thing or two about hospitality in
the grand manner, but the mood here is
decidedly more cutting edge. This is Stilton
country, so Cropwell Bishop with quince paste
might look appealing.

Chef Daniel Jimminson **Seats** 46 **Open** All Year
Parking 40 **Notes** Children welcome

◾ LINCOLNSHIRE

GRANTHAM
MAP 11, SK93

Harry's Place
◉◉ CLASSIC FRENCH

01476 561780 | 17 High Street, Great Gonerby, NG31 8JS

Now in its fourth decade of operations, Harry and Caroline Hallam's place retains the 1980s ethos with which it began: a domestic dinner-party feel in their converted farmhouse, from the era when nobody knew what a website was. The short, handwritten menu has been built of long-standing dishes honed to a pitch of straightforward but effective refinement.

Chef Harry Hallam **Seats** 10 **Closed** 25-26 December, **Prices from** S £14.50, M £39.50, D £9 **Parking** 4 **Notes** Vegetarian dishes, No children under 5 years

HORNCASTLE
MAP 17, TF26

Magpies Restaurant with Rooms
◉◉ BRITISH, EUROPEAN

01507 527004 | 73 East Street, LN9 6AA

In a terrace of 200-year-old cottages, Magpies has decor of duck-egg blue, with mirrors, candlelight and drapes over the bay windows. After enjoyable savoury courses, if you've got room, finish with a trio of desserts: chocolate mousse, espresso crème brûlée and dark chocolate fondant.

Chef Andrew Gilbert **Seats** 34 **Closed** 26-30 December and 1-8 January **Notes** Vegetarian dishes, Children welcome

HOUGH-ON-THE-HILL
MAP 11, SK94

The Brownlow Arms
◉◉ BRITISH

01400 250234 | High Road, NG32 2AZ

www.thebrownlowarms.com

This Lincolnshire village inn has come up in the world, being as elegantly appointed as an interiors magazine country house, with tapestry-backed chairs and gilt-framed mirrors in a panelled dining room. Meanwhile, attentive, friendly service puts everyone at their ease.

Chef Ruaraidh Bealby **Seats** 80, Private dining 26 **Closed** 25-26 December, 1 January **Prices from** S £6.25, M £19.95, D £7.50 **Parking** 26 **Notes** Vegetarian dishes, No children under 8 years

LACEBY
MAP 17, TA20

Best Western Oaklands Hall Hotel
◉ MODERN BRITISH

01472 872248 | Barton Street, DN37 7LF

www.thecomfyduck.com

The balustraded red-brick mansion, built in 1877, sits in five acres of landscaped parkland between the Wolds and the Humber and makes a pleasant spot for the full country-house experience. Dining takes place in the Comfy Duck Bistro, which goes for a modern brasserie look and delivers inventive modern British comfort food.

Closed 26 December

LINCOLN
MAP 17, SK97

The Lincoln Hotel
◉ MODERN BRITISH **V**
01522 520348 | Eastgate, LN2 1PN
www.thelincolnhotel.com
Just a stone's throw away from Lincoln's
12th-century cathedral, The Green Room has a
striking, design-led interior, with candles and
fresh flowers adding a nice homely touch. The
atmosphere is relaxed but the small restaurant
retains an air of formality.

Chef Dale Gill **Seats** 30, Private dining 12 **Open** All Year
Parking 54 **Notes** Children welcome

The Old Bakery
◉◉ MODERN INTERNATIONAL
01522 576057 | 26–28 Burton Road, LN1 3LB
www.theold-bakery.co.uk
Ivano and Tracey de Serio's restaurant with
rooms is a homely place, with the feel of a
farmhouse kitchen. A five-course taster menu
offers a comprehensive tour, and desserts
include white chocolate and pistachio ganache
with vanilla pannacotta and delicately flavoured
star anise ice cream.

Chef Ivano de Serio **Seats** 65, Private dining 40
Closed 26 December, 1–16 January and 1st week August
Notes Vegetarian dishes, Children welcome

Tower Hotel
◉◉ MODERN INTERNATIONAL
01522 529999 | 38 Westgate, LN1 3BD
www.lincolntowerhotel.com
In the Bailgate district of the cathedral quarter,
the Tower benefits from all the charm of
medieval Lincoln. The backbone of its operation
is finely detailed, up-to-date cooking while gels,
dusts and purées in profusion show
understanding of fashionable textural variety.

Chef Mike Watts **Seats** 48 **Closed** 25–26 December,
1 January **Prices from** S £5.50, M £16.50, D £6
Notes Vegetarian dishes, Children welcome

Washingborough Hall Hotel
◉◉ MODERN BRITISH
01522 790340 | Church Hill, Washingborough, LN4 1BE
www.washingboroughhall.com
Set in three acres of a sleepy Lincolnshire
village, with a garden to provide herbs for the
kitchen, Washingborough delivers all you would
hope for in a Georgian manor turned country-
house hotel. The smart Dining Room exudes
quietly understated class.

Chef Mark Cheseldine, Anthony Smith **Seats** 50, Private
dining 110 **Open** All Year **Prices from** S £5.95, M £13.95,
D £5.95 **Parking** 40 **Notes** Vegetarian dishes, Children
welcome

The White Hart
◉ MODERN BRITISH
01522 563290 | Bailgate, LN1 3AR
www.whitehart-lincoln.co.uk
The old hotel is a feature of the historic quarter
of Lincoln, with splendid views of one of
England's greatest cathedrals, and the castle not
far off. Inside, a suave contemporary look brings
wood flooring and large mirrors to the Grille
restaurant and bar, where dark wood tables look
the part.

Chef Myles Mumby **Seats** 88, Private dining 100 **Open** All
Year **Prices from** S £5.25, M £12.95, D £6.25 **Parking** 40
Notes Vegetarian dishes, Children welcome

LOUTH
MAP 17, TF38

The Masons Arms Hotel *NEW*
◉ MODERN BRITISH
01507 621200 | Cornmarket, LN11 9PY
www.the-masons-arms.com
This 18th-century market town inn has been
lovingly refurbished with 21st-century comforts
and a stylishly uncluttered contemporary decor
blending seamlessly with period charm. Parquet
floors, pale wood tables and ceramic tile friezes
are the backdrop for uncomplicated rustic food
that scores a hit with its gutsy flavours and
refreshing lack of fussiness.

Chef Roman Ganenko **Seats** 58, Private dining 30
Open All Year **Prices from** S £6.50, M £9.50, D £7
Notes Vegetarian dishes, Children welcome

MARKET RASEN
MAP 17, TF18

The Advocate Arms
◉◉ MODERN EUROPEAN, BRITISH
01673 842364 | 2 Queen Street, LN8 3EH
www.advocatearms.co.uk
The 18th-century restaurant with rooms in the centre of town has a contemporary finish and aims to impress with boutique styling and an open-plan interior. In the main restaurant, the output is broadly modern British, with some inventive combinations and plenty to satisfy any traditionalists.

Chef Josh Kelly **Seats** 65, Private dining 20 **Parking** 6 **Notes** Vegetarian dishes, Children welcome

SCOTTER
MAP 17, SE80

The White Swan
◉ MODERN BRITISH
01724 763061 | 9 The Green, DN21 3UD
www.whiteswanscotter.com
The whitewashed façade looks the very image of the coaching inn that The White Swan once was, but indoors the restaurant conforms to modern expectations with neutral shades, pale wood and glass panels. The approach is decidedly unaffected, with hospitable service matched by appealing, well-executed food.

Chef Matthew Horsefield **Seats** 120, Private dining 40 **Parking** 25 **Notes** Vegetarian dishes, Children welcome

SCUNTHORPE
MAP 17, SE81

San Pietro Restaurant Rooms
◉◉ MODERN MEDITERRANEAN
01724 277774 | 11 High Street East, DN15 6UH
www.sanpietro.uk.com
Pietro Catalano, who hails from Sicily, has created a restaurant with rooms in a former windmill that combines the best of Italian hospitality with a touch of boutique swagger. A first course dish of ballotine of rabbit and foie gras shows ambition.

Chef Pietro Catalano, Chris Grist **Seats** 80, Private dining 12 **Closed** 25–26 December and bank holiday Mondays **Prices from** S £6.75, M £16.95, D £6.95 **Parking** 22 **Notes** Vegetarian dishes, Children welcome

SLEAFORD
MAP 12, TF04

The Bustard Inn & Restaurant
◉ MODERN BRITISH
01529 488250 | 44 Main Street, South Rauceby, NG34 8QG
www.thebustardinn.co.uk
The bar, with an open fireplace, flagstones and real ales, is the hub of this Grade II listed inn. A typical main might be two ways with beef (fillet and rillette), accompanied by Madeira sauce, a fricassée of greens, pommes Anna and wild mushrooms.

Chef Phil Lowe **Seats** 66, Private dining 12 **Open** All Year **Prices from** S £6, M £11, D £6 **Parking** 18 **Notes** Vegetarian dishes, Children welcome

SOUTH FERRIBY
MAP 17, SE92

The Hope and Anchor Pub
◉◉ MODERN BRITISH
01652 635334 | Sluice Road, DN18 6JQ
www.thehopeandanchorpub.co.uk
Tucked amidst creeks and moorings, the panoramic views from the patio and restaurant encompass the waterways and nearby Humber Bridge. An appealingly, updated 19th-century inn, with exposed brickwork and a log-burning stove, this is a popular stop not only for birdwatchers and dog-walkers but those seeking good bistro-style food.

Closed 27–30 December and 1st week in January (check website)

STALLINGBOROUGH
MAP 17, TA11

Stallingborough Grange Hotel
◉ ENGLISH, EUROPEAN *V*
01469 561302 | Riby Road, DN41 8BU
www.stallingboroughgrange.co.uk
Set in an 18th-century thatched building with modern extensions, this hotel restaurant takes an informal view of things with its oak panelling, bare brickwork, unclothed tables and garden views. When it comes to the food, local produce shows up well in capable dishes.

Chef Daniel Blow **Seats** 72, Private dining 26 **Closed** 26 December and 1 January **Prices from** S £6.50, M £12.50, D £6.95 **Parking** 80 **Notes** Children welcome

Winteringham Fields

◉◉◉◉ MODERN BRITISH, EUROPEAN ⚱ NOTABLE WINE LIST

01724 733096 | 1 Silver Street, DN15 9ND

www.winteringhamfields.co.uk

The wilds of Lincolnshire near the Humber estuary are not where you'd expect to find a top-flight restaurant with rooms, but Colin and Bex McGurran's inspiring place has long been a destination for culinary excellence. They have their own farm producing honey, free-range eggs, and seasonal fruit, veg and herbs, the rest is sourced diligently from local suppliers. The restaurant has a confident identity, done out in an eye-catching contemporary style, with natural textures and designer touches, and watched over by a formally-attired team who make you feel at home. Whether you choose from the carte, or go for the six- or eight-course tasting menus, expect creative modern food which maintains the integrity of the splendid produce – the likes of cod with smoked mussels, fennel salad and lemon butter sauce, then a tried-and-tested combo of venison with parsnip purée and spiced red cabbage.

Chef Colin McGurran Seats 60, Private dining 12 Closed 2 weeks Christmas Parking 20 Notes Vegetarian dishes, Children welcome

STAMFORD
MAP 11, TF00

The Bull & Swan at Burghley
⊚ TRADITIONAL BRITISH
01780 766412 | High Street, St Martins, PE9 2LJ
www.thebullandswan.co.uk
The old stone inn used to be a staging post for coaches on the Great North Road and is nowadays an informal dining pub. Within are beams, stone walls, rugs on dark wood floors and caramel-coloured leather dining chairs. Regional produce is the backbone.

Open All Year

The Oak Room
⊚ TRADITIONAL BRITISH *V*
01780 750750 | The George of Stamford, 71 St Martins, PE9 2LB
www.georgehotelofstamford.com
History seeps from the pores of every mellow stone of this venerable coaching inn, which once fed and watered passengers on the Great North Road. The oak-panelled restaurant is a magnificent room with an old-world feel, and its menus are steadfastly traditional too.

Chef Paul Reseigh **Seats** 90, Private dining 46 **Open** All Year **Prices from** S £9, M £19.95, D £9.40 **Parking** 110 **Notes** No children under 8 years

The William Cecil
⊚⊚ MODERN BRITISH
01780 750070 | High Street, St Martins, PE9 2LJ
www.thewilliamcecil.co.uk
The hotel is an interesting amalgam of three Georgian houses built at different times, named after the Elizabethan statesman otherwise known as Lord Burghley. It's a clever blend of old and new, the panelling done in lighter colours, with booth seating in the restaurant.

Chef Craig McCready **Seats** 72, Private dining 100 **Open** All Year **Prices from** S £7, M £15.50, D £7.50 **Parking** 70 **Notes** Vegetarian dishes, Children welcome

WINTERINGHAM
MAP 17, SE92

Winteringham Fields
⊚⊚⊚⊚ MODERN BRITISH, EUROPEAN ▮ NOTABLE WINE LIST
See opposite

WOODHALL SPA
MAP 17, TF16

Petwood
⊚ MODERN BRITISH
01526 352411 | Stixwould Road, LN10 6QG
www.petwood.co.uk
Once a private residence, this secluded mansion opened as a hotel in 1933 and guests have included King George VI. It was also home of the legendary 617 Dambusters Squadron and proudly retains its links to aviation history. The formal dining room offers refined, ambitious dishes.

Chef Philip Long **Seats** Private dining 16 **Parking** 140 **Notes** Children welcome

WOOLSTHORPE
MAP 11, SK83

Chequers Inn
⊚ MODERN BRITISH
01476 870701 | Main Street, NG32 1LU
www.chequersinn.net
A beautifully preserved 17th-century inn, the Chequers stands cheek-by-jowl with Belvoir Castle in a pastoral spot where Lincolnshire meets two other counties. Interiors are a blend of old and new, with brasserie-style tables and banquettes in the dining room, while the pub retains its rustic ambience.

Chef Keith Martin **Seats** 70, Private dining 20 **Open** All Year **Parking** 35 **Notes** Vegetarian dishes, Children welcome

LONDON

Index of London Restaurants

This index shows Rosetted restaurants in alphabetical order, followed by their postal district or Greater London location, plan/map references and page number in the guide. London plans are found on pages 208–218 and maps are at the back of the guide.

London Plan 2

A   **B**   **C**   **D**   **E**

5   **4**   **3**   **2**   **1**

0	250	500 metres
0	250	500 yards

Maida Vale

Westbourne Green

St John's Wood

Lord's (Middlesex CCC & MCC)

PADDINGTON

PADDINGTON STATION

Bayswater

Lisson Grove

Kurobuta

The Hyde

Angelus Restaurant

Nipa, Island Grill & Bar (Royal Lancaster London)

Kensington Gardens

Clarke's

Min Jiang, Park Terrace Restaurant (Royal Garden)

━━━ Congestion Charge and Ultra Low Emission Zone boundary
● Restaurant
● AA Award Winner

London Plan 3

0	250	500 metres
0	250	500 yards

London Plan 4

0 — 250 — 500 metres
0 — 250 — 500 yards

Bayswater

The Hyde

St James

Angelus Restaurant

Nipa,
Island Grill & Bar
(Royal Lancaster London)

Kensington Gardens

Speke's Monument

Peter Pan Statue

Physical Energy Statue

Round Pond

Police Station

Ranger's Lodge

Serpentine Bridge

The Long Water

Isis Statue

The Lido

The Serpe

Embassy of Slovak Republic

Federation

Embassy of Nepal

Time Flies Clock Tower

Embassy of Russia

Embassy of Lebanon

Clarke's

Fox Primary School

Kensington Palace

Kensington Palace Green

Serpentine Gallery

Bandstand

St Govor's Well

Diana Princess of Wales Memorial Fountain

Albert Memorial

Romanian Embassy

Israel Embassy

Min Jiang,
Park Terrace Restaurant
(Royal Garden)

Kensington & Chelsea Town Hall

St Mary Abbots

St Mary Abbots CE Primary School

Zaika of Kensington

The Milestone Hotel

Brunello

Polish Institute & Sikorski Museum

Kensington Road

Kensington Gore

Royal College of Art

Royal Albert Hall

Royal Geographical Society

Imperial College London

Knightsbridge

High Street Kensington

Heythrop College

190 Queen's Gate
by Daniel Galmiche

Royal College of Music

Imperial College London

Imperial College London

The Oratory

Kitchen W8

Thomas's Day School

St Alban's Grove

Launceston Place

Imperial College London

Science

Royal College of Art

Victoria & Albert

Police Station

Chantry Square

Darwin Centre

Natural History

Baden Powell House

Health Centre

Cromwell

Superstore

Olives Restaurant

Gloucester Road

Bombay Brasserie

South Kensington

Our Lady of Victories RC Primary School

Lycée Français Charles de Gaulle

Admiral Codrington

Bo Lan Restau

Claude Bosi at Bibendum

Earl's Court Station

Earl's Court

Cambio de Tercio

Capote y Toros

Le Colombier

Royal Marsden

Elystan Street

Oratory RC Primary School

Tom's Kitchen - Chelsea

Earls Court Exhibition Centre

St Cuthbert & St Matthias CE Primary School

Boufield Primary School

Royal Brompton

CHELSEA

West Brompton Station

St Luke's

Hampshire School, Chelsea

Sports Centre

West Brompton

Servite RC Primary School

Maze Grill Park Walk

Chelsea & Westminster

Carlyle's House

Ambulance Station

Brompton Cemetery

Medlar Restaurant

Albert Bridge

A B C D E

6 5 4 3 2 1

London Plan 5

| 0 | | 250 | | 500 metres |
| 0 | | 250 | | 500 yards |

Restaurants shown on map: Ekte, KYM'S, Café Spice Namaste, Chamberlain's Restaurant, Fenchurch Restaurant, La Dame de Pic, Mei Ume, Swan, Shakespeare's Globe, Roast, Oblix, Hutong, Ting, Le Pont de la Tour, Restaurant Story, Pizarro

Congestion Charge and Ultra Low Emission Zone boundary

● **Restaurant**

● **AA AWARD Winner**

London Plan 6

0 — 250 — 500 metres
0 — 250 — 500 yards

POPLAR

South Bromley

Canary Wharf

Quadrato

Plateau

Roka

The Market Brasserie,
Peninsula Restaurant

Congestion Charge and Ultra Low Emission Zone boundary
● Restaurant

A **B** **C** **D** **E**
① **②** **③** **④** **⑤** **⑥**

■ LONDON

LONDON E1

BRAT *NEW*
PLAN 3, J4

◉◉ BRITISH

First Floor, 4 Redchurch Street, E1 6JL
www.bratrestaurant.com

The USP of this high-flying restaurant up on the top floor of a former boozer is simple: source the finest ingredients and cook them with pinpoint precision on a wood-fired grill. The results are terrific, and it all takes place in a wood-panelled, shabby-chic room with the roaring grill taking centre stage amid the hubbub of enthusiastic diners.

Chef Tomos Parry **Seats** 60 **Open** All Year
Prices from S £3.50, M £18, D £4.50 **Notes** Vegetarian dishes, Children welcome

Café Spice Namasté
PLAN 3, J1

◉ INDIAN, PAN-ASIAN

020 7488 9242 | 16 Prescot Street, E1 8AZ
www.cafespice.co.uk

Set in an imposing red-brick Victorian Gothic building, the interior of this vibrant Indian has brightly-painted walls and colourful fabrics that are matched by Cyrus Todiwala's refined, confidently spiced, inventive modern food, which draws on his Parsee roots and the best seasonal British ingredients.

Chef Cyrus Todiwala **Seats** 120 **Closed** Christmas and bank holidays **Prices from** S £8, M £18, D £6.95
Notes Vegetarian dishes, Children welcome

Canto Corvino
PLAN 3, H3

◉◉ MODERN ITALIAN

020 7655 0390 | 21 Artillery Lane, E1 7HA
www.cantocorvino.co.uk

Canto Corvino ('song of the raven') brings modern Italian style to Spitalfields, with artwork on rough-hewn walls, comfortable chairs at well-spaced tables, soft lighting and a lively atmosphere. The menu is as fashionable as the surroundings, divided into eight sections of modestly portioned dishes.

Closed Christmas, New Year

The Culpeper
PLAN 3, J2

◉ TRADITIONAL, BRITISH

020 7247 5371 | 40 Commercial Street, E1 6LP
www.theculpeper.com

This lively gastro pub occupies a handsome Victorian boozer rejuvenated in hipster-friendly post-industrial style with bare-brick walls and a healthy dollop of period detail. The jam-packed ground-floor bar does an appealing line in

switched-on modern food, while the first-floor Kitchen restaurant offers home-grown and European flavours on a thoroughly modern menu.

Chef Pawel Ojdowski **Closed** 1 week Christmas
Prices from S £7, M £13, D £6.50 **Notes** Vegetarian dishes, Children welcome

Galvin HOP
PLAN 3, H3

◉◉ MODERN BRITISH, INTERNATIONAL

020 7299 0404 | 35 Spital Square, E1 6DY
www.galvinrestaurants.com

In trendy Spitalfields, Galvin HOP has reinvented itself and now takes a modern bistro approach. The buzzy venue has kept its burnished copper tanks above the bar brimming with Czech Pilsner whilst giving the place a facelift with brightly colourful seating and pale wood tables. The traditional three-course lunch format segues to a repertoire of small and larger sharing plates.

Chef Jeff Galvin **Seats** 70, Private dining 30
Closed 25–26 December and 1 January
Prices from S £7, M £14, D £7 **Notes** Vegetarian dishes, Children welcome

Galvin La Chapelle
PLAN 3, H3

◉◉◉ FRENCH, EUROPEAN *V* ⁑ NOTABLE WINE LIST

020 7299 0400 | St Botolph's Hall, 35 Spital Square, E1 6DY
www.galvinrestaurants.com

Sweeping stone archways, marble pillars and arched windows soaring 30 metres to the roof rafters of the converted red-brick Victorian St Botolph's girls' school provide a suitably jaw-dropping setting for the Galvin brothers' high-flying City venue. The cooking rises to the occasion, conforming immaculately to the Galvin genre: polished classical French cuisine buffed up with a light, modern gloss. Uncluttered, fine-tuned and pretty on the plate it is too – a fish cake of cod brandade poshed up with the luxury of lobster chunks and bisque foam being a case in point. Main course is another winner, matching roast suprême of Landes chicken with heavenly buttery mash, fresh peas and chard, crisp onions, trompette de mort mushrooms and a fathoms-deep jus, while fish dishes could see Cornish red mullet teamed with celeriac and wasabi, apple consommé, razor clam and hazelnut. To finish, top-drawer pastry skills distinguish a roast provençal apricot tart served with elderflower and rosemary custard.

Chef Jeff Galvin **Seats** 110, Private dining 16
Closed 24–26 December and 1 January
Prices from S £17.50, M £32, D £10.50 **Notes** Children welcome

Lyle's
PLAN 3, J4

◉◉ MODERN BRITISH *V*

020 3011 5911 | Tea Building, 56 Shoreditch High Street,
E1 6JJ

www.lyleslondon.com

Lyle's coolly austere warehouse good looks –
think whitewashed brick walls, subway tiles and
industrial pendant lights – have made it a must-
visit outfit since it first opened. The food
certainly delivers on expectations, with some
lesser-used gutsy cuts of meat and innovative
combinations.

Chef James Lowe **Seats** 48 **Closed** Bank holidays,
Christmas, New Year **Prices from** S £9, M £23, D £9
Notes Children welcome

Super Tuscan
PLAN 3, H3

◉ ITALIAN

020 7247 8717 | 8a Artillery Passage, E1 7LJ

www.supertuscan.co.uk

The cheery Italian enoteca in a Dickensian
Spitalfields' alley is a hang-loose setting for
inspired classic Italian home cooking. Antipasti
sharing platters of salamis and/or cheeses are
obvious ways to pique the appetite. Expect
hearty mains such as chargrilled veal chop with
rosemary-spiked potatoes.

Chef Nick Grossi **Seats** 30 **Closed** Christmas and New
Year **Prices from** S £4, M £12.95, D £6 **Notes** Vegetarian
dishes, Children welcome

LONDON E2

Brawn
PLAN 3, K5

◉◉ TRADITIONAL EUROPEAN ⚑ NOTABLE WINE LIST

020 7729 5692 | 49 Columbia Road, E2 7RG

www.brawn.co

Set among a strip of artisanal shops, the corner-
sited restaurant is a hard-edged, pared-back
neighbourhood outfit. The trendy interior goes
for an unadorned look of whitewashed brickwork,
high ceilings, and plain café tables and retro
chairs, plus the de rigueur open kitchen.

Chef Ed Wilson, Doug Rolle **Seats** 70 **Closed** Christmas,
New Year and bank holidays **Prices from** S £8, M £14,
D £7 **Notes** Vegetarian dishes, Children welcome

Marksman
PLAN 3, K6

◉◉ MODERN BRITISH

020 7739 7393 | 254 Hackney Road, E2 7SJ

www.marksmanpublichouse.com

What was once a run-down boozer, this was
taken over by chefs Tom Harris and Jon
Rotheram, both of whom previously worked at
influential London restaurant St John. Restored
to its former glory as a traditional pub

downstairs, the first-floor restaurant is of a
minimalist style.

Chef Tom Harris, Jon Rotheram **Seats** 45, Private
dining 12 **Closed** 25-28 December **Notes** Vegetarian
dishes, Children welcome

LONDON E8

Pidgin
PLAN 1, G4

Rosettes suspended MODERN BRITISH *V*

020 7254 8311 | 52 Wilton Way, E8 1BG

www.pidginlondon.com

*The Rosette award for this establishment has
been suspended due to a change of chef and
reassessment will take place in due course.* Set in
a Hackney terrace, Pidgin could hardly be more
of the moment. It's a small, rough-and-ready
looking venue in which bare twigs adorn the
walls beneath a bottle shelf, and bentwood chairs
at café tables give notice that nobody expects
you to come in your finery.

Chef Greg Clarke **Seats** 27 **Closed** Christmas **Notes** No
children under 5 years

MEET THE CHEF

Tom Brown
CORNERSTONE
BY TOM BROWN
London, E9, page 222

**What are the vital ingredients for
a successful kitchen?**
Passion and hard work, it's a cliché but true.

What inspired you to become a chef?
Having grown up in Cornwall I was lucky
enough to be exposed to some of the best
seafood in the UK from a very early age.

What are your favourite foods/ingredients?
Seasonality is the main criteria in all my
ingredients – and seafood, obviously!

**What's your favourite dish on the current
menu and why?**
Mackerel pâté, it's been on the menu for a
little while but it's just so tasty and keeps
on evolving.

LONDON E9

**AA Restaurant of the Year for London
2019–20**

Cornerstone by Chef Tom Brown NEW

PLAN 1, G4

⍟⍟⍟ MODERN BRITISH, SEAFOOD *V*

020 8986 3922 | 3 Prince Edward Road, E9 5LX

www.cornerstonehackney.com

A highly-talented young chef with an impressive CV choosing edgy Hackney Wick for their first solo venture might sound a little left-field, but Tom Brown (a Nathan Outlaw protégé and previous head chef of Outlaws at the Capital) has done exactly this, a fact that only makes Cornerstone all the more fascinating. This new seafood joint is making big waves. The vibe is super cool, light and relaxed; a handsome monochrome, industrial look with retro bow-back chairs and black tabletops and dominant central-hub kitchen. Confidently exposed, Brown's team turns out dazzling seafood sharing-plates in the simple but brilliantly executed genre, backed by standout ingredients, flavour and balance. Take a sensational opener of pickled oyster served with celery, dill and subtle kick of horseradish, followed perhaps by headlining whole, sparkling-fresh John Dory (on the bone), again simply delivered with a silky roast chicken butter sauce. Round-off proceedings with a classy dark chocolate fondant, orange and whisky. Bubbly, informed service hits a high note too.

Chef Tom Brown, Christian Sharp **Prices from** S £4.50, M £30, D £10 **Notes** Children welcome

The Empress

PLAN 1, G4

⍟⍟ MODERN BRITISH

020 8533 5123 | 130 Lauriston Road, Victoria Park, E9 7LH

www.empresse9.co.uk

This Victorian tavern fits right into its buzzy Victoria Park location. Red chesterfields, fashionable retro lighting and bare-brick walls are suitably à la mode, and when it comes to food, the kitchen (headed up by an ex L'Ortolan man) delivers honest stuff made with quality ingredients.

Closed 25–26 December

LONDON E14

Plateau

PLAN 6, B3

⍟ MODERN FRENCH

020 7715 7100 | 4th Floor, Canada Place, Canada Square, Canary Wharf, E14 5ER

www.plateau-restaurant.co.uk

Bag a window table to enjoy the incredible view over Canary Wharf from this fourth-floor restaurant with minimalist decor and an open-plan kitchen. A skilful pastry cook is behind a crisp pastry case for salted caramel and chocolate tart with raspberry coulis.

Closed 25 December, 1 January

Quadrato

PLAN 6, A3

⍟ ITALIAN

020 7510 1999 | Canary Riverside Plaza, 46 Westferry Circus, Canary Wharf, E14 8RS

www.canaryriversideplaza.com

Ensconced in a glossy white riverside hotel among the high-rise buildings of Canary Wharf, contemporary chic reigns in the Quadrato restaurant, while a terrace is a welcome bonus for fine weather dining. Simplicity is the watchword in an eclectic modern menu.

Open All Year

Roka Canary Wharf

PLAN 6, C3

⍟⍟ JAPANESE

020 7636 5228 | 1st Floor, 40 Canada Square, E14 5FW

www.rokarestaurant.com

A cool, ultra-modern interior of natural woods befits the setting in Canada Square. Contemporary Japanese robatayaki cuisine is the deal, based on the robata grill (diners sitting alongside can watch the chefs silently working), with first-class fresh produce the kitchen's stock-in-trade.

Closed 25 December, 1 January

LONDON EC1

Anglo
PLAN 3, D3

◉◉◉ MODERN BRITISH *V*

020 7430 1503 | 30 St Cross Street, EC1N 8UH

www.anglorestaurant.com

The anonymous grey frontage and stripped-back interior neutrality of bare tables, pendant lights and concrete floor are very much of the moment at this high-flying venue near Hatton Garden. Mark Jarvis's approach is all about celebrating splendid British ingredients – the clue's in the name – so expect cooking that matches contemporary creativity with a colourful, high-impact look on the plate. If time is tight at lunch, slot in the three-course option, otherwise settle in for one of the tasters – it's all defined by a deft lightness of touch but without reining in on big flavours. Home-made sourdough with yeasted butter and punchy intros of smoked haddock on a nori cracker and a cone of duck liver parfait and walnut get the tastebuds dancing for cured salmon with fish broth and croûtons. Main course brings premium Goosnargh chicken with chestnut and celeriac, its richness lifted by pickled trompette mushrooms to produce something remarkable. A pre-dessert of cheese and onion on malt loaf leads on to a grand finale of sticky toffee pudding with lightly smoked caramel.

Chef Mark Jarvis **Seats** 32 **Closed** 24 December, 2–3 January and bank holidays **Notes** Vegetarian dishes, No children

The Bleeding Heart
PLAN 3, D3

◉ MODERN FRENCH

020 7242 2056 | Bleeding Heart Yard, off Greville Street, EC1N 8SJ

www.bleedingheart.co.uk

Named after the Dickensian courtyard where 17th-century 'It girl' Lady Elizabeth Hatton was killed by her jealous lover, this intimate cellar restaurant has atmosphere in spades, making it a hot spot for business lunches and romantic dinners. The kitchen deals in hearty Anglo-French fare.

Closed Christmas and New Year (10 days)

Le Café du Marché
PLAN 3, E3

◉ FRENCH

020 7608 1609 | Charterhouse Mews, Charterhouse Square, EC1M 6AH

www.cafedumarche.co.uk

The popularity of this classic cross-Channel country auberge-style venue remains undiminished. Bare-brick walls, French posters and candlelit tables set the tone in the rustic-chic converted Victorian warehouse. Food-wise, expect unreconstructed French provincial dishes on an ever-changing carte backed up by daily specials – honest, peasant cooking built on fresh, well-sourced materials.

Chef Tony Pineda **Seats** 120, Private dining 65 **Closed** Christmas, New Year, Easter and bank holidays **Notes** Vegetarian dishes, Children welcome

Chez Mal Brasserie
PLAN 3, E3

◉ MODERN BRITISH

020 3750 9402 | Malmaison Charterhouse Square, 18–21 Charterhouse Square, Clerkenwell, EC1M 6AH

www.malmaison.com

Like other hotels in the group, this branch is done out in best boutique fashion, with dramatic crimson and purple interiors, a sultrily lit bar and a brasserie in deep brown tones. The order of the day is lively modern British cooking with interesting variations.

Open All Year

The Clove Club

PLAN 3, H5

◉◉◉ MODERN BRITISH **V**

020 7729 6496 | Shoreditch Town Hall, 380 Old Street, EC1V 9LT

www.thecloveclub.com

The Victorian pomp of old Shoreditch Town Hall has been reinvented as an arts venue and this rather chic, trend-conscious eatery. In step with the hipster-central location, the place goes for a pared-back look – white walls, wooden floors and tables, and a tiled open kitchen in a white, high-ceilinged space have a certain elegance still, but it's the cutting-edge production of the kitchen that creates most notice. A multi-course taster is the principal business, though there's also a shorter six-course option, and an entry-point four-course lunch, all bursting with clever ideas realised with top-flight technical skill. Flame-grilled mackerel comes pointed up with yogurt and kafir lime, then Cornish Thornback ray with cedrat lemon and sauce maltaise. On the meat front, pork jowl is matched with tart bursts from cider vinegar gel and apple balsamic. If you're not up for wine pairings, try a selection of soft drinks or ambient teas to go with the dishes.

Chef Isaac McHale, Oli Williamson **Seats** 55 **Closed** 2 weeks at Christmas and New Year **Notes** Children welcome

Club Gascon

PLAN 3, E3

◉◉◉ FRENCH **V**

020 7600 6144 | 57 West Smithfields, EC1A 9DS

www.clubgascon.com

The former Lyons tea room on a corner in the Smithfield district has been home to Pascal Aussignac's innovative restaurant for over 20 years. Dealing in a contemporary small-plate dining version of the culinary heritage of the chef-patron's native south-west France, it was a trail-blazer when it opened, and still manifests plenty of energy amid the rather sedate marbled walls and formal service of the setting. Start with a cylinder of pressed foie gras in a layer of concentrated crab jelly with piperade dip and a savoury crab canelé. Even more bewitching is a serving of monkfish with garnishes in camouflage colours, fashioned from truffles, parsley and beetroot, as well as brittle pork crackling, alongside a bowl of pork and fish stock consommé. Sweet things run from sublime prune jam with orange Armagnac cream to peach soufflé in a cup dusted with Earl Grey with cleansing lime and mint sorbet.

Chef Pascal Aussignac **Seats** 42, Private dining 10 **Closed** Christmas, New Year, bank holidays **Prices from** S £17, M £25, D £10 **Notes** Children welcome

Comptoir Gascon

PLAN 3, E3

◉ TRADITIONAL EUROPEAN

020 7608 0851 | 61-63 Charterhouse Street, EC1M 6HJ

www.comptoirgascon.com

Comptoir deals in the gutsy food of south-west France, delivering simple comfort-driven cooking with full-on flavours. The decor fits the bill with its modern-rustic vibe; exposed brickwork and ducting, dinky elbow-to-elbow wooden tables, while the miniscule deli counter offers supplies to take away.

Chef Pascal Aussignac **Seats** 45 **Closed** 25-31 December, bank holidays **Prices from** S £5, M £9.75, D £5.50 **Notes** Vegetarian dishes, Children welcome

The Green

PLAN 3, D4

◉ TRADITIONAL BRITISH

020 7490 1258 | 29 Clerkenwell Green, EC1R 0DU

www.thegreenclerkenwell.com

The corner-sited Green conforms to the trendy gastro pub template with its mismatched tables and chairs, art-laden walls and battery of real ales at the bar. Light streams in through big windows upon a lively crew whose attention is focussed on the perky menu of fuss-free dishes that impress with their big flavours.

Chef Andy Prince **Seats** 35, Private dining 45 **Closed** 1 week at Christmas **Prices from** S £6, M £13, D £6 **Notes** Vegetarian dishes, Children welcome

Luca

PLAN 3, E4

◉ ITALIAN

020 3859 3000 | 88 St John Street, EC1M 4EH

www.luca.restaurant

Another sizeable venue on the bustling entrepôt of St John Street, Luca is that quintessentially millennial proposition, a restaurant using regional British produce in menus that look to Italy. Sharing plates for mixing and matching, and a boisterous, well-stocked bar are also on trend.

Chef Robert Chambers **Seats** 80, Private dining 10 **Closed** Christmas **Prices from** S £11, M £28, D £9 **Notes** Vegetarian dishes, Children welcome

The Modern Pantry Clerkenwell   PLAN 3, E4

◉◉ MODERN, FUSION

020 7553 9210 | 47–48 St John's Square, Clerkenwell, EC1V 4JJ

www.themodernpantry.co.uk

Set in two listed Georgian townhouses on St John's Square, this breezy all-day eatery is an intimate, relaxed backdrop for a lively trek through the world of fusion cooking. Expect influences from around the globe, delivered in inspired combinations and stimulating contrasts of flavour and texture.

Chef Anna Hansen, Robert McLeary **Seats** 110, Private dining 60 **Closed** Christmas, New Year and Summer Bank Holiday **Notes** Vegetarian dishes, Children welcome

The Montcalm London City at   PLAN 3, G4
The Brewery

◉ TRADITIONAL BRITISH

020 7614 0100 | 52 Chiswell Street, EC1Y 4SB

www.themontcalmlondoncity.co.uk

Samuel Whitbread built up one of the UK's foremost beer brands on this spot, and part of his one-time Georgian brewery has been converted into this swanky hotel. There are a couple of dining options in situ, all entirely in keeping with the Georgian setting.

Closed Christmas, New Year and bank holidays

Moro   PLAN 3, D4

◉ MEDITERRANEAN, NORTH AFRICAN

020 7833 8336 | 34–36 Exmouth Market, EC1R 4QE

www.moro.co.uk

Taking its cue from Spain via North Africa to the eastern Mediterranean, Sam and Samantha Clark's Moorish-inspired food draws in hordes who spill out onto pavement tables in fine weather. You can perch at the bar washing down tapas with splendid sherries or sink into a harem-style bolster cushion at one of the closely-packed tables. Friendly staff keep it all together, while inventive menus deliver colourful dishes of big flavours.

Closed Christmas to New Year, bank holidays

Plate NEW   PLAN 3, G5

◉◉ MODERN BRITISH

020 3837 3000 | M by Montcalm London Shoreditch Tech City, 151–157 City Road, EC1V 1JH

www.mbymontcalm.co.uk

Located on the first floor of the M by Montcalm in London's Shoreditch, this modern space is a large open-plan room. The staff are a great asset – casual and attentive in serving up the crowd-pleasing modern British food which offers a mix of simplicity and innovation. The best tables are by the windows.

Chef Arnaud Stevens **Open** All Year **Notes** Vegetarian dishes, No children

St John   PLAN 3, E3

◉◉ BRITISH

020 7251 0848 | 26 St John Street, EC1M 4AY

www.stjohnrestaurant.com

St John has earned its reputation as a pilgrimage spot for British foodies. In business for a quarter of a century in a stark, functional space in a former Georgian smokehouse by Smithfield Market, the 'nose-to-tail' eating philosophy championing unglamorous, lesser-used cuts has inspired a generation of chefs to this robust, gutsy style of cookery.

Chef Steve Daron **Seats** 120, Private dining 18 **Closed** 25–26 December, 1 January, bank holidays **Prices from** S £9, M £16, D £4.40 **Notes** Vegetarian dishes, Children welcome

Smiths of Smithfield,   PLAN 3, E3
No.3 Restaurant & Terrace

◉◉ EUROPEAN

020 7251 7950 | 67–77 Charterhouse Street, EC1M 6HJ

www.smithsofsmithfield.co.uk/no3

Smack opposite Smithfield Market, Smith's top-floor venue offers rooftop views of the City skyscrapers from its long, light-filled room through full-drop sliding glass doors and dream-ticket, fine-weather terrace. White linen, designer chairs, semi-circular leather banquettes and unstuffy service are spot on, while the kitchen produces light, modern, dishes of flair and flavour.

Closed 25–26 December and 1 January

The Zetter NEW   PLAN 3, E4

◉◉ MODERN BRITISH

020 7324 4455 | 86–88 Clerkenwell Road, EC1M 5RJ

www.thezetter.com/food-and-drink

An all-day restaurant on the ground-floor of a hip Clerkenwell hotel; the ingredient-driven menu offers plenty of modern British staples, from a starter of pressed terrine of confit duck and foie gras with pickled plums to a main course of roasted Gigha halibut, St Austell Bay mussels, charlotte potatoes and cucumber.

Chef Ben Boeynaems **Seats** 40 **Open** All Year **Prices from** S £7, M £15, D £7.50 **Notes** Vegetarian dishes, Children welcome

LONDON EC2

Aviary Restaurant
PLAN 3, G4

◎ MODERN BRITISH

020 3873 4000 | Montcalm Royal London House, 22-25 Finsbury Square, EC2A 1DX

www.montcalmroyallondoncity.co.uk

Ten floors above Finsbury Square in the heart of the City, this ultra-modern restaurant with a centralised bar and excellent roof terrace features two stuffed peacocks and sundry birdcages, which explain the restaurant's name. The main draw, of course, is the British brasserie-style food.

Open All Year

Boisdale of Bishopsgate
PLAN 3, H3

◎ TRADITIONAL BRITISH, FRENCH, SCOTTISH

020 7283 1763 | Swedeland Court, 202 Bishopsgate, EC2M 4NR

www.boisdale.co.uk

Down a Dickensian alley near Liverpool Street station, this Boisdale occupies an atmospheric vaulted basement. The soundtrack is live jazz, and the cooking is simple stuff founded on thoroughbred - often Scottish - meats and seafood, so starters include smoked salmon, or roast Blackface haggis.

Closed Christmas, 31 December, 1 January and bank holidays

City Social
PLAN 3, H2

◎◎◎ MODERN EUROPEAN *V* ⧅ NOTABLE WINE LIST

020 7877 7703 | Tower 42, EC2N 1HQ

www.citysociallondon.com

A dedicated lift whisks you up to the 24th floor of Tower 42 for wraparound views of the cityscape, taking in the Gherkin, the Cheesegrater and the Shard. The setting is no slouch either - a glamorous contemporary art deco-inspired space with rosewood panelling, horseshoe booths, leather banquettes, mirrored ceiling and brass table lamps. The food is equally spectacular - inventive, detailed and bursting with entertaining combinations of taste and texture - courtesy of Paul Walsh, who brings intelligence and top-flight technical craftsmanship to the classically founded modern European cooking. An opener of pig's trotter croquettes with crispy black pudding, apple textures and Madeira sauce sets the bar high, but it's easily upstaged by a staggeringly fine plate of rabbit saddle, wrapped in Parma ham, stuffed with trompette mushrooms and tarragon, and pointed up with spelt and silky purées of lovage and black garlic. At the end, a sensational raspberry soufflé comes with white chocolate ice cream is worth waiting for.

Chef Jason Atherton, Paul Walsh, Daniel Welna **Seats** 90, Private dining 24 **Closed** 25 December, 1 January and Bank holidays **Prices from** S £15, M £24, D £6.50 **Notes** Children welcome

Coq d'Argent
PLAN 3, G2

◎◎ FRENCH *V*

020 7395 5000 | 1 Poultry, EC2R 8EJ

www.coqdargent.co.uk

A stylish, modern, sharp-suit confection that comes properly dressed for the accomplished, big-flavoured French cooking and City skyscraper views. Menus boast bags of luxury for City high rollers; from oysters, lobster or caviar to deep-wallet mains like slabs of prime beef.

Chef Damien Rigollet **Seats** 150 **Closed** Christmas and winter bank holidays **Prices from** S £11, M £22, D £8 **Notes** Children welcome

Duck & Waffle
PLAN 3, H2

◎◎ BRITISH, EUROPEAN

020 3640 7310 | 110 Bishopsgate, EC2N 4AY

www.duckandwaffle.com

The view from the 40th floor of the City's Heron Tower is pretty amazing, and Duck & Waffle can sort you out for breakfast, lunch, dinner, cocktails, a late supper, in a casual space open 24/7. Food takes a broad sweep through contemporary European ideas.

Open All Year

Eastway Brasserie
PLAN 3, H3

◎ EUROPEAN

020 7618 7400 | Andaz London Liverpool Street, 40 Liverpool Street, EC2M 7QN

eastwaybrasserie.co.uk

There are numerous eating places to choose from here, including this take on a New York brasserie, with its own entrance, an open-to-view kitchen and massed ranks of tables. Open all day from breakfast to dinner, the carte offers up a wide selection of classic dishes.

Chef Sam Dunleavy **Seats** 96 **Open** All Year **Prices from** S £8, M £16, D £7 **Notes** Vegetarian dishes, Children welcome

Leroy NEW
PLAN 3, H4
◉◉ EUROPEAN
020 7739 4443 | 18 Phipp Street, EC2A 4NU
www.leroyshoreditch.com
The formula is on-trend – a spartan room of neutral hues and bare wood with an open kitchen and a short menu that reads like a shopping list of good things. Leroy's attraction is its simple approach to food – high quality produce, cooked precisely and no frills presentation in a buzzy, tightly-packed venue with switched-on service.

Chef Sam Kamienko Seats 48 Closed Christmas, New Year, bank holidays Prices from S £3, M £9, D £5 Notes Vegetarian dishes, Children welcome

Manicomio City
PLAN 3, F2
◉ MODERN ITALIAN
020 7726 5010 | Gutter Lane, EC2V 8AS
www.manicomio.co.uk/city/
The city branch of Manicomio occupies a Sir Norman Foster-designed glass building with a buzzy ground-floor terrace and café-bar (open from breakfast) and a sleek first-floor restaurant dressed up with a decor as sober as the suited-and-booted city types at its tables. Light and fresh contemporary Italian cooking that pays due respect to the provenance, seasonality and quality of its ingredients is the deal here.

Closed 1 week at Christmas

Merchants Tavern
PLAN 3, H4
◉◉ MODERN EUROPEAN
020 7060 5335 | 36 Charlotte Road, EC2A 3PG
www.merchantstavern.co.uk
The converted Victorian warehouse certainly plays its part in delivering the Tavern's on-cue character, tucked just off the main drag in cool Shoreditch. With Angela Hartnett as one of the owners, there's a sure touch; from fashionable bar with log burner to the restaurant with open kitchen beyond. The uncomplicated, confident cooking delivers British flavours with a nod to France and the Med.

Chef John Mcteer Seats 120, Private dining 22 Closed 25-26 December, 1 January Prices from S £8, M £16, D £7 Notes Vegetarian dishes, Children welcome

Miyako
PLAN 3, H3
◉ JAPANESE
020 7618 7100 | Andaz London Liverpool Street, 40 Liverpool Street, EC2M 7QN
www.londonliverpoolstreet.andaz.hyatt.com/en/hotel/dining/Miyako.html
Miyako is within the Andaz London hotel, although it has its own entrance where queues form at lunchtime for takeaway boxes. The restaurant itself has a cool, uncluttered look, thanks to large windows, walls veneered in pale wood and bamboo, and black-lacquered tables and chairs.

Chef Kosei Sakamoto Seats 24 Closed Christmas, New Year Prices from S £3, M £7, D £6.50 Notes Vegetarian dishes, Children welcome

Popolo Shoreditch
PLAN 3, H5
◉◉ ITALIAN, MEDITERRANEAN
020 7729 4299 | 26 Rivington Street, EC2A 3DU
www.popoloshoreditch.com
A fashionable and young crowd are drawn to this small, modern restaurant that's spread over two levels. The service is informal but the staff are very knowledgeable, and you can sit at the bar to view the chefs producing excellent regional Italian tapas-style dishes.

Chef Jonathan Lawson Seats 33 Closed 24 December to 2 January Prices from S £4.50, M £12, D £7 Notes Vegetarian dishes, Children welcome

SAGARDI London
PLAN 3, H4
◉ BASQUE 𝑽
020 3802 0478 | Cordy House building, 95 Curtain Road, EC2A 3BS
www.sagardi.co.uk
Specialising in the cooking of the Basque country, Sagardi features a glass-walled meat-hanging room, wood-fired grilling and a copiously stocked wine wall. Steaks and pintxos (Basque tapas), plus fish from northern Spanish waters, comprise a menu replete with flavourful protein. The signature desserts include pastel vasco, a densely textured, crisp-shelled cake.

Chef Iñaki López de Viñaspre Seats Private dining 30 Open All Year Notes Children welcome

SUSHISAMBA London
PLAN 3, H2

◉◉ JAPANESE, BRAZILIAN, PERUVIAN

020 3640 7330 | 110 Bishopsgate, EC2N 4AY

www.sushisamba.com

The glass lift whizzes up to the 38th floor of Heron Tower in a few queasy seconds, but Sushisamba offers nothing but pleasure to the digestion. Japan, Brazil and Peru provide inspiration for a fusion of straight-up sushi and all-day grazing plates of high-quality ingredients.

Open All Year

LONDON EC3

Caravaggio
PLAN 3, H2

◉ MODERN ITALIAN

020 7626 6206 | 107–112 Leadenhall Street, EC3A 4AF

caravaggiorestaurant.co.uk

Ornate ceilings, art deco light fittings and an imposing staircase leading to a mezzanine gallery lend a 1930s pizzazz to this Italian in a former banking hall. The pace is full-on at lunch, while evenings are more chilled. This is food of simplicity and flavour.

Chef Alban Gura **Seats** 150 **Closed** Christmas and bank holidays **Prices from** S £7.60, M £19, D £7 **Notes** Vegetarian dishes, Children welcome

Chamberlain's Restaurant
PLAN 3, H2

◉ MODERN BRITISH, SEAFOOD

020 7648 8690 | 23–25 Leadenhall Market, EC3V 1LR

www.chamberlainsoflondon.co.uk

Spread over several floors amid the Victorian splendour of Leadenhall Market, Chamberlain's buzzes with the power-lunch crowd from the city skyscrapers. There's an all-weather terrace beneath the market's glass roof, while windows in the buzzy dining room and more intimate mezzanine make for good people-watching.

Closed Christmas, New Year and bank holidays

La Dame de Pic
PLAN 3, H1

◉◉◉ FRENCH 𝑉 NOTABLE WINE LIST

020 3297 3799 | Four Seasons Trinity Square, 10 Trinity Square, EC3N 4AJ

www.ladamedepiclondon.co.uk

Anne-Sophie Pic may not be a household name on this side of la Manche, but she has earned her place in French culinary history at her renowned restaurant Maison Pic in the Rhône Valley in south-east France. Her base for conquering the UK's foodies is a sleek space done out with leather, wood and mirrors in the swanky Four Seasons Hotel by Tower Hill, and her fine-tuned culinary imagination produces some powerful and unexpected flavour combinations in the

contemporary French style. The cooking is really on song in a starter of Cornish crab, steamed with sobacha and dill pannacotta, with a fab Corsican clementine jelly. John Dory meunière with a purée of coco de paimpol haricot beans, sage and coffee-infused dashi is a beautifully constructed main course, and an elaborate dessert of smooth blackberry coulis, sorbet and fresh blackberry, with sencha and Sakanti chocolate mousse spiked with cubes of sencha jelly makes for an impressive finale.

Chef Anne-Sophie Pic, Luca Piscazzi **Seats** 50, Private dining 14 **Open** All Year **Prices from** S £23, M £38, D £14 **Notes** Children welcome

Fenchurch Restaurant
PLAN 3, H1

◉◉ MODERN EUROPEAN 𝑉 NEW

0333 772 0020 | Sky Garden, 1 Sky Garden Walk, EC3M 8AF

skygarden.london/fenchurch-restaurant

Up on the 35th floor of the Walkie Talkie tower, wraparound city views are a real draw at this sleek contemporary restaurant cantilevered over the tourist-magnet Sky Garden. Happily, the food is no mere afterthought, thanks to the high-level craft and creativity that goes into an appealing menu of modern European cooking.

Seats Private dining 16 **Prices from** S £14, M £27.50 **Notes** Children 15 years and under are required to proceed straight to the restaurant from 6pm weekdays and 9pm weekends

The Fortnum's Bar & Restaurant at Royal Exchange NEW
PLAN 3, G2

◉ CLASSIC AND MODERN BRITISH

020 7734 8040 | The Courtyard, The Royal Exchange, EC3V 3LR

Surrounded by glittering boutiques in the neoclassical majesty of the Royal Exchange building, this glossy outpost of Fortnum's offers an all-day menu replete with luxurious ingredients, as well as an easygoing line-up of classic and modern British dishes. Take a seat at the central island bar counter or go for a table in the roped-off area.

Mei Ume
PLAN 3, H1

◉◉ JAPANESE, CHINESE

020 3297 3799 | Four Seasons Trinity Square, 10 Trinity Square, EC3N 4AJ

www.meiume.com

Mei Ume is an impossibly chic Asian restaurant, showcasing dishes from China and Japan. Part of the incredibly impressive Ten Trinity Square hotel, the high-ceilinged dining room, with its pillars and curved banquettes, is a suitable venue for authentic dishes with a modern slant.

Chef Tong Truong **Seats** 50, Private dining 12 **Open** All Year **Prices from** S £5, M £20, D £9 **Notes** Vegetarian dishes, Children welcome

LONDON EC4

Bread Street Kitchen
PLAN 3, F2
◉◉ BRITISH, EUROPEAN
020 3030 4050 | 10 Bread Street, EC4M 9AJ
www.breadstreetkitchen.com
At this cavernous, high-decibel, high-octane city-slicker operation, courtesy of Gordon Ramsay Holdings, expect a soaring, warehouse-like space that mixes retro and modern looks with art deco references and the feel of a film set from Fritz Lang's *Metropolis*. Battalions of servers dressed in black ricochet to and fro, all friendly, engaging and on the ball, delivering quick-fire dishes from a lengthy all-day roster.

Open All Year

Chinese Cricket Club
PLAN 3, D1
◉ CHINESE
0871 942 9190 | Crowne Plaza London – The City, 19 New Bridge Street, EC4V 6DB
www.chinesecricketclub.com
Occupying a neutral modern space enlivened with cricketing memorabilia, CCC combines modern techniques with traditional and authentic Szechuan flavours. For example, from the dim sum list come three light and fluffy steamed dumplings packed with minced chicken, prawn and spinach with a fiery dipping sweet chilli sauce.

Closed Christmas and Easter

Diciannove
PLAN 3, E1
◉◉ ITALIAN
0871 942 9190 | Crowne Plaza London – The City, 19 New Bridge Street, EC4V 6DB
www.diciannove19.com
The slick Italian operation at the Crowne Plaza City branch looks like the upscale café of a smart contemporary art gallery, all gleaming uncovered surfaces, striped upholstery, and a bar lit in throbbing sunny yellow. Save room for warm amarena cherries, ricotta and sweet pistachios.

Closed Christmas, 24–30 January, Easter and bank holidays

Ekte *NEW*
PLAN 3, G1
◉◉ NORDIC
020 3814 8330 | 2-8 Bloomberg Arcade, EC4N 8AR
ektelondon.co.uk
Ekte's Nordic kitchen – with its chilled-out Scandi good looks, upbeat service and healthy values – stands out from the corporate crowd. The light, cosily minimalist space includes some communal tables so maybe kick off with a few plates of smørrebrød (open sandwiches; perhaps curried herring served with celery, apple and boiled egg). Also open for breakfast.

KYM'S *NEW*
PLAN 3, G1
◉◉ CHINESE
020 7220 7088 | 19 Bloomberg Arcade, EC4N 8AR
www.kymsrestaurant.com
Andrew Wong certainly has cooking in his DNA, and his second venture, set in the Bloomberg Arcade, is worth seeking out. Its designer interior looks sexy with its dark wood, leather, and crushed-velvet banquettes, while the food brings clever, up-to-date takes on regional cuisine, with an emphasis on Chinese-style roasting on the barbecue.

Chef Andrew Wong **Seats** 130, Private dining 40 **Notes** Vegetarian dishes, No children

Vanilla Black
PLAN 3, D2
◉◉ MODERN VEGETARIAN *V*
020 7242 2622 | 17-18 Tooks Court, EC4A 1LB
www.vanillablack.co.uk
Tucked down an alley off Chancery Lane, Andrew Dargue and Donna Conroy's slick restaurant is a million miles from the lentil bake school of vegetarianism. A minimalist contemporary look blends with dark floorboards, antique framed photos and rustic pine tables.

Chef Andrew Dargue **Seats** 45 **Closed** 2 weeks at Christmas and New Year, bank holiday Mondays **Notes** Children welcome

LONDON N1

Frederick's Restaurant
PLAN 1, F4

⊛ MODERN BRITISH

020 7359 2888 | 106–110 Islington High Street, Camden Passage, Islington, N1 8EG

www.fredericks.co.uk

Celebrating its 50th birthday in 2019, the Victorian façade of this much-loved restaurant opens up into a smart bar and capacious conservatory dining area done out with painted and plain brick walls and clothed tables; statement abstract art on the walls adds to the stylish ambience. The wide-ranging roster of light, modern pan-European dishes is a real crowd pleaser.

Closed Christmas, New Year and bank holidays

The Frog Hoxton
PLAN 3, H5

⊛⊛⊛ MODERN BRITISH V♥ NOTABLE WINE LIST

020 3813 9832 | 45/47 Hoxton Square, N1 6PD

www.thefroghoxton.com

Adam Handling deploys the techno arsenal in exciting modern cooking fizzing with ambition and creativity. It all happens in a casual space that fits the Hoxton mood with bare tables and polished concrete floors, the ambience ramped up by the buzz of a centrepiece open kitchen and a beaty rock-and-roll soundtrack. Slathered onto top-class sourdough, the signature chicken butter with crispy skin pieces and intense roasting juices jolts the tastebuds into life for a starter of pig's head terrine with zippy pineapple and chilli chutney. Main course celebrates spring via pink and tender lamb rump matched with black garlic purée, crispy artichoke and sour cream. Desserts keep the vibrant flavours and textures coming with a technically adept dish involving dark chocolate, malt and lemon. Ticking all the right boxes for sustainability and homage to seasonal materials, the carte and seven-course tasters offer plenty for veggie and vegan modes, and a savvy drinks list is strong on pairing artisan beers with food.

Chef Adam Handling, Jamie Park Seats 60, Private dining 20 Closed 25–26 December Prices from S £8, M £15, D £10 Notes Children welcome

Hicce NEW
PLAN 1, F4

⊛⊛ BRITISH, SCANDINAVIAN, MEDITERRANEAN

020 3869 8200 | 102 Stable Street, Coal Drops Yard, King's Cross, N1C 4DQ

www.hicce.co.uk

Part of the Coal Drops Yard development in King's Cross, this second-floor restaurant occupies a reinvented Victorian warehouse with bare brick walls and high-beamed roof. From the vast open kitchen with its BBQ grills, modern European dishes emerge – perhaps cured salmon, wasabi and apple, followed by octopus, peperonata, cured egg yolk and almonds.

Chef Pip Lacey Seats 70, Private dining 24 Open All Year Notes Vegetarian dishes, Children welcome until 9pm on Friday and Saturday

Prawn on the Lawn NEW
PLAN 1, F4

⊛ SEAFOOD, TAPAS

020 3302 8668 | 292–294 St Paul's Road, N1 2LH

prawnonthelawn.com

You can almost smell the sea at this no-frills temple to fish – a bright and breezy space with subway tiles, exposed brick, big windows and paper-clothed tables. Choose the freshest fish you could ask for listed on a daily-changing small plate blackboard, or fish sourced from day boats and West Country markets from the fishmonger's counter.

Chef Patrizia Pesavento, Rick Toogood Seats 32, Private dining 16 Closed 23 December to 6 January Prices from S £7.50, M £7.50, D £6.50 Notes Vegetarian dishes, Children welcome

Radici
PLAN 1, F4

⊛⊛ ITALIAN

020 7354 4777 | 30 Almeida Street, Islington, N1 1AD

www.radici.uk

Francesco Mazzei's restaurant is located opposite the Almeida Theatre, so it's a great spot to pop into before or after the theatre. It's a big room with a large bar and busy open kitchen that creates a great atmosphere. Service is attentive without being stuffy.

Closed 26 December, 1 January

St Pancras by Searcys
PLAN 3, B6

⊛ BRITISH

020 7870 9900 | Grand Terrace, Upper Concourse, St Pancras International, N1C 4QL

stpancrasbysearcys.co.uk

With Eurostar trains outside the windows, you might expect the new menu to give a nod to their destinations, but no. British place names proliferate, as in Portland crab cake, Scottish sherry-soaked salmon, Lake District beef cheek, Cornish plaice fillet and grilled Goosnargh chicken breast. And unquestionably British too is blackberry fool for dessert.

Chef Colin Layfield Seats 160, Private dining 35 Closed 25 December, 1 January Prices from S £4.50, M £13.50, D £7 Notes Vegetarian dishes, Children welcome

Smokehouse
PLAN 1, F4

◉ MODERN AMERICAN

020 7354 1144 | 63–69 Canonbury Road, Islington, N1 2DG

www.smokehouseislington.co.uk

The Smokehouse is an old Islington boozer reborn as a temple to the elemental, Fred Flintstone principle of subjecting hunks of meat to fire and wood-smoke. In the yard are three giant smokers, and global culinary influences add punch, fire and spice.

Closed 24–26 December

Trullo
PLAN 1, F4

◉◉ ITALIAN

020 7226 2733 | 300–302 St Paul's Road, N1 2LH

www.trullorestaurant.com

Just off Highbury Corner, Trullo is a cracking little place, the setting for honest, ingredients-driven modern Italian cooking and a menu that changes with every sitting. Antipasti run to full-bore ideas such as ox tongue with agretti and anchovy. Finish with excellent almond tart.

Closed 25 December to 3 January

LONDON NW1

The Gilbert Scott
PLAN 3, B5

◉◉◉ MODERN BRITISH ⚑ NOTABLE WINE LIST

020 7278 3888 | St Pancras Renaissance Hotel, Euston Road, NW1 2AR

www.thegilbertscott.com

The Victorian era of the train was in full swing when the grand Midland Hotel opened back in 1873, but our illustrious forbears didn't have Eurostar trains that run non-stop to the Continent. Now spectacularly restored as the St Pancras Renaissance Hotel, it is once more a London landmark at the heart of the rejuvenated Kings Cross quarter. The place is a masterpiece of Victorian Gothic opulence, all columns, wedding-cake cornicing and vast windows, that makes the perfect setting for a statement restaurant in the Marcus Wareing stable. His signature British-focused menus take prime UK produce and a soupçon of French style to deliver a well-crafted, gently contemporary repertoire that opens with pressed chicken and truffle terrine with pickled morels and mushroom ketchup, followed by roast cod with grilled squid, sea aster and pea shoots. To finish, an artfully constructed chocolate pavé comes with salted caramel and popcorn.

Chef Michael D'Adomo Seats 130, Private dining 18 Notes Vegetarian dishes, Children welcome

Michael Nadra Primrose Hill
PLAN 1, E4

◉◉ MODERN EUROPEAN

020 7722 2800 | 42 Gloucester Avenue, NW1 8JD

www.restaurant-michaelnadra.co.uk

Nadra cooks on-the-money dishes of global cuisine, a reach that extends from tuna tartare and salmon céviche, through Ibérico presa (shoulder steak) and belly, wild mushrooms and mash in Madeira jus, to an apple and pear version of kataifi, the Greek shredded pasta dish.

Closed 24–26 December, 1 January

Odette's
PLAN 1, E4

◉◉◉ MODERN BRITISH, EUROPEAN 𝑽

020 7586 8569 | 130 Regent's Park Road, NW1 8XL

www.odettesprimrosehill.com

Primrose Hill has always had its own distinct identity, centred on the smart parade of shops and delis along Regent's Park Road, and Odette's has been part of this evolving scene since the late 1970s. Anybody looking to get a fix on the concept of the 'neighbourhood restaurant', look no further. An open-air dining terrace conjures a sensation of the countryside out of the north London air, and the interior walls are crammed with diverting prints. Bryn Williams has moved with the times to the extent of offering a vegetarian tasting menu among the repertoire, but the core of his operation is elevated French bistro food of readily comprehensible appeal. Crème fraiche and wild garlic tart with English asparagus and peas might lead on to Cornish turbot with brisket, consommé, cockles and sea herbs. Look out for the Welsh cheeses, accompanied by fruit chutney and Nain`s bara brith, to finish.

Chef Bryn Williams, Tom Dixon Seats 70, Private dining 20 Closed 2 weeks from 24 December Prices from S £8, M £19, D £8 Notes Children welcome

Pullman London St Pancras
PLAN 3, A5

◉ MODERN EUROPEAN 𝑽

020 7666 9000 | 100–110 Euston Road, NW1 2AJ

www.accorhotels.com/5309

This sleek hotel restaurant continues the cross-Channel link by refuelling Eurostar travellers at St Pancras International, five minutes away. This is a clean-cut 21st-century space constantly thrumming with activity. An open kitchen and Josper grill turn out an eclectic repertoire of uncomplicated modern European dishes.

Chef Carmelo Carnevale Seats 92 Open All Year Notes Children welcome

The Winter Garden
PLAN 2, F3

◎◎ MODERN EUROPEAN

020 7631 8000 | The Landmark London,
222 Marylebone Road, NW1 6JQ
www.landmarklondon.co.uk/dining/winter-garden
The Winter Garden is open all day, and the mood
changes with the hour (and the weather), for it is
in the heart of the eight-storey atrium that forms
the nucleus of The Landmark London. It's an
impressive spot for classically minded modern
food drawing ideas from the Continent.

Chef Gary Klaner **Seats** 90 **Open** All Year
Prices from S £8, M £18, D £8 **Parking** 40
Notes Vegetarian dishes, Children welcome

LONDON NW3

Manna
PLAN 1, E4

◎ INTERNATIONAL, VEGAN

020 7722 8028 | 4 Erskine Road, Primrose Hill,
NW3 3AJ
www.mannav.com
Open for over 50 years, this pioneer in gourmet
vegetarian and vegan dining sits in a residential
street in well-heeled Primrose Hill. Relaxed decor
has a touch of class. Carefully sourced produce
is turned into vibrantly colourful dishes that take
inspiration from far and wide.

Chef Robin Swallow, Marcin Janicki, Ioan Maftei
Seats 50 **Closed** Christmas and New Year
Prices from S £7, M £14, D £7 **Notes** Children welcome

LONDON SE1

The Anchor & Hope
PLAN 5, E5

◎ BRITISH, EUROPEAN

020 7928 9898 | 36 The Cut, SE1 8LP
www.anchorandhopepub.co.uk
Rock up at this rollicking Waterloo gastro pub
and try your luck for a table in the dining area.
Every bit a proper no-frills boozer, food at the
Anchor & Hope fits the no-nonsense mood, with
wine served in tumblers and big-hearted dishes
on a menu that changes each session.

Closed 25 December to 1 January and bank holidays

Brasserie Joël
PLAN 5, C5

◎◎ MODERN FRENCH

020 7620 7200 | Park Plaza Westminster Bridge
London, SE1 7UT
brasseriejoel.co.uk
Park Plaza's dining options centre on a French
venue called Brasserie Joël, a monochrome
space with a large tree in the middle and funky
music filling the air. A mix of traditional and
lightly modernised French dishes brings plenty of
lustre to the brasserie-style menu.

Chef Franck Katemesha **Seats** 180, Private dining 80
Open All Year **Prices from** S £7, M £13, D £6
Notes Vegetarian dishes, Children welcome

Chino Latino London
PLAN 5, C3

◎◎ MODERN PAN ASIAN, PERUVIAN

020 7769 2500 | Plaza on the River London,
18 Albert Embankment, SE1 7TJ
www.chinolatino.eu/london
The London outpost of the east Asian/South
American fusion venture is to be found in the
Plaza on the River London on the South Bank. A
thoroughgoing glitziness sees an illuminated pink
wall-sculpture preside over a soberly grey-toned
dining room with the feel of a theatre set.

Open All Year

See advertisement opposite

Florentine Restaurant *NEW*
PLAN 5, D4

◎ BRITISH, ITALIAN

0845 450 2145 | Park Plaza London Waterloo,
6 Hercules Road, SE1 7DP
www.parkplaza.co.uk/london-hotel-gb-se1-7dp/
gbwater
A short walk from the South Bank's attractions
and London Waterloo, this all-day contemporary
restaurant and bar is a buzzy and informal
setting for crowd-pleasing Mediterranean
brasserie-style food. Flatbreads come freshly
baked from the wood-fired oven, while the open
kitchen deals in straight-up steaks and an
appealing roster of uncomplicated, fresh and
vibrant dishes.

Chef Nicolas Blanc **Seats** 70 **Open** All Year
Prices from S £7, M £13, D £5 **Notes** Vegetarian
dishes, Children welcome

MODERN PAN-ASIAN CUISINE AND LATIN BAR ON LONDON'S SOUTH BANK

FIND US
18 Albert Embankment
London SE1 71J

CONTACT
+44 207 769 2500
london@chinolatino.co.uk
chinolatino.eu

@chinolatinoeu

LONDON SE1 continued

Hutong
PLAN 5, G6

◉◉ NORTHERN CHINESE **V**

020 3011 1257 | Level 33, The Shard,
31 St Thomas Street, SE1 9RY
www.hutong.co.uk
The view from the 33rd floor of The Shard is
stunning, particularly at night with the
shimmering lights below. The room is a bit of a
looker itself, with red lanterns and an open-to-
view wood-fired oven where ducks are cooking
and drying, ready for the classic two-stage
Peking-style presentation.

Chef Fei Wang **Seats** 130, Private dining 26 **Closed** 25
December, 1 January **Prices from** S £10.50, M £29.50,
D £6.50 **Notes** Children welcome

Oblix
PLAN 5, G6

◉ MODERN INTERNATIONAL

020 7268 6700 | Level 32, The Shard,
31 St Thomas Street, SE1 9RY
www.oblixrestaurant.com
It goes without saying: the views from the 32nd
floor of The Shard are terrific. Oblix holds its own
too, with its slick, brasserie vibe, open kitchen,
cool lounge bar and vibrant food that's driven by
the grill and Josper oven.

Closed 25 December

The Oxo Tower Restaurant
PLAN 3, D1

◉◉ MODERN BRITISH

020 7803 3888 | 8th Floor, Oxo Tower Wharf,
Barge House Street, SE1 9PH
www.oxotowerrestaurant.com
On the eighth floor of the old Oxo building, this
bar, brasserie and restaurant overlooks the river
and St Paul's Cathedral, a world-class vista which
never fails to impress. The cooking is modern
British with a bit of globetrotting into Asian
territory. Afternoon tea and cocktails too.

Closed 25 December

Park Plaza County Hall London
PLAN 5, C5

◉ MODERN ITALIAN

020 7021 1919 | 1 Addington Street, SE1 7RY
www.parkplazacountyhall.com
Inside the snazzy modern hotel next to County
Hall on the South Bank, L'Italiano restaurant is on
a mezzanine level and has bags of style, including
great views through the large glass wall. The
heart of the culinary action is a wood-fired oven.

Open All Year

Pizarro
PLAN 5, H4

◉◉ TRADITIONAL SPANISH

020 7378 9455 | 194 Bermondsey Street, SE1 3TQ
www.josepizarro.com/restaurants/pizarro
Whole hams hanging at a Spanish tile-frieze bar,
warm wood textures, and chefs at an open
plancha are a nod to an Iberian mood, while a
stripped back aesthetic appeals to local
trendsters. At Pizarro, the tapas formula has
evolved into gutsier regional fare.

Closed 4 days at Christmas

Le Pont de la Tour
PLAN 5, J6

◉◉ MODERN FRENCH

020 7403 8403 | The Butlers Wharf Building,
36d Shad Thames, SE1 2YE
www.lepontdelatour.co.uk
The name translates as Tower Bridge, and that's
what lies before you, a blue-chip view framed by
the City skyscrapers, whether you're sitting out
on the riverside terrace or indoors soaking up
the vista through floor-to-ceiling windows in the
sleek art-deco-style dining room. The well-
executed food is rooted in the French classics
and doesn't stint on luxury ingredients.

Open All Year

Restaurant Story
PLAN 5, J5

◉◉◉◉◉ MODERN BRITISH **V** NOTABLE WINE LIST

020 7183 2117 | 199 Tooley Street, SE1 2JX
www.restaurantstory.co.uk
After a makeover in 2018, Restaurant Story now
sports a simple-yet-refined look involving
polished concrete floors, tablecloths and a
ceiling adorned with bird mobiles. It's a bijou
space, where full-drop windows flood the place
with light, and chefs do their thing in an open
kitchen. One of the capital's more intensively
experimental practitioners, chef-patron Tom
Sellers learned his trade in some stellar kitchens
including Tom Aikens here in London, Thomas
Keller at Per Se in New York and René Redzepi's
Noma in Copenhagen. As the name suggests,
everything here tells a story, and while the menu
concept isn't applied too thickly, you can expect
hyper-modern food full of revelatory twists, turns
and outstanding technique. Forget any idea of a
quick meal: the drill at lunch is eight courses,
rising to 10 for dinner, so settle in and appreciate
the well-paced, informed and intelligent service
– an essential element of the experience, since
menu descriptions reveal little of the highly
worked detail in every dish.

A volley of clever and innovative 'snacks' among them a Proustian trip back to childhood via sourdough bread and a beef fat dripping candle, or an 'Oreo' cookie comprising goats' cheese mousse and malt vinegar powder, sets the ball rolling, before a fabulous concoction of golden beetroot, caviar and potato blinis. Further down the line, a plump roasted langoustine keeps company with a rich bisque and burnt apple purée, while the principal meat dish matches tender pigeon with ratte potato purée, rainbow chard and a punchy pigeon sauce with walnuts. 'Paddington Bear' is a transition from savoury to sweet, uniting marmalade pain perdu with cardamom parfait, grated foie gras and Sauternes, before various desserts conclude with variants of almond (cream, ice cream, butter, caramelised nuts) deftly aromatised with dill snow. The drinks list is equally of the moment, championing fragrantly botanical cocktails, modern wines and rare gin brands.

Chef Tom Sellers Seats 35 Closed August Bank Holiday weekend, 2 weeks Christmas Notes No children under 6 years

Roast
PLAN 5, G6

◉ BRITISH

020 300 66111 | The Floral Hall, Borough Market, Stoney Street, SE1 1TL

www.roast-restaurant.com

Lording it above the global gourmet paradise of Borough market, Roast occupies the ornate Victorian Floral Hall, relocated from the old Covent Garden and, with pigeon's-eye views of the market, St Paul's Cathedral and The Shard, it's a fantastic setting. In true market fashion, it's open for breakfast too.

Chef Paul Shearing, Ian Howard Seats 120 Closed 25–26 December, 1 January Prices from S £8.50, M £19, D £6.75 Notes Vegetarian dishes, Children welcome

Skylon
PLAN 5, C6

◉ MODERN BRITISH

020 7654 7800 | Royal Festival Hall, Southbank Centre, SE1 8XX

www.skylon-restaurant.co.uk

Knock-out Thames-side views and its setting inside the Royal Festival Hall ensure that Skylon rocks. A real looker, the Southbank set up incorporates a hotspot centrepiece bar, swish grill and stellar restaurant, with chandelier-style lighting, soaring pillars, dramatic flower displays and low-slung contemporary seating.

Closed 25 December

Swan, Shakespeare's Globe NEW
PLAN 3, F1

◉◉ MODERN BRITISH

020 7928 9444 | 21 New Globe Walk, South Bank, SE1 9DT

www.swanlondon.co.uk/restaurant/

Offering camera-clicking views across the Thames to Paul's, the smartly refurbished Swan has a hit on its hands. Sitting above its bustling ground-floor bar, the more formal restaurant is a light-filled room dominated by its lead-light Thames-side windows. Here, modern British cooking is underpinned by classic French references.

Ting
PLAN 5, G6

◉◉ BRITISH, EUROPEAN, ASIAN

020 7234 8008 | Shangri-La Hotel at The Shard, London, 31 St Thomas Street, SE1 9QU

www.ting-shangri-la.com

The Shangri-La occupies the 34th to 52nd floors of The Shard, so the full-drop windows in Ting, the restaurant on level 35, pack quite a punch. The dining room is elegant, with a Chinoiserie feel, and the modern European menu has Asian influences.

Open All Year

Union Street Café
PLAN 5, E6

◉◉ ITALIAN, MEDITERRANEAN

020 7592 7977 | 47-51 Great Suffolk Street, SE1 0BS

www.gordonramsay.com/union-street-cafe

This café's casual, urban-chic warehouse sheen, with funky lighting, buffed concrete, striking artwork and an open kitchen, is a big hit, as is the cooking, driven by the best market produce. Skilled simplicity and a confident, light, modern touch keep the food high on flavour.

Open All Year

LONDON SE10

Craft London
PLAN 1, H3

◉◉ MODERN BRITISH

020 8465 5910 | Peninsula Square, SE10 0SQ
www.craft-london.co.uk

On the piazza among the throngs funnelling into the O2, Craft London is a thoroughly 21st-century operation comprising a café, bar, restaurant and shop in a curvy construction of glass and steel. British artisanal ingredients are given of-the-moment treatments by a creative team who deliver inspiring plates of classy ideas.

Chef Stevie Parle, Richard Blackwell **Seats** 90
Closed Christmas **Prices from** S £8, M £18, D £7
Notes Vegetarian dishes, Children welcome

The Market Brasserie NEW
PLAN 6, E3

◉ MODERN INTERNATIONAL

020 8463 6868 | InterContinental London – The O2,
1 Waterview Drive, SE10 0TW
www.iclondon-theo2.com

Views of the curving River Thames and bright lights of Canary Wharf skyscrapers through full-drop windows provide a big-city backdrop for dining in this stylish cosmopolitan brasserie. Expect prime British produce to form the backbone of hearty grills and modern European dishes prepared with a touch of culinary theatre in the open kitchen.

Chef Johan Rox **Seats** 200 **Open** All Year
Prices from S £6.50, M £17, D £5 **Notes** Vegetarian dishes, Children welcome

Peninsula Restaurant
PLAN 6, E3

◉◉◉ MODERN EUROPEAN *V*

020 8463 6868 | InterContinental London – The O2,
1 Waterview Drive, SE10 0TW
www.peninsula-restaurant.com

It's all happening on the Greenwich Peninsula, which has gradually been transformed into a smart London quarter with its own cultural milieu, and a swish InterContinental Hotel to boot. The Peninsula Restaurant on the second floor has views of the whole district, with Canary Wharf hovering behind it, and amid the sleek contemporary design, a menu of cutting-edge cooking completes the picture. The influences are from modern and classic European cuisines and this has created a menu reflective of the spice, exotic fruit and fresh fish trade that passed through East London's docks to be sold at London's Billingsgate. Highlights of the menu include excellent melt-in-the-mouth and flavoursome Wagyu beef with a silky-smooth celeriac purée and black garlic. The service is very well managed – there's a good team in place offering diligent service with good knowledge and recommendations offered throughout.

Chef Aurelie Simon **Seats** 60, Private dining 24
Closed Bank holidays, for private hire **Parking** 220
Notes Children welcome

LONDON SE22

Franklins
PLAN 1, F2

◉ BRITISH

020 8299 9598 | 157 Lordship Lane, East Dulwich,
SE22 8HX
www.franklinsrestaurant.com

British produce is celebrated zealously at Franklins, an exemplary neighbourhood eatery that combines the virtues of a pubby bar and a buzzy bistro at the rear that's all exposed brick, big Victorian mirrors and paper-clothed tables with an open view into the kitchen. Don't overlook the knockout treacle tart.

Chef Ralf Wittig **Seats** 42, Private dining 24
Closed 25–26 and 31 December, 1 January
Prices from S £7.50, M £14.50, D £7 **Notes** Vegetarian dishes, Children welcome

LONDON SE23

Babur
PLAN 1, G2

◉◉ MODERN INDIAN

020 8291 2400 | 119 Brockley Rise, Forest Hill, SE23 1JP
www.babur.info

Babur has been a pioneer of modern Indian cuisine since 1985, its contemporary approach bolstered by a classy brasserie look. The cooking continues to deliver original ideas, backed by spice-friendly wine recommendations for each dish. Quality ingredients are the bedrock, judiciously spiced and delivered with well-dressed presentation.

Chef Jiwan Lal **Seats** 72 **Closed** 26 December
Prices from S £6.75, M £14.95, D £5.25 **Parking** 15
Notes Vegetarian dishes, Children welcome
See advertisement opposite

A smart,
comfortable,
space with
fantastic food

babur

119 Brockley Rise, Forest Hill, London SE23 1JP
020 8291 2400
www.babur.info mail@babur.info
www.facebook.com/BaburRestaurant www.twitter.com/BaburRestaurant

Céleste at The Lanesborough

PLAN 4, G5

◉◉◉ FRENCH, INTERNATIONAL

020 7259 5599 | Hyde Park Corner, SW1X 7TA

www.oetkercollection.com/destinations/the-lanesborough/restaurants-bars/restaurants/celeste

A grand old mansion on Hyde Park Corner, The Lanesborough's world-class level of luxury and service tends to be the preserve of celebs and oligarchs. Assuming you're not up for its stratospherically priced rooms with a personal butler thrown in, you can buy into the hotel's glamour by dining at Céleste – not as inaccessible as you might think if you go for the set-price menu du jour – beneath a glass-domed ceiling and shimmering chandeliers. The cooking is in the modern French style, blending classic techniques with a contemporary eye for light, fresh flavours in supremely elegant dishes that celebrate first-class British ingredients: exquisite halibut is matched with a riot of Jerusalem artichoke – crushed, puréed, crispy skin, and in a truffle-dusted bon bon – and deftly aromatised with truffle shavings and chicken jus. Caramelised red apple, green apple sorbet, pine nut crumble and elderflower mousse provide a classy finish.

Chef Steeven Gilles, Eric Frechon **Seats** 100, Private dining 12 **Open** All Year **Parking** 25 **Notes** Vegetarian dishes, Children welcome

Le Chinois at Millennium Knightsbridge

PLAN 4, F4

◉ CHINESE

020 7201 6330 | 17 Sloane Street, Knightsbridge, SW1X 9NU

www.millenniumhotels.com/knightsbridge

The Millennium is a modern Sloaneland hotel aimed at the style-conscious. Darkwood and plum-coloured pillars, as well as a row of birdcage light fittings, make a bright backdrop to the refined Cantonese-based cooking on offer, which veers between textbook traditionalism and newer ideas.

Open All Year

Chutney Mary
PLAN 4, J6

@@ MODERN INDIAN

020 7629 6688 | 73 St James's Street, SW1A 1PH
www.chutneymary.com

Glamorously set in stylish St James's, Chutney Mary feels like it has always been here. A smart doorman sets the tone, likewise the glittering Pukka Bar for cocktails. But its main dining room behind is the real jewel in the crown. The creative Indian cuisine runs to inspiring combinations with luxurious touches and well-dressed presentation. Superb service and wines.

Chef Achal Aggarwal **Seats** 112, Private dining 32 **Open** All Year **Notes** Vegetarian dishes, No children under 10 years at lunch Monday to Friday, 4–10 years at early dinner, must leave by 8pm

See advertisement on page 281

The Cinnamon Club
PLAN 5, A4

@@ MODERN INDIAN

020 7222 2555 | The Old Westminster Library, 30–32 Great Smith Street, SW1P 3BU
www.cinnamonclub.com

Former public buildings often make good venues, particularly those built with a bit of empire pomp, like the old Westminster Library with its handsome façade, book-lined galleries and high-end feel. Here, classy modern Indian cooking combines Asian and European techniques to deliver bang-on flavours.

Chef Vivek Singh, Rakesh Ravindran **Seats** 130, Private dining 60 **Closed** Bank holidays (some) **Prices from** S £9, M £21.50, D £9 **Notes** Vegetarian dishes, Children welcome

Colbert
PLAN 4, G3

@ FRENCH *V*

020 7730 2804 | 50–52 Sloane Square, Chelsea, SW1W 8AX
www.colbertchelsea.com

Inspired by the grand boulevard cafés of Paris, the Colbert is a very popular Sloane Square destination and bustles with a wonderful feel-good vibe from breakfast to late evening. The lengthy all-day menu offers something for every occasion. The essence of the cooking is clean simplicity, defined by premium ingredients and flavour. The street-side alfresco tables are a hot ticket.

Chef Adam Middleton **Seats** 140 **Closed** Christmas **Notes** Children welcome

Dinner by Heston Blumenthal
PLAN 4, F5

@@@@ BRITISH ♪ NOTABLE WINE LIST

020 7201 3833 | Mandarin Oriental Hyde Park, 66 Knightsbridge, SW1X 7LA
www.dinnerbyheston.co.uk

Within the Mandarin Oriental Hotel in Knightsbridge, a surprisingly unelaborate dining room is kitted out with unclothed tables, with views over Hyde Park as well as a centrally sited kitchen with open frontage allowing diners occasional glimpses behind the scenes. What Heston Blumenthal has created here is the culinary equivalent of a research institute, with dishes from British history – often quite distant history at that – offering quite as much novelty to today's globalised standard palate as the avant-garde goings-on at The Fat Duck.

The starter known as Rice and Flesh dates from the troubled reign of Richard II and is in essence a painstakingly timed saffron risotto topped with mouthfuls of tender calf's tail richly glazed in red wine. Then perhaps pause at the late Georgian era for 21-day-aged Hereford beef with mushroom ketchup and thrice-fried chips, perhaps followed by a gloriously elaborate raspberry tart lathered with Jersey cream, its sponge injected with olive oil, topped with corpulent raspberries filled with lovage cream and a pebble of gorgeously intense raspberry sorbet. A classic booze-sodden tipsy cake is garnished with sticky spit-roasted pineapple for a touch of exotic climes, while the cheeses come with gently spiced apple and plum chutney.

Chef Ashley Palmer-Watts **Seats** 110, Private dining 12 **Closed** late August **Prices from** S £22, M £39, D £17.50 **Notes** Vegetarian dishes, No children under 4 years

The English Grill
PLAN 4, H4

@@ MODERN BRITISH

020 7834 6600 | The Rubens at the Palace, 39 Buckingham Palace Road, SW1W 0PS
www.redcarnationhotels.com

This elegant dining room is part of a hotel that has been run by the same family since 1912. Banquette seating along one wall provides views of large glass doors into the kitchen, where classic cooking techniques are employed for a menu that appeals to all.

Chef Ben Kelliher **Seats** 65, Private dining 60 **Open** All Year **Prices from** S £9, M £24, D £9 **Notes** Vegetarian dishes, Children welcome

Enoteca Turi
PLAN 1, D2

◉◉ MODERN ITALIAN 🔖 NOTABLE WINE LIST

020 7730 3663 | 87 Pimlico Road, SW1W 8PH

www.enotecaturi.com

Run by the same family since 1990, Enoteca Turi has moved to Chelsea. The focus is on regional Italian flavours, with the menu highlighting the origins of each dish - Campania, Piedmont etc. The whole place buzzes with life and the wine list champions Italian wines.

Chef Massimo Tagliaferri **Seats** 75, Private dining 28
Closed 25-26 December, 1 January
Prices from S £13.50, M £18.50, D £7.50
Notes Vegetarian dishes, Children welcome

Estiatorio Milos
PLAN 2, K1

◉◉ GREEK, MEDITERRANEAN, SEAFOOD

020 7839 2080 | 1 Regent Street, St James's, SW1Y 4NR

www.estiatoriomilos.com

The august surroundings of deep windows with voile coverings, frosted-glass lighting and white linen here make a handsome backdrop for its modern Greek food. The cooking is full of both sea-fresh savour and hearty meaty robustness.

Chef Costas Spiliadis **Notes** Vegetarian dishes, No children

The Game Bird at The Stafford London
PLAN 4, J6

◉◉ CLASSIC BRITISH 𝑽🔖 NOTABLE WINE LIST

020 7518 1234 | 16-18 St James's Place, SW1A 1NJ

www.thegamebird.com

Tucked away in a discreet street near Green Park, The Stafford is a luxurious St James's address that is worth tracking down. The kitchen takes top-notch British produce, subjects it to contemporary treatments and comes up with ambitious dishes glowing with Mediterranean colour.

Chef Jozef Rogulski **Seats** 60, Private dining 44 **Open** All Year **Prices from** S £11.50, M £14.50, D £9.50
Notes Vegetarian dishes, Children welcome

GBR NEW
PLAN 4, J6

◉◉ MODERN, CLASSIC BRITISH 𝑽

020 7491 4840 | DUKES London, 35 St James's Place, SW1A 1NY

www.dukeshotel.com

Buttoned banquettes, mirrored walls, herringbone parquet and high leather stools at the marble-topped bar add up to a glam setting in this classy all-day Mayfair eatery. The initials stand for Great British Restaurant, in case you were wondering, and that's a clear pointer to the kitchen's inventive and up-to-date style of cooking.

Chef Nigel Mendham **Seats** 56, Private dining 14
Closed 25 December evening **Prices from** S £8, M £16, D £8 **Notes** Children welcome

The Goring
PLAN 4, H4

Rosettes suspended TRADITIONAL BRITISH 𝑽🔖 NOTABLE WINE LIST

020 7396 9000 | Beeston Place, SW1W 0JW

www.thegoring.com

The Rosette award for this establishment has been suspended due to a change of chef and reassessment will take place in due course.
Belgravia's Goring Hotel is a class act, and a family-owned one at that. Its century-long service to this elegant quarter of London has seen the titled and the improvident pass through its portals, and treated with flawless civility one and all. Brushing aside all thought of brutal modernism, the lustrous dining room is bathed in light from Swarovski chandeliers of an evening. As we go to press, Nathan Outlaw, is set to offer simple seafood dishes that showcase the best of Cornish seafood and produce in the form of the brand new Siren restaurant.

Chef Nathan Outlaw **Seats** 70, Private dining 50 **Open** All Year **Parking** 7 **Notes** Children welcome

Hai Cenato
PLAN 4, H4

◉◉ NEW YORK ITALIAN

020 3816 9320 | Cardinal Place, 2 Sir Simon Milton Square, SW1E 5DJ

www.haicenato.co.uk

The restaurateur with the Midas touch, Jason Atherton, brings New York-Italian casual dining to the shiny Nova complex opposite Victoria Station. Huge glass windows and a buzzy, on-trend interior decked-out with red banquette seating displays obvious style, though the main focal point is the large theatre kitchen and its pizza ovens. The roster of sourdough pizzas is impressive.

Closed Bank holidays

Ikoyi *NEW*

PLAN 2, K1

◉◉◉ MODERN WEST AFRICAN

020 3583 4660 | 1 St James's Market, SW1Y 4AH

www.ikoyilondon.com

Set in the St James's Market development just south of Piccadilly, Ikoyi, the name of an affluent Lagos neighbourhood in Nigeria, has been grabbing the column inches for its exciting interpretations of West African cuisine. The modern, glass-fronted space has clean-lined pale-wood good looks, with dangling clay lamps, bright artwork and gold-coloured banquette seating catching the eye, while its dinky bar offers views into the semi-open kitchen. Youthful, well-informed service hits just the right note, likewise the uptempo it-place vibe. Chef-patron Jeremy Chan presents highly innovative, intriguing small plates that deliver his translation of West African cuisine, punctuated by heat, bold flavour, high-skill and unusual ingredients... think cassava, banga or asaro. 'Blind tasting Menus' might include the signature 'plantain and smoked scotch bonnet' with raspberry salt, or perhaps 'hake and velouté' served with ground elder, spring greens, sorrel and kelp oil, while 'Ibèrico, hazelnut and clam' comes with nettles and mandarin sweet potato asaro, and the umami-rich 'jollof rice with crab custard' and wild garlic. To finish, 'wild rice (ice cream), mango' and fonio biscuit. Inventive cocktails catch the eye along the way too.

Chef Jeremy Chan **Closed** Sundays

Il Convivio

PLAN 4, G3

◉◉ MODERN ITALIAN

020 7730 4099 | 143 Ebury Street, SW1W 9QN

www.ilconvivio.co.uk

A family-owned Italian in a Georgian townhouse, Il Convivio is a favourite of the Belgravia set. Its name is inspired by a Dante poem, which translates as 'a meeting over food and drink', and lines from his verse are inscribed on the walls.

Chef Yari Mollica **Seats** 65, Private dining 14
Closed Christmas, New Year and bank holidays
Notes Vegetarian dishes, Children welcome

See advertisement below

LONDON SW1 continued

Kahani NEW

PLAN 4, G3

◉◉ MODERN INDIAN V

020 7730 7634 | 1 Wilbraham Place, SW1X 9AE

kahanirestaurants.com

Just off Sloane Square, this upmarket and stylish restaurant uses prime British ingredients for its contemporary Indian dishes. The innovative style is typified by a starter of chargrilled Scottish scallop with star anise and spiced raw mango thuvayal. For mains, there's venison keema, shallots, fenugreek leaves and truffle naan bread.

Chef Peter Joseph **Seats** 110, Private dining 12 **Open** All Year **Prices from** S £3, M £10, D £6 **Notes** Children welcome

Lorne Restaurant

PLAN 4, J3

◉◉ MODERN BRITISH, EUROPEAN

020 3327 0210 | 76 Wilton Road, SW1V 1DE

www.lornerestaurant.co.uk

If you're looking to enjoy excellent cuisine in a relaxed atmosphere in central London, Lorne makes a fine choice. The restaurant has a bright and airy feel, with calming decor. Sommelier Katie Exton has created a wine list for enthusiasts of every taste and pocket.

Chef Peter Hall **Seats** 44

Closed 24 December–1 January, bank holiday Mondays **Prices from** S £9, M £20, D £7 **Notes** Vegetarian dishes, Children welcome

Marcus

PLAN 4, G5

◉◉◉◉◉ MODERN EUROPEAN, BRITISH V 🍷NOTABLE WINE LIST

020 7235 1200 | Wilton Place, Knightsbridge, SW1X 7RL

www.marcusrestaurant.com

A few top restaurateurs can expect recognition from their first name alone; Southport-born Marcus Wareing is one. From a standing start at the Savoy when he was 18, he quickly rose through the grills and griddles to become an acknowledged maestro in the vanguard of his craft, a great professional trainer and a TV celebrity chef. Here in Knightsbridge's Berkeley Hotel in 2008, he opened Marcus, which since then has proved itself eminently capable of punching above its weight, even for such a top establishment. The dining room's contemporary styling is an amalgam of rich, greyish patterned carpets, muted light glowing off burnished wood panelling, trendy prints, and tables laid with crisp white cloths, on which burn small tealights in smart opaque white glass bowls. Dining options are flexible, with a range offering light lunch up to eight-course tasting menus. As an example, take the three-course carte, which gets the ball rolling with roast native lobster, English wasabi and Oscietra caviar, before advancing to rack, loin and confit belly of Herdwick lamb with beetroot, chanterelle and pesto; and ending with bitter chocolate mousse, cardamom fudge and pickled cherry. Moving on, the seasonal Taste of Spring tasting menu might feature slow-cooked egg with wild garlic and Mr Little's Yetholm Gypsy potato (named for the man who in 1899 allegedly introduced it to the Scottish Borders town); then skate roasted on the bone with chicken butter and sea vegetable; smoked pork cheek with piccalilli, and bacon broth; and mango, meadowsweet and yogurt. Wine flights come in two levels: Sommelier's Selection and, for an additional outlay, the Prestige Selection, both of course fully bearing out the AA's Notable Wine List award. The management makes a point of warning that, while there is no formal dress code, sportswear is unacceptable.

Chef Marcus Wareing **Seats** 90, Private dining 16 **Notes** No children under 8 years

Osteria Dell'Angolo

PLAN 5, A4

◉ ITALIAN

020 3268 1077 | 47 Marsham Street, SW1P 3DR

www.osteriadellangolo.co.uk

The neutral tones of this Westminster Italian bring an air of Mediterranean sophistication to Marsham Street. Leather seating and white linen add class, and large windows fill the space with light, while a glass-panelled wall offers a glimpse of the chef in action as staff deliver regional classics and inventive modern interpretations, with simplicity and flavour to the fore.

Chef Demian Mazzocchi **Seats** 80, Private dining 22 **Closed** Christmas, New Year, last 2 weeks August and bank holidays **Prices from** S £8, M £14, D £6 **Parking** 6 **Notes** Vegetarian dishes, Children welcome

Park Plaza Victoria London

PLAN 4, J3

◉◉ ITALIAN

020 7769 9771 | 239 Vauxhall Bridge Road, SW1V 1EQ

www.tozirestaurant.co.uk

Now refurbished, this vibrant Italian restaurant and bar serves classic Venetian cicchetti dishes from the open kitchen. With its full-length windows and original Fiat 500 at the entrance, the room is sleek and modern with lots of natural wood and neutral colours.

Open All Year

Roux at Parliament Square

⊚⊚⊚ **MODERN EUROPEAN** *V* ⚑NOTABLE WINE LIST

020 7334 3737 | Parliament Square, SW1P 3AD
www.rouxatparliamentsquare.co.uk

In a regal Georgian building that's home to the Royal Institution of Chartered Surveyors, this outpost of the Roux empire restaurant offers refined cooking in elegant surroundings. Its duo of dining rooms sport a fetching mix of modernity and clubby restraint, run by impeccably correct and professional staff. The kitchen here is headed up by Steve Groves, a prodigious talent in his own right, whose interpretation of the Roux house style delivers light, modern, smartly-engineered dishes that merge British, French and broader European ideas with a dash of innovation here and there, as in a starter of Dorset crab with apple, fermented chilli and dashi. Mains course stars superb Berkshire pork supported by turnip, barley and tarragon, or perhaps sea trout pointed up with cucumber, caviar and dill. It all looks pretty as a picture on the plate too, right through to the Manjari chocolate delice with hazelnut and crème fraîche ice cream.

Chef Steve Groves **Seats** 60, Private dining 27 **Closed** Christmas, New Year and bank holidays **Notes** Children welcome

Petrichor Restaurant
PLAN 4, J6

◉◉ MODERN EUROPEAN

020 7930 2111 | The Cavendish London,
81 Jermyn Street, SW1Y 6JF
www.thecavendish-london.co.uk
The Cavendish is as chic as can be, with a
plethora of striking paintings. The dining room
may look over St James's, but conjures in its
name the scent of freshly moistened earth
after the first rains. The kitchen draws on
thoroughbred suppliers for materials.

Chef Nitin Pawar **Seats** 80, Private dining 70
Closed 25–26 December and 1 January
Prices from S £6.50, M £16.50, D £5 **Parking** 60
Notes Vegetarian dishes, Children welcome

Pétrus
PLAN 4, G5

◉◉◉ MODERN FRENCH V✦ NOTABLE WINE LIST

020 7592 1609 | 1 Kinnerton Street, Knightsbridge,
SW1X 8EA
www.gordonramsay.com/petrus
Restaurant Gordon Ramsay in Royal Hospital
Road may well be the flagship of Mr Ramsay's
empire, but Pétrus runs it a very close second
when it comes to delivering dynamic modern
French food. The dining room is a sophisticated
space with hues of copper, beige, silver, and
splashes of claret red as a nod to the namesake
wine, and well-spaced tables dressed up for the
business of fine dining around a centrepiece
walk-in glass wine room bristling with starry
vintages. Now headed up by Russell Bateman,
the kitchen interprets the Ramsay style
confidently, with classic techniques and
combinations rather than novelty to the fore, as
in the roast veal sweetbreads that combine with
castelfranco radicchio, almond, lemon and truffle
in a stunning opener. Next up, superb Cornish
monkfish is counterpointed by squash,
chanterelle and ginger. To finish, a quenelle of
roast hazelnut ice cream is slotted into a
masterful praline soufflé at the table.

Chef Russell Bateman **Seats** 55, Private dining 8
Closed 26–28 December **Notes** Children welcome no
children's menu or facilities

Quaglino's
PLAN 4, J6

◉ EUROPEAN

020 7930 6767 | 16 Bury Street, SW1Y 6AJ
www.quaglinos-restaurant.co.uk
Once the favoured watering-hole Evelyn Waugh
and the future Edward VIII, Quaglino's is a
masterpiece of art deco style on the cruise-ship
scale, complete with golden-lit staircase to
tempt out your inner Gloria Swanson. Flavours
simply shine from the plate.

Quilon
PLAN 4, J4

◉◉ INDIAN ✦ NOTABLE WINE LIST

020 7821 1899 | 41 Buckingham Gate, SW1E 6AF
www.quilon.co.uk
With its own entrance in the swish St James'
Court hotel, Quilon's chic, ultra-modern interior
looks the part for a venue that sits in the top
flight of London's Indian restaurants. The
kitchen's focus is on the cuisine of India's south-
west region, mixing traditional and inventive
ideas, with top-class materials forming the
backbone of the output.

Chef Sriram Aylur **Seats** 90, Private dining 16
Closed 25 December **Prices from** S £12, M £12, D £10
Notes Vegetarian dishes, Children welcome

The Rex Whistler Restaurant NEW
PLAN 5, B3

◉◉ MODERN BRITISH, EUROPEAN ✦ NOTABLE WINE LIST

020 7887 8825 | Lower Floor, Tate Britain, Millbank,
SW1P 4JU
**www.tate.org.uk/visit/tate-britain/rex-whistler-
restaurant**
Rex Whistler's mural 'The Expedition in Pursuit of
Rare Meats' covers the four walls of Tate Britain's
restaurant and keeps you pleasantly distracted
as you peruse the seasonally changing menus.
There are some very good techniques on display
here – each complementing the quality of the
produce on offer. The wine list is highly prized
and sommelier recommendations are available.

Chef Alfio Laudani **Seats** 70 **Closed** 24–26 December
Prices from S £8.50, M £18, D £7 **Notes** Vegetarian
dishes, Children welcome

Roux at Parliament Square
PLAN 5, B5

@@@ MODERN EUROPEAN ***V*** 🍷 NOTABLE WINE LIST

See page 245

The Royal Horseguards
PLAN 5, B6

@ MODERN BRITISH

020 7451 9333 | 2 Whitehall Court, SW1A 2EJ
www.guoman.co.uk

This grand old pile was home to the Secret Service in World War I, and now makes an upmarket base when visiting London's attractions. Its posh restaurant comes kitted out with plush banquettes and deals in appealing modern brasserie-style food with its roots in French classics.

Open All Year

Sake No Hana
PLAN 4, J6

@@ MODERN JAPANESE

020 7925 8988 | 23 Saint James's Street, SW1A 1HA
www.sakenohana.com

Part of the Hakkasan stable, this sleek Japanese restaurant is a striking L-shaped space with a wood lattice ceiling, bamboo columns and windows hung with screens. Perch at the sushi counter, or sit at low-slung leather banquettes for a menu offering both contemporary and traditional dishes.

Closed 25-26 December and New Year

Santini Restaurant
PLAN 4, H4

@ TRADITIONAL ITALIAN

020 7730 4094 | 29 Ebury Street, SW1W 0NZ
www.santinirestaurant.com

The traditional values of a family-run Italian restaurant underpin this glossy Belgravia darling, and Latin style runs all the way from the sleek and bright interior to the waiters and the wine list. Impeccably sourced seasonal ingredients treated with a light touch are at the core.

Closed Christmas, 1 January

Seven Park Place by William Drabble
PLAN 4, J6

@@@@ MODERN FRENCH

020 7316 1600 | St James's Hotel and Club, 7-8 Park Place, SW1A 1LP
www.stjameshotelandclub.com

Tucked away in St James's, the eponymously titled five-star hotel and club is home to one of London's most seductive dining opportunities, where the incomparable William Drabble has been producing dynamic and creative modern French cuisine since 2009. The dining room is a gem, small but perfectly formed, shimmering with rich, warm colours and bold contemporary artworks.

The set lunch is a great introduction to William's work for anyone on a budget (two choices at each course), with an all-conquering Menu Gourmand at the other end of the spectrum (including a choice of three wine flights or a juice pairing). First-rate ingredients from trusted suppliers lead the way on the à la carte menu that might take you from plump, generously-sized seared scallops with crisp courgette fritters and lettuce and basil purée, via saddle of Lune Valley lamb, with garlic purée, baby artichokes, broad beans and tomatoes, to a fresh, ripe peach dessert, with Lancashire yogurt mousse, almond crumble and zingy lemon verbena sorbet.

The technical virtuosity on display is impressive from start to finish, with attention to texture, flavour and temperature. The wine 'book' excels in France and does more than justice to the rest of the world.

Chef William Drabble Seats 34, Private dining 35
Open All Year Notes Vegetarian dishes, No children

Wild Honey
PLAN 4, K6

Rosettes suspended FRENCH

020 7968 2900 | 6 Waterloo Place, SW1Y 4AN
www.wildhoneystjames.co.uk

After 12 successful years in Mayfair, the well-respected chef patron Anthony Demetre moves Wild Honey into the Sofitel London St James on the former site of The Balcon restaurant. Head Chef Simon Woodrow will collaborate on menus which will continue the French-based contemporary, seasonal cooking for which Wild Honey became so well known.

Open All Year

Zafferano

PLAN 4, F4

◉◉ MODERN ITALIAN

020 7235 5800 | 15 Lowndes Street, SW1X 9EY

www.zafferanorestaurant.com

Zafferano has always held its head high among the upper echelons of the UK's contemporary Italians since Giorgio Locatelli opened the place back in 1995. The kitchen gives classic dishes a sophisticated spin and well-sourced ingredients remain at the heart of it all.

Chef Daniele Camera Seats 140, Private dining 26
Closed 25 December Prices from S £14.50, M £15.50,
D £8.50 Notes Vegetarian dishes, Children welcome

LONDON SW3

Admiral Codrington

PLAN 4, E3

◉ BRITISH, EUROPEAN

020 7581 0005 | 17 Mossop Street, SW3 2LY

www.theadmiralcodrington.co.uk

The Cod is a proper pub with real ales at the pumps, red leather stools and a wee terrace for supping outside. It's also a dining address with cosy booths, pretty banquettes and interesting wallpapers, plus private rooms upstairs. The menu offers globally-inspired stuff.

Chef Benjamin Cucis-Bourbon Seats 40, Private
dining 22 Prices from S £7.50, M £15, D £2
Notes Vegetarian dishes, Children welcome

Bo Lang Restaurant

PLAN 4, E3

◉ CHINESE

020 7823 7887 | 100 Draycott Avenue, SW3 3AD

www.bolangrestaurant.co.uk

A seductive Chelsea hangout for lovers of dim sum, this take on the teahouse theme is set in a moodily lit space with lanterns dangling. The extensive tea menu backs up a dim sum roster offering the likes of pork char sui steamed buns, or saffron scallop and cod dumplings, while main courses are no less accomplished.

Open All Year

Claude Bosi at Bibendum

PLAN 4, E3

◉◉◉◉◉ MODERN FRENCH *V*

0207 581 5817 | Michelin House, 81 Fulham Road, SW3 6RD

www.bibendum.co.uk

One of the world's oldest trademarks, Bibendum is the official mascot of Michelin, the French tyre company. This unusual post-Art Nouveau building in South Ken was once their UK headquarters. How appropriate then that since 2016, a Frenchman, Claude Bosi, has been head chef here. And how fitting too that old adverts featuring the pneumatic Bib carried the words *nunc est bibendum*, meaning 'now is the time to drink'. The building's exterior is decorated with tiles featuring early 20th-century racing cars; there are more inside in what, believe it or not, used to be a tyre-fitting bay. An ornate pillared entrance leads into the ground-floor, all-day Oyster Bar, with stairs up to a beautiful dining room, its stained-glass window in cobalt blues depicting our inflatable friend on his bicycle. From Thursday to Saturday a three-course lunch offers 36-month-old parmesan custard, followed by Galician beef fillet with coffee and pickled walnuts, then Gariguette strawberries with elderflower and strawberry sauce. Sunday lunchtimes and Wednesday-to-Sunday evenings present a signature nine-course tasting menu, which is worth quoting in full: it opens with Bibendum egg, then proceeds to duck jelly with special selection caviar; Cornish cock crab; seasonal nosotto (risotto with a root veg not rice) with chicken oysters, 24-month-old Comté and Lancashire mead; Cornish turbot à la Grenobloise; French veal sweetbread; pickled walnuts and macadamia nut purée; Brittany rabbit, langoustine and artichoke barigoule; crème fraîche with Alphonso mango and Corsican pomelo; and finally asparagus with white chocolate, black olive and coconut. Things are simpler in the Oyster Bar, where prawn and avocado cocktail might be followed by moules marinière and chips, or fillet steak au poivre, before a dessert of apple and rhubarb crumble and custard. Four caviars, including Beluga Tsar Imperial, are served with blinis and crème fraîche. The mainly French and Italian wine list has just one from the New World, a Californian Zinfandel.

Chef Claude Bosi Closed 23–26 December, 1–7 January,
14–22 April Prices from S £22, M £25, D £15
Notes Children welcome

Le Colombier
PLAN 4, D2

◎ TRADITIONAL FRENCH

020 7351 1155 | 145 Dovehouse Street, SW3 6LB

www.le-colombier-restaurant.co.uk

Le Colombier is the epitome of the old-school neighbourhood French restaurant, its blue-canopied terrace is a hot ticket, while the dining room is an equally sunny confection of cream and blues. Unfussy, unashamedly classic French brasserie-style dishes are so familiar they hardly need their translations.

Chef Philippe Tamet **Seats** 70, Private dining 28 **Open** All Year **Prices from** S £6.90, M £20.90, D £8.50 **Notes** Vegetarian dishes, No children

Elystan Street
PLAN 4, E3

◎◎◎ MODERN BRITISH V ⬛ NOTABLE WINE LIST

020 7628 5005 | 43 Elystan Street, Chelsea, SW3 3NT

www.elystanstreet.com

An expansive, light-flooded space with chairs in two colours at bare-topped tables is the location for Phil Howard's Chelsea operation, a sophisticated take on informal contemporary eating. His cooking, as befits his many years at The Square, displays a level of fine-tuned attention to detail in every element of a dish, from the skin-thin pasta of chicken and butternut ravioli with hazelnut pesto in chicken jus to the gently caramelised Orkney scallops that garnish a roasted fillet of sea bream with puréed broccoli and glazed salsify. Meat is of a high order too, perhaps Cumbrian rib-eye with a stuffed field mushroom, puréed shallots and potato galette in red wine. Peppered vanilla and bayleaf ice cream makes an asssertive accompaniment to properly glutinous pear Tatin, while the Brillat-Savarin cheesecake is already legendary, its Seville orange glaze adding tang, its ice cream humorously flavoured with toast.

Chef Philip Howard, Toby Burrowes **Seats** 64, Private dining 14 **Closed** Christmas **Prices from** S £15, M £25, D £12 **Notes** Children welcome

The Five Fields
PLAN 4, F3

◎◎◎◎ MODERN BRITISH V ⬛ NOTABLE WINE LIST

See page 250

Hans' Bar & Grill *NEW*
PLAN 4, F3

◎ MODERN BRITISH

020 7730 7000 | 11 Cadogan Gardens Hotel, 11 Cadogan Gardens, Chelsea, SW3 2RJ

Part of a luxury townhouse hotel on a Chelsea square, Hans' has its own entrance and slots in comfortably among the upscale shops on Pavilion Road. The place has smart contemporary looks – bare brickwork, low-slung banquettes and tasteful hues – and food to match on an appealing all-day menu of modern British dishes.

Chef Adam England **Seats** 102, Private dining 16 **Open** All Year **Prices from** S £7, M £13, D £7 **Notes** Vegetarian dishes, Children welcome

Manicomio Chelsea
PLAN 4, F3

◎ MODERN ITALIAN

020 7730 3366 | 85 Duke of York Square, Chelsea, SW3 4LY

www.manicomio.co.uk/chelsea

Manicomio presents a cool, calming image, with its darkwood floor, leather banquettes, dark blue walls and eye-catching artwork. Contemporary Italian cooking is the deal, with key ingredients imported from the motherland and a menu evenly divided between fish and meat.

Closed Christmas and New Year

The Restaurant at The Capital
PLAN 4, F5

Rosettes suspended BRITISH

020 7591 1202 | Basil Street, Knightsbridge, SW3 1AT

www.capitalhotel.co.uk

The Rosette award for this establishment has been suspended due to a change of chef and reassessment will take place in due course. The restaurant showcases British-inspired cuisine using local and seasonal ingredients sourced from trusted suppliers.

Open All Year

The Five Fields

◉◉◉◉ MODERN BRITISH *V* NOTABLE WINE LIST

020 7838 1082 | 8–9 Blacklands Terrace, SW3 2SP

www.fivefieldsrestaurant.com

Perfectly in keeping with the Chelsea postcode, The Five Fields is the very template of discretion and elegance. The place might be billed as a 'neighbourhood restaurant', but images of a casual, budget eatery are wide of the mark – it exudes the kind of designer class that comes with a rather swish location, just off Sloane Square. Chef-patron Taylor Bonnyman, head chef Marguerite Keogh and the team continue to deliver intelligent and thrilling contemporary food based on outstanding ingredients. Expect artfulness and accuracy in equal measure in stunning looking plates, whether you go for the set-price menu or the eight-course tasting extravaganza. A starter of sea bass might arrive with rhubarb, curry and onion, while short rib is taken to another level with its accompaniments of parsnip, blackcurrant and grape mustard. Slick service and a cleverly compiled wine list seal the deal.

Chef Taylor Bonnyman, Marguerite Keogh **Seats** 40, Private dining 10 **Closed** Christmas, 2 weeks January, 2 weeks August **Notes** No children

LONDON SW3 continued

Restaurant Gordon Ramsay
PLAN 4, F1

◉◉◉◉ FRENCH *V*

020 7352 4441 | 68 Royal Hospital Road, SW3 4HP

www.gordonramsayrestaurants.com

Over 20 years since it opened in Royal Hospital Road, the flagship of the Gordon Ramsay global empire remains a strong contender in London's high-end dining scene. The dining room is surprisingly intimate – just 45 or so seats – with clean-lined, art deco-influenced looks and plush, pastel-hued tones giving a sophisticated sheen to the space. As for the kitchen team, Matt Abé has been running things here for more than a decade. What keeps this venue in the premier league is its rejection of pointless experimentation and tawdry effects: what you get is superb ingredients, harmoniously combined and executed with pin-sharp precision.

A starter of scallop tartare with yuzu, lovage and Tokyo turnip, or ravioli of lobster, langoustine, salmon and sorrel could be followed by roast pigeon with beetroot, shallot and buckwheat. Desserts maintain the impeccably haute tone via Yorkshire rhubarb soufflé, or caramelised apple tarte Tatin with Tahitian vanilla ice cream.

The fixed-price lunch menu is the best entry point for anyone looking for the RGR experience on a budget (relatively speaking). Pitch-perfect service is supervised by Jean-Claude Breton, and sommelier James Lloyd and his team steer the way through a roll-call of the world's best producers.

Chef Matt Abé **Seats** 45 **Closed** 1 week at Christmas **Notes** Children welcome

Tom's Kitchen – Chelsea
PLAN 4, E2

◉◉ TRADITIONAL BRITISH

020 7349 0202 | 27 Cale Street, Chelsea, SW3 3QP

www.tomskitchen.co.uk/chelsea

Well placed for the still trendy Fulham and King's Roads, the decor here is modern, the ceilings high, the kitchen open-plan and the service good. Note that all starters and mains are for sharing, and as the menu recommends three to four dishes per person, don't be surprised if the prices raise an eyebrow.

Open All Year

LONDON SW4

Bistro Union
PLAN 1, E2

◉◉ BRITISH

020 7042 6400 | 40 Abbeville Road, Clapham, SW4 9NG

www.bistrounion.co.uk

This is exactly the sort of easy-going neighbourhood eatery we'd all like on our patch. You can perch on wooden bar stools, choosing from a menu of on-trend nibbles hand-written onto a roll of brown paper. What leaves the kitchen is built with British-led ingredients.

Chef Adam Byatt **Seats** 40 **Closed** 24-27 December **Prices from** S £6, M £18, D £6 **Notes** Vegetarian dishes, Children welcome

The Dairy
PLAN 1, E2

◉◉ MODERN BRITISH, EUROPEAN *V*

020 7622 4165 | 15 The Pavement, Clapham, SW4 0HY

www.the-dairy.co.uk

From the outside, this buzzy operation looks unremarkable, but step inside and you'll find a friendly, welcoming and popular place, with a pared-back decor. The cooking is clever and innovative, producing well-crafted dishes that are impeccably seasonal and full of big, clear flavours. Small plates are the deal here.

Chef Robin Gill **Seats** 40 **Closed** Christmas **Prices from** S £5.50, M £12.50, D £7 **Notes** Vegetarian dishes, Children welcome

Sorella *NEW*
PLAN 1, F2

◉ ITALIAN

020 7720 4662 | 148 Clapham Manor Street, Clapham, SW4 6BX

www.sorellarestaurant.co.uk

Chef-restaurateur Robin Gill of The Dairy fame has relaunched his former The Manor into this cracking little neighbourhood Italian that genuinely celebrates the Mediterranean attitude to cooking, eating and socialising. Tucked away off the main drag, its stripped back, casual look is right on-trend. Expect uncomplicated, produce-led dishes big on flavour and generosity.

Trinity Restaurant

PLAN 1, E2

◉◉◉ BRITISH, EUROPEAN ⬤ NOTABLE WINE LIST

020 7622 1199 | 4 The Polygon, Clapham, SW4 0JG

www.trinityrestaurant.co.uk

In the Old Town, just a short stroll from Clapham Common tube, Adam Byatt's stellar neighbourhood restaurant is a good reason to move to SW4. The outdoor terrace and cool, understated tones inside, complete with open-to-view kitchen, are very much what modern London dining is about, watched over by a slick service team who are all wised-up about the menu and maintain a relaxed mood throughout proceedings. The inventive modern European cooking has its feet firmly grounded in French classicism, with careful balanced dishes that impress with their invention and satisfy with their deceptive simplicity. Crispy trotters make an impressive opener, with zingy sauce gribiche, cider mayonnaise and crackling. Main course brings sensational wild turbot, given simple bonne femme treatment to let its quality shine, alongside fresh morels and silky creamed potatoes pointed up with wild garlic. Dessert is salt caramel heaven, in the form of wobbly custard tart and intense ice cream.

Chef Adam Byatt **Seats** 50 **Closed** 24–27 December and 1–2 January **Notes** Vegetarian dishes, No children under 10 years

Tsunami

PLAN 1, F2

◉ JAPANESE

020 7978 1610 | 5–7 Voltaire Road, SW4 6DQ

www.tsunamiclapham.co.uk

This branch of Tsunami appeals to crowds of thirty-somethings eager for first-class sushi and sashimi and slick modern Japanese fusion food. Okay, the open-planned space may be hard-edged and high-decibel, but it's really sociable, with the kitchen delivering fresh, skilful, smart-looking classic-meets-contemporary dishes designed for sharing and grazing.

Chef Ken Sam **Seats** 75 **Closed** 24–26 December, 1 January **Prices from** S £5.60, M £11.50, D £4 **Notes** Vegetarian dishes, Children welcome

LONDON SW5

Cambio de Tercio

PLAN 4, C2

◉◉ MODERN SPANISH **V**

020 7244 8970 | 163 Old Brompton Road, SW5 0LJ

www.cambiodetercio.co.uk

Folding full-length glass windows open Tercio up to the street, while inside there's a dark, intimate feel – black slate floors, mustard yellow and fuchsia pink walls hung with striking modern artworks. The food is equally colourful and good looking, ranging from traditional tapas to more innovative dishes.

Chef Alberto Criado **Seats** 90, Private dining 18 **Closed** 2 weeks at Christmas, New Year, 15–31 August **Parking** 10 **Notes** Children welcome

Capote y Toros

PLAN 4, C2

◉ SPANISH **V**

020 7373 0567 | 157 Old Brompton Road, SW5 0LJ

www.cambiodetercio.co.uk

A few doors away from sibling Cambio de Tercio, Capote y Toros describes itself as a tapas, ham and sherry bar. It has vivid decor with photographs of matadors and hams hanging from the ceiling above the bar. Live flamenco music adds to the fun.

Chef Luis Navacerrada Lanzadera **Seats** 25 **Closed** Christmas **Notes** Children welcome

LONDON SW6

The Harwood Arms

PLAN 1, E3

◉◉ BRITISH **V**

020 7386 1847 | 27 Walham Grove, Fulham, SW6 1QR

www.harwoodarms.com

On an unassuming backstreet in trendy Fulham, the stylish Harwood Arms is one of Britain's top gastro pubs. Inside, you could almost forget you're in London, with photos of outdoor country pursuits hung on grey and cream walls, and rustic wooden tables. On the menu, first class, carefully-sourced English produce that's cooked with confidence.

Chef Sally Abé **Seats** 60 **Closed** 24–26 December **Prices from** S £13.50, M £29.50, D £11.50 **Notes** Children welcome

LONDON SW7

Bombay Brasserie
PLAN 4, C3

◎◎ INDIAN

020 7370 4040 | Courtfield Close, Courtfield Road, SW7 4QH

www.bombayb.co.uk

This glamorous South Ken institution (first opened back in 1982) still packs in the crowds for its authentic, melting-pot Mumbai (one-time Bombay) pan-Indian cuisine. Reworked modern interiors evoke that Raj-era spirit. The kitchen deals in freshly-ground, lightly toasted spices to impart maximum flavour.

Chef Prahlad Hegde **Seats** 185, Private dining 16 **Closed** 25 December **Prices from** S £12, M £19, D £10 **Notes** Vegetarian dishes, Children welcome

Brunello
PLAN 4, C5

◎ MODERN ITALIAN

020 7368 5700 | Baglioni Hotel London, 60 Hyde Park Gate, Kensington Road, Kensington, SW7 5BB

www.baglionihotels.com

The opulent restaurant at the Baglioni Hotel facing Kensington Gardens is a haven of Italian chic, done In parquet and monochrome tiles, with chairs in lemon leather, and giant mirrored baubles suspended from the ceiling. Classic Italian cooking is what this international chain trades in.

Open All Year

Olives Restaurant
PLAN 4, C3

◎ ITALIAN

020 7331 6308 | Millennium Bailey's Hotel London Kensington, 140 Gloucester Road, SW7 4QH

www.olivesrestaurant.co.uk

The elegantly restored Victorian townhouse hotel in upmarket South Kensington is handy for the museums as well as some serious shopping. The main dining room, Olives, a long narrow room with unclothed tables and pastel-shaded upholstery, goes for a pared-down look, the better to offset the uncomplicated Italian cooking on offer.

Open All Year

190 Queen's Gate by Daniel Galmiche
PLAN 4, C4

◎◎ BRITISH, FRENCH **V**

020 7584 6601 | The Gore, 190 Queen's Gate, SW7 5EX

www.gorehotel.com

Close to the Royal Albert Hall, this venerable venue features a wood-panelled cocktail bar where the launch party for the Rolling Stones' *Beggars Banquet* album was held. French maître Galmiche oversees proceedings in the chandeliered, gilt-mirrored dining room, where modernised classic English dishes are served.

Chef Daniel Galmiche, Helder Andrade **Seats** 45, Private dining 60 **Open** All Year **Prices from** S £9, M £19, D £8 **Notes** Children welcome

Zuma
PLAN 4, F5

◎◎ MODERN JAPANESE

020 7584 1010 | 5 Raphael Street, Knightsbridge, SW7 1DL

www.zumarestaurant.com

An effortlessly cool playground of the beau monde, super glossy Zuma appeals to lovers of contemporary Japanese food and slick design. The vibe is high octane, buoyed by the buzzing front bar-lounge offering 40 different sakes. A lengthy roster of in-vogue sharing plates feature; the sushi is exemplary.

Closed 25 December

LONDON SW8

FIUME
PLAN 4, H1

◎◎ ITALIAN

020 3904 9010 | Circus West, Battersea Power Station, SW8 5BN

www.fiume-restaurant.co.uk

This modern restaurant within the Battersea Power Station redevelopment offers a stripped-back decor with industrial decor plus an open-plan kitchen with a pizza oven that takes centre stage. The seasonally changing menus offer Italian dishes from Sardinia with a modern twist. A full wine list with a well-stocked bar and a cocktail menu backs it all up.

Chef Francesco Mazzei, Francesco Chiarelli **Seats** 90 **Open** All Year **Prices from** S £7, M £10.50, D £6.50 **Notes** Vegetarian dishes, Children welcome

LONDON SW10

Maze Grill Park Walk
PLAN 4, C1

◉ MODERN AMERICAN, JAPANESE

020 7495 2211 | 11 Park Walk, SW10 0AJ

www.gordonramsayrestaurants.com/maze-grill-park-walk

On one side of the room at Maze Grill Park Walk is a neat line of marble tables at olive-green banquettes, on the other is a long bar. The place takes inspiration from Manhattan grill rooms, so beef is king here.

Open All Year

Medlar Restaurant
PLAN 4, D1

◉◉◉ MODERN EUROPEAN ▲ NOTABLE WINE LIST

020 7349 1900 | 438 King's Road, Chelsea, SW10 0LJ

www.medlarrestaurant.co.uk

At the World's End end of Kings Road, Medlar's pavement terrace is a pull in fine weather; inside the place goes for a discreet simplicity, with mint-green banquettes, cheery splashes of modern art, and crisply clothed tables reflected in distressed mirror panels. Cheery staff create an easygoing ambience, while the kitchen deals in modern European dishes that deploy a broad range of top-class components in well-defined precision. Tagliatelle with braised oxtail, chestnuts, chanterelles and crosnes open proceedings with an impressive interplay of textures and crystal-clear flavours. There's a similarly refreshing lack of faff, too, with a full-on main course starring wild Scottish venison, the rump served ruby red and tender alongside braised shoulder, crushed carrot and swede, cime di rapa and pickled walnut. At the end, a classic rendition of tarte Tatin is as good as you're likely to encounter anywhere, particularly when it's matched with the cleansing tang of crème fraîche ice cream.

Chef Joe Mercer Nairne **Seats** 85, Private dining 28 **Closed** Christmas and 1 January **Notes** Vegetarian dishes, Children welcome

LONDON SW11

London House
PLAN 1, E3

◉◉ MODERN BRITISH 1, E3

020 7592 8545 | 7-9 Battersea Square, Battersea Village, SW11 3RA

www.gordonramsayrestaurants.com/london-house

Smack on the corner of lovely Battersea Square, Gordon Ramsay's neighbourhood restaurant and bar is just the outfit everyone would love on their doorstep. The kitchen's creative modern British brasserie-style repertoire displays the same unmistakeable gloss; think simplicity, precision, flavour and flair.

Open All Year

LONDON SW14

Rick Stein, Barnes
PLAN 1, D2

◉ SEAFOOD

020 8878 9462 | 125 Mortlake High Street, Barnes, SW14 8SN

www.rickstein.com/eat-with-us/barnes/

The Stein empire's first foray into London sees bottle-green banquettes and brass edged tables add class to the conservatory-style space. The globetrotting menu parades fish and seafood dishes inspired by Rick Stein's TV travels: simple, light-touch treatments that let the top-class ingredients do the talking.

Open All Year

LONDON SW17

Chez Bruce
PLAN 1, E2

◎◎◎ MODERN BRITISH NOTABLE WINE LIST

020 8672 0114 | 2 Bellevue Road, Wandsworth
Common, SW17 7EG
www.chezbruce.co.uk

Overlooking leafy Wandsworth Common, the
discreet aubergine-coloured frontage of Bruce
Poole's high-flying neighbourhood restaurant sits
discreetly in a parade of shops. A beacon of top-
notch culinary achievement since 1995, the place
doesn't need a celebrity chef, a social media
storm or a glossy West End location to bring in
the punters, preferring the unshouty approach of
a white-walled dining room hung with tasteful
art, furnished with linen-clad tables on
herringbone parquet floors, and alive with the
civilized hum of people revelling in splendid
gastronomy. It's a setting that suits Poole's
unfussy but highly classy cooking to perfection,
the roots of the modern European menu deeply
imbedded in France and the Mediterranean. Start
with the visceral punch of sautéed duck hearts
with pearl barley, roast new season garlic,
smoked sausage and parsley, then move on to
the indulgent sensuality of roast pork and trotter
sausage with a peerless supporting cast of
girolles, lardons, coco de Paimpol beans and
salsa verde. To finish, there's a cheeseboard
humming with ripeness, or a chocoholic's delight
of warm chocolate pudding with praline parfait.

Chef Bruce Poole, Matt Christmas **Seats** 75, Private
dining 16 **Closed** 24–26 December and 1 January
Notes Vegetarian dishes, Children at lunch only

LONDON SW19

The Fox & Grapes
PLAN 1, D2

◎ TRADITIONAL BRITISH

020 8619 1300 | 9 Camp Road, Wimbledon, SW19 4UN
www.foxandgrapeswimbledon.co.uk

On the edge of Wimbledon Common, the
18th-century Fox & Grapes has morphed into a
contemporary food-oriented pub with an airy
open-plan interior of oak floors, wood panelling,
and chunky bare wooden tables, and mismatched
chairs wrapped around a central island bar.

Open All Year

Hotel du Vin Wimbledon
PLAN 1, D1

◎ MODERN BRITISH, EUROPEAN

020 8879 1464 | Cannizaro House, West Side,
Wimbledon Common, SW19 4UE
www.hotelduvin.co.uk

Located in Cannizaro House, an eye-poppingly
posh late-Georgian mansion, this Bistro du Vin is
split into two areas, the main part being the
orangery. From the menu you might start with
scallop ceviche marinated in lime juice, salt,
sugar, pomegranate, chilli and coriander and
follow with sole meunière.

Open All Year

The Light House Restaurant
PLAN 1, D1

◎ MODERN INTERNATIONAL, EUROPEAN

020 8944 6338 | 75–77 Ridgway, Wimbledon, SW19 4ST
www.lighthousewimbledon.com

The Light House is a beacon of fresh seasonal
cooking just a short stroll from Wimbledon
Common. Appealing menus of fresh, modern
bistro-style dishes are the deal, with plenty of
sunny, Mediterranean flavours being cooked up
in the open kitchen.

Closed 25–26 December, 1 January

The White Onion
PLAN 1, D1

◎◎ CONTEMPORARY FRENCH

020 8947 8278 | 67 High Street, Wimbledon, SW19 5EE
www.thewhiteonion.co.uk

This smart-casual bistro fits the bill for its well-
heeled neighbourhood. With a sleek look of deep
teal blue and white walls, bright modern
artworks, buttoned leather banquettes and bare
wood tables, it's a suitable setting for sparkily
confident modern French cooking that gives star
billing to excellent seasonal ingredients.

Chef Frédéric Duval, Ondrej Hula **Seats** 68, Private
dining 22 **Closed** 30 July to 15 August and 24 December
to 10 January **Prices from** S £9.50, M £15, D £8
Notes Vegetarian dishes, Children welcome

LONDON W1

Alain Ducasse at The Dorchester PLAN 4, G6

@@@@ CONTEMPORARY, MODERN FRENCH *V* ❧ NOTABLE WINE LIST

020 7629 8866 | The Dorchester, 53 Park Lane, W1K 1QA

www.alainducasse-dorchester.com

The notion of the maître cuisinier overseeing a flotilla of exclusive dining rooms across the known world may seem a little forbidding in these straitened times, but it remains a powerful exemplar of what aspirational restaurateuring is about. Alain Ducasse undoubtedly fits the model to a T, and The Dorchester makes a suitably grand setting for the London iteration of his culinary practice. It's an understated space, let it be said, elegant enough to be sure, but essentially pitched at the neutral end of the spectrum, the pierced curvilinear screen that shields the entrance distantly suggesting British post-war abstract sculpture.

The kitchen here is the preserve of Jean-Philippe Blondet, who supervises a menu that remains a beacon of constancy in a changing culinary landscape. These are dishes burnished to a high degree of accomplishment through long acquaintance, from the crab tourteau with celeriac and caviar, through medallion of farmhouse veal and sweetbreads with carrots, to the rum-laced babas to finish. That is not to suggest that the menu doesn't develop – look to Anjou pigeon with aubergine and lemon balm for a peek into the unfamiliar. The Menu Jardin vegetarian six-courser may be a pleasant surprise in the context. The quartet of French cheeses with individual dressings should not be missed.

Chef Jean-Philippe Blondet, Thibault Hauchard, Alberto Gobbo **Seats** 82, Private dining 30 **Closed** 1st week in January, Easter weekend, 3 weeks in August, 26–30 December **Parking** 20 **Notes** Vegetarian dishes, No children under 10 years

Alyn Williams at The Westbury PLAN 2, H1

@@@@ MODERN EUROPEAN *V* ❧ NOTABLE WINE LIST

See opposite

Amaranto at Four Seasons Hotel London at Park Lane PLAN 4, G6

@@ ITALIAN *V*

020 7319 5206 | Hamilton Place, Park Lane, W1J 7DR

www.fourseasons.com/london/dining/restaurants/amaranto_restaurant

Four Seasons stands in modern grandeur at Hyde Park Corner, a distinctly plutocratic node of London. In the restaurant, carefully-crafted Italian dishes embrace the simplicity that everyone seeks in Italian food. The garden terrace is just the ticket in the summer.

Chef Romuald Feger **Seats** 62, Private dining 10 **Open** All Year **Prices from** S £11, M £12, D £8 **Notes** Children welcome

Antidote PLAN 2, J2

@ MODERN EUROPEAN

020 7287 8488 | 12a Newburgh Street, W1F 7RR

www.antidotewinebar.com

Tucked away in a fashionably 'off-the-radar' cobbled lane behind Carnaby Street, Antidote offers the perfect fix for organic/biodynamic wine lovers and foodies alike. Upstairs, above its bustling wine bar, the dining room is a relaxed oasis and the kitchen delivers seasonal modern ideas that work thanks to great ingredients and a light touch.

Seats 45 **Closed** Christmas and bank holidays **Prices from** S £7, M £19, D £6 **Notes** Vegetarian dishes, Children welcome

---

MEET THE CHEF

Oli Marlow

ROGANIC

London, W1, page 272

What inspired you to become a chef?
I realised from an early age how much pleasure I got from eating and found that cooking food can bring so much pleasure to others. I love the fact that in this industry you can never stop learning with the amount of cuisines and styles around the world.

What are the vital ingredients to a successful kitchen?
Having a clear goal or an ambition for what you want the establishment to achieve. Having a driven and passionate team. If you employ passionate people who are pulling in the same direction anything is possible.

What are your favourite foods/ingredients?
A good sandwich, pizza, burgers. The less fuss the better. My favourite ingredients are good shellfish - with good shellfish you don't have to do much, the natural flavours are so incredible and unique.

Alyn Williams at The Westbury

⊛⊛⊛⊛ **MODERN EUROPEAN** 𝑽 ⚭ NOTABLE WINE LIST
020 7183 6426 | 37 Conduit Street, W1S 2YF
www.alynwilliams.com

Alyn Williams continues to explore his own territory at an address that is a fixture among the A-list of Mayfair's five-star hotels. Expect impeccably correct, seamless and unobtrusive service in a glossy space where burnished darkwood panels, huge mirrors and romantic, subtly-backlit alcoves make a confidence-inspiring backdrop for the culinary fireworks to come. Williams has evolved a highly personal take on modern European cuisine, so beetroot, smoked eel, ricotta and pecan combine in an opener of faultlessly composed flavours and textures.

A main course showcasing Cartmel Valley venison alongside roasted and pickled celeriac, black pudding purée and trompette mushrooms also produces seductive results. Dessert brings the simple perfection of blackberries in various forms with marjoram Ice cream. The three-course set lunch offers staggering value for cooking of this class in such a ritzy setting.

Chef Alyn Williams **Seats** 65, Private dining 20 **Closed** 1st 2 weeks January, last 2 weeks August **Notes** Children welcome

Aqua Kyoto
PLAN 2, J2

◉◉ CONTEMPORARY JAPANESE
020 7478 0540 | 240 Regent Street, W1B 3BR
www.aquakyoto.co.uk
The rooftop views from the terrace of this
modern Japanese outfit on the top floor of the
former Dickins & Jones building are great, and
Aqua Kyoto's dining room shimmers with
contemporary style, complementing the knife-
wielding theatre of a sunken centrepiece sushi
bar and robata grill.

Chef Paul Greening **Seats** 110, Private dining 10
Closed 25–26 December and 1 January
Prices from S £4.50, M £15, D £7.50 **Notes** Vegetarian
dishes, Children welcome

Aqua Nueva
PLAN 2, J2

◉◉ MODERN SPANISH
020 7478 0540 | 5th Floor, 240 Regent Street, W1B 3BR
www.aquanueva.co.uk
A lift whizzes you up from ground-floor street life
to jet-set high life at this slick fifth floor
restaurant where people come to see and be
seen while grazing on contemporary renditions
of tapas based on top-class Spanish ingredients.
Pick from a bilingual menu.

Chef Yahir Gonzalez **Seats** 100, Private dining 80
Closed 25–26 December and 1 January
Prices from S £5.50, M £13, D £8 **Notes** Vegetarian
dishes, Children welcome

The Arch London
PLAN 2, F2

◉ MODERN BRITISH
020 7724 0486 | 50 Great Cumberland Place, W1H 7FD
www.thearchlondon.com
Just a short stroll from Marble Arch, The Arch is
a charming hotel spread over seven Georgian
townhouses. A stone oven comes into its own
with some main courses, from game pie to whole
sea bass with orange and rosemary butter.

Chef Gary Durrant **Seats** 66, Private dining 48 **Open** All
Year **Prices from** S £7.50, M £16.50, D £8
Notes Vegetarian dishes, Children welcome

Barrafina Dean Street
PLAN 2, K2

◉◉ SPANISH
020 7813 8016 | 26–27 Dean Street, W1D 3LL
www.barrafina.co.uk
Tapas is the name of the game here at this
bustling plate-glass corner site. The no booking
policy means queues are likely but, once In, you
perch elbow-to-elbow at the marble counter and
tuck into rapid-fire small plates bursting with
flavour. The maximum group size is four.

Chef Angel Zapata Martin **Seats** 28 **Closed** Bank
holidays **Prices from** S £2.80, M £7 **Notes** Vegetarian
dishes, Children welcome

Beck at Brown's
PLAN 2, J1

◉◉ MODERN ITALIAN, INTERNATIONAL
020 7518 4004 | Albemarle Street, Mayfair, W1S 4BP
www.roccofortehotels.com/hotels-and-resorts/
browns-hotel/restaurants-and-bars/beck-at-
browns
Beck at Brown's dining space has been
reimagined by Olga Polizzi to feature high
wooden panelling and large mirrors that create a
clubby atmosphere and a striking frieze of
tropical foliage and colourful birds to add a
sense of fun. Heinz Beck's seasonally changing
menus of classical Italian dishes accompany
a wine list ably nurtured by the enthusiast
Itallian sommilier.

Chef Heinz Beck, Heros de Agostinis **Seats** 80 **Open** All
Year **Prices from** S £12, M £24, D £12 **Notes** Vegetarian
dishes, Children welcome

Bellamy's
PLAN 2, H1

◉ FRENCH
020 7491 2727 | 18–18a Bruton Place, W1J 6LY
www.bellamysrestaurant.co.uk
Bellamy's effortlessly classy good looks and
slickly professional service epitomise the chic,
timeless French brasserie genre. Leather
banquettes, tasteful French artworks, white linen
and staff in bow ties and waistcoats add to the
authentic look. The kitchen excels in simple,
clear-flavoured dishes. Fabulous all-French
wines, an afternoon oyster bar and a chic
evening cocktail bar complete the experience.

Chef Stéphane Pacoud **Seats** 70 **Closed** Christmas,
New Year, bank holidays **Prices from** S £9, M £22,
D £8.50 **Notes** Vegetarian dishes, Children welcome

Benares Restaurant

PLAN 2, H1

@ @ MODERN INDIAN *V*

020 7629 8886 | 12a Berkeley Square, W1J 6BS

www.benaresrestaurant.com

In the heart of Mayfair, this restaurant has the buzz of a glamorous nightclub but takes a serious approach when it comes to dining. Combining high-end British ingredients with spices and aromatics the Anglo-Indian cooking always excites with its innovative ideas, precise technique and enticing presentation.

Chef Brinder Narula **Seats** 120, Private dining 36 **Closed** 25 December, 1 January **Prices from** S £14, M £26, D £8 **Notes** No children under 8 years after 7pm

Bentley's Oyster Bar & Grill

PLAN 2, J1

@ BRITISH, IRISH

020 7734 4756 | 11–15 Swallow Street, W1B 4DG

www.bentleys.org

Now over a hundred years old, the illustrious oyster bar is a highly popular, feel-good rendezvous, its canopied terrace a hot ticket for slithering-fresh fish and seafood on a balmy day. Prices lean toward West End scary, but then the ingredients are second to none, the service slick and the wines a superb bunch.

Closed 25 December and 1 January

Berners Tavern

PLAN 2, J2

@ @ MODERN BRITISH

020 7908 7979 | The London EDITION, 10 Berners Street, W1T 3NP

www.bernerstavern.com

This palatial space with a magnificent plaster ceiling, chandelier, and walls crowded with pictures, is nothing like a tavern. Jason Atherton oversees the cooking, which is in his contemporary brasserie style. Restyled classics such as lobster and prawn cocktail get things going nicely.

Chef Phil Carmichael, Jason Atherton **Seats** 145, Private dining 14 **Open** All Year **Prices from** S £12, M £20, D £9 **Notes** Vegetarian dishes, Children welcome

Blanchette

PLAN 2, J2

@ MODERN, TRADITIONAL FRENCH TAPAS *V*

020 7439 8100 | 9 D'Arblay Street, Soho, W1F 8DR

www.blanchettesoho.co.uk

Opened by three brothers from across the Channel, Blanchette delivers imaginative bistro-style French cuisine served as sharing plates. The charcuterie and cheese selections show what this place is all about – salami-style Rosette de Lyon and truffled saucisson from the Rhône region, plus ewes-milk Tomme de Corse and Fourme d'Ambert among the fromages.

Chef Tam Storrar, William Alexander **Seats** 54, Private dining 14 **Prices from** S £5, M £10.25, D £6.25 **Notes** Children welcome

Bocca di Lupo

PLAN 2, K1

@ ITALIAN

020 7734 2223 | 12 Archer Street, W1D 7BB

www.boccadilupo.com

High-energy, high-octane and great fun, Bocca di Lupo rocks. Grab a stool at the long marble bar's 'chef's counter' to enjoy the culinary theatre, or head straight to the restaurant area proper, with its polished wood tables and feature lighting.

Closed 25 December and 1 January

Casita Andina

PLAN 2, K1

@ PERUVIAN

020 3327 9464 | 31 Great Windmill Street, Soho, W1D 7LP

www.andinalondon.com/casita

Canteen eating in the Peruvian style has to be another Soho first. Housed in a building that was a bolthole for actors and artists over the years, the Casita maintains links with its past – at least until the food starts emerging in dazzlingly array.

Open All Year

Cecconi's

PLAN 2, J1

@ @ TRADITIONAL ITALIAN

020 7434 1500 | 5a Burlington Gardens, W1S 1EP

www.cecconis.co.uk

Cecconi's is a classic, from the glamorous Mayfair crew slurping cocktails and cicchetti at the island bar to the black-and-white humbug-striped marble floors, green leather upholstery and slick Italian staff. Dedication to top-class seasonal produce is clear, and it's simply prepared to deliver full-on flavours.

Closed Christmas and New Year

The Chesterfield Mayfair

PLAN 4, H6

@ @ TRADITIONAL BRITISH

020 7491 2622 | 35 Charles Street, Mayfair, W1J 5EB

www.chesterfieldmayfair.com

A fine Georgian property jam-packed with antiques and run with a touch of old-school charm. A suckling pig's cheek croquette looks pretty, with a sliver of black pudding and sweetcorn purée. There's a pre-theatre menu, and afternoon tea is served in the conservatory.

Open All Year

China Tang at The Dorchester

PLAN 4, G6

◉◉ CLASSIC CANTONESE

020 7319 7088 | 53 Park Lane, W1K 1QA
www.chinatanglondon.co.uk

This opulent homage to 1930s Shanghai, now with new carpets, upholstery and wallpaper, elevates classic Cantonese cuisine to a higher level; remember, though this is The Dorchester, so don't expect normal high-street prices. Familiar-sounding, nevertheless, are dim sum, vegetarian soups, roast duck mixed platter, and Szechuan peppercorn-braised Dover sole. Vegetarian, halal and gluten free options are all available.

Chef Chong Choi Fong **Seats** 120, Private dining 80 **Closed** 24–25 December **Prices from** S £6, M £16, D £8 **Notes** Vegetarian dishes, Children under 10 years allowed until 8pm

Clipstone

PLAN 2, H3

◉◉ MODERN EUROPEAN

020 7637 0871 | 5 Clipstone Street, W1W 6BB
www.clipstonerestaurant.co.uk

Clipstone is the more casual sibling of the high-rolling Portland. The corner site has an informal vibe with an open kitchen and cheery, unstuffy service keeping things on course. The menu revolves around bistro-esque sharing plates of simplicity, precision and flavour, bound by a seasonal accent.

Chef Stuart Andrew **Seats** 35 **Closed** Christmas and New Year **Prices from** S £9, M £19, D £7 **Notes** Vegetarian dishes, Children welcome

The Colony Grill Room

PLAN 2, G1

◉ BRITISH, AMERICAN *V*

020 7499 9499 | The Beaumont, 8 Balderton Street, Mayfair, W1K 6TF
www.colonygrillroom.com

On the south side of Oxford Street, not far from Selfridges, The Beaumont is a burnished slice of Mayfair elegance. The dining room's grill concept sees crustacea, grills and steaks arrive as simply honest, hearty fare, all delivered in a richly decorated room with an art deco theme. A number of dishes are prepared at the table to add further theatre.

Chef Christian Turner **Seats** 100, Private dining 45 **Open** All Year **Prices from** S £9.75, M £19.50, D £7.75 **Notes** Vegetarian dishes, Children welcome

Corrigan's Mayfair

PLAN 2, G1

◉◉◉ BRITISH, IRISH *V* NOTABLE WINE LIST

020 7499 9943 | 28 Upper Grosvenor Street, W1K 7EH
www.corrigansmayfair.co.uk

Richard Corrigan's Mayfair flagship delivers a real feel of old-school grandeur in a dining room that is as buffed-up and glossy as you'd expect in the blue-chip postcode. Take in the sleek art deco-style looks and sink into plush navy-blue leather seats and banquettes at linen-clothed tables, while the front-of-house team are as slick as they come. Corrigan's Anglo-Irish food is refined and robust, classical certainly, big on flavour and grounded in honest-to-goodness gutsiness. To kick off, go for grilled mackerel with heavenly oyster cream and the sour kick of apple and gooseberry. Main-course Welsh lamb arrives pink, as meltingly tender as you'd like, with smoky aubergine purée, wilted spinach and fresh peas, while a dessert of pannacotta with zingy passionfruit gel and silky coconut sorbet is equally on the money. With a six-course tasting menu, plus a seasonal set lunchtime menu, and a stellar wine list, Corrigan's is a class act from top to bottom.

Chef Richard Corrigan, Aidan McGee **Seats** 85, Private dining 30 **Closed** 25 December, bank holidays **Prices from** S £16, M £36, D £9 **Notes** Children welcome

Coya

PLAN 4, H6

◉◉ MODERN PERUVIAN

020 7042 7118 | 118 Piccadilly, Mayfair, W1J 7NW
www.coyarestaurant.com

With its open kitchen, a céviche counter, a charcoal grill and a glamorous pisco bar, Coya is a hive of Peruvian-inspired activity. Expect classy food full of entertaining South American and Japanese fusion flavours and some spot-on ingredients in the mix.

Chef Sanjay Dwiveve **Seats** 110, Private dining 12 **Closed** 25 December **Prices from** S £8, M £18, D £9 **Notes** Vegetarian dishes, Children welcome

CUT at 45 Park Lane
PLAN 4, G6

⊛⊛⊛ MODERN AMERICAN *V*

020 7493 4554 | 45 Park Lane, W1K 1BJ

www.dorchestercollection.com/en/london/45-park-lane

The Park Lane glitz of a swanky hotel in the Dorchester stable makes a suitably top-end joint for one of US chef and restaurateur Wolfgang Puck's über-glam international steakhouses. With an extravagant decor of glitterball chandeliers, swathes of curtain, burnished wooden panels and a full set of Damien Hirst 'Psalm' artworks, no-one could fault the jet-set vibe of this temple to top-grade beef sourced from all over the world. Take your pick: Australian and Japanese Wagyu, South Devon Angus, USDA rib-eye steak with fries, all expertly aged, sold by weight, and precision timed on the grill, with eight sauces – Armagnac and green peppercorn, Argentinian chimichurri, or wasabi yuzu kosho butter, say – to go with it. Don't fancy all that red meat? Not a problem, as the menu runs to seared scallops, or steamed sea bass 'Hong Kong' style. Warm dark chocolate Valrhona soufflé is a suitable finish.

Chef David McIntyre **Seats** 70, Private dining 14 **Open** All Year **Prices from** S £14, M £28, D £14 **Notes** Children welcome

Davies and Brook *NEW*
PLAN 2, H1

020 7494 4170 | Brook Street, Mayfair, W1K 4HR

www.claridges.co.uk

As we went to press, Claridges announced that chef Daniel Humm and restaurateur Will Guidara of 'Make It Nice Hospitality' will take the helm at the hotel's new restaurant, set to open in summer 2019. Hopefully, exciting things await.

Chef Daniel Humm

Dehesa
PLAN 2, J1

⊛ SPANISH, ITALIAN

020 7494 4170 | 25 Ganton Street, W1F 9BP

www.saltyardgroup.co.uk/dehesa

Dehesa comes from the same stable as Salt Yard and Opera Tavern and, like them, is a charcuterie and tapas bar serving up a lively hybrid of Spanish and Italian dishes. It's a small, buzzy place where you sit elbow-to-elbow at high-level tables.

Chef William Breese **Seats** 40, Private dining 13 **Closed** 24–26 and 31 December and 1 January **Prices from** S £4.50, M £6.50, D £6.50 **Notes** Vegetarian dishes, Children welcome

Dinings
PLAN 2, E3

⊛⊛ JAPANESE, EUROPEAN

020 7723 0666 | 22 Harcourt Street, W1H 4HH

www.dinings.co.uk

There's scarcely room to swing a chopstick here, but the exquisitely-crafted array of Japanese tapas is the draw. The creative kitchen fuses Japanese and modern European dishes, so check out the blackboard specials, then tackle the lengthy menu by sharing a selection of small but perfectly-formed dishes.

Closed 24–26 December, 31 December and 1 January

Ember Yard
PLAN 2, J2

⊛⊛ SPANISH, ITALIAN

020 7439 8057 | 60–61 Berwick Street, W1F 8SU

www.emberyard.co.uk

Ember Yard is the latest in the chain of uptempo tapas outfits that have been trending in the capital. The food comes inspired by Spain (the Basque country in particular) and Italy, and is smoked or cooked simply on a Basque-style wood and charcoal grill.

Closed 25–26 December

L'Escargot
PLAN 3, A2

⊛⊛ FRENCH, MEDITERRANEAN

020 7439 7474 | 48 Greek Street, W1D 4EF

www.lescargotrestaurant.co.uk

This near-century-old Soho institution serves the rich comforts of classic French cuisine. Occupying a fine Georgian townhouse once home to the Duke of Portland, L'Escargot's sumptuous colours and serious art collection set an elegant old-school scene for cooking that reassures, comforts and thrills from the off.

Chef James Tyrrell **Seats** 80, Private dining 60 **Closed** 25–26 December, 1 January **Prices from** S £8, M £18, D £8 **Notes** Vegetarian dishes, No children under 10 years

Galvin at The Athenaeum
PLAN 4, H6

⊛⊛ MODERN, CLASSIC BRITISH

020 7640 3333 | 116 Piccadilly, W1J 7BJ

www.athenaeumhotel.com

The Athenaeum Hotel's restaurant is another outpost in London chefs Chris and Jeff Galvin's empire. For the first time they've stepped away from their trademark French-inspired menus in favour of an array of menus including afternoon tea and private dining, and feature a modern take on classic British dishes.

Chef William Lloyd Baker **Seats** 90, Private dining 70 **Open** All Year **Prices from** S £8, M £16, D £7.50 **Notes** Vegetarian dishes, No children

Galvin at Windows Restaurant & Bar

PLAN 4, G6

@@@ MODERN FRENCH 𝑉⚑ NOTABLE WINE LIST

020 7208 4021 | London Hilton on Park Lane, 22 Park Lane, W1K 1BE
www.galvinatwindows.com

Of the many different versions of glamour, one of the headiest is eating in the sky, especially when it begins with a voluble greeting from TV celeb host, Fred Sirieix, star of Channel 4's *First Dates*. The views from up here are bracing, with London laid out like an architectural model during the day, and as a filigree of lights after dark. Joo Won produces a dazzling style of Asian-inflected modern European cuisine that scores many a hit. The menu du jour is a bit of a bargain at this level, and might begin with kimchi risotto topped with a slow-cooked egg, sprinkled with spring onions, sesame seeds and parmesan shavings. Then comes pan-fried fillet of sea bass with artichokes, rocket and salted anchovies, or perhaps fillet of Scotch beef with braised short rib, bone marrow and foie gras. Draw things to a satisfying close with pear soufflé, warm salted caramel fudge and cinnamon ice cream.

Chef Joo Won, Chris Galvin **Seats** 130 **Open** All Year **Notes** Vegetarian dishes, Children welcome

Gauthier Soho

PLAN 3, A1

@@@ MODERN FRENCH 𝑉⚑ NOTABLE WINE LIST

020 7494 3111 | 21 Romilly Street, W1D 5AF
www.gauthiersoho.co.uk

Alexis Gauthier's charmingly unmodernised Regency townhouse restaurant, with its iron railings and glossy black front door, certainly stands out from the regular Soho crowd; you even have to ring the bell or knock to enter. Inside, the light-filled first-floor dining room aptly conveys its charm, with original fireplace, striking artworks and tall windows. This is the elegant backdrop for Gauthier's appealing prix-fixe roster that runs the full gambit of carte, lunch and tasting menus (including vegan options) boosted by classy between-course action, plus impressive breads and a sparkling wine list. Take a classy duck and cep ravioli lunch opener, teamed with sautéed girolles, mushroom salad and a duck jus, while roast fillet of sparkling-fresh sea bream is complemented by sweet-and-sour root vegetables, sautéed sea aster and a top-notch fish velouté. Okay, each dish maybe labelled with a calorie count, but

don't hold back on the heavenly dark chocolate tart (70% grand cru) and yogurt sorbet.

Chef Gerard Virolle, Alexis Gauthier **Seats** 60, Private dining 32 **Closed** Christmas, bank holidays **Notes** Children welcome

Le Gavroche Restaurant

PLAN 2, G1

@@@ FRENCH 𝑉

020 7408 0881 | 43 Upper Brook Street, W1K 7QR
www.le-gavroche.co.uk

For over half a century Le Gavroche has been synonymous with classic French cuisine while also playing its part in developing the UK's own culinary identity, thanks to the A-list chefs who have learned the perfection of the traditional ways in its kitchen, then taken their own path. Situated in a smart Mayfair basement, the room sticks to a refined and graceful look that is entirely in keeping with the kind of flawlessly courteous service that has all but disappeared from London's 21st-century dining rooms. Two generations of the Roux family have built a culinary empire on classical French cuisine of the Escoffier era, with discreetly applied modernist notes to tastes and textures, and Michel Roux Jnr, a genially familiar figure from foodie TV, is only too happy to make a tour of the dining room towards the end of service, dressed in his pristine whites, for the selfies. Dishes as straightforward as roasted sea-fresh scallops with fresh peas, pea purée, cured pork and crispy pork crumb are virtuoso displays of culinary artistry, while main-course saddle of Herdwick lamb with turnip, beetroot and fennel is the ultimate in meaty comfort food.

Chef Michel Roux Jnr **Seats** 60, Private dining 6 **Closed** Christmas, New Year and bank holidays **Notes** Children welcome

Goodman

PLAN 2, J1

@ BRITISH, CLASSIC AMERICAN

020 7499 3776 | 26 Maddox Street, W1S 1QH
www.goodmanrestaurants.com

There's plenty of red meat action going on for die-hard carnivores in this upscale New York-inspired steakhouse serving prime slabs of US and UK beef. Choose your cut, from rib-eye, through bone-in sirloin to porterhouse, and it arrives precision timed and served with béarnaise, pepper or Stilton sauces.

Closed Christmas, New Year, bank holidays

The Greenhouse
PLAN 4, H6

◉◉◉◉ MODERN FRENCH *V* ⓝ NOTABLE WINE LIST

020 7499 3331 | 27a Hay's Mews, Mayfair, W1J 5NY
www.greenhouserestaurant.co.uk

A succession of top-flight chefs has headed up the kitchen at The Greenhouse over the decades, cementing its place in the premier league of the UK's culinary destinations. Alex Dilling took the reins in 2018, and keeps standards in rarefied territory with his refined, hyper-focused take on contemporary cooking. The Mayfair mews location promises discreet, high-end pleasures, approached along a decked pathway through a delightful, tranquil garden – sadly, alfresco dining is not on the cards. Inside, the soothing decor establishes a connection with nature via views of the garden from the serenely stylish dining room; restful shades of beige and ivory are offset by dark wood floors, tables dressed in pristine white linen, and a feature wall with a filigree display of tree branches to echo the garden theme.

Things start with a precise and intricate presentation – spheres of velvety foie gras parfait pointed up with lemongrass gel, marinated Cévennes onion, lemon thyme leaves and mushrooms dusted with cep powder. Then there's rabbit loin, wrapped in the gentle smokiness of Alsace bacon and matched with wild mustard leaf, a pasta shell filled with confit rabbit shoulder, and a glossy mustard-spiked jus. Dessert could be an elegant confection involving coconut, Piedmont hazelnut and white chocolate.

Chef Alex Dilling **Seats** 60, Private dining 12 **Closed** Christmas, bank holidays **Notes** Children welcome

Gridiron by COMO *NEW*
PLAN 4, H6

◉◉ GRILL

020 7447 1000 | COMO Metropolitan London, Old Park Lane, W1K 1LB
www.comohotels.com/metropolitanlondon

One of several dining possibilities at this urbane Park Lane hotel, Gridiron is a quietly luxurious grill restaurant. Sit up close and personal with the fiery action at the marble counter overlooking the open kitchen, or park at a leather seat or banquette to tuck into precision-seared meats and fish of the highest quality.

The Grill at The Dorchester
PLAN 4, G6

◉◉ MODERN BRITISH

020 7317 6531 | Park Lane, W1K 1QA
www.dorchestercollection/london/the-dorchester

There's a been a Grill Room at the Dorchester since 1931 and today's version is a shimmering and elegant room. Save room for one of the delicious desserts, and try once of the famous sweet soufflés (sticky toffee, for example with salted caramel ice cream). Or try a classic Sunday Roast experience with carvings done tableside on the trolley.

Chef Guy Fenton **Seats** 65 **Parking** 20 **Notes** Vegetarian dishes, Children welcome

GYMKHANA
PLAN 4, J6

◉◉ CONTEMPORARY INDIAN *V*

020 3011 5900 | 42 Albermarle Street, W1S 4JH
gymkhanalondon.com

At the time of going to press Gymkhana was closed due to a fire – please check their website for further details. Gymkhana may look like a colonial-era Indian gentlemen's club with its dark oak panelling, marble tables in rattan-trimmed booths, swishing ceiling fans, and boar's head on the wall, but there's nothing retro about its inventive new-wave Indian cooking.

Chef Karam Sethi, Sid Ahuja **Seats** 90, Private dining 15 **Closed** Christmas, 1 January **Notes** Children welcome until 7pm

Hakkasan
PLAN 2, K2

◉◉ MODERN CHINESE

020 7927 7000 | 8 Hanway Place, W1T 1HD
www.hakkasan.com

Escape the Oxford Street crowds in this chic basement and you're immediately seduced by its modern Chinoiserie design, super-cool cocktail bar and uptempo, nightclubby vibe. Innovative new-wave and classic Cantonese dishes cover all bases, and luxury ingredients abound. A heavyweight wine list and an exciting cocktail selection completes the picture.

Closed 25 December

Hakkasan Mayfair

PLAN 2, H1

◉◉◉ MODERN CANTONESE, CHINESE
020 7907 1888 | 17 Bruton Street, W1J 6QB
www.hakkasan.com

The Mayfair branch of the now global Hakkasan chain is discretely tucked away just off Berkeley Square and certainly exemplifies the brands super-cool DNA, with its contemporary mix of seductive design and dazzling east-meets-west Cantonese cuisine. A long entrance corridor leads to the ground-floor dining room with its smart low-slung leather seating and sexy bar, while downstairs is a more intimate, nightclubby space enclosed by intricately carved wood screens. Wherever you sit, a high-gloss high-octane approach abounds; from the slick, informed service to the kitchen's vibrant reimaginings of traditional Cantonese dishes, all immaculately dressed to thrill and delivered with polished technique and tip-top ingredients. Divine dim sum encompasses the likes of caviar-dotted abalone and chicken shu mai to royal king crab jade dumplings. House speciality mains take in roasted silver cod with champagne and honey to spicy prawn with lily bulb and almond, or melt-in-the-mouth stir-fry black pepper rib-eye beef with merlot. Desserts prolong the thrill factor; think yuzu tart with burnt meringue, confit citrus and yuzu ice cream. The fixed-price lunch is considered a steal at this pitch.

Chef Tong Chee Hwee, Tan Tee Wei **Seats** 220, Private dining 16 **Closed** 25 December **Prices from** S £9, M £19, D £8 **Notes** Vegetarian dishes, Children welcome

Heddon Street Kitchen

PLAN 2, J1

◉ MODERN BRITISH *V*
020 7592 1212 | 3-9 Heddon Street, Regent Street Food Quarter, W1B 4BD
www.heddonstreetkitchen.co.uk

In a pedestrianised oasis just off Regent Street, Ramsay's contemporary take on the brasserie theme spreads over two floors, mingling industrial chic with macho leather and wood textures that suit the local vibe. The all-day menu aims to please all comers.

Chef Dario Catapano **Seats** 180, Private dining 12 **Open** All Year **Notes** Vegetarian dishes, Children welcome

Hélène Darroze at The Connaught

PLAN 2, H1

◉◉◉◉ FRENCH *V*
020 3147 7200 | Carlos Place, W1K 2AL
www.the-connaught.co.uk

Four generations, including Hélène herself, have worked in the Darroze family restaurant in Acquitaine. After graduating, she worked for top chef Alain Ducasse in Monaco, before opening her own restaurant in Paris, then joining The Connaught. She now shuttles weekly between the two capitals to keep a close eye on both. Her French culinary craft is showcased amid the splendour of Iranian designer India Mahdavi's sophisticated interior, with Damien Hirst artworks on the wall, and glass cloches displaying the visual appeal of the ingredients found in her cooking. With places to sip champagne, tuck into a magnificent afternoon tea, or dine pretty much any time of the day, it's a truly high-class location. Menus reveal the source of each dish's main element, thus a weekday lunch lobster hails from St Ives in Cornwall; the lamb from the Rhug Estate in Corwen, north Wales; and a dessert's rhubarb is grown in West Yorkshire's famous Rhubarb Triangle. Looking more closely at a couple of dishes reveals the full extent – apart from the actual eating – of her approach: lobster is served with highly prized Pertuis green asparagus, morel and vin jaune d'Arbois; and the highest grade (A5) of Wagyu beef with parsnip, arabica coffee and sansho pepper. Unlike some places, vegetarians are no mere afterthought, with dedicated menus offering, for example, Italian acquerello rice with white asparagus, seaweed and lemon; and beetroot with capers and balsamic vinegar. Pre-ordained wine flights may be added at a price, or you can select your own, maybe with the help of one of the team of sommeliers, who will advise on whether to select a Left or Right Bank Bordeaux, or talk you through the whites from the Weingut Keller Collection, one of Germany's truly great estates. Service at every stage strikes a pleasing balance between slick professionalism and relaxed confidence.

Chef Hélène Darroze **Seats** 60, Private dining 100 **Notes** No children under 7 years

Hide – Ground NEW

PLAN 4, H6

◉◉ MODERN BRITISH *V*

020 3146 8666 | 85 Piccadilly, W1J 7NB

www.hide.co.uk/restaurant/ground

This multi-floor dining operation features an all-day dining operation on the 'Ground' floor. No expense has been spared with the refit of this swanky restaurant and there's lots of attention to detail. The floor-to-ceiling windows look onto the street and Green Park beyond. The slick polished service presents modern British/European fare. A vast, oak staircase transports you to 'Above', the fine-dining restaurant upstairs. There's also a bar called 'Below'.

Chef Ollie Dabbous **Seats** 100, Private dining 16 **Closed** 25 December, 1 January **Prices from** S £18, M £26, D £4 **Notes** Children welcome

HIX Soho

PLAN 2, J1

◉ BRITISH *V*

020 7292 3518 | 66–70 Brewer Street, W1F 9UP

www.hixrestaurants.co.uk/restaurant/hix-soho

The mothership of Mark Hix's restaurant empire pays homage to Brit Art with an eclectic collection of works by celebrated artists like Damien Hirst and Sarah Lucas, while the patriotic brasserie fare celebrates seasonality and the UK's splendid regional produce.

Chef Rodrigo Agapito **Seats** 70, Private dining 10 **Closed** 25–26 December and 1 January **Prices from** S £4.50, M £17.50, D £2 **Notes** Children welcome

Indian Accent

PLAN 2, J1

◉◉ MODERN INDIAN

020 7629 9802 | 16 Albemarle Street, Mayfair, W1S 4HW

www.indianaccent.com

With outposts in New Delhi and New York, this swanky Mayfair sibling brings merit to London's vibrant, high-end Indian dining scene. Opposite Brown's Hotel, its dining space, spread over two floors, is a magnet for the international jet-set. The decor mirrors the deep wallets.

Open All Year

Inko Nito NEW

PLAN 2, J2

◉ MODERN JAPANESE

020 3959 2650 | 55 Broadwick Street, Soho, W1F 9QS

inkonitorestaurant.com

A smoking robata grill is the engine room at the heart of this buzzy Japanese eatery. For close-up cheffy action, go for one of the seats at the counter, otherwise settle at one of the blond wood tables in the capacious dining room. The food offers a creative take on Japanese classics, and the mood is upbeat.

Chef Christian Onia **Closed** 25 December **Notes** Vegetarian dishes, Children welcome

Jamavar

PLAN 2, H1

◉◉ INDIAN

020 7499 1800 | 8 Mount Street, Mayfair, W1K 3NF

www.jamavarrestaurants.com

A smart Mayfair location suits this stylish restaurant. It's spread over two floors, with dark wood tables and Indian-inspired artwork and brass-framed mirrors. Staff are efficient and friendly, and menus showcase a wide array of flavours from across India.

JW Steakhouse

PLAN 2, G1

◉ AMERICAN

020 7399 8460 | Grosvenor House Hotel, Park Lane, W1K 7TN

www.jwsteakhouse.co.uk

The expansive JW brings American-style steakhouse dining to the Grosvenor House in an ambience of black and white ceramic floor tiles and parquet, dressers and a menu offering variations of cuts and sauces. The beef is either thoroughbred USDA-approved or grass-fed Aberdeen Angus.

Open All Year

Kai Mayfair

PLAN 4, G6

◉◉ MODERN CHINESE

020 7493 8988 | 65 South Audley Street, W1K 2QU

www.kaimayfair.co.uk

This swanky Chinese restaurant is decorated in glossy Mayfair style, with arty photographs on the walls. Judicious use of spicing and seasoning, and subtle combinations of flavours and textures are hallmarks. The menu opens unusually with desserts, showing how seriously they are taken here.

Closed 25–26 December and 1 January

KANISHKA *NEW*
PLAN 2, J1

ⓖⓖ MODERN INDIAN *V*

020 3978 0978 | 17–19 Maddox Street, W1S 2QH

www.kanishkarestaurant.co.uk

Atul Kochhar's sophisticated restaurant just a short stroll from Bond Street focuses on regional cooking from the north-east of India. A meal might begin with smoked chilli-spiced diver scallops paired with textures of cauliflower. For main course, roasted Gressingham duck breast appears with smoked tomato sauce, potato salad and crispy poha.

Chef Shishir Kumarsinha **Open** All Year **Prices from** S £10, M £18 **Notes** No children

The Keeper's House
PLAN 2, J1

ⓖ MODERN BRITISH

020 7300 5881 | Royal Academy of Arts, Burlington House, Piccadilly, W1J 0BD

www.keepershouse.org.uk

Originally a grace-and-favour residence in the 19th century for the steward of the Royal Academy collections, The Keeper's House has an intimate restaurant tucked away in its basement. Done out with green felt walls, cream leather buttoned banquettes and dramatic classical friezes, it's a stylish space to indulge in a menu of light-touch modern British and European cooking.

Kitchen Table
PLAN 2, J3

ⓖⓖⓖ MODERN BRITISH *V*

020 7637 7770 | 70 Charlotte St, W1T 4QG

kitchentablelondon.co.uk

Advance through the hot dogs and champagne going on out front, and behind a curtain at the back is what feels like a secret gourmands' club, where devotees gather round a counter for an up-close interface with the sizzles and scents of a kitchen in full gear. A multi-course tasting menu chalked up in abbreviations on the board is the drill, delivering small morsels of outstanding, always surprising food. Highlights include a crab bisque with matching custard crowned with Thai basil; rhubarb-wrapped mackerel on seaweed salsa and horseradish cream; and the fascinating contrasts of ribboned squid cooked in chicken fat and topped with preserved gooseberry. Fruit with fish is a confirmed trend as when sea bass appears with elderberry, and there's also a needle-sharp clementine sauce with the pigeon. Desserts then maintain the pace by exploring apples and pears in dazzling variety, the former appearing with sorrel granita, shortbread and chamomile custard.

Chef James Knappett **Seats** 20 **Closed** Christmas and summer (check website for details) **Notes** No children

Kitty Fisher's
PLAN 4, H6

ⓖⓖ MODERN BRITISH

020 3302 1661 | 10 Shepherd Market, W1J 7QF

www.kittyfishers.com

Closely packed tables and stools at the bar offer diners two options in this low-lit, atmospheric, Bohemian-style restaurant with red velvet banquettes, retro light fittings and candles. The modern British food is driven by what's available at the market on the day.

Chef George Barson **Seats** 36 **Closed** 25 December, 1 January and bank holidays **Prices from** S £4, M £22, D £6 **Notes** Vegetarian dishes, Children welcome

Laurent at Café Royal *NEW*
PLAN 2, J1

ⓖⓖ SUSHI, GRILL

020 7406 3333 | Hotel Café Royal, 68 Regent Street, W1B 4DY

www.hotelcaferoyal.com

On the first floor of the glamorous Hotel Café Royal, this spiffy Regent Street restaurant rises to the occasion with a handsome decor of bronze and grey hues, chocolate brown leather seats and a showpiece Murano glass chandelier. The menu keeps skinnies happy with delicate sushi and sashimi, while at the same time satisfying carnivores with grilled prime beef.

Levant
PLAN 2, G2

ⓖ LEBANESE, MIDDLE EASTERN

020 7224 1111 | Jason Court, 76 Wigmore Street, W1U 2SJ

www.levant.co.uk

Levant delivers the authentic flavours of the Middle East, along with an exotic Aladdin's-cave decor of rich fabrics, carved wood, candlelight and lamps. Small plates for grazing and sharing are the way to start, while freshly cooked meat dishes are succulent and full of flavour.

Closed 25–26 December

Lima
PLAN 2, K3

ⓖⓖ MODERN PERUVIAN

020 3002 2640 | 31 Rathbone Place, Fitzrovia, W1T 1JH

www.limalondongroup.com/fitzrovia

Named after Peru's capital, this trendy, high-octane restaurant brings a refined take on that country's contemporary cuisine to the West End. Excellent British and Peruvian ingredients are the backbone, all handled confidently and skilfully to produce pretty little plates of knockout flavours.

Chef Robert Ortiz, Virgilio Martinez **Seats** 70 **Closed** Christmas **Prices from** S £9, M £20, D £8 **Notes** Vegetarian dishes, No children under 12 years after 7pm

Locanda Locatelli

PLAN 2, G2

◉◉◉ ITALIAN ● NOTABLE WINE LIST

020 7935 9088 | 8 Seymour Street, W1H 7JZ

www.locandalocatelli.com

TV star Giorgio Locatelli's culinary career began by the shore of Lake Comabbio in the Lombardy region of northern Italy, a provenance that attunes him precisely to one of the prevalent currents of British gastronomy. Italian classical cooking, gently modernised but staying true to its principles of honesty and simplicity, will never lack for devotees. Curving booth seating in stone-coloured leather, etched glass screens and mirrors make for an ambience of refined civility, naturally, but the generously proportioned tables are designed with convivial family dining in mind. Traditionally structured menus open with compendious antipasti salads, before pasta makes its appearance, perhaps via spaghetti with octopus. Principal dishes command the attention with majestic fish – monkfish with walnut and caper sauce – or pan-fried calf's kidneys with potato purée and stewed lentils. Finish with tiramisù, naturally, or perhaps bayleaf pannacotta, orange, basil and grapefruit compôte with lemon biscuit and green olives.

Chef Giorgio Locatelli **Seats** 85, Private dining 50 **Closed** 24-26 December, 1 January **Prices from** S £14.50, M £17, D £8.50 **Notes** Vegetarian dishes, Children welcome

The Mandeville Hotel

PLAN 2, G2

◉ MODERN BRITISH

020 7935 5599 | Mandeville Place, W1U 2BE

www.mandeville.co.uk

Understated contemporary decor and a calming ambience are the hallmarks of this stylish boutique hotel, while unclothed tables and bottle-green banquettes set the tone in the restaurant. Familiar-sounding Black Forest cake and apple tart Tatin can be found on the menu.

Open All Year

The Mayfair Chippy

PLAN 2, G1

◉ BRITISH

020 7741 2233 | North Audley Street, W1K 6WE

www.mayfairchippy.com

As a pairing, Mayfair and Chippy breaks new ground, and so it should. This wealthy quarter of W1 has as much right to a quintessentially British fish and chip restaurant as anywhere else. And it certainly looks the part too.

Chef Pete Taylor, Desiree Inezhaley **Seats** 45, Private dining 14 **Closed** 25 December and 1 January **Prices from** S £3.25, M £8.25, D £5.25 **Notes** Vegetarian dishes, Children welcome

Mele e Pere

PLAN 2, J1

◉ ITALIAN

020 7096 2096 | 46 Brewer Street, Soho, W1F 9TF

www.meleepere.co.uk

'Apples and Pears' looks a riot of colour and conviviality on its Soho corner. At ground-floor level is a café area, but the main dining goes on downstairs in a dynamic, russet-walled basement room. Italian sharing plates are the principal draw to start, with San Daniele ham and gnocchi, deep-fried squid and smoked aïoli, or beef carpaccio with pecorino among the offerings.

Chef Andrea Mantovani **Seats** 90 **Closed** 25-26 December and 1 January **Notes** Vegetarian dishes, Children welcome

Mere

PLAN 2, J3

◉◉◉ MODERN EUROPEAN V ● NOTABLE WINE LIST

020 7268 6565 | 74 Charlotte Street, W1T 4QH

www.mere-restaurant.com

You may know Monica Galetti best from her terrifying appearances as a judge on *MasterChef: The Professionals*, but she's also a former Michel Roux Jr/Le Gavroche protégée and Mere, (pronounced 'Mary' – a play on the French for mother and Monica's mother's name) is her restaurant. It's classily understated; a sophisticated, grown-up space, with a smart bar at ground level, while downstairs the dining room is unexpectedly light, thanks to its double-height glass frontage. The cooking is contemporary French-European with Western Samoan and Kiwi touches, and the expected consummate skill and attention to detail comes with a refined approach, backed by flavour and panache. Take an opener of springy tender octopus, with a sweet-sharp tomato reduction and caper condiment, finished with parsley oil, or perhaps a star-turn squab pigeon main (soft pink roasted breast and crispy skinned leg), with peach (adding a balanced sweetness), girolles and Earl Grey. Service is informed, professional but relaxed, and the wine list is a corker.

Chef Monica Galetti **Seats** 60, Private dining 10 **Closed** Bank holidays **Prices from** S £13, M £23, D £11 **Notes** Children welcome

Le Meridien Piccadilly

PLAN 2, J1

@ MODERN BRITISH

020 7734 8000 | 21 Piccadilly, W1J 0BH

www.lemeridienpiccadilly.com

Within Le Meridien is a series of vast public rooms, including the impressive Terrace and Baran atrium-style space with a curved glass ceiling, columns and dark wood tables. The menu features grills from Red Poll rib-eye to lamb cutlets, but there's plenty more of interest.

Open All Year

Mews of Mayfair

PLAN 2, H1

@ MODERN BRITISH

020 7518 9388 | 10-11 Lancashire Court, New Bond Street, Mayfair, W1S 1EY

www.mewsofmayfair.com

The Mayfair set converge on this stylish bar and restaurant, hidden from the Bond Street crowds on a narrow cobbled alleyway. With its terrace tables and roll-back doors, it feels more Mediterranean than West End. The cocktail bar and basement lounge make a glam statement.

Chef Andrew Bennet **Seats** 70, Private dining 28 **Closed** 25 December **Prices from** S £7.50, M £12, D £6 **Notes** Vegetarian dishes, Children welcome

The Montagu Kitchen

PLAN 2, F2

@@ MODERN BRITISH

020 7299 2037 | Hyatt Regency London – The Churchill, 30 Portman Square, W1H 7BH

themontagurestaurant.co.uk

Located within a five-star hotel, this all-day dining destination features a relaxed and welcoming environment and serves up seasonally changing menus of smart, modern British ideas using British produce. There are great views over Portman Square and it's all just a short walk from Oxford Street and Marylebone.

Chef **Seats** 60 **Open** All Year **Prices from** S £12, M £21, D £7 **Notes** Vegetarian dishes, Children welcome

Murano

PLAN 4, H6

@@@@ MODERN EUROPEAN, ITALIAN INFLUENCE ● NOTABLE WINE LIST

020 7495 1127 | 20 Queen Street, W1J 5PP

www.muranolondon.com

Lurking amid office buildings on the business side of Mayfair, Angela Hartnett's upscale Italian is all about creature comforts, with yielding upholstery and thick carpets, mirrored surfaces and dark wood trim in a punctiliously well-patrolled room. Simplicity and freshness may be the Italian watchwords as ever, but often those impressions disguise a great deal of preliminary labour, as here where each dish is fine-tuned to a supremely satisfying pitch. Look at the sheer-textured pasta in a starter of pumpkin tortelli in sage butter, its filling silky, the final touch of genius a scattering of smashed amaretti. Fish could be beautifully tender pollock in parsley velouté with charred calçot onion and spicy 'nduja crumble, or there may be a winter warmer of melting venison loin in its own ragù, with smooth celeriac purée, red cabbage and delicate gnocchi. In spring, Herdwick lamb comes into its own, the braised neck and sweetbreads served with the sharpening element of goat curd and a slew of freshly popped peas. For dessert, there's an irresistible Amalfi lemon tart, served slightly warm and sharp enough to produce a pleasurable sucking-in of cheeks, or the signature pistachio soufflé with luxurious hot chocolate sauce.

Chef Angela Hartnett, Emily Brightman **Seats** 46, Private dining 12 **Closed** Christmas **Notes** Vegetarian dishes, Children welcome

The Ninth

PLAN 2, K3

@@@ MODERN FRENCH, MEDITERRANEAN

020 3019 0880 | 22 Charlotte Street, W1T 2NB

www.theninthlondon.com

New York-born chef-patron (and TV regular) Jun Tanaka has over two decades of working in starry kitchens. There's uncomplicated logic behind the outfit's name, as it's simply the ninth place he's worked in, but here he shuns fine-dining pretension for relaxed good looks and a menu of stand-out sharing plates that shout precision, flavour and flair. Spread across two floors with a bar on each, the decor scores high in the stripped-back cool stakes, with exposed brick walls, decorated concrete and floorboards and eye-catching statement pieces. Leather banquettes and café-style chairs provide chilled-out comforts alongside mahogany or white marble-topped tables. The light Mediterranean menu is underpinned by Tanaka's classic French background, and bursts with refined simplicity, confidence, flavour and seasonality. Take grilled pink-perfection lamb cutlets teamed with anchovy and charred hispi cabbage, or perhaps wild sea bass (with a basil crust) accompanied by salsify and tardivo (Italian radicchio). The fixed-price lunch menu is a steal.

Chef Jun Tanaka **Seats** 84, Private dining 22 **Closed** Bank holidays **Prices from** S £9, M £19, D £9 **Notes** Vegetarian dishes, Children welcome

Nobu Berkeley ST
PLAN 4, H6

@@ JAPANESE, PERUVIAN
020 7290 9222 | 15 Berkeley Street, W1J 8DY
www.noburestaurants.com
Nobu draws in the Mayfair fashionistas who come for the see-and-be-seen buzz of the bar, or the cool minimalist restaurant. Traditionalists can head straight for the sushi bar, or for some fun DIY dining with chefs supervising your efforts around a sunken hibachi grill.

Chef Mark Edwards, Rhys Cattermoul **Seats** 180 **Closed** 25 December **Notes** Vegetarian dishes, Children welcome

Nobu Old Park Lane
PLAN 4, H6

@@ JAPANESE, PERUVIAN
020 7447 4747 | COMO Metropolitan London, Old Park Lane, W1K 1LB
www.noburestaurants.com
Since opening 33 years ago, Nobu's brand of Japanese-Peruvian cooking remains highly popular. Classics include hot yellowtail sashimi with jalapeño, and cold baby tiger shrimp with three different sauces. On the seemingly endless menu too are sushi, grilled or stir-fried yakimono dishes, and omakase – tasting dishes that the chef chooses. Anticucho rib-eye steak is a Peruvian representative.

Chef Mark Edwards, Hideki Maeda **Seats** 160, Private dining 40 **Closed** 25 December, 1 January **Notes** Vegetarian dishes, Children welcome

NOPI
PLAN 2, J1

@ MEDITERRANEAN
020 7494 9584 | 21–22 Warwick Street, W1B 5NE
www.nopi-restaurant.com
Inspired by the sun-drenched cuisines of the Middle East, North Africa and the Mediterranean, owner Yotam Ottolenghi's cooking is creative stuff; bursting with punchy flavours and delivered in dishes made for sharing in an all-white brasserie-style space, or in the basement.

Closed 25–26 December, 1 January

Novikov Asian Restaurant
PLAN 4, H6

@ CHINESE, PAN-ASIAN
020 7399 4330 | 50a Berkeley Street, W1J 8HA
www.novikovrestaurant.co.uk
The Asian venue of Russian restaurateur Arkady Novikov's see-and-be-seen Mayfair food palace offers a palate-tingling cornucopia of pan-Asian dishes. A busy team of chefs behind a glass wall among mounds of super-fresh produce

resembling an Asian street market takes centre-stage in the slick brasserie-style space.

Chef Luca Malacarne **Seats** 149 **Closed** 25 December **Prices from** S £5.50, M £16.25, D £9 **Notes** Vegetarian dishes, No children under 12 years after 9pm

Novikov Italian Restaurant
PLAN 4, H6

@ ITALIAN
020 7399 4330 | 50a Berkeley Street, W1J 8HA
www.novikovrestaurant.co.uk
Once you've navigated the street-level security guards and glam meet-and-greet ladies, the extravagant Novikov operation's Italian venue sprawls across a vast basement, where cornucopian buffet displays and a wood-fired oven dazzle on arrival. The Italian cooking is surprisingly rustic and simple.

Chef Marco Torri **Seats** 200, Private dining 40 **Closed** 25 December **Prices from** S £16.50, M £18.50, D £8.50 **Notes** Vegetarian dishes, No children under 12 years after 9pm

Orrery
PLAN 2, G3

@@@ MODERN FRENCH *V*
020 7616 8000 | 55–57 Marylebone High Street, W1U 5RB
www.orrery-restaurant.co.uk
Perched on top of the Conran store, Orrery displays a similar penchant for clean-lined contemporary design. A stalwart of the Marylebone dining scene, it still cuts a dash with its classy good looks, polished service and skilful, modern take on classical French cuisine. Refurbished in 2018, it's a stylish space, lit by a full-length skylight and arched windows giving leafy views over Marylebone church gardens; a roof terrace adds further to its appeal. Igor Tymchyshyn's refined classic and modern French dishes exercise a powerful pull too, taking in a flavour-packed seafood raviolo in lobster bisque as a luscious way in, or perhaps cured sea bass with cucumber, horseradish and kumquat. Alluring main courses are similarly well conceived and beautifully presented, as seen in poached salmon with mushroom purée, crisp polenta and watercress velouté, or perhaps a classic idea such as tournedos Rossini with celeriac and sauce périgourdine. To conclude, the sweet delights of white chocolate and elderflower mousse are balanced with poached peach, sorbet and coulis, but the pungently ripened cheese trolley is worth exploring before you get there.

Chef Igor Tymchyshyn **Seats** 110, Private dining 16 **Closed** 26–28 December, 1 January, Easter Monday, Summer Bank Holiday **Notes** Children welcome

The Palomar

PLAN 2, K1

◉◉ MODERN JERUSALEM

020 7439 8777 | 34 Rupert Street, W1D 6DN

www.thepalomar.co.uk

Quick-fire dishes that take inspiration from the Levant, North Africa and southern Spain are the deal in this high-octane operation in Theatreland. It's first come, first served for ringside seats at the open kitchen counter, where the Josper oven works overtime, delivering full-on, sun-drenched flavours to eager diners.

Seats 50 **Closed** 25-26 December **Prices from** S £5.40, M £10, D £3.80 **Notes** Vegetarian dishes, Children welcome

Park Chinois

PLAN 4, H6

◉◉ CHINESE

020 3327 8888 | 17 Berkeley Street, Mayfair, W1J 8EA

parkchinois.com

Dine amidst Salon de Chine's plush French Chinoiserie, or in Club Chinois' underground entertainment hideaway. The dinner menu starts with some eye-wateringly-priced caviars, then dim sums and soups before reaching the likes of crispy satay chicken with tamarind; steamed Kamchatka king crab with Shaoxing wine and rice noodles; and even 35-day-aged Irish rib-eye with king soya.

Chef Lee Che Liang **Seats** 230, Private dining 12 **Closed** 25 December **Prices from** S £9, M £23 **Notes** Vegetarian dishes, No children under 8 years

Picture

PLAN 2, H3

◉◉ MODERN EUROPEAN *V*

020 7637 7892 | 110 Great Portland Street, W1W 6PQ

www.picturerestaurant.co.uk

Set up by three talented deserters from the acclaimed Arbutus/Wild Honey stable, this switched-on outfit presses all the on-trend buttons. It has that sleek, neutral modern look – grey walls, abstract images, oak floors, and food that's more cheffy than the brown-paper menus, accessible pricing, or casually dressed staff might suggest. The kitchen deals in fresh, pretty-as-a-picture, 'small plates' spiked with flavour and flair.

Chef Alan Christie, Colin Kelly **Seats** 55 **Closed** Christmas, bank holidays **Prices from** S £10, M £15, D £6 **Notes** Children welcome

Pied à Terre

PLAN 2, J3

◉◉◉ MODERN FRENCH *V* NOTABLE WINE LIST

020 7636 1178 | 34 Charlotte Street, W1T 2NH

www.pied-a-terre.co.uk

A top dining destination since the early 1990s, David Moore's Pied à Terre is a Fitzrovia elder statesman. The bijou dining room has had a redesign, rich jewel colours adding an air of luxury and sophistication to white linen clad tables. The cooking is bang-on-trend; inventive, dressed-to-thrill dishes of finesse, refinement and precision. New head chef Asimakis Chaniotis has made the kitchen his own, and can even be found delivering dishes to tables in the modern style. On the carte, you'll find the signature starter – smoked quail with celeriac, truffle, Piedmont hazelnut and confit egg yolk – to be followed, perhaps, by honey-glazed lemon sole with asparagus, baby artichokes, morels and wild garlic foam. Desserts are a delight; look for Gariguette strawberries, orange cake, and 100% chocolate mousse with strawberry and basil sorbet. The encyclopaedic wine list offers a galaxy of stars as well as value, while service is professional yet friendly and unstuffy.

Chef Asimakis Chaniotis **Seats** 40, Private dining 16 **Closed** 2 weeks at Christmas and New Year **Notes** Children welcome

Plum Valley

PLAN 2, K1

◉ CHINESE

020 7494 4366 | 20 Gerrard Street, W1D 6JQ

www.plumvalleyrestaurant.co.uk

Plum Valley stands out on Gerrard Street with its sleek black frontage and inside it has a dark, minimalist contemporary gloss. Service is brisk but friendly. The mainstay of the menu is classic Cantonese stuff, with familiar old favourites and some perky modern ideas, too.

Closed 25 December

Podium

PLAN 4, G6

◉◉ MODERN EUROPEAN

020 7208 4022 | London Hilton on Park Lane, 22 Park Lane, W1K 1BE

www.podiumrestaurant.com

This swish all-day eatery in the Park Lane Hilton fits the bill when you're tootling around Mayfair and fancy a relaxed pit-stop with an eclectic, comfort-oriented menu. The kitchen delivers the goods via unpretentious and well-executed modern European dishes constructed from well-sourced materials, while the service team do their bit with friendly professionalism.

Open All Year

Pollen Street Social

PLAN 2, H2

◉◉◉◉◉ MODERN BRITISH **V** 🍷 NOTABLE WINE LIST
020 7290 7600 | 8–10 Pollen Street, W1S 1NQ
www.pollenstreetsocial.com

Since becoming Britain's 'Best Young Chef' in 1996, Jason Atherton has never looked back. Not only has he gathered an ever-growing list of prestigious awards, but he has opened restaurants and bars around the globe, from the Philippines to St Moritz, and from Shanghai to New York City. He also has a portfolio of venues in London, but Pollen Street Social remains the capital's flagship. Squeezed down a Mayfair side street, so narrow you could step from pavement to pavement, it's jolly handy for when it's time to seek refuge from arduous West End shopping expeditions. Inside, the impression of a classy, contemporary look stems largely from the wooden floors, linen-clothed tables and white walls punctuated by modern British artworks, while a glass-fronted pass to the kitchen adds to the mix. Atherton's concept is 'relaxed fine dining', although it's left to head chef Dale Bainbridge and his team to produce the inventive interpretations which look so good on the plate that briefly it seems almost sacrilegious to disturb them by tucking in. With produce arriving from across Britain, including Orkney oysters, Cumbrian suckling pig, Cornish sea bass and Norfolk quail, there are plenty of temptations on the set lunch, the eight-course tasting menu, the carte and the vegetarian and vegan options. Page space precludes highlighting much: suffice to say a typical carte selection might include Paignton Harbour crab salad with apple, coriander, lemon purée and brown crab on toast; Wye Valley asparagus with morels stuffed with Creedy Carver chicken mousse and Madeira jus; and dry-aged Lake District beef fillet with aubergine and miso purée, roasted garlic and snails. Veggies might head for Isle of Wight tomato tartare with verjus granita and sourdough croûtons; or roasted celeriac risotto with woodland mushrooms, truffle, aged parmesan, garlic and parsley.

Chef Jason Atherton, Dale Bainbridge **Seats** 52, Private dining 12 **Closed** Bank holidays **Prices from** S £17.50, M £34.50, D £13 **Notes** Children welcome

Portland

PLAN 2, H3

◉◉◉ MODERN BRITISH 🍷 NOTABLE WINE LIST
020 7436 3261 | 113 Great Portland Street, W1W 6QQ
www.portlandrestaurant.co.uk

The Portland scores high in the understated cool stakes. The modern clean-lined, upbeat dining room has an intimate, self-effacing note, its Scandi-style darkwood tables and chairs illuminated by dangling retro lighting, while white walls are cheered by large, pastel-shade contemporary artworks leading the eye to the keynote open kitchen at the back. The culinary action, headed by Zach Elliot-Crenn, is the big draw with chefs bringing-out dishes to the table. This faultless modern take on new-Brit cuisine delivers in spades; brimming with innovation and seasonality, a classy lightness of touch, balanced and eye-catching presentation, but, above all, flavour. Picking highlights is impossible, but take an opener of hot-smoked Lincolnshire eel topped with golden beetroots, pears and herring roe, or perhaps sparkling-fresh pollock drenched in squid ink with white sprouting broccoli and sea vegetables. Finish in style with a baked apple terrine, hazelnut ice cream and lemon thyme soft-serve. Service is spot-on, while the wine list is a labour of love with excellence by-glass too.

Chef Zach Elliot-Crenn, Martin Labron-Johnson **Seats** 36, Private dining 16 **Closed** 23 December to 3 January **Prices from** S £13, M £24, D £12 **Notes** Vegetarian dishes, Children welcome

Quo Vadis

PLAN 2, K2

◉◉ MODERN BRITISH
020 7437 9585 | 26–29 Dean Street, W1D 3LL
www.quovadissoho.co.uk

Tan banquettes, modern art and mirrors on the walls and stained-glass windows provide the backdrop for accomplished cooking at this Soho stalwart, with the kitchen favouring the modern British style. Flavour combinations are well considered so dishes maintain interest without over-elaboration.

Chef Jeremy Lee **Seats** 26, Private dining 32 **Closed** Bank holidays (excluding Good Friday), 25 December, 1 January **Notes** Vegetarian dishes, Children welcome

The Riding House Café

PLAN 2, J3

◉ MODERN EUROPEAN
020 7927 0840 | 43–51 Great Titchfield Street, W1W 7PQ
www.ridinghousecafe.co.uk

This big, high-decibel, all-day operation has an urban brasserie vibe. Head for a swivel seat at the white-tiled island bar overlooking the open kitchen or park at a long refectory table, or if you don't do communal dining, there's a separate space with a more intimate mood. A flexible menu of small plates and modern brasserie dishes is on offer.

Closed 25–26 December and 1 January

The Ritz Restaurant
PLAN 4, J6

◉◉◉ BRITISH, FRENCH *V*

020 7300 2370 | 150 Piccadilly, W1J 9BR

www.theritzlondon.com

When César Ritz opened his latest hotel at the northern tip of Green Park in 1906, it bade fair to become one of the capital's most opulent lodgings, and so it would remain, from the Entente Cordiale to Cool Britannia. At its heart is the stunningly beautiful dining room, lined with French windows along the park side, topped with a ceiling fresco of sunlit clouds, overseen by a gilded statue of a reclining Poseidon. Many of the principles of the haute cuisine of yesteryear live on in John Williams' renditions of classics like Dover sole véronique, veal fillet with asparagus, wild garlic and Madeira, or the Mont Blanc dessert with its chestnut and rum ice cream. There are more contemporary dishes, too, and full vegan and vegetarian menus. Even if you don't opt for the crêpes suzette, hand-flamed by the maître d' at your table, you've got to hope somebody nearby does.

Chef John T Williams MBE **Seats** 90, Private dining 60 **Open** All Year **Parking** 10 **Notes** Children welcome

Roganic
PLAN 2, G3

◉◉◉◉ MODERN BRITISH *V* NOTABLE WINE LIST

020 337 06260 | 5-7 Blandford Street, Marylebone, W1U 3DB

www.roganic.uk

The original pop-up Roganic was such a barnstorming success that Simon Rogan came back to Marylebone with a more permanent set-up in 2018, and the place is now firmly established as a go-to venue for foodies. The new incarnation occupies a spartan space of bronze and white textured concrete walls, linen-clothed tables and design-classic chairs. As in Rogan's other ventures, the kitchen is tuned in to nature, and its stunning ingredients – some sourced from his own Lake District farm – are delivered by head chef Oli Marlow and his team in highly technical, precisely engineered miniatures. Tasting menu fans are in for a small-plate cavalcade of eight or 12 courses, but if you're not in for the long haul, the four-course set lunch is a steal – the inspired cooking driven by flavour, freshness and balance. Taking the budget route, things get going with a blue cheese croquette supported by black garlic, cubes of sea trout and a tomato juice of remarkable purity.

Next up, duck comes three ways, the breast timed to perfection and served with cauliflower purée, pear and raspberry, braised leg matched with cabbage, and seared duck hearts highlighted with prune chutney and potato mousse. To finish, there's a sublime fig ice cream with sorrel crisps and snow.

Chef Oli Marlow, Simon Rogan **Seats** 42 **Closed** 1st week January, last week August, last week December **Notes** No children under 6 years at lunch or under 12 years at dinner

Roka Charlotte Street
PLAN 2, J3

◉◉◉ JAPANESE

020 7580 6464 | 37 Charlotte Street, W1T 1RR

www.rokarestaurant.com

A magnet for the fashion and media darlings of Fitzrovia since 2004, this super-cool flagship of the Roka brand shows that London diners still have a big appetite for stylish contemporary Japanese robatayaki cooking. The light-flooded room's plate-glass frontage looks into a lively scene of chunky hardwood furniture around the beating heart of the robata counter, where ringside views of the kitchen action exert a strong pull. The menu's fusion temptations run to black cod, crab and crayfish dumplings, seared yellowtail with sakura leaf and daikon, or Wagyu tempura maki with karashi ponzu and oscietra caviar. As for the robata offerings, heavenly pork belly comes with punchy hoisin sauce and pickled apple, lamb cutlets with Korean spices, or sea bream fillet with ryotei miso and red onion. Desserts pull off an exciting fusion of East and West: witness dark chocolate and green tea pudding with crunchy Jivara and pear ice cream. If choosing for yourself is a trial, there's a tasting menu (with a vegan option), and an enthusiastic service team who are on hand to demystify any alien terminology.

Chef Hamish Brown **Seats** 350, Private dining 20 **Closed** Christmas **Notes** Vegetarian dishes, Children welcome

Roka Mayfair
PLAN 2, G1

◉◉◉ MODERN JAPANESE

020 7305 5644 | 30 North Audley Street, W1K 6ZF

www.rokarestaurant.com

The Mayfair branch of London's Roka group is just a short stroll from Oxford Street, so it proves a top draw for high-gloss contemporary Japanese food lovers and shoppers in the day, and the trendy, fashionable cocktail set after dusk. The focus is squarely on the large central robata grill, where prized counter seats offer ringside action of the chefs in the engine room that drives the high-energy buzz. The menu offers Roka favourites from the robata, like black cod marinated in yuzu miso, or perhaps salmon fillet teriyaki with sansho salt, while the comfort rice hotpot with Japanese mushrooms, mountain vegetables and shaved truffle offers an equal umami-rich kick. Precision tempura includes an eye-catching array of assorted vegetables served with spicy yuzu sauce, while a galaxy of top-notch sushi and sashimi might include beef tartare with black truffle sponge. A tasting menu, switched-on service, and an extensive sake list (with tasting notes) means its fans are in for a treat too.

Chef André Camilo **Seats** 113, Private dining 24
Closed 25 December **Prices from** D £7
Notes Vegetarian dishes, Children welcome

Roti Chai   PLAN 2, G2
◉ MODERN INDIAN
020 7408 0101 | 3 Portman Mews South, W1H 6AY
www.rotichai.com
A restaurant of two halves, Roti Chai takes its inspiration from the lively street food of the Indian sub-continent. The ground-floor, canteen-style Street Kitchen serves small plates, while the basement Dining Room offers more refined nouveau Indian cooking and has a smart contemporary look. Expect a modern take on Indian flavours.

Open All Year

Roux at The Landau   PLAN 2, H3
◉◉ MODERN EUROPEAN, FRENCH **V**
020 7636 1000 | The Langham, London, Portland Place, W1B 1JA
rouxatthelandau.com
Relaunched with a new look in early 2018, there's now more of a brasserie feel to proceedings with leather banquettes and snugs plus a marble-topped oyster and charcuterie island in the middle. The panelled oval restaurant is still a highlight of the hotel with excellent food and wine service.

Chef Nicolas Pasquier **Seats** 100, Private dining 18
Prices from S £9, M £16, D £8 **Notes** Children welcome

Sabor   PLAN 2, J1
◉◉ SPANISH
020 3319 8130 | 35-37 Heddon Street, Mayfair, W1B 4BR
www.saborrestaurants.co.uk
Sabor (translating as 'flavour') delivers an authentic regional experience via its trio of dining options; from diminutive tapas bar to dining-counter restaurant facing a high-energy open kitchen. Otherwise, head up the spiral staircase to the asador's communal tables (you'll need to book) for more regional delights.

Chef Nieves Barragán Mohacho **Open** All Year
Notes No children

Salt Yard   PLAN 2, J3
◉◉ ITALIAN, SPANISH
020 7637 0657 | 54 Goodge Street, W1T 4NA
www.saltyard.co.uk
This buzzy restaurant deals in small-but-perfectly formed plates of vibrant food with a Spain-meets-Italy theme. The bar is the place for a glass of fizz with a plate of cured meats, or take a seat and graze, tapas-style, through a mix of the familiar and creative.

Chef Nick Rochford, Joe Howley **Seats** 80 **Closed** 24-26 December, 31 December, 1 January **Notes** Vegetarian dishes, Children welcome

Sartoria   PLAN 2, J1
◉ ITALIAN **V**
020 7534 7000 | 20 Savile Row, W1S 3PR
www.sartoria-restaurant.co.uk
Appropriately set in the fine suiting and booting world of Savile Row, Sartoria is an immaculately turned-out operation with a classy interior and switched-on, upbeat service from staff dressed to look the part. The menu straddles classic and contemporary Italian cooking.

Chef Francesco Mazzei **Seats** 100, Private dining 50
Closed 25-26 December, 1 January, Easter Monday, bank holidays **Prices from** S £11.50, M £17, D £8
Notes Vegetarian dishes, Children welcome

Scott's   PLAN 2, G1
◉◉ SEAFOOD **V**
020 7495 7309 | 20 Mount Street, W1K 2HE
www.scotts-restaurant.com
Glamour fills Scott's, from its charming service to the eye-catching mountain of seafood on ice in the swanky champagne bar. Apart from celebrities, there are mosaics, mirrors, oak-panelled walls, leather seats, and modern artworks to catch the eye, plus a menu brimming with top-notch seafood.

Chef Dave McCarthy **Seats** 150, Private dining 40
Closed 25-26 December **Notes** Children welcome

PLAN 2, J1

Sketch (The Gallery)

◉◉◉ **MODERN EUROPEAN**

020 7659 4500 | 9 Conduit Street, W1S 2XG

www.sketch.london/the-gallery

Virtuoso cooking in an artist-designed restaurant

Behind the facade of a Grade II listed townhouse in Mayfair lurks something a little surprising. Built at the end of the 18th century, the place may look at first glance like a bastion of traditional values, but within you'll find a venue as avant-garde as any in the capital. With an approach to interior design that doesn't so much push the envelope as shred it into a million tiny pieces and use it as a decorative feature, super-cool Sketch makes quite a style statement beneath its soaring cupola roof: an explosion of candy pink designer glam from designer India Mahdavi mingles with Brit artist David Shrigley's whimsical cartoonish artworks filling the walls, and well-heeled, beautiful people taking selfies on low-slung, candy-pink sponge finger-like barrel chairs and banquettes.

Über-chef Pierre Gagnaire's food doesn't stint on creativity either, with vibrancy, sheer skill and a sense of fun evident

> "... vibrancy, sheer skill and a sense of fun evident throughout"

throughout, opening in contemporary European mode with a super-light ham tart with celeriac, sweetcorn and pink grapefruit fondue, or perhaps prawns macerated in orange manzanilla gel with red quinoa and amaranth cake. Sophisticated technique, along with an intuitive grasp of flavours also distinguishes a main-course of clarified butter-poached sea bass served with tender squid and bitter green herbs in a dramatic black squid ink sauce enriched with Parmesan cream. If you're in the mood for something meaty, duck breast might be flavoured with rosemary and supported by an eclectic cast of red cabbage jam with

blackcurrant, cured Bigorre pork fat, salmis sauce, crunchy pommes gaufrettes, the tart kiss of tamarillo sorbet, and whisky gel. Desserts are also highly technical workouts: a pink meringue shell is filled with Manjari 64% dark chocolate mousse and Ice cream, raspberry sauce, toasted hazelnuts, cocoa jelly and strawberry ganache. The wine list is stacked with expensive thoroughbred bottles that are more than up to the job of enhancing the complex flavour profiles of the food.

Chef Pierre Gagnaire, Frederic Don
Seats 126
Closed 25 December
Prices from S £15, M £17, D £6
Notes Vegetarian dishes, Children welcome

PLAN 2, J1

Sketch (Lecture Room & Library)

◉◉◉◉◉ **MODERN EUROPEAN** *V* NOTABLE WINE LIST

020 7659 4500 | 9 Conduit Street, W1S 2XG

www.sketch.london

Highly conceptualised food from a modern master

Something rather extraordinary lies in wait behind the sober façade of this Grade II listed townhouse in Mayfair. This is a dining room that sets the pulse racing: with its lavish red, pink, orange and gold colour scheme, padded cream leather walls and all-round air of theatricality, it's a suitably unforgettable spot for some ground-breaking cuisine. The menus – à la carte and tasting – reveal dishes of complexity and imagination, in fact the lengthy menu descriptions can only hint at the mind-boggling extravagance of what you're in for. The skill of this kitchen is beyond question: the French modern master Pierre Gagnaire still devises all menus here, with head chef Johannes Nuding aiming to encompass a dizzyingly wide range of ingredients and techniques in a multitude of small plates.

An opening salvo, 'Italian Spirit', comprises thin slices of veal fillet with

"... a beautiful progression of complementary flavours, appealing textures and visual impact."

Nocellara olive oil and Cremona fruit mustard, then stracciatella with tomato marmalade and wild fennel seeds, followed by smoked raw gambero rosso prawns, black Venere rice and parmesan, and a final fusillade of potato gnocchi with osso buco jus, Parma ham and Taggiasco olives. Yep, it's a lot to take in for sure, but the result is a beautiful progression of complementary flavours, appealing textures and visual impact.

The way the components work together produces an undeniable alchemy in mains too – a duck workout might bring a whole roasted salt chamber-aged bird with Szechuan peppercorns, tamarind jus,

pistachios, a medley of radishes, turnip tops with horseradish, and duck foie gras terrine. Desserts follow a similar multi-faceted route, guided by an intuitive understanding of flavours: choose a theme – 'Almost Spring', say – and a riot of little dishes ensues: a volley of Yorkshire rhubarb preparations, then early season strawberries served as a Pavlova, followed by asparagus bavaroises and tips with tarragon, and a finale of lemon parfait coated in almond paste.

Chef Pierre Gagnaire, Johannes Nuding
Seats 50, Private dining 40
Closed 2 weeks August, 2 weeks December, 1 January and bank holidays
Prices from S £45, M £50, D £20
Notes No children under 6 years

LONDON W1 continued

Sexy Fish

PLAN 2, H1

◉◉ ASIAN, SEAFOOD

020 3764 2000 | Berkeley Square House,
Berkeley Square, W1J 6BR
www.sexyfish.com
Be prepared for jaw-dropping interiors of marble
with aquatic-themed artworks by big names, and
a water wall cascading behind the bar. The feel is
glittering art deco with bags of bling, but it's not
all style over substance: the kitchen sends out a
well-executed roster of Asian-inspired fish and
seafood, while Japanese whisky, cocktails and
champagne add fizz.

Closed 25-26 December

Sketch (The Gallery)

PLAN 2, J1

◉◉◉ MODERN EUROPEAN

See pages 274-275

Sketch (Lecture Room & Library)

PLAN 2, J1

◉◉◉◉ MODERN EUROPEAN **V**◖ NOTABLE WINE LIST

See pages 276-277

Sketch (The Parlour)

PLAN 2, J1

◉◉ MODERN EUROPEAN

020 7659 4500 | 9 Conduit Street, W1S 2XG
www.sketch.london/the-parlour
The more casual of the trio of eating options at
style-conscious Sketch is The Parlour. It's a
funky, theatrical and rather glamorous boudoir-
style take on an all-day café serving breakfast,
then an appealing roster of European comfort
food from lunch until teatime (there's no booking,
just turn up) before morphing into a lively
evening cocktail bar with DJs.

Chef Pierre Gagnaire, Frederic Don **Seats** 50 **Closed** 25
December **Prices from** S £11, M £11, D £8
Notes Vegetarian dishes, Children welcome
See advertisement below

Social Eating House

PLAN 2, J2

◉◉◉ MODERN BRITISH **V** NOTABLE WINE LIST

020 7993 3251 | 58–59 Poland Street, W1F 7NS
www.socialeatinghouse.com

The Poland Street iteration of Jason Atherton's burgeoning empire looks very much the Soho part, the rather anonymous frontage leading into a racy cavern of bare brick walls and distressed leather stools at the copiously stocked bar. Draw up a bentwood chair at a café table if you prefer, for a menu that begins with sharing jars of smoked houmous and spiced aubergine, or confit duck rillettes with mango and coriander. The main menu deals in three-dimensional combinations that are more off the wall than at other Atherton venues, from octopus with charcoal mayonnaise and Padrón pepper in green sauce, to treacled côte de porc and salt-baked white carrot for a main course that also incorporates cime di rapa and a spicy nut granola. Hake is smoked over applewood and served in seaweed butter with cured trout caviar and Charlottes, and anything can be further dolled up with a supplementary addition of truffle.

Chef Paul Hood **Seats** 75, Private dining 8 **Closed** 25–26 December and bank holidays **Prices from** S £12.50, M £29, D £9 **Notes** Children welcome

The Square

PLAN 2, H1

◉◉◉ MODERN FRENCH **V**

020 7495 7100 | 6–10 Bruton Street, Mayfair, W1J 6PU
www.squarerestaurant.com

The sense of having stepped into a contemporary art space makes a powerful initial impact at The Square, where monochrome abstracts and a strange headless sculptural group form the mise en scène for one of Mayfair's longest-running high fliers. Clément Leroy, formerly of Chantilly, cooking alongside his wife Aya Tamura, maintains the French-oriented style of the cuisine, which is as haute as it is moderne, with novel and challenging ideas coming thick and fast on the four-course menu format. Main courses are essays in delicately considered balance, perhaps John Dory with sea urchin and lychees, or the superlative matured meats that might be a three-way serving of 55-day aged pork, or 28-day Cumbrian beef fillet à la royale. If you're still feeling pretty royale at dessert stage, look to a creation of grand cru chocolate with pistachios and red shiso leaf, or salt-crusted pineapple with kombu caramel.

Chef Clément Leroy **Seats** 80, Private dining 18 **Closed** 24–26 December, 1 January **Notes** Children welcome

Street XO

PLAN 2, J1

◉◉ INTERNATIONAL **V**

020 3096 7555 | 15 Old Burlington Street, W1S 2JR
www.streetxo.com/london

With its neon signage and pumping music, nobody could accuse this frenetic Mayfair restaurant and cocktail bar of lacking atmosphere. Descend the golden staircase to the black-and-red basement, where the cutting-edge fusion cooking is as vibrant as the decor, and small plates plunder the global larder.

Chef Dabiz Muñoz **Closed** 25–26 December, 1 January **Notes** Vegetarian dishes, Children welcome

Tamarind

PLAN 4, H6

◉◉ INDIAN **V**

020 7629 3561 | 20 Queen Street, Mayfair, W1J 5PR
www.tamarindrestaurant.com

Tamarind has been through a thorough transformation and now features a basement and first-floor restaurant. Downstairs, the open kitchens provide theatre and atmosphere, while upstairs natural light and a central cocktail bar feature while banquettes and booth seating frame the room. Many dishes are designed to be shared and the modern Indian cooking looks to subtle and delicate flavours and cooking methods from across the sub-continent.

Chef Karunesh Khanna **Seats** 145, Private dining 10 **Closed** 25–26 December and 1 January **Prices from** S £8, M £20, D £9 **Notes** No children under 10 years at dinner

10 Greek Street

PLAN 3, A2

◉◉ MODERN BRITISH, EUROPEAN

020 7734 4677 | W1D 4DH
www.10greekstreet.com

A Soho bistro reinvented for the present age, the lively cooking at number 10 has plenty to say for itself. Fish dishes in two sizes, such as gurnard with Jerusalem artichokes and black pudding, or mackerel chermoula with pomegranate and pistachio, indicate a flexible approach.

Chef Cameron Emirali **Seats** 30, Private dining 12 **Closed** 24–26 December, 1 January **Notes** Vegetarian dishes, Children welcome

Texture Restaurant

PLAN 2, F2

◎◎◎◎ MODERN EUROPEAN *V*

020 7224 0028 | 4 Bryanston Street, W1H 7BY

www.texture-restaurant.co.uk

Texture is a compelling mix of Scandinavian style and traditional English charm. The former is down to the sheer blinding talent of Agnar (Aggi) Sverrisson, an Icelander who has brought his prodigious culinary talent to London and created one of the most divertingly appealing addresses in town. The latter is down to the splendid Georgian proportions of the space. It is this fusion of simple design and big-scale grandeur that makes dining chez Sverrisson such an appealing prospect. The cooking is a kind of fusion too, with Icelandic influences gliding through the modern European menu. Choose from the à la carte or tasting menus, which include fish and vegan versions. There is a lightness of touch in the cooking, a genuine depth of flavour achieved, and without the overuse of cream, butter (zero in the savoury courses) or sugar. In an opening course, Anjou pigeon comes with sweetcorn, shallot, bacon popcorn and red wine essence, while mains might include best end and shoulder of Icelandic lamb with peas, Jersey Royals and mint, or Cornish turbot with oscietra caviar, shellfish, wasabi and lemon verbena. The wine list shows the same level of attention to detail as the food, with great advice on hand if required.

Chef Agnar Sverrisson **Seats** 52, Private dining 16 **Closed** 2 weeks at Christmas, 1 week at Easter, 2 weeks in August **Prices from** S £19.50, M £37.50, D £13.50 **Notes** Children welcome

Trishna

PLAN 2, G3

◎◎ INDIAN

020 7935 5624 | 15–17 Blandford Street, W1U 3DG

www.trishnalondon.com

Trishna takes a minimalist decorative line in two dining rooms done out with oak floors and tables, painted brickwork, mirrored walls, and hues of cream and duck-egg blue. The kitchen celebrates the coastal cuisine of south-west India in fresh, flavour-packed contemporary dishes.

Closed 24–27 December, 1–3 January

Twist

PLAN 2, F3

◎◎ MEDITERRANEAN TAPAS

020 7723 3377 | 42 Crawford Street, W1H 1JW

www.twistkitchen.co.uk

Lively, intimate and fun, this Marylebone-hinterland 'kitchen and tapas' is smack-on-cue. The in-vogue, pared-back look keeps things relaxed while the Spanish-style tiled open kitchen draws top focus. The chefs bring together Italian roots with Spanish and other Mediterranean influences in small-plate dishes of intelligent simplicity and freshness that allow flavours and textures to shine.

Chef Eduardo Tuccillo **Seats** 75, Private dining 35 **Closed** Christmas, 1 January, Easter, last 2 weeks in August, some bank holidays **Notes** Vegetarian dishes, Children welcome

Umu

PLAN 2, H1

◎◎◎ JAPANESE

020 7499 8881 | 14–16 Bruton Place, W1J 6LX

www.umurestaurant.com

With its smart Mayfair address, Umu's fans are prepared to pay handsomely for high-definition food of lightness and bracing freshness, and the stylishness with which the package is achieved. Enter the discreet push-button sliding door and a greeting is called out in the best tradition of Japanese hospitality, the calm interior inspired by upmarket Kyoto kaiseki joints, all delicate wood screens and sub-dued lighting acting as a foil to the precision knifework of the kitchen brigade. The food is firmly anchored in traditional ways, with Bento-box lunches and various set menus removing the need to agonise over the extensive main menu, the former opening with a precise assemblage of seasonal vegetables and shiitake mushrooms with edamame purée and red miso powder, before going on with a selection of stunning fish and seafood dishes, ringing with resonant freshness and pinpoint seasoning, among them sea bass and tuna sashimi, and lightly grilled Dover sole with tangy fermented vegetables and the umami kick of bonito flakes. If budget is not an issue, seasonal Kaiseki menus deliver a world of sparkling-fresh fish and gold-standard meats.

Chef Yoshinori Ishii **Seats** 64, Private dining 10 **Closed** Christmas, New Year and bank holidays **Notes** Vegetarian dishes, Children welcome

THREE OF THE VERY BEST
INDIAN RESTAURANTS

Amaya

This award winning Indian Grill offers intense flavours with an innovative twist, in a theatrical open kitchen setting. Michelin star.

Halkin Arcade, Lowndes Street
Knightsbridge, London SW1X 8JT
T: 020 7823 1166
E: amaya@realindianfood.com

Private dining room seats 14

CHUTNEY MARY

The rich setting, interesting art and romantic candles are secondary details in London's haven of great Indian contemporary food.

Weekend brunch at £35.

73 St James's Street
London SW1A 1PH
T: 020 7629 6688
E: chutneymary@realindianfood.com

Two private dining rooms seat 30 and 16

VEERASWAMY
1926

Classical dishes, lovingly prepared and beautifully served in sumptuous surroundings overlooking Regent Street. The oldest Indian restaurant in the world. Michelin starred.

Mezzanine Floor, Victory House
1st floor, 99 Regent Street
London W1B 4RS
T: 020 7734 1401
E: veeraswamy@realindianfood.com

Private dining room seats 24

LONDON W1 continued

Vasco & Piero's Pavilion Restaurant

PLAN 2, J2

® MODERN ITALIAN

020 7437 8774 | 15 Poland Street, W1F 8QE

www.vascosfood.com

This stalwart of the Soho dining scene has been plying its trade since 1971 but has a modern, clean-lined and arty look. The handwritten menu changes after each serving, so seasonality is a given. Rustic, home-style cooking delivers clear flavours; splendid pasta is made fresh.

Chef Vasco Matteucci **Seats** 50, Private dining 36 **Closed** Bank holidays **Prices from** S £6.50, M £18.50, D £7 **Notes** Vegetarian dishes, No children under 5 years

Veeraswamy Restaurant

PLAN 2, J1

®® INDIAN

020 7734 1401 | Mezzanine Floor, Victory House, 99 Regent Street, W1B 4RS

www.veeraswamy.com

The granddaddy of the UK's Indian restaurants, this lavishly elegant first-floor venue on Regent Street is a hotspot for tourists keen to try Britain's adopted culinary exotica. The kitchen puts creative spin on subcontinental stalwarts via smoked chicken tikka with garam masala and mace, or delves into the regional repertoire with Keralan seafood moilee.

Open All Year

See advertisement on page 281

The Wolseley

PLAN 4, J6

® TRADITIONAL EUROPEAN *V*

020 7499 6996 | 160 Piccadilly, W1J 9EB

www.thewolseley.com

The Wolseley fizzes with energy. Staff rush about, customers chatter, and that's the case all day long beneath its cathedral-like vaulted ceiling, from breakfast through to evening meals. Timeless brasserie classics are the deal and the all-day concept fits the bill whether you're after savoury satisfaction or a sweet treat.

Chef David Stevens **Seats** 150, Private dining 14 **Open** All Year **Prices from** S £6.75, M £12.75, D £2.75 **Notes** Children welcome

Yauatcha

PLAN 2, J2

®® MODERN CHINESE

020 7494 8888 | 15 Broadwick Street, W1F 0DL

www.yauatcha.com

A colourful array of pâtisserie opens the show in Yauatcha's ground-floor 'tea house', but in the basement dining room things are lively and loud. The menu impresses with its exciting blend of traditional Cantonese favourites and more intriguing contemporary compositions.

Closed 24–25 December

Zoilo

PLAN 2, G2

®® ARGENTINIAN

020 7486 9699 | 9 Duke Street, W1U 3EG

www.zoilo.co.uk

The mayhem of Oxford Street is close by but feels miles away in this racy outpost of South American cuisine. Bare brick walls, crimson banquettes and a midnight-blue palette around a central bar lined with counter seats make a chic backdrop to dynamic food inspired by Argentina's regions, from Patagonia to Mendoza. Sharing is the name of the game.

Chef Diego Jacquet **Seats** 48, Private dining 12 **Closed** Christmas and bank holidays **Prices from** S £4.50, M £14.90, D £7.90 **Notes** Vegetarian dishes, Children welcome

LONDON W2

Angelus Restaurant

PLAN 2, D1

® MODERN FRENCH

020 7402 0083 | 4 Bathurst Street, W2 2SD

www.angelusrestaurant.co.uk

A former pub which was transformed into a classy Parisian-style brasserie by renowned sommelier, Thierry Tomasin, Angelus Restaurant continues to impress with its luxe, art nouveau-inspired finish and ambitious, modern French cooking. The wine list offers some seriously good drinking opportunities.

Closed 24–25 December

LONDON W2 continued

The Hyde
PLAN 2, D2

◉ MODERN BRITISH

020 7479 6600 | Roseate House London, 3 Westbourne Terrace, Lancaster Gate, Hyde Park, W2 3UL
www.roseatehouselondon.com
A boutique hotel occupying a row of townhouses a short walk from Paddington railway station, Roseate House is just a block away from Hyde Park and ideal for exploring central London's attractions. The hotel's contemporary food is worth a detour.

Chef Daniel Pocz-Nagy **Seats** 25 **Open** All Year **Prices from** S £6.95, M £12.95, D £5.95 **Parking** 9 **Notes** No children

See advertisement on page 283

Island Grill & Bar
PLAN 2, D1

◉◉ MODERN BRITISH, EUROPEAN

020 7551 6070 | Royal Lancaster London, Lancaster Terrace, W2 2TY
www.islandrestaurant.co.uk
Island Grill & Bar is on the ground floor of the hotel with views over the busy road to Hyde Park opposite. Go for something from the grill – perhaps a steak with béarnaise or pork cutlets – or try salmon in a saffron-infused consommé.

Open All Year

Kurobuta
PLAN 2, E2

◉ JAPANESE

020 7920 6440 | 17-20 Kendal Street, Marble Arch, W2 2AW
www.kurobuta-london.com
A modern, stripped-down look with dark and moody colours, exposed industrial ducting and wood-slab tables, plus a lively musical policy make Kurobuta a popular, buzzy place. Inspired by Japan's izakaya taverns, the kitchen takes a Japanese fusion approach and chucks a few lively global ideas in the mix for good measure.

Chef Francico **Seats** 100 **Open** All Year **Notes** Vegetarian dishes, Children welcome

Nipa
PLAN 2, D1

◉◉ TRADITIONAL THAI

020 7551 6039 | Royal Lancaster London, Lancaster Terrace, W2 2TY
www.niparestaurant.co.uk
Opposite Hyde Park, in the Thai-owned Royal Lancaster hotel, an all-female, all-Thai kitchen balances the five main flavours in a comprehensive offering of appetisers, soups, salads, curries, pan-fried dishes, rices and noodles. Examples are crisp-fried prawn dumplings; a mixed seafood curry, beef with onions, mushrooms and oyster sauce; and stir-fried chicken with chillies. Set menus avoid making difficult decisions.

Chef Sanguan Parr **Seats** 55 **Notes** Vegetarian dishes, Children welcome

LONDON W4

Restaurant Michael Nadra
PLAN 1, D3

◉◉ MODERN EUROPEAN

020 8742 0766 | 6-8 Elliott Road, Chiswick, W4 1PE
www.restaurant-michaelnadra.co.uk
A stalwart of the Chiswick dining scene, this classy restaurant's pan-European fixed-price repertoire offers bags of interest. Rabbit ballotine and cromesquis are combined with baby turnip, fresh peas and pea purée and fired up with a well-judged glow from spicy Italian 'nduja sauce.

Chef Michael Nadra **Seats** 55 **Closed** 24-28 December and 1 January **Prices from** S £9, M £21, D £8.50 **Notes** Vegetarian dishes, Children welcome

La Trompette
PLAN 1, D3

◉◉ MODERN EUROPEAN ⚑ NOTABLE WINE LIST

020 8747 1836 | 5-7 Devonshire Road, Chiswick, W4 2EU
www.latrompette.co.uk
This neighbourhood restaurant par excellence has been playing to packed houses since 2001. The mood is relaxed, with a broad glass frontage looking in to a classy interior where white linen and a neutral colour palette meet bright abstract artworks. There's a cracking wine list, and the kitchen has a light, creative and pretty modern European outlook.

Chef Rob Weston **Seats** 88, Private dining 16 **Closed** 25-26 December and 1 January **Notes** Vegetarian dishes, Children welcome at lunch only

Le Vacherin
PLAN 1, D3

◉◉ FRENCH *V*

020 8742 2121 | 76-77 South Parade, W4 5LF

www.levacherin.com

Le Vacherin brings a hit of Gallic bonhomie to Chiswick, saving you a trip across the Channel when you're in the mood for some classic French cooking. The place has the look of a smart neighbourhood bistro, simple things are done well by a skilful kitchen, and the prix-fixe menu is particularly good value in any language.

Chef Marc Wainwright **Seats** 72, Private dining 36 **Closed** Bank holidays **Prices from** S £8.50, M £14.50, D £5.50 **Notes** Children welcome in private dining room

LONDON W6

L'Amorosa
PLAN 1, D3

◉ ITALIAN, BRITISH

020 8563 0300 | 278 King Street, Ravenscourt Park, W6 0SP

www.lamorosa.co.uk

This neighbourhood restaurant on Hammersmith's main drag has a man with pedigree at the stoves in the shape of ex-Zafferano head chef Andy Needham. The setting is smart-casual - darkwood floors, polished wood tables, buttoned brown leather banquettes and cream-painted walls hung with modern art.

Chef Andy Needham **Seats** 40 **Closed** 1 week Christmas, 2 weeks August, bank holidays **Prices from** S £7, M £14, D £6 **Notes** Vegetarian dishes, Children welcome

Anglesea Arms
PLAN 1, D3

◉ CLASSIC MEDITERRANEAN

020 8749 1291 | 35 Wingate Road, Ravenscourt Park, W6 0UR

www.angleseaarmspub.co.uk

London does street-corner gastro-pubs like this so well. Way back, landlords of the Anglesea in quiet Brackenbury Village could never have conceived of offering anything like today's duck and pistachio terrine, cornichons and capers, and seafood and chorizo paella with langoustine, king prawns, mussels, clams and squid. Works by local artists adorn its 'long brick wall'.

Chef Jasnobio Fardin **Seats** 37 **Closed** 24-26 December **Prices from** S £7, M £17, D £7 **Notes** Vegetarian dishes, Children welcome until 7.30pm

The River Café
PLAN 1, D3

◉◉◉ ITALIAN

020 7386 4200 | Thames Wharf Studios, Rainville Road, W6 9HA

www.rivercafe.co.uk

Not many would have predicted when Ruth Rogers and the late Rose Gray opened here in the 1980s that their cheering Italian café on the riverside in residential Hammersmith would still be going strong, well into the 21st century. And yet. The timeless appeal of Mediterranean food constructed from unimpeachable ingredients, to which only the least complicating treatments are given, tells a story all of its own. A quartet of whole young squid emerge from the chargrill with their sea savour intact, the dressing a little rocket and chilli and as much lemon as you feel like squeezing. Similarly, the flawless crisp-skinned sea bass cooked over coals with wood-roasted yellow peppers, olives and spinach is a banner-waving exemplar of the style, as are meats such as marinated lamb leg with braised chicory and grilled peppers. Finish with moistly alluring pear and almond tart alongside a slick of crème fraîche.

Chef Ruth Rogers, Sian Wyn Owen, Joseph Trivelli **Seats** 120, Private dining 18 **Closed** 24 December to 1 January **Prices from** S £19, M £36, D £10 **Parking** 29 **Notes** Vegetarian dishes, Children welcome

LONDON W8

Clarke's
PLAN 4, A6

◉◉ MODERN BRITISH, ITALIAN

020 7221 9225 | 124 Kensington Church Street, W8 4BH

www.sallyclarke.com

Sally Clarke's eponymous restaurant is a quietly elegant affair, with walls hung with abstract art. They take the best, freshest produce available in the markets and from Sally's own garden each day to focus on making it all taste resoundingly of itself, with Italian accents.

Chef Michele Lombardi, Gabrielle Marzo **Seats** 90, Private dining 30 **Closed** 8 days Christmas and New Year, 1 week August **Prices from** S £8.50, M £26.50, D £8.50 **Notes** Vegetarian dishes, Children welcome

Kitchen W8

PLAN 4, A4

◉◉◉ MODERN BRITISH ◢ NOTABLE WINE LIST

020 7937 0120 | 11-13 Abingdon Road, Kensington, W8 6AH

www.kitchenw8.com

Okay, it maybe tucked away just a few paces off fashionable Kensington High Street and lends its name to its up-scale postcode, but the 'Kitchen' shrewdly delivers a winning neighbourhood-character format, albeit high calibre, to these well-heeled parts. Inside follows the theme; a smart, relaxed, light, contemporary confection of warm pastel shades interspersed with modernist artworks and oval mirrors, while stylish seating, white linen and friendly, efficient service seal that neighbourhood-cum-destination vibe. Appealing menus fit the bill from the off, the kitchen delivering light, clean, well-presented modern dishes with a strong emphasis on flavour and seasonality. Perhaps open with a breast of quail teamed with Scottish girolles, summer truffles, corn and almonds, while main event sea-fresh roasted John Dory, served with coco bean ragù, pancetta and caramelised cauliflower, might rock your boat too. Desserts fly the flag for fruit, perhaps poached greengage plums with stem ginger, yogurt and almond, but also go rich; witness a warm chocolate croustade, salt caramel and lime. The fixed-price lunch/early-evening menu offers real value, while wines score high too.

Chef Mark Kempson **Seats** 75, Private dining 14
Closed 25-26 December, bank holidays
Prices from S £8.95, M £17, D £6.95 **Notes** Vegetarian dishes, Children welcome

Launceston Place

PLAN 4, C4

◉◉◉ MODERN EUROPEAN 𝒱 ◢ NOTABLE WINE LIST

020 7937 6912 | 1a Launceston Place, W8 5RL

www.launcestonplace-restaurant.co.uk

There's no obvious clue that the well-groomed Georgian townhouse on the corner of a leafy little residential Kensington street is anything more than just another smart-neighbourhood eatery, but gastronomes know that this is a destination worth seeking out. The interior design is certainly in keeping with the postcode, with the series of spaces done out in shades of grey with splashes of colour coming from the modern artworks on the walls. Light, modern cooking, courtesy of the talented young chef, Ben Murphy, delivers clever combinations of texture and bold flavour, all deftly engineered with invention and flair and dressed-to-thrill presentation. Roast celeriac stars in an impressive opener alongside a gutsy vegetable ragout ramped up with truffle, mint oil and emulsion, and parmesan. Next up, superlative halibut shines in the company of grelot onion, potato terrine and a potent jus. To finish, pear in various forms is matched with maple mousse and crunchy pecan feuilletine.

Chef Ben Murphy **Seats** 50, Private dining 12
Closed Christmas **Prices from** S £14, M £16, D £10
Notes Vegetarian dishes, Children welcome

The Milestone Hotel

PLAN 4, B5

◉◉ MODERN BRITISH

020 7917 1000 | 1 Kensington Court, W8 5DL

www.milestonehotel.com

Formed from three red-brick Victorian townhouses, this venerable hotel in affluent Kensington offers old-school service in the elegant, wood-panelled dining room, right down to the roast-of-the-day trolley. Start with lobster and Devon crab topped with caviar and move on to Suffolk lamb cooked three ways; or whole piri-piri baby chicken.

Chef **Seats** 30, Private dining 8 **Open** All Year
Prices from S £14, M £19, D £9 **Notes** Vegetarian dishes, Children welcome

Min Jiang

PLAN 4, B5

◉◉◉ CHINESE

See pages 288-289

See advertisement opposite

Min Jiang

◉◉◉ **CHINESE**
020 7361 1988 | Royal Garden Hotel, 2–24 Kensington High Street, W8 4PT
www.minjiang.co.uk

Seen from up on the 10th floor of the swanky Royal Garden Hotel, the splendid views across the treetops of Hyde Park and Kensington Gardens to the city skyscrapers spearing the skyline are worth the price of a lunch at Min Jiang. That magnificent cityscape is no longer such a draw after dark, of course, but the strikingly stylish dining room featuring blue-and-white Chinese porcelain, red lacquered walls hung with black-and-white photos, and tables swathed in crisp white linen is a fine sight, and the service is professional and ready with guidance on the ins and outs of the menu. Whatever the time of day, the food doesn't take a backseat to the opulent surroundings.

Upscale Chinese cuisine in five-star hotels is not always the best idea – you may find yourself eating sweet-and-sour pork at about ten times what it would cost in Chinatown – but here, authenticity in ingredients, seasonings and timings is assured. Dim sum is a star attraction, and there are some interesting meat-free options such as tofu with morel

mushrooms in black bean sauce. A great dish of sliced pork belly with crispy fried bean curd and pillowy steamed buns makes a simple but harmonious beginning, while sweetcorn soup with blue swimmer crab meat is also a good bet. Among main courses, grilled rack of lamb comes with garlic-infused soy sauce, or you might go for roasted chicken with five spice salt and refined ginger saucing to unleash its wonderful flavours.

The kitchen does a very fine rendition of wood-fired Beijing duck in the classic two servings, but you'll need to order this in advance. If you're in the mood for fish, there may be pan-fried black cod in XO sauce with asparagus. There are

> "Whatever the time of day, the food doesn't take a backseat to the opulent surroundings."

thoughtfully constructed desserts too, as the creative modern approach here produces coconut treacle pudding with spiced pineapple compôte for an outstanding finish.

Chef Weng Han Wong
Seats 80, Private dining 20
Open All Year
Parking 200
Notes Vegetarian dishes, Children welcome

See advertisement on page 287

LONDON W8 continued

Park Terrace Restaurant

PLAN 4, B5

◉◉ MODERN EUROPEAN

020 7937 8000 | Royal Garden Hotel,
2-24 Kensington High Street, W8 4PT
www.parkterracerestaurant.co.uk

Overlooking Kensington Gardens through a wall of floor-to-ceiling glass, the upmarket contemporary decor in the Royal Garden Hotel's restaurant reflects the park-life theme, with a natural colour palate, wood veneer and large black-and-white images of trees. The modern cooking is light, clear-flavoured and uncomplicated, and shows commitment to local British suppliers and seasonality.

Open All Year

See advertisement opposite

Zaika of Kensington

PLAN 4, B5

◉◉ INDIAN *V*

020 7795 6533 | 1 Kensington High Street, W8 5NP
www.zaikaofkensington.com

Comfortably in step with its postcode, this high-end Indian in a former bank has the feel of a Raj-era gentlemen's club, with its high ceilings, oak panels and colonial pictures. Taking classic, Moghul-inspired north Indian dishes as its starting point, the kitchen conjures scintillating, authentic flavours.

Chef Shekhar Daniel Rozario **Seats** 100, Private dining 30 **Closed** 25-26 December, 1 January
Prices from S £7.50, M £14.50, D £6 **Notes** Children welcome

LONDON W11

Core by Clare Smyth

PLAN 1, E3

◉◉◉◉◉ BRITISH *V* 🍷 NOTABLE WINE LIST

020 3937 5086 | 92 Kensington Park Road, W11 2PN
www.corebyclaresmyth.com

When she was 15, Clare Smyth took a holiday job in a restaurant near her County Antrim home, an experience that inspired her to become a chef. But she did better than that, becoming one of the UK's most acclaimed chefs, following a career that took in senior roles with Terence Conran, Alain Ducasse and Gordon Ramsay, who made her chef-patron of his eponymous Chelsea restaurant. She left Ramsay in 2017 for her first solo venture here at Core. As well as receiving many culinary awards, she has also been made an MBE. The stripped-back setting is as polished as the superlative service and food that are the restaurant's highlights; fine glassware, cutlery and crockery, yes, although tablecloths and carpets have been dispensed with. Smyth, and her kitchen team, work behind a glass partition, from where emerges beautifully crafted, delicious artisanal food, as in her Core Classics, typically roasted monkfish with Morecambe Bay shrimps, Swiss chard and brown butter; and duck and red grapes with thyme, honey and Nepalese timut pepper. She also offers a Core Seasons menu, on which you'll find trademark specialities like a starter of morel and asparagus tart with wild garlic and vin jaune; mains of lamb hogget and mutton with celtuce, savory and black cardamom; and Cornish brill with oysters, cucumber and caviar. And to finish, what Smyth calls a 'Core-teser', which on the plate translates as chocolate with malt and hazelnut. Wine pairings, chosen from the 450-bin wine list, are available to accompany these menus. The final offering is a set menu affording the opportunity at lunch or dinner to enjoy Isle of Mull scallop tartare with sea vegetable consommé; oxtail stuffed Roscoff onion with beef short rib; and lemonade parfait with honey and yogurt. A Chef's Table tasting menu dinner for eight to 10 people makes a great gift.

Chef Clare Smyth, Jonny Bone **Seats** 54
Closed Christmas, New Year **Notes** No children

E&O

PLAN 1, D4

◉ PAN-ASIAN

020 7229 5454 | 14 Blenheim Crescent, Notting Hill, W11 1NN
www.rickerrestaurants.com

E&O is trend-central with the Notting Hill fashionistas. The decor is casually scuffed these days, but the high-octane vibe (ramped-up by a lively bar) puts the experience-factor in overdrive. The young-at-heart pack the place for the fashionable, well-executed pan-Asian cuisine, plus great cocktails.

Closed 25-26 December, 1-2 January, Summer Bank Holiday

LONDON W11 continued

Edera
PLAN 1, D3

⊕ MODERN ITALIAN

020 7221 6090 | 148 Holland Park Avenue, W11 4UE

www.edera.co.uk

Decked out on tiered levels, with light walls hung with big mirrors and linen-dressed tables, this minimally-styled Holland Park eatery pulls in a well-heeled crowd for its fashionable Sardinian-accented Italian cooking. The kitchen team certainly know their stuff, keeping things simple and straightforward.

Closed 24 December to 1 January

The Ledbury
PLAN 1, E4

⊕⊕⊕⊕ MODERN BRITISH 𝑽 ⭐ NOTABLE WINE LIST

020 7792 9090 | 127 Ledbury Road, W11 2AQ

www.theledbury.com

With its gathered curtains and smooth parquet floor, The Ledbury has something of the air of a room that might be cleared for dancing later on. Contemporary light fittings and battalions of finely attentive staff contribute a soft glow to the proceedings, not exactly the impression you might expect from the faintly forbidding dark exterior. Brett Graham has been one of Notting Hill's prime movers in recent years, bringing highly accomplished modern sensibilities to plates that manage to look dazzling without recourse to fuss and foam, and deliver waves of striking and memorable flavour.

The standard menu is a four-course format, perhaps encompassing bracing sea bream tartare with oyster cream, Avruga and frozen wasabi for an initial vivid hit, followed by a much earthier dish of gently warmed bantam egg with celeriac, crisped ham, sliced chestnut mushrooms and shaved truffle. More mushrooms – chanterelles now – might turn up in a main dish of fallow venison with textures of Violina pumpkin and smoked bone marrow, before the signature dessert, an oblong of crunchy-topped brown sugar tart accompanied by assertively spicy ginger ice cream. For the full Ledbury experience, go nuts with the comprehensive eight-course taster. The quality wine list adds class.

Chef Brett Graham **Seats** 55 **Closed** 25-26 December, Summer Bank Holiday **Notes** No children under 12 years

LONDON W14

Cibo
PLAN 1, D3

⊕⊕ ITALIAN

020 7371 2085 | 3 Russell Gardens, W14 8EZ

www.ciborestaurant.net

The epitome of the authentic neighbourhood Italian, long-serving Cibo is a big hit with savvy Holland Park-ers. Breads and nibbles raise expectation from the off, and pasta is the real deal too. This is skilful Italian cooking showing respect of prime ingredients, flavour and precision timing.

Chef Piero Borrell **Seats** 50, Private dining 14 **Closed** Christmas, Easter Bank Holidays **Notes** Vegetarian dishes, Children welcome

LONDON WC1

The Montague on the Gardens
PLAN 3, B3

⊕ BRITISH

020 7612 8416 | 15 Montague Street, Bloomsbury, WC1B 5BJ

www.montaguehotel.com

The bowler-hatted doorman at the entrance is a clue that this is a classy boutique hotel, on a quiet street near the British Museum. Its Blue Door Bistro is a welcoming and informal dining room, decorated with a frieze depicting London in around 1850.

Chef Martin Halls **Seats** 40, Private dining 100 **Open** All Year **Prices from** S £7, M £20, D £7 **Notes** Vegetarian dishes, Children welcome

Otto's
PLAN 3, C4

⊕⊕ CLASSIC FRENCH

020 7713 0107 | 182 Gray's Inn Road, WC1X 8EW

www.ottos-restaurant.com

Small, intimate and owner-run, this old-school French restaurant feels like it has been around for decades. As befits a traditional French restaurant, the wine list is hefty in both range and price and the food displays confident cooking skills and high-quality ingredients. Leave room for classic puds such as tarte Tatin or Grand Marnier soufflé.

Chef Michael Boquiren **Seats** 45, Private dining 30 **Closed** Christmas, Easter, bank holidays **Notes** Vegetarian dishes, No children under 8 years

Rosewood London
PLAN 3, C3

⊕⊕ MODERN EUROPEAN

020 3747 8620 | 252 High Holborn, WC1V 7EN

www.rosewoodhotels.com/london

This magnificent building on High Holborn is a fine setting, and the old East Banking Hall with its soaring marble pillars is an elegant restaurant. The Mirror Room offers a relaxed and social dining experience.

Open All Year

LONDON WC2

Balthazar
PLAN 3, B1

🍴 FRENCH, EUROPEAN

020 3301 1155 | 4–6 Russell Street, WC2B 5HZ

www.balthazarlondon.com

The London offshoot of the legendary New York brasserie has played to packed houses right from the start. It's a real looker, with mosaic floors, art deco lighting, leather banquettes and antique mirrors. The places buzzes from breakfast through to lunch, afternoon tea and dinner, seven days a week.

Chef Robert Reid **Seats** 175, Private dining 60 **Closed** 25 December **Notes** Vegetarian dishes, Children welcome

Barrafina Adelaide Street
PLAN 3, B1

🍴🍴 MODERN SPANISH

10 Adelaide Street, WC2N 4HZ

www.barrafina.co.uk

Tapas is the name of the game here and the place is cool and packed to the rafters. The no booking policy means queues are likely and, once in, you sit at the marble counter and tuck into small plates full of flavour. There are daily specials galore, superb cured meats and lots of things you've maybe not tried before.

Chef Angel Zapata Martin **Seats** 29, Private dining 32 **Closed** Christmas, New Year, bank holidays **Prices from** S £2.80, M £7 **Notes** Vegetarian dishes, Children welcome

Barrafina Drury Lane
PLAN 3, B2

🍴🍴 SPANISH

43 Drury Lane, WC2B 5AJ

www.barrafina.co.uk

A lively repertoire of classic and modern tapas dishes and the perfect spot to grab and graze through a few little plates of big flavours in the pre- and post-theatre slots. There's a no-bookings policy here and it takes groups of up to four people.

Chef Angel Zapata Martin **Seats** 31, Private dining 24 **Closed** 25–26 December, 1 January, bank holidays **Notes** Vegetarian dishes, Children welcome

Café Murano Covent Garden
PLAN 3, C1

🍴🍴 ITALIAN

020 7240 3654 | 36 Tavistock Street, WC2E 7PB

www.cafemurano.co.uk

A long-raftered room with dark grey banquettes and an adjoining pastificio and coffee shop fits its Covent Garden location like a glove, with pre- and post-theatre menus on offer and a bustling lunchtime trade too. Northern Italian dishes under the aegis of Angela Hartnett are the stock-in-trade here.

Open All Year

Christopher's
PLAN 3, C1

🍴 CONTEMPORARY AMERICAN

020 7240 4222 | 18 Wellington Street, Covent Garden, WC2E 7DD

www.christophersgrill.com

This elegant eatery on the fringes of Covent Garden features a grand staircase, winding up from the uptempo street-level Martini Bar, while corniced high ceilings tower over the airy dining room, where chairs and banquettes in grey and lemon deliver bags of contemporary swagger.

Closed Christmas and 1 January

MEET THE CHEF

Ben Murphy

LAUNCESTON PLACE

London, W8, page 286

What inspired you to become a chef?
To be honest, I never aspired to become a chef, after losing out from a professional football career, food technology at school was the only subject I achieved well in, and honestly turned up to. Cooking was never the plan, I've been very fortunate with the path of my journey to where I am today.

What are the vital ingredients for a successful kitchen?
Salt! Knowing the difference between what is too salty and not seasoned enough is vital. We don't serve salt and pepper on the table, so tasting of all ingredients is crucial.

What are your favourite foods/ingredients?
Everything on my menu is what I like. Staying within the seasons is important, it's the same as fashion. Utilising the best possible produce I can get my hands on.

Cigalon

PLAN 3, D2

◉ MEDITERRANEAN

020 7242 8373 | 115 Chancery Lane, WC2A 1PP
www.cigalon.co.uk
Cigalon's classy dining room certainly evokes memories of sun-drenched South of France dining rather than the dry legal world of Chancery Lane. But it's not all style over substance. The kitchen focuses on the grill to deliver its sunny, seasonal Provençal menu.

Closed Christmas, New Year, bank holidays

Clos Maggiore

PLAN 3, B1

◉◉◉ FRENCH, MEDITERRANEAN ◗ NOTABLE WINE LIST

020 7379 9696 | 33 King Street, Covent Garden, WC2E 8JD
www.closmaggiore.com
The official 'world's most romantic restaurant' isn't just a Valentine's Day pitch. Clos Maggiore is in the mood for love all year round, and to that end sports a fantastical decor reminiscent of a permanent Japanese cherry blossom festival in the hot-ticket glass-ceilinged courtyard area. The setting may be soft focus but there's nothing whimsical about the cooking: ingredients are well sourced and skilfully handled, with easy-on-the-eye presentations adding to the lustre. Traditionalists will encounter plenty of decadent depth in silky-smooth chicken liver and foie gras parfait with red onion and ginger marmalade and toasted hazelnut bread. At main course, slow-cooked Berkshire pork neck and shredded ham hock are partnered with braised lettuce, capers, raisins and an intense pork sauce, while fish fans could be seduced by oven-roasted turbot with a casserole of Paimpol beans, mussels and courgette. Desserts are a beguiling proposition too – perhaps caramelised Valrhona chocolate sensation with burnt honey ice cream and Armagnac jelly.

Chef Marcellin Marc **Seats** 70, Private dining 23
Closed 24-25 December **Prices from** S £11.90, M £23.50, D £8.90 **Notes** Vegetarian dishes, No children under 3 years at lunch

Cora Pearl *NEW*

PLAN 3, B1

◉◉ MODERN BRITISH

020 7324 7722 | 30 Henrietta Street, Covent Garden, WC2E 8NA
www.corapearl.co.uk
Named after a 19th-century courtesan, this second restaurant from the team behind Mayfair's Kitty Fisher's occupies an elegant Covent Garden townhouse. Modern comfort food is the form here, a meal beginning with cow's curd agnolotti, pea and truffle, continuing with plaice, fennel and brown shrimps. Finish with 'milk and cookies'.

Chef George Barson **Open** All Year **Prices from** S £3.50, M £18, D £5 **Notes** Vegetarian dishes, No children

Frenchie Covent Garden

PLAN 3, B1

◉◉ FRENCH, EUROPEAN *V*

020 7836 4422 | 16 Henrietta Street, WC2E 8QH
www.frenchiecoventgarden.com
Located in the heart of Covent Garden, this is the UK brasserie of chef-patron Gregory Marchand who splits his time chiefly between his Paris restaurant and here. The menus are straightforward, yet full of quality and the accuracy of the cooking is very high.

Chef Gregory Marchand **Seats** 72, Private dining 20
Closed 25 December, 1 January **Prices from** S £14, M £25, D £8 **Notes** Children welcome

Frog by Adam Handling

PLAN 3, B1

◉◉◉ MODERN BRITISH *V*◗ NOTABLE WINE LIST

020 7199 8370 | 34-38 Southampton Street, WC2E 7HF
www.frogbyadamhandling.com
Adam Handling's chic venue in Covent Garden is a dream of contemporary design, with bare wood floor, black granite tables, floor-to-ceiling street views and an open kitchen, exactly the disposition London expects to see when eating out today. The bar downstairs gets reliably buzzing of an evening. Artworks add eye-catching lustre to the place, including a depiction of Piccadilly Circus, and Handling's menus offer momentous, technically accomplished dishes that make big statements. Thinly sliced salt-baked celeriac comes with sweet dates, a slow-cooked egg yolk, shredded apple, powdered mushroom and lime for an impressive opening balancing-act, before lamb comes three ways – a Wellington of the loin with charred cabbage,

spelt risotto with breaded neck, wild garlic and parmesan, and a slow ragout of the shoulder topped with creamy mash – for a virtuoso main-course performance. The closing turn could be mango and coconut cheesecake. Pre- and post-theatre menus are a useful resource.

Chef Adam Handling, Steven Kerr **Prices from** S £17, M £27, D £12 **Notes** Children welcome

The Ivy   PLAN 3, A1

◉ BRITISH, INTERNATIONAL

020 7836 4751 | 1–5 West Street, Covent Garden, WC2H 9NQ

www.the-ivy.co.uk

The curtain opened on this Theatreland dining institution over a century ago and it's still a classy act. Looking as elegant as ever, the room's original harlequin stained-glass windows, green leather banquettes, mirrors and eye-catching modern artwork set the scene for a wide-ranging menu of classic British and international food.

Closed 25–26 December, 1 January

J. Sheekey & J. Sheekey Atlantic Bar   PLAN 3, A1

◉ SEAFOOD *V*

020 7240 2565 | 32–34 St Martin's Court, WC2N 4AL

www.j-sheekey.co.uk

This enduring and much-loved seafood restaurant in the heart of Theatreland began life as a humble seafood stall in the 1890s. Today it's a seafood and oyster bar, offering a menu dealing in straightforward fish and shellfish dishes whose impeccable credentials speak for themselves.

Chef Andy McLay **Seats** 114 **Closed** 25–26 December, 1 January **Notes** Children welcome

Kaspar's Seafood Bar & Grill   PLAN 3, C1

◉ BRITISH, JAPANESE SEAFOOD

020 7836 4343 | The Savoy, Strand, WC2R 0EU

www.fairmont.com/savoy-london/dining/kaspars

The centrepiece of Kaspar's striking, art deco-inspired dining room is the seafood and oyster bar. You won't meet Kaspar there, but if you are part of a table of 13, a sculpted cat can make numbers up to 14, maintaining an old Savoy tradition and putting superstition to rest.

Open All Year

Kerridge's Bar & Grill   PLAN 5, B6

◉◉◉ MODERN BRITISH

020 7321 3244 | Corinthia Hotel London, 10 Northumberland Avenue, WC2N 5AE

www.kerridgesbarandgrill.co.uk

After thoroughly colonising Marlow with his big-hearted, refined and yet inherently simple cooking, Tom Kerridge has picked a glossy venue in a super-posh hotel for his first big-city venture. There's red leather, brass and art to ogle at in a cavernous room whose decor is more clubby than pubby. As you'd expect from the jovial TV chef, the food is a celebration of Britishness, importing the culinary generosity from The Hand and Flowers via dishes that are big on flavour and impact – a starter of Cornish crab vol-au-vent dressed with mayonnaise, apple and avocado purée, all brought into vivid focus by a luxuriant crab bisque, being a case in point. Main course brings the gamey delights of Ramsbury Estate venison with carrot in various guises, coriander emulsion, and a side of venison chilli topped with aerated cheese sauce and crisp barley. To finish, a lush custard tart is enriched with brown butter and balanced with the astringency of buttermilk ice cream.

Chef Tom Kerridge

Lima Floral   PLAN 3, B1

◉◉ MODERN PERUVIAN

020 7240 5778 | 14 Garrick Street, WC2E 9BJ

www.limalondongroup.com/floral

Lima's Covent Garden outpost offers a more casual setting than its Fitzrovia flagship, but the blast of South American vivacity is still a big draw. Peru pretty much invented the potato, and that fine tuber originally grown at 4,000 metres turns up in the mains.

Chef Patricia Roig **Seats** 70, Private dining 12 **Closed** Christmas **Prices from** S £6, M £15, D £6 **Notes** Vegetarian dishes, Children welcome

Margot
PLAN 3, B2

◉◉ ITALIAN **V**

020 3409 4777 | 45 Great Queen Street,
Covent Garden, WC2B 5AA

www.margotrestaurant.com

The dining room of this suave Italian looks as
sharp as an Armani suit with its black leather
banquettes and abstract artworks, and the slick
service purrs along like clockwork. The seasonal
menu is full of promise, with classic
combinations and masterful home-made pasta.

Chef Alessio Piras **Seats** 105, Private dining 32
Closed 25 December **Prices from** S £7.50, M £18.50,
D £6 **Notes** Children welcome

Mon Plaisir Restaurant
PLAN 3, B2

◉ TRADITIONAL FRENCH

020 7836 7243 | 19–21 Monmouth Street, WC2H 9DD

www.monplaisir.co.uk

The unapologetically 1940s-themed Parisian-
bistro look of the original front dining room here
conjures a suitably retro cross-Channel mood
with close-set tables and resolutely French
service, while beyond there's a series of lighter,
cosy rooms including a mezzanine-style loft. The
menu presents safe and respectable traditional
Gallic food.

Seats 100, Private dining 25 **Closed** Christmas, New
Year, bank holidays **Prices from** S £6.95, M £16, D £5.75
Notes Vegetarian dishes, Children welcome

The National Dining Rooms
PLAN 3, A1

◉ MODERN BRITISH

020 7747 2525 | Sainsbury Wing, The National Gallery,
Trafalgar Square, WC2N 5DN

www.peytonandbyrne.co.uk

Overlooking Trafalgar Square from the National
Gallery, this sleek all-day operation never
struggles to fill its tables, but there's a lot more
to the cooking than a simple pit-stop when you're
checking out the art. Unfussy modern dishes
draw on well-sourced seasonal materials.

Chef Kristofer Serfozo **Seats** 84 **Closed** 24–26
December, 1 January **Prices from** S £6, M £12, D £6.50
Notes Vegetarian dishes, Children welcome

The Northall
PLAN 5, B6

Rosettes suspended BRITISH

020 7321 3100 | Corinthia Hotel London,
10a Northumberland Avenue, WC2N 5AE

www.thenorthall.co.uk

The Northall is dedicated to all things British,
with the produce of artisan growers and
breeders showcased in the modern national
culinary style. Seasonality is key. As we went to
press André Garrett takes over the reins as
executive chef so expect great things to come
– one to watch.

Chef André Garrett **Open** All Year

The Opera Tavern
PLAN 3, C1

◉◉ SPANISH, ITALIAN

020 7836 3680 | 23 Catherine Street, Covent Garden,
WC2B 5JS

www.operatavern.co.uk

This classic old London pub, has become a
relaxed, two-storeyed tapas joint with the
restaurant on the upper level and an intimate
bar, with high stools, on the ground floor. You
could go three-course if you're an old stickler,
but little dishes are the principal bill of fare and
they pack quite a punch.

Closed 25 December, 1 January

Roka Aldwych
PLAN 3, C2

◉◉ CONTEMPORARY JAPANESE

020 7294 7636 | 71 Aldwych, WC2B 4HN

www.rokarestaurant.com

Roka is characterised by top-drawer ingredients,
with the freshest of seafood, to-the-second
timings and artful presentation. The speciality is
robatayaki: contemporary-style Japanese
barbecued food. Puddings include Japanese
pancakes with banana, toffee and black sugar
syrup, and cherry blossom ice cream
accompanying almond crème brûlée.

Closed 25 December

Savoy Grill
PLAN 3, C1

◉◉ BRITISH

020 7592 1600 | 1 Savoy Hill, Strand, WC2R 0EU

www.gordonramsayrestaurants.com

A handsome art deco room with lustrous
panelling, antiqued mirrors, chandeliers and
velvet banquettes, the Savoy's iconic Grill has
always been the place to see and be seen. Built
on classic Anglo-French foundations, the cooking
aims for comfort.

Open All Year

Spring
PLAN 3, C1
◎◎ EUROPEAN
020 3011 0115 | New Wing, Somerset House,
Lancaster Place, WC2R 1LA
www.springrestaurant.co.uk
After winning much acclaim at the rustic
glasshouse restaurant of Petersham Nurseries,
Skye Gyngell has brought her trademark style to
the grander stage of Somerset House. The
regularly-changing Mediterranean menu delivers
good-looking plates of seasonal fare with
flavours that shine. Though prices are high, a
fixed-price lunch option eases the bottom line.

Chef Skye Gyngell Closed 24–29 December

Terroirs
PLAN 3, B1
◎ MEDITERRANEAN, FRENCH
020 7036 0660 | 5 William IV Street, Covent Garden,
WC2N 4DW
www.terroirswinebar.com
A buzzy, split-level affair with an old-school
bistro look: enter on the ground floor, the
downstairs space is dominated by a big zinc-
topped bar, and eat where you like. The style is
provincial French cooking with a modern edge
and a nod towards the Mediterranean. Dishes are
never over-complicated, and flavours are
forthright and hearty.

Chef Simon Barnett Seats 120, Private dining 50
Closed Christmas, New Year, Easter and bank holidays
Prices from S £8, M £18.50, D £8 Notes Vegetarian
dishes, Children welcome

Tredwells
PLAN 3, B1
◎◎ MODERN BRITISH V 🍷 NOTABLE WINE LIST
020 3764 0840 | 4a Upper St Martin's Lane,
Covent Garden, WC2H 9NY
www.tredwells.com
Tredwells spreads over three floors with a
basement cocktail bar and two airy, retro-looking
dining rooms lit by large windows. The menu
describes itself as 'modern London cooking'
which translates as good-quality British
ingredients which have been livened up with
globetrotting flavours.

Chef Chantelle Nicholson Seats 150, Private dining 60
Closed 25–26 December, 1 January Prices from S £7,
M £18, D £4 Notes Children welcome

Yen London NEW
PLAN 3, C1
◎◎ TRADITIONAL, MODERN JAPANESE V
020 3915 6976 | 190 Strand, 5 Arundel Street,
WC2R 3DX
www.yen-london.co.uk
A buzzy open kitchen and sushi preparation
counter provide plenty of culinary action to
watch in this smartly minimal Japanese
restaurant set in an impressive double-height
space. Bowls of freshly-made soba (buckwheat)
noodles are the speciality; elsewhere, simplicity
and skilled execution are key in a roster of
flavour-packed mains and expertly-crafted
tempura, sushi and sashimi.

Chef Hiro Kihiyama Seats 75, Private dining 18
Closed Christmas, 1 January (variable) Notes Vegetarian
dishes, Children welcome

■ GREATER LONDON

BARNET
MAP 6, TQ29
Savoro Restaurant with Rooms
◎ MODERN EUROPEAN, BRITISH
020 8449 9888 | 206 High Street, EN5 5SZ
www.savoro.co.uk
Behind a rather quaint-looking shop front, the
restaurant has a cool, contemporary interior.
'Simple execution of good technique' is the
kitchen's mantra, with everything made in-house.
Puddings are no afterthought when among them
might be lemon crème brûlée with raspberries
and ginger shortbread.

Chef Yiannis Avramidis Seats 100, Private dining 50
Closed 1 January, 1 week New Year Parking 6
Notes Vegetarian dishes, Children welcome

BROMLEY
Chapter One
PLAN 1, H1
◎◎◎ MODERN EUROPEAN V
See page 298

BROMLEY   PLAN 1, H1

Chapter One

◉◉◉ MODERN EUROPEAN **V**
01689 854848 | Farnborough Common, Locksbottom, BR6 8NF
www.chapteronerestaurant.co.uk

Situated snugly on the suburban cusp of Kent, Andrew McLeish's relaxing venue looks discreetly upmarket, with crisply linened tables and gastronomic prints setting a refined tone. Whether you go for the six-course taster, the carte, or the remarkably wallet-friendly menu du jour, McLeish strikes an inviting balance here between assured modern European cooking and the pressing need to offer value. Pressed terrine of pig's head with a crispy croquant, gribiche sauce and mustard dressing makes for a punchy opener, while main course brings roast Barbary duck breast alongside crisp Anna potatoes, orange braised chicory, red cabbage and duck jus. There's an effortless understanding of combinations throughout the dishes, and dessert fits the bill with indulgent Valrhona chocolate marquise vividly offset by boozy griottine cherries and cherry sorbet.

Chef Andrew McLeish Seats 120, Private dining 55 Closed 2–4 January Parking 70 Notes Children welcome

HADLEY WOOD

MAP 6, TQ29

West Lodge Park Hotel

⊚ MODERN BRITISH

020 8216 3900 | Cockfosters Road, EN4 0PY

www.bealeshotels.co.uk

The Beale family's West Lodge stands in 35 acres of tranquil grounds, including an arboretum. Paintings by Mary Beale, a 17th-century ancestor, hang in the restaurant named after her, where dinner might be seared tuna, fennel and kohlrabi pickle; venison, roasted baby parsnips and braised blackberries; and Bramley apple pie, salted caramel ice cream and blackberry coulis.

Chef Wayne Turner **Seats** 92, Private dining 110 **Open** All Year **Parking** 75 **Notes** Vegetarian dishes, Children welcome

HEATHROW AIRPORT

La Belle Époque

PLAN 1, A3

⊚⊚ MODERN FRENCH

020 8757 5029 | Sofitel London Heathrow, Terminal 5, Wentworth Drive, London Heathrow Airport, TW6 2GD

www.la-belle-epoque.co

There's something a touch counter-intuitive about looking for seriously good cooking in the environs of Heathrow Airport, but put aside your preconceptions and head over the covered walkway from Terminal 5 into the swanky Sofitel hotel. With its lush hues of purple and royal blue, La Belle Époque offers a suave change of mood from the airport mayhem.

Chef Mark Lawton **Seats** 86, Private dining 20 **Closed** Christmas, bank holidays **Prices from** S £11, M £26, D £9.50 **Parking** 400 **Notes** Vegetarian dishes, Children welcome

Hilton London Heathrow Airport Terminal 5

MAP 6, TQ07

⊚ BRITISH, INTERNATIONAL

01753 686860 | Poyle Road, Colnbrook, SL3 0FF

www.heathrowt5.hilton.com

Open all day and located on the mezzanine level of this hotel by Terminal 5, with views over the lobby, The Gallery's long, globally inspired menu features dishes that recall an altogether more pastoral existence, with dishes from the farm, the field and the sea.

Chef Jasbeer Dawar **Seats** 203 **Open** All Year **Prices from** S £6.50, M £19.95, D £7.50 **Parking** 480 **Notes** Vegetarian dishes, Children welcome

Mr Todiwala's Kitchen

MAP 6, TQ07

⊚⊚ PORTUGUESE, INDIAN, PAN-ASIAN

01753 686860 | Hilton London Heathrow Airport Terminal 5, Poyle Road, Colnbrook, SL3 0FF

www.hilton.com/heathrowt5

Cyrus Todiwala (he of Café Spice Namaste) brings pan-Indian style to this airport hotel, in a clinically white atmosphere of lime-washed floors and café-style furnishings. Highly spiced, vividly seasoned food is the perfect antidote to corporate anonymity. Don't overlook the vegetarian dishes.

Chef Cyrus Todiwala, Arun Dev **Seats** 80, Private dining 6 **Closed** Christmas **Prices from** S £7.25, M £18.50, D £7.50 **Parking** 480 **Notes** Vegetarian dishes, Children welcome

Urban Brasserie NEW

MAP 6, TQ07

⊚⊚ MODERN BRITISH

020 3971 4411 | Crowne Plaza London Heathrow – T4, 1 Swindon Road, Terminal 4, London Heathrow Airport, TW6 3FJ

www.cpheathrowt4.com

Heathrow Airport isn't the most obvious spot to look for accomplished modern British cooking, but that's just what this smart hotel brasserie delivers, and it's easy to reach by foot from Terminal 4. Served in an airy space with grey leather seats, pale wood tables and a soothing ambience, the eclectic menu includes grills and Asian street food.

Vivre Restaurant

PLAN 1, A3

⊚ INTERNATIONAL

020 8757 5027 | Sofitel London Heathrow, Terminal 5, Wentworth Drive, London Heathrow Airport, TW6 2GD

www.sofitelheathrow.com

The Sofitel at Heathrow Terminal 5 boasts more decent eating than many airport hotels. As an alternative to the fine French goings-on in La Belle Époque, Vivre offers informal dining in an open-plan room of colourful contemporary design. The kitchen team are on view at their wokking and pizza-throwing, and service puts everyone at their ease. The large menu changes seasonally, but is reliably built around a core of firm favourites.

Chef Carl Stockenstrom **Seats** 235 **Open** All Year **Prices from** S £7, M £14, D £6.50 **Parking** 200 **Notes** Vegetarian dishes, Children welcome

KEW

The Glasshouse
PLAN 1, C3

◉◉◉ MODERN INTERNATIONAL ⚑NOTABLE WINE LIST

020 8940 6777 | 14 Station Parade, TW9 3PZ
www.glasshouserestaurant.co.uk
This perennially popular neighbourhood restaurant stands out in the parade of shops near Kew Gardens tube station. From the same stable as Chez Bruce in Wandsworth and La Trompette in Chiswick, its pedigree shines through from the off, with unshowy neutral tones, textured walls, white linen, polished-wood floors and colourful abstract artworks giving the space a smart modern sheen. But the main draw here is classy contemporary cooking that hits the high notes without seeming to try too hard, with head chef Gregory Wellman leading the team in producing prettily presented dishes high on precision, flavour and intelligent simplicity. Big, gutsy flavours can be expected in main-course lamb rump and belly with baby artichokes, potato gnocchi, anchovy, rosemary and garlic. Dessert is equally impressive: creamy malt custard with almond ice cream and cocoa nib. The wine list is a corker, and lunch a steal for cooking of this level.

Chef Gregory Wellman **Seats** 60 **Closed** 24–26 December, 1 January **Notes** Vegetarian dishes, Children accepted at lunch only

PINNER

Friends Restaurant
PLAN 1, C3

◉ BRITISH, FRENCH

020 8866 0286 | 11 High Street, HA5 5PJ
www.friendsrestaurant.co.uk
Occupying a 500-year-old timbered building in Betjeman's suburban Metro-Land, Friends' devoted local fan base turns up for top-grade meat and fish handled with skill and sound modern thinking. Perhaps seared scallops with parsnip purée, black pudding crumble, crispy bacon and truffle foam for your opener.

Chef Stelian Scripcariu **Seats** 40, Private dining 14 **Open** All Year **Prices from** S £5.75, M £17.95, D £6.50 **Notes** Vegetarian dishes, Children welcome

RICHMOND UPON THAMES

Bacco Restaurant & Wine Bar
PLAN 1, C2

◉ ITALIAN

020 8332 0348 | 39–41 Kew Road, TW9 2NQ
www.bacco-restaurant.co.uk
This smart independent Italian has built a loyal local fan base, who come for its lively ambience

and the straight-talking classic cooking. There's a decked terrace out on the pavement, and inside it's all bare floorboards and colourful artwork. Mains deliver the likes of oven-roasted cod with chickpea and chorizo stew.

Chef Gian Francesco **Seats** 70, Private dining 25 **Closed** Christmas, New Year and bank holidays **Prices from** S £8.50, M £15, D £5 **Notes** Vegetarian dishes, Children welcome

Bingham Riverhouse
PLAN 1, C2

◉◉◉ MODERN BRITISH ⚑NOTABLE WINE LIST

020 8940 0902 | 61–63 Petersham Road, TW10 6UT
www.binghamriverhouse.com
Occupying a handsome pair of Georgian townhouses, with gorgeous Thames views making the covered balcony a hot ticket for alfresco dining during the summer, the Bingham sports a boutique look straight out of an interiors magazine. Easy-on-the-eye neutral hues and an ambience of calm set the tone in the elegantly relaxed dining room – it's all very comfortable indeed, and Andrew Cole is a skilful chef who coaxes sharply-defined flavours and textures from top-drawer materials in his well-conceived modern British creations. An appealing starter of chicken terrine with baby leeks, pickled shemeji mushrooms and black truffle mayonnaise is a perfect balance of flavours. At main, roasted hake comes draped with peppered lardo, accompanied by a light haricot bean cassoulet and white pudding. Last but not least, a creative reworking of rhubarb trifle, with tender jelly, light sponge and excellent compôte is topped with a light mascarpone mousse, sorbet and delicious crispy ginger.

Chef Andrew Cole **Seats** 82, Private dining 110 **Open** All Year **Parking** 20 **Notes** Vegetarian dishes, Children welcome

La Buvette
PLAN 1, C2

◉ FRENCH, MEDITERRANEAN *V*

020 8940 6264 | 6 Church Walk, TW9 1SN
www.labuvette.co.uk
Down a leafy walkway off the high street, La Buvette is a winner all year round, whether you're out at one of the courtyard tables or ensconced indoors, where chequered tablecloths and sunny yellow walls foster a cosy old-school bistro ambience. Expect a cross-Channel menu of uncomplicated classic French dishes backed up by daily specials.

Chef Buck Carter **Seats** 50 **Closed** 25–26 December, 1 January, Good Friday, Easter Sunday **Prices from** S £6, M £14.50, D £5.75 **Notes** Children welcome

The Dysart Petersham

PLAN 1, C2

◉◉ TRADITIONAL EUROPEAN *V*
020 8940 8005 | 135 Petersham Road, Petersham,
TW10 7AA
www.thedysartpetersham.co.uk
The Dysart occupies a 1904 Arts and Crafts
building with original leaded windows and
wooden window frames facing south over
Richmond Park. Sunshine streams in on bright
days, and a low-key jazz soundtrack floats
around the elegant room. Kenneth Culhane's
confident and sure-footed cooking delivers some
fascinating, intricately detailed dishes full of
subtle interplays of taste and texture.

Chef Kenneth Culhane **Seats** 45, Private dining 40
Closed 25 December, 1 week January, 1 week August
Prices from S £8.50, M £24.50, D £8.50 **Parking** 30
Notes No children after 8pm

Petersham Nurseries Café

PLAN 1, C2

◉◉ MODERN BRITISH, ITALIAN
020 8332 8665 | Church Lane, Petersham Road,
TW10 7AB
www.petershamnurseries.com
This busy one-off restaurant is a romantically
quirky, shabby-chic place, with its dirt floor and
mismatched tables and chairs, but that's all part
of the fun. The kitchen sends out a weekly-
changing menu of modern Italian-accented ideas
with fresh produce plucked from the garden.

Chef Ambra Papa **Seats** 120, Private dining 20
Closed 25-27 December **Prices from** S £13, M £25.50,
D £6 **Notes** Vegetarian dishes, Children welcome

The Petersham Restaurant at The Petersham Hotel

PLAN 1, C2

◉◉ MODERN *V*
020 8940 7471 | Nightingale Lane, TW10 6UZ
www.petershamhotel.co.uk
Benefiting from panoramic views of the famous
bend in the River Thames and surrounding
Petersham Meadows, enjoy the warm and
welcoming atmosphere, attentive service and
smartly dressed tables. The menus offer
seasonal dishes at good value. Try the
Petersham champagne.

Chef Jean-Didier Gouges **Seats** 90, Private dining 30
Closed 25 December **Prices from** S £9, M £19, D £9
Parking 45 **Notes** Children welcome

RUISLIP

The Barn Hotel

PLAN 1, A5

◉◉ MODERN FRENCH
01895 636057 | West End Road, HA4 6JB
www.thebarnhotel.co.uk
An expansive modern boutique hotel handy for
inward-bound travellers at Heathrow, The Barn
might sound rather agricultural, but stands in
fact in three acres of attractive landscaped
gardens. A Jacobean effect has been created in
the dark-panelled dining room, Hawtrey's.

Open All Year

SURBITON

The French Table

PLAN 1, C1

◉◉ MODERN FRENCH 🍷 NOTABLE WINE LIST
020 8399 2365 | 85 Maple Road, KT6 4AW
www.thefrenchtable.co.uk
Tucked away in leafy Maple Road, The French
Table is a smart neighbourhood outfit.
Dressed-to-impress modern French cooking
punches above its weight on a fixed-price
repertoire buoyed by a five-course taster. Breads
are a triumph, while pastry impresses too – no
surprise with its sibling boulangerie/patisserie
bang next door.

Chef Eric Guignard **Seats** 60, Private dining 32
Closed 25 December to 4 January, 17 August to
4 September **Notes** Vegetarian dishes, Children
welcome

TWICKENHAM

A Cena

PLAN 1, C2

◉ MODERN ITALIAN
020 8288 0108 | 418 Richmond Road, TW1 2EB
www.acena.co.uk
Just the sort of informal neighbourhood bistro-
style Italian we'd all like on our patch, A Cena
dishes up comforting, authentic cooking made
with minimum fuss in a dining room done out
with a woody mix of dark floorboards, church
pew furniture and white walls hung with mirrors.
The kitchen makes a good job of classic dishes.

Closed Christmas and bank holidays

■ MERSEYSIDE

FRANKBY
MAP 15, SJ28

Riviera at Hillbark
◉◉ FRENCH, MEDITERRANEAN

0151 625 2400 | Hillbark Hotel & Spa, Royden Park,
CH48 1NP

www.rivierarestaurant.co.uk

This all-mod-cons spa hotel features a light-filled
Riviera dining room, which embraces a sweeping
Mediterranean arc all the way from Nice to
Liguria, presented in the grazing format of little
and large dishes, courtesy of a super-cool
modern brasserie service.

Open All Year

HESWALL
MAP 15, SJ28

Burnt Truffle
◉ MODERN BRITISH

0151 342 1111 | 106 Telegraph Road, CH60 0AQ

www.burnttruffle.net

The sibling of the Sticky Walnut in Chester, Burnt
Truffle follows a very similar and effective
contemporary bistro vibe with its roster of
intelligently updated classics, and good-looking
decor featuring natural textures of wood, stone
and slate. Expect inventive, well-executed dishes
and bold flavours.

Closed 25–26 December

LIVERPOOL
MAP 15, SJ39

The Art School Restaurant, Liverpool
◉◉ MODERN INTERNATIONAL *V* 🍷 NOTABLE WINE LIST

0151 230 8600 | 1 Sugnall Street, L7 7EB

www.theartschoolrestaurant.co.uk

Local food hero Paul Askew has brought
thoroughgoing British culinary modernism to
Liverpool, in the stunning Victorian setting of the
light-filled lantern room of what was once the
Home for Destitute Children. Dishes are carefully
composed, full of imaginative juxtapositions, and
confidently rendered.

Chef Paul Askew Seats 48, Private dining 28
Closed 25–26 December, 1–7 January, 3–11 August
Notes Children under 12 years welcome until 7.30pm

Chez Mal Brasserie
◉ MODERN BRITISH

0151 229 5000 | Malmaison Liverpool,
7 William Jessop Way, Princes Dock, L3 1QZ

www.malmaison.com

On the landward side of Princes Dock,
Malmaison's first purpose-built hotel is a
landmark for the maritime city. Echoing the city's
industrial heritage, the exposed bricks, lighting
gantries and air ducts of the double-height
brasserie, are balanced by warm, plush, purple
and black furnishings.

Open All Year

The London Carriage Works
◉◉ MODERN BRITISH

0151 705 2222 | Hope Street Hotel, 40 Hope Street,
L1 9DA

www.thelondoncarriageworks.co.uk

The stripped-back interior of the old workshop at
The London Carriage Works is a very modern
setting with large windows to give a view of the
street action. The menu makes much of
provenance and there's a satisfying regional
flavour to the food.

Chef Mike Kenyon Seats 60, Private dining 110 Open All
Year Prices from S £6.50, M £17.50, D £7.50
Notes Vegetarian dishes, Children welcome

Mowgli
◉ INDIAN

0151 708 9356 | 69 Bold Street, L1 4EZ

www.mowglistreetfood.com

Restauranteur Nisha Katona brings Indian street
and domestic food to Liverpool, in a space with
rough-edged Stateside appeal. High-concept
recreations of popular subcontinental dishes
begin with the likes of chat bombs, crisp potato
shells with chickpeas, spices and yogurt
garnished with pomegranate.

Closed 25–26 December, 1 January

Panoramic 34

◉ MODERN EUROPEAN

0151 236 5534 | 34th Floor, West Tower, Brook Street, L3 9PJ

www.panoramic34.com

Panoramic 34 offers stunning views from the 34th floor – the city, the Mersey flowing out to sea and the mountains of north Wales. The lift takes you to a sleek, modern dining room with floor-to-ceiling windows and the menu features a contemporary take on classic dishes.

Chef Dominic Grundy **Seats** 80 **Closed** 25–26 December, 1 January **Prices from** S £9, M £17, D £8.50
Notes Vegetarian dishes, No children under 8 years at dinner

Röski Restaurant *NEW*

◉◉ MODERN BRITISH

0151 708 8698 | 16 Rodney Street, L1 2TE

www.roskirestaurant.com

MasterChef: The Professionals' 2012 winner Anton Piotrowski's restaurant is a smart venue located in the bustling Georgian quarter of Liverpool. The main kitchen is in the basement, and there are exciting plans to develop a 'chef's table' down there. The tasting menu format has a notable focus on early seasonality and look out for the great value lunch. Reservations and good time-keeping are definitely necessary.

60 Hope Street Restaurant

◉ MODERN BRITISH *V*

0151 707 6060 | 60 Hope Street, L1 9BZ

www.60hopestreet.com

A Liverpool dining fixture for two decades, this popular Georgian townhouse restaurant still pulls in the crowds. Occupying a convenient spot close to the Philharmonic Hall, the unfussy decor is reflected in the simple, seasonal modern food, which puts an international spin on well-sourced British ingredients.

Chef Neil Devereux **Seats** 90, Private dining 40
Closed 26 December **Prices from** S £7.95, M £14.95, D £6.95 **Notes** Children welcome

OXTON
MAP 15, SJ28

Fraiche

◉◉◉ MODERN FRENCH, EUROPEAN *V* NOTABLE WINE LIST

0151 652 2914 | 11 Rose Mount, CH43 5SG

www.restaurantfraiche.com

The discrete frontage of Fraiche, in the Wirral conservation village of Oxton, gives no clue as to the feast for the senses that awaits within. Dining chez Marc Wilkinson is almost as much as a thrilling visual experience as it is one of taste, with the LED lighting changing throughout the meal, and projected images of the seasons helping to set the mood. What arrives on the plate is a visual treat, too, an array of creative presentations that will make you smile and gasp with amazement. First and foremost, the sense most stimulated will be taste, as Marc and his team deliver a highly personal experience that takes in contemporary cooking techniques while never losing sight of the produce itself – top-drawer ingredients from start to finish.

An opening salvo from the six-course signature menu might be Nordic smoked salmon, bringing together bergamot cream and pineapple granité in a compelling combination, with fresh sea herbs, followed by celeriac textures with ceps and pears. Fresh fish is handled with skill, a fabulous piece of brill, say, with crisp rice noodles and a spot-on dashi broth, plus smoked yogurt and more sea herbs. Next up, Loire Valley quail stars in another course with beetroot and kohlrabi, and a wee bit of black pudding, and among sweet courses, toasted coconut flakes and foam come with yuzu gel and shards of sesame tuiles. It's a joyful journey of texture and flavour, led by a hands-on chef who can be seen at the pass, ensuring the superb standard is maintained. The wine list has lots of interesting options at the lower end of the price spectrum alongside some outstanding vintages.

Chef Marc Wilkinson **Seats** 12, Private dining 12
Closed 25 December, 1 January, 2 weeks August
Notes No children under 8 years

PORT SUNLIGHT

Riviera at Leverhulme

◎◎ FRENCH, MEDITERRANEAN

0151 644 6655 | Leverhulme Hotel, Central Road, CH62 5EZ

www.rivierarestaurant.co.uk

Lord Leverhulme opened the place in 1907 as a cottage hospital for soap works employees at his Port Sunlight garden village, and who wouldn't find their health restored amid such exquisite art deco surroundings? The comprehensive French-Mediterranean menu is a mix of small and large plates that come to the table 'as and when ready'.

Open All Year

SOUTHPORT

Bistrot Vérité

◎◎ FRENCH, INTERNATIONAL

01704 564199 | 7 Liverpool Road, Birkdale, PR8 4AR

www.bistrotverite.co.uk

Marc and Michaela Vérité's place is the essence of a neighbourhood bistro. The tables are closely packed, the staff are clued-up, and the place generates a contented buzz. Start perhaps with baked crab thermidor and move on to roast haunch of red deer with pear and fois gras cromesquis and red wine jus.

Chef Marc Vérité **Seats** 45 **Closed** 1 week February and 1 week August **Prices from** S £6, M £14, D £7 **Notes** Vegetarian dishes, Children welcome

Gusto Trattoria

◎ MODERN ITALIAN

01704 544255 | 58–62 Lord Street, PR8 1QB

www.gustotrattoria.co.uk

Gusto is a trattoria with a nice line in cheerful bonhomie and some good and proper Italian cooking. The two rooms are looked over by the charming service team and the open kitchen adds to the buzz of the place. The food does not attempt to reinvent the wheel, just to do things properly. The pizzas are very good.

Chef Giorgio Lamola **Seats** 38 **Open** All Year **Prices from** S £4.95, M £6.95, D £4.95 **Notes** Vegetarian dishes, Children welcome

Vincent Café and Restaurant

◎◎ MODERN EUROPEAN

01704 883800 | Vincent Hotel, 98 Lord Street, PR8 1JR

www.thevincenthotel.com

This is the place to be in the evening, with lights dimmed and candles lit. Tables are closely packed and floor-to-ceiling windows look onto bustling Lord Street (alfresco dining is an option). The menu roams around Britain and Europe before arriving in Japan with some platters of authentic sushi and sashimi.

Chef Ian Moss **Seats** 85, Private dining 40 **Open** All Year **Prices from** S £6, M £12, D £6.50 **Parking** 50 **Notes** Vegetarian dishes, Children welcome

THORNTON HOUGH

The Lawns Restaurant at Thornton Hall

◎◎◎ MODERN EUROPEAN *V*

0151 336 3938 | Neston Road, CH63 1JF

www.lawnsrestaurant.com

On the fringes of the pretty Wirral village of Thornton Hough, this classy spa hotel exudes an unerring sense of occasion, making it a big hit for weddings or landmark days in the calendar. At its heart is The Lawns Restaurant, occupying a grand room with a harmonious mix of old and new – teardrop chandeliers, fancy plasterwork and ornate wood carvings set against dark contemporary tones and unclothed tables. The kitchen is on song, sending out modernist dishes that team prime regional ingredients with a resourceful range of techniques. The workmanship is impressive whether in a starter of hand-dived scallops teamed with smoked eel, salt-baked kohlrabi and apple in various forms, or a main course starring suckling pig – the loin, braised belly and crisped pig's ear helped along by white asparagus, Roscoff onion and the carefully managed contrast of rhubarb compôte and liquorice. Finish with an inventive trio of garriguette strawberries, baked yogurt and matcha tea.

Chef Richard Collingwood **Seats** 45, Private dining 24 **Prices from** S £13, M £25, D £12 **Parking** 250 **Notes** No children under 12 years after 6pm

■ NORFOLK

BAWBURGH
MAP 13, TG10

The Kings Head Bawburgh
◉◉ MODERN BRITISH
01603 744977 | Harts Lane, NR9 3LS
www.kingsheadbawburgh.co.uk
The pub itself dates from the early 17th century, but the king in question is Edward VII (born 1841), chosen for his reputation as a bon viveur. There are real ales and the likes of fish and chips up for grabs, plus low oak beams, real fires and plenty of character. Its reputation as a dining pub is confirmed by its well-judged output.

Chef Jake Armes, Geoff Smith, Max Emmerson
Seats 62, Private dining 18 Open All Year
Prices from S £6, M £13, D £5 Parking 30
Notes Vegetarian dishes, Children welcome

BLAKENEY
MAP 13, TG04

The Blakeney Hotel
◉ MODERN BRITISH
01263 740797 | The Quay, NR25 7NE
www.blakeneyhotel.co.uk
Those who like to be by the sea need look no further: this is in a perfect spot on the quay, with magnificent views over the estuary to Blakeney Point Area of Outstanding Natural Beauty. Well-sourced raw materials underpin the operation in the sea-facing restaurant.

Closed 25-27 December

Morston Hall
◉◉◉◉ MODERN BRITISH V ◆ NOTABLE WINE LIST
01263 741041 | Morston, Holt, NR25 7AA
www.morstonhall.com
Galton and Tracy Blackiston's 17th-century country house is truly an idyllic escape from the daily grind. The old manor is handsome without being overly grand, and your hosts are passionate about the area and its magnificent produce. The conservatory dining room makes a soothing setting, especially when the sun is out and the French doors are open. Dinner is served at a single setting, so it's aperitifs at 7pm before heading through to the dining room at 8pm where a single menu awaits.

The seven-course tasting menu presents refined classical technique with contemporary verve and intricate yet seemingly effortless presentation. An opening salvo might be stuffed partridge, wrapped in pancetta to keep it moist, with buttery, silky endive purée providing a welcome mellow sweetness. Timing of Herdwick lamb is spot on, while roasted root vegetables add a lovely earthiness; light, crisply golden haggis complements the dish perfectly. At dessert, a pear and honey tart with delicate, crisp pastry and subtly spiced poached pears is balanced by a quenelle of cream, oats and crushed nuts and finished with a honeycomb tuille. Add cheese from the trolley if you can. The wine list covers the globe and has lots of gems among its pages, and you're in safe hands if you opt for the wine flight.

Chef Galton Blackiston, Greg Anderson Seats 50
Closed 3 days at Christmas, January Parking 50
Notes Children welcome

BRANCASTER STAITHE
MAP 13, TF74

The White Horse
◉◉ MODERN BRITISH
01485 210262 | PE31 8BY
www.whitehorsebrancaster.co.uk
Here, the big skies of north Norfolk can be viewed over platefuls of fantastic regional produce, a sight made even better from a table in the conservatory area. In a location such as this, diners are bound to have fish and seafood in mind. Local meat fans might find their eye focusses on pheasant breast, red cabbage, fondant, kale, hazelnuts and jus.

Chef Fran Hartshorne Seats 100 Open All Year
Prices from S £7, M £28, D £7 Parking 30
Notes Vegetarian dishes, Children welcome

BURNHAM MARKET
MAP 13, TF84

North Street Bistro NEW
◉◉ BRITISH, EUROPEAN
01328 730330 | 20 North Street, PE31 8HG
www.20northstreet.co.uk
A warm welcome is guaranteed at this relaxed and intimate bistro occupying a converted chapel with high ceilings, bare floorboards, unclothed wooden tables and a minimalist white decor. The kitchen serves up a weekly-changing menu of no-nonsense, clear-flavoured food that draws on classic French techniques combined with top-notch British produce.

Chef Dan Fancett Seats 26 Closed 1st week October, last 3 weeks January Prices from S £6.50, M £12, D £2
Notes Vegetarian dishes, Children welcome, no children's menu – smaller dishes only

Socius NEW

◉◉ MODERN BRITISH V

01328 738307 | 11 Foundry Place, PE31 8LG

www.sociusnorfolk.co.uk

Socius is Latin for joining in/partaking, and that's the essence of this new restaurant where the dishes are designed to share and the theme is very much modern British tapas. Well-chosen, locally sourced produce is the order of the day. The open-plan kitchen/restaurant has a contemporary feel and the team are very friendly and demonstrate a high degree of professionalism.

Chef Dan Lawrence **Seats** 54, Private dining 30
Closed 2nd and 3rd week of January
Prices from S £5.50, M £10.50, D £7.50 **Parking** 186
Notes Vegetarian dishes, Children welcome

COLTISHALL
MAP 13, TG21

Norfolk Mead Hotel

◉◉ MODERN BRITISH

01603 737531 | Church Lane, NR12 7DN

www.norfolkmead.co.uk

This handsome old house in the heart of the Norfolk Broads is looking dapper with its contemporary, country-chic finish. The smart restaurant follows the theme, seamlessly blending period features with an uncluttered style – white walls, abstract artworks, and simple flower arrangements. On the food front, the kitchen hauls in fine local ingredients and offers a vibrant modern British menu.

Chef Anna Duttson, Damien Woollard **Seats** 40, Private dining 22 **Open** All Year **Parking** 45 **Notes** Vegetarian dishes, Children welcome

CROMER
MAP 13, TG24

The Grove Cromer

◉◉ BRITISH, SEAFOOD

01263 512412 | 95 Overstrand Road, NR27 0DJ

www.thegrovecromer.co.uk

A private path leads through woodland to the beach from this north Norfolk hotel, a substantial white Georgian house partly covered in creepers.

In the restaurant, it's all about clear, fresh flavours. You might try Norfolk cheeses with quince jelly as an alternative to dessert.

Chef Reis Khalil **Seats** 48, Private dining 30
Closed January (phone to check) **Parking** 15
Notes Vegetarian dishes, Children welcome

Sea Marge Hotel

◉◉ MODERN BRITISH

01263 579579 | 16 High Street, Overstrand, NR27 0AB

www.mackenziehotels.com

The Sea Marge is a family-run Edwardian hotel of great charm with terraced lawns sitting just above the coastal path, and glorious marine views from the panelled dining room. Chocolate and ginger terrine with salted caramel ice cream makes a satisfying dessert option.

Chef Rene Ilupar **Seats** 80, Private dining 40 **Open** All Year **Prices from** S £7, M £14.50, D £6.25 **Parking** 50
Notes Vegetarian dishes, Children welcome

The White Horse Overstrand

◉◉ MODERN EUROPEAN, BRITISH

01263 579237 | 34 High Street, Overstrand, NR27 0AB

www.whitehorseoverstrand.co.uk

In a pretty village a short walk from the sea, this Victorian inn's restaurant occupies a converted barn, given a modern look within flint walls and oak ceiling trusses. The kitchen's a hive of industry, making everything on the premises, from breads to ice creams.

Chef Nathan Boon **Seats** 80, Private dining 40 **Open** All Year **Prices from** S £5.50, M £14, D £5 **Parking** 6
Notes Vegetarian dishes, Children welcome

FLEGGBURGH
MAP 13, TG41

The Kings Arms NEW

◉◉ MODERN, TRADITIONAL

01493 368333 | Main Road, NR29 3AG

www.kingsarmsfleggburgh.com

This 19th-century red-brick pub in the village of Fleggburgh is split across a few areas with a bar feel to the front and a slightly more formal style dining area to the side with clothed tables. Service is attentive and professional with a gastro pub feel to proceedings.

Open All Year

GREAT YARMOUTH
MAP 13, TG50

Imperial Hotel
◉ MODERN BRITISH *V*
01493 842000 | North Drive, NR30 1EQ
www.imperialhotel.co.uk
Generations of the Mobbs family have run the Imperial since the 1930s, when one of its attractions was being seated at separate tables. Today, frosted glass panels demonstrate that separate tables are still the elevated norm. Classic dishes from the brasserie repertoire are the stock-in-trade.

Chef Peter Clarke, Daniel Lawrence **Seats** 60, Private dining 140 **Closed** 24–28 and 31 December
Prices from S £7, M £14, D £7 **Parking** 45 **Notes** Children welcome

The Prom Hotel
◉ CONTEMPORARY BRITISH
01493 842308 | 77 Marine Parade, NR30 2DH
www.promhotel.co.uk
Overlooking the seafront, the Prom is on Marine Parade. Strollers is its attractively furnished restaurant, with a bar that's perfectly positioned for pre-meal drinks. Yarmouth's trawler fleet has all but disappeared, but fish and seafood still have their place on the menu.

Chef Leigh Schofield **Seats** 40 **Open** All Year
Prices from S £6.50, M £11.50, D £6.40 **Parking** 30
Notes Vegetarian dishes, Children welcome

GRIMSTON
MAP 12, TF72

Congham Hall Country House Hotel
◉◉ MODERN BRITISH, EUROPEAN *V*
01485 600250 | Lynn Road, PE32 1AH
www.conghamhallhotel.co.uk
This Georgian house has gorgeous gardens, a swish spa and a restaurant full of period charm. A herb garden produces an astonishing 400 varieties. French windows look onto the garden, while the cooking that arrives at pristine linen-clad tables is gently modern in outlook.

Chef James O'Connor **Seats** 50, Private dining 20
Open All Year **Prices from** S £8, M £21, D £8 **Parking** 50
Notes Children welcome

HEACHAM
MAP 12, TF63

Heacham Manor Hotel
◉ MEDITERRANEAN, EUROPEAN
01485 536030 | Hunstanton Road, PE31 7JX
www.heacham-manor.co.uk
The wide-open skies of Norfolk's fabulous coast make Heacham Manor an attractive prospect, and the place even comes with a coastal golf course. Built as an Elizabethan manor, the hotel has been brought smartly up-to-date and the conservatory-style Mulberry Restaurant has been extended and modernised.

Open All Year

HETHERSETT
MAP 13, TG10

Park Farm Hotel
◉ MODERN BRITISH
01603 810264 | NR9 3DL
www.parkfarm-hotel.co.uk
Park Farm Hotel and its spa and conference facilities are surrounded by 200 acres of beautiful open countryside. The contemporary, open-plan Seasons Restaurant looks out over the gardens while uniformed staff deliver the kitchen's well-presented and well-timed modern British fare.

Open All Year

HOLT
MAP 13, TG03

The Lawns
◉ MODERN EUROPEAN
01263 713390 | 26 Station Road, NR25 6BS
www.lawnshotelholt.co.uk
A small hotel dating from Georgian times, The Lawns offers a number of dining options: bar, conservatory, restaurant and south-facing garden. It's a warm and friendly place, reflected in a menu of largely comfortingly reassuring dishes pinned on East Anglian produce.

Chef Leon Brookes, Harry Hadley **Seats** 60 **Open** All Year **Prices from** S £6.50, M £12.50, D £6.50 **Parking** 18
Notes Vegetarian dishes, Children welcome

The Pheasant Hotel & Restaurant

◉ MODERN BRITISH

01263 588382 | Coast Road, Kelling, NR25 7EG

www.pheasanthotelnorfolk.co.uk

With the never ending beaches and marshland of the north Norfolk coast on hand, The Pheasant is plumb in one of the country's most fashionable resort areas. Cooking is modern British, with seafood a strong suit. Afternoon teas are an abiding part of The Pheasant's appeal.

Chef David Carter **Seats** 78, Private dining 30 **Open** All Year **Prices from** S £7.50, M £14.50, D £8 **Parking** 50 **Notes** Vegetarian dishes, Children welcome

---

HUNSTANTON
MAP 12, TF64

Caley Hall Hotel

◉ MODERN BRITISH

01485 533486 | Old Hunstanton Road, PE36 6HH

www.caleyhallhotel.co.uk

Built around a manor dating from 1648, Caley Hall is a short walk to the wide beaches on The Wash, a twitcher's paradise. Its restaurant, in a former stable block, is a relaxing-looking room. It's a popular place offering precisely cooked, quality East Anglian produce.

Chef Chris Brown **Seats** 80 **Closed** 22–26 December **Prices from** S £4.50, M £12.50, D £4.95 **Parking** 50 **Notes** Vegetarian dishes, Children welcome

The Neptune Restaurant with Rooms

◉◉◉ MODERN EUROPEAN

01485 532122 | 85 Old Hunstanton Road, Old Hunstanton, PE36 6HZ

www.theneptune.co.uk

Just a short hop from the coast, The Neptune still has the look of an old inn, with its creeper-covered Georgian façade, but it's a top-notch restaurant with rooms these days. Much of the glorious regional bounty around these parts finds its way into Kevin Mangeolles' kitchen and onto a fixed-price carte and full-works tasting menu. The dining room is a smart, intimate space, with a neutral colour scheme and tables dressed in white linen. The cooking has classical roots, loads of good ideas and those local ingredients to the fore; Brancaster mussels, for example, with Serrano ham and apple, or Norfolk quail and truffle terrine. Main course suckling pig is accompanied by cabbage, butternut squash and dauphine potato, while British and French cheeses come with biscuits and grape chutney, or there might be almond iced nougat with

strawberry, coconut and lime. The smart wine list has good options by the glass and half bottle.

Chef Kevin Mangeolles **Seats** 20 **Closed** 3 weeks January, 1 week May, 1 week November and 26 December **Parking** 6 **Notes** No children under 10 years

---

LODDON
MAP 13, TM39

The Loddon Swan

◉◉ MODERN BRITISH

01508 528039 | 23 Church Plain, NR14 6LX

www.theloddonswan.co.uk

Close to the stunning River Chet, this 18th-century coaching inn retains traditional charm along with 21st-century styling. While much is made of local sourcing of ingredients, the menu mixes modern British dishes with Mediterranean classics.

Closed 26 December

NORTH WALSHAM
MAP 13, TG23

Beechwood Hotel

◉◉ MODERN BRITISH V

01692 403231 | 20 Cromer Road, NR28 0HD

www.beechwood-hotel.co.uk

Hospitality is top of the agenda at this charming country house hotel, with hands-on owners and plenty of staff ensuring that guests are well looked after. The kitchen sources most ingredients from within 10 miles of the hotel and sends out contemporary British ideas.

Chef Steven Norgate **Seats** 60 **Prices from** S £7.50, M £15.50, D £4.95 **Parking** 20 **Notes** Children welcome

---

NORWICH
MAP 13, TG20

Benedicts

◉◉◉ MODERN BRITISH V

01603 926080 | 9 St Benedicts Street, NR2 4PE

www.restaurantbenedicts.com

Norwich is firmly established on the UK's foodie firmament thanks to Benedicts, a switched-on operation where pared-back, Scandi-chic looks tick all the boxes of a big-city venue and make a suitably modernist setting for chef-patron Richard Bainbridge's innovative contemporary cooking. Devotees of Great British Menu may remember that Bainbridge was the 2015 dessert winner, so diners can be assured of exciting 21st-century food with stimulating combinations of excellent materials. A starter of Thornage Hall beetroot tartare comes with confit egg yolk, pickled onion and chervil, or you might prefer Norfolk partridge, spätzle, chestnut and pomegranate. For main, there might be Skrei cod with parsnip, roasted onions and shellfish bisque. To finish, Nanny Bush's trifle (the GBM winning dish) with milk jam remains as a signature finisher, or you might go for the splendid treacle tart with caramelised pecans and vanilla. There's a seasonal à la carte, six- or eight-course tasting options, and a daily changing set lunch which offers remarkable value.

Chef Richard Bainbridge **Seats** 40, Private dining 16 **Closed** 29 July to 14 August, 23 December to 8 January **Notes** Children welcome

Best Western Annesley House Hotel
⊛⊛ MODERN BRITISH
01603 624553 | 6 Newmarket Road, NR2 2LA
www.bw-annesleyhouse.co.uk
Standing just outside the old city walls, Annesley's landscaped gardens impart a country-house feel, and an old vine supplies sweet red grapes to garnish the cheese plates. Perhaps try the roast guinea fowl with confit garlic and braised baby gem for the main course.

Chef Saul King **Seats** 30 **Closed** Christmas **Prices from** S £6.75, M £19.50, D £6.75 **Parking** 29 **Notes** Vegetarian dishes, Children welcome

Brasted's
⊛⊛ MODERN EUROPEAN
01508 491112 | Manor Farm Barns, Fox Road, Framingham Pigot, NR14 7PZ
www.brasteds.co.uk
In the village of Framingham Pigot, Brasted's occupies a converted barn, a charming room of raftered ceiling, oak floor and brick walls. Sure-footed experience brings the complex food together. A starter might be poached ray wing with grape gel, steamed clams and chorizo and truffle cream.

Open All Year

See advertisement on page 310

Farmyard NEW
⊛⊛ MODERN BRITISH
01603 733188 | 23 St Benedicts Street, NR2 4PF
www.farmyardrestaurant.com
Driven by a passion for Norfolk's finest produce, the team at this ultra-modern, minimalist bistro in the heart of the city are on a roll. Everything is cooked from scratch in the open kitchen, with a charcoal-fired oven playing its part. A daily-changing menu delivers contemporary, innovative combinations with knockout textures, flavours and presentation.

Chef John Walker **Seats** 52 **Prices from** S £6, M £13, D £6.50 **Notes** Vegetarian dishes, Children welcome

Maids Head Hotel
⊛⊛ MODERN BRITISH
01603 209955 | Tombland, NR3 1LB
www.maidsheadhotel.co.uk
The brick-built hotel in the city centre lays claim to being the UK's oldest, having been feeding and watering East Anglian travellers for 800 years. Dining goes on in a glassed-in courtyard with a quarry-tiled floor and simple wooden tables.

Chef Magic Pomierny **Seats** 100, Private dining 130 **Open** All Year **Prices from** S £8, M £17, D £8 **Parking** 60 **Notes** Vegetarian dishes, Children welcome

Roger Hickman's Restaurant
⊛⊛⊛ MODERN BRITISH V 𝟏 NOTABLE WINE LIST
01603 633522 | 79 Upper St Giles Street, NR2 1AB
www.rogerhickmansrestaurant.com
The location, in a quiet cul-de-sac near the cathedral, may be discreet, but Roger Hickman's calm and comfortable restaurant is a popular place, a refined and elegant setting for original artworks, smartly laid tables, and confident, attentive service. The modern British cooking is equally refined, stylishly presented and demonstrates a fine grasp of technique and seasonal opportunities. The wine list is well worth exploring, and fixed-price menus and tasting options are offered at both lunch and dinner. You might begin with a heritage carrot salad with lemon yogurt and dukkah crumb, or blowtorched mackerel with mackerel mousse, the flavours of gooseberry and horseradish a sharp contrast to the fish. Main course roast partridge comes with truffle mash, parsnips, sprouts and bacon, while butternut squash gnocchi with shiitake mushroom, cavolo nero and sage and chestnut crumb is an excellent wintery vegetarian option. A dessert of forced rhubarb with blood orange cake, custard and ginger ice cream shows spring is reassuringly just over the horizon.

Chef Roger Hickman **Seats** 40, Private dining 18 **Closed** 2 weeks in January **Notes** Children welcome

Stower Grange
⊛ MODERN BRITISH
01603 860210 | 40 School Road, Drayton, NR8 6EF
www.stowergrange.co.uk
The ivy-covered country house in its own wooded grounds a few miles out of Norwich is a charming family-run hotel where contemporary cooking based on quality ingredients aims to satisfy rather than startle. Try crisp-skinned sea bass with wild mushrooms, beetroot and puréed onions as a main course.

Closed 26-30 December

BRASTED'S

MULTI-AWARD WINNING
Fine Dining

*O*ur award winning a la carte menus offer locally sourced ingredients and produce, resulting in traditional British dishes with a modern European twist. As a fine dining restaurant, service and food are paramount, resulting in the ultimate dining experience.

Restaurant Opening Times

Thursday, Friday & Saturday
6.30pm till 10.00pm

Thursday & Friday lunchtime
12.00pm till 2.30pm

Contact Us

01508 491112   brasteds.co.uk   Manor Farm Barns, Framingham Pigot, Norwich NR14 7PZ

NORWICH continued

Thailand Restaurant
◉ THAI
01603 700444 | 9 Ring Road, Thorpe St Andrew, NR7 0XJ
www.thailandnorwich.co.uk
Plants and hanging baskets add dash to the exterior of this well-established restaurant. Inside, the decor is as busy as the bamboo-framed upholstered seats are busy with customers: drapes over the windows, statues in niches, friezes on beams and lots of greenery.

Closed 25 December

Warwick Street Social
◉◉ MODERN BRITISH
01603 627687 | 2 Warwick Street, NR2 3LD
www.warwickstsocial.co.uk
In Norwich's Golden Triangle, the WSS has contemporary style. The Norfolk-inspired British cuisine is pretty modern too: sea-salt crackling belly pork with charred tenderloin then a lip-smacking finale of dark chocolate fondant with salted caramel purée and amaretti ice cream.

Chef Daniel Smith, Lewis Peck Seats 95, Private dining 45 Closed 25 December Prices from S £7, M £12.50, D £6.50 Notes Vegetarian dishes, Children welcome

REEPHAM
MAP 13, TG12
The Dial House NEW
◉◉ MODERN BRITISH
01603 879900 | Market Place, NR10 4JJ
www.thedialhouse.org.uk
Occupying a splendid Georgian house, The Dial House offers a series of character spaces running from a chandelier-hung main dining room to a garden room with a terrace, and a cellar with bare brick walls. Wherever you choose, expect sparky modern cooking from a kitchen that likes to bang the drum for regional ingredients.

SHERINGHAM
MAP 13, TG14
Dales Country House Hotel
◉◉ BRITISH, EUROPEAN
01263 824555 | Lodge Hill, Upper Sheringham, NR26 8TJ
www.mackenziehotels.com
This step-gabled Victorian mansion has period charm in spades, although the cooking in Upchers restaurant takes a rather more contemporary European view of things. With the

briny so near, a fillet of sea bass is a good bet, or try lamb kofta with spiced aubergine caviar.

Chef Rene Ilupar Seats 70, Private dining 40 Open All Year Prices from S £7, M £16.50, D £6.25 Parking 50 Notes Vegetarian dishes, Children welcome

SNETTISHAM
MAP 12, TF63
The Rose & Crown
◉ MODERN BRITISH
01485 541382 | Old Church Road, PE31 7LX
www.roseandcrownsnettisham.co.uk
The interior of this country inn is all twisty passageways, low beams, flagged floors, and a busy bar. It isn't unknown for locals to dine here three or four times a week, returning for the likes of seared scallops with cauliflower and tonka bean purée.

Open All Year

STOKE HOLY CROSS
MAP 13, TG20
The Wildebeest
◉◉ MODERN EUROPEAN
01508 492497 | 82–86 Norwich Road, NR14 8QJ
www.thewildebeest.co.uk
Set in a tranquil village, The Wildebeest continues to be a haven of refined eating, now in the skilful hands of chef-patron Daniel Smith. The interior is rich with beams, aged floorboards, wood-topped tables and leather-clad dining chairs. Much produce comes from a nearby farm.

Chef Daniel Smith, Charlie Wilson Seats 80 Closed 25–26 December Prices from S £7.95, M £16.50, D £7.95 Parking 30 Notes Vegetarian dishes, Children welcome

THETFORD
MAP 13, TL88
The Mulberry NEW
◉ MEDITERRANEAN, ENGLISH
01842 824122 | 11 Raymond Street, IP24 2EA
www.mulberrythetford.co.uk
This intimate restaurant in the heart of Thetford makes good use of local ingredients but looks to the Mediterranean for its inspiration on the plate. Go for the king prawn bruschetta, garlic prawns, tomato, chickpea, tarragon and lobster butter, perhaps followed by aged Norfolk beef sirloin tagliata with rocket, parmesan and red wine jus.

Chef Nathan Coleman Seats 45, Private dining 20 Open All Year Prices from S £7, M £12, D £7 Notes Vegetarian dishes, Children welcome

TITCHWELL   MAP 13, TF74

Titchwell Manor Hotel

◉◉◉ **MODERN EUROPEAN** *V*
01485 210221 | PE31 8BB
www.titchwellmanor.com

Extensive repertoire in a delightful coastal hotel

Now in their fourth decade at the helm of
Titchwell Manor, Margaret and Ian Snaith
have their gorgeous boutique hotel firing
on all cylinders. Positioned in an idyllic spot
on the north Norfolk coast, where
stretching sands spiked with marram grass
unroll to the sea and the great pale sky, it
is a location worth travelling for. The name
of the place might suggest a grandiose
pile, but the hotel is built around a red-
brick Victorian farmhouse, with chic
interiors of vibrant patterns and colour
combinations in fabrics and carpets. The
light-flooded Conservatory restaurant
looks over the walled garden, where much
of the kitchen's seasonal veg, fruit and
herbs are grown.

Chris Mann's cooking is adventurous,
modern stuff built on his uncommon
culinary ability and exciting dexterity with
flavours and textures. Innovative
combinations, thoughtful presentations

> "Innovative combinations, thoughtful presentations and clearly defined flavours can be seen from the off"

and clearly defined flavours can be seen from the off in a starter of resonantly full-on foie gras and cocoa terrine, the richness offset by Yorkshire rhubarb compôte, lapsang souchong syrup and home-made brioche, or perhaps a restorative beef consommé with short rib, caper jam and gruyère toast. Pedigree meats are the foundations of main courses, as seen in the Gloucestershire Old Spots pork that comes in three cuts, helped along by pear and wild garlic, or the crispy-skinned, tenderly pink Creedy Carver duck breast accompanied by confit leg, orange sauce, golden beetroot and thyme. Fish is imaginatively handled too, as when turbot turns up with crab bisque, pommes dauphine enriched with cod's roe, sea vegetables and nasturtium.

For the grand finale, chocolate marquise is as luscious as you'd hope for, and comes with the balancing tartness of silky crème fraîche ice cream and blood orange; otherwise, try the signature golden Titchwell trifle, a seriously grown-up version bursting with intriguing textures and flavour contrasts, incorporating rhubarb, honey and caramel-flavoured golden chocolate.

Chef Eric Snaith, Chris Mann
Seats 80
Open All Year
Prices from S £7, M £14, D £7
Parking 50
Notes Vegetarian dishes, Children welcome

THORNHAM
MAP 12, TF74

The Chequers Inn
⚫ MODERN BRITISH

01485 512229 | High Street, PE36 6LY

www.chequersinnthornham.com

This pretty village inn dates back to the 16th century and its location on the north Norfolk coast makes it a popular spot for people heading to the beautiful beaches of Brancaster and Holkham. Contemporary but rustic, the restaurant attracts locals as well as visitors.

Open All Year

The Lifeboat Inn
⚫ TRADITIONAL BRITISH *V*

01485 512236 | Ship Lane, PE36 6LT

www.lifeboatinnthornham.com

Down a quiet lane behind the church, this charming, white-painted inn has been providing hospitality for more than 500 years. The terrace is a tranquil spot to enjoy a pint in summer, while the coastal location means local seafood gets a strong showing.

Chef Nik Hoare **Seats** 140, Private dining 18 **Open** All Year **Prices from** S £6.50, M £14.75, D £6.95 **Parking** 60 **Notes** Children welcome

TITCHWELL
MAP 13, TF74

Titchwell Manor Hotel
⚫⚫⚫ MODERN EUROPEAN *V*

See pages 312–313

WIVETON
MAP 13, TG04

Wiveton Bell
⚫⚫ MODERN BRITISH

01263 740101 | The Green, Blakeney Road, NR25 7TL

www.wivetonbell.co.uk

An authentic Georgian country pub on the village green, the Bell is near Blakeney and the salt marshes of north Norfolk and is done up in light and airy modern fashion. The cooking has a pleasingly traditional air about it.

Closed 25 December

WYMONDHAM
MAP 13, TG10

Number Twenty Four Restaurant
⚫ MODERN BRITISH

01953 607750 | 24 Middleton Street, NR18 0AD

www.number24.co.uk

Grade II listed, this comfortably furnished restaurant has been hewn out of a row of Georgian cottages and it retains a smart but homely feel to it. The atmosphere is welcoming, with efficient, friendly staff, and the regularly-changing, thoughtfully constructed menus are stylish and appealing.

Chef Jonathan Griffin **Seats** 50, Private dining 50 **Closed** 26 Decemnber, 1 January **Notes** Vegetarian dishes, Children welcome

■ NORTHAMPTONSHIRE

DAVENTRY
MAP 11, SP56

Fawsley Hall Hotel & Spa
⚫⚫ MODERN BRITISH

01327 892000 | Fawsley, NN11 3BA

www.handpickedhotels.co.uk/fawsleyhall

Plantagenets, Tudors and Georgians all played a part in the beguiling architectural mishmash seen today, and it screams 'grand' with its oak panels, stone arches and the Cedar Restaurant. However, a feeling of intimacy pervades the place, and the kitchen deals in imaginative 21st-century ideas.

Chef Richard Walker **Seats** 70, Private dining 20 **Open** All Year **Parking** 140 **Notes** Vegetarian dishes, Children welcome

KETTERING
MAP 11, SP87

Barton Hall Hotel
⚫⚫ TRADITIONAL BRITISH

01536 515505 | Barton Road, Barton Seagrave, NN15 6SG

www.bartonhall.com

A charming hotel surrounded by splendid gardens and a Grade I listed orangery, Barton Hall dates from the 16th century. The hotel's Vines Brasserie is a welcoming place with informal service matched by unclothed tables and modern background music to create a relaxed setting for the innovative cooking.

Open All Year

Kettering Park Hotel & Spa
⚫ MODERN BRITISH

01536 416666 | Kettering Parkway, NN15 6XT

www.ketteringparkhotel.co.uk/food-drink

Kettering Park belies its business park location by having plenty of charm with its real fire and sunny terrace. Local Melton Mowbray pies and Leicestershire cheeses make an appearance, but the menu takes a global approach. Wild boar Scotch egg could precede roasted cod with smoked bacon and white wine sauce.

Chef Steven White **Seats** 90, Private dining 40 **Closed** 25-26 December, 1 January (excluding residents and pre-bookings) **Prices from** S £6, M £15, D £7 **Parking** 200 **Notes** Vegetarian dishes, Children welcome

KETTERING

MAP 11, SP87

Rushton Hall Hotel and Spa

◉◉◉ **MODERN BRITISH**
01536 713001 | Rushton, NN14 1RR
www.rushtonhall.com

The black sheep of the illustrious family who built Rushton Hall in the 15th century was a player in the Gunpowder Plot, and the magnificent pile was the later inspiration for Dickens' Satis House in *Great Expectations*. These days it earns a crust as a stately leisure retreat with all the trappings of a grand country hotel. The Tresham Restaurant – named after the former owners, including the ill-fated plotter – has relocated to a new spot, and makes a refined and elegant setting for Adrian Coulthard's precise and refined modernist cooking. Smoked ham hock, chicken and foie gras are allied in a carefully composed pressing, with lovage mayonnaise, pickled onion petals and potato crisps. Main course brings pan-fried halibut with brown shrimps, gnocchi, cucumber, tomato and butter sauce, the happy colours reflecting the summer seasonality. The 1593 Brasserie is the more informal dining option.

Chef Adrian Coulthard **Seats** 40, Private dining 60 **Open** All Year **Parking** 140 **Notes** Vegetarian dishes, No children under 12 years

NASSINGTON

The Queens Head Inn

◉ MODERN BRITISH

01780 784006 | 54 Station Road, PE8 6QB

www.queensheadnassington.co.uk

On the banks of the River Nene, this delightful mellow stone inn does a solid line in muscular modern cooking built on locally sourced ingredients. The 200-year-old hostelry still functions as a pub, but food drives the action with a charcoal-fired Josper grill taking pride of place in the kitchen. If you're up for some serious meat action, the steaks are impeccably sourced.

Open All Year

NORTHAMPTON

The Hopping Hare

◉◉ MODERN, TRADITIONAL *V*

01604 580090 | 18 Hopping Hill Gardens, Duston, NN5 6PF

www.hoppinghare.com

Spacious, thoughtfully decorated and furnished, with an informal and atmospheric dining room and a popular bar. The modern, and inventive, British culinary output changes with the seasons – Balmoral venison loin bolognese with Szechuan pepper; shepherd's pie; hake fillet roasted in Marmite butter; crispy almond milk polenta, and daily chef's specials.

Chef Darren Curson **Seats** 80 **Open** All Year
Prices from S £4.95, M £12.95, D £6.95 **Parking** 40
Notes Children welcome

See advertisement below

OUNDLE
MAP 11, TL08

The Talbot
◉ BRITISH

01832 273621 | New Street, PE8 4EA

www.thetalbot-oundle.com

If The Talbot looks ancient, that's maybe because its stone façades, mullioned windows and grand timber staircase were recycled from Fotheringhay Castle in the 17th century. Nowadays, it does a brisk trade as a hotel, coffee house and eatery, aka the restaurant.

Open All Year

WEEDON BEC
MAP 11, SP65

Narrow Boat at Weedon
◉◉ MODERN BRITISH

01327 340333 | Stowe Hill, A5 Watling Street, NN7 4RZ

www.narrowboatatweedon.co.uk

It's not actually on the water, but plenty of boats moor by this popular gastro pub. It offers watery rural views, and serves food in the bar and the restaurant. The kitchen offers everything from pub classics, stone-baked pizzas, and up-to-date ideas in the restaurant.

Chef Liam Bolger **Seats** 100, Private dining 40 **Closed** 26 December **Prices from** S £7, M £16, D £6 **Parking** 40 **Notes** Vegetarian dishes, Children welcome

WHITTLEBURY
MAP 11, SP64

Murrays
◉◉ MODERN BRITISH, EUROPEAN

01327 850489 | Whittlebury Hall, NN12 8QH

www.whittleburyhall.com

This plush neo-Georgian hotel with a Rolls Royce of a spa and a sophisticated restaurant is just a Ferrari's roar away from Silverstone. While the slick front-of-house team help diners relax in the slow lane, the kitchen hits top gear with modern British cooking.

Closed selected dates at Christmas, 31 December

■ NORTHUMBERLAND

BAMBURGH
MAP 21, NU13

Waren House Hotel
◉◉ MODERN, TRADITIONAL BRITISH

01668 214581 | Waren Mill, NE70 7EE

www.warenhousehotel.co.uk

Tradition is the watchword in the kitchen of this classic country-house hotel, starting with diligent sourcing of the region's finest ingredients, which are brought together in a broadly modern British style. Dishes are well conceived and the fish cookery is handled with aplomb.

Chef Steven Owens **Seats** 30 **Open** All Year **Parking** 15 **Notes** Vegetarian dishes

BERWICK-UPON-TWEED
MAP 21, NT95

Magna
◉ INDIAN

01289 302736 | 39 Bridge Street, TD15 1ES

www.magnatandooriberwick.co.uk

Close to the bridge over the Tweed at the lower end of the walled town, Magna has earned a reputation for top-notch Indian cooking since it opened in 1982. Occupying a grand Victorian building, bright red chairs and colourful murals add a cheery glow to the place. The menu offers familiar curry-house staples making admirable use of local produce.

Chef Oliul Khan, Suman Ahmed **Seats** 85, Private dining 40 **Open** All Year **Prices from** S £3.95, M £8.50, D £3.50 **Parking** 60 **Notes** Vegetarian dishes, Children welcome

Queens Head
◉ MODERN MEDITERRANEAN

01289 307852 | Sandgate, TD15 1EP

www.queensheadberwick.co.uk

A traditional hotel overlooking Sandgate in the old part of Berwick, the Queens Head is a place with ambition. The principal dining room has a stripped wood floor, old beams and well-spaced tables, a relaxing place for upscale pub cooking founded on sound culinary logic.

Chef Gillet Libau, Alistair McGregor, Joanne Greenaway **Seats** 58 **Open** All Year **Prices from** S £5.25, M £12.95, D £6.25 **Notes** Vegetarian dishes, Children welcome

BLANCHLAND

MAP 18, NY95

The Lord Crewe Arms Blanchland

@ TRADITIONAL BRITISH

01434 675469 | The Square, DH8 9SP

www.lordcrewearmsblanchland.co.uk

Built for the residents of Blanchland Abbey in the 1100s, this wonderfully historic inn has served everyone from monks to lead miners. It seems unlikely that the latter would have been interested in the architecture, not least the vaulted stone crypt, now an atmospheric bar.

Open All Year

CHATHILL

MAP 21, NU12

Doxford Hall Hotel & Spa

@ MODERN BRITISH

01665 589700 | NE67 5DN

www.doxfordhall.com

Doxford Hall's restaurant has chandeliers in ornate ceilings, a stone fireplace, deep-red walls and menus reflecting 21st-century dining expectations. Seared scallops with two croquettes of slowly cooked pig's cheek and celeriac remoulade is just one possible starter of intense, distinct flavours.

Open All Year

CORNHILL-ON-TWEED

MAP 21, NT83

Tillmouth Park Country House Hotel

@ MODERN BRITISH

01890 882255 | TD12 4UU

www.tillmouthpark.co.uk

On the border between England and Scotland, this lovely Victorian hotel is surrounded by 15 acres of landscaped grounds. The menu in the Library Dining Room looks to classically-based modern British food with international influences. Begin with a South African-inspired venison bobotie before a chargrilled rib-eye steak with whisky sauce.

Chef Mike Struthers Seats 40, Private dining 20 Closed 26-28 December and January to March Parking 50 Notes Vegetarian dishes, Children welcome

HEXHAM

MAP 21, NY96

The Barrasford Arms

@ BRITISH

01434 681237 | Barrasford, NE48 4AA

www.barrasfordarms.co.uk

Close to Hadrian's Wall in the tranquil village of Barrasford, this ivy-clad country inn has three dining rooms kitted out with rustic furniture. The kitchen works to a modern British template, the emphasis firmly placed on produce from local estates and punchy flavours.

Chef Michael Eames Seats 60, Private dining 10 Closed 25 December, 1 January Prices from S £6, M £13, D £6.50 Parking 30 Notes Vegetarian dishes, Children welcome

Langley Castle Hotel

@@ CONTEMPORARY BRITISH, FRENCH

01434 688888 | Langley, NE47 5LU

www.langleycastle.com

At the Langley Castle restaurant you'll find a creative and modern output delivered via a table d'hôte menu; expect dishes based on top quality, seasonal ingredients sourced from the Northumberland area. The kitchen's aim is to produce straightforward flavoursome food without unnecessary distractions.

Chef Mark Percival Seats 48, Private dining 28 Open All Year Parking 57 Notes Vegetarian dishes, Children welcome

LONGHORSLEY

MAP 21, NZ19

Macdonald Linden Hall, Golf & Country Club

@ MODERN BRITISH

01670 500000 | NE65 8XF

www.macdonaldhotels.co.uk/lindenhall

This late-Georgian manor house sits in 450 acres amid views of the Cheviots and wild Northumberland landscapes. The upscale Dobson Restaurant – warm autumnal tones of russet and brick-red, linen-clothed tables and relaxed, professional service – makes a refined setting for well-conceived dishes.

Open All Year

MATFEN

MAP 21, NZ07

Matfen Hall

@@ MODERN BRITISH

01661 886500 | NE20 0RH

www.matfenhall.com

Matfen Hall, a creation of the Victorian era, within 300 acres of parkland, today offers all modern amenities. The panelled library, replete with shelves of old volumes, does duty as the dining room. The contemporary menus make a neat counterpoint to the surroundings.

Open All Year

MORPETH
MAP 21, NZ18

Eshott Hall

◎◎ BRITISH, EUROPEAN

01670 787454 | Eshott, NE65 9EN

www.eshotthall.co.uk

Eshott Hall is a compact boutique hotel in a handsome Georgian property – a perfect base from which to explore the National Park and end the day with dinner in the elegant restaurant, with its soothing gold colour scheme and a fire in cooler weather.

Closed Private functions

NEWTON-ON-THE-MOOR
MAP 21, NU10

The Cook and Barker Inn

◎ BRITISH

01665 575234 | NE65 9JY

www.cookandbarkerinn.co.uk

With great views of the Cheviot Hills and the coast from its elevated location, The Cook and Barker has turned from a traditional inn to a stylish place. Exposed brickwork, beams with fairy lights, upholstered chairs and wooden tables add up to a sophisticated look.

Open All Year

STOCKSFIELD
MAP 21 NZ06

The Duke of Wellington Inn

◎ MODERN BRITISH

01661 844446 | Newton, NE43 7UL

www.thedukeofwellingtoninn.co.uk

'The Wellie', an 18th-century country inn, has much appeal, and the views from the bar and restaurant are magnificent, especially so from the terrace on a sunny day. The menu is concise, but you'll still find a decent range of modern British dishes.

Open All Year

■ NOTTINGHAMSHIRE

BARNBY MOOR
MAP 16, SK68

Restaurant Bar 1650

◎ MODERN BRITISH

01777 705121 | Ye Olde Bell Hotel & Spa, DN22 8QS

www.yeoldebell-hotel.co.uk

This hotel offers beauty therapies aplenty, and lots of room for functions. There's a bistro in the St Leger bar, but the main event is the oak-panelled Restaurant Bar 1650, with its art deco style in the bar area and modern chandeliers to add a touch of glamour.

Chef Karl Davison Seats 40, Private dining 200 Open All Year Prices from S £8.50, M £13.50, D £8 Parking 200 Notes Vegetarian dishes, Children welcome

BLIDWORTH
MAP 16, SK55

The Black Bull

◎◎ MODERN BRITISH

01623 490222 | Main Street, NG21 0QH

www.blackbullblidworth.co.uk

Not far from Sherwood Forest and Byron's Newstead Abbey is this classic Georgian timbered inn. Sand-blasted beams, a brick fireplace and checkered carpeting make for a modernised but still homely atmosphere for showcasing some creatively witty cooking. The inventive pace is sustained to the end.

Open All Year

FARNDON
MAP 17, SK75

Farndon Boathouse

◎◎ MODERN BRITISH

01636 676578 | Off Wyke Road, NG24 3SX

www.farndonboathouse.co.uk

The leafy banks of the River Trent make an interesting contrast to the contemporary exposed ducting, industrial-style lighting, stone floors and glazed frontage of the stylish Boathouse. The kitchen uses modern cooking techniques such as sous-vide, to squeeze every molecule of flavour from the ingredients.

Open All Year

GUNTHORPE
MAP 11, SK64

Tom Browns Brasserie

◎◎ MODERN BRITISH

0115 966 3642 | The Old School House, Trentside, NG14 7FB

www.tombrowns.co.uk

The homage to Thomas Hughes' plucky Victorian schoolboy denotes the fact that this large riverside building was a place of education in the 19th century. No risk of having to face school dinners here now, though, this is a robustly complex, well-considered brasserie cooking in the modern style.

Open All Year

NOTTINGHAM

MAP 11, SK53

Alchemilla

◉◉◉ MODERN BRITISH 𝑽 ⁴ NOTABLE WINE LIST

0115 941 3515 | 192 Derby Road, NG7 1NF

alchemillarestaurant.uk

Curving brick vaulted ceilings with big skylights, and a feature wall of vivid green moss set the scene in this high-flying newcomer to Nottingham's flourishing restaurant scene. Brought to life from a long-derelict coaching inn – much of the renovation work done by the chef, Alex Bond, himself – Alchemilla feels like an enveloping organic space with its simple wooden tables and open kitchen. Expect of-the-moment cookery that, while not remotely vegetarian, shifts attention more squarely onto the vegetable elements within tasting menus bristling with on-trend ingredients in intriguing combinations. Tender squid strips, hen of the woods mushrooms, buttermilk and black garlic add up to a playful take on carbonara, while grain risotto comes dressed in three-year-old parmesan and truffle. A main meat dish partners spot-on venison with quince and puréed pumpkin. Striking desserts continue the innovative mood, matching Peruvian marigold sorbet with apple granita and espuma, and tangy cultured cream.

Chef Alex Bond **Seats** 48, Private dining 9 **Closed** 31 July to 13 August **Notes** No children

Byrons *NEW*

◉ MODERN

0115 950 0566 | Colwick Hall Hotel, Racecourse Road, NG2 4BH

colwickhallhotel.com

Named for poet Lord Byron, whose ancestral home this grand Georgian pile once was, the informal bar and brasserie goes for a more up-to-date look with its cream leather chairs and darkwood floors and tables. The kitchen follows suit, offering an appetising menu of modern, uncomplicated ideas that aims to please all comers.

Open All Year

Hart's Kitchen

Hart's aims to provide a thoroughly professional blend of skilled service and modern British cooking in a stylish and comfortable interior with emphasis on simple but fantastic, fresh ingredients. Head chef Martin Sludd uses only the best quality ingredients, often locally sourced in simple striking combinations.

Hart's Hotel, Standard Hill, Park Row, Nottingham NG1 6GN
Tel: 0115 988 1900 • www.hartsnottingham.co.uk

Hart's Kitchen

◉◉ MODERN BRITISH

0115 988 1900 | Hart's Hotel, Standard Hill, Park Row,
NG1 6GN

www.hartsnottingham.co.uk

Hart's is a welcoming restaurant with an
approachable, weekly-changing menu. The space
within the hotel is well set out and there's a good
use of lighting and partitioning. Crisp linen
napkins and cloths topped with sparkling
stemware set the scene for the modern British
food - clean and simple with fresh ingredients.
Look out for the wine list.

Chef Martin Sludd **Closed** 1 January

See advertisement opposite

MemSaab Restaurant

◉◉ INDIAN

0115 957 0009 | 12-14 Maid Marian Way, NG1 6HS

www.mem-saab.co.uk

A gigantic venue of 200 covers, there's a real
vibrancy about this unique Nottingham
establishment. A signature starter comes in the
form of tandoori ostrich, roasted in garlic and red
chilli. Meats benefit from the tenderising
influence of slow cooking.

Chef Majid Ashraf **Seats** 200, Private dining 60
Closed 25 December **Prices from** S £5.25, M £9.95,
D £4.95 **Notes** Vegetarian dishes, Children welcome

See advertisement on page 322

Merchants Restaurant

◉ MODERN EUROPEAN

0115 948 4414 | Lace Market Hotel,
29-31 High Pavement, NG1 1HE

www.lacemarkethotel.co.uk

The Lace Market Hotel occupies a handsome
Georgian townhouse, carefully restored and
retaining much of its period detail. The elegant
Merchants Restaurant is a light and airy room
with large sash windows, walls dotted with
vibrant modern art, and a confident, modern
European menu.

Open All Year

Park Plaza Nottingham

◉◉ PAN-ASIAN

0115 947 7444 | 41 Maid Marian Way, NG1 6GD

www.chinolatino.eu

Latin America meets the Far East in this
Nottingham branch of the Park Plaza. Set across
two levels, this buzzy restaurant and bar fuses
pan-Asian cooking with international cuisine on
the globe-trotting menu. Thai and Korean dishes
appear in mains.

Chef Manol Dmitrov **Seats** 70 **Closed** 25-26 December
Prices from S £3, M £14.50, D £5 **Parking** 30
Notes Vegetarian dishes, Children welcome

Restaurant Sat Bains with Rooms

◉◉◉◉◉ MODERN BRITISH *V* ◉ NOTABLE WINE LIST

0115 986 6566 | Lenton Lane, Trentside, NG7 2SA

www.restaurantsatbains.com

Satwant Singh Bains, to give the chef-patron his
full name, chose rather an unexpected location
for his restaurant. Not only is it outside the city
centre, it's in a handsomely converted Victorian
farmhouse and outbuildings down a narrow lane,
with the River Trent flowing behind. Sat's
reputation has elevated him to the ranks of this
country's super-chefs and if you want to know
what makes him tick, pick up - buy, that is, while
you're here - a copy of *Too Many Chiefs Only One
Indian*, his autobiographical cookbook featuring
the recipes behind his seven- and 10-course
tasting menus. He also explains how important is
the research, development and creativity that
goes into them. And the produce itself - for
example, around 40 per cent of the veg and
herbs that end up on the tables come from the
urban garden outside created by Ken Holland,
one of the UK's top growers. There's a small
courtyard, ideal for a pre- or post-prandial drink,
as well. Dining options are several: Chef's Table,
with dishes served by the very chefs you may
well have watched preparing them; Kitchen
Bench, where you sit on high chairs within the
main body of the pastry kitchen while, again, the
chefs themselves look after you; the
Conservatory, and the main restaurant itself.
How the dishes are presented will undoubtedly
be one of the table's talking points. A sample
seven-course menu might begin with smoked eel
from Louth; and continue with roast veal
sweetbread; crispy potato, caviar and samphire
velouté; dry-aged beef; turnip dashi; a tomato
'jammy dodger' to take your taste buds from
savoury to sweet; and a dish called 'Lenton Lane',
apparently inspired by the lane you'll have driven
down, although how is not immediately revealed.
Wine flights ensure food and drink matches are
as perfect as everything else.

Chef Sat Bains **Seats** 46, Private dining 8 **Closed** 2
weeks in December to January, 1 week in April, 2 weeks
in August **Parking** 16 **Notes** No children under 8 years

TWO AA ROSETTES
FOR CULINARY EXCELLENCE

MEMSAAB
RESTAURANT

Harden's

2018
MICHELIN

Winner

Best Front of House Team

Nottinghamshire Restaurant of the Year Runner up

Nottingham Restaurant & Bar Awards 2018

PRIVATE DINING • CANAPÉ & DRINKS RECEPTIONS
CELEBRATION DINNERS • OUTSIDE CATERING
£13.95 EARLY EVENING MENU AVAILABLE

**Observer
FoodMonthly
Awards**
In association with
Cuisinart

Runner up
**Best Restaurant 2014
2013, 2012, 2011**

curry life **Best Achiever 2015
BUSINESS ACHIEVEMENT AWARDS**

Nottingham's Best Independent Business 2014

COBRA **The Cobra Good Curry Guide Awa**
Best in the East Midlands 2014

BRITISH **British Curry Awards 2014 Winn**
Curry Awards **Best Restaurant in The Midlands**

2016 Winner
Best Indian Restaurant
NOTTINGHAMSHIRE
FOOD & DRINK AWARDS
2015 Winner Best Asian Experience

Post IN PARTNERSHIP WITH
FRASER BROWN

POST **indian
RESTAURANT
of the YEAR**

0115 957 0009 12-14 MAID MARIAN WAY, NOTTINGHAM NG1 6HS WWW.MEM-SAAB.CO.UK CONTACT@MEM-SAAB.CO

NOTTINGHAM continued

World Service

◉◉ MODERN BRITISH ▮ NOTABLE WINE LIST

0115 847 5587 | Newdigate House, Castle Gate, NG1 6AF
www.worldservicerestaurant.com

Renaissance-styled Newdigate House was built in 1675. Its idiosyncratic interior mines a colonial vein, the warm orange and copper hues of the main dining room offset with oriental artefacts: Buddha heads, Indian statuary and objets d'art in vitrines. The cooking has a gentle East-meets-West theme.

Chef James Nicholas **Seats** 80, Private dining 34
Closed 26 December and 1–7 January **Prices from** S £6, M £16.95, D £6.50 **Notes** Vegetarian dishes, No children under 12 years at dinner

---

RETFORD
MAP 17, SK78

Blacksmiths

◉ MODERN BRITISH

01777 818171 | Town Street, Clayworth, DN22 9AD
www.blacksmithsclayworth.com

A beautifully revamped inn in a village dating back to the 12th century, Blacksmiths is still a local pub, but with three attractively furnished bedrooms and a restaurant serving divertingly modern food, it's also a destination worth crossing county lines to visit.

Closed 1st week January

■ OXFORDSHIRE

BANBURY
MAP 11, SP44

Banbury Wroxton House Hotel

◉◉ MODERN BRITISH

01295 730777 | Wroxton St Mary, OX15 6QB
www.wroxtonhousehotel.com

Wroxton House is a honey-stone beauty in a photogenic thatched village. Its restaurant occupies what was a row of cottages; all oak beams, columns and an inglenook fireplace. Table settings are smart and the kitchen turns out thoughtful modern brasserie dishes, founded on classic combinations.

Chef Rob Marshall **Seats** 60, Private dining 90
Parking 70 **Notes** Vegetarian dishes, Children welcome

The White Horse

◉◉ TRADITIONAL BRITISH, FRENCH INFLUENCE

01295 812440 | 2 The Square, Kings Sutton, OX17 3RF
www.whitehorseks.co.uk

This old pub has been given a makeover that, while creating a clean, modern look, still ensures that you are reminded of its past. Clearly popular, it has received regional food accolades for its British and European cooking. Perhaps choose breast and leg of Loomswood duck with carrot, cumin and lentil dhal as a main, and lemon cheesecake with stem-ginger ice cream to finish.

Chef Hendrik Dutson **Seats** 45, Private dining 7
Closed 25 December **Prices from** S £6, M £14.95, D £5.50 **Parking** 14 **Notes** Vegetarian dishes, Children welcome

---

BURFORD
MAP 5, SP21

The Angel at Burford

◉ CLASSIC BRITISH

01993 822714 | 14 Witney Street, OX18 4SN
www.theangelatburford.co.uk

Just off the main street in pretty Burford, this welcoming Cotswold stone inn oozes character. Perfectly kept pints of Hook Norton lure drinkers to the cosy and bustling bar, with the all-day bar menu offering sandwiches, burgers and a charcuterie board alongside the main carte.

Open All Year

The Bay Tree Hotel
@ MODERN BRITISH
01993 822791 | Sheep Street, OX18 4LW
www.cotswold-inns-hotels.co.uk/baytree
Built in Cotswold stone, this is a stylishly
appointed place and a menu of modern-classic
English food. Try perhaps scallops on cauliflower
purée, then Ruby White 36-day aged beef with
truffle fries.

Chef Shawn Lovegrove **Seats** 70, Private dining 30
Open All Year **Parking** 55 **Notes** Vegetarian
dishes, Children welcome

The Lamb Inn
@@ MODERN BRITISH
01993 823155 | Sheep Street, OX18 4LR
www.cotswold-inns-hotels.co.uk/lamb
Beautifully cosy and comfortable, with flagstone
floors and open fires, The Lamb is your
quintessential Cotswold inn, set in a quaint
market town. The dining room, with its grey walls
and skylight, makes a very classy setting for their
chic food – complex, precise seasonal dishes.

Open All Year

CHECKENDON
MAP 5, SU68

The Highwayman
@ MODERN, TRADITIONAL BRITISH
01491 682020 | Exlade Street, RG8 0UA
www.thehighwaymaninn-checkendon.co.uk
Tucked away in a secluded hamlet, this rambling
16th-century inn is all brickwork, beams and
wood-burner in a huge inglenook. Fine ales are
on tap in the pubby bar, and all bases are covered
in the food department by steaks from the grill,
and home-made pies.

Chef Paul Burrows, Evelyne Martin **Seats** 85, Private
dining 40 **Closed** 25 December, 1 January **Parking** 30
Notes Vegetarian dishes, Children welcome

CHINNOR
MAP 5, SP70

The Sir Charles Napier
@@ MODERN BRITISH, EUROPEAN *V* NOTABLE WINE LIST
01494 483011 | Sprigg's Alley, OX39 4BX
www.sircharlesnapier.co.uk
Hidden down rural Oxfordshire lanes, this
sublime flint-and-brick inn is named after the
19th-century British Army general who became
commander-in-chief in India. Menus feature
hedgerow and field-sourced herbs, mushrooms,

berries and game. You can eat inside, on the
vine-covered terrace or under the cherry trees.

Chef Liam Leech **Seats** 75, Private dining 45
Closed 25-27 December **Prices from** S £10.50,
M £24.50, D £9.50 **Parking** 60 **Notes** No children
under 6 years at dinner

FARINGDON
MAP 5, SU29

Magnolia
@@ MODERN BRITISH
01367 241272 | Sudbury House, 56 London Street,
SN7 7AA
www.sudburyhouse.co.uk
Close to the M4 between Swindon and Oxford,
this smart hotel occupies an enviable spot on the
edge of the Cotswolds. The contemporary
Magnolia is the more informal of the hotel's two
restaurants and the room is dominated by the
open kitchen with a wood-burning stove.

Chef Nick Bennett **Seats** 120, Private dining 40 **Open** All
Year **Prices from** S £6, M £14.50, D £7 **Parking** 100
Notes Vegetarian dishes, Children welcome

FYFIELD
MAP 5, SU49

The White Hart
@@ MODERN BRITISH
01865 390585 | Main Road, OX13 5LW
www.whitehart-fyfield.com
Built as a chantry house, The White Hart offers
traditionally-based British food with
contemporary flourishes. Sharing boards of fish,
meze or antipasti might take your fancy. Dessert
could be a study in cherry, with purée, tuile,
sorbet and Kirsch-soaked fruit accompanying
pistachio cake.

Open All Year

GREAT MILTON
MAP 5, SP60

Belmond Le Manoir aux Quat'Saisons
@@@@@ MODERN FRENCH *V* NOTABLE WINE LIST
01844 278881 | Church Road, OX44 7PD
www.belmond.com/hotels/europe/uk/oxfordshire/
belmond-le-manoir-aux-quat-saisons
Besançon-born Raymond Blanc bought this
beautiful 15th-century manor in 1983, opening it a
year later as a country house hotel and
restaurant. He still runs it today, although it is
owned by the Belmond hotel and leisure group.
With luxurious bedroom suites, it stands at the

heart of glorious grounds with sculptures, an orchard, a Japanese tea garden and a bounteous, organic kitchen garden. It should be no surprise that Blanc remains the life force of the place, with his long-standing executive head chef Gary Jones, chef-pâtissier Benoit Blin, and their amazing teams, loyally alongside him. The dining experience is never less than utterly pleasurable, from the warm greeting and the charming attention to, of course, the delicious, classic French cuisine that has made Le Manoir's five-, six-and seven-course menus, with vegetarian and vegan options, such a gastronomic success. In addition is the three-course carte - Spécialités du Moment, as they say here – beginning with warm duck liver, gingerbread, clementine curd and garden sorrel; or langoustine with truffle and Jerusalem artichoke. Those choosing to follow the langoustine with fish might consider braised Cornish turbot with scallop, cucumber and wasabi; while an alternative of salt-baked pigeon with bacon and Madeira jus would definitely be worth going for too. Continuing in the same peerless vein are desserts such as seasonal pear almondine with caramel croustillant and ginger sauce; and exotic fruit raviole with kaffir lime and coconut jus. And there's a children's menu too. Perhaps understandably the French led wine list has just a few candidates from the New World. Up to 50 guests can be accommodated in the private dining room in La Belle Epoque wing. Cookery and gardening schools add to Le Manoir's mix, enabling everyone a chance to take knowledge home, together with wonderful memories.

Chef Raymond Blanc OBE, Gary Jones, Benoit Blin **Seats** 80, Private dining 50 **Parking** 60 **Notes** Children welcome

HENLEY-ON-THAMES

MAP 5, SU78

The Baskerville

@ CLASSIC EUROPEAN **V**
0118 940 3332 | Station Road, Lower Shiplake, RG9 3NY
www.thebaskerville.com
This Baskerville is a handsome beast, a contemporary kind of inn that offers beer and bar snacks, comfortable rooms, and a restaurant that produces serious modern British grub. Pub classics like steak, ale and mushroom pie and Sunday roasts play to the gallery.

Chef Jamie Herridge **Seats** 58, Private dining 12 **Closed** 1 January **Prices from** S £7, M £15, D £7 **Parking** 15 **Notes** Vegetarian dishes, Children welcome until 7pm on Friday and Saturday (non-resident)

Hotel du Vin Henley-on-Thames

@ EUROPEAN
01491 848400 | New Street, RG9 2BP
www.hotelduvin.com
Hotel du Vin always chooses impressive buildings, and the Henley branch is no exception: a Thames-side Georgian property that was the HQ of Brakspears brewery. Bistro classics plus a few less standard dishes are what to expect, all cooked just as they should be.

Open All Year

Orwells

@@@@ MODERN BRITISH **V**
0118 940 3673 | Shiplake Row, Binfield Heath, RG9 4DP
www.orwellsrestaurant.co.uk
The whitewashed Georgian pub stands on a country road in the unruffled environs of Binfield Heath, but this is no mere pie-and-a-pint operation. Liam Trotman and Ryan Simpson have between them transformed the place into a beacon of modern British gastronomy, to the extent of being around 75% self-sufficient in fresh produce in the summer months, and filling every interior nook and cranny with tables so that the emphasis is very much on dining.

There are new-fangled ideas aplenty, but allied to highly burnished classical technical skills, seen in an opener of flavour-drenched, lightly cooked mackerel with pickled cucumber and ozone-fresh sea veg. Acknowledgement of the original pub ethos is evident in a dish that builds a slew of shredded ham hock with a runny egg yolk, bitter endive and dots of fiery mustard on an underlay of crumbled black pudding. For main, there could be seared cod on shredded trombConcino squash with sprouts and chicken jus, or wonderfully tender muntjac venison with its little cottage pie, sprouting broccoli and wild garlic. A moistly seductive bitter orange marmalade frangipane tart with blood-orange ice cream is a dessert with class, or consider the luscious honey sponge with yogurt, granola and sultanas.

Chef Ryan Simpson, Liam Trotman **Seats** 35, Private dining 16 **Closed** 2 weeks beginning January and 2 weeks beginning September **Prices from** S £10, M £26, D £9 **Parking** 30 **Notes** Children welcome

Shaun Dickens at The Boathouse

🟢🟢🟢 MODERN BRITISH *V*

01491 577937 | Station Road, RG9 1AZ

www.shaundickens.co.uk

As you'd hope from the monicker, the River Thames pursues its unhurried course past the decked terrace and glass frontage of this stylishly converted boathouse. Having honed his skills in some top kitchens, including Le Manoir aux Quat'Saisons and Per Se in New York, Shaun Dickens has his name above the door and his creative, contemporary food on the menu in a smartly neutral modern space, watched over by an engaging service team. Shaun is passionate about the ingredients he uses, building strong links with farmers and producers, which bears fruit in what arrives on the plate. Confit Loch Duart salmon arrives with compressed cucumber, lemon peel purée, pickled shallots and confit potato, while main-course Merrifield Farm duck comes perfectly pink and crisp-skinned alongside a crisp caraway and onion pastilla, mustard leaf, charred onion and rich duck jus. The invention and impressive presentation continues into a finale of rich dark chocolate parfait, chocolate streusel and blood orange.

Chef Shaun Dickens, James Walshaw **Seats** 45 **Open** All Year **Prices from** S £10, M £21, D £9 **Notes** Children welcome

KINGHAM   MAP 10, SP22

The Kingham Plough

🟢🟢 MODERN BRITISH

01608 658327 | The Green, OX7 6YD

www.thekinghamplough.co.uk

An idyllic honey-hued stone inn on the green of a pretty Cotswolds village, the Plough presents a quintessentially English picture. Inside, the place has the sort of stylish rustic-chic decor – all venerable beams and exposed stone walls – that you'd hope for in a foodie pub, but kids and Fido are welcome so there's no standing on ceremony.

Chef Iain Dixon **Seats** 54 **Closed** 25 December **Prices from** S £8, M £17, D £7 **Parking** 30 **Notes** Vegetarian dishes, Children welcome

The Wild Rabbit

🟢🟢🟢 MODERN BRITISH *V*

01608 658389 | Church Street, OX7 6YA

thewildrabbit.co.uk

A stone-built, wisteria-draped Cotswold country inn on a village corner makes an appealing prospect when its outdoor tables under the sunshades fill up. Allied with the Daylesford Estate, an expansive organic farming business, it makes a virtue of the natural approach, with horsehair mattresses in the guest rooms and a menu informed by nose-to-tail butchery and locally grown produce. Scottish mackerel with heritage beetroot, English wasabi and bittercress is a sound opening move, or you might plunge into a compendious Daylesford market garden salad with creamed curds, pickled walnut dressing and croûtons. The Wild Rabbit might be miles from the sea, but you'll still find Cornish bream, or butter-poached cod with confit leek, sea herbs and potted brown shrimps, or there might be roast cauliflower with Israeli couscous, semi-dried grape and gingerbread. There are temptations galore at the finishing line, including Wye Valley rhubarb with almond frangipane, and rhubarb sorbet.

Chef Nathan Eades **Seats** 50, Private dining 20 **Open** All Year **Prices from** S £13, M £22.50, D £8.50 **Parking** 15 **Notes** Children welcome

MILTON COMMON   MAP 5, SP60

The Oxfordshire

🟢 MODERN BRITISH

01844 278300 | Rycote Lane, OX9 2PU

www.theoxfordshire.com

Whether you're at this new-build hotel in the Chilterns for golf or pampering, the Sakura restaurant has sweeping views of the course and countryside from its picture windows as a backdrop to a broad-ranging menu of modern dishes spiked with global influences.

Chef Craig Heasley **Seats** 50, Private dining 40 **Closed** Christmas, New Year **Notes** Vegetarian dishes, Children welcome

MURCOTT   MAP 11, SP51

The Nut Tree Inn

🟢🟢 MODERN EUROPEAN *V* NOTABLE WINE LIST

01865 331253 | Main Street, OX5 2RE

www.nuttreeinn.co.uk

The old stone walls and gnarled beams are a venerable backdrop for contemporary dishes that are designed to tease maximum flavour from exemplary ingredients. A salad of the Nut Tree's own garden roots with vegetable crisps is an appealing, simple opener to be followed by perhaps an Indian-spiced treatment of cod garnished with almonds and raisins.

Chef Michael North, Mary North **Seats** 70, Private dining 36 **Closed** 27 December for 2 weeks **Prices from** S £13, M £15, D £9 **Parking** 30 **Notes** Children welcome

OXFORD

MAP 5, SP50

Bear & Ragged Staff

◉ MODERN, CLASSIC BRITISH

01865 862329 | Appleton Road, Cumnor, OX2 9QH

www.bearandraggedstaff.com

The Bear offers an appealing mixture of traditional atmosphere and contemporary design. Masses of artwork on cool green walls in the dining room offset the roughcast stone, and forward-thinking menus offer trend-conscious British food. Create a themed board with ingredients from sea, garden and butchery.

Chef Ben Flynn **Seats** 160 **Open** All year
Prices from S £6, M £14, D £5.75 **Parking** 30
Notes Vegetarian dishes, Children welcome, no children's menu - smaller portions

The Cherwell Boathouse *NEW*

◉ MODERN ENGLISH

01865 552746 | Bardwell Road, OX2 6ST

cherwellboathouse.co.uk

With swans and punts paddling by on the River Cherwell, it's no wonder that this Victorian boathouse restaurant is one of the city's cherished institutions. Waterside tables are at a premium on fine days; inside, the ambience is cosy and humming with the chatter of happy diners tucking into a menu of inventive, modern British ideas.

Chef Paul Bell **Seats** 65, Private dining 45 **Closed** 24 December evening to 31 December lunch
Prices from S £6, M £17.75, D £6 **Parking** 15
Notes Vegetarian dishes, Children welcome

The Oxford Kitchen

◉◉◉ **MODERN BRITISH** *V*

01865 511149 | 215 Banbury Road, Summertown, OX2 7HQ
www.theoxfordkitchen.co.uk

Bustling, contemporary neighbourhood venue

The place may look like an unassuming neighbourhood eatery by a bus-stop on the Banbury Road in Summertown, but appearances can be deceptive – there's rather more to the culinary goings-on in The Oxford Kitchen than first meets the eye. Its chef, Paul Welburn worked under some of the luminaries of British cuisine, including Gary Rhodes and Richard Corrigan, and has done TV time too on *The Great British Menu*. His bustling venue has plenty of unbuttoned character, with comfortable brown banquettes and unclothed tables set against bare brick walls hung with funky artworks inside, and tables outside the aubergine-hued frontage for sunny days. It all adds up to a relaxed setting for high-flying modern bistro eating that extends to seven menus, including ample choice for meat avoiders, and a cracking value two- or three-course set lunch option with bread and bottled water thrown in.

> "Welburn's cooking takes its cues from the seasons, deploying fine British ingredients in combinations full of inventive élan"

Welburn's cooking takes its cues from the seasons, deploying fine British ingredients in combinations full of inventive élan, thus you might start with a perfectly balanced trio of cured Loch Duart salmon with beetroot sorbet and horseradish emulsion, or a more gutsy opener of rabbit terrine matched with curry emulsion, raisin purée and puffed rice. Main courses are executed with the same vivid panache, whether it's pork collar, perhaps served with chorizo, romesco and charred cabbage, or fish such as roast pollock given robust bourguignon treatment, together with Roscoff onion and béarnaise. Presentations are no less exuberant and dramatic, and the balance of flavours always strong and true in vegetarian ideas too, perhaps mushroom tea with caramelised onion and Welsh rarebit, or spinach and ricotta tortellini bathed in green sauce, and enriched with duck egg yolk.

Puddings put a thoughtful, satisfying spin on intuitive flavour combinations with constructions such as vanilla custard with cinnamon pastry, rhubarb sorbet, pickled rhubarb and ginger parkin gel.

Chef Paul Welburn
Seats 80, Private dining 50
Closed 1st 2 weeks January
Notes Children welcome

See advertisement on page 327

Cotswold Lodge Hotel

⊛ BRITISH, EUROPEAN

01865 512121 | 66a Banbury Road, OX2 6JP

www.cotswoldlodgehotel.co.uk

This stately Victorian villa is replete with period style, all high ceilings, sweeping staircases and expansive bay windows, but given a modern facelift. The kitchen deals in contemporary food with clear European accents, but you might choose to end with a plate of tempting Oxfordshire cheeses.

Chef Andrew Carr **Seats** 50, Private dining 120 **Open** All Year **Prices from** S £6.50, M £15.95, D £6.95 **Parking** 40 **Notes** Vegetarian dishes, Children welcome

Gee's Restaurant

⊛ MEDITERRANEAN

01865 553540 | 61 Banbury Road, OX2 6PE

www.gees-restaurant.co.uk

Gee's continues to delight townies and gownies on the northern edge of the city centre. The bright glasshouse setting sees potted olive trees and lightweight café-style furniture in a room flooded with natural light, and the style is very satisfying Mediterranean-influenced modern brasserie cooking.

Chef Russell Heeley **Seats** 74 **Open** All Year **Prices from** S £6.95, M £15.95, D £6.50 **Notes** Vegetarian dishes, Children welcome

No.1 Ship Street

⊛ MODERN BRITISH, BRASSERIE

01865 806637 | Ship Street, OX1 3DA

www.no1shipstreet.com

Tucked away in a side street, this smartly decorated restaurant creates a cosy atmosphere with its polished copper-topped tables, wooden chairs, creative lighting and soft ambient music. The Ground Floor dining space (there's a bar upstairs) offers modern British, brasserie-style food and a good selection of wines.

Chef Owen Little **Seats** 64, Private dining 30 **Closed** 25–26 December and 1 January **Prices from** S £6.50, M £13, D £6 **Notes** Vegetarian dishes, Children welcome

The Oxford Kitchen

⊛⊛⊛ MODERN BRITISH *V*

See pages 328–329

See advertisement on page 327

The Mason Arms

⊛⊛ BRITISH

01993 656238 | Artist Residence Oxfordshire, Station Road, OX29 6XN

themasonarms.co.uk

'A traditional English inn with an eccentric twist' is how this pub describes itself. Tucked away in the countryside just outside Oxford, the atmosphere is friendly and menus are a subtle, contemporary interpretation of British produce and flavours. A Scotch egg with the pub's own brown sauce goes down well with a pint.

Open All Year

The English Restaurant

⊛⊛ MODERN BRITISH

01865 890714 | The Crazy Bear, Bear Lane, OX44 7UR

www.crazybeargroup.co.uk

We often comment on Tudor inns carefully converted to preserve their original character, but a different approach has been adopted here. Pink cushioned walls, a leopard-print carpet, big steel mirrors and a kind of herringbone overhead wine store set the scene for what's on offer. The contemporary brasserie food majors in comfort-oriented classics.

Open All Year

Thai Thai at The Crazy Bear

⊛⊛ MODERN THAI

01865 890714 | Bear Lane, OX44 7UR

www.crazybeargroup.co.uk

Crazy Bear's first outfit occupies a Tudor inn in an Oxfordshire village. As well as a British dining room, it boasts a Thai restaurant with crimson velvet beams, scatter cushions and tables that resemble brass platters balanced on boxes. There are forays beyond Thailand too.

Open All Year

SWINBROOK
MAP 10, SP21

The Swan Inn
⚜ MODERN BRITISH
01993 823339 | OX18 4DY
www.theswanswinbrook.co.uk
The wisteria-clad, 16th-century Swan is the quintessential village pub, with an orchard to the rear and the Windrush River running by. The kitchen sources seasonal ingredients with care (traceability is a big deal here), and knows how to turn it into some skilfully rendered dishes.

Closed 25-26 December

TOOT BALDON
MAP 5, SP50

The Mole Inn
⚜⚜ MODERN EUROPEAN
01865 340001 | OX44 9NG
www.themoleinn.com

In a quiet village on the outskirts of Oxford, The Mole Inn is everything a country inn should be, adorned with framed mirrors and run by a casual but professional team. A starter of devilled lamb's kidneys with chargrilled ciabatta might be followed by rump of lamb, pea and mint mash, grain mustard cabbage and roast garlic.

Chef Johnny Parke **Seats** 70 **Closed** 25 December **Prices from** S £5, M £12, D £7 **Parking** 40 **Notes** Vegetarian dishes, Children welcome

WANTAGE
MAP 5, SU38

The Star Inn
⚜⚜ MODERN BRITISH
01235 751873 | Watery Lane, Sparsholt, OX12 9PL
www.thestarsparsholt.co.uk
Inside this solid 300-year-old inn in the quintessentially English village of Sparsholt, all is decluttered and open plan with chunky wooden furniture and plain white walls, and the food has a suitably modern accent. So, start perhaps with salt-cured beef brisket and bacon terrine.

Open All Year

WATLINGTON
MAP 5, SU69

The Fat Fox Inn
⚜ MODERN BRITISH
01491 613040 | 13 Shirburn Street, OX49 5BU
www.thefatfoxinn.co.uk
The Fat Fox lurks in a small market town on the edge of the Chilterns, and is a proper old country inn with an inglenook fireplace and wood-burning stove. The frequently changing menu offers hearty portions of rustic, unfussy food with the right amount of modern tweaking.

Closed 25 December

WITNEY
MAP 5, SP31

Hollybush Witney
⚜ BRITISH
01993 708073 | 35 Corn Street, OX28 6BT
www.hollybushwitney.com
The Hollybush is a buzzy gastro pub run by a youthful team that successfully delivers the gastronomy part without neglecting that essential pub side of the equation. There are real ales at the hand pumps and a menu that comes up with pub classics.

Chef Kevin Jones **Seats** 71, Private dining 35 **Open** All Year **Prices from** S £8, M £14.50, D £7 **Notes** Vegetarian dishes, Children welcome

WOODSTOCK
MAP 11, SP41

Macdonald Bear Hotel

◉◉ MODERN, TRADITIONAL BRITISH

01993 811124 | Park Street, OX20 1SZ

www.macdonaldhotels.co.uk/bear

This former coaching inn has its origins in the Middle Ages, although the kitchen clearly has its fingers on the pulse of today's tastes. Fish gets a decent airing, puddings can be a visual delight, and the kitchen's attention to detail even extends to canapés.

Open All Year

WOOTTON
MAP 11, SP41

The Killingworth Castle

◉◉ CLASSIC BRITISH *V*

01993 811401 | Glympton Road, OX20 1EJ

www.thekillingworthcastle.com

The inn has been an integral part of its community since the 1630s. When the Alexanders (who also run the Ebrington Arms near Chipping Campden) took over in 2012, the old place received the investment it needed, while retaining its earthy charm and period character. Organic beers are brewed on site.

Chef Will Patterson, Darral Warner **Seats** 70, Private dining 20 **Closed** 25 December **Parking** 40 **Notes** Vegetarian dishes, Children welcome

■ RUTLAND

CLIPSHAM
MAP 11, SK91

The Olive Branch

◉◉ BRITISH, EUROPEAN *V*

01780 410355 | Beech House, Main Street, LE15 7SH

www.theolivebranchpub.com

Home-grown and foraged herbs and berries play a big part here, alongside local farm meats, English Channel fish and Norfolk shellfish. Daily-changing menus offer pan-fried pigeon breast with braised lentils; hake with mussels and curry sauce; rump of lamb with sweetbreads; and orzo pasta with chargrilled shallots. Forced Yorkshire rhubarb is a popular tailpiece.

Chef Sean Hope **Seats** 45, Private dining 20 **Closed** 31 December, 1 January **Prices from** S £7.50, M £14.75, D £7 **Parking** 15 **Notes** Children welcome

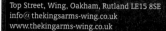

KING'S ARMS INN & RESTAURANT

The Kings Arms Inn's laid back, relaxed ambiance is complemented by award-winning cuisine created by Head Chef and Partner James Goss.

Our ethos is dedicated to providing the finest food in the area, locally sourced and produced in house. Villagers and visitors will be found side by side creating that wonderful country pub community feel.

Our friendly team serves traditional, artisan and innovative pub fare, surrounded by beamed ceilings, flagstone floors and open fires.

The Bar is brimming with a large selection of homemade snacks from the pub's Jimmy's Rutland Smokehouse. Awaiting visitors are a selection of well-kept local real ales, regional and local ciders, fruit pressés and traditional soft drinks. A comprehensive wine list boasts some 30 served by the glass of which we are especially proud.

The Inn has 8 en-suite rooms, 4 in the old Bake House and 4 in the slightly newer Orchard Houses. 2 of the large rooms can either be triple or twin occupancy. Excluding the single room, the remaining spacious accommodation all has either double or king size beds.

Top Street, Wing, Oakham, Rutland LE15 8SE
info@thekingsarms-wing.co.uk
www.thekingarms-wing.co.uk

OAKHAM
MAP 11, SK80

Barnsdale Lodge Hotel

⊛ MODERN BRITISH

01572 724678 | The Avenue, Rutland Water,
North Shore, LE15 8AH

www.barnsdalelodge.co.uk

To one side of the Earl of Gainsborough's Exton estate, this is a handsome country seat on the shore of Rutland Water, with a main dining room, garden room and alfresco courtyard. It's host to simple modern British menus featuring produce from the vegetable garden.

Chef David Bucrowicki **Seats** 120, Private dining 200
Open All Year **Prices from** S £6.95, M £14.25, D £5.95
Parking 250 **Notes** Vegetarian dishes, Children welcome

Fox & Hounds

⊛⊛ MODERN BRITISH, EUROPEAN

01572 812403 | 19 The Green, Exton, LE15 8AP

www.afoxinexton.co.uk

Overlooking the green in the pretty village of Exton, this former coaching inn has been feeding people since the 17th century. A smart pub with rooms, it retains plenty of original character although the food is thoroughly contemporary. The puddings are worth exploring.

Open All Year

Hambleton Hall

⊛⊛⊛⊛ MODERN BRITISH **V** NOTABLE WINE LIST

See pages 334–335

UPPINGHAM
MAP 11, SP89

The Lake Isle

⊛⊛ BRITISH, FRENCH

01572 822951 | 16 High Street East, LE15 9PZ

www.lakeisle.co.uk

The property may be 350 years old but the cooking at this restaurant-with-rooms is thoroughly modern. Global influences are apparent across the menu, with a starter of Timothy Taylor ale-cured English Parma ham, poached duck egg and asparagus soldiers followed by sea bream, clams, samphire and lemon sorrel pesto.

Chef Stuart Mead **Seats** 40, Private dining 16
Closed 1 January, bank holidays **Parking** 6
Notes Vegetarian dishes, No children

WING
MAP 11, SK80

Kings Arms Inn & Restaurant

⊛⊛ TRADITIONAL BRITISH

01572 737634 | 13 Top Street, LE15 8SE

www.thekingsarms-wing.co.uk

Beamed ceilings, flagstone floors, open fires and rustic wooden tables characterise the bar and restaurant. Try the grilled teriyaki beef starter; and for a main course, the ling cod with poached langoustines; or the fallow deer leg steak with venison salami. 'Lunch for Less' on pheasant schnitzel with peas and fries; or fish pie with seasonal vegetables.

Chef James Goss **Seats** 32 **Open** All Year
Prices from S £7, M £17, D £7 **Parking** 20
Notes Vegetarian dishes, Children welcome

See advertisement opposite

Hambleton Hall

◉◉◉◉ **MODERN BRITISH** *V* ● NOTABLE WINE LIST

01572 756991 | Hambleton, LE15 8TH

www.hambletonhall.com

Simple but powerfully effective country house cooking

Hambleton was built by a Victorian chap who made his fortune in brewing and rather fancied a place to stop over when enjoying the hunting in this part of the country. He picked a good spot that got even better when Rutland Water reservoir was opened in 1976. It remains a handsome property, its public rooms full of lively colour and opulent fabric, and the major attraction of spectacularly good dining in the soft-focus elegance of its dining room.

Aaron Patterson has made a major contribution to Hambleton's charms, heading up the kitchen since 1992 after some handy time spent in the stellar kitchens of Raymond Blanc and Anton Mosimann. Patterson has always favoured an understated, essentially ungimmicky approach, with pure, true flavours allowed to speak up in their own right – a style of cooking that everyone can appreciate but lacks nothing in technical flourish.

Opening courses are bold and bright – perhaps salmon gravad lax with horseradish ice cream and ginger caviar of crystal clarity, or chicken liver and foie gras parfait with fig for traditionalists. Thoroughbred meats and impeccably fresh fish are the foundations of main courses that gain lustre from ingenious textural balancing of their elements, so you might follow that with a masterful reworking of beef sirloin with roast potatoes, Yorkshire pudding and horseradish mayonnaise, or superb fillet of turbot with clams, fennel, orange and an invitingly fragrant lovage risotto.

The dessert repertoire offers a masterclass in technical know-how, delivering such delights as coconut and lime nougat glacé with spiced pineapple, or

> "Patterson has always favoured an understated, essentially ungimmicky approach"

a flavour-drenched quince and honey soufflé served with almond ice cream. A separate vegetarian menu might centre on artichoke tartlet with a poached egg and hollandaise, and wild mushroom tagliatelle with grappa sauce. Look to the sommelier for sound advice from the magisterial 400-bin wine list; service all round is irreproachable.

Chef Aaron Patterson
Seats 60, Private dining 40
Open All Year
Parking 40
Notes No children under 5 years

■ SHROPSHIRE

BISHOP'S CASTLE
MAP 15, SO38

The Coach House
◉◉ MODERN BRITISH

01588 650846 | Norbury, SY9 5DX
www.coachhousenorbury.com
Four miles from the market town of Bishop's
Castle, this delightful 18th-century inn stands in
the centre of a pretty conservation village in the
beautiful Onny Valley. Once you've had a pint of
local ale in the bar, head to the dining area for a
meal that might feature monkfish, salmon and
mussels poached in shellfish sauce with rouille
and purple sprouting broccoli.

Chef Harry Bullock **Seats** Private dining 25
Closed January, 9–25 June, 13–22 October
Prices from S £7, M £14, D £7 **Parking** 8
Notes Vegetarian dishes, No children under 5 years

IRONBRIDGE
MAP 10, SJ60

Number Ten
◉ MODERN BRITISH

01952 432901 | White Hart, The Wharfage, TF8 7AW
www.whitehartironbridge.com
Set just beyond Abraham Darby's famous bridge,
the White Hart is located deep in the Severn
Gorge and surrounded by reminders of the
industrial revolution. Their Number Ten
restaurant is a fine dining option with large
windows that look out to the river.

Chef Kate Bradley **Seats** 40, Private dining 40 **Closed** 25
December **Notes** Vegetarian dishes, Children are
welcome with certain restrictions (early dining times,
menu adaptions).

Restaurant Severn
◉ MODERN BRITISH

01952 432233 | 33 High Street, TF8 7AG
www.restaurantsevern.co.uk
This small restaurant blends in with the terrace
of souvenir and tea shops facing Abraham
Darby's Iron Bridge World Heritage Site. Inside,
however, the bare wooden floors, unclothed
tables and high-backed toffee-brown leather
chairs make for an intimate brasserie look.

Chef Michelle Drayton, Cameron Barden **Seats** 30,
Private dining **Open** All Year **Notes** Vegetarian
dishes, No children under 5 years

LUDLOW
MAP 10, SO57

The Charlton Arms
◉ MODERN BRITISH

01584 872813 | Ludford Bridge, SY8 1PJ
www.thecharltonarms.co.uk

You can eat and drink not only by, but above, the
River Teme here, because the lower of two
outdoor decks projects over it; the views are
delightful. On the modern British menu, a good
selection of dishes includes ham hock Scotch
egg with piccalilli coulis; and pan-fried hake fillet
with crab and chorizo croquettes.

Chef Krisztian Balogh **Seats** 40 **Closed** 25 December
Parking 30 **Notes** Vegetarian dishes, Children welcome

The Cliffe at Dinham
◉◉ MODERN BRITISH

01584 872063 | Halton Lane, Dinham, SY8 2JE
www.thecliffeatdinham.co.uk
A handsome red-brick Victorian mansion beside
the River Teme with views across to Ludlow
Castle, The Cliffe has morphed into a stylish
restaurant with rooms with a breezily modern
approach to its interior decor. Sporting sage-
green walls, bare floorboards and unclothed
tables, the restaurant is a suitably contemporary
spot for the kitchen's modern bistro dishes.

Chef Ian Pugh **Seats** 60, Private dining 30 **Closed** 25–26
December **Prices from** S £6, M £16.50, D £6 **Parking** 30
Notes Vegetarian dishes, Children welcome

The Clive Arms

◉ MODERN BRITISH

01584 856565 | Bromfield, SY8 2JR

www.theclive.co.uk

Once the home of Clive of India, then a pub, this brick-built Georgian house has been imaginatively appointed. Seasonality dictates the modern British menu, which may feature pickled wild mushrooms with chicken liver parfait with toasted sourdough bread.

Chef Peter Mills **Seats** 90 **Open** All Year **Parking** 80 **Notes** Vegetarian dishes, Children welcome

Fishmore Hall

◉◉◉ MODERN BRITISH

01584 875148 | Fishmore Road, SY8 3DP

www.fishmorehall.co.uk

It's hard to believe that this handsome Georgian country pile just outside the foodie hub of Ludlow was falling apart until its current owners restored it to the porticoed, pristine white boutique bolt-hole (with a spa tucked away in the garden) that we see today. Housed in an orangery extension, Forelles restaurant enjoys views of the rolling Shropshire hills as a backdrop to the classic country-house cuisine. As you'd hope, it's all built on pedigree materials sourced from within a 30-mile radius (apart from seafood, of course, which comes from Brixham and Skye). You might begin with soft and tender quail, served with butternut squash filled with chorizo cubes, pomegranate seeds, goats' curd and shallots, before moving on to an excellent piece of fresh, bright turbot, served with chicken wing, sweetcorn, crab gnocchi, lemongrass and dashi. Old-school and dramatic, baked Alaska is flamed at the table and has a filling of pistachio, peach and cardamom.

Chef Joe Gould **Seats** 60, Private dining 20 **Closed** 2-13 January **Parking** 30 **Notes** Vegetarian dishes, Children welcome, no children's menu

Old Downton Lodge

◉◉◉◉ MODERN BRITISH

01568 771826 | Downton on the Rock, SY8 2HU

www.olddowntonlodge.com

A short drive from foodie Ludlow, Old Downton Lodge is a rural idyll overlooking the hills of the Welsh Marches. Originally a farmhouse and cider mill, the country-chic restaurant with rooms comprises a fascinating cluster of buildings – medieval, half-timbered, Georgian – around a courtyard filled with herbs and flowers. Dating from Norman times, the restaurant has the feel of a medieval great hall with its stone walls,

tapestry and chandelier. Dinner takes the form of daily-changing six- and nine-course menus or a three-course market menu, all built on local, home-grown and foraged produce of the highest order. Head chef Karl Martin's cooking is defined by its inherent simplicity, precision and intuitive balance, kicking off with a combo of cauliflower, onion and parmesan of remarkable depth to pave the way for Wagyu beef boosted with blue cheese, broccoli and walnut. These are highly original compositions where everything is there for a good reason: main courses see lobster counterpointed with cherry tomato fondue, caviar and Thai basil, then a superlative pork medallion is matched with braised gem lettuce, winberries and peas. The results are impressive all the way through to thought-provoking desserts of Muscovado mousse with blueberries, peanut and sorrel, and rice pudding with elderflower, strawberry and tarragon.

Chef Karl Martin **Seats** 25, Private dining 60 **Closed** Christmas **Parking** 20 **Notes** Vegetarian dishes, No children

MARKET DRAYTON
MAP 15, SJ63

Goldstone Hall

◉◉ MODERN BRITISH ◗ NOTABLE WINE LIST

01630 661202 | Goldstone Road, TF9 2NA

www.goldstonehall.com

The two stand-out elements to Goldstone Hall are its magnificent gardens and ambitious restaurant. The kitchen garden is a major part of the operation, providing seasonal produce, and dishes are bright and modern while avoiding jumping on the bandwagon of every contemporary fashion.

Chef Liam Philbin **Seats** 60, Private dining 14 **Open** All Year **Parking** 70 **Notes** Vegetarian dishes, Children welcome

MUCH WENLOCK
MAP 10, SO69

Raven Hotel

◉◉ MODERN BRITISH

01952 727251 | 30 Barrow Street, TF13 6EN

www.ravenhotel.com

Raven Hotel is a former coaching inn dating from the 17th century with plenty of period charm, with venerable beams, log fires and hand-pulled ales available in the bar. On the dining front, though, things are positively 21st century, for the kitchen turns out smart, modern dishes.

Closed 25-26 December

MUNSLOW
MAP 10, SO58

Crown Country Inn
◉◉ MODERN BRITISH
01584 841205 | SY7 9ET
www.crowncountryinn.co.uk
In an Area of Outstanding Natural Beauty, the
Crown dates from Tudor times and was first
licensed in 1790. The kitchen has a 'Local to
Ludlow' policy that might include a reworking of
breakfast for black pudding croquettes with
Boston beans, bacon and 'fried bread'.

Closed some days during Christmas

NORTON
MAP 10, SJ70

The Hundred House
◉ BRITISH, FRENCH
01952 580240 | Bridgnorth Road, TF11 9EE
www.hundredhouse.co.uk
Run by the Phillips family since the mid-1980s,
The Hundred House is brimful of character and
personality. The handsome Georgian coaching
inn has stylish bedrooms, a bar serving pretty
nifty pub grub, and a brasserie and restaurant
producing classy dishes based on tip-top
regional ingredients, many from the house's own
bountiful gardens.

Chef Stuart Phillips **Seats** 80, Private dining 34 **Open** All
Year **Parking** 60 **Notes** Vegetarian dishes, Children
welcome

OSWESTRY
MAP 15, SJ22

Pen-y-Dyffryn Country Hotel
◉◉ MODERN BRITISH
01691 653700 | Rhydycroesau, SY10 7JD
www.peny.co.uk
A construction company built the rectory, church
and village school here in 1840. Nowadays, the
church is on the Welsh side of the border and the
rectory is in England. With sweeping views over
the valley, it is traditionally furnished in a
country-house style.

Chef Alex Lloyd **Seats** 25 **Closed** 20 December to
21 January **Parking** 18 **Notes** Vegetarian dishes, No
children under 3 years

Sebastians
◉◉ FRENCH **V**
01691 655444 | 45 Willow Street, SY11 1AQ
www.sebastians-hotel.com
In a 17th-century inn, full of cossetting beamed
character, but not stuck in the past. Monthly-
changing menus (with complimentary appetiser
and sorbet before mains) take you through three
courses of well-crafted, Gallic-influenced ideas,
with an appetiser to set the ball rolling, and a
refreshing sorbet before mains.

Chef Mark Fisher **Seats** 45 **Closed** 25-26 December,
1 January and all bank holiday Mondays **Parking** 6
Notes No children under 10 years

Wynnstay Hotel
◉◉ BRITISH
01691 655261 | Church Street, SY11 2SZ
www.wynnstayhotel.com
The Wynnstay's Four Seasons restaurant
produces modern British cooking based on
reinvented versions of dishes taken from the
Wynnstay's 1960s menus. Try the delights of pea
and mint velouté followed by pan-seared
Gressingham duck breast à l'orange perhaps.

Open All Year

SHREWSBURY
MAP 15, SJ41

Albright Hussey Manor Hotel & Restaurant
◉ MODERN BRITISH
01939 290571 | Ellesmere Road, Broad Oak, SY4 3AF
www.albrighthussey.co.uk
This Tudor hotel with strangely unmatched wings
(built only 35 years apart) is stocked with
fascinating antiques, both martial and domestic.
Confident, contemporary food is served up in a
beamed room with mullioned windows and a
pleasing coral-pink colour scheme.

Open All Year

Henry Tudor House Restaurant and Bar

◉ MODERN BRITISH *V*

01743 361666 | Henry Tudor House, Barracks Passage, SY1 1XA

www.henrytudorhouse.com

Among the town's oldest half-timbered buildings, HTH's whimsical interior boasts a Parisian-style zinc bar bathed in ever-changing coloured light, while elegant chandeliers in the conservatory shine through delicate iron birdcages. The all-day menu offers a range of classics, while things are more elaborate in the evenings.

Chef Chris Conde, Dan Smith **Seats** 34, Private dining 18 **Closed** 25-26 December, 1 January **Prices from** S £5.50, M £12, D £6.50 **Notes** Vegetarian dishes, Children welcome

House of the Rising Sun

◉ MODERN INTERNATIONAL *V*

01743 588040 | 18 Butcher Row, SY1 1UW

www.hotrs.co.uk

This restaurant is tucked away down a narrow lane, where in medieval times butchers plied their trade. The two dining areas vary greatly – upstairs is very clubby with dark walls and geisha-inspired artwork, while the ground floor is more open plan with long tables. The staff are well informed and clearly passionate about the food on offer – imagine Asian street food meets Spanish tapas.

Chef Llam Watton **Seats** 52 **Closed** 25-26 December, 1 January **Prices from** S £4.25, M £8.50, D £6.50 **Notes** Vegetarian dishes, Children welcome

Lion & Pheasant Hotel

◉◉ BRITISH *V*

01743 770345 | 49-50 Wyle Cop, SY1 1XJ

www.lionandpheasant.co.uk

This coaching inn has stood since the 16th century and before the street called Wyle Cop became a bridge over the River Severn. Its period façade gives way to a contemporary New England-style interior, with neutral tones and tongue-and-groove-panelling combining harmoniously with the brickwork and beams.

Chef Paul Downes **Seats** 35, Private dining 45 **Closed** 25-26 December **Parking** 14 **Notes** Children welcome

The Mytton and Mermaid

◉ MODERN BRITISH *V*

01743 761220 | Atcham, SY5 6QG

www.myttonandmermaid.co.uk

Alongside the River Severn, this handsome Grade II listed building has a dining room that's partially separated from the large open-plan bar but the atmosphere flows well across both areas. The modern British menu is split between pub favourites and specials which often lean towards the Far East as in the Vietnamese Bahn mi salad.

Chef Chris Burt **Seats** 80, Private dining 18 **Open** All Year **Prices from** S £6, M £13.50, D £5 **Parking** 60 **Notes** Children welcome

The Peach Tree Restaurant

◉ MODERN BRITISH, ASIAN FUSION *V*

01743 355055 | 18-21 Abbey Foregate, SY2 6AE

www.thepeachtree.co.uk

Modern flavours with influences from the East share the menu with more traditional dishes at this 15th-century building opposite Shrewsbury Abbey. Kick off with chicken liver pâté, onion jam and artisan toast, then on to mains like wild salmon with miso butter crust, and a Korean barbecue rice noodle salad.

Chef Matthew Parry **Seats** 96, Private dining 80 **Open** All Year **Prices from** S £3.95, M £9.95, D £3.95 **Notes** Children welcome

The Royalist Restaurant

◉ MODERN, CLASSIC

01743 499955 | Prince Rupert Hotel, Butcher Row, SY1 1UQ

www.princeruperthotel.co.uk

As befits a former home of the grandson of King James I, the Grade II listed Prince Rupert Hotel is a regal affair surrounded by cobbled streets and Tudor buildings. With tapestries and suits of armour, the oak-panelled Royalist Restaurant provides a medieval ambience.

Chef Mike Peters **Seats** 85, Private dining 16 **Open** All Year **Prices from** S £6, M £16, D £7 **Notes** Vegetarian dishes, Children welcome

TELFORD
MAP 10, SJ60

Chez Maw Restaurant
◉◉ MODERN BRITISH

01952 432247 | The Valley Hotel, Ironbridge, TF8 7DW

www.chezmawrestaurant.co.uk

On the bank of the Severn in Ironbridge, and barely a rivet's throw from the bridge, The Valley Hotel was owned by Arthur Maw and his family, suppliers of ceramic tiles, hence the name of its smart restaurant; there's an outside terrace for a pre-dinner drink.

Chef Barry Workman **Seats** 50, Private dining 30
Closed 26 December to 2 January **Parking** 100
Notes Vegetarian dishes, Children welcome

Hadley Park House
◉ MODERN BRITISH

01952 677269 | Hadley Park, TF1 6QJ

www.hadleypark.co.uk

The origins of Hadley Park remain shrouded in mystery, but it seems likely to have been built in the mid-Georgian era, the 1770s perhaps. The conservatory extension dining room in the form of Dorrells is dedicated to the elegant pursuit of regionally sourced British cooking.

Closed 26 December

UPTON MAGNA
MAP 10, SJ51

The Haughmond
◉◉ MODERN BRITISH **V**

01743 709918 | Pelham Road, SY4 4TZ

www.thehaughmond.co.uk

With a smart makeover a few years back, there's a contemporary feel to this traditional village inn. Family-run, it retains a pubby atmosphere, while drawing diners from afar. Classics can be enjoyed in the bar, while the Basil's restaurant offers a fine-dining experience.

Chef Martin Board **Seats** 48, Private dining 20 **Open** All Year **Prices from** S £7, M £14, D £8 **Parking** 30
Notes Children welcome

■ SOMERSET

AXBRIDGE
MAP 4, ST45

The Oak House
◉◉ CLASSIC BRITISH

01934 732444 | The Square, BS26 2AP

www.theoakhousesomerset.com

Parts of the Oak House date from the 11th century. Inside, a stylish mix of old and new places it at the boutique end of the design spectrum. Steaks are cooked on the grill – 10oz rib-eye, say – and arrive with triple-cooked chips.

Open All Year

BATH
MAP 4, ST76

Bailbrook House Hotel
◉◉ MODERN BRITISH **V**

01225 855100 | Eveleigh Avenue, London Road West, BA1 7JD

www.bailbrookhouse.co.uk

Bailbrook is a handsome Georgian country mansion done out in classy contemporary boutique style. Its Cloisters Restaurant is the fine-dining option, an intimate split-level space. Flavours counterpoint well in fish dishes such as halibut fillet with pea and bacon fricassée, Jersey Royals and girolles.

Chef Michael Ball **Seats** 54, Private dining 14 **Open** All Year **Prices from** S £8, M £17, D £9 **Parking** 100
Notes Children welcome

The Bath Priory Hotel, Restaurant & Spa
◉◉◉ MODERN EUROPEAN, FRENCH **V**

01225 331922 | Weston Road, BA1 2XT

http://www.thebathpriory.co.uk

Built in 1835 on land owned by the priory of Bath Abbey, the present-day, family-owned hotel and spa is a tranquil place on the western side of the Georgian city, dedicated to the full range of creature comforts, from massages to modern cuisine, the latter courtesy of much-travelled executive chef Michael Nizzero. The dining room is all neutral hues and white linen, a relaxing setting for confident British cooking with a sense of style. A three-course meal might begin simply, with smoked Loch Duart salmon, avocado, crème fraîche and caviar, or Cornish crab with the fresh flavours of celery and lovage. A Dover sole main is accompanied by cauliflower, sea vegetables and sorrel, or perhaps you might choose fillet of beef with carrot purée, fondant potato, red wine and tarragon sauce. Finish with salted caramel fondant and banana, or the fresh spring flavours of poached rhubarb and vanilla cream with citrus croûtons and sorbet.

Chef Michael Nizzero **Seats** 50, Private dining 72 **Open** All Year **Parking** 40 **Notes** No children under 12 years

The Chequers

◉◉ MODERN BRITISH

01225 360017 | 50 Rivers Street, BA1 2QA

www.thechequersbath.com

The Chequers has been providing drink and victuals since 1776. Food is the core of the operation, and everything is made from scratch. Why not step outside the box with something like seared scallops with smoked pork belly, cauliflower, candied lime and cumin velouté?

Open All Year

The Circus Restaurant

◉ MODERN EUROPEAN *V*

01225 466020 | 34 Brock Street, BA1 2LN

www.thecircusrestaurant.co.uk

In a prime location between two of Bath's most iconic locations, The Circus and the Royal Crescent, this is an upmarket all-day eatery, with high-ceilinged dining rooms offering a bold, modern setting for the monthly-changing, seasonally-inspired menu, based on fine West Country produce.

Chef Alison Golden, Tom Bally, Ash Saman **Seats** 50, Private dining 32 **Closed** 3 weeks from 24 December **Prices from** S £6, M £11.50, D £4.50 **Notes** No children under 10 years

Dan Moon at the Gainsborough Restaurant

◉◉◉ MODERN BRITISH *V*

01225 358888 | Beau Street, BA1 1QY

www.thegainsboroughbathspa.co.uk

If it's a blowout stay in Bath you're after, its hotels don't come with a more blue-blooded pedigree than The Gainsborough Bath Spa. Named after the eponymous artist, an erstwhile Bath resident, the place spreads across a handsome Grade II listed building dating from the 18th century. Looking elegantly understated with its unclothed tables, blue-and-white walls and caramel leather seats, the dining room is a suitably contemporary setting for Dan Moon's impeccably up-to-date British food. Expect bright, fresh combinations and entertaining textures, all soundly rooted in an intuitive grasp of how things work together, as seen in openers such as smoked fillet of beef with pané quail egg, foie gras, celeriac remoulade and pickled vegetables. A main of butter-poached halibut

with asparagus, parmesan broth, broad bean purée and lobster is a very well-conceived and attractive dish, while a dessert of buttermilk pannacotta with Yorkshire rhubarb, honeycomb and granola is a fine conclusion.

Chef Daniel Moon **Seats** 70 **Open** All Year **Notes** Children welcome

The Dower House Restaurant

◉◉◉ MODERN BRITISH *V* ⬛⬛⬛

See pages 342-343

The Hare & Hounds

◉ MODERN BRITISH

01225 482682 | Lansdown Road, BA1 5TJ

www.hareandhoundsbath.com

The Hare & Hounds is an enticing bolt-hole with glorious views from its hilltop location just north of Bath. Huge leaded windows look over the terrace, flooding light over a smart interior of wood tables, chairs, panelling and floors. It's relaxed and informal, but the kitchen has a serious commitment to food and draws on top-grade produce.

Chef Chris Lynn **Seats** 106, Private dining 12 **Open** All Year **Prices from** S £4, M £12, D £5 **Parking** 30 **Notes** Vegetarian dishes, Children welcome

Macdonald Bath Spa

◉◉ MODERN BRITISH *V*

01225 444444 | Sydney Road, BA2 6JF

www.macdonald-hotels.co.uk/bathspa

A majestic Georgian façade sets a grand tone, running through to the Vellore Restaurant in the original ballroom, where pillars and a high-domed ceiling add to a stately air; engaging staff and a helpful sommelier keep things on track, and the kitchen delivers unfussy dishes.

Chef Jonathan Machin **Seats** 80, Private dining 120 **Open** All Year **Prices from** S £7, M £18, D £9 **Parking** 160 **Notes** Children welcome

The Marlborough Tavern

◉◉ MODERN BRITISH

01225 423731 | 35 Marlborough Buildings, BA1 2LY

www.marlborough-tavern.com

This straight-talking foodie pub has a pleasingly unstuffy vibe and local ales and ciders on tap. Fare could be as simple as home-made burgers or fish and chips, or at the more gastro end, a five-course tasting menu with matching wines.

Open All Year

The Dower House Restaurant

◉◉◉ MODERN BRITISH *V* 🍷 NOTABLE WINE LIST

01225 823333 | The Royal Crescent Hotel & Spa, 16 Royal Crescent, BA1 2LS
www.royalcrescent.co.uk

Strong contemporary cooking behind the Royal Crescent

The Dower House Restaurant has always been up among Bath's most elegant addresses. Sitting smack in the centre of the sweeping Georgian landmark that is Bath's iconic Royal Crescent, it looks over the acre of immaculate landscaped gardens behind the namesake luxury hotel. As you'd expect in a hotel of this calibre, it's refined, elegant and comfortable, with flowers on well-spaced tables, thickly carpeted floor, soft furnishings of blue and gold, silk wallpapers, and French windows opening on to the garden –perfect for pre-dinner drinks on balmy days. Service is on the formal side, with uniformed staff knowledgeable and willing, while a sommelier is on hand to help with choosing wines from an international treasure trove.

Head chef David Campbell's culinary style might be described as a modern take on classic themes, but that fails to do full justice to the high degree of creativity and

imagination – as well as labour intensiveness – of his cooking. Things are sharp and precise from the off, featuring big flavours and the all-important inventive touch in starters such as the duck liver that comes spiked with pink peppercorn, alongside smoked pigeon, ginger and gingerbread, the additional note of Yorkshire rhubarb supplying the perfect tart foil to all that richness, or soy-cured mackerel, say, which arrives in a well-considered medley of avocado wasabi, cucumber, black garlic and crispy seaweed.

Main courses are equally dedicated to delivering the essence of each ingredient, whether it's loin and braised belly of superlative organic pork with sage and apple quinoa, apple sauce and pork skin crumb, or fish in the form of roasted sea bass supported by scallops, beetroot,

"David Campbell's culinary style might be described as a modern take on classic themes"

smoked eel, hay-baked potato, smoked roe cream and horseradish. The dessert course could be a bracing trio of blood orange tart, poached rhubarb and ginger ice cream, while a classic mélange of flavours brings together iced coffee parfait, caramel-scented Dulcey chocolate mousse and milk ice cream.

Chef David Campbell
Seats 60, Private dining 30
Open All Year
Parking 17
Notes No children under 12 years after 8pm

Menu Gordon Jones

@@ MODERN BRITISH

01225 480871 | 2 Wellsway, BA2 3AQ

www.menugordonjones.co.uk

Gordon Jones has form in Bath, having run the Royal Crescent Hotel kitchen, but here he's doing his own thing in an unassuming little spot with foodies beating down the door to enjoy what's put before them. The main concepts here are surprise and anticipation.

Chef Gordon Jones **Closed** 35 days a year (variable)

The Olive Tree at the Queensberry Hotel

@@@ MODERN BRITISH *V* 💷 NOTABLE WINE LIST

See pages 346–347

The Scallop Shell

@ BRITISH

01225 420928 | 22 Monmouth Place, BA1 2AY

www.thescallopshell.co.uk

Behind a sky-blue frontage not far from Queen Square, this popular venue offers a versatile range of fish and seafood dishes in a relaxed café-style format where food is ordered at the counter. Freshness is everything at The Scallop Shell. There is no separate dessert menu, just one sweet thing per day.

Chef Garry Rosser, Peter Horn **Seats** 85 **Closed** 25–26 December, 1 January **Notes** Vegetarian dishes, Children welcome

Woods Restaurant

@ MODERN BRITISH, FRENCH

01225 314812 | 9-13 Alfred Street, BA1 2QX

www.woodsrestaurant.com

Woods stands in a very 'Bath' setting, occupying the ground floor of five Georgian townhouses, and its comfortable bistro look is pretty much timeless. The cooking is broadly European, with French and Italy to the fore, and a British flavour here and there.

Closed 25-26 December

BRIDGWATER

MAP 4, ST23

Walnut Tree Hotel

@ TRADITIONAL BRITISH

01278 662255 | North Petherton, TA6 6QA

www.walnuttreehotel.com

The handsome former coaching inn is to be found in the town of North Petherton near Bridgwater, with the Quantock Hills not far. A traditional pub ambience prevails in the bar, and

there is a cream-walled, airy dining room bright with fresh flowers and candles.

Chef Dan Rawlison-Wheller **Seats** 36, Private dining 100 **Open** All Year **Prices from** S £5, M £11, D £5.50 **Parking** 60 **Notes** Vegetarian dishes, Children welcome

CHARD

MAP 4, ST30

Lordleaze Hotel *NEW*

@ BRITISH, EUROPEAN

01460 61066 | Henderson Drive, Forton Road, TA20 2HW

lordleazehotel.com

Fashioned from an 18th-century farmhouse, this friendly country hotel basks in bucolic West Country tranquillity. An airy conservatory-style dining room overlooking the gardens is the appealing setting for a menu of uncomplicated dishes cooked with care by a kitchen that hauls in the best local produce it can lay its hands on.

Chef Joe Nagy **Seats** Private dining 100 **Open** All Year **Prices from** S £3.50, M £12.50, D £2.50 **Parking** 50 **Notes** Vegetarian dishes, Children welcome

CHEDDAR

MAP 4, ST45

The Bath Arms

@@ MODERN BRITISH

01934 742425 | Bath Street, BS27 3AA

www.batharms.com

Smack in the centre of Cheddar village and within footslogging distance of the eponymous gorge and caves, The Bath Arms has kept faith with those essential pubby virtues - real ales, a genuine welcome and great food. The kitchen turns out some impressive culinary action.

Open All Year

CHEW MAGNA

MAP 4, ST56

The Pony and Trap

@@ MODERN BRITISH *V*

01275 332627 | Knowle Hill, BS40 8TQ

www.theponyandtrap.co.uk

Chef/owner Josh Eggleton, who is remembered for his 2014 performance on the TV show *The Great British Menu*, is the driving force behind this revitalised 200-year-old country cottage pub in lush Chew Valley countryside. Ingredients arrive on the plate fresh from the herb and vegetable garden.

Chef Josh Eggleton **Seats** 64 **Closed** 25-26 December **Prices from** S £8.50, M £18, D £8 **Parking** 40 **Notes** Vegetarian dishes, Children welcome

CORTON DENHAM
MAP 4, ST62

The Queens Arms
◉◉ MODERN BRITISH
01963 220317 | DT9 4LR
www.thequeensarms.com
This mellow stone 18th-century inn is set amid buxom hills on the Somerset-Dorset border, and a glance at the menu shows a clear love for local produce and a creative mind. The dining room is a cosy space with bare boards, dark walls and mis-matched, unclothed tables.

Chef Alec Hollingsworth Seats 78, Private dining 45 Open All Year Prices from S £7, M £17, D £7.50 Parking 20 Notes Vegetarian dishes, Children welcome

DULVERTON
MAP 3, SS92

Woods Bar & Restaurant
◉◉ MODERN BRITISH, FRENCH *V*
01398 324007 | 4 Banks Square, TA22 9BU
www.woodsdulverton.co.uk
On the edge of Exmoor, Woods is a pub cunningly disguised on the outside to look like a café. The interior scene is cheered with a log fire in winter, and wooden partitions roughly divide the place between the drinking of local ales and the eating of locally-sourced food. The kitchen offers intricately worked modern British cooking.

Chef Ed Herd Seats 40 Closed 25 December Prices from S £6.50, M £11.50, D £6.50 Notes Children welcome

DUNSTER
MAP 3, SS94

The Luttrell Arms Hotel
◉◉ BRITISH
01643 821555 | Exmoor National Park, TA24 6SG
www.luttrellarms.co.uk
Located within the delightful setting of this 15th-century hotel, the restaurant offers relaxed and comfortable dining and a pleasing combination of traditional style with a more modern country-house feel. Hearty portions from an inspiring menu might include beef Wellington with truffle mash or poached fillet of turbot.

Chef Barrie Tucker Seats 45, Private dining 20 Open All Year Notes Vegetarian dishes, Children welcome

FIVEHEAD
MAP 4, ST32

Langford Fivehead
◉◉ MODERN BRITISH *V*
01460 282020 | Lower Swell, TA3 6PH
www.langfordfivehead.co.uk
The Tudor manor house at Lower Swell stands in seven acres of mature grounds, full of cedars, box and yew. A contemporary dining room with modern artworks has a relaxed feel, and elegantly simple farm-to-plate eating is the order of the day.

Chef Olly Jackson Seats 22, Private dining 12 Closed 22 December-2 January, 27 July-9 August Parking 12 Notes Vegetarian dishes, No children under 8 years

FLAX BOURTON
MAP 4, ST56

Backwell House
◉◉ MODERN BRITISH
01275 794502 | Farleigh Road, BS48 3QA
www.backwellhouse.co.uk
Backwell House is a splendid Georgian mansion with a walled garden - elegant and stylish throughout, the place has a relaxed and welcoming ambiance. The kitchen is all about seasonality and the daily-changing menus feature fish and shellfish from Brixham and Cornwall, local game in the autumn and fruit and vegetables from their own organic garden.

Open All Year

HOLCOMBE
MAP 4, ST64

The Holcombe Inn
◉◉ BRITISH, INTERNATIONAL, FRENCH
01761 232478 | Stratton Road, BA3 5EB
www.holcombeinn.co.uk
The Holcombe is a textbook country inn with fires, local ales and amicable staff. Regional ingredients, including the produce of its own garden, supply the menus of mostly traditional fare. Desserts get creative with a raspberry and nougat parfait choc ice to accompany a Valrhona brownie.

Chef Shane Vant Seats 65 Open All Year Prices from S £6.75, M £17, D £6.95 Parking 30 Notes Vegetarian dishes, Children welcome

BATH

The Olive Tree at the Queensberry Hotel

◉◉◉ MODERN BRITISH 𝑽 ⬤ NOTABLE WINE LIST

01225 447928 | Russell Street, BA1 2QF

www.olivetreebath.co.uk

Accomplished cooking in chic, boutique Georgian hotel

Owners Laurence and Helen Beere have transformed their magnificent Georgian townhouse – built for the 8th Marquess of Queensbury in 1771, incidentally – into a top-ranking boutique hotel, driven by a passion for hospitality and a keen eye for interior aesthetics. Down in the basement rooms, but none the worse for that, The Olive Tree restaurant bathes in a light, minimalist look that's a fitting stage for Chris Cleghorn's dynamic contemporary cooking. After honing his craft in some top-flight kitchens (stints chez James Sommerin, Michael Caines and Heston Blumenthal to name but three), his eclectic approach and sharp technical skills are showcased here via five- and seven-course seasonal tasting menus, including vegetarian, vegan and dairy-free variations, and an admirably flexible approach allows you to cherry-pick a starter, main course and dessert if you're not up for the full-on

"... the modern British dishes are all built on the finest West Country produce delivered in intuitive flavour combinations"

tasting experience. Whichever route you take, the modern British dishes are all built on the finest West Country produce delivered in intuitive flavour combinations.

Finely tuned starters might see raw scallops pointed up with horseradish, pink grapefruit and dill, or tagliatelle fragrant with Périgord truffle, 30-month-aged parmesan and lardo. The meat department comes up with ideas such as fallow deer matched with barbecued cauliflower, golden raisins, sprouts and bitter chocolate, while other creations could be robustly treated fish, perhaps brill poached on the bone with turnip, hispi cabbage, shrimp and salted lemon. If you're giving

meat a swerve, intelligently composed dishes such as beetroot with Perl Las blue cheese, pecan and salted lemon, or macaroni with asparagus, cheddar, hen of the woods mushrooms and hazelnuts are a lesson in texture and well-matched flavours. Scintillating desserts bring a final flourish of tastes and textures – dark chocolate mousse, say, with yogurt sorbet and olive, or garriguette strawberry with mascarpone, yuzu and vanilla meringue. The wine list offers an eclectic international selection that bears the owners' hands-on stamp.

Chef Chris Cleghorn
Seats 60, Private dining 30
Closed 1 week January, 1 week April, 1st week August and 1st week November
Prices from S £17.50, M £30, D £12.50
Notes Children welcome

HUNSTRETE
MAP 4, ST66
THE PIG near Bath
◎◎ MODERN BRITISH ▲ NOTABLE WINE LIST

01761 490490 | Hunstrete House, Pensford, BS39 4NS

www.thepighotel.com

Well positioned between Bristol and Bath, this chilled shabby-chic country-house hotel is proud of its walled garden, which supplies much of the produce on the menu. Elephant garlic, chive crumpet and bacon jam might be followed by chargrilled pork tomahawk, garden greens, Somerset cider brandy and mustard sauce and triple-cooked chips.

Chef Jack Stallard **Seats** 90, Private dining 22 **Open** All Year **Prices from** S £6, M £12, D £7.50 **Parking** 50 **Notes** Vegetarian dishes, Children welcome

KINGSDON
MAP 4, ST52
The Kingsdon Inn *NEW*
◉ MODERN BRITISH, ITALIAN INFLUENCES

01935 840543 | Nr Somerton, TA11 7LG

kingsdoninn.co.uk

Once a cider house, this pretty thatched pub is furnished with stripped pine tables, cushioned farmhouse chairs and enough open fires to keep everywhere well warmed. The three charmingly decorated, saggy-beamed rooms have a relaxed and friendly feel. A menu of revamped English comfort dishes and Italian-accented ideas is a key part of the Kingsdon's appeal.

LITTON
MAP 4, ST55
The Litton *NEW*
◉ BRITISH, EUROPEAN *V*

01761 241554 | BA3 4PW

www.thelitton.co.uk

The Litton's stylish interior is light and airy with bare stone walls, wood-burning stove, chesterfields, mix and match furniture and, definitely worth admiring, a long bar that's made from one solid piece of elm. There's also a whisky bar, terrace and gardens. The up-to-the-minute cooking is firmly rooted in the changing seasons.

Chef Ryan Brokenbrow **Seats** 140, Private dining 8 **Open** All Year **Prices from** S £5, M £12.50, D £6.50 **Parking** 50 **Notes** Children welcome

MIDSOMER NORTON
MAP 4, ST65
Best Western Plus Centurion Hotel
◎◎ MODERN BRITISH

01761 417711 | Charlton Lane, BA3 4BD

www.centurionhotel.co.uk

The restaurant in this modern family-run hotel is an inviting space, with a bright conservatory extension and menus full of appealing options. So, if you have room you'll want to conclude with one of the choose-me puddings such as an assiette of Yorkshire rhubarb, or caramelised pear rice pudding.

Chef Sean Horwood **Seats** 60, Private dining 120 **Closed** 25-26 December **Prices from** S £6, M £15, D £6 **Parking** 164 **Notes** Vegetarian dishes, Children welcome

MILVERTON
MAP 3, ST12
The Globe
◉ MODERN BRITISH

01823 400534 | Fore Street, TA4 1JX

www.theglobemilverton.co.uk

The Globe is still very much a pub, but it's a strong food destination too. The food is up-to-date country-pub fare and Sundays bring on traditionally garnished roasts – beef topside, lamb leg, pork –with roasties and Yorkshire puddings.

Open All Year

MONKSILVER
MAP 3, ST03
The Notley Arms Inn
◉ CLASSIC BRITISH

01984 656095 | Front Street, TA4 4JB

www.notleyarmsinn.co.uk

Chesterfields at an open fire, a mix of dining chairs and pew-style seating, and attentive staff add to the enjoyable experience of a visit to this whitewashed village inn. The kitchen turns out eloquently flavoured, well-executed dishes as well as some pub classics.

Open All Year

NORTH WOOTTON
MAP 4, ST54

Crossways Inn
⬤ MODERN BRITISH
01749 899000 | Stocks Lane, BA4 4EU
www.thecrossways.co.uk
A thoroughly contemporary kind of inn these days, the 18th-century Crossways looks much the same as it always has from the outside, but a 21st-century makeover has opened-up the place. It's the kind of inn where you can eat what you want where you want.

Chef Tom Ollis **Seats** 100, Private dining 86 **Open** All Year **Prices from** S £6, M £12, D £6.50 **Parking** 120 **Notes** Vegetarian dishes, Children welcome

OAKHILL
MAP 4, ST64

The Oakhill Inn
⬤ MODERN BRITISH
01749 840442 | Fosse Road, BA3 5HU
www.theoakhillinn.com
An ancient stone-built inn with hanging baskets is many people's idea of old England, and The Oakhill looks the part. The food itself edges more firmly into modern British territory than hitherto, although devotees of pub classics such as bubble-and-squeak have not been abandoned.

Closed 25 December

SHEPTON MALLET
MAP 4, ST64

Charlton House Hotel & Spa
⬤⬤ MODERN BRITISH
01749 342008 | Charlton Road, BA4 4PR
www.bannatyne.co.uk
On the fringes of the town centre, this grand, stone manor combines period charm and contemporary style. A menu of modern dishes includes global flavours. Start with pan-fried octopus, cauliflower purée, smoked chorizo and pickled pear before confit leg and roasted breast of duck with dauphinoise potatoes, shallot purée and spinach.

Chef Martin Baker **Seats** 60, Private dining 80 **Open** All Year **Prices from** S £7, M £13, D £7 **Parking** 70 **Notes** Vegetarian dishes, Children welcome

SOMERTON
MAP 4, ST42

The Devonshire Arms
⬤ MODERN BRITISH
01458 241271 | Long Sutton, TA10 9LP
www.thedevonshirearms.com
This Georgian former hunting lodge turned restaurant with rooms is a convivial hub where people pop in for a jar of ale or cider in the bar, or for a full meal in the restaurant. Warm-weather alfresco dining is pleasant in the courtyard and walled garden.

Closed 25-26 December

STON EASTON
MAP 4, ST65

Ston Easton Park Hotel
⬤⬤ BRITISH, FRENCH **V**
01761 241631 | BA3 4DF
www.stoneaston.co.uk
A grand Palladian mansion with sumptuous antique-packed interiors in 36 acres of grounds landscaped by Humphry Repton – including a Victorian walled kitchen garden that provides seasonal, organic fruit, veg, herbs and edible flowers – Ston Easton is a real delight. The team deliver light and confident modern country house-style cooking, bursting with luxurious ingredients, intense flavours and pin-sharp presentations.

Chef Ashley Lewis **Seats** 40, Private dining 80 **Open** All Year **Prices from** S £14, M £20, D £14 **Parking** 60 **Notes** No children under 8 years at dinner

TAUNTON
MAP 4, ST22

Augustus
⬤⬤ BRITISH, FRENCH **V**
01823 324354 | 3 The Courtyard, St James Street, TA1 1JR
www.augustustaunton.co.uk
The repeated shrilling of the phone serves notice of the popularity of Richard Guest's stylish, friendly courtyard restaurant in the town centre. There's a pared-down, contemporary look, with white-painted brick walls and unclothed, dark wood tables complementing the equally modern brasserie-style food.

Chef Richard Guest **Seats** 40 **Closed** 25 December, 1 January **Notes** Children welcome

Castle Bow Restaurant

@@@ MODERN BRITISH

01823 328328 | The Castle at Taunton, Castle Green, TA1 1NF

castlebow.com

Still in the ownership of the Chapman family, The Castle hotel is the jewel in Taunton's crown, sitting smothered in purple wisteria in the centre of town. Once more firing on all cylinders in the culinary stakes, the principal dining room, Castle Bow, is the preserve of Liam Finnegan. He draws on the Castle's own orchard and herb garden, as well as meticulously selected local suppliers, to furnish a menu of vigorous modern British dishes that achieve real impact. Pasta work is good, as in an opener of Brixham crab tortellini scented with sea herbs, lemongrass and lime, while Quantock rabbit stars in a robust production with goose liver, celeriac and piccalilli. For main, there might be Exmoor venison with parsnip and red cabbage, opulently sauced in whisky, or a carefully considered fish dish such as Lyme Bay cod and grilled octopus in an assertive array of chicory, quince, bacon and tartare sauce. That orchard produce then turns up as apple mousse with pear and cinnamon ice cream, or there could be orange mascarpone cheesecake with macadamias and yogurt sorbet.

Chef Liam Finnegan **Seats** 30 **Closed** 7-24 January, 25 December **Prices from** S £10, M £19, D £5 **Parking** 44 **Notes** Vegetarian dishes, No children under 5 years

The Mount Somerset Hotel & Spa

@@@ BRITISH *V*

01823 442500 | Lower Henlade, TA3 5NB

www.mountsomersethotel.co.uk

Set in four acres of beautiful grounds and gardens, a cosseting air of luxury pervades the Mount Somerset, a fine Regency hotel with splendid views across the Quantock and Blackdown Hills. Inside, you'll find all the original features you could wish for, from impressive fireplaces and a statement staircase to chandeliers and magnificent plasterwork. In the kitchen, head chef Mark Potts ensure his menus bring a stylish and contemporary air to the high-ceilinged dining room. Dishes are nicely judged, often featuring herbs, fruit and vegetables from the hotel's own garden. A starter of perfectly cooked poached lobster tail is enhanced by fresh mango and mango mayonnaise, with coconut and coriander, while a main of roast halibut with crispy chicken wings, salsify and charred, puréed

and caramelised onion is a beautifully constructed, elegant dish. Finish with goats' curd cheesecake with a punchy blackcurrant compôte and blackcurrant leaf ice cream.

Chef Mark Potts **Seats** 60, Private dining 50 **Open** All Year **Prices from** S £17.50, M £26.50, D £9.50 **Parking** 100 **Notes** Children welcome

TINTINHULL

MAP 4, ST41

Crown & Victoria

@ BRITISH

01935 823341 | Farm Street, BA22 8PZ

www.thecrownandvictoria.co.uk

This is the kind of country pub that spurs urbanites to up sticks and move to a rural idyll. It's a proper pub, with a changing rota of ales and a serious approach to food. The kitchen keeps things local, seeking out organic, free-range ingredients for the tempting dishes.

Chef Jean Paul De Ronne, Daniel Hillyard, Oliver Harrison **Seats** 100, Private dining 45 **Open** All Year **Prices from** S £6.25, M £10.50, D £5.95 **Parking** 50 **Notes** Vegetarian dishes, Children welcome

WELLS

MAP 4, ST54

Best Western Plus Swan Hotel

@@ MODERN BRITISH

01749 836300 | Sadler Street, BA5 2RX

www.swanhotelwells.co.uk

Once a coaching inn, The Swan is in the heart of Wells, close to the cathedral. The panelled restaurant is a smart and comfortable affair, with a short but ingenious menu. Check out the warm honey and stout tart for dessert.

Chef Adam Kennington **Seats** 50, Private dining 90 **Open** All Year **Parking** 30 **Notes** Vegetarian dishes, Children welcome

Goodfellows

@@ MEDITERRANEAN, EUROPEAN

01749 673866 | 5 Sadler Street, BA5 2RR

www.goodfellowswells.co.uk

Look for the plum-coloured façade in the town centre. If it's first thing, breakfast is on hand in the café, or you might have a Danish and cappuccino for elevenses. Otherwise, sign up for some distinguished seafood-led cookery in the adjoining restaurant.

Closed 25-27 December and 1 January

YEOVIL

MAP 4, ST51

Little Barwick House

◉◉◉ MODERN BRITISH 🍷 NOTABLE WINE LIST

01935 423902 | Barwick, BA22 9TD

www.littlebarwickhouse.co.uk

This charming Georgian dower house is the perfect setting for a family-run restaurant with rooms. Public areas are relaxed and comfortable, and the Ford family (Tim and son Olly in the kitchen, wife Emma out front) have worked hard to create a delightfully civilized setting for their classically-based, thoughtfully considered and precisely constructed dishes. The airy, gracious dining room overlooks the garden, and menus concentrate on wonderfully fresh produce, including fish from Cornwall. Menus are straightforward, and the main ingredient in each dish is given plenty of room to shine, admirably demonstrated by a main course of saddle of wild roe deer, cooked pink, with braised red cabbage, rösti potato and beetroot purée. Finish with pear and plum crumble, posset and tart with stem ginger ice cream, packed full of interest and flavour, each element working harmoniously together. The wine list is exceptionally good.

Chef Timothy Ford **Seats** 40 **Closed** New Year, 2 weeks in January **Parking** 25 **Notes** Vegetarian dishes, No children under 5 years

■ STAFFORDSHIRE

HOAR CROSS

MAP 10, SK12

The Ballroom Restaurant

◉ MODERN BRITISH

01283 575671 | Hoar Cross Hall, Maker Lane, DE13 8QS

www.hoarcross.co.uk

Guests at this 17th-century stately home in 50 deeply rural acres flock to the rather grand Ballroom, but not just for its food. Huge chandeliers hang from its lofty ceilings, the wallpaper is William Morris, the table settings are faultless, and the garden views are delightful. Modern British menus are brief, but appealing.

Chef Tom Biddle **Open** All Year **Notes** Vegetarian dishes, No children

LEEK

MAP 16, SJ95

Three Horseshoes Country Inn & Spa

◉◉ CLASSIC BRITISH

01538 300296 | Buxton Road, Blackshaw Moor, ST13 8TW

www.threeshoesinn.co.uk

The stone-built inn overlooked by lowering gritstone outcrops in the southern stretches of the Peak District covers many bases. Original oak beams, exposed brick walls and dark slate tiles are matched to create contemporary styling, with an open-to-view kitchen augmenting the dynamic atmosphere.

Open All Year

LICHFIELD

MAP 10, SK10

Swinfen Hall Hotel

Rosettes suspended MODERN BRITISH

01543 481494 | Swinfen, WS14 9RE

www.swinfenhallhotel.co.uk

The Rosette award for this establishment has been suspended due to a change of chef and reassessment will take place in due course.
Dating from 1757, this splendid mansion, complete with columns and pediment, is set in 100 acres of parkland, including a walled kitchen garden, deer park and formal gardens – hard to believe it's just half an hour from Birmingham's city centre. A careful restoration has created a stylish hotel, with elegant bedrooms and fine public areas with many period features. The oak-panelled dining room, with its ornate ceiling and heavily-swagged drapes, enjoys views across the terrace and gardens to the deer park.

Chef Bruce Cheyne **Seats** 45, Private dining 22 **Closed** 26 December and 1 January **Prices from** S £11, M £24, D £10 **Parking** 80 **Notes** Vegetarian dishes, Children welcome

STAFFORDSHIRE

STAFFORD
MAP 10, SJ92

The Moat House
🌸🌸 MODERN BRITISH *V*

01785 712217 | Lower Penkridge Road, Acton Trussell, ST17 0RJ

www.moathouse.co.uk

The Moat House is indeed moated, a part-timbered manor dating from the 14th century. Main courses on the seasonally-changing carte can be complex too but equally satisfying. For dessert try Turkish delight cheesecake with rose water gel and chocolate sorbet.

Chef James Cracknell **Seats** 120, Private dining 150 **Closed** 25 December **Prices from** S £6.25, M £15, D £6.50 **Parking** 200 **Notes** Vegetarian dishes, Children welcome

The Shropshire Inn
🌸 TRADITIONAL BRITISH

01785 780904 | Newport Road, Haughton, ST18 9HB

www.theshropshireinnhaughton.co.uk

The family-run Shropshire hasn't decamped to Staffordshire, but has stood firm while county boundaries have flowed around it. Its physiognomy is a little different these days, with full-length windows looking on to the garden, and gathered curtains in the dining area creating an upscale ambience.

Chef Steve Kirkham **Seats** 100 **Open** All Year **Prices from** S £5.25, M £12.95, D £6.25 **Parking** 60 **Notes** Vegetarian dishes, Children welcome

■ SUFFOLK

ALDEBURGH
MAP 13, TM45

Brudenell Hotel
🌸🌸 MODERN BRITISH, EUROPEAN

01728 452071 | The Parade, IP15 5BU

www.brudenellhotel.co.uk

This privately owned hotel is virtually on Aldeburgh's beach so, naturally enough, seafood tops the bill, freshly delivered along with free-range meat each morning. Whole dressed crab with salad, new potatoes and lemon mayonnaise is just one of the tasty options.

Open All Year

Regatta Restaurant
🌸 MODERN BRITISH

01728 452011 | 171 High Street, IP15 5AN

www.regattaaldeburgh.com

In a fine building in the town centre, this long-running restaurant specialises in fresh fish and seafood, often locally landed. Daily specials support the carte, opening with Mediterranean fish soup and rouille, then continues with home-smoked whole prawns in garlic mayo; bradan rost (roasted salmon) with chilli chutney; and roast chicken breast in Parma ham.

Chef Robert Mabey **Seats** 90, Private dining 20 **Closed** 24–26 and 31 December, 1 January **Prices from** S £4.50, M £12, D £5.50 **Notes** Vegetarian dishes, Children welcome

The White Lion Hotel
🌸 BRITISH, FRENCH

01728 452720 | Market Cross Place, IP15 5BJ

www.whitelion.co.uk

Sitting in beachfront splendour by the shingle banks of Aldeburgh's strand, The White Lion deals in unpretentious brasserie dining, built on fine Suffolk ingredients – in fact, sourcing doesn't get more local than the fish landed a few steps away on the beach.

Open All Year

BILDESTON
MAP 13, TL94

The Bildeston Crown
🌸🌸🌸 MODERN AND CLASSIC BRITISH

01449 740510 | 104–106 High Street, IP7 7EB

www.thebildestoncrown.com

The Bildeston Crown has all the chocolate-box charm you'd hope for in a 15th-century former coaching inn, although there's a very 21st-century take on things these days, which means boutique bedrooms, an atmospheric beamed bar, a smart restaurant and classy food ranging from pub classics to more modern ideas from a kitchen that's firing on all cylinders. Chef Chris Lee's understanding of how flavours work together results in outstanding dishes, whether you go for something pubby from the Classics menu – a Red Poll cheese burger poshed up with foie gras and truffle mayo, say – or look to the Select menu and open with cumin-roasted scallop with cauliflower and apple. Main courses such as loin of local rabbit with duck liver, beetroot, fennel and endive, or hake fillet with curried mussels and coriander demonstrate mastery of both texture and taste. Flavours punch above their weight in deserts too, particularly when warm chocolate mousse is matched with ginger ice cream.

Chef Chris Lee **Seats** 100, Private dining 34 **Open** All Year **Prices from** S £9, M £18, D £8 **Parking** 20 **Notes** Vegetarian dishes, Children welcome

BROME

MAP 13, TM17

Best Western Brome Grange Hotel

◉ MODERN BRITISH

01379 870456 | Norwich Road, Nr Diss, IP23 8AP
www.bromegrangehotel.co.uk

It's easy to imagine horse-drawn carriages sweeping into the central courtyard of this 16th-century former coaching inn, with plenty of period details remaining inside and out. The Courtyard Restaurant, however, is a light and contemporary affair with vivid colours and well-spaced dark wood tables.

Chef Matthew Cooke Seats 60, Private dining 28 Open All Year Prices from S £5.95, M £10.95, D £5.95 Parking 120 Notes Vegetarian dishes, Children welcome

BURY ST EDMUNDS

MAP 13, TL86

The Angel Hotel

◉◉ MODERN BRITISH V

01284 714000 | Angel Hill, IP33 1LT
www.theangel.co.uk

Overlooking the cathedral and abbey walls, The Angel is a quintessential Georgian coaching inn with a creeper-curtained façade. Inside, the generous spaces have been overlaid with a contemporary boutique look. The Eaterie's kitchen shows equally 21st-century sensibilities in its repertoire of upbeat brasserie food.

Seats 85, Private dining 16 Open All Year
Prices from S £6, M £14, D £6 Notes Children welcome

Best Western Priory Hotel

◉ MODERN BRITISH, INTERNATIONAL

01284 766181 | Mildenhall Road, IP32 6EH
www.prioryhotel.co.uk

A peaceful atmosphere reigns throughout the Priory, including in the Garden Room restaurant, which offers soft lighting and a comforting feeling of being looked after by endlessly helpful staff. The kitchen produces dishes that pull in inspiration from all over the known world.

Chef Matthew Cook Seats 90, Private dining 28 Open All Year Prices from S £3, M £10.95, D £5.95 Parking 60 Notes Vegetarian dishes, Children welcome

The Leaping Hare Restaurant & Country Store

◉◉ CLASSIC, TRADITIONAL

01359 250287 | Wyken Vineyards, Stanton, IP31 2DW
www.wykenvineyards.co.uk

Set on a 1,200-acre farm complete with Shetland sheep and Red Poll cattle, plus a vineyard, The Leaping Hare occupies a splendid 400-year-old barn with a high raftered ceiling. What the farm doesn't provide is locally sourced, with fish landed at Lowestoft.

Chef Simon Woodrow Seats 47 Closed 2 weeks at Christmas reopening 6–8 January Prices from S £6.95, M £14.95, D £4.95 Parking 50 Notes Vegetarian dishes, Children welcome

Maison Bleue

◉◉ MODERN FRENCH

01284 760623 | 30–31 Churchgate Street, IP33 1RG
www.maisonbleue.co.uk

The Maison flies the tricolour for proudly French seafood cuisine in the bustling heart of the town. The place is teemingly popular, indicating that the taste for unreconstructed Gallic cooking never went away. Meat dishes include beef featherblade which is a cut above.

Closed January, 2 weeks in summer

1921 Angel Hill

◉◉ MODERN BRITISH

01284 704870 | IP33 1UZ
www.nineteen-twentyone.co.uk

It may occupy a timbered period building in the historic heart of Bury St Edmunds, but there's nothing old-fashioned about the modern British food here. Seasonal and local ingredients are at the fore in dishes like hay-smoked duck breast, rhubarb and celeriac, and fillet of coley, parsley root, snails and garlic velouté.

Chef Zack Deakins Seats 50, Private dining 14 Closed 23 December to 8 January Prices from S £8, M £17, D £8 Notes Vegetarian dishes, Children welcome

Pea Porridge

◉◉ MODERN BISTRO

01284 700200 | 28–29 Cannon Street, IP33 1JR
www.peaporridge.co.uk

Two cottages dating from 1820 have been converted into this unpretentious restaurant where 'simplicity' is key, although plenty of expertise goes into the cooking. Snails with bone marrow, bacon, parsley, capers and garlic is a great way to kick things off.

Closed 2 weeks September and 2 weeks Christmas

The White Horse

◉ MODERN BRITISH

01284 735760 | Rede Road, Whepstead, IP29 4SS

www.whitehorsewhepstead.co.uk

This stylishly made over, mustard-yellow village inn sits comfortably at the gastro pub end of the spectrum, but without losing any of the features one hopes for – smart and cosy rooms with a copper-sheathed bar serving Suffolk ales, a huge inglenook and country-style tables.

Open All Year

CAVENDISH

MAP 13, TL84

The George

◉◉ MODERN BRITISH

01787 280248 | The Green, CO10 8BA

www.thecavendishgeorge.co.uk

This handsome, timbered 16th-century George is rooted into the fabric of its ancient Suffolk village. There are beams and bare-brick walls, but the understated neutral shades and classy cream seats combine in a tasteful, modern interior. The kitchen deals in no-nonsense modern comfort food with big, bold Mediterranean-inflected flavours that keep a keen eye on the seasons.

Closed 25 December, 1 January

DUNWICH

MAP 13, TM47

The Ship at Dunwich

◉ MODERN BRITISH

01728 648219 | St James Street, IP17 3DT

www.shipatdunwich.co.uk

Climbing foliage adorns this red-brick pub in a coastal village. Surrounded by heathland and nature reserves, with a beach on hand and Southwold nearby, it's got the lot, including a garden with an ancient fig tree and a courtyard for outdoor dining.

Chef Liam Davidson **Seats** 70, Private dining 35 **Open** All Year **Parking** 20 **Notes** Vegetarian dishes, Children welcome

FRESSINGFIELD

MAP 13, TM27

Fox & Goose Inn

◉◉ MODERN BRITISH

01379 586247 | Church Road, IP21 5PB

www.foxandgoose.net

The beamed restaurant upstairs in Fressingfield's timber-framed, 16th-century village inn specialises in creative, modern cooking driven by north Suffolk's abundant larder. An opener of pork belly with piccalilli and watercress might precede chump of lamb with beetroot, fondant potato, spinach, fennel and salsa verde. Finish with banana tarte Tatin.

Chef P Yaxley, M Wyatt **Seats** 70, Private dining 35 **Closed** 25-30 December, 2nd week January for 2 weeks **Prices from** S £8, M £18, D £7.50 **Parking** 15 **Notes** Vegetarian dishes, No children under 6 years at dinner

HINTLESHAM

MAP 13, TM04

Hintlesham Hall Hotel

◉◉ MODERN BRITISH *V*

01473 652334 | George Street, IP8 3NS

www.hintleshamhall.com

Hintlesham Hall is a beautifully proportioned Grade I listed building of three wings, the façade a 1720 addition to the 16th-century core. The kitchen displays originality not commonly seen in such surroundings, producing thoughtfully-constructed and elegant dishes eminently suited to the stylish dining room.

Chef Alan Ford **Seats** 80, Private dining 80 **Prices from** S £12, M £25, D £9 **Parking** 80 **Notes** No children under 12 years at dinner

HORRINGER

MAP 13, TL86

The Ickworth

◉◉ MODERN MEDITERRANEAN *V*

01284 735350 | IP29 5QE

www.ickworthhotel.co.uk

Frederick Hervey, 4th Earl of Bristol, who lived here in the early 18th century, commissioned the impressive Rotunda to house his treasures. Overlooking the Italianate gardens is Frederick's, the candlelit restaurant named after him, which has its delights too, notably its British food with international influences, from chickpea tagine with tabouleh to Chateaubriand.

Chef George Aldus **Seats** 78, Private dining 34 **Open** All Year **Prices from** S £8, M £16.50, D £9 **Parking** 50 **Notes** Children welcome

INGHAM
MAP 13, TL87

The Cadogan Arms
◉ TRADITIONAL BRITISH

01284 728443 | The Street, IP31 1NG

www.thecadogan.co.uk

Flexibility is key in this smartly appointed former coaching inn, whether you just want a jar of real ale in the bar, a grazing board to snack on, or a full-blown meal. The decor is stylish with subdued lighting, upholstered sofas and chair.

Closed 25-26 December

IPSWICH
MAP 13, TM14

Mariners
◉◉ FRENCH, MEDITERRANEAN *V*

01473 289748 | Neptune Quay, IP4 1AX

www.marinersipswich.co.uk

Built as a gunboat in Bruges in 1899, it was sunk in 1940, became a hospital ship in the 1950s and was an Italian restaurant in Ipswich before becoming a French brasserie. Mains might be pan-fried fillet of Scottish salmon with creamy wild mushroom Carnaroli risotto.

Chef Frederic Lebrun Seats 80, Private dining 30 Closed January Notes Children welcome

milsoms Kesgrave Hall
◉◉ MODERN INTERNATIONAL

01473 333741 | Hall Road, Kesgrave, IP5 2PU

www.milsomhotels.com

Still deep in woodland after more than 200 years, this hotel restaurant's open kitchen is the source of modern international dishes, typically smoked haddock fishcake with a soft-boiled egg centre; and pan-fried Creedy Carver duck breast with beetroot and sour cherries. Lastly, maybe yogurt pannacotta, raspberries and basil. No dress code, and no booking necessary.

Chef Stuart Oliver, Aaron Skerritt Seats 150, Private dining 24 Open All Year Prices from S £6.50, M £14, D £6.95 Parking 150 Notes Vegetarian dishes, Children welcome

Salthouse Harbour Hotel
◉◉ MODERN BRITISH

01473 226789 | No 1 Neptune Quay, IP4 1AX

www.salthouseharbour.co.uk

A harbourside warehouse makeover with eye-popping interior collisions of lime-green and violet, the Salthouse deals in brasserie food with look-at-me flavours. A gin and tonic arrives later than is conventional perhaps, in a dessert of

apple and Hendrick's jelly, with cucumber sorbet and lime granita.

Chef Luke Bailey Seats 70 Open All Year Prices from S £5, M £12, D £5 Notes Vegetarian dishes, Children welcome

IXWORTH
MAP 13, TL97

Theobald's Restaurant
◉◉ MODERN BRITISH

01359 231707 | 68 High Street, IP31 2HJ

www.theobaldsrestaurant.co.uk

Converted from a whitewashed Tudor inn in the early 1980s, Theobald's pulls in diners with its consistency and attention to detail. Ancient beams abound and tables are dressed in pristine white. There's a monthly-changing carte, and locally reared meats and East Anglian fish are the mainstays.

Chef Simon Theobald Seats 32 Closed 10 days in spring/summer Notes Vegetarian dishes, No children under 8 years at dinner

LAVENHAM
MAP 13, TL94

The Great House NEW
◉◉ FRENCH

01787 247431 | Market Place, CO10 9QZ

www.greathouse.co.uk

In a 14th-century former house on Market Place, this elegant restaurant with rooms brings a genuine flavour of France to historic Lavenham. Local raw materials are transformed into creative Gallic dishes like rack of lamb, buttered golden turnips, local asparagus, mange tout, garlic and rosemary jus. Service is efficient and attentive.

Chef Guillaume Dericq Notes No children

The Swan at Lavenham Hotel and Spa
◉◉ MODERN, TRADITIONAL *V* NOTABLE WINE LIST

01787 247477 | High Street, CO10 9QA

www.theswanatlavenham.co.uk

Dating back to the 15th century, this characterful, asymmetrical timbered building is full of beams and period charm. The main restaurant is the Gallery, named for the medieval minstrels' balcony that can still be seen. The setting might be historic but the food is modern.

Chef Justin Kett Seats 90, Private dining 40 Open All Year Prices from S £7.95, M £13.90, D £7.95 Parking 50 Notes No children under 5 years

LOWESTOFT
MAP 13, TM59

The Crooked Barn Restaurant
◉◉ MODERN BRITISH

01502 501353 | Ivy House Country Hotel, Ivy Lane, Beccles Road, Oulton Broad, NR33 8HY
www.ivyhousecountryhotel.co.uk
A 16th-century barn, its ceiling exposed to the rafters, is the destination eatery of Ivy House Country Hotel, set in 20 acres of grounds on Oulton Broad. The kitchen makes excellent use of the region's produce in some eclectic dishes.

Closed 19 December to 6 January

NEWMARKET
MAP 12, TL66

Bedford Lodge Hotel & Spa
◉ BRITISH, MEDITERRANEAN

01638 663175 | Bury Road, CB8 7BX
www.bedfordlodgehotel.co.uk
This one-time Georgian hunting lodge offers plenty of top-end facilities to satisfy the modern epicure. The red-hued dining room sticks to a modern British mantra, starting perhaps with chicken liver parfait and moving on to seared fillet of Denham venison, smoked game sausage, celeriac dauphinoise and roasted baby turnips.

Chef Sean Melville **Seats** 60, Private dining 150 **Open** All Year **Prices from** S £7, M £19, D £7.50 **Parking** 120 **Notes** Vegetarian dishes, Children welcome

The Packhorse Inn
◉◉ MODERN BRITISH

01638 751818 | Bridge Street, Moulton, CB8 8SP
www.thepackhorseinn.com
Close to the racing at Newmarket, this modern country inn still pulls in local drinkers but it's the classy, inventive cooking that attracts foodies from far and wide. Suffolk produce is treated with respect in the kitchen and impressive pastry skills are evident in desserts.

Chef Win Hai (Sunny) Lau **Seats** 65, Private dining 32 **Open** All Year **Parking** 30 **Notes** Vegetarian dishes, Children welcome

Tuddenham Mill
◉◉◉ MODERN BRITISH **V**
See pages 358–359

ORFORD
MAP 13, TM45

The Crown & Castle
◉◉ ITALIAN, BRITISH **V**

01394 450205 | IP12 2LJ
www.crownandcastle.co.uk
There's genuine character to the spaces within this easy-going, rustic-chic restaurant, where pastel colours blended in a modern palette help create a relaxed vibe. The daily-changing menu has an Italian accent, featuring the fashionable Venetian small plates, cicchetti, alongside flavour-driven dishes that showcase the region's excellent ingredients.

Chef Rob Walpole **Seats** 50, Private dining 10 **Closed** 25–26 and 31 December, 1 January **Prices from** S £6.50, M £16.90, D £8 **Parking** 17 **Notes** No children under 8 years at dinner

SIBTON
MAP 13, TM36

Sibton White Horse Inn
◉◉ MODERN BRITISH

01728 660337 | Halesworth Road, IP17 2JJ
www.sibtonwhitehorseinn.co.uk
This fascinating pub's Tudor origins – low ceilings, mighty ships' timbers, quarry tiles – are impossible to miss. The bar has a raised gallery, an elegant dining room and a secluded courtyard. The kitchen produces globally influenced modern cooking that's won a heap of awards.

Closed 25–26 December

SOUTHWOLD
MAP 13, TM57

The Crown NEW
◉ MODERN BRITISH

01502 722275 | 90 High Street, IP18 6DP
www.thecrownsouthwold.co.uk
The grand Georgian portico on Southwold's high street looks imposing, but once inside, bare floorboards and mismatched tables and chairs give The Crown a relaxed and pubby ambience. The kitchen draws on the local larder for a crowd-pleasing menu of uncomplicated modern British food, backed by a great roll-call of Adnams' beers and wines.

Chef Stephen Duffield, Robert Mace **Seats** 68, Private dining 30 **Open** All Year **Prices from** S £7, M £16.50, D £7.50 **Parking** 17 **Notes** Vegetarian dishes, Children welcome

The Still Room Restaurant NEW
◉◉ MODERN BRITISH **V**

01502 722186 | The Swan, Market Place, IP18 6EG
theswansouthwold.co.uk/food-drink/still-room-restaurant
The 17th-century Swan is the jewel in the Adnams empire's crown, and it's looking pretty buff after a top-to-toe refurb. Blending contemporary panache with its Georgian features, The Still Room's light and airy, modern and funky design references the house brewery and small-batch

distillery as a backdrop to some inventive contemporary cooking.

Chef Rory Whelan **Seats** 50, Private dining 16 **Open** All Year **Prices from** S £8, M £18, D £8 **Notes** Children welcome

Sutherland House
◉◉ MODERN BRITISH, SEAFOOD
01502 724544 | 56 High Street, IP18 6DN
www.sutherlandhouse.co.uk
A period property of genuine charm, Sutherland House has wooden beams, ornate ceilings, coving and real fireplaces, with fixtures and fittings creating a chic finish. Likewise, the cooking impresses with its modern ambitions, passion for top-quality seafood and loyalty to locally-sourced ingredients.

Closed 25 December and 2 weeks January

STOKE-BY-NAYLAND
MAP 13, TL93

The Angel Inn
◉ MODERN BRITISH
01206 263245 | Polstead Street, CO6 4SA
www.angelinnsuffolk.co.uk
A charming hostelry with quarry-tiled floors, exposed red-brick walls and a double-height ceiling in the dining area with oak beams and the original well. There are quality meats, like saddle and confit leg of rabbit, while veggies might opt for chickpea and bean curry.

Chef Mark Allen **Seats** 80, Private dining 12 **Open** All Year **Prices from** S £5, M £13, D £6 **Parking** 20 **Notes** Vegetarian dishes, Children welcome

The Crown
◉◉ MODERN BRITISH
01206 262001 | CO6 4SE
www.crowninn.net
Five centuries old and now a classy boutique inn offering monthly-changing modern British menus supplemented by daily fish deliveries. Dinner might start with pigeon breast, roasted cauliflower purée, shallots and crispy prosciutto; continue with pan-roasted salmon, seared scallop, cockle and prawn. For dessert, banana cake is partnered by dulce de leche and coffee ice cream.

Chef Nick Beavan **Seats** 125, Private dining 14 **Closed** 25-26 December **Prices from** S £5.75, M £10.50, D £7 **Parking** 49 **Notes** Vegetarian dishes, Children welcome

SUDBURY
MAP 13, TL84

The Black Lion
◉◉ MODERN BRITISH
01787 312356 | The Green, Long Melford, CO10 9DN
www.theblacklionhotel.com
The Chestnut Group's imposing Black Lion has rapidly made a name for itself. There's no doubt that the discerning people of Suffolk have taken in a big way to the restaurant and its modern British cuisine.

Open All Year

The Case Restaurant with Rooms
◉ MEDITERRANEAN
01787 210483 | Further Street, Assington, CO10 5LD
www.thecaserestaurantwithrooms.co.uk
This charming country inn has a cosy little restaurant with a wood-burning stove, darkwood tables and ceiling beams; also there's a café and deli. Host-led hospitality is the key to its success as well as the quality of the cooking. Puddings hit the mark.

Chef Barry and Antony Kappes **Seats** 40 **Open** All Year **Prices from** S £5.95, M £12.95, D £3.95 **Parking** 30 **Notes** Vegetarian dishes, Children welcome

THORPENESS
MAP 13, TM45

Thorpeness Hotel
◉ MODERN BRITISH
01728 452176 | Lakeside Avenue, IP16 4NH
www.thorpeness.co.uk
The heathland golf course adjacent to the sea was opened in 1922 and there are views over the third tee from the traditional and roomy restaurant (there's also a wood-panelled bar and a terrace with a watery vista). The daily-changing menu keeps things relatively simple.

Open All Year

WESTLETON
MAP 13, TM46

The Westleton Crown
◉◉ MODERN BRITISH *V*
01728 648777 | The Street, IP17 3AD
www.westletoncrown.co.uk
This hotel, restaurant and pub, between Aldeburgh and Southwold, has its roots in the 12th century. 'Hearty yet sophisticated' cooking is the kitchen's aim and ambition doesn't falter among puddings: expect chocolate and pistachio cake with chocolate sorbet and cherries.

Chef James Finch **Seats** 85, Private dining 50 **Open** All Year **Parking** 50 **Notes** Children welcome

Tuddenham Mill

@@@ MODERN BRITISH *V*

01638 713552 | High Street, Tuddenham St Mary, IP28 6SQ

www.tuddenhammill.co.uk

Innovative regional cooking and a waterwheel taking centre stage

From the outside, the weatherboarded 18th-century mill looks solid enough to carry on its grinding career today, but a peek inside the doors reveals a seductive modern boutique hotel. Meticulous renovation means its heritage remains intact – the fast-flowing stream that turned its waterwheel is now a thriving wildlife habitat, while the impressive cast-iron wheel that was once its beating heart is atmospherically lit within glass walls to form a diverting centrepiece to the first-floor restaurant. With its framework of exposed beams, bare black tables, gauzy curtain partitions and bucolic views over the millpond, it's a classy setting for chef-patron Lee Bye's confident cooking.

As a local lad, he's in touch with his East Anglian roots and has an instinctive feel for combining ingredients from the surrounding region to striking effect, thus a typical opener strikes a balance between

no-nonsense gutsiness and contemporary refinement via meltingly tender pig's cheek matched with Italian coppa, rhubarb and chard. Another clever construction might see barbecued heritage carrots topping the bill, supported by pheasant leg, lovage and seeds. Cleverly constructed main courses owe their success to intricate detail and careful execution – hogget rump and kidney, say, partnered with parsley and pea sauce, penny leaf and golden ale, while fish dishes such as Gigha halibut with potato dauphinoise, sherry cream and black cabbage are equally well handled. Imaginative meat-free ideas should keep vegetarians entertained with the likes of roasted artichoke with carrot, wild honey and coastal herbs.

Desserts are executed with memorable dexterity, bringing entertaining plays of flavour and texture in ideas such as

'... an instinctive feel for combining ingredients from the surrounding region to striking effect"

croissant pudding with rum-soaked raisins, star anise, and vanilla ice cream, or bitter chocolate marquise counterpointed by flat white ice cream and sugared pistachios; for a savoury finish, there are fine British artisanal cheeses with Garibaldi biscuits and chutney. If you're just passing by for a pitstop, set lunch menus offer cracking value.

Chef Lee Bye
Seats 54, Private dining 36
Open All Year
Prices from S £8, M £24, D £8.50
Parking 40
Notes Children welcome

WOODBRIDGE

MAP 13, TM24

The Crown at Woodbridge

◉◉ MODERN EUROPEAN

01394 384242 | 2 Thoroughfare, IP12 1AD

www.thecrownatwoodbridge.co.uk

A stylish 21st-century inn, the look here is decidedly boutique, combining 16th-century features with contemporary design ethos. The kitchen raids the Suffolk larder for its unfussy, big-hearted modern cooking.

Open All Year

Seckford Hall Hotel

◉◉ MODERN EUROPEAN, BRITISH

01394 385678 | IP13 6NU

www.seckford.co.uk

Approached by a sweeping drive, this Tudor pile impresses with its creeper-curtained brick façade. Culinary style is classical country house with a contemporary sensibility and the dessert menu offers old-school comforts.

Open All Year

MEET THE CHEF

Steve Drake

SORREL

Dorking, page 361

What inspired you to become a chef?
I love the constant learning and development of dishes, ingredients and how we operate. When I was a kid we didn't eat well at home, so when I went to work in a local restaurant I was suddenly exposed to many new things I hadn't tried before. I was hooked.

What are the vital ingredients for a successful kitchen?
Teamwork is vital to operate the kitchen but working together creatively as a team is just as important. Whether it's collaborating on new dishes or an element of service, everyone needs to contribute even in a small way. We don't exclude anyone.

What are your favourite foods/ingredients?
I don't have a favourite ingredient but I love cooking with vegetables. I try not to follow the latest trends that come and go and prefer to stick to what I feel works best for the dish.

The Unruly Pig

◉ BRITISH, ITALIAN *V*

01394 460310 | Orford Road, Bromeswell, IP12 2PU

www.theunrulypig.co.uk

Just five minutes from the market town of Woodbridge, this 16th-century pub is a lovely spot to enjoy a pint beneath original oak beams. Despite its age, The Unruly Pig has a contemporary look and feel with shabby-chic decor, a modern European menu, and relaxed, friendly service.

Chef Dave Wall **Seats** 90, Private dining 22
Closed 25 December **Prices from** S £6, M £11.25, D £7
Parking 40 **Notes** Children welcome

YAXLEY

MAP 13, TM17

The Auberge

◉◉ MODERN EUROPEAN

01379 783604 | Ipswich Road, IP23 8BZ

www.the-auberge.co.uk

Ancient beams, panelling and exposed brickwork dating back to medieval times are clear evidence that this was an inn for many centuries, but the name describes today's modern restaurant with rooms. The dining room is darkly intimate and French influences underpin modern, skilfully rendered food.

Chef John Stenhouse, Mark and Helena Bond **Seats** 60, Private dining 20 **Parking** 25 **Notes** Vegetarian dishes, Children welcome

■ SURREY

BAGSHOT

MAP 6, SU96

The Brasserie at Pennyhill Park

◉◉ MODERN BRITISH

01276 471774 | Pennyhill Park, London Road, GU19 5EU

www.exclusive.co.uk

The Brasserie is an informal and relaxed eating space with a muted colour palette and stone walls to set the scene and the mobile buffet stations offer a never-ending variety of food throughout the day from breakfast through to dinner.

Open All Year

Matt Worswick at The Latymer

◉◉◉◉ MODERN EUROPEAN *V*

01276 471774 | Pennyhill Park, London Road, GU19 5EU

www.exclusive.co.uk

The original 19th-century mansion has been extended over the years, but it's still the heart and soul of the place, and it is where you'll find Matt Worswick at The Latymer, one of the UK's most compelling contemporary restaurants. It's a genteel and luxurious space with panelled walls and rich fabrics. In this formal and elegant setting comes food of diverting modernity, with contemporary cooking techniques showcased on five- or seven-course tasting menus. The very best seasonal produce finds its way to the table and everything looks just beautiful as it is set gently before you.

An opener of just-poached Colchester oyster brings a lovely taste of the sea, with lightly pickled apple providing contrast. Playfulness with temperature brings a delicate cold celeriac rémoulade with a warm truffle concealed in its depths. Next up, a beautiful cep risotto offers different levels of mushroomy earthiness, a brilliant contrast to the rémoulade. Following that, tender breast of Goosnargh duck with duck liver is a perfectly balanced dish. Matt Worswick never lets the fabulous produce get lost along the way, which is true right up to desserts such as a delicate vanilla and blackberry bavarois. The wine list is a global tour de force.

Chef Matt Worswick **Seats** 46, Private dining 8 **Closed** 1st 2 weeks January **Parking** 500 **Notes** No children under 12 years

CAMBERLEY
MAP 6, SU86

Macdonald Frimley Hall Hotel & Spa
BRITISH, EUROPEAN
01276 413100 | Lime Avenue, GU15 2BG
www.macdonaldhotels.co.uk/frimleyhall

The handsome mansion not far off the M3 was home to William Valentine Wright, the man who gave Britain Coal Tar Soap. Its Linden restaurant has an intimate candlelit ambience in the evenings. Thoroughbred Scottish steaks are a popular feature, as are the intriguing desserts.

Open All Year

CHOBHAM
MAP 6, SU96

Stovell's
MODERN EUROPEAN NOTABLE WINE LIST
01276 858000 | 125 Windsor Road, GU24 8QS
www.stovells.com

This old inn wears its age on its sleeve, with a timbered façade under red slate roof and a beamed interior with open fireplaces and mind-your-head ceilings. It makes a diverting setting for high-end creative cooking, sourced locally and presented with confident artistry. A domed terrine of pig trotter, ham hock and apple is garnished with pickled red onion and carrot for a robust opener to poached cod with brown shrimps and samphire from the set lunch menu.

Elsewhere, it might be venison carpaccio with ash-baked beetroot as a prelude to properly hung seasonal roast grouse in blackberry jus with the sharpening flavours of endive, fennel and pomegranate. Side-dishes are hard to avoid adding, when they might include charred broccoli dressed in anchovy and chilli. Two-tone Valrhona chocolate mousse, caramelised banana and seductive milk ice cream is a classy finale or go for artisanal English and French cheeses.

Chef Fernando Stovell **Seats** 60, Private dining 16 **Closed** 19-25 August **Parking** 20 **Notes** Vegetarian dishes, Children welcome

DORKING
MAP 6, TQ14

Sorrel
MODERN BRITISH NOTABLE WINE LIST
01306 889414 | 77 South Street, RH4 2JU
sorrelrestaurant.co.uk

The setting for Steve Drake's domain certainly doesn't lack character: the stylishly reworked 300-year-old building wears its age gracefully, with its wonky beams, wood floors, and linen-clad tables laid with fine glassware adding to the all-round feel of a classy operation. It's a restaurant to suit our times, classy yet relaxed, the cooking exciting and thoroughly modern. Drake has form with creative contemporary ways when it comes to making an impact with his seasonal, ingredients-led compositions.

Via a cracking value set lunch and five-and nine-course tasting menus, the kitchen delivers inspirational dishes starting with an impeccably seasonal celebration of spring – asparagus, say, transformed by the salty punch of sea purslane, lardo and the balancing sourness of fermented tomatoes and verjus. Ingredients are combined in thoughtful and stimulating ways in main courses, perhaps superb sea bass, its natural flavour enhanced with the judicious accompaniments of wild garlic, bouillabaisse sauce, turnips and fish bread, or lamb with courgette caviar and marjoram milk. Flavours are judged just so, through to fragrant finales, which could see a strawberry-based workout pointed up with black pepper biscuit, coconut and lemon verbena, or the imaginative pairing of Earl Grey and ginger bringing an exquisite touch to an utterly delicious rhubarb and custard millefeuille.

Chef Steve Drake, Richard Giles **Seats** 40 **Closed** 21 December to 5 January **Parking** 10 **Notes** Vegetarian dishes, Children welcome

EAST MOLESEY

Petriti's Restaurant
PLAN 1, B1

◉◉ MODERN EUROPEAN V

020 8979 5577 | 98 Walton Road, KT8 0DL

www.petritisrestaurant.co.uk

Tucked away in suburban East Molesey, not far from Henry VIII's Hampton Court palace, Petriti's is king in these parts. Smart in its relaxing hues of grey and cream, with matching modern seating and white linen, the dining room is enlivened by colourful artworks.

Chef Sokol Petriti **Seats** 55 **Closed** 1–15 January **Notes** No children under 6 years

EGHAM
MAP 6, TQ07

The Estate Grill at Great Fosters

◉◉ MODERN BRITISH

01784 433822 | Stroude Road, TW20 9UR

www.greatfosters.co.uk

The Estate Grill chefs use Old Spots pigs reared in the grounds and honey from the apiary, as well as Cumbrian fell-bred lamb. Sharing platters are a possibility – charcuterie to start and a selection of the estate-reared pork for main.

Chef Rob Chasteauneuf **Seats** 44, Private dining 20 **Open** All Year **Prices from** S £9, M £20, D £8 **Parking** 200 **Notes** Vegetarian dishes, Children welcome

The Lock Bar and Kitchen at The Runnymede on Thames

◉ MODERN

01784 220999 | Windsor Road, TW20 0AG

www.runnymedehotel.com/food-drink/the-lock-bar-kitchen/

The scene could hardly be more *Wind in the Willows*, with the Thames burbling by, and outdoor tables and parasols set out by Bell Weir lock that lends its name to the kitchen and bar. The parquet-floored brasserie room has a light, breezy ambience.

Chef Adesh Bissonauth **Seats** 60 **Open** All Year **Parking** 300 **Notes** Vegetarian dishes, Children welcome

The Tudor Room

Rosettes suspended MODERN EUROPEAN V

01784 433822 | Great Fosters, Stroude Road, TW20 9UR

www.greatfosters.co.uk

The Rosette award for this establishment has been suspended due to a change of chef and reassessment will take place in due course.

Great Fosters is a many-gabled red-brick Tudor mansion that once lay within the bounds of Windsor Great Park, and was originally the home of Sir John Dodderidge, James I's solicitor-general. Its 50 acres of gardens and parkland provide ample space for strolling, and make it a popular local resource for stylish weddings, but the main dining room is an unexpectedly intimate space of just seven tables, with sconce lights on russet silk-lined walls and a large dramatic 17th-century Flemish tapestry, all reflected in an expansive mirror.

Chef Tony Parkin **Seats** 24 **Closed** 2 weeks in January, 1 week at Easter, 2 weeks in August **Parking** 200 **Notes** Children welcome

EPSOM
MAP 6, TQ26

Dastaan

◉◉ INDIAN

020 8786 8999 | 447 Kingston Road, Ewell, KT19 0DB

www.dastaan.co.uk

Forget the low-key location off a traffic-mobbed dual carriageway in Epsom's hinterland, Dastaan is a neighbourhood gem and anything but your regular curry house. There's an open kitchen and the heady whiff of spices, and the atmosphere's much more Mumbai café than Surrey Indian. Even better, the intelligently compact menu delivers a succession of authentic flavours bursting with freshness, finesse and attitude.

Chef Sanjay Gour, Nand Kishor **Seats** 56 **Closed** New Year **Prices from** S £5.85, M £7.95, D £4.95 **Notes** No children

GUILDFORD
MAP 6, SU94

The Jetty

◉ CLASSIC BRITISH

01483 792300 | Guildford Harbour Hotel, 3 Alexandra Terrace, High Street, GU1 3DA

www.guildford-harbour-hotel.co.uk

Located within the Harbour Hotel, The Jetty has a separate entrance leading into a jolly ambience of sand- and sea-coloured seating. These signifiers announce a seafood bar and grill, the appealing menus built around main courses such as herby crab-crusted cod with creamy mash and peas.

Open All Year

Surrey

The Mandolay Hotel

@@ MODERN EUROPEAN

01483 303030 | 36–40 London Road, GU1 2AE

www.guildford.com

The restaurant of this smart hotel certainly looks swish, and the kitchen delivers a menu suffused with creativity. You might start with a very tasty roast partridge with boudin and round off with a spot-on dessert of chocolate fondant with pistachio ice cream

Chef David Fodor **Seats** 60, Private dining 300 **Open** All Year **Prices from** S £8, M £17, D £7 **Parking** 25 **Notes** Vegetarian dishes, Children welcome

OTTERSHAW

MAP 6, TQ06

Foxhills Club & Resort

@@ MODERN, CLASSIC BRITISH *V*

01932 704471 | Stonehill Road, KT16 OEL

www.foxhills.co.uk

A short hop from Heathrow, this Victorian manor comes with a championship golf course, a spa and multifarious sporting pursuits spread around its 400-acre estate to help work up an appetite for contemporary, ingredient-led cooking in the Manor Restaurant. A starter of pressed pigeon might precede a main course of venison.

Chef Paul Green **Seats** 100, Private dining 40 **Open** All Year **Parking** 200 **Notes** Vegetarian dishes, Children welcome

REDHILL

MAP 6, TQ25

Nutfield Priory Hotel & Spa

@@ MODERN BRITISH *V*

01737 824400 | Nutfield, RH1 4EL

www.handpickedhotels.co.uk/nutfieldpriory

Standing in 12 acres on Nutfield Ridge, the Priory is classic Victorian neo-Gothic, dating from the 1870s. The Cloisters has mullioned windows offering expansive views over the grounds and lake, and makes an appropriate backdrop for a refined, modern take on country-house cooking.

Chef Alec Mackins **Seats** 60, Private dining 60 **Open** All Year **Prices from** S £7, M £19, D £7 **Parking** 100 **Notes** Children welcome

RIPLEY

MAP 6, TQ05

The Anchor

@@ MODERN BRITISH

01483 211866 | High Street, GU23 6AE

www.ripleyanchor.co.uk

Dating back to the 16th century, the old brick-and-timber building's interior sympathetically blends old and new – think beams and exposed brick meets pastel tones and trendy leatherette seating, while a cosy snug, bar and alfresco courtyard add kudos. Light, adept, pretty, modern dishes fit the bill.

Chef Michael Wall-Palmer **Seats** 46, Private dining 8 **Closed** 25 December and 1 January **Prices from** S £7, M £16, D £7 **Parking** 14 **Notes** Vegetarian dishes, Children welcome

The Clock House

@@@ MODERN BRITISH *V*

01483 224777 | High Street, GU23 6AQ

www.theclockhouserestaurant.co.uk

Located on well-healed Ripley's pretty High Street, the dining room and adjoining bar here has been jazzed up; all on-cue clean lines and pastel shades of sage and grey set against stripped-back old wall timbers and tall street-side windows, while white linen reveals its fine-dining credentials. Fred Clapperton's refined, creative modern cooking revolves around a choice of fixed-price menus, including tasting and vegetarian options. The watchwords here are lightness and flavour, with fresh, confidently engineered, well-dressed dishes that include some unusual combinations; take stunning Norwegian Skrei cod with its melting white flaky flesh, served with carrot, alexanders (horse parsley) and vadouvan (a French curry spice blend) combined here with crispy puffed rice and lentils. Openers, like wonderful smoked eel, hit a flavour high too, delivered with leek, cockles and horseradish. Finish with white chocolate, compressed pineapple, candied pistachios and chamomile ice cream, while formal-code canapés, petits fours and in-house breads are classy too. The walled garden is a bonus for alfresco drinks.

Chef Fred Clapperton **Seats** 40 **Closed** 1 week in January, 1 week after Easter, 2 weeks in August, 1 week at Christmas **Parking** 2 **Notes** Children welcome

STOKE D'ABERNON
MAP 6, TQ15

Oak Room
◎◎ MODERN BRITISH
01372 843933 | Woodlands Park Hotel,
Woodlands Lane, KT11 3QB
www.handpickedhotels.co.uk/woodlandspark
Built in 1885 by William Bryant of the safety
match dynasty, this magnificent pile is set in
landscaped gardens and the grandeur extends to
the oak-panelled restaurant. Provenance drives
the menu, a typical meal starting with duck and
goose liver terrine before sea bream, baby squid,
samphire and red pepper marmalade.

Chef John Stephens **Seats** 36, Private dining 150
Open All Year **Prices from** S £7, M £14, D £7 **Parking** 150
Notes Vegetarian dishes, Children welcome

WARLINGHAM
MAP 6, TQ35

India Dining
◎◎ MODERN INDIAN
01883 625905 | 6 The Green, CR6 9NA
www.indiadining.co.uk
India Dining features a stylish cocktail bar, black
leatherette banquettes, polished-wood tables
and highly contemporary artworks. The authentic
pan-Indian cooking takes an equally creative,
modern and upmarket approach. Maybe start
with monkfish tikka, cooked in the tandoor, its
peppy spicing not overwhelming the sparkling-
fresh fish.

Closed 1 January

WEYBRIDGE
MAP 6, TQ06

Brooklands Hotel
◎◎ BRITISH, EUROPEAN
01932 335700 | Brooklands Drive, KT13 0SL
www.brooklandshotelsurrey.com
This thrillingly modern structure overlooks the
first purpose-built car-racing circuit in the world,
opening back in 1907. There's a creative modern
brasserie feel to the food, with the kitchen team
keenly producing dishes that arrive on the plate
dressed to thrill.

Chef Adam McLaren **Seats** 120, Private dining 150
Open All Year **Prices from** S £7.50, M £16.50, D £8.50
Parking 120 **Notes** Vegetarian dishes, Children welcome

WONERSH
MAP 6, TQ04

Oak Room Restaurant
◎◎ MODERN BRITISH
01483 893361 | Barnett Hill Hotel, Blackheath Lane,
GU5 0RF
www.alexanderhotels.co.uk/barnett-hill
A striking Queen Anne-style building set within
26 tranquil acres of woodlands and lovely
gardens, the Barnett Hill Hotel is conveniently
located just a 10-minute drive from Guildford.
The wood-panelled Oak Room Restaurant
overlooks a terrace and well-manicured lawns
and it's an elegant setting for the contemporary
British food.

Chef David James **Seats** 32 **Closed** 1–9 January
Prices from S £8, M £19, D £8 **Parking** 50
Notes Vegetarian dishes, Children welcome

■ EAST SUSSEX

ALFRISTON
MAP 6, TQ50

Deans Place
◎◎ MODERN BRITISH
01323 870248 | Seaford Road, BN26 5TW
www.deansplacehotel.co.uk
Once part of an extensive farming estate, Deans
Place, with its elegant modern decor, makes a
refreshing backdrop to the Victorian gardens and
charming riverside location, while the stylish
Dining Room offers the full-dress experience of
fine table linen and glassware.

Open All Year

BATTLE
MAP 7, TQ71

The Powder Mills Hotel
◎◎ MODERN BRITISH V
01424 775511 | Powdermill Lane, TN33 0SP
www.powdermillshotel.com
Powder Mills was once the site of a major
gunpowder-making operation that helped
defeat Napoleon. It stands in 150 acres of lush
parkland with a seven-acre fishing lake.
The owner's Springer spaniels sometimes
welcome arrivals and dining takes place in the
Orangery Restaurant.

Chef Neil Bennett **Seats** 90, Private dining 20 **Open** All
Year **Prices from** S £6.95, M £17.50, D £7 **Parking** 100
Notes No children under 10 years at dinner

BRIGHTON & HOVE   *MAP 6, TQ30*

The Chilli Pickle

◉ REGIONAL INDIAN

01273 900383 | 17 Jubilee Street, BN1 1GE

www.thechillipickle.com

The Chilli Pickle's open-plan interior works a casual, rustic look, with chunky wooden tables, blond-wood floors and vivid splashes of colour while full-length glass walls create the impression of dining alfresco. The vibe is breezy and buzzy, and the menu gives subcontinental clichés a swerve.

Chef Alun Sperring **Seats** 140 **Closed** 25–26 December **Prices from** S £5.50, M £11, D £4.50 **Notes** Vegetarian dishes, Children welcome

etch. by Steven Edwards

◉◉◉ MODERN BRITISH ***V*** 🍷 NOTABLE WINE LIST

01273 227485 | 216 Church Road, Hove, BN3 2DJ

www.etchfood.co.uk

The man leading the young team in this exciting new-generation Brit eatery is a former BBC *MasterChef: The Professionals* winner, and since he set up shop at the western end of Hove's main drag in 2017, the cooking has really gathered momentum. The space is cool with its midnight-blue walls, brass-edged tables and open kitchen adding to a buzzy air of all-round vitality. Monthly-changing set menus of five, seven or nine courses have their heart in Sussex produce, and, the palate primed with an umami hit from Marmite brioche with seaweed butter, creative and intricately detailed combos score hit after hit, among them sea bass with cauliflower in various incarnations, apple, capers and shrimps, then outstanding South Downs smoked venison loin, with a crisp samosa of haunch, plus pickled, roasted and puréed squash. As for sweet ideas, cranberry Bakewell tart is matched with cinnamon ice cream, cranberry gel and poached and puréed pear.

Chef Steven Edwards, George Boarer **Seats** 32, Private dining 8 **Closed** Christmas and New Year **Notes** No children under 8 years

GB1 Restaurant

◉◉ MODERN BRITISH, SEAFOOD

01273 224300 | The Grand Brighton, 97–99 Kings Road, BN1 2FW

www.grandbrighton.co.uk/dining-en.html

Turn your back on the stunning Italianate Victorian design at this seafront landmark and enter the cool, clean lines of the GB1 restaurant. Seafood is the thing, with a menu as bright and contemporary as the surroundings. Meat-eaters can choose from a selection of grills.

Chef Alan White **Seats** 90 **Open** All Year **Prices from** S £7, M £14, D £6 **Notes** Vegetarian dishes, Children welcome

The Ginger Dog

◉ MODERN BRITISH

01273 620990 | 12–13 College Place, BN2 1HN

www.thegingerdog.com

A once run-down corner pub in Kemp Town village was made over to create clean white walls and bright pink banquettes in the main dining area. To finish a meal, go for oat junket, with caramelised banana, toffee sponge and candied pecans.

Closed 25 December

MEET THE CHEF

Steven Edwards
ETCH. BY STEVEN EDWARDS
Brighton & Hove

What inspired you to become a chef?
The love of eating was my biggest inspiration. From a young age I have always enjoyed different foods and flavours. I would say it was a lunch at Le Manoir that inspired me to be a chef though. I was, and still am, in awe of what they do.

What are the vital ingredients for a successful kitchen?
Great produce, a solid team and direction. All three need to work hand in hand.

What are your favourite foods/ingredients?
My favourite ingredient at the moment is onion. Its sounds strange but I love making a feature of it rather than just using it to bulk out dishes, stocks and soups. It's very versatile and can be a dish on its own.

What's your favourite dish on the current menu and why?
Sea trout and cockle. It's really unique as we serve cured sea trout with cockle ice cream, battered cockles and dill. I love the freshness and contrast in textures and temperatures in the dish.

The Gingerman Restaurant

◉◉ MODERN BRITISH

01273 326688 | 21a Norfolk Square, BN1 2PD

www.gingermanrestaurants.com

The Gingerman is committed to dynamic modern British cooking with an inventive slant, notably incorporating touches of the Maghreb tradition. Typical dishes are maple-glazed pigeon breast with pine nuts and dates; vegetarian duck egg curry with a dosa, lemon pickle and green chutney, and a soufflé for two.

Chef Ben McKellar, Mark Charker **Seats** 32 **Closed** 2 weeks from New Year's eve **Notes** Vegetarian dishes, Children welcome

Hotel du Vin Brighton

◉ TRADITIONAL BRITISH, FRENCH

01273 718588 | 2-6 Ship Street, BN1 1AD

www.hotelduvin.com

The Brighton branch of the chain has all the expected Francophile touches, its walls adorned with posters and risqué pictures, leather-look banquettes running back to back down the centre and small wooden tables. A glance at the menu reveals more than your average bistro fare.

Open All Year

Isaac at

◉◉ MODERN BRITISH

07765 934740 | 2 Gloucester Street, BN1 4EW

www.isaac-at.com

'Local' and 'seasonal' is the mantra in this ambitious, pocket-sized outfit in the trendy North Laine quarter – even the wines are from Sussex vineyards. Serving just 20 or so diners from an open kitchen in a stripped-back space, the venue fits the youthful Brighton mood, and the food keeps step with modern trends.

Chef Isaac Bartlett-Copeland **Seats** 20, Private dining 22 **Notes** No children under 13 years

The Little Fish Market

◉◉◉ MODERN, FISH

01273 722213 | 10 Upper Market Street, Hove, BN3 1AS

www.thelittlefishmarket.co.uk

Tucked away in a little side street off Hove's Western Road, chef-patron Duncan Ray's modest little operation certainly punches above its weight. After stints at The Fat Duck and Pennyhill Park, here he works alone in the kitchen, and the results speak for themselves: stunning local and sustainable seafood cooked with exemplary attention to detail, accuracy and an intelligent creative edge. The setting is a light-filled space done out with a bare-bones contemporary look – neutral colours, bright, seafood-themed local art, wooden tables and quarry-tiled floors, and it is comfortable and atmospheric in the evening, with a charming solo server managing front of house for the 20 lucky diners. The tersely-worded fixed-price menu offers five no-choice courses and delivers dishes of pure seafood flavour, witness outstanding scallops pointed up with caper and cauliflower purées and crunchy beer-battered raisins. The bright, clean flavours continue in stunning turbot with crab cannelloni, sea herbs and shellfish sauce.

Chef Duncan Ray **Seats** 22 **Closed** 1 week in March, 2 weeks in September, Christmas **Notes** Vegetarian dishes, No children under 12 years

The Salt Room

◉ MODERN, SEAFOOD

01273 929488 | 106 Kings Road, BN1 2FU

www.saltroom-restaurant.co.uk

In a prime location on the seafront, this is a smart, contemporary space, with a terrace for alfresco dining. The atmosphere is buzzing, the black-clad staff friendly, and the large dining room the perfect setting for modern British cooking. Specials are chalked up on blackboards, and simple presentation allows the main ingredient to shine.

Chef Dave Mothersil **Seats** 80, Private dining 16 **Closed** 25-26 December **Prices from** S £5, M £12, D £3 **Notes** Vegetarian dishes, Children welcome

64 Degrees

◎◎ MODERN BRITISH

01273 770115 | 53 Meeting House Lane, BN1 1HB

www.64degrees.co.uk

Tucked – squeezed more like – down a narrow, flint-walled alley, this compact and bijou restaurant is, appropriately perhaps, into small-plate dining, the idea being tapas-style sharing. Its open kitchen prepares four each of the menu's fish, veg and meat options, such as squid ink agnolotti; cauliflower with cocoa nibs mole; and pork shoulder taco.

Chef Michael Bremner **Seats** 20 **Closed** 25–26 December, 1 January **Prices from** S £7, M £12.50, D £8 **Notes** Vegetarian dishes, No children under 16 years after 9pm

See advertisement below

Terre à Terre

◎ MODERN VEGETARIAN *V*

01273 729051 | 71 East Street, BN1 1HQ

terreaterre.co.uk

This trendsetting restaurant serves creative, classy veggie-vegan food. It's just back from the seafront, and the pared-back dining area stretches back to a small terrace. The service team can help with the eccentric menu's sometimes baffling descriptions. Inspiration comes from around the globe.

Chef A Powley, P Taylor **Seats** 110 **Closed** 25–26 December **Prices from** S £7.95, M £16.75, D £9.50 **Notes** Children welcome

CAMBER

MAP 7, TV91

The Gallivant

◎◎ MODERN BRITISH

01797 225057 | New Lydd Road, TN31 7RB

www.thegallivant.co.uk

Overlooking the Camber shoreline near Rye, The Gallivant has its heart in New England, where that laid-back eastern seaboard style translates as oceans of space, light wood, and café furniture. Sourcing from within a 10-mile radius is an especially good idea when the radius takes in such impeccable stuff.

Open All Year

Brighton's social dining hotspot, centred in the heart of the iconic lanes, serving a dynamic menu of sharing plates. Request a spot at the pass where you can interact with the chefs in the open kitchen while they create your dishes

53 Meeting House Lane
Brighton
BN1 1HB

01273 770115

64Degrees.co.uk

DITCHLING
MAP 6, TQ31

The Bull
@ MODERN BRITISH
01273 843147 | 2 High Street, BN6 8TA
www.thebullditchling.com
In the heart of Ditchling, The Bull has been a community hub for centuries, as the inglenook fire, half-timbered walls and old beams testify. The newly-built restaurant has a buzzing brasserie feel and the modern British cooking uses some produce so local that's its grown in their kitchen garden.

Chef Steve Sanger Seats 120, Private dining 20 Open All Year Prices from S £7, M £13, D £7 Parking 40 Notes Vegetarian dishes, Children welcome

EASTBOURNE
MAP 6, TV69

Langham Hotel
@ MODERN BRITISH
01323 731451 | 43-49 Royal Parade, BN22 7AH
www.langhamhotel.co.uk
The often-sparkling English Channel is just over the road from the hotel's conservatory dining room. Some dishes are old school, like farmhouse chicken and pork terrine; South Downs lamb with colcannon potatoes; and treacle tart with vanilla custard, but some definitely modern British ones show through, such as cod steak with pak-choi, mussels, prawns and scallion broth.

Chef Michael Titherington Seats 24, Private dining 120 Notes Vegetarian dishes, Children welcome

The Mirabelle Restaurant
@@ MODERN, CLASSIC EUROPEAN
01323 412345 | The Grand Hotel, King Edwards Parade, BN21 4EQ
www.grandeastbourne.com
The Grand Hotel embodies glorious Victorian Empire pomp. The Mirabelle Restaurant makes an appropriately ritzy showing with cloches, trolleys and attentive service. But there's nothing passé about the kitchen's contemporary take on flavour combinations and textures, with dishes revealing modern European thinking and fine-tuned techniques.

Chef Stephanie Malvoisin Seats 50 Closed 2-16 January Parking 70 Notes Vegetarian dishes, Children welcome, no children's menu

EAST CHILTINGTON
MAP 6, TQ31

Jolly Sportsman
@ MODERN, CLASSIC
01273 890400 | Chapel Lane, BN7 3BA
www.thejollysportsman.com
Located deep in the South Downs hinterland, a GPS comes in handy for hunting down this weatherboarded country inn. There's a cosy bar area with casks on trestles and a rustic-chic restaurant. The kitchen delivers full-flavoured, contemporary cooking.

Chef Vincent Fayat Seats 80, Private dining 20 Closed 25 December Prices from S £6.75, M £14.75, D £6.75 Parking 35 Notes Vegetarian dishes, Children welcome

FOREST ROW
MAP 6, TQ43

The Anderida Restaurant
@@ MODERN BRITISH
01342 824988 | Ashdown Park Hotel & Country Club, Wych Cross, RH18 5JR
www.ashdownpark.com
Ashdown Park is a magnificent Victorian pile in acres of grounds, and The Anderida Restaurant, with its elegant drapes, sparkling glassware, double-clothed tables and grand piano, is a fine setting for cooking that is a sophisticated take on both classical and contemporary.

Chef Andrew Wilson Seats 120, Private dining 160 Open All Year Prices from S £10.50, M £22, D £10.50 Parking 120 Notes Vegetarian dishes, Children welcome

RYE
MAP 7, TQ92

Mermaid Inn
@@ BRITISH, TRADITIONAL FRENCH
01797 223065 | Mermaid Street, TN31 7EY
www.mermaidinn.com
British and French-style food is the deal at this black-and-white timbered, one-time smugglers' inn. One way to start, beneath the ships' timber beams, is with pheasant leg gnocchi, wild mushrooms, roasted onions, squash and sherry, followed by roasted guinea fowl breast with confit leg suet pudding, white onion, golden beetroot, pancetta and leeks.

Chef Benjamin Fisher Seats 64, Private dining 14 Open All Year Parking 26 Notes Vegetarian dishes, Children welcome

See advertisement opposite

Webbe's at The Fish Café

◉ MODERN, SEAFOOD

01797 222226 | 17 Tower Street, TN31 7AT

www.webbesrestaurants.co.uk

A brick-built warehouse constructed in 1907 houses this modern seafood restaurant. Exposed brickwork, high ceilings and fish-related artwork all feed in to the buzz of the ground-floor dining room where the chefs work their magic in the open-plan kitchen. Fish is king here, but meat eaters and veggies won't feel left out.

Chef Matthew Drinkwater **Seats** 52, Private dining 60 **Closed** 25-26 December, 2-17 January **Prices from** S £6.50, M £13.50, D £6.50 **Notes** Vegetarian dishes, Children welcome

TICEHURST

MAP 6, TQ63

Dale Hill Hotel & Golf Club

◉ MODERN EUROPEAN

01580 200112 | TN5 7DQ

www.dalehill.co.uk

With its pair of 18-hole courses, golf may be top of the agenda, but hill views and a pair of restaurants are reason enough for non-players to visit. The fine-dining Wealden View restaurant is the star attraction; modern European cooking is par for this particular course.

Chef Lloyd Walker **Seats** 60, Private dining 24 **Prices from** S £7, M £18, D £7 **Parking** 220 **Notes** Vegetarian dishes, Children welcome

UCKFIELD

MAP 6, TQ42

Buxted Park Hotel

◉◉ MODERN EUROPEAN *V*

01825 733333 | Buxted, TN22 4AY

www.handpickedhotels.co.uk/buxtedpark

Offering the full country-house package, the hotel has hosted eminent guests, including William Wordsworth and Marlon Brando, and indeed many others. Celebrity or not, diners will enjoy good, honest modern European dishes, including textures of Cornish crab, pickled rhubarb and avocado purée; pork fillet and belly with tomato and olive croquettes; and chocolate and banana fondant.

Chef Mark Carter **Seats** 40, Private dining 120 **Open** All Year **Prices from** S £7, M £21, D £7 **Parking** 100 **Notes** Children welcome

---

UCKFIELD continued

East Sussex National Golf Resort & Spa

◉◉ MODERN BRITISH

01825 880088 | Little Horsted, TN22 5ES

www.eastsussexnational.co.uk

Overlooking the greens and the South Downs, the vast Pavilion Restaurant offers a concise menu with plenty of choice. Start, perhaps, with the earthy flavours of rabbit and leek terrine with pistachios, carrot and sourdough bread. Dishes throughout the menu bring out upfront flavours without being gimmicky.

Open All Year

Horsted Place

◉◉ MODERN BRITISH

01825 750581 | Little Horsted, TN22 5TS

www.horstedplace.co.uk

In 1850, Gothic Revivalist architect Augustus Pugin was commissioned to work his wonders here, hard on the heels of his design for the interior of the new Palace of Westminster. Outside are 1,100 acres of verdant Sussex countryside. Inside is a rich green dining room.

Chef Nicholas Hall **Seats** 40, Private dining 80 **Closed** 1st week January **Prices from** S £9.90, M £23, D £9.50 **Parking** 50 **Notes** Vegetarian dishes, No children under 7 years

WESTFIELD
MAP 7, TQ81

The Wild Mushroom Restaurant

◉◉ MODERN BRITISH

01424 751137 | Woodgate House, Westfield Lane, TN35 4SB

www.wildmushroom.co.uk

A converted 19th-century farmhouse surrounded by countryside just outside Hastings, Paul and Rebecca Webbe's restaurant is part of a local mini-empire. Original features like flagged floors and low beams impart a smart country feel to the ground-floor restaurant, helped along by friendly service. Sharp, contemporary cooking is the name of the game.

Chef Paul Webbe, Christopher Weddle **Seats** 40 **Closed** 25 December, 2 weeks beginning of January **Prices from** S £6.95, M £14.50, D £8.95 **Parking** 20 **Notes** Vegetarian dishes, Children welcome

WILMINGTON
MAP 6, TQ50

Crossways

◉◉ MODERN BRITISH

01323 482455 | Lewes Road, BN26 5SG

www.crosswayshotel.co.uk

Set in the South Downs National Park, the elegant restaurant in this Georgian country-house hotel sticks to a monthly-changing, four-course menu that appeals to locals and visitors alike. There's always a fish of the day, and meat dishes include roast rack of lamb with port, redcurrant and rosemary sauce.

Chef David Stott **Seats** 24 **Closed** 24 December to 24 January **Parking** 20 **Notes** Vegetarian dishes, No children under 12 years

■ WEST SUSSEX

ALBOURNE
MAP 6, TQ21

The Ginger Fox

◉◉ MODERN BRITISH, EUROPEAN

01273 857888 | Muddleswood Road, BN6 9EA

thegingerfox.com

The Brighton-based Ginger group of restaurants and refashioned pubs has given its country bolt-hole a stripped-down look with parquet and slate floors, chunky tables and brown leather banquettes, plus a beer-garden and raised beds where the Fox's own vegetables are grown. The menu mixes English staples with modern European thinking.

Chef Ben McKellar, Mark Bradley **Seats** 62, Private dining 22 **Closed** 25 December **Prices from** S £8.50, M £15, D £5.50 **Parking** 40 **Notes** Vegetarian dishes, Children welcome

AMBERLEY
MAP 6, TQ01

Amberley Castle
◉◉◉ CLASSIC EUROPEAN **V**
01798 831992 | BN18 9LT
www.amberleycastle.co.uk
Looking like the kind of place you'd happily pay the National Trust for the chance to look around, the Castle is a nearly millennium-old fortification at the foot of the South Downs that did time as a Royalist stronghold in the Civil War. Anywhere that is entered via a portcullis has more than a touch of class, an impression reinforced by the dining rooms with their armoury, tapestries, barrel-vault ceilings and lancet windows. Paul Peters produces assertive modern dishes with plenty to say for themselves, from amuse bouche of mushroom arancini and cheese gougère onwards. You might begin with a nicely-constructed scallop dish with caramelised cauliflower, hazelnut, golden raisin, caper, apple and Amberley ver jus. Main courses of wild sea bass, or veal, (loin, cheek and sweetbread) are thoughtfully conceived and full of flavour. Bring things to a close with a beautiful pistachio bavarois with grapefruit and banana.

Chef Paul Peters **Seats** 56, Private dining 12 **Open** All Year **Parking** 40 **Notes** No children under 8 years

ARUNDEL
MAP 6, TQ00

The Parsons Table
◉◉ BRITISH, EUROPEAN
01903 883477 | 2 & 8 Castle Mews, Tarrant Street, BN18 9DG
theparsonstable.co.uk
Picture-perfect Arundel, laid out prettily beneath its majestic castle, is home to this bright, airy venue named not after a local cleric but the chef-patron. White walls and unclothed light wood tables furnish a neutral backdrop to thoroughgoing modern British culinary wizardry.

Chef Lee Parsons **Seats** 34 **Closed** 24-28 December, February half term, Summer Bank Holiday to start of school term **Prices from** S £7.75, M £15.25, D £6.50 **Notes** No children

The Town House
◉◉ MODERN **V**
01903 883847 | 65 High Street, BN18 9AJ
www.thetownhouse.co.uk
This smart restaurant with rooms is a place of enormous charm, its intimate dining room brought into the 21st century with high-backed black chairs, wooden floors and mirrors with funky striped frames. The kitchen takes the best of Sussex produce as the foundation.

Chef Lee Williams **Seats** 24 **Closed** 25-26 December, 1 week March, 1 week August, 2 weeks November **Prices from** S £7.50, M £19, D £6 **Notes** Children welcome

BOSHAM
MAP 5, SU80

The Millstream Hotel & Restaurant
◉◉ MODERN BRITISH
01243 573234 | Bosham Lane, PO18 8HL
www.millstreamhotel.com
Built of red brick and flint, this charming hotel was originally three 17th-century workmen's cottages. On a balmy evening, the lawned gardens with ducks quacking along the millstream make an idyllic spot for drinks. The kitchen stays abreast of modern trends while keeping traditionalists happy.

Open All Year

See advertisement on page 371

CHICHESTER
MAP 5, SU80

Chichester Harbour Hotel
◉ BRITISH, SEAFOOD
01243 778000 | 57 North Street, PO19 1NH
www.chichester-harbour-hotel.co.uk
In the heart of Chichester, this hotel presents a sober, red-brick Georgian exterior, but inside the designers have unleashed a riot of boutique style. Murray's Restaurant is a split-level dining room that works a classy colonial look with palm trees, touchy-feely fabrics, exposed floorboards and unclothed dark wood tables. Brasserie-style menus tick the right boxes.

Chef David Hunt **Seats** 58, Private dining 98 **Open** All Year **Prices from** S £6, M £11, D £6 **Parking** 28 **Notes** Vegetarian dishes, Children welcome

Earl of March
◉ MODERN BRITISH
01243 533993 | Lavant Road, PO18 0BQ
www.theearlofmarch.com
Just a short drive out of Chichester, this 18th-century coaching inn looks out over the South Downs. There's a small patio garden, but most of the action takes place inside, in the large dining area or the snug bar area with a fire and sofas.

Closed 25 December

Halliday's

◉◉ MODERN BRITISH

01243 575331 | Watery Lane, Funtington, PO18 9LF
www.hallidays.info

At the foot of the South Downs in the peaceful village of Funtington, Halliday's occupies three flint-fronted thatched cottages dating from the 13th century. Chef and owner Andy Stephenson sources first-rate produce from the local area, shown off to advantage in his seasonally-changing menus.

Chef Andrew Stephenson **Seats** 26, Private dining 12
Closed 1 week March, 2 weeks August
Prices from S £8.25, M £19.50, D £7.50 **Parking** 12
Notes Vegetarian dishes, Children welcome

Potager Restaurant

◉◉ MODERN BRITISH *V*

01243 784995 | Crouchers Hotel, Birdham Road, PO20 7EH
www.crouchershotel.co.uk

Over the past two decades as a stalwart of the Chichester dining scene, Crouchers has traded upwards from a simple B&B to a smart modern hotel near Dell Quay and the marina. Desserts maintain the high standards, as shown by the well-balanced flavours and textures.

Chef David Smith **Seats** 80, Private dining 22 **Open** All Year **Prices from** S £6, M £15.50, D £7 **Parking** 40
Notes Children welcome

Richmond Arms

◉◉ ECLECTIC

01243 572046 | Mill Road, West Ashling, PO18 8EA
www.therichmondarms.co.uk

The whitewashed Richmond is one of the glories of West Ashling, a peaceful village at the foot of the South Downs, only five minutes from Chichester. Daily specials are written up on the blackboard, and there's a wood-fired oven for traditional pizzas. Indeed, the extensive menus look far and wide for inspiration.

Chef William Jack **Seats** 36, Private dining 60
Prices from S £7, M £16, D £7 **Parking** 9
Notes Vegetarian dishes, Children welcome

The Royal Oak

◉ CONTEMPORARY BRITISH

01243 527434 | Pook Lane, East Lavant, PO18 0AX
www.royaloakeastlavant.co.uk

A whitewashed village inn on a narrow lane in East Lavant, near Chichester, The Royal Oak is refreshingly allowed all its original character inside, with red-brick and flint walls and tiled and timbered floors. Modern pub cooking is supplemented by daily specials. Sunday lunches are a local main attraction.

Chef James Bailey **Open** All Year **Prices from** S £6.95, M £14, D £6.95 **Notes** Vegetarian dishes, Children welcome

CHILGROVE
MAP 5, SU81

The White Horse

◉ BRITISH, EUROPEAN

01243 519444 | High Street, PO18 9HX
www.thewhitehorse.co.uk

This stylish pub boasts plenty of quirky touches, right down to sheepskin throws on the high-backed benches and deer skulls, some of which sport sunglasses and scarves. A meal here showcases some modern British cooking of considerable poise and confidence.

Open All Year

GATWICK AIRPORT
MAP 6, TQ24

Arora Hotel Gatwick

◉ MODERN BRITISH

01293 530000 | Southgate Avenue, Southgate, RH10 6LW
www.arorahotels.com

Despite its name, this smart modern hotel is in Crawley town centre and its Grill restaurant is worth a visit in its own right. It's an airy open-plan room with clean-lined contemporary looks and diligently sourced British produce. Straight-up steaks keep the carnivores happy.

Chef Tony Staples **Seats** 70, Private dining 15 **Closed** 25 December **Parking** 210 **Notes** Vegetarian dishes, Children welcome

Langshott Manor

◉◉◉ MODERN EUROPEAN *V*

01293 786680 | Langshott Lane, RH6 9LN

www.langshottmanor.com

Not every hotel within striking distance of Gatwick bears the marks of corporate anonymity. A Tudor mansion faced in exquisitely laid red brickwork with original beams and mullioned windows is a sight for travel-weary eyes if ever there was, not least for its garden tables under the trees, and Langshott's Elizabethan interiors – all low ceilings and blazing fireplaces – have been discreetly augmented with the accoutrements of the modern hotel. In the Mulberry Restaurant, views over the grounds are a welcome complement to Phil Dixon's assured and stylish country-house cooking. A gentle richness characterises many of his dishes, meats are out of the top drawer and desserts aim to seduce with lashings of chocolate, caramel and coffee in the enveloping forms of mousses and soufflés, or there might be roasted peanut parfait, with 'textures of banana' – that's caramelised, dried and in the form of banana cake.

Chef Phil Dixon **Seats** 55, Private dining 60 **Open** All Year **Parking** 30 **Notes** Children welcome

Sofitel London Gatwick

◉◉ FRENCH

01293 567070 | North Terminal, RH6 0PH

www.sofitel.com

An impressive central atrium makes a massive impact at this smart hotel close to Gatwick's North Terminal. The menu at La Brasserie, with its neatly laid tables and its contemporary artworks, takes a modern British path, with a French accent.

Chef David Woods **Seats** 120 **Open** All Year **Prices from** S £8.95 **Parking** 565 **Notes** Vegetarian dishes, Children welcome

GOODWOOD
MAP 6, SU80

The Goodwood Hotel

◉◉ MODERN BRITISH

01243 775537 | PO18 0QB

www.goodwood.com

Part of the 12,000-acre Goodwood Estate, the Farmer, Butcher, Chef restaurant at this luxurious hotel uses pork, lamb and beef from the estate's organic home farm. Although there are plenty of fish and vegetarian options on the menu, home-reared meat dominates.

Chef Mark Forman **Seats** 84, Private dining 50 **Open** All Year **Prices from** S £7.50, M £17, D £7.50 **Parking** 200 **Notes** Vegetarian dishes, Children welcome

HASSOCKS
MAP 6, TQ21

The Glass House Restaurant & Terrace

◉ MODERN BRITISH

01273 857567 | Wickwoods Country Club Hotel & Spa, Shaveswood Lane, Albourne, BN6 9DY

www.wickwoods.co.uk

The contemporary Glass House Restaurant at Wickwoods Country Club Hotel & Spa occupies an orangery overlooking the landscaped grounds. The crowd-pleasing modern British menu includes local steaks cooked on the chargrill, burgers and ribs, although there's plenty of other options to choose from.

Chef James Villiers **Seats** 50, Private dining 24 **Closed** 25 December **Prices from** S £7, M £10.95, D £6.50 **Parking** 160 **Notes** Vegetarian dishes, No children

HAYWARDS HEATH
MAP 6, TQ32

Jeremy's at Borde Hill

◉◉ MODERN EUROPEAN, PAN-ASIAN

01444 441102 | Balcombe Road, RH16 1XP

www.jeremysrestaurant.com

It is hard to imagine a more idyllic setting than this contemporary restaurant in Borde Hill Gardens. Occupying a stylishly converted stable block overlooking the Victorian walled garden and south-facing terrace, it's a wide open, bright space. The kitchen delivers bold flavours and vibrant food.

Chef Jimmy Gray **Seats** 55, Private dining 120 **Closed** after New Year for 14 days **Prices from** S £10, M £30, D £8 **Parking** 30 **Notes** Vegetarian dishes, Children welcome

HORSHAM
MAP 6, TQ13

Restaurant Tristan

◉◉◉ MODERN BRITISH, FRENCH *V* NOTABLE WINE LIST

01403 255688 | 3 Stan's Way, East Street, RH12 1HU

www.restauranttristan.co.uk

The building, in the heart of old Horsham, may be 16th century, but chef-patron Tristan Mason's food is bang up-to-date. The first-floor dining room blends ancient and modern with panache, its striking beamed vaulted ceiling, wall timbers and oak floorboards sitting alongside sleek contemporary decor. As is often the way with this kind of innovative, creative, technically skilful cooking, menus make a virtue of conciseness, listing the components of each composition, but whether you go for three, four, six or eight courses, you can be sure that the full gamut of taste categories, textural contrasts and temperatures will be deployed. Clever stuff, then, but this isn't just about techno flim-flam; having trained with Marco Pierre White, Mason's ideas are solidly grounded in classic French technique. Fish and meat combinations are favoured, as in the crisp chicken wings and turbot that arrive beautifully cooked alongside trompette mushroom foam and jelly, and parsley root purée and crisps.

Chef Tristan Mason **Seats** 34 **Closed** 25–26 December, 1–2 January **Notes** No children under 10 years

KIRDFORD
MAP 6, TQ02

The Half Moon Inn
◉◉ MODERN BRITISH
01403 820223 | Glasshouse Lane, RH14 0LT
www.halfmoonkirdford.co.uk
Owned by TV presenter and international model Jodie Kidd, it ticks all the 'quintessential village pub' boxes – oak beams, red-brick floors, an inglenook fireplace and friendly staff. A tasty, indeed attractively presented, opener is salmon and langoustine ravioli with rich shellfish cream, peas and broad beans, and decorated with pub garden flowers.

Open All Year

LICKFOLD
MAP 6, SU92

The Lickfold Inn
◉◉◉ BRITISH *V*
01789 532535 | GU28 9EY
www.thelickfoldinn.co.uk
This Tudor inn with its eye-catching facing in herringboned red brick is an upstairs-downstairs operation. On the ground floor, village drinkers are regaled with hand-pumped ales, while the first floor, with its exposed brickwork and dark beams, is consecrated to modern dining. Aspirational the food may be, but not at the expense of remembering its surroundings, by

offering a slice of venison and game pie with a fruity jelly lining, garnished with puréed and roasted quince, as a loin-girding starter. Balance that with a fish main course such as expertly timed cod with brown shrimps and spinach in brown butter, with delightful sharp notes coming from pickled and barbecued fennel, or perhaps truffled gnocchi with wild mushrooms and hazelnuts. The must-have dessert is lemon curd sponge cake with stunning milk ice-cream and a milk cracker, to which honey from the Lickfold's own beehive is added at the table.

Chef Tom Sellers, Graham Squire **Seats** 40 **Closed** 25 December **Prices from** S £8, M £24, D £6 **Parking** 20 **Notes** Children welcome

LODSWORTH
MAP 6, SU92

The Halfway Bridge Inn
◉ MODERN BRITISH
01798 861281 | Halfway Bridge, GU28 9BP
www.halfwaybridge.co.uk
This classy 18th-century roadside inn makes an inviting pitstop after a hike on the South Downs Way or a leisurely perusal of Petworth's antique emporia. The ambience is friendly and unbuttoned, while the kitchen deals in pub classics given a contemporary tweak.

Chef Clyde Hollett **Seats** 55, Private dining 16 **Open** All Year **Prices from** S £6.50, M £14.50, D £7 **Parking** 30 **Notes** Vegetarian dishes, Children welcome

LOWER BEEDING
MAP 6, TQ22

The Camellia Restaurant at South Lodge
◉◉ BRITISH
01403 891711 | Brighton Road, RH13 6PS
www.exclusive.co.uk
A handsome Victorian mansion hotel where starters range from slow-braised octopus to feta pannacotta by way of duck terrine, and main courses wander merrily from Sussex beef fillet to pistachio falafel via pan-fried halibut with mussels. Navigating from berries, vanilla and cream to cheese and fruit could easily mean passing through sticky toffee pudding.

Chef Jamie Gibson **Seats** 100, Private dining 140 **Open** All Year **Prices from** S £9, M £19.50, D £8.50 **Parking** 200 **Notes** Vegetarian dishes, Children welcome

The Pass Restaurant

Rosettes suspended BRITISH, JAPANESE *V*

01403 891711 | South Lodge, Brighton Road, RH13 6PS

www.exclusive.co.uk

The Rosette award for this establishment has been suspended due to a change of chef and reassessment will take place in due course. Many establishments offer a chef's table for those who like to glean plating and garnishing tips from the professionals, but at the South Lodge hotel's Pass Restaurant, chef's tables are all there are. And quite the show it is, with seating for over two dozen, watching the action in the flesh or on plasma-screen monitors, depending which way you're facing.

Chef Tom Kemble **Seats** 28 **Closed** 1st 2 weeks January **Parking** 200 **Notes** No children

ROWHOOK
MAP 6, TQ13

The Chequers Inn

⊛ BRITISH

01403 790480 | RH12 3PY

thechequersrowhook.com

A proper village local with flagstones, oak beams, chunky wooden tables, open fires and well-kept real ales on hand pump. The Chequers has been around since the 15th century, but it is in tune with modern tastes, with no pretensions, just bang-on-the-money modern ideas.

Chef Yves Noel, Tim Neal **Seats** 40 **Closed** 25 December **Parking** 40 **Notes** Vegetarian dishes, Children welcome

RUSPER
MAP 6, TQ23

Ghyll Manor

⊛ MODERN BRITISH

0330 123 0371 | High Street, RH12 4PX

www.ghyllmanor.co.uk

A timbered manor house in picture-perfect Sussex countryside, Ghyll Manor is an ideal retreat from the city. Inside, an appealing mixture of period features and modern styling creates a harmonious impression. The kitchen team maintains a steady hand at the tiller for assured country-house cooking.

Open All Year

SIDLESHAM
MAP 5, SZ89

The Crab & Lobster

⊛⊛ MODERN BRITISH

01243 641233 | Mill Lane, PO20 7NB

www.crab-lobster.co.uk

The whitewashed 17th-century pub is an upscale restaurant with rooms, and looks spruce from top to bottom. On the edge of the Pagham Harbour nature reserve, it offers a stylish restaurant that aims to impress with ambitious, top-notch modern British food.

Chef Dan Storey, Clyde Hollett **Seats** 54 **Open** All Year **Prices from** S £8.75, M £17, D £7.50 **Parking** 12 **Notes** Vegetarian dishes, Children welcome

TANGMERE
MAP 6, SU90

Cassons Restaurant

⊛⊛ MODERN BRITISH

01243 773294 | Arundel Road, PO18 0DU

www.cassonsrestaurant.co.uk

Chef-patronne Viv Casson ran a successful restaurant in France, so you can expect Gallic culinary influences to her work. Inside, the place gains character from the huge inglenook and low-beamed ceilings, while the modern menu takes in classically influenced ideas. Super-fresh crab from nearby Selsey often appears on the menus.

Chef Viv Casson, Gary Mures **Seats** 36, Private dining 14 **Closed** Christmas to New Year **Prices from** S £9.25, M £24, D £9.25 **Parking** 30 **Notes** Vegetarian dishes, Children welcome

TILLINGTON
MAP 6, SU92

The Horse Guards Inn

⊛⊛ TRADITIONAL BRITISH

01798 342332 | Upperton Road, GU28 9AF

www.thehorseguardsinn.co.uk

The Horse Guards is a relaxed and friendly pub dating back 350 years, with open fires, wooden tables, beams and a boarded floor. It's a foodie destination with a daily-changing menu showcasing what's been bought or foraged locally or dug up from the garden.

Chef Lee Conan **Seats** 55, Private dining 18 **Closed** 25-26 December **Prices from** S £6.50, M £13.50, D £6 **Notes** Vegetarian dishes, Children welcome

TURNERS HILL
MAP 6, TQ33

AG's Restaurant at Alexander House Hotel

◉◉◉ BRITISH, FRENCH **V**

01342 714914 | East Street, RH10 4QD

www.alexanderhouse.co.uk

With 120 acres of Sussex countryside all to itself, Alexander House is in a Goldilocks spot, close enough to Gatwick Airport for those jetting in and out, but tranquil enough as a getaway in its own right. The handsome red-brick hotel has glam bedrooms, a spa to pamper you into submission, and two smart dining options. Royal-blue upholstery and white linen reinforce the fine dining mood in AG's, the principal dining room. The kitchen has all dietary bases covered with vegetarian, vegan and dairy-free versions of set-price and tasting menus, and the cooking is contemporary, with striking combinations of ingredients and heaps of visual artistry. First off, scallops are teamed with miso, kimchi, sesame dressing, radishes and a seaweed cracker. Next up, herb-crusted lamb cannon with moist and tender braised belly wrapped in crisp potato, with confit garlic, hispi cabbage and mint jellies. Look out for the excellent Marmite bread.

Chef Darrel Wilde **Seats** 30, Private dining 12 **Open** All Year **Parking** 100 **Notes** No children at dinner

Reflections at Alexander House

◉◉ MODERN BRITISH

01342 714914 | Alexander House Hotel & Utopia Spa, East Street, RH10 4QD

www.alexanderhouse.co.uk

The handsome 17th-century mansion has moved into boutique territory after a thoroughly modern makeover, with pampering facilities to delight spa enthusiasts and a buzzy brasserie – Reflections – to lift the spirits still further (the fine-dining option is AG's Restaurant).

Open All Year

WEST CHILTINGTON
MAP 6, TQ01

The Roundabout

◉ BRITISH

01798 817336 | Monkmead Lane, RH20 2PF

www.southcoastinns.co.uk

One of several buildings in the tranquil village of West Chiltington designed in the 1920s and 1930s by sculptor Reginald Wells, the Tudor-style Roundabout has a traditional, beamed restaurant with drapes and red carpet is an elegant setting for the modern British cooking.

Chef Andrew Lee **Open** All Year **Notes** No children

WEST HOATHLY
MAP 6, TQ33

Gravetye Manor Hotel

◉◉◉◉ MODERN BRITISH **V** NOTABLE WINE LIST

See pages 378–379

WORTHING
MAP 6, TQ10

Indigo Seafood & Grill

◉ MODERN BRITISH, EUROPEAN **V**

01903 230451 | Ardington Hotel, Steyne Gardens, BN11 3DZ

www.indigorestaurant.info

Just outside the town centre, and a few minutes' walk from the seafront, Indigo is a contemporary seafood and grill restaurant. Red leather banquettes and lavish chandeliers add a luxurious touch to the proceedings, although the vibrant, globally-influenced food is simple and well-defined.

Chef Luca Mason, John Wheatland **Seats** 80, Private dining 120 **Closed** 25 December to 4 January **Prices from** S £6, M £15, D £6 **Notes** Children welcome

WEST HOATHLY   MAP 6, TQ33

Gravetye Manor Hotel

◉◉◉◉ MODERN BRITISH *V* NOTABLE WINE LIST
01342 810567 | Vowels Lane, RH19 4LJ
www.gravetyemanor.co.uk

Dynamic modern cooking in a brand new dining room

The Elizabethan mansion was built by one Richard Infield as a little something for his new bride. Their initials appear above the garden entrance, and the place still works its soft-focus romantic magic 400 years later, delivering the upscale country house experience in spades with its interiors of lavish panelling and intricate plasterwork mouldings brought into the 21st century alongside elegant modern comforts. A century ago, the place was owned by the great Victorian landscaper William Robinson, who laid out its acres of grounds in the style still seen today.

Gravetye closed for several months in order to build the stylish new dining room for George Blogg to showcase his dynamic contemporary British cooking, and the results have brought wow factor in spades. Floor-to-ceiling glass walls open up views of those glorious gardens, whose walled sections provide a plentiful seasonal

> "Expect a modernist style that explores creative combinations of flavour and textural contrasts"

bounty that inspires what turns up on your plate. Expect a modernist style that explores creative combinations of flavour and textural contrasts, starting with roasted Norfolk quail, the breast and leg perfectly timed and delivered in an innovative presentation involving fresh diced pear, quince purée, a rich and elegant liver parfait, and seeded granola for textural interest. Flavours are sharply defined and true in a fish course starring splendid loin of south coast haddock with parsnip purée, crisp chicken skin and Savoy cabbage, all made glamorous by the addition of black truffle and a glossy roasted chicken sauce of mesmerising

fragrance, while meat might be represented by a tomahawk cut of local venison given smoky barbecued depth by wood grilling, and served with butternut squash, ceps and chestnuts.

Desserts aim for deep satisfaction in the form of a masterclass forced rhubarb soufflé with stem ginger ice cream. A compendious, globe-spanning wine list delivers plenty to please, ranging from the local Sussex terroir to pedigree vintages that will catch the eye of the big spenders.

Chef George Blogg
Seats 60, Private dining 30
Open All Year
Parking 40
Notes No children under 7 years

■ TYNE & WEAR

GATESHEAD   *MAP 21, NZ26*

Eslington Villa Hotel *NEW*
◎ MODERN *V*

0191 487 6017 | 8 Station Road, Low Fell, NE9 6DR
www.eslingtonvilla.co.uk
Originally built for a Victorian industrialist,
today's hotel retains bags of period features,
allied with contemporary verve and character.
Dining goes on mainly in a light and airy
conservatory extension with tiled floor and
commanding views over the lawns, as well as in
the interior room behind it.

Chef Jamie Walsh **Seats** 94, Private dining 40
Closed 25–26 December, 1 January **Prices from** S £6,
M £16, D £5 **Parking** 30 **Notes** Vegetarian
dishes, Children welcome

NEWCASTLE UPON TYNE   *MAP 21, NZ26*

The Broad Chare *NEW*
◎ MODERN BRITISH

0191 211 2144 | 25 Broad Chare, NE1 3DQ
www.thebroadchare.co.uk
Located just off the Quayside, this new kind of
'old' pub features stripped back rustic wood and
exposed stone. Nothing fancy, nothing fussy, but
great beer with quality produce simply put
together to maximise flavour. The specials board
changes on a regular basis. Local produce is
used to good effect.

Chef Dan Warren **Seats** 54 **Closed** 25–26 December,
1 January **Prices from** S £6.50, M £10.50, D £6
Notes Vegetarian dishes, Children welcome

Cal's Own
◎ ITALIAN, MEDITERRANEAN

0191 281 5522 | 1–2 Holly Avenue West, Jesmond,
NE2 2AR
www.calsown.co.uk
When you're up for a slice of pizza nirvana, this
family-run joint delivers the authentic goods,
courtesy of a hand-built wood-fired pizza oven
imported from Naples sitting centre stage amid a
no-nonsense setting of unclothed tables and
bare brick walls. Pukka regional salami, hams
and cheeses are sourced meticulously from Italy.
Tapas-style starters change daily.

Chef Calvin Kitchin **Seats** 65, Private dining 20
Closed 25–26 December **Prices from** S £4.95, M £7.85,
D £2.95 **Parking** 2 **Notes** Vegetarian dishes, Children
welcome

Horton Grange Country House Hotel
◎ CLASSIC BRITISH

01661 860686 | Berwick Hill, Ponteland, NE13 6BU
www.hortongrange.co.uk
Set within a privately owned Grade II country
house hotel the open-plan restaurant boasts
some elegant touches with high quality
crockery on the well-spaced tables. A meal
here showcases some ambitious modern
British cooking.

Chef Mark Young **Seats** 60, Private dining 40 **Open** All
Year **Prices from** S £6.25, M £18.95, D £6.25 **Parking** 50
Notes Vegetarian dishes, Children welcome

Hotel du Vin Newcastle
◎ BRITISH, FRENCH ◢ NOTABLE WINE LIST

0191 229 2200 | Allan House, City Road, NE1 2BE
www.hotelduvin.com
The converted red-brick Edwardian warehouse
of the Tyne Tees Steam Shipping Company
enjoys commanding views of the city's many
bridges, while, as might be expected from this
well-established chain, the restaurant has the
look of a French bistro, with dark wood floors
and wooden-topped tables.

Chef Kevin Bland **Seats** 86, Private dining 22
Prices from S £5.50, M £12.50, D £5.95 **Parking** 15
Notes Vegetarian dishes, Children welcome

House of Tides
◉◉◉◉ MODERN BRITISH V NOTABLE WINE LIST
See pages 382–383

Jesmond Dene House
◉◉ MODERN BRITISH, EUROPEAN
0191 212 3000 | Jesmond Dene Road, NE2 2EY
jesmonddenehouse.co.uk
Part of the allure of Jesmond Dene House is that it has the feel of a grand country house sitting in a tranquil wooded valley, yet is actually within the city limits of Newcastle. There is refinement, creativity and skill in the execution of dishes.

Chef Danny Parker **Seats** 80, Private dining 24 **Open** All Year **Prices from** S £9.50, M £15.50, D £10.50 **Parking** 64 **Notes** Vegetarian dishes, Children welcome

Peace and Loaf
◉◉ MODERN BRITISH
0191 281 5222 | 217 Jesmond Road, Jesmond, NE2 1LA
www.peaceandloaf.co.uk
In the fashionable Jesmond district of Newcastle, this is a thoroughly 21st-century place, with wood floors and brick walls offset by quirky decorative touches. Bag a table on the mezzanine floor for views of the kitchen pass and the folks below. The menus deal in avant-garde brasserie food with an imaginative edge.

Chef David Coulson **Seats** 53 **Closed** 24–27 December, 1–3 January **Notes** Vegetarian dishes, Children welcome

21
◉ MODERN BRITISH V
0191 222 0755 | Trinity Gardens, Quayside, NE1 2HH
www.21newcastle.co.uk
Located just off the Quayside, the spacious, glass-fronted brasserie is popular with the area's office folk but also with the people who 'do lunch'. Bright and welcoming, it remains as buzzy as ever, with slick and smooth service. The appealing modern brasserie-style dishes playing a big part in the attraction.

Chef Chris Dobson **Seats** 130, Private dining 44 **Closed** 25–26 December, 1 January **Prices from** S £6.60, M £17, D £6.50 **Notes** Children welcome

Ury Restaurant
◉ INDIAN V
0191 232 7799 | 27 Queen Street, NE1 3UG
www.uryrestaurants.com
An ury is a clay pot used for storing preserved food, a traditional feature of Keralan homes in south India, which is where the regional specialities hail from in this large, exuberantly decorated restaurant just off the quayside. Mains run from turmeric-spiked lamb cooked with coconut and curry leaves to chemmeen masala.

Chef Yusuf Mukkat, Naseer Chennad **Seats** 80, Private dining 25 **Open** All Year **Prices from** S £4.50, M £7, D £3 **Parking** 2 **Notes** Children welcome

NORTH SHIELDS *MAP 21, NZ36*

The Staith House
◉ MODERN BRITISH
0191 270 8441 | NE30 1JA
www.thestaithhouse.co.uk
Since it was taken over by former *MasterChef: The Professionals* finalist John Calton, this venerable pub on the regenerated North Shields fish quay has established itself as a foodie hotspot. Rubbing shoulders with the fish merchants, the quality of the piscine produce is beyond question.

Chef John Calton, James Laffan **Seats** 45 **Closed** 25–26 December **Prices from** S £5, M £12.50, D £5 **Parking** 10 **Notes** Vegetarian dishes, No children after 7.30pm

TYNEMOUTH *MAP 21, NZ36*

Buddha Lounge
◉ PAN-ASIAN
0191 270 8990 | 76 Front Street, NE30 4BP
www.buddhaloungetynemouth.co.uk
The setting is memorable: a converted church where a huge Buddha statue surveys a galleried upper floor beneath the soaring timber roof. Local ingredients and seafood from day boats shine through, appearing in vibrant ideas that take their cue from Indian, Japanese, Thai and Chinese cuisines.

Chef Xiaokun Chen **Seats** 92 **Closed** 25 December **Notes** Vegetarian dishes, Children welcome

NEWCASTLE UPON TYNE

MAP 21, NZ26

House of Tides

◉◉◉◉ MODERN BRITISH 𝐕 NOTABLE WINE LIST

0191 230 3720 | 28-30 The Close, NE1 3RF

www.houseoftides.co.uk

Gourmet paradise down by the riverside

It's fair to say that born-and-bred Geordie Kenny Atkinson's contemporary restaurant has put this previously neglected quarter of the city, in the immediate shadow of the Tyne Bridge, back on the modern map. Set within a beautifully restored, Grade 1-listed 16th-century former merchant's townhouse, his much-accoladed, two-storey operation lights up the scene with a bare wood ambience for cocktails and modern dining, to a soundtrack of rock favourites of the past 20 years. Those signing up for the tasting menu upstairs should be prepared to receive their cutlery in one compendious clatter, as part of an experience that aims from the get-go for true distinctiveness. While acknowledging the north east, the modern British tasting menus also draw inspiration from further afield, as in dream canapés, including a parmesan churro with smoked cod's roe tart. Other potential highlights include

mussels and sea purslane on baby leeks with caviar, and then an intermediate serving of Cerney Ash cheese with broccoli, confit potato, pine-nuts and shaved truffle. Meat is top-drawer, as in the meltingly tender beef fillet that comes with crumbed sweetbreads, confit shallots, dots of black garlic purée and lovage in a rich beef jus, or if at this point you'd prefer seafood, try scallop with pork belly, sweetcorn and lardo. Desserts play variations of texture and temperature, such as apple parfait sandwiched by almond tuiles and the scent of marigold alongside sweet croissant ice cream. On the other hand, a simple selection of British cheeses might be just the ticket. Proudly moulded with the letters HoT, the salted caramel petits fours are made with lovely dark bitter chocolate dusted with gold. Although there's absolutely no need,

While acknowledging the north east, the modern British tasting menus also draw inspiration from further afield

feel free to go off-piste from the carefully chosen wine pairings with something else from the excellent list that showcases Atkinson's favourites from around the world.

Chef Kenny Atkinson
Seats 50, Private dining 12
Closed See website for closure dates
Parking 70
Notes No children under 9 years

■ WARWICKSHIRE

ALDERMINSTER
MAP 10, SP24

The Bell at Alderminster
◉ BRITISH
01789 450414 | Shipston Rd, CV37 8NY
www.thebellald.co.uk
Part of the Alscot Estate, The Bell is a free house with classy bedrooms and a bar stocked with the estate's own ales, and a restaurant, now extended to cover two floors, that successfully brings contemporary elements into the traditional space. Service is upbeat.

Open All Year

Ettington Park Hotel
◉◉ MODERN, TRADITIONAL BRITISH
01789 450123 | CV37 8BU
www.handpickedhotels.co.uk/ettingtonpark
A magnificent example of mid-Victorian Gothic architecture, Ettington Park stands in 40 acres of grounds in the Stour Valley. The interior bursts with antiques and walls hung with paintings, plus several friezes. Staff are friendly as they serve up some modern contemporary cooking.

Open All Year

ANSTY
MAP 11, SP48

Macdonald Ansty Hall
◉ BRITISH
024 7661 2888 | Main Road, CV7 9HZ
www.macdonald-hotels.co.uk/anstyhall
Ansty Hall is a handsome, red-brick 17th-century mansion house set in eight acres of grounds. The emphasis is on British food wrought from good-quality seasonal produce, cooked without pretension and served without undue fanfare or fuss.

Open All Year

ARMSCOTE
MAP 10, SP24

The Fuzzy Duck
◉◉ SEASONAL, MODERN BRITISH
01608 682635 | Ilmington Road, CV37 8DD
www.fuzzyduckarmscote.com
This upmarket gastro pub is looking pretty swanky these days after a makeover that made the most of the original character of the place (it's been doing the business as a coaching inn since the 18th century) and injected a bit of contemporary style.

Chef Ben Tynan **Seats** 60, Private dining 20
Prices from S £7.50, M £13, D £6.50 **Parking** 15
Notes Vegetarian dishes, Children welcome

HENLEY-IN-ARDEN
MAP 10, SP16

The Bluebell
◉◉ MODERN, CLASSIC
01564 793049 | 93 High Street, B95 5AT
www.thebluebell-henley.co.uk
The Bluebell occupies a half-timbered coaching inn on Henley's uncommercialised High Street. Within are uneven flagged floors, beamed ceilings, draught beers in the bar and an enterprising restaurant menu. Expect interesting starters along the lines of braised pig's cheek with lobster bisque.

Open All Year

Cheal's NEW
◉◉ MODERN EUROPEAN V
01564 793856 | 64 High Street, B95 5BX
www.chealsofhenley.co.uk
The black-and-white timbered façade of Cheal's slots in unobtrusively among the wonky beamed buildings of the affluent 'Henley Mile' high street. Inside, the dining room is as you'd hope, all gnarly beams and tables dressed up smartly with white linen. The kitchen sends out confident, flavour-driven dishes with sound classical foundations and contemporary verve.

Chef Matt Cheal **Seats** 30, Private dining 12
Closed 25-26 December, 1 January **Prices from** S £15, M £29, D £11 **Notes** Children welcome

ILMINGTON
MAP 10, SP24

The Howard Arms
◉ BRITISH
01608 682226 | Lower Green, CV36 4LT
www.howardarms.com
History seeps from every stone of the Howard, a 400-year-old inn on a Warwickshire village green to the south of Stratford. A big old stone fireplace, weathered armchairs and unclothed tables make for a relaxing ambience, and the cooking is in the modern country-pub mould.

Chef Gareth Rufus **Seats** 45 **Open** All Year
Prices from S £7.50, M £15, D £7.50 **Parking** 20
Notes Vegetarian dishes, Children welcome

KENILWORTH
MAP 10, SP27

The Cross at Kenilworth

⊕⊕⊕ MODERN BRITISH V ⚑ NOTABLE WINE LIST

01926 853840 | 16 New Steet, CV8 2EZ

www.thecrosskenilworth.co.uk

This whitewashed 19th-century inn has had a new lease of life under the auspices of Andreas Antona. Tasteful modern refurbishment makes the most of its beams and exposed brickwork, with warm tones, dark wood and polished tables entirely in tune with the pubby mood. The cooking has its roots in classic European ideas and delivers a touch of modern refinement whilst not turning its nose up at steak and chips with onion rings on the same menu. A big-hitting opener partners crispy duck egg with beer-cured ham, caramelised celeriac, intense cep purée and a rich and glossy chicken jus. Next up, a piggy plateful of pork belly, tender cheek and a croquette of head meat is helped along by crackling, smoked onion, salted apple purée, sage jus and braised barley, while caramelised white chocolate sauce poured into hazelnut praline soufflé alongside blood orange ice cream provides a final flourish.

Chef Adam Bennett **Seats** 74, Private dining 12 **Closed** 25-26 December, 1 January **Prices from** S £11, M £27, D £11 **Parking** 25 **Notes** Children welcome

LEAMINGTON SPA (ROYAL)
MAP 10, SP38

The Brasserie at Mallory Court Hotel

⊕⊕ MODERN BRITISH V

01926 453939 | Harbury Lane, Bishop's Tachbrook, CV33 9QB

www.mallory.co.uk

As well as the main dining room, Mallory Court boasts a more contemporary-looking brasserie just a short stroll from the main house, serving modern European and traditional British classic food. No mere adjunct to the main action, this is a fine venue in its own right, with art deco-style lines and glass-topped wicker tables.

Chef Paul Evans **Seats** 80, Private dining 24 **Open** All Year **Parking** 100 **Notes** Children welcome

The Dining Room at Mallory Court Hotel

⊕⊕⊕ MODERN BRITISH V

See page 386

Queans Restaurant

⊕ MODERN EUROPEAN

01926 315522 | 15 Dormer Place, CV32 5AA

www.queans-restaurant.co.uk

This is a delightful establishment with a good deal of genteel charm, where a smartly neutral decor meets an appealing menu of unpretentious dishes based on high-quality regional produce. Save room for a dessert of strawberry and pink champagne cheesecake.

The Tame Hare

⊕ MODERN BRITISH

01926 316191 | 97 Warwick Street, CV32 4RJ

www.thetamehare.co.uk

Understated on the outside, this is contemporary restaurant with wooden floors, soft downlighting and a mirrored wall that creates the illusion of a large space. The modern British menu follows the seasons and the short descriptions of the dishes can keep you guessing.

Closed 2 weeks in January and 2 weeks in the autumn

SHIPSTON ON STOUR
MAP 10, SP24

The Red Lion

⊕ TRADITIONAL BRITISH

01608 684221 | Main Street, Long Compton, CV36 5JS

www.redlion-longcompton.co.uk

Built as a coaching stop in 1748, The Red Lion is a textbook country inn, right down to its inglenook fireplace, settles and eclectic furniture and local artwork. The cooking takes traditional pub food to a higher level, both in terms of preparation and presentation.

Chef Sarah Keightley **Seats** 70 **Closed** 25 December **Parking** 70 **Notes** Vegetarian dishes, Children welcome

STRATFORD-UPON-AVON
MAP 10, SP25

Hallmark Hotel The Welcombe

⊕ MODERN BRITISH, FRENCH

0330 028 3422 | Warwick Road, CV37 0NR

www.hallmarkhotels.co.uk

The formal garden outside this splendid Victorian house brings a stately presence to the Jacobean-style property. The restaurant matches the setting with its grandeur. Start perhaps with a pre-dinner drink in the lounge and eat alfresco if the weather is good. The concise menu offers a contemporary take on classic country-house cuisine.

The Dining Room at Mallory Court Hotel

@@@ MODERN BRITISH *V*

01926 330214 | Harbury Lane, Bishop's Tachbrook, CV33 9QB

www.mallory.co.uk

A charming manor house not far from Leamington Spa, set in 10 acres of grounds including a kitchen garden where they grow some of the produce for the restaurant, Mallory Court has a comfortable country-house feel with plump sofas and wooden floors adorned with Chinese rugs. There are lovely garden and countryside views from the smart, panelled restaurant, where floral drapes and elegantly dressed tables all add up to a classy setting – ideal for the smart, grown-up cooking style. Backing the seasonal carte and daily-changing set price menus there's a seven-course taster, and vegetarians also get their own menu. You might kick things off with a cleanly presented roasted quail breast, home-grown sweetcorn, with game consommé and delicate herbs. Move on to pan-braised wild turbot, with pickled, puréed and roasted cauliflower, a nicely conceived combination of textures, before finishing with a delightfully refined flavour of a tarte Tatin with baked apple terrine, and milk ice cream.

Chef Paul Evans **Seats** 56, Private dining 14 **Open** All Year **Parking** 100 **Notes** Children welcome

STRATFORD-UPON-AVON continued

Hotel du Vin Stratford upon Avon NEW

◉ BISTRO

01789 613685 | 7–8 Rother Street, CV37 6LU

www.hotelduvin.com/locations/
stratford-upon-avon

Set in a building dating from Georgian times, this branch of the HdV chain combines blond wood tables and midnight-blue banquettes to stylish effect in its sleek contemporary bistro. Expect classic French favourites such as snails in garlic butter, then sea bass en papillotte, and tarte au citron for pudding.

Open All Year

Macdonald Alveston Manor

◉ MODERN BRITISH

01789 205478 | Clopton Bridge, CV37 7HP

www.macdonald-hotels.co.uk/alvestonmanor

A Tudor manor house a few minutes from the centre of the Shakespeare action in Stratford, Alveston brims with old-school charm. When you've wearied of minimalism in glass and steel, the gnarled oak beams and mullioned windows of the Manor dining room suddenly look luxurious.

Chef Sunil Kumar **Seats** 110, Private dining 40 **Open** All Year **Prices from** S £7.50, M £14.50, D £7.50 **Parking** 120 **Notes** Vegetarian dishes, Children welcome

No 44 Brasserie on The Waterside

◉◉ MODERN BRITISH *V*

01789 298682 | The Arden Hotel, Waterside, CV37 6BA

www.theardenhotelstratford.com

Just across the river from the theatres of the Royal Shakespeare Company, this contemporary brasserie offers a champagne bar and enterprising modern cooking. Expect fashionable twists on the classics – for example a dessert of dark chocolate pavé with a deconstructed garnish of griottine cherries, cherry sorbet and Chantilly cream.

Chef Don Hilario **Seats** , Private dining 28 **Open** All Year **Notes** Children welcome

Salt

◉◉◉ MODERN BRITISH *V*

01789 263566 | 8 Church Street, CV37 6HB

www.salt-restaurant.co.uk

Three cheers for crowdfunding, without which the lucky residents of Stratford-upon-Avon

would be without this high-flying addition to the local gastronomic scene. The bijou dining room is shoehorned into a snug space, all low beams, bare brick and wood and a tiny open kitchen. Chef-patron Paul Foster brings a sound pedigree from world-class kitchens, conveying a clear passion for the very best ingredients and a sound grasp of contemporary cooking techniques in his captivating à la carte and tasting menus. His clear vision of how flavours and textures work together is amply demonstrated in a vibrant dish of cured halibut with pickled cucumber, grapes, almonds and sea purslane, all deftly offset with suave dill emulsion. Meat is also handled with impressive dexterity, as in a pairing of deeply flavoured Herdwick hogget shoulder and tender lamb rump served with minted goats' curd, charred hispi cabbage and pickled onion.

Chef Paul Foster **Seats** 35 **Closed** Christmas **Notes** Children welcome

WARWICK
MAP 10, SP26

The Brasserie

◉ MODERN BRITISH

01926 843111 | Ardencote, The Cumsey, Lye Green Road, Claverdon, CV35 8LT

www.ardencote.com

The all-day dining venue at Ardencote, The Brasserie, is another string to the bow of this establishment. Situated in an extension to the original grand Victorian house, the Brasserie is open for light lunches and sandwiches, and ups the ante in the evening.

Open All Year

Tailors Restaurant

◉◉ MODERN BRITISH

01926 410590 | 22 Market Place, CV34 4SL

www.tailorsrestaurant.co.uk

In a pint-sized room centred on an old brick fireplace, the cooking is complex, with much technical skill. The seafood cocktail consists of prawns and brown shrimps, Marie Rose dressing deep-fried in breadcrumbs, red pepper purée and a gel of preserved lemon; all in all a conceptual triumph.

Chef Dan Cavell, Mark Fry **Seats** 30 **Closed** Christmas **Notes** Vegetarian dishes, No children under 8 years at lunch, 10 years at dinner

WISHAW
MAP 10, SP19

The Belfry
@ MODERN BRITISH, EUROPEAN
01675 238600 | B76 9PR
www.thebelfry.com
The Belfry has more than 300 bedrooms, a nightclub and four eating places, including the lively Ryder Grill. Enjoy views across the famous Brabazon golf course, and in summer relax on its outdoor terrace. Steaks, chargrills and spit-roasts, fish and lobster are the stock in trade.

Chef Robert Bates **Seats** 220, Private dining 16 **Open** All Year **Prices from** S £7, M £19, D £7 **Parking** 1000 **Notes** Vegetarian dishes, Children welcome

■ WEST MIDLANDS

BALSALL COMMON
MAP 10, SP27

Nailcote Hall
@ TRADITIONAL EUROPEAN
024 7646 6174 | Nailcote Lane, Berkswell, CV7 7DE
www.nailcotehall.co.uk
Built on the eve of the Civil War, Nailcote is a stately home on a modest scale, with 15 acres of grounds containing what are reputedly some of England's oldest yew trees. Old-school service extends to tableside steak-flambéing, but otherwise the mood is modern.

Closed 31 December

BIRMINGHAM
MAP 10, SP08

Adam's
@@@ MODERN BRITISH V NOTABLE WINE LIST
0121 643 3745 | New Oxford House, 16 Waterloo Street, B2 5UG
www.adamsrestaurant.co.uk
Originating as a peripatetic pop-up, Adam and Natasha Stokes' restaurant moved into its permanent residence in early 2016 and set about making itself at home. The principal dining room on the ground floor is a distinctly elegant space with large annular light fittings, unclothed tables and comfortable seating. Service moves with discreet efficiency over the thick-pile carpet, delivering thrillingly presented dishes of confident and refined modern British food. An opening course of accurately timed monkfish comes with thinly tempura-battered eel, Roscoff onion petals and slivered grapes, as well as a foam-light onion purée with capers and dill, as a possible prelude to breast and smoked heart of duck with hispi cabbage, shiitakes and parsley root, or rare-breed Hampshire pork with black pudding, quince and crisp-topped potato terrine. The tasting menu aims to win you over with eight ingeniously constructed dishes, and there are some imaginative wine pairings to accompany.

Chef Adam Stokes, Tom Shepherd **Seats** 34, Private dining 16 **Closed** 2 weeks in summer, 3 weeks at Christmas **Notes** Children welcome

Carters of Moseley
@@@ MODERN BRITISH V
0121 449 8885 | 2c Wake Green Road, Moseley, B13 9EZ
cartersofmoseley.co.uk
Tucked away in a row of shops in one of Birmingham's more tranquil quarters, Brad Carter's place is an understated venue with minimal plain walls doing nothing to distract from the activity in the open kitchen, the built-in wine cabinets exercising their own allure. An unabashedly direct culinary approach brings on an intro course of razor clams blitzed with Old Winchester cheese, with peppery red dulse to garnish. That's followed by halibut cooked sous-vide with spots of black garlic purée, anointed at the table with vivid green leek oil. To precede the meat, there could be a bowl of creamy mash in gravy with smoked bone marrow, and then the butter-soft aged red venison arrives, honour-guarded by tart quince purée and roast squash. A poached Cox's apple in fluid caramel with fragrant meadowsweet ice cream completes the show. Don't forget to try the Tamworth pork fat butter with bread.

Chef Brad Carter **Seats** 32 **Closed** 1–17 January, 24 April to 3 May and 3–23 August **Parking** 4 **Notes** No children under 8 years

Chez Mal Brasserie
@ MODERN, TRADITIONAL
0121 246 5000 | Malmaison Birmingham, 1 Wharfside Street, The Mailbox, B1 1RD
www.malmaison.com
The Malmaison team bring their brand of boutique swagger to this place in The Mailbox, a swanky shopping and eating venue. The Brasserie, with its floor-to-ceiling windows and contemporary finish, is a relaxed and lively spot offering a menu of globally inspired contemporary dishes.

Open All Year

Circle Restaurant Birmingham Hippodrome

◉ MODERN BRITISH

0844 338 9000 *(Calls cost 4.5p per minute plus your phone company's access charge)* | B5 4TB

www.birminghamhippodrome.com/plan-your-visit/food-drink/circle-restaurant

Pre-theatre dining doesn't get much closer to curtain-up than at this large, open-plan restaurant on the second floor of the Hippodrome. You can even save your dessert for the interval; a uniquely quirky and thoughtful touch. Service is friendly and the modern British cooking is confident.

Chef Melissa Menns **Seats** 95, Private dining 25 **Closed** Non-performance days, 25 December, 1 January **Notes** Vegetarian dishes, Children welcome

Harborne Kitchen *NEW*

◉◉ MODERN BRITISH *V*

0121 439 9150 | 175 High Street, Harborne, B17 9QE

www.harbornekitchen.com

A neighbourhood restaurant with an already very excellent local reputation, this former butcher's shop has been transformed into a modern and bright dining venue with a bar area at the front. The kitchen is open plan and a tiled wall is also used as a white board to run the service. The restaurant team of three are welcoming and knowledgeable. A small garden to the rear provides seasonal fruit and vegetables.

Chef Jamie Desogus, Craig Shepherd **Seats** 50, Private dining 12 **Closed** 4 times a year, see website **Notes** Children welcome

Hotel du Vin & Bistro Birmingham

◉ BRITISH, FRENCH

0121 200 0600 | 25 Church Street, B3 2NR

www.hotelduvin.com

Light floods through the tall windows of this hotel dining room in Birmingham's financial area. The Gallic-inspired decor is backed up by a menu of bistro classics. A typical meal could begin with steak tartare, followed by roast cod with braised Puy lentils, button onions and pancetta, and finish with crème brûlée.

Chef Greg Pryce **Seats** 85, Private dining 108 **Open** All Year **Prices from** S £8.50, M £14.50, D £5.95 **Notes** Vegetarian dishes, Children welcome

Lasan Restaurant

◉◉ INDIAN

0121 212 3664 | 3–4 Dakota Buildings, James Street, St Paul's Square, B3 1SD

www.lasangroup.co.uk

Set in the Jewellery Quarter, Lasan is a stylish contemporary Indian restaurant. A vibrant atmosphere pervades the light and spacious split-level dining room, where the menu takes a broad sweep across the Indian subcontinent to deliver regional authenticity alongside modern fusion touches.

Chef Khalid Khan, Munayam Khan **Seats** 85 **Closed** 25 December, 1 January **Notes** Vegetarian dishes, Children welcome

Opus Restaurant

◉◉ MODERN BRITISH

0121 200 2323 | 54 Cornwall Street, B3 2DE

www.opusrestaurant.co.uk

In letters six-foot high across its wide street windows, Opus declares its presence to the city's business execs, lunching shoppers and evening diners. The attraction Is the modern British cooking, represented by pan-seared wild halibut; roasted duck breast; truffled wild mushroom Wellington; a five-course tasting menu; and a new one-course express lunch.

Chef Ben Ternent **Seats** 85, Private dining 32 **Closed** between Christmas and New Year, bank holidays **Notes** Vegetarian dishes, Children welcome

See advertisement on page 390

Purnell's

◉◉◉ MODERN BRITISH ⚑ NOTABLE WINE LIST

0121 212 9799 | 55 Cornwall Street, B3 2DH

purnellsrestaurant.com

Glynn Purnell's personality shines through on his menus, where playful puns and little details give insight Into his development as a chef. The building in the financial district has been on a journey as well, and it's looking fine and dandy right now; the old red-brick warehouse has surely never looked so dapper within – a fashionably muted colour palette with the occasional splash of something more daring, and stylish artworks. In this smart and confident setting, Glynn's menus include a fixed-price carte and tasting menus: '10 Years In the Making', 'Brummie Tapas', and 'A Purnell's journey...', the latter featuring the BBC *Great British Menu*-winning monkfish masala (which is also a regular on the carte). Main courses extend to Wiltshire pork belly, paired with burnt apple purée and confit turnip, while desserts might be burnt English surprise (a rhubarb and custard number also seen on *Great British Menu*). The impressive wine list features staff favourites.

Chef Glynn Purnell **Seats** 45, Private dining 12 **Closed** 1 week Easter, Christmas and New Year **Notes** Vegetarian dishes, No children under 10 years

Simpsons

⊛⊛⊛ MODERN BRITISH **V**

0121 454 3434 | 20 Highfield Road, Edgbaston, B15 3DU

www.simpsonsrestaurant.co.uk

The gradual evolution of Simpsons has been one of the more fascinating journeys of the Birmingham dining scene over the years. Housed in a Georgian mansion in well-heeled Edgbaston, it has been made over into a thoroughly modern dining space, all wood and stone textures in an expansive airy room that looks out on to the landscaped garden. There's also a chef's table in the middle of the kitchen action, and the Eureka development hub, where members of the brigade are encouraged to unleash their creative skills. The result is cooking of bright, sculpted flavours and inspired combinations, as in mains such as cheek and bavette of Aberdeenshire beef in a charcoal emulsion with salsify, nasturtiums and shallots. Taster menus distil the carte into seven stages of loveliness, ending perhaps with passionfruit curd and yogurt sorbet, followed by Guanaja chocolate with blood orange and burnt marmalade ice cream.

Chef Luke Tipping **Seats** 70, Private dining 14 **Closed** Bank holidays **Parking** 12 **Notes** Children welcome

The Wilderness

⊛⊛⊛ BRITISH **V**

0121 233 9425 | 27 Warstone Lane, Jewellery Quarter, B18 6JQ

www.wearethewilderness.co.uk

Tucked down an alleyway in the jewellery quarter, The Wilderness is an atmospheric venue with skylight panels and an open kitchen, decked with foliage to bring a sense of sylvan repose to city eating. Top-class British produce supplemented by foraged ingredients and seasonal goodies from their own allotment provide the building-blocks and underpinning them is a sharp grasp of flavour and sound technique that delivers playful, inspired modern cooking. A dramatic opener of venison tartare with beetroot purée, parsley shoots, sweet shallot and the pungency of wasabi emulsion paves the way for a sharply executed dish of tempura monkfish with a hint of garlic and chilli and a light and fresh accompaniment of sorrel, elderflower emulsion, gherkin and pickled pickled parsnip powder. Desserts experiment with multi-layered, often savoury flavours, as in the miso ice cream matched with sesame caramelised filo pastry,

white wine-infused apple balls and richly buttery salted caramel.

Chef Stuart Deeley, Alex Claridge **Seats** 20
Closed Christmas, New Year **Notes** No children under 12 years

HOCKLEY HEATH
MAP 10, SP17

Nuthurst Grange Hotel
@@ MODERN BRITISH
01564 783972 | Nuthurst Grange Lane, B94 5NL
www.nuthurst-grange.com
Nuthurst's long tree-lined avenue approach leads to a brick-built Victorian mansion in private woodland, so allow time for exploring. A judicious balance of culinary modernism and traditional ideas is evident on the menus. Dishes have a lot in them but manage not to look crowded.

Open All Year

SOLIHULL
MAP 10, SP17

AA Wine Award for England and Overall Wine Award Winner 2019–20

Hampton Manor
@@@@ MODERN BRITISH V NOTABLE WINE LIST
01675 446080 | Swadowbrook Lane, Hampton-in-Arden, B92 0EN
www.hamptonmanor.com
Towers and turrets mark the spot within the 45 acres of land surrounding this impressive stately manor, built by a son of Sir Robert Peel. These days it's a divertingly stylish restaurant with rooms, with a kitchen garden providing its bounty and the dynamic contemporary cooking of Rob Palmer in the offing. The design of the place is timelessly tasteful; the part-panelled dining room is a mix of traditional comfort and contemporary sophistication, while the staff are just as engaging as the setting. The format sees three tasting menus vying for your attention – two four-course options, the more expensive of which features Wagyu beef – and a full-throttle seven-course menu that includes all the bells and all the whistles.

Flavour combinations are not designed to shock, and what arrives on the plate is creative, pretty as a picture, and never less than delicious. A starter of tomato and burata may be simple but it's absolutely delicious, with fabulous depth and clarity of flavour from just-picked tomatoes. A single perfectly-timed langoustine is brought warmth from ginger and textural interest from crispy leeks, and main courses might include smoked eel with kohlrabi and samphire, or Wagyu beef served with joyously fresh and sweet garden carrots and black garlic.

Chef Rob Palmer **Seats** 28, Private dining 14 **Closed** 21 December to 6 January **Parking** 30 **Notes** No children under 12 years

The Regency Hotel
@ MODERN, CLASSIC
0121 745 6119 | Stratford Road, Shirley, B90 4EB
www.corushotels.com/solihull
Less than 20 minutes from Birmingham Airport and the NEC, The Regency is a well-positioned base for visitors, but the hotel's stylish restaurant appeals equally to Solihull locals. A contemporary space with its own courtyard, the restaurant offers inventive British dishes inspired by international flavour combinations.

Chef Nigel Cooke **Seats** 64, Private dining 20 **Open** All Year **Prices from** S £5.50, M £11.95, D £4.95 **Parking** 320 **Notes** Vegetarian dishes, Children welcome

SUTTON COLDFIELD (ROYAL)
MAP 10, SP19

The Bridge at New Hall
@@ MODERN BRITISH
0121 378 2442 | Walmley Road, B76 1QX
www.handpickedhotels.co.uk/newhall
Before Birmingham's suburban sprawl engulfed the village of Sutton Coldfield, this 800-year-old moat house stood in empty countryside. Nowadays, it's cushioned from the hurly-burly by 26 acres of grounds. The Bridge Restaurant is the top-end dining option, where mullioned stained-glass windows blend with modern decor.

Chef Matthew Brookes **Seats** 52, Private dining 12 **Open** All Year **Parking** 60 **Notes** Vegetarian dishes, Children welcome

The Oak Room Restaurant

◉◉ MODERN BRITISH *V*

0121 308 3751 | Moor Hall Hotel & Spa, Moor Hall Drive, Four Oaks, B75 6LN

www.moorhallhotel.co.uk

A family-run country-house hotel set in parkland, Moor Hall's panelled Oak Room restaurant has a real sense of grandeur and lovely views over the grounds, including the golf course. The contemporary British cooking from a young kitchen team emphasises quality ingredients.

Chef Nigel Parnaby **Seats** 70, Private dining 30 **Open** All Year **Prices from** S £6, M £14, D £6.50 **Parking** 170 **Notes** Children welcome

WALSALL

MAP 10, SP09

Restaurant 178

◉◉ MODERN BRITISH *V*

01922 455122 | Fairlawns Hotel & Spa, 178 Little Aston Road, Aldridge, WS9 0NU

www.fairlawns.co.uk

Well placed to reach virtually anywhere in the West Midlands, the spa hotel near Walsall is family-owned and a refreshing antidote to corporate anonymity. The dining room, Restaurant 178, is the place to sample an extensive Market Menu of modern British ideas that change with the seasons.

Chef Chris Morris **Seats** 80, Private dining 100 **Closed** 25-26 December, 1 January **Parking** 120 **Notes** Children welcome

WOLVERHAMPTON

MAP 10, SO99

Bilash

◉ INDIAN, BANGLADESHI

01902 427762 | 2 Cheapside, WV1 1TU

www.thebilash.co.uk

Bilash has been pushing beyond the confines of mere curry since 1982. The stylishly clean-cut interior works neutral colour palette with cream chairs, seating booths, tables with crisp white linen and walls hung with sparkling mirrors, a smart contemporary setting.

Chef Sitab Khan **Seats** 48, Private dining 30 **Closed** 25-26 December, 1 January **Prices from** S £7.90, M £14.90, D £6.90 **Parking** 15 **Notes** Vegetarian dishes, Children welcome

Drawing Room, Bar and Grill

◉◉ MODERN EUROPEAN

01902 752055 | The Mount Hotel Country Manor, Mount Road, Tettenhall Wood, WV6 8HL

www.themount.co.uk

In a stately Victorian mansion overlooking the canal, the dining room wears a more understated modern look. Expect brasserie buzz rather than a country-house whispering gallery, and food that satisfies most modern tastes. Chocolate and raspberry delice sprinkled with amaretti crumbs is a classy finisher.

Chef Craig Thomas **Seats** 38, Private dining 100 **Parking** 120 **Notes** Vegetarian dishes, Children welcome

■ WILTSHIRE

BEANACRE

MAP 4, ST96

Beechfield House Restaurant

◉◉ MODERN BRITISH

01225 703700 | SN12 7PU

www.beechfieldhouse.co.uk

A charming, privately-owned hotel in eight beautiful acres with its own arboretum. At dinner there's a good selection of carefully prepared dishes, including, as a starter, Scottish smoked salmon with caperberries; to be followed by Cornish cod with dressed linguine and brown shrimp; braised duck leg and smoked sausage; or roasted gnocchi with sun-dried tomatoes.

Chef Tony O'Neill **Seats** 70, Private dining 20 **Closed** 1 January **Prices from** S £7.50, M £22, D £8 **Parking** 70 **Notes** Vegetarian dishes, Children welcome

The George

...ere are three unique dining spaces to choose from at this Wiltshire inn, so whether ...u want to cosy up by the inglenook fire on a chesterfield, or watch the team of chefs ...he theatre kitchen or catch up with friends in the pantry dining room, there's a spot ...every occasion. Supper is best started with a G&T, the bar boasts a healthy selection, ...ore browsing the à la carte menu of modern British and European influenced ...hes. Experienced head chef and owner Alex Venables oversees the classically trained ...gade. Expect favorites such as beef Wellington, executed with skill and style. The whole ...perience can be topped off with a night in one of the charming bedrooms.

67 Woolley Street, Bradford on Avon, Wiltshire BA15 1AQ

01225 865650 **W:** thegeorgebradfordonavon.co.uk **E:** info@thegeorgebradfordonavon.co.uk

BOX

MAP 4, ST86

The Northey Arms

🏵 BRITISH, EUROPEAN

01225 742333 | Bath Road, SN13 8AE

www.ohhpubs.co.uk

Looking rather swish these days, this old stone-built inn has been brought up to full 21st-century spec with seagrass chairs and boldly-patterned wallpaper in the split-level dining area. Locally-reared 32-day-aged steaks get star billing; perhaps a 14oz T-bone if you're feeling peckish.

Closed 25-26 December

BRADFORD-ON-AVON

MAP 4, ST86

The Bunch of Grapes NEW

🏵🏵 MODERN BRITISH

01225 938088 | 14 Silver Street, BA15 1JY

www.thebunchofgrapes.com

Very much a food-oriented hostelry in the contemporary vein, The Bunch of Grapes has a dapper pared-back decor with a rich blue finish, bare wood tables and floors – a look that's more bistro than boozer. The kitchen draws on high quality ingredients to deliver a modern British menu full of up-to-date ideas and big flavours.

Chef Tony Casey **Seats** 80, Private dining 28 **Open** All Year **Prices from** S £6.50, M £12.95, D £6.50 **Notes** Vegetarian dishes, Children welcome

The George

🏵🏵 MODERN BRITISH

01225 865650 | 67 Woolley Street, BA15 1AQ

www.thegeorgebradfordonavon.co.uk

Once three houses from the Georgian era, now a comfortably spacious pub with modern and period furnishings, chesterfields, winged armchairs and four open fires. From the open-fronted kitchen come modern British dishes like confit duck leg with haggis bubble-and-squeak; black bream fillet; George's bacon and kimchi burger; and ricotta and spinach gnocchi.

Chef Alex Venables **Seats** 90, Private dining 16 **Closed** 25 December **Prices from** S £6.50, M £14.50, D £5.50 **Parking** 11 **Notes** Vegetarian dishes, Children welcome

See advertisement on page 393

The Restaurant at Woolley Grange NEW

🏵🏵 MODERN

01225 864705 | Woolley Grange Hotel, Woolley Green, BA15 1TX

www.woolleygrangehotel.co.uk

While the ethos of this upmarket, family-friendly, country-house hotel is certainly attuned to the needs of its younger guests, the fine dining restaurant provides an adults-only sanctuary when you need a little peace and quiet. A cosy space done out in soothing neutral shades, it makes a fitting backdrop for well-executed modern British cooking.

Chef Jethro Lawrence **Open** All Year **Prices from** S £8, M £20, D £8 **Notes** Vegetarian dishes, Children welcome

CALNE

MAP 4, ST97

Strand Room

🏵🏵 MODERN BRITISH

01249 812488 | The Lansdowne, The Strand, SN11 0EH

www.lansdownestrand.co.uk

Dating from the 16th century, The Lansdowne pub is owned by Arkell's Brewery and the Strand Room restaurant is at the very heart of the place. The modern cooking keeps things simple on the plate, allowing local produce to shine.

Chef Joel Lear **Seats** 50, Private dining 12 **Closed** 25 December **Prices from** S £6, M £12, D £7 **Notes** Vegetarian dishes, Children welcome

The White Horse

🏵🏵 MODERN BRITISH

01249 813118 | Compon Bassett, SN11 8RG

www.whitehorse-comptonbassett.co.uk

Named after the equine figure cut into the chalk at nearby Cherhill, this charming old inn dates from the 18th century. The menu reflects the different eating areas – bar and gardens, or restaurant – or put another way, from beer-battered haddock to, say, Wiltshire pork cutlet with pan-fried polenta cake and roasted fennel.

Chef Ben Reid **Seats** 42 **Open** All Year **Prices from** S £6, M £12.50, D £6 **Parking** 36 **Notes** Vegetarian dishes, No children after 8pm

See advertisement opposite

THE WHITE HORSE INN

COMPTON BASSETT

Nestled in the beautiful Wiltshire countryside, we are a traditional Free House with good homemade food and welcoming accommodation.

CASTLE COMBE
MAP 4, ST87

The Bybrook at The Manor House, an Exclusive Hotel & Golf Club

◉◉◉ MODERN BRITISH 𝑉 NOTABLE WINE LIST

01249 782206 | SN14 7HR

www.exclusive.co.uk

Set in 365 acres of parkland, the 14th-century manor house ticks all the right boxes for Cotswolds exclusivity. Named after the river that flows through the grounds, The Bybrook restaurant does a nice line in heritage and class with its mullioned windows, sober colours and pristine white linen, but there's nothing old-fashioned about the food here – Rob Potter's cooking is defined by well-thought-out and enterprising ideas, clear flavours and razor-sharp accuracy. It's all based on top-drawer ingredients, often sourced from the vicinity, and what doesn't carry the 'local' tag is tracked with due diligence – the Loch Duart salmon, for example, confit citrus-cured and served with marinated garden beetroot, Yukon Gold potatoes and silky smooth horseradish mousse. Next up, line-caught Cornish sea bass with a hazelnut pesto topping, served with crushed new season Jerusalem artichoke, roast ceps, curly kale and chicken jus. The sure-footed display ends with blackberry Brillat-Savarin cheesecake, blackberry jelly, confit lemon and blackberry sorbet.

Chef Robert Potter **Seats** 60, Private dining 100 **Open** All Year **Parking** 100 **Notes** No children under 11 years

COLERNE
MAP 4, ST87

The Brasserie

◉◉ MODERN BRITISH

01225 742777 | Lucknam Park Hotel & Spa, SN14 8AZ

www.lucknampark.co.uk

The Brasserie is the less formal dining option at Lucknam Park. Located within the walled garden, with a wall of glass of its own, it has a classy finish and serves up high-end food from its open kitchen and a wood-burning oven.

Chef Hywel Jones **Seats** 40 **Open** All Year **Parking** 80 **Notes** Vegetarian dishes, Children welcome

Restaurant Hywel Jones by Lucknam Park

◉◉◉ MODERN BRITISH 𝑉 NOTABLE WINE LIST

01225 742777 | Lucknam Park Hotel & Spa, SN14 8AZ

www.lucknampark.co.uk

Lucknam Park is a beautiful, symmetrical Palladian mansion, set in 500 acres of unspoilt parkland. For the last 30 years it has been a splendidly luxurious hotel and spa, offering an indulgent escape from the daily grind into a world of elegant country-house living. From the mile-long drive lined with beech trees to the delightful public spaces, it's all effortlessly sumptuous. The dining room, with its curved walls, cloud-painted ceiling and pristine double-clothed tables, is the perfect setting for Hywel Jones' sophisticated, focused cooking. This is not fanciful stuff at the whim of fashion, but mature and well directed, where great produce is treated with respect. To begin, heritage beetroot comes with buffalo ricotta tart and Wiltshire truffle, and a main course of roast Bwlch Farm venison is supported by miso and ginger roast hispi cabbage and plum chutney. Butter roast pear with buttermilk sorbet and walnut wafers is a fine way to finish.

Chef Hywel Jones **Seats** 70, Private dining 28 **Open** All Year **Parking** 80 **Notes** No children under 5 years

CORSHAM
MAP 4, ST87

Guyers House Hotel

◉◉ MODERN EUROPEAN, BRITISH

01249 713399 | Pickwick, SN13 0PS

www.guyershouse.com

An elegant country house in handsome grounds with a relaxing dining room patrolled by friendly staff, and menus with a real sense of creative élan. Save room for an up-to-the-minute Earl grey and lavender crème brûlée with pistachio brittle and mullet wine sorbet.

Closed 30 December to 3 January

The Methuen Arms

◉◉◉ BRITISH, ITALIAN

01249 717060 | 2 High Street, SN13 0HB

www.themethuenarms.com

In 1805, the former Red Lion took the Methuen family's name when it was rebuilt in Bath stone with three storeys and a fine portico. The period character looms large within thanks to elm floorboards, flagstones, rugs, log fires and walls hung with local prints and etchings, and there's a real energy about the place these days, particularly in the kitchen where Leigh Evans delivers modern British food that satisfies on all levels with its clearly defined, confident flavours and thoughtful textural interplay. The finest local produce, including goodies from the kitchen garden, underpin it all. A feisty starter unites lamb belly and sweetbreads with artichokes, hazelnut, gem lettuce and mint, while main course sees a superlative slab of halibut alongside the forthright flavours of girolles, parsnips, braised beef and truffle mash. Vivacious flavours continue through to a dessert of burnt passionfruit cream with mango salsa, crisp coconut and coconut ice cream.

Chef Leigh Evans **Seats** 60, Private dining 50 **Open** All Year **Prices from** S £7.50, M £15, D £7 **Parking** 40 **Notes** Vegetarian dishes, Children welcome

CRICKLADE
MAP 5, SU09

The Red Lion Inn
◉ MODERN BRITISH

01793 750776 | 74 High Street, SN6 6DD
www.theredlioncricklade.co.uk
A 17th-century inn with cosy beams, log fires and real ales from its own Hop Kettle microbrewery. Food is taken as seriously as beer – the pub rears pigs, and veggies come from locals' allotments. Choose the bar or the contemporary country-chic dining room.

Closed 25-26 December

DEVIZES
MAP 4, SU06

The Peppermill
◉◉ BRITISH *V*

01380 710407 | 40 St John's Street, SN10 1BL
www.peppermilldevizes.co.uk
This family-run restaurant with rooms impresses with its contemporary, feel-good menu. In the evening you might start with BBQ-infused, slow-roasted pork belly with carrot 'slaw', or potted shrimps with home-made brioche. It is a popular place so it's worth booking ahead.

Chef Leon Sheppard **Seats** 60 **Open** All Year **Prices from** S £6, M £15, D £6 **Parking** 5 **Notes** Children welcome

EDINGTON
MAP 4, ST95

The Three Daggers
◉◉ MODERN BRITISH

01380 830940 | Westbury Road, BA13 4PG
www.threedaggers.co.uk
A pub with its own microbrewery, farm and farm shop, The Three Daggers has plenty to offer locals and destination diners. Bare tables, mismatched wooden chairs, exposed brick and heritage colours add to the informal country pub feel, as does the seasonal modern cooking.

Open All Year

FOXHAM
MAP 4, ST97

The Foxham Inn
◉ MODERN BRITISH

01249 740665 | SN15 4NQ
www.thefoxhaminn.co.uk
Dinner is served in both the small bar and the purpose-built restaurant at this red-brick country inn. There's variety aplenty on the enticing menu, with starters including snails with noodles in a light soya broth. Dishes have clear, distinct flavours.

Chef Neil Cooper **Seats** 60 **Closed** 1st 2 weeks January **Prices from** S £7, M £13.95, D £7 **Parking** 16 **Notes** Vegetarian dishes, Children welcome

HORNINGSHAM
MAP 4, ST84

The Bath Arms at Longleat
◉ MODERN BRITISH

01985 844308 | Longleat Estate, BA12 7LY
www.batharms.co.uk
A creeper-covered stone building, The Bath Arms is in a delightfully picturesque village within the Longleat Estate. The kitchen takes pride in sourcing produce from within 50 miles of the estate, all the bread is made in-house, and dishes keep within broadly British parameters.

Open All Year

LACOCK
MAP 4, ST96

Sign of the Angel
◉◉ BRITISH *V*

01249 730230 | 6 Church Street, SN15 2LB
www.signoftheangel.co.uk
This 500-year-old, timbered inn is the very personification of classy Cotswold charm. Low-beamed ceilings, walk-in fireplaces and cosy nooks and crannies are all present and correct, and candlelit tables add to the cossetting mood. On the food side, the kitchen takes local sourcing very seriously.

Chef Jon Furby **Seats** 50, Private dining 16 **Open** All Year **Prices from** S £6.50, M £17, D £6.50 **Notes** Children welcome

LITTLE BEDWYN
MAP 5, SU26

The Harrow at Little Bedwyn
◉◉◉ MODERN *V*
See pages 398–399

The Harrow at Little Bedwyn

◉◉◉ MODERN *V*
01672 870871 | SN8 3JP
www.theharrowatlittlebedwyn.com

Highly polished cooking with the accent on fun

The Harrow sounds like a rustic gastro pub and although it does indeed look like many red-brick, creeper-clad Victorian country inns, its well-earned status as a food and wine lover's mecca becomes apparent once you're inside. Tastefully modernised, the tone is deeply relaxing in the best country manner, the dining room a white-linened space with high-backed black chairs and artworks on pale walls. Chef-patron Roger Jones has made a name for the place by buying only natural and free-range produce of remarkable quality, much of it from artisan growers and traders, and treating it with exemplary skill and simplicity.

Multi-course menus are the order of the day, with tasters in six or eight stages, the latter also available in vegetarian and vegan modes, plus a five-course lunch offering. Dishes are clutter free and everything tastes of what it is, so the eight-course workout might open with

"Dishes are clutter free and everything tastes of what it is"

cured salmon pointed up with ewe cheese curd and Siberian cavlar, while venison tartare relies on the sheer quality of the meat for its impact. Elsewhere, foraged herbs and chilli squid make a flavour-packed accompaniment to Cornish line-caught lemon sole, before the main course arrives in the form, perhaps, of roast free-range quail with foie gras and Puy lentils.

Dessert could be a majestically airborne strawberry soufflé, or perhaps an imaginative chocolate and coffee-based confection. If you're on the meat-free trail, expect a parade of equally imaginative dishes extending from an aromatic Périgord truffle risotto with cep cream, through to a Mediterranean spread of grilled aubergine with honey, paprika, grilled halloumi and smoked tomatoes. To say that wine is taken very seriously here is a massive understatement, and the expert pairings with the menus – with the option of upgrading to Coravin servings of the likes of decades-old Mosel Riesling, mature-vine burgundies and aged Napa Cabernet – are reliably spot-on.

Chef Roger Jones, John Brown
Seats 34
Closed Christmas and New Year
Notes Children welcome

MALMESBURY   *MAP 4, ST98*

Best Western Mayfield House Hotel *NEW*
@ BRITISH

01666 577409 | Crudwell, SN16 9EW

www.mayfieldhousehotel.co.uk

Sympathetically extended over the centuries, Mayfield House started life as a farmhouse in the 18th century. The restaurant is a traditionally decorated space in converted outbuildings, done out in bright and cheery style with simple white walls and linen-clothed tables. Service is genuinely friendly, and the kitchen brigade deals in uncomplicated ideas built on well-sourced materials.

Chef James Gilbert **Seats** 80, Private dining 30 **Open** All Year **Prices from** S £6.50, M £14.95, D £6.50 **Parking** 20 **Notes** Vegetarian dishes, Children welcome

---

The Dining Room
@@@@ MODERN BRITISH, ASIAN INFLUENCES *V*

01666 822888 | Whatley Manor Hotel and Spa, Easton Grey, SN16 0RB

www.whatleymanor.com

A feeling of anticipation builds as the gated entrance opens into Whatley Manor's cobbled courtyards of honeystone Cotswold buildings – and that's as it should be because the Victorian manor house has long sat in the top flight of the UK's country house hotels. The Dining Room is rightly at the heart of the Whatley experience, an understated modern space, with cream walls, bare floors and a generously spaced tables. Niall Keating leads the kitchen team here and his refined contemporary cooking draws inspiration from Asia and France – this is serious food, realised with ambition, confidence and panache.

Delivered via a 12-course tasting menu, including a vegetarian version, phenomenal precision and flavours are there from the off in lobster custard and meaty chicken broth pointed up with caviar, then the umami explosion of raw oyster with seaweed mignonette dressing. Produce is, naturally, as good as you can get, and flavours and textures come pin sharp, whether it's a delicate composition of salmon with turnip, ham and caviar, or the big, bold hit of pigeon with kohlrabi, spiced date purée and horseradish. A barrage of desserts offers ideas such as matcha with yogurt and milk crisp, and wine flights of revelatory pairings line up to enhance the whole experience further.

Chef Niall Keating **Seats** 46, Private dining 30 **Open** All Year **Parking** 120 **Notes** No children under 12 years

The Refectory
@ MODERN, CLASSIC EUROPEAN

01666 822 344 | The Old Bell Hotel, Abbey Row, SN16 0BW

oldbellhotel.co.uk

Originally a hostelry in the 13th century for dignitaries visiting Malmesbury Abbey, The Old Bell is possibly England's oldest hotel. Behind its largely wisteria-covered Edwardian exterior is a rich architectural mix, uncompromised by contemporary interior decor and furnishings. Some dishes belong in gastro-pub territory while others have classic heritage.

Chef Gordon Jones **Seats** 52, Private dining 16 **Open** All Year **Prices from** S £7.50, M £13, D £6 **Parking** 40 **Notes** Vegetarian dishes, Children welcome

---

MEET THE CHEF

Niall Keating

THE DINING ROOM

Malmesbury

What inspired you to become a chef?
At a young age, I took a job in the kitchen of my local gastro pub. The people that I met there, the buzz of working as a team, and the encouragement that I received made me pursue a career as a chef.

What are the vital ingredients for a successful kitchen?
Gathering the right team of people around you and sharing your vision with them, so they can understand your passion and motivation. For my first two years at Whatley Manor, we were operating with a nearly defunct kitchen, and still managed to achieve four Rosettes. It was tough, but we could see beyond that, and now we have a stunning new kitchen.

What are your favourite foods/ingredients?
We are having a lot of fun at the moment with our kitchen garden produce – peas, broad beans, corn, beetroot, carrots, and lettuces. Our neighbouring farmer Tom Wakefield produces fantastic quality organic Aberdeen Angus beef.

MARLBOROUGH
MAP 5, SU16

Three Tuns Freehouse
⊛ BRITISH

01672 870280 | 1 High Street, Great Bedwyn, SN8 3NU
www.tunsfreehouse.com
A welcoming and dog-friendly pub on the edge of the Savernake Forest, the Three Tuns combines the traditional charms of a local village inn with an excellent selection of carefully prepared tempting dishes. Everything from bread to ice cream is made on the premises.

Chef James Wilsey **Seats** 48, Private dining 34 **Closed** 25 December **Prices from** S £6.50, M £13.50, D £2.50 **Parking** 11 **Notes** Vegetarian dishes, No children after 8pm

PEWSEY
MAP 5, SU16

Red Lion Freehouse
⊛⊛⊛ MODERN BRITISH

01980 671124 | East Chisenbury, SN9 6AQ
www.redlionfreehouse.com
Along a narrow lane in a slip of a Wiltshire village, Guy and Brittany Manning's thatched pub is what most of us hope to find in a country inn. Inside, a big brick fireplace and bare-boarded floors, with menus chalked up on blackboards, set the tone, and the place is run with appreciable charm and cheer. The regionally based menus of sharply defined country cooking are extremely appealing. Chestnut soup with Brussels leaves, bacon lardons and chives might raise the curtain for wild mushroom and celeriac pithivier with Burbage shiitakes and brown butter, or roast quail crown with medjool date and foie gras samosa, king carrots, glazed Roscoff onion and dukkah. At the end, there might be classic crème brûlée, or stem ginger baked Alaska with poached Yorkshire rhubarb. Sunday lunches are a locally revered amenity, and the breakfasts are a thing of beauty too.

Chef Guy and Brittany Manning **Seats** 45, Private dining 23 **Open** All Year **Prices from** S £8.50, M £20, D £8.50 **Parking** 14 **Notes** Vegetarian dishes, Children welcome

RAMSBURY
MAP 5, SU27

The Bell at Ramsbury
⊛⊛ MODERN BRITISH, EUROPEAN

01672 520230 | The Square, SN8 2PE
www.thebellramsbury.com
A whitewashed coaching inn dating back 300 years, The Bell is a popular pitstop for walkers and visitors to nearby Marlborough. It has its own brewery, distillery and smokehouse, with much of the produce used in the kitchen coming from the estate and walled garden.

Closed 25 December

ROWDE
MAP 11, SP75

The George & Dragon
⊛⊛ SEAFOOD

01380 723053 | High Street, SN10 2PN
www.thegeorgeanddragonrowde.co.uk
This Tudor coaching inn in the unassuming village of Rowde has a reputation as a destination dining venue. The rustic country finish is part of its charm, while the menu makes a speciality of seafood hauled in from the boats at St Mawes in Cornwall.

Closed 25 December

SOUTH WRAXALL
MAP 4, ST86

The Longs Arms
⊛⊛ SEASONAL MODERN BRITISH

01225 864450 | BA15 2SB,
www.thelongsarms.com
Across the road from the church in the picturesque village of South Wraxall, The Longs Arms is a welcoming stone-built pub with traditional flagstone floors and a wood-burning stove in the fireplace. Everything here is made on the premises including the delicious bread.

Chef Robert Allcock **Seats** 46, Private dining 38 **Closed** 3 weeks January and 2 weeks September **Prices from** S £6, M £13.50, D £2.25 **Parking** 15 **Notes** Vegetarian dishes, Children welcome

SWINDON

MAP 5, SU18

The Angel

◉ MODERN BRITISH

01793 851161 | 47 High Street, Royal Wootton Bassett, SN4 7AQ

www.theangelhotelwoottonbassett.co.uk

Ancient oak panelling and flagstone floors confirm the pedigree of this veteran coaching inn, which continues life as a high-street hub of local goings-on into the 21st century. The kitchen keeps up with the times, sending out starters such as seared pigeon breast accompanied by a Merlot-poached pear.

Open All Year

TOLLARD ROYAL

MAP 4, ST91

King John Inn

◉◉ BRITISH

01725 516207 | SP5 5PS

www.kingjohninn.co.uk

You might expect a Victorian country inn on the Wiltshire-Dorset border to be a good bet for hearty English food, and the King John obliges. The chef is there all the way from field to plate, shooting most of the game himself.

Open All Year

WARMINSTER

MAP 4, ST84

The Milking Parlour

◉◉ SEASONAL BRITISH

01225 777393 | The Moonraker Hotel, Trowle Common, BA14 9BL

www.moonrakerhotel.com

Its age given away by beams, thick walls, fireplaces and stone floor, this was once the 500-year-old Moonraker Hotel's milking barn. A large kitchen garden, orchard and on-site smokery are key to the menus' offerings. The five-course tasting menu is highly tempting.

Chef Xavier Picquenot **Open** All Year **Notes** No children

WARMINSTER

MAP 4, ST84

The Bishopstrow Hotel & Spa

◉◉ MODERN BRITISH

01985 212312 | Borenam Road, BA12 9HH

www.bishopstrow.co.uk

Surrounded by 27 acres of grounds alongside the River Wylye, this creeper-clad Regency mansion is now a glossy country-house hotel with a cool contemporary spa. The kitchen team creates vibrant contemporary menus, supported by top-class ingredients from the estate and local area.

Open All Year

■ WORCESTERSHIRE

ABBERLEY

MAP 10, SO76

The Elms Country House Hotel & Spa

◉◉ MODERN BRITISH

01299 896666 | Stockton Road, WR6 6AT

www.theelmshotel.co.uk

Dating from 1710, this grand Queen Anne manor house has been a country house hotel since 1946, with 10 acres of grounds including tennis courts and croquet lawns. Produce from the hotel's kitchen garden forms the basis of seasonal menus in the elegantly-styled fine dining Brookes restaurant.

Seats 50, Private dining 60 **Open** All Year **Parking** 150 **Notes** Vegetarian dishes, No children after 7.30pm

The Manor Arms

◉ MODERN BRITISH

01299 890300 | The Village, WR6 6BN

www.themanorarms.co.uk

Originally dating from the 17th century, today's pub is a valuable part of the community, appreciated by locals and visitors alike (note the six classy bedrooms). The traditional decor inside is entirely in keeping and the finish is smart but informal.

Open All Year

BEWDLEY

MAP 10, SO77

The Mug House Inn

◉ MODERN BRITISH

01299 402543 | 12 Severnside North, DY12 2EE

www.mughousebewdley.co.uk

This Georgian inn is an entirely pleasing place, with hanging baskets adorning the white façade, and views of river traffic on the Severn. Lively ideas see a dessert of 'Pimm's Mess', a mash-up of meringue, cream, Pimm's syrup, strawberries, mint and cucumber sorbet.

Chef Drew Clifford, Mark Rhoden **Seats** 26, Private dining 12 **Closed** 25 December **Prices from** S £6, M £15.95, D £5.75 **Notes** Vegetarian dishes, No children under 10 years

Royal Forester Country Inn

◉ MODERN EUROPEAN

01299 266286 | Callow Hill, DY14 9XW

www.royalforesterinn.co.uk

This historic inn has ancient beams and plenty of nooks and crannies, but with boutique bedrooms and an on-trend bar, it chimes with our times.

The restaurant is the setting for classically-inspired dishes featuring Cornish seafood and some items foraged by the chef himself.

Chef Mark Hammond **Seats** 60, Private dining 18 **Open** All Year **Prices from** S £5.50, M £12, D £6.95 **Parking** 25 **Notes** Vegetarian dishes, Children welcome

BROADWAY
MAP 10, SP03

The Back Garden

◉◉◉ MODERN V

01386 852711 | Dormy House Hotel, Willersey Hill, WR12 7LF

www.dormyhouse.co.uk

Owned by the same family for over 40 years, Dormy House perches on a hill above Broadway, its origins as a 17th-century farmhouse evident in its golden stones, beams and panelling; these days the place is a swish bolt-hole with looks worthy of an interiors magazine, plus the de rigueur spa for 21st-century hedonists. Done out in sleek, modern style, the airy Garden Room looks through floor-to-ceiling windows onto a verdant backdrop. Culinary director, Martin Burge and head chef Sam Bowser have created a concept where every single dish showcases the best of the Cotswolds. Delivered by menus of cleverly constructed, contemporary British dishes, dinner might begin with smoked haddock tart with pickled onion, confit egg yolk and parsley oil, followed by braised beef cheek with pointed cabbage, cauliflower purée and king oyster mushrooms. Blackcurrant and custard doughnuts are a suitably indulgent finale.

Chef Sam Bowser **Seats** 50, Private dining 14 **Open** All Year **Parking** 70 **Notes** Children welcome

The Broadway Hotel

◉◉ TRADITIONAL BRITISH

01386 852401 | The Green, High Street, WR12 7AA

www.cotswold-inns-hotels.co.uk/broadway

The Broadway Hotel, overlooking the green, has its roots in the 16th century, so Tattersall's Brasserie, in a contemporary light-filled atrium, is in sharp contrast to its traditional surroundings. The kitchen focuses on quality seasonal produce and has an assured sense of what will work.

Chef Eric Worger **Seats** 60 **Open** All Year **Prices from** S £6.50, M £17.50, D £6.50 **Parking** 15 **Notes** Vegetarian dishes, Children welcome

The Fish

◉◉ BRITISH

01386 858000 | Farncombe Estate, WR12 7LJ

www.thefishhotel.co.uk

The sea is miles away, no river flows past, for The Fish is named after the hill on which it stands, because monks once cured fish in caves on the hillside. Forming part of a 400-acre estate, today's boutique hotel has an informal Scandi-chic style restaurant.

Chef Jon Ingram

Foxhill Manor NEW

◉◉ MODERN CLASSIC

01386 852711 | Farncombe Estate, WR12 7LJ

www.foxhillmanor.com

Foxhill Manor is a relaxed and home-away-from-home where the residents-only dining can be taken anywhere in the property, be it an intimate table for two or while catching a movie in the cinema room – even discussions with the chef are encouraged. The brasserie-style, modern, classic cooking has a focus on high quality ingredients and there's a compact well-chosen wine list too.

Chef Richard Thorpe **Open** All Year **Parking** 15 **Notes** Vegetarian dishes, No children under 12 years

MO NEW

◉◉◉ MODERN BRITISH

01386 852711 | Dormy House Hotel, Willersey Hill, W12 7LF

www.dormyhouse.co.uk

Up on the hill above Broadway, that quintessential Cotswolds honeypot, Dormy House started life as a humble farmhouse in the 17th century but has morphed into a slinky designer retreat with a glossy spa. The place is also a beacon of culinary pleasures, the latest addition being MO, an intimate and interactive dining experience that takes place around a marble-topped counter in a cosy space with a pineapple-themed decor. With just a dozen guests to serve, the chefs can deliver a remarkable level of precision in the seven-course exploration of tastes and textures. Expect technical showmanship and plenty of theatre and fun, starting with scrambled duck egg served in the shell with Jerusalem artichoke foam and grated truffle. Along the way, charcoal-grilled prawns turn up with rich bisque and lemon curd, while tender monkfish comes with black curry sauce and mung beans, and smoked rose veal fillet is matched with maple-glazed salsify and sprouting broccoli. The virtuoso performance ends with a confection of orange, rhubarb and cheesecake.

Chef Sam Bowser **Seats** 12 **Closed** Monday to Tuesday, lunch all week

Russell's

@@ MODERN BRITISH

01386 853555 | 20 High Street, WR12 7DT

www.russellsofbroadway.co.uk

In a prime spot on the High Street of this pretty, touristy village, Russell's is smartly decked out in contemporary style. Puddings get heads turning: a light plum soufflé, say, with subtle Earl Grey pannacotta, poached plums and frothy almond foam.

Chef Jorge Santos **Seats** 60, Private dining 14 **Closed** Bank holiday Mondays and 1 January **Prices from** S £7, M £15, D £7 **Parking** 7 **Notes** Vegetarian dishes, Children welcome

---

CHADDESLEY CORBETT   MAP 10, SO87

Brockencote Hall Country House Hotel

@@@ MODERN BRITISH *V*

01562 777876 | DY10 4PY

www.brockencotehall.com

Victorian Brockencote stands in 70 acres of landscaped gardens and parkland overlooking the waters of its ornamental lake. The place has been made over with a light touch that blends original features with a sprinkle of contemporary pizzazz. Sweeping pastoral views are best appreciated from either a seat in the Colonial lounge-bar or a table in the linen-swathed elegance of the Chaddesley dining room, or if you are going about things in the right spirit, one after the other. Tim Jenkins is in charge of the gastronomic show, setting high standards with precisely executed modern dishes – an opener of pan-fried scallops with pickled quince and chestnut velouté being a case in point. Main courses might see roasted venison loin next to Jerusalem artichoke, Oxford Blue cheese and elderberry jus, and technical dexterity is once again in abundance at dessert, when iced muscovado parfait with pear textures is a beautifully presented dish.

Chef Tim Jenkins **Seats** 40, Private dining 16 **Open** All Year **Parking** 50 **Notes** Children welcome

---

EVESHAM   MAP 10, SP04

Best Western Salford Hall Hotel NEW

@ BRITISH, FRENCH, ASIAN *V*

01386 871300 | Abbots Salford, WR11 8UT

www.salfordhall.co.uk

Originally built to put up monks travelling to nearby Evesham Abbey, Salford Hall is replete with historic charm, not least in its dining room, where oak-panelling, mullioned windows and a walk-in fireplace make for an atmospheric setting. The food is rather more contemporary, dipping into the global larder for inspiration.

Chef Mihály Bencsik **Seats** Private dining 40 **Open** All Year **Prices from** S £4.95, M £14.95, D £5.95 **Parking** 50 **Notes** Children welcome

See advertisement opposite

Fleur de Lys Brasserie NEW

@ MODERN BRITISH

01386 765611 | The Wood Norton, Worcester Road, WR11 4YB

www.thewoodnorton.com

In a mansion built in 1897 by the exiled Duke of Orléans, the Fleur de Lys Brasserie overlooks the terrace and gardens through large windows. The place goes for a casual mood, but its magnificent oak panelling lends a sense of occasion as you tackle an enticing menu of uncomplicated modern British dishes and straight-up grills.

MALVERN   MAP 10, SO74

L'Amuse Bouche Restaurant

@@ MODERN FRENCH *V*

01684 572427 | The Cotford Hotel, 51 Graham Road, WR14 2HU

www.cotfordhotel.co.uk

Built in the mid-19th century as a summer bolt-hole for the Bishop of Worcester, The Cotford Hotel is still in the rest-and-recreation business, its chapel now L'Amuse Bouche Restaurant. A main course might be slow-braised Welsh lamb with sweet Burgundy jus.

Chef Christopher Morgan, Craig Englefield **Seats** 40 **Open** All Year **Prices from** S £7.50, M £17.50, D £8.75 **Parking** 12 **Notes** Children welcome

Colwall Park Hotel

@@ MODERN BRITISH

01684 540000 | Walwyn Road, Colwall, WR13 6QG

www.colwall.co.uk

Colwell Park is a half-timbered inn on the borders of Herefordshire and Worcestershire. In a chapel-like dining room, the menu of locally reared meats, Evesham fresh produce and own-grown herbs is full of modern style where mains could be tenderloin and belly of superlative pork, teamed with a black pudding Scotch egg and apple purée.

Chef Richard Dixon **Seats** 24, Private dining 20 **Open** All Year **Prices from** S £6.75, M £18.25, D £6.95 **Parking** 30 **Notes** Vegetarian dishes, Children welcome

The Cottage in the Wood

◉◉ MODERN BRITISH

01684 588860 | Holywell Road, Malvern Wells,
WR14 4LG

www.cottageinthewood.co.uk

This delightful Georgian property has a
panoramic view across the Severn Valley from its
position high up on a wooded hillside. The aptly
named Outlook Restaurant makes the best of its
situation while the kitchen's rather refined,
classically inspired yet modern output is a
distraction in itself.

Chef Mark Redwood **Seats** 80, Private dining 50 **Open** All
Year **Prices from** S £6, M £9, D £6 **Parking** 45
Notes Vegetarian dishes, Children welcome

Holdfast Cottage Hotel

◉ TRADITIONAL, MODERN BRITISH

01684 310288 | Marlbank Road, Welland, WR13 6NA

www.holdfast-cottage.co.uk

Built in the 17th century and extended by the
Victorians, Holdfast Cottage Hotel is surrounded
by magnificent gardens with spectacular views
of the Malvern Hills. The hotel is an ideal base to
explore Worcester, Gloucester and Hereford and
there is a no-frills approach to cooking.

The Inn at Welland NEW

◉ MODERN CLASSIC *V*

01684 592317 | Hook Bank, WR13 6LN

www.theinnatwelland.co.uk

Firmly established on the local foodie map, this
rural pub sports a smart country-chic look in
shades of grey, with flagstone floors, tasteful
fabrics and chunky furniture. The view of the
Malvern Hills from the garden terrace is a slice of
heaven on a sunny day. Expect well-crafted
modern food with clear flavours and heaps of
local input.

Chef Hanjo Veenstra **Seats** 75 **Closed** 1st week January
Prices from S £5.90, M £14.90, D £6.90 **Parking** 40
Notes Children welcome

The Malvern

◉ MODERN BRITISH

01684 898290 | Grovewood Road, WR14 1GD

www.themalvernspa.com

The Malvern, the first spa resort in the town,
opened in 1910. Its brasserie is a fresh-looking
space of neutral tones, wooden tables and a tiled
floor. You might start a meal with Indian flavours
of pan-fried scallops on squash purée with an
onion bhaji.

Open All Year

OMBERSLEY
MAP 10, SO86

The Venture In Restaurant
◉◉ BRITISH, FRENCH
01905 620552 | Main Road, WR9 0EW
www.theventurein.co.uk

Behind the half-timbered façade of this
15th-century property is a bar with a open fire,
comfortable sofas and low tables and a
restaurant with bags of ancient character from
its ceiling beams and standing timbers.
Chef-patron Toby Fletcher stamps his style on
the Anglo-French repertoire.

Chef Toby Fletcher **Seats** 32, Private dining 32
Closed 25 December to 1 January, 2 weeks summer,
2 weeks winter **Parking** 15 **Notes** Vegetarian dishes, No
children

TENBURY WELLS
MAP 10, SO56

Pensons NEW
◉◉◉ MODERN BRITISH
01885 410321 | Pensons Yard, WR15 8RT
www.pensons.co.uk

A labour-of-love project has transformed derelict
farm buildings into this high-flying newcomer.
Pensons occupies a stripped-back, barn-like
space with sturdy rafters soaring to the vaulted
roof, bare brickwork and a stylishly minimalist
Scandi-inspired decor. With a kitchen garden,
as well as beehives, foraged goodies and
superlative materials from the surrounding
Netherwood Estate and local producers to draw
from, the food is unquestionably ingredients led,
and luckily Lee Westcott's team know how to
transform it all into creative and unpretentious
dishes full of contemporary verve. Sea-fresh,
raw scallop is served with yeast mayonnaise,
apple, kale pesto and monk's beard in an
exquisitely crafted starter, then the deeply meaty
bass notes of braised ox cheek are harmonised
with white kale and the sweet and sour contrasts
of puréed, roasted and pickled carrot. The
creative, of-the-moment ideas continue into a
dessert of luscious chocolate crémeux matched
with sweet beetroot sorbet and the balancing
tartness of damson preserve.

Chef Lee Westcott **Seats** Private dining 14
Notes Children welcome - must select from main menu

■ EAST RIDING OF YORKSHIRE

BEVERLEY
MAP 17, TA03

The Pipe and Glass
◉◉ MODERN BRITISH **V** ◤NOTABLE WINE LIST
01430 810246 | West End, South Dalton, HU17 7PN
www.pipeandglass.co.uk

The rustic bar has a smart finish with
chesterfield chairs and sofas, and a wood-
burning stove, while the restaurant is dominated
by horse-themed prints and chunky wooden
tables. The industrious and creative team in the
kitchen deliver arresting options - that all seems
entirely in keeping with the setting and chimes
with the times.

Chef James Mackenzie **Seats** 100, Private dining 28
Closed 25 December, 2 weeks January
Prices from S £7, M £11.50, D £7.50 **Parking** 60
Notes Children welcome

The Westwood Restaurant
◉◉ MODERN BRITISH **V**
01482 881999 | New Walk, HU17 7AE
www.thewestwood.co.uk

Owned by twins Matt and Michelle Barker, the
Westwood began life as a courthouse and the
building is full of character. Decorated in dark
colours with copper and gold highlights, it has a
contemporary feel, with an open kitchen and a
terrace for outdoor dining. The kitchen produces
confident modern British cooking, with simple,
effective flavour combinations.

Chef Matt Barker **Seats** 70, Private dining 20 **Closed** 27
December to 15 January **Prices from** S £6.95, M £15.95,
D £7.95 **Parking** 32 **Notes** Children welcome

■ NORTH YORKSHIRE

ALDWARK
MAP 19, SE46

Aldwark Manor Golf & Spa Hotel
CLASSIC BRITISH
01347 838146 | YO61 1UF
www.qhotels.co.uk/our-locations/aldwark-manor-golf-spa-hotel-york

When you're all done with golf and pampering, the contemporary, split-level brasserie of this grand Victorian manor in 120 acres of parkland will see you right on the gastronomic front. The kitchen delivers tasty combinations and there's a bustling vibe with attentive and engaging staff.

Chef Lucy Hyder **Seats** 85, Private dining 18 **Closed** 25 December, 31 December **Prices from** S £6, M £13, D £6 **Parking** 200 **Notes** Vegetarian dishes, Children welcome

ARKENGARTHDALE
MAP 18, NY90

Charles Bathurst Inn
BRITISH
01748 884567 | DL11 6EN
www.cbinn.co.uk

The CB – to its friends – is named after a Georgian parliamentarian, and the beamed dining room is done out with pale wood and generously spaced tables. Local farmers and fishermen supply its seasonally-changing menus of modern Yorkshire cooking.

Closed 25 December

ASENBY
MAP 19, SE37

Crab & Lobster Restaurant
MODERN BRITISH *V*
01845 577286 | Crab Manor, Dishforth Road, YO7 3QL
www.crabandlobster.co.uk

The Crab & Lobster Restaurant offers various settings in which to dine, from a garden terrace to a room hung with a profusion of fishing nets and pots. Traditional seafood specialities cooked with flair include fresh plump blue-shelled mussels in a hearty marinière.

Chef Steve Dean, Stephen Thomas **Seats** 85, Private dining 16 **Open** All Year **Prices from** S £7, M £14, D £9 **Parking** 80 **Notes** Children welcome

AUSTWICK
MAP 18, SD76

The Traddock
MODERN BRITISH
01524 251224 | Settle, LA2 8BY
www.thetraddock.co.uk

The Yorkshire Dales extend gloriously all around the character stone house, where a vigorous rendition of British modernism is the stock-in-trade, with overlays of various Mediterranean traditions. A white-truffled pumpkin and chestnut risotto is one way to start a meal.

Chef Thomas Pickard **Seats** 36, Private dining 16 **Open** All Year **Prices from** S £6.95, M £18.25, D £7.15 **Parking** 20 **Notes** Vegetarian dishes, Children welcome

AYSGARTH
MAP 19, SE08

The Aysgarth Falls
MODERN
01969 663775 | DL8 3SR
www.aysgarthfallshotel.com

When you're exploring the Yorkshire Dales, schedule a pitstop at this traditional pub with rooms in the pretty village of Aysgarth, whether it's for a pint of locally brewed Black Sheep ale or a meal in the contemporary restaurant overlooking the lovely garden.

BAINBRIDGE
MAP 18, SD99

Yorebridge House
MODERN BRITISH *V* NOTABLE WINE LIST
See pages 408–409

BIRSTWITH
MAP 19, SE25

The Station Hotel
MODERN BRITISH *V*
01423 770254 | Station Road, HG3 3AG
www.station-hotel.net

The Station is a venerable building in a village on the edge of Nidderdale, near Harrogate. The pick of the eating areas is the smart room that looks over the garden, but the main menu is served throughout. Classical cooking is given a high shine by Tim Bradley and his team.

Chef Tim Bradley **Seats** 60 **Open** All Year **Prices from** S £5.25, M £12.95, D £5.95 **Parking** 30 **Notes** Children welcome

BAINBRIDGE

MAP 18, SD99

Yorebridge House

◉◉◉ MODERN BRITISH V♦ 🍷 NOTABLE WINE LIST

01969 652060 | DL8 3EE

www.yorebridgehouse.co.uk

High-impact modern dining in the former headmaster's house

Dating from the dawn of the 17th century, the old Yorebridge grammar school is deeply rooted into this gorgeous location, although the present schoolhouse and headmaster's residence date from around 1850. Today, the trim greystone buildings make a living as a fine country hotel, with the luxuriant Yorkshire Dales unfolding all around, and Yorebridge's five acres bracketed by the rivers Bain and Ure flowing peacefully by. The public areas and guest rooms have been boutiqued to perfection, while an understated neutral contemporary style fits the bill in the dining room.

Dan Shotton and his brigade champion the region's produce in menus that reflect ambition and a desire to impress via modern British ideas executed with skill and creativity, but without undue complication. The kitchen's flair for comforting, intuitive flavour combinations

"The kitchen's flair for comforting, intuitive flavour combinations is clear from the off"

is clear from the off, as when chalk stream trout is lifted by crab and the earthy note of beetroot, or when beef carpaccio is teamed with salt-baked kohlrabi and deftly aromatised with truffle. Intense flavours show up in mains too, in well-balanced combinations of, say, Wensleydale pork with carrot and chicory jam, or Nidderdale chicken with morels and purple sprouting broccoli. Likewise, fish is sourced from trusted local suppliers, and might appear in the shape of superb halibut with cauliflower and dashi consommé.

Before moving on to dessert, you might consider the outlay on an impressive array of British cheeses to be money well spent,

particularly as they include some fine local specimens from Swaledale or the Wensleydale creamery, served with imaginative accompaniments of quince, pickled grapes and lavoche crispbread. The finale might be a virtuoso workout based on luxuriant 72% chocolate accessorised with hazelnut and milk. If you're an aficionado of rhubarb, you're in the right county, and could find it teaming up with white chocolate in support of a retro 'Caramac' parfait.

- -

Chef Daniel Shotton
Seats 35, Private dining 18
Open All Year
Parking 30
Notes Children welcome

- -

BOLTON ABBEY
MAP 19, SE05

The Burlington Restaurant
◉◉◉◉ MODERN BRITISH V

01756 718100 | The Devonshire Arms Hotel & Spa, BD23 6AJ

www.thedevonshirearms.co.uk

The Devonshire Arms may sound like a cosy village pub but is actually a country house hotel set in 30,000 acres of the Duke of Devonshire's estate, and The Burlington Restaurant is the star of the show, where chef Paul Leonard delivers food of craft and creativity, making good use of the estate's excellent produce (dining during the game season is a good idea) and the kitchen garden for herbs, vegetables and fruits.

Presented in various tasting menus (there's a veggie version too), in addition to the fixed price menu, his dishes are colourful, full of presentational artistry and precisely composed flavours, opening with salt-baked beetroot, perhaps, with smoked goats' cheese and beer vinegar, or langoustine with pig's cheek, fennel and granola. Meat and fish are handled with top-level skills, whether it's Yorkshire Shorthorn beef with spring fresh asparagus, morels and wild garlic, or superlative halibut from Gigha with spring peas, hispi cabbage and mussels.

The final flourish delivers wonderful flavours, whether Gariguette strawberries with sweet cicely and custard, or figs with yogurt and pistachio. The cheeses, too, are remarkable, selected direct from individual farms. Nibbles and amuses punctuate the whole experience in imaginative style.

Chef Paul Leonard **Seats** 60, Private dining 90 **Closed** Christmas and New Year (open residents only) **Parking** 100 **Notes** Children welcome

The Devonshire Brasserie & Bar
◉ TRADITIONAL BRITISH

01756 710710 | The Devonshire Arms Hotel & Spa, BD23 6AJ

www.thedevonshirearms.co.uk

The Devonshire Arms has a lot going for it, from its fabulous position on the 30,000-acre estate, the luxe bedrooms and the high-end restaurant, but don't forget about the Brasserie & Bar. The menu deals in upscale modern brasserie food, with a Yorkshire flavour.

Open All Year

BURNSALL
MAP 19, SE06

The Devonshire Fell
◉◉ MODERN BRITISH V

01756 729000 | BD23 6BT

www.devonshirefell.co.uk

The informal, friendly service here feeds into the easy-going vibe of The Devonshire Fell. The please-all menus are driven by quality ingredients, with simple pubby classics such as fish and chips or steaks thrown into the mix. There's a very good use of quality, local produce and the dishes are honest and well balanced.

Chef Rob Harrison **Seats** 40, Private dining 70 **Open** All Year **Prices from** S £6.95, M £10.95, D £5.95 **Parking** 40 **Notes** Children welcome

EASINGWOLD
MAP 19, SE56

George at Easingwold NEW
◉ MODERN BRITISH

01347 821698 | Market Place, YO61 3AD

www.the-george-hotel.co.uk

Smack on Easingwold's cobbled square, the George is the epitome of a traditional Georgian former coaching inn. It offers plenty of open fires, wooden beams, exposed brickwork and an informal mood alongside hearty pub classics and more modern food. Check out the ever-evolving specials board to see what the season's bounty has brought into the kitchen.

Chef Matthew Rennie, Richard Brooks **Seats** 40 **Closed** 25 December **Prices from** S £5.25, M £12, D £5.75 **Parking** 10 **Notes** Vegetarian dishes, Children welcome

GILLING EAST
MAP 19, SE67

The Fairfax Arms
◉◉ CLASSIC BRITISH

01439 788212 | Main Street, YO62 4JH

www.thefairfaxarms.co.uk

Popular with the local farming community, The Fairfax guards the village crossroads, one of which leads to Gilling Castle, prep school for the well-known Ampleforth College. The pub's black-beamed, open-plan bar and dining area leads out to a beer garden bordered by a stream.

Chef Ben Turner **Seats** 90, Private dining 50 **Open** All Year **Prices from** S £5.50, M £15.95, D £5.50 **Parking** 12 **Notes** Vegetarian dishes, Children welcome

GOATHLAND
MAP 19, NZ80

Mallyan Spout Hotel

◉ MODERN BRITISH

01947 896486 | YO22 5AN

www.mallyanspout.co.uk

Named after the tumbling 70-ft waterfall behind the hotel, the Mallyan Spout clings comfortingly to a traditional style of furnishing and decor – textured wallpaper, mirrors, high-backed upholstered chairs, that sort of thing. Old and New World wines are well balanced on the 50-bin list.

Chef Ross Oram **Seats** 50, Private dining 12
Closed 25-26 December **Prices from** S £5.95, M £12.95, D £6.50 **Parking** 30 **Notes** Vegetarian dishes, Children welcome

GOLDSBOROUGH
MAP 19, SE35

Goldsborough Hall

◉◉ BRITISH

01423 867321 | Church Street, HG5 8NR

www.goldsboroughhall.com

Princess Mary, one of the Queen's aunts, lived in this 1620s stately home until 1929. The Dining Room is small, with formally laid tables, a baby grand, and a splendid marble fireplace. White-gloved staff serve from the informal Garden menu, a seven-course taster, or the carte.

Chef Adam Thur **Seats** 60, Private dining 110
Closed 24-26 December **Parking** 50 **Notes** Vegetarian dishes, Children welcome

GRASSINGTON
MAP 19, SE06

Grassington House

◉◉ MODERN BRITISH

01756 752406 | 5 The Square, BD23 5AQ

www.grassingtonhouse.co.uk

The parquet-floored restaurant in this stone-built Georgian house in the market square is known for its traditional dishes prepared the modern way. Proof is found throughout the menu, so try starting with seared scallop and glazed pork belly, then Thirsk lamb rump with aubergine and roast red pepper, or pure and simple beer-battered sustainable fish of the day.

Chef John Rudden **Seats** 40 **Closed** 25 December
Prices from S £5.95, M £13.95, D £6.50 **Parking** 20
Notes Vegetarian dishes, Children welcome

GUISBOROUGH
MAP 19, NZ61

Gisborough Hall

◉ MODERN BRITISH *V*

01287 611500 | Whitby Lane, TS14 6PT

www.gisborough-hall.com

The hall is an imposing creeper-covered country-house hotel situated in well-kept grounds, and Chaloner's restaurant occupies a large space with pillars and a fireplace in what was once the billiard room. The kitchen team turns out some rather interesting dishes.

Chef David Sotheran **Seats** 75, Private dining 36
Open All Year **Prices from** S £6.75, M £18.50, D £6.75
Parking 180 **Notes** Children welcome

HAROME
MAP 19, SE68

The Star Inn

◉◉ MODERN BRITISH *V* ⓵ NOTABLE WINE LIST

01439 770397 | YO62 5JE

www.thestaratharome.co.uk

This thatched pub in a moorland village boasts a rustic bar, a dining room with chunky tables, a real fire and knick-knacks galore, and a more modern restaurant. The country cooking places a high premium on big, rugged flavours, seen in a main of grilled fillet of John Dory with Jerusalem artichoke purée, salsify, a lobster fritter, a poached egg yolk and celeriac ash.

Chef Andrew Pern, Steve Smith **Seats** 70, Private dining 10 **Open** All Year **Parking** 30 **Notes** Children welcome

HARROGATE
MAP 19, SE35

Clocktower

◉◉ MODERN BRITISH

01423 871350 | Rudding Park, Follifoot, HG3 1JH

www.ruddingpark.co.uk/dine/clocktower

Rudding Park's Clocktower boasts food that's worth a detour. It's all vibrant, colourful spaces, from the long limestone bar to the grand conservatory with its Catalonian olive tree, and a dining room complete with an eye-catching pink glass chandelier.

Chef Eddie Gray **Seats** 110, Private dining 14 **Open** All Year **Prices from** S £8.50, M £18.50, D £9.50
Parking 350 **Notes** Vegetarian dishes, Children welcome

Horto Restaurant

Rosettes suspended MODERN BRITISH *V*

See page 412

Horto Restaurant

Rosettes suspended **MODERN BRITISH V**

01423 871350 | Rudding Park, Follifoot, HG3 1JH

www.ruddingpark.co.uk/dine/horto-restaurant

The Rosette award for this establishment has been suspended due to a change of chef and reassessment will take place in due course.

Restaurants where the gardener gets equal billing with the chef are rare beasts indeed, but that's the case here at Horto, set in the 300 acres of landscaped gardens and woodland of Rudding Park, a classy spa and golfing hotel. The steward of the productive kitchen garden, Adrian Reeve, works in perfect synergy with the team to create dishes built on unimpeachable seasonal freshness. Choose between the concise carte or seven-course taster for food that brings together this peerless produce in exciting and adventurous ways. The menu restricts descriptions to three-word listings, thus scallop might be paired with potato and caviar, or superb Cornish turbot with mussel and parsnip. The umami notes of wakame seaweed and parmesan typically add depth to a principal dish of pork tortellini, while Nidderdale mallard is supported, perhaps, by beetroot and pear.

Seats 45 **Open** All Year **Prices from** S £12, M £27, D £12 **Parking** 350 **Notes** Children welcome

Hotel du Vin & Bistro Harrogate
◉ BRITISH, FRENCH, EUROPEAN
01423 856800 | Prospect Place, HG1 1LB
www.hotelduvin.com/locations/harrogate
The Harrogate outpost of the HdV chain occupies a luxuriously converted terrace of eight Georgian townhouses opposite the 200-acre Stray Common. With hops around the windows and mustard-coloured walls, the place bears the group's corporate stamp, and the kitchen makes a virtue of simplicity.

Open All Year

Studley Hotel
◉◉ PACIFIC RIM, THAI
01423 560425 | 28 Swan Road, HG1 2SE
www.orchidrestaurant.co.uk
In the Studley Hotel's Orchid restaurant, a multinational brigade of chefs delivers authentic regional flavours in an eclectic pan-Asian melting pot of cuisines. Mango and darkwood interiors divided by Japanese lattice-style screens make for a classy contemporary setting.

Chef Kenneth Poon **Seats** 72, Private dining 20 **Closed** 25-26 December **Prices from** S £5.90, M £10.90, D £6 **Parking** 15 **Notes** Vegetarian dishes, Children welcome

West Park Hotel
◉ TRADITIONAL BRITISH
01423 524471 | West Park, HG1 1BJ
www.thewestparkhotel.com
This contemporary boutique hotel occupies a lovely spot overlooking the Harrogate Stray, an open area of 200 acres of grassland in the centre of the historic spa town. In the comfortable modern dining room or in the alfresco courtyard, everything looks good on the plate.

Chef Pawel Cekala **Seats** 70, Private dining 55 **Open** All Year **Prices from** S £5.95, M £11.95, D £4.95 **Notes** Vegetarian dishes, Children welcome

White Hart Hotel
◉ CLASSIC BRITISH
01423 505681 | 2 Cold Bath Road, HG2 0NF
www.whiteharthotelharrogate.com
The White Hart is a Harrogate landmark, having provided bed and sustenance to travellers since the Georgian era. The Fat Badger Grill is its main eating space, serving up classic British food with a bit of a contemporary twist.

Chef Richard Ferebee **Seats** 100, Private dining 90 **Open** All Year **Prices from** S £5.95, M £9.50, D £6.50 **Parking** 80 **Notes** Vegetarian dishes, Children welcome

HAWES
MAP 18, SD88
Simonstone Hall
◉ MODERN BRITISH *V*
01969 667255 | Simonstone, DL8 3LY
www.simonstonehall.com
An old stone manor house, built to last, Simonstone Hall is a country-house hotel with a few contemporary surprises in store. The rural aspect may be timeless, and the decor soothingly traditional, but the restaurant's food is very much of our times.

Chef Sean Gavin **Seats** 40, Private dining 22 **Open** All Year **Prices from** S £6, M £12, D £6 **Parking** 30 **Notes** Children welcome

HELMSLEY
MAP 19, SE68
Black Swan Hotel
◉◉◉ CLASSIC BRITISH, FRENCH *V*
01439 770466 | Market Place, YO62 5BJ
www.blackswan-helmsley.co.uk
Set in a trio of ancient houses spanning the centuries from Elizabethan to Georgian to Victorian, the Black Swan is still a focal point of this lovely little market town in the 21st century, albeit with a rather smart country-chic look these days to offset the old-world charm of its open fires and antiques. The Gallery restaurant (so named because it doubles up as a daytime gallery showcasing original artworks for sale) is where head chef Matt Tyler gets to show off his skills and creative flair. Respecting the integrity of top-drawer ingredients is one of the secrets, as seen in a starter that pairs a beautiful salad of heritage tomatoes with deliciously fresh burrata mozzarella. Next up, whole lemon sole from Whitby, with cucumber, dill and brown shrimp butter, and to round things off nicely, dark chocolate fondant comes with native cherries and cherry ripple ice cream.

Chef Matt Tyler **Seats** 65, Private dining 50 **Open** All Year **Prices from** S £9.50, M £18, D £9.50 **Parking** 40 **Notes** Children welcome

Feversham Arms Hotel & Verbena Spa
◉◉ MODERN BRITISH
01439 770766 | 1-8 High Street, YO62 5AG
www.fevershamarmshotel.com
Sophisticated cooking built on fine regional ingredients is the order of the day here in The Weathervane Restaurant. The seared scallop with warm apple jelly, black pudding and smoked roe emulsion seems appropriate for a hotel in an affluent market town.

Open All Year

The Pheasant Hotel

◉◉ MODERN BRITISH **V** NOTABLE WINE LIST

01439 771241 | Mill Street, Harome, YO62 5JG
www.thepheasanthotel.com

The award-rich Pheasant, once the blacksmith's, village shop and barns, overlooks the duckpond in the charming village of Harome. The contemporary, even adventurous, cooking style produces carpaccio of braised octopus; butter-poached Isle of Gigha halibut; 60-day-aged salt beef sirloin; and warm chocolate tart with blackcurrant leaf ice cream.

Chef Peter Neville **Seats** 60, Private dining 30 **Open** All Year **Prices from** S £11, M £20, D £11 **Parking** 15 **Notes** Children welcome

---

HETTON   *MAP 18, SD95*

The Angel at Hetton

◉◉◉◉ MODERN EUROPEAN **V**

01756 730263 | BD23 6LT
angelhetton.co.uk

This 500-year-old inn has always had food at the heart of everything. In the vanguard of the gastro pub movement back in the 1980s, The Angel was among the first pubs to bin the chicken-in-a-basket mentality and offer inspired, imaginative cooking and serious wines. It remains a dining destination to this day, and the future certainly looks bright since Michael Wignall (formerly of Gidleigh Park) took over. A makeover has injected a brighter style to the warren-like interior to chime with the classy new culinary regime; like the food, it's certainly not pubby in the traditional sense of the word.

Wignall crafts complex dishes, layering crystal-clear flavours and textures into finely balanced creations, as seen in a starter of 72-hour-cooked suckling pig with puréed and roasted parsnip, wafer-thin crackling and sublime cider-enriched jus. Main course powers

ahead with fillet of aged Yorkshire beef alongside caramelised onion, wild garlic and forest mushrooms, and carrots boosted by cumin and coriander, or there might be turbot in the robust company of charred leeks and purée, cep velouté and Madeira sauce. A splendid dessert of über-rich treacle tart with crunchy caramelised walnuts and Dark Horse Brewery beer-flavoured ice cream is cut by the deftly managed sharpness of lemon curd.

Chef Michael Wignall **Seats** 65, Private dining 24 **Closed** 25 December, 2 weeks January **Prices from** S £9.50, M £21.95, D £6.95 **Parking** 40 **Notes** Vegetarian dishes, Children welcome

---

HOVINGHAM   *MAP 19, SE67*

The Worsley Arms Hotel

◉◉ BRITISH

01653 628234 | High Street, YO62 4LA
www.worsleyarms.co.uk

This Victorian hotel is well positioned in a pretty village set against a backdrop of the spectacular Howardian Hills. With its red walls, white linen and floral drapes, the restaurant is an elegant and traditional setting for fine-tuned dishes.

Open All Year

KETTLEWELL   *MAP 18, SD97*

King's Head Restaurant

◉ MODERN BRITISH **V**

01756 761600 | The Green, BD23 5RD
www.thekingsheadkettlewell.co.uk

This owner-run inn is a great base for leisure guests and keen walkers alike. Meals can be enjoyed in the cosy bar area beside an open roaring fire. It's all very seasonal and the blackboard-style menu allows for frequent changes and the best of local produce – expect a lot of game. Honest food, very well done.

Chef Michael Pighills, George Pighills **Seats** 34 **Closed** 1 week in November, 2 weeks in January **Prices from** S £6, M £14, D £7.50 **Notes** Children welcome

---

KIRKBY FLEETHAM   *MAP 19, SE29*

Black Horse Inn

◉ MODERN BRITISH

01609 749010 | 7 Lumley Lane, DL7 0SH
www.blackhorseinnkirkbyfleetham.com

A short spin from the whirling traffic at Scotch Corner, this stone-built traditional inn pushes all the right buttons for a northern country hostelry. The main dining room overlooks the back garden and delivers classic and modern British dishes.

Chef David Davies **Seats** 60, Private dining 12 **Open** All Year **Prices from** S £3.95, M £10.95, D £6.50 **Parking** 100 **Notes** Vegetarian dishes, Children welcome

KNARESBOROUGH
MAP 19, SE35

General Tarleton Inn
@@ MODERN BRITISH

01423 340284 | Boroughbridge Road, Ferrensby, HG5 0PZ

www.generaltarleton.co.uk

At this well-established, handsome, 18th-century coaching inn, the emphasis for their menus in the smart bar-brasserie and Orangery is on high-quality ingredients, skilfully prepared. Popcorn king prawns in crisp tempura batter with sriracha and tomato mayonnaise is an innovative opener which might precede Goosnargh duckling, black pudding, rhubarb and foie gras.

Chef John Topham **Seats** 64, Private dining 40 **Open** All Year **Prices from** S £5.95, M £14.50, D £6.50 **Parking** 40 **Notes** Vegetarian dishes, Children welcome

MASHAM
MAP 19, SE28

Samuel's at Swinton Park
Rosettes suspended MODERN BRITISH

01765 680900 | Swinton, HG4 4JH

www.swintonestate.com

The Rosette award for this establishment has been suspended due to a change of chef and reassessment will take place in due course. With its baronial tower and castellated walls hung with creeper, Swinton Park makes quite an impression. Within, there's no let up in its opulent public areas festooned with antiques and family portraits, and millions have been lavished on grafting on a glitzy spa. Samuel's restaurant is the jewel in its culinary crown, a suitably grand space, with its high gilded ceilings, carved fireplace and views onto the 20,000-acre estate. The kitchen celebrates the produce from Swinton's four acres of walled kitchen garden and the local area.

Seats 60, Private dining 20 **Closed** 2 days January **Parking** 80 **Notes** Vegetarian dishes, No children under 8 years at dinner

The Terrace
@ MODERN, INTERNATIONAL

01765 680900 | Swinton Park, HG4 4JH

www.swintonestate.com

The Swinton Park estate is well known for the impressive Samuel's in the main hotel, but if you're looking for casual dining with a relaxed atmosphere then The Terrace restaurant serves a globally inspired menu served throughout the day and there's a cosy bar area with a range of cocktails. The seasonally changing menus are focused around small gazing plates.

Chef Sam Miller **Seats** 50 **Open** All Year **Prices from** S £7, M £12, D £5 **Parking** 50 **Notes** Vegetarian dishes, Children welcome

MIDDLESBROUGH
MAP 19, NZ41

Chadwicks Inn Maltby
@@ MODERN BRITISH *V*

01642 590300 | High Lane, Maltby, TS8 0BG

www.chadwicksinnmaltby.co.uk

In a quiet village on the edge of the North Yorks Moors, you can dine either in the bar, with its wood-burner and sofas, or in the comfortable restaurant. Wherever, the dinner menu guarantees your full attention by listing Whitby crab and curry; pan-roasted Neasham beef with oxtail dumpling; and Hartlepool-landed halibut with lobster ravioli.

Chef Steven Lawford **Seats** 47 **Closed** 26 December and 1 January **Prices from** S £6, M £22, D £6 **Parking** 50 **Notes** Children welcome

MIDDLETON TYAS
MAP 19, NZ20

The Coach House
@@ ENGLISH, MEDITERRANEAN *V*

01325 377977 | Middleton Lodge, DL10 6NJ

www.middletonlodge.co.uk

The Coach House restaurant with its smart, rustic finish, soothing natural colours and a ceiling opened to the rafters, it is a stylish spot to tuck into fine Yorkshire produce treated with respect. The hard-working kitchen has a sure touch, with main courses such as soy-glazed duck with sweet potatoes and toasted seeds.

Chef Gavin Swift **Seats** 100, Private dining 20 **Open** All Year **Parking** 100 **Notes** Children welcome

Forge NEW

◉◉◉ CONTEMPORARY BRITISH **V**

01325 377977 | Middleton Lodge, DL10 6NJ

www.middletonlodge.co.uk/forge-restaurant

Forge restaurant and the collection of rooms around it, "The Dovecot" are the latest addition to this always improving estate. Set apart from the Coach House (itself a notable venue), the wonderful walled garden and the main estate house, this offers a slightly different experience. Dining in Forge is a real experience for the senses with Gareth Rayner serving up innovative, ultra seasonal menus featuring estate produce. The concise descriptions of the tasting menu give little indication of the delights to come – say, torched halibut, mussel broth; and white chocolate, cherry, marigold, almond.

Chef Gareth Rayner **Seats** 50 **Open** All Year **Parking** 100 **Notes** Children welcome

OLDSTEAD

MAP 19, SE57

The Black Swan at Oldstead

◉◉◉◉ MODERN BRITISH **V**

01347 868387 | YO61 4BL

www.blackswanoldstead.co.uk

Down on the farm on the edge of the North York Moors, is where the Banks family calls home. With foraging forays to supplement the growing of fresh produce, it's a very modern enterprise, which is to say it has taken on many of the attributes of the rural life of 200 years ago. James Banks runs a tight ship out front, while his brother Tommy works wonders in the kitchen. It's worth a wander around the kitchen gardens to get a handle on how your dinner will eventually come together. The tasting menu, which is the standard bill of fare, opens with the customary nibbles, and posts notice of the intent straight away: mussel and wood sorrel; Jerusalem artichoke; a langoustine with caramelised whey. You're offered sour butter to spread on your sourdough bread, then it's on to raw Oldstead deer, followed by scallop with razor clam and rhubarb wild ferment. There's more fermentation in the next dish, celeriac this time, which accompanies monkfish, followed by the signature beetroot, cooked for five hours in beef fat. There's aged sirloin with onion and lovage, and then cheese, which is optional, before rhubarb and clotted cream, hay and Topaz apples, and a final savoury of root vegetable toast.

Chef Tommy Banks, Will Lockwood **Seats** 50 **Open** All Year **Parking** 20 **Notes** No children under 10 years

OSMOTHERLEY

MAP 19, SE49

The Cleveland Tontine

◉◉ MODERN BRITISH, FRENCH **V**

01609 882671 | Staddlebridge, DL6 3JB

www.theclevelandtontine.com

Once an overnight stop for travellers using the London to Sunderland mail coach, this has been an iconic restaurant for the past four decades. Now modernised for contemporary diners, the candlelit dining room oozes atmosphere with its stone fireplace and rustic carvings.

Chef Luke Taylor **Seats** 88, Private dining 50 **Open** All Year **Prices from** S £7.25, M £13.95, D £5.95 **Parking** 60 **Notes** Vegetarian dishes, Children welcome

PICKERING

MAP 19, SE78

The White Swan Inn

◉ MODERN, TRADITIONAL

01751 472288 | Market Place, YO18 7AA

www.white-swan.co.uk

This charming, stone-built inn is very much at the heart of Pickering life and the kitchen philosophy is all about good Yorkshire produce. Rare-breed meats, Whitby fish and veg from the allotment all feature proudly in assured dishes like roast rump of local lamb with dauphinoise potatoes, charred carrots and mint jelly.

Chef Darren Clemmit **Seats** 50, Private dining 30 **Open** All Year **Prices from** S £6, M £14, D £8 **Parking** 45 **Notes** Vegetarian dishes, Children welcome

SALTBURN-BY-THE-SEA

MAP 19, NZ62

Brockley Hall Boutique Hotel & Fine Dining Restaurant

◉◉ MODERN BRITISH **V**

01287 622179 | Glenside, TS12 1JS

www.brockleyhallhotel.com

Located close to the seafront in the heart of Saltburn, this hotel has been lovingly restored, and the restaurant has a dark and opulent theme that works really well. For dessert how about a wickedly sweet apple tart Tatin, apple textures and ginger?

Chef Scott Miller **Seats** 60, Private dining 20 **Closed** 25–26 December **Prices from** S £5.50, M £10.95, D £5.95 **Parking** 14 **Notes** Children welcome

See advertisement opposite

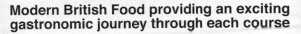

BROCKLEY HALL
BOUTIQUE HOTEL · SALTBURN

Modern British Food providing an exciting gastronomic journey through each course

Brockley Hall Boutique Hotel and Restaurant is situated in the beautiful town of Saltburn-by-the Sea, which has just been recognised as one of the top 10 places to live in Britain.

Saltburn is famous for its pier, water powered funicular cliff lift and Victorian pleasure gardens as well as its vibrant arts scene and huge variety of eating places celebrated in the annual food festival.

Brockley Hall is a beautiful Victorian building which has been restored in an individual and quirky style with a range of double, twin and family rooms and individually designed suites with freestanding feature baths, perfect for romantic breaks.

The hotel has a spectacular restaurant in which to enjoy our award winning fine dining menu, we also serve well known favourites from our à la carte menu. Our delightful hand painted conservatory and sumptuous lounge are ideal for sampling our lunch menu and handcrafted afternoon teas.

Our restaurant was awarded 2 AA Rosettes in the first year of opening for its fine dining menu.

Our head chef, Scott Miller, and his team of talented and inventive chefs will take you on a journey of taste with our unique menus which make the most of fabulous, locally sourced, ingredients. We are working with some of the UK's finest wine suppliers to provide exciting wines to complement your dining experience.

www.brockleyhallhotel.com

Reservations: 01287 622179

SCARBOROUGH
MAP 17, TA08

Clark's Restaurant NEW
◉ MODERN BRITISH

01723 447373 | 40 Queen Street, YO11 1HQ

www.clarksrestaurant.co.uk

A very tempting frontage is your gateway into this neighbourhood restaurant where the tables are made from Singer sewing machine bases. The room is dominated by the bar/servery and a big display of gins, including products from Scarborough and Yorkshire breweries. Locally-caught lobsters are a feature of the menus, which are seasonal and dependent on the catch of the day.

Chef Rob Clark **Seats** 30, Private dining 16 **Closed** 6–14 January and 5–11 November **Prices from** S £3.50, M £16.50, D £7 **Notes** Vegetarian dishes, Children welcome

Lanterna Ristorante
◉ ITALIAN, SEAFOOD

01723 363616 | 33 Queen Street, YO11 1HQ

www.lanterna-ristorante.co.uk

It has been honoured by Italian newspaper *La Stampa* as 'the English temple of Italian cuisine', which seems an extraordinary accolade for an unassuming, albeit heartily convivial restaurant. Chef-patron, tireless Giorgio Alessio, oversees a venue done out in reds, oranges, sunny yellow and sky-blue.

Chef Giorgio Alessio **Seats** 35 **Closed** 2 weeks in October, 25–26 December, 1 January **Prices from** S £7.95, M £15.50, D £7.50 **Notes** Vegetarian dishes, Children welcome

SCAWTON
MAP 19, SE58

The Hare Inn
◉◉◉ MODERN BRITISH **V**

01845 597769 | YO7 2HG

www.thehare-inn.com

The 13th-century Hare wears its age well, with a fresh whitewashed exterior, and a pleasantly understated split-level dining room of rough-hewn stone walls and unclothed tables. In case you weren't aware of the place's status as a culinary beacon, the exclusively tasting menu format (six or eight courses) is a heads-up that standard pub fare is not served here. Expect complexity and creativity in equal measure, and materials sourced from the pick of local suppliers in dishes full of dramatic flair. Things get going with stone bass alongside mussels, dill oil and wakame, progressing through a highly detailed two-way workout starring mackerel, and then a sumptuous main course of duck breast

and confit leg with creamy Tunworth cheese and richly truffled jus. The signature pre-dessert of nitro-frozen mascarpone balls with milk ice cream, honeycomb and a tricksy techno garnish of egg and honey makes a perfect precursor to a final dessert of raspberries with lemon verbena ice cream and gel.

Chef Paul Jackson **Seats** 16 **Closed** Annual holidays vary (see The Hare Inn website for details) **Parking** 12 **Notes** No children

SKIPTON
MAP 18, SD95

Macleod's Restaurant NEW
◉◉ MODERN BRITISH **V**

01756 748080 | The Coniston Hotel Country Estate and Spa, Coniston Cold, BD23 4EA

www.theconistonhotel.com

A host of leisure activities and spa pampering at this swish country house hotel on the 1,400-acre Coniston Estate will ensure your appetite is honed for some accomplished cooking. The culinary heart of the enterprise is Macleod's Restaurant, where you can expect charming old-school service and refined dishes that pack a contemporary punch.

Chef Simon Bolsover **Seats** 50, Private dining 30 **Open** All Year **Prices from** S £9.50, M £23, D £9.50 **Parking** 150 **Notes** Children welcome

See advertisement opposite

TIMBLE
MAP 19, SE15

The Timble Inn
◉◉ MODERN BRITISH **V**

01943 880530 | LS21 2NN

www.thetimbleinn.co.uk

Retaining all that makes a village pub such an asset, this Grade II listed, 18th-century coaching inn is squirrelled away in the beautiful Washburn Valley inside the Nidderdale Area of Outstanding Natural Beauty. Five miles from the Yorkshire Dales National Park, it's a popular pit stop for walkers in search of a pint of local ale. Warmed by a real fire, the comfortable restaurant showcases prime regional ingredients.

Chef Jamie Cann **Seats** 45, Private dining 12 **Open** All Year **Prices from** S £8, M £15, D £8 **Parking** 10 **Notes** No children under 10 years

WEST WITTON
MAP 19, SE08

The Wensleydale Heifer
◉ MODERN BRITISH, SEAFOOD *V*

01969 622322 | Main Street, DL8 4LS

www.wensleydaleheifer.co.uk

Dining on super-fresh fish and seafood isn't the first thing that comes to mind when you're in the heart of the beautiful Yorkshire Dales National Park, but this chic 17th-century inn with boutique rooms draws foodies from far and wide for its piscine pleasures.

Chef Craig Keenan **Seats** 70 **Open** All Year **Prices from** S £9.75, M £16.75, D £8.50 **Parking** 30 **Notes** Children welcome

WHITBY
MAP 19, NZ81

Estbek House
◉◉ MODERN BRITISH

01947 893424 | East Row, Sandsend, YO21 3SU

www.estbekhouse.co.uk

Overlooking the North Sea just north of Whitby, Estbek House is perfectly positioned to source its materials from the chilly waters out front and the rolling moors behind. It all takes place in a handsome Regency house that operates as a restaurant with charming rooms.

Chef Tim Lawrence **Seats** 40, Private dining 20 **Closed** 1 January to 10 February **Parking** 6 **Notes** Children welcome

The Star Inn The Harbour NEW
◉ BRITISH, SEAFOOD *V*

01947 821900 | Langborne Road, YO21 1YN

www.starinntheharbour.co.uk

An ideal harbourside location is the setting for this spacious restaurant with its delightfully styled fishing/nautical-themed interior. Catch-of-the-day fish and meat specials, sometimes from local game, feature. A separate ice cream parlour provides the desserts, but is also open to non-restaurant clientele. All in all it's very tempting indeed.

Chef Matthew Leivers, Ryan Osborne **Seats** 123, Private dining 10 **Closed** Certain periods in January **Prices from** S £6, M £12, D £6 **Notes** Children welcome

YARM
MAP 19, NZ41

The Conservatory
◉◉ MODERN BRITISH *V* ✦ NOTABLE WINE LIST

01642 789000 | Judges Country House Hotel, Kirklevington Hall, TS15 9LW

www.judgeshotel.co.uk

Dating from 1881, the Judges Country House Hotel occupies a magnificent edifice within 22 acres of well-maintained grounds that include a walled kitchen garden. The dining room is appointed in keeping with the age and the style of the property, with double-clothed tables set with silver cutlery and fresh flowers, and large windows as standard in the conservatory area. Service is on the formal side, but staff are friendly and keen to engage. First-class ingredients underpin the kitchen's output.

Chef Dave McBride **Seats** 30, Private dining 50 **Open** All Year **Prices from** S £9.50, M £27.50, D £7.50 **Parking** 110 **Notes** Vegetarian dishes, Children welcome

Crathorne Hall Hotel
◉ MODERN BRITISH

01642 700398 | Crathorne, TS15 0AR

www.handpickedhotels.co.uk/crathorne-hall

While the decor and furnishings of The Leven Restaurant are all early 20th century – oak half-panelled walls, heavy drapes at the tall sash windows, oil paintings, and a gilt-edged coffered ceiling – the cuisine tends towards modern British sensibilities, with sound, classical technique on display throughout the seasons.

Open All Year

YORK
MAP 16, SE65

The Bow Room Restaurant at Grays Court NEW
◉◉ MODERN BRITISH

01904 612613 | Chapter House Street, YO1 7JH

www.grayscourtyork.com

A great 'find' for any would-be diner in central York, The Bow Room Restaurant is part of the historic Grays Court, the oldest continuously inhabited house with links back to the 11th century. The long gallery (it's 90ft!) is delightful and features a bay window with views out to the city walls and the hotel garden. The impressive kitchen garden supplies the all-day food options, which features good contemporary British dishes.

Chef Joseph Clapham **Seats** 24 **Closed** 24-27 December **Notes** Vegetarian dishes, No children

Dean Court Hotel

◉ MODERN BRITISH

01904 625082 | Duncombe Place, YO1 7EF

www.deancourt-york.co.uk

Sitting on the corner of Petergate, Dean Court is an amalgam of Victorian buildings originally put up to house clergy at the Minster. Today, the dining room is a clean-lined, light-coloured contemporary space. The modern styling gives a clue to the orientation of the cooking.

Chef Benji Thornton **Seats** 60, Private dining 40
Open All Year **Prices from** S £5.25, M £12.25, D £4.95
Notes Vegetarian dishes, Children welcome

The Grange Hotel

◉◉ MODERN

01904 644744 | 1 Clifton, YO30 6AA

www.grangehotel.co.uk

The Ivy Brasserie in the cellar of this elegant hotel combines contemporary design with original features dating back to its Georgian roots. The kitchen has a modern attitude and showcases Yorkshire producers in dishes like Whitby crab and prawn ravioli, perhaps followed by roast pork fillet and croquette, apple, leek and sweet potato.

Chef Will Nicol **Seats** 60, Private dining 70 **Open** All Year
Prices from S £6.95, M £16.50, D £6.50 **Parking** 19
Notes Vegetarian dishes, Children welcome

Guy Fawkes Inn

◉ BRITISH

01904 466674 | 25 High Petergate, YO1 7HP

www.guyfawkesinnyork.com

The gunpowder plotter was born here in 1570, in the shadow of York Minster. It is a darkly atmospheric den with an interior akin to stepping into an 'old master' painting, with log fires, wooden floors, gas lighting, and lots of cosy nooks and crannies.

Chef Adrian Knowles **Seats** 34 **Open** All Year
Prices from S £4.95, M £12.95, D £6.95
Notes Vegetarian dishes, Children welcome

Hotel du Vin & Bistro York

◉ EUROPEAN, FRENCH

01904 557350 | 89 The Mount, YO24 1AX

www.hotelduvin.com

The York billet of the HdV group is a late Georgian townhouse in the vicinity of the Minster's Gothic splendour and the city racecourse. Bare tables and wooden floor fit in with the unbuttoned ethos, and the menu offers sturdy French domestic fare with minimal flounce.

Open All Year

Hudsons

Rosettes suspended MODERN BRITISH 𝑉

01904 380038 | The Grand Hotel & Spa, York, Station Rise, YO1 6HT

www.thegrandyork.co.uk

The Rosette award for this establishment has been suspended due to a change of chef and reassessment will take place in due course. The grand old Edwardian pile by the city's medieval walls started life as the headquarters of the North Eastern Railway and its handsome features and lavish scale were ripe for reinvention as today's luxurious hotel. The place boasts the sort of swish facilities we expect in the 21st century – classy bedrooms, a glossy spa, and an elegant cocktail bar for a sharpener before dining in Hudson's, a brasserie-style venue with a sophisticated sheen and professional service to match.

Seats 24 **Closed** 25 December (check website for additional closure dates) **Notes** No children

The Judge's Lodging

◉ MODERN BRITISH

01904 638733 | 9 Lendal, YO1 8AQ

www.judgeslodgingyork.co.uk/food-drink

The Georgian townhouse hard by the Minster has been reinvented as a modern inn of much character with a plethora of eating and drinking options. Dining can be elegantly panelled or domestic-cosy, and the all-day menus offer a wide range of international favourites.

Chef Katie Hoskins **Seats** 100 **Open** All Year
Notes Vegetarian dishes, Children welcome

Middlethorpe Hall & Spa

@@ MODERN BRITISH ♦ NOTABLE WINE LIST

01904 641241 | Bishopthorpe Road, Middlethorpe, YO23 2GB

www.middlethorpe.com

This majestic old building stands in 20 acres of gardens and parkland. The kitchen offers a fashionable surf 'n' turf combination of diver-caught roasted scallop with sticky pork belly, kohlrabi and apple purée. The cracking wine list offers good advice on food and wine matching.

Chef Ashley Binder **Seats** 60, Private dining 56 **Open** All Year **Prices from** S £11.50, M £24, D £8 **Parking** 70 **Notes** Vegetarian dishes, No children under 6 years

Oxo's on The Mount

@@ MODERN EUROPEAN *V*

01904 619444 | Mount Royale, 119 The Mount, YO24 1GU

www.oxosrestaurantyork.com

Cobbled together from a pair of Regency-era houses, Mount Royale brings a country-house atmosphere to the city. The kitchen combines simple flavours to good effect. Save room for lemon pannacotta with milk ice cream, honey, almonds and oat crumb.

Chef Russell Johnson **Seats** 70, Private dining 18 **Prices from** S £5.95, M £16.95, D £7.95 **Parking** 15 **Notes** Children welcome

The Park Restaurant

@@@ MODERN, TRADITIONAL BRITISH *V*

01904 540903 | Marmadukes Town House Hotel, 4–5 St Peters Grove, Bootham, YO30 6AQ

www.marmadukestownhousehotelyork.com

Marmadukes is a boutique townhouse hotel of the latest vintage, conjured from a Victorian gentleman's residence a little way from the medieval city walls. Antique furniture fills the public spaces, and The Park Restaurant is a bright conservatory space with a skylight and glass frontage, grey wood tables and matching walls hung with modern artworks. The drill here is Adam Jackson's four- or seven-course dinner menu, an extended showcase of quality Yorkshire produce and the kind of ingredient-centred approach that brings the concentrated best out of all elements in a dish. Principal components of each course are listed on the menu, which might open with sea trout, hispi and wasabi. Successful compositions include venison with carrot and red cabbage, pork with onion and wild garlic, and a simple but memorable dessert of blood orange,

chocolate and malt. For a supplement, there's the option of a cheese course, perhaps deliciously oozy Vacherin Mont d'Or with truffle honey.

Chef Adam Jackson **Seats** 24, Private dining 25 **Closed** 1–16 January, 12–20 April, 2–10 August and 25–29 October **Parking** 12 **Notes** No children

The Refectory Kitchen & Terrace *NEW*

@ MODERN BRITISH

01904 653681 | The Principal York, Station Rd, YO24 1AA

www.phcompany.com/principal/york-hotel

Located within the Victorian-built Principal York Hotel next to the railway station, the orangery-style Refectory Kitchen & Terrace goes to great lengths to showcase Yorkshire produce. Crispy cayenne-spiced calamari with crab and chive mayonnaise and a 'surf 'n' turf' of cod fillet and pig's cheek are typical of the modern British style on offer here.

Chef Rhys Jackson **Seats** 94 **Open** All Year **Parking** 100 **Notes** Vegetarian dishes, Children welcome

Skosh

@@ MODERN, INTERNATIONAL

01904 634849 | 98 Micklegate, YO1 6JX

www.skoshyork.co.uk

Skosh has made a big splash on the local and national food radar. Occupying a former shop in central York, a slate grey and vivid yellow colour scheme adds a bright and cheery vibe, as does the jeans and T-shirt attire of the relaxed staff.

Chef Neil Bentinck **Seats** 45 **Closed** 25–26 December, 1 week January, 2 weeks September **Prices from** S £5, M £10, D £3.50 **Notes** Vegetarian dishes, Children welcome

The Star Inn The City

@ MODERN BRITISH

01904 619208 | Lendal Engine House, Museum Street, YO1 7DR

www.starinnthecity.co.uk

This former pump engine house in a stunning riverside setting in the centre of York has been redeveloped into a modern bustling restaurant. There are various dining spaces, including a terrace and a cellar, but overall the decor has a pub-like feel.

Chef Monty Kanev **Seats** 140, Private dining 36 **Open** All Year **Prices from** S £6, M £14, D £6 **Notes** Vegetarian dishes, Children welcome

■ SOUTH YORKSHIRE

SHEFFIELD   *MAP 16, SK38*

1855 Restaurant

◉ CONTEMPORARY BRITISH

0114 252 5480 | Copthorne Hotel Sheffield, Sheffield
United Football Club, Bramall Lane, S2 4SU
www.millenniumhotels.co.uk/copthornesheffield
Bramall Lane, home of Sheffield United FC, is
also home to the Copthorne Hotel. The stylishly
contemporary 1855 Restaurant Is close to the
stadium and five minutes from The Crucible
Theatre. The menu offers broad appeal and the
on-trend British dishes have a pronounced
Yorkshire accent.

Open All Year

Jöro Restaurant

◉◉◉ BRITISH, SCANDINAVIAN *V*

0114 299 1539 | Krynkl, 294 Shalesmoor, S3 8UL
www.jororestaurant.co.uk
A converted shipping container off a roundabout
on the outskirts of Steel City doesn't sound too
inviting a prospect, but Jöro's urban edginess is
bang in tune with the contemporary trend for
neo-Nordic-influenced eating. Inside, the space
has a minimalist feel with bare wood floors and
tables decorated with flowers and baby
vegetables, the buzz of an open kitchen adding
to the convivial vibe. Despite the urban
surrounds, the kitchen team maintains a close
bond to nature, working with local farms and
foragers to provide a steady flow of seasonal
materials, and the small plate concept
encourages diners to try a salvo of different
dishes. Expect pin-sharp techniques and
combinations that pack a punch, starting with a
perfect piece of mackerel in miso-boosted broth
alongside kohlrabi pickled in buttermilk whey,
intensely sweet and smoky wood-fired onions,
and roasted yeast purée, followed by mallard
with red cabbage ketchup and blackcurrant jam.

Chef Luke French **Seats** 40 **Notes** Children welcome

Juke and Loe *NEW*

◉ MODERN BRITISH

01142 680271 | 617 Ecclesall Road, S11 8PT
www.jukeandloe.com
This small shop-fronted restaurant is situated in
a trendy area of Sheffield and serves up modern
British fare in a relaxed and informal
atmosphere. Expect rustic-style wooden tables
and contemporary, seasonal dishes which are
good on flavour and natural presentation.

Closed 1 week January and 1 week August

Nonnas

◉ MODERN ITALIAN *V*

0114 268 6166 | 535–541 Ecclesall Road, S11 8PR
www.nonnas.co.uk
Nonnas is a bustling, good-natured Italian
restaurant with friendly staff, café-style
marble-topped tables and green walls. This is an
imaginative kitchen turning out properly cooked,
highly original dishes. Among accomplished
secondi there might be the vivid combinations of
Merlot-braised oxtail with beetroot mash and
horseradish canederli (bread dumplings) and
grilled sea bass fillet with borlotti bean and
tomato stew and rosemary aïoli.

Chef Ross Sayles **Seats** 80, Private dining 30 **Closed** 25
December and 1 January **Prices from** S £5.75, M £14.50,
D £7 **Notes** Children welcome

Rafters Restaurant

◉◉ MODERN BRITISH

0114 230 4819 | 220 Oakbrook Road, Nethergreen,
S11 7ED
www.raftersrestaurant.co.uk
After more than two decades, Rafters contInues
to deliver the goods as a Sheffield dining
hotspot. Located on the first floor of a shop in a
leafy neighbourhood, the contemporary, grey-
hued room is smart and formal, while the set
menu is packed with interesting combinations.

Chef Thomas Lawson **Seats** 34 **Closed** 26 August to
2 September, 23–30 December **Notes** Vegetarian
dishes, No children under 10 years

Whitley Hall Hotel

◉◉ MODERN BRITISH

0114 245 4444 | Elliott Lane, Grenoside, S35 8NR
www.whitleyhall.com
Surrounded by rolling countryside, Whitley Hall is
a solid stone mansion dating from the 16th
century, set in 20 acres of immaculate grounds.
The restaurant may have a whiff of formality, but
the kitchen keeps ahead of the game with a
thoroughly modern menu.

Open All Year

WORTLEY
MAP 16, SK39

Ruddy Duck Restaurant
@@ BRITISH

0114 2882100 | Wortley Hall, S35 7DB
www.wortleyhall.org.uk

Wortley Hall is a grand Regency building in golden stone, with pillars and portico, set in 26 acres of lovely gardens and splendid parkland. The walled garden provides some of the fruit and veg used in the restaurant, where modern British cooking is underpinned by classic techniques.

Closed 25–26 December and 1 January

The Wortley Arms
@ MODERN BRITISH

0114 288 8749 | Halifax Road, S35 7DB
www.wortley-arms.co.uk

The Wortley Arms is an appealing spot for a pint of local ale and some modern gastro-pub cooking. Timeless staples (beer-battered fish and chips with home-made tartare sauce, or gammon steak with griddled pineapple) rub shoulders with more up-to-date ideas.

Open All Year

◼ WEST YORKSHIRE

BRADFORD
MAP 19, SE13

Prashad
@@ INDIAN VEGETARIAN V

0113 285 2037 | 137 Whitehall Road, Drighlington, BD11 1AT
www.prashad.co.uk

There is strong competition in Bradford when it comes to authentic Indian cooking, but Prashad's meat-free repertoire ensures a loyal local following. A mural depicting an Indian street scene provides a vibrant look, and food has its roots in the vegetarian cuisine of the Gujarat.

Chef Minal Patel Seats 75, Private dining 10 Closed 25 December Prices from S £6.20, M £11.25, D £6.95 Parking 26 Notes Children welcome

HALIFAX
MAP 19, SE02

Holdsworth House Hotel
@ TRADITIONAL BRITISH

01422 240024 | Holdsworth Road, Holmfield, HX2 9TG
www.holdsworthhouse.co.uk

Creeper-covered Holdsworth House was built during the reign of Charles I and boasts a suitably Jacobean interior. The restaurant overlooks the secluded formal gardens and it's a charming setting to enjoy precisely cooked dishes like ham hock, apple and parsley terrine, followed by roasted guinea fowl supreme. Sunday lunches are classic affairs.

Chef Adam Harvey Seats 45, Private dining 120 Parking 60 Notes Vegetarian dishes, Children welcome

Shibden Mill Inn
@@ MODERN BRITISH V

01422 365840 | Shibden Mill Fold, Shibden, HX3 7UL
www.shibdenmillinn.com

With milling abandoned long ago, it's left to the beams and exposed stone to remind us of its history. An inviting menu covers a lot of ground, ranging from a starter such as cured chalk stream trout, to mains like 65-day salt-aged pavé of beef with ox-cheek crumble; and vegetarian cauliflower arancini.

Chef William Webster Seats 80, Private dining 12 Open All Year Prices from S £7, M £14, D £7 Parking 60 Notes Children welcome

See advertisement opposite

HAWORTH
MAP 19, SE03

The Dining Room NEW
@@ BRITISH

01535 645726 | Ashmount Country House, Mytholmes Lane, BD22 8EZ
www.ashmounthaworth.co.uk

The contemporary cooking at Ashmount Country House is well focused on the best of local and Yorkshire produce – enjoyable flavours are a highlight. The dining takes place in a relaxed atmosphere, complete with log fire, in two rooms, both with views to the front of the house. Staff are very friendly and attentive.

Open All Year

HUDDERSFIELD
MAP 16, SE11

315 Bar and Restaurant
@@ MODERN V

01484 602613 | 315 Wakefield Road, Lepton, HD8 0LX
www.315barandrestaurant.co.uk

This place brings a touch of metropolitan chic to Huddersfield. The menu bursts with bright, modern ideas such as crab and lobster mousse wrapped in nori with ginger, lime and coriander dressing to start. Main courses are no less original and puddings are attractively presented.

Chef Jason Neilson Seats 90, Private dining 115 Open All Year Prices from S £5.75, M £19.50, D £7.50 Parking 97 Notes Children welcome

AN AWARD WINNING COUNTRY INN
NESTLED IN THE FOLD OF THE GLORIOUS SHIBDEN VALLEY.

OFTEN DESCRIBED AS A HIDDEN GEM,
TUCKED AWAY DOWN COUNTRY LANES,
THIS AWARD WINNING SEVENTEENTH
CENTURY INN IS THE PERFECT
COUNTRY ESCAPE.

Halifax, West Yorkshire, HX3 7UL. 01422365840

www.shibdenmillinn.com

ILKLEY
MAP 19, SE14

Box Tree

◉◉◉ MODERN, CLASSIC INTERNATIONAL 𝗩 NOTABLE WINE LIST

01943 608484 | 35-37 Church Street, LS29 9DR

www.theboxtree.co.uk

The Box Tree has been a name to conjure with since it first opened in the 1960s, and this traditional stone building, one of the oldest in Ilkley, is recognisable by its jolly hanging baskets and flower-filled front garden. The lounges and dining rooms have undergone an update, but it still has an air of luxury. Simon Gueller's classically-inspired food is bang on and firmly up to date, with refined dishes showing an elegant grasp of modern style. Dinner might begin with a delicious amuse bouche of mushroom velouté with parmesan and tarragon, followed by a starter of scallop with fennel, cucumber and capers in a fine bisque. Main course leg and breast of duck is accompanied by turnip, alliums, honey and soy. Dishes are beautifully presented and flavours clear and uncluttered. At dessert, look out for the seasonal soufflés – spring might bring a rhubarb version, with rhubarb compôte and vanilla ice cream.

Chef Simon Gueller, Samira Effa **Seats** 50, Private dining 20 **Closed** 27–31 December, 1–8 January **Notes** No children under 5 years at lunch, 10 years at dinner

LEEDS
MAP 19, SE23

Calverley Grill

◉ MODERN BRITISH 𝗩

0113 282 1000 | Oulton Hall, Rothwell Lane, Oulton, LS26 8HN

www.oultonhallhotel.co.uk

Surrounded by beautiful Yorkshire countryside, this handsome 18th-century mansion is well positioned for junction 30 of the M62. Named after the championship golf course outside, the elegant Calverley Grill is at the heart of the hotel and offers soundly conceived British menu that follows the seasons.

Chef Stephen Collinson **Seats** 150, Private dining 16 **Open** All Year **Parking** 300 **Notes** Vegetarian dishes, Children welcome

Chez Mal Brasserie

◉ MODERN BRITISH

0113 398 1000 | Malmaison Leeds, 1 Swinegate, LS1 4AG

www.malmaison.com

The Malmaison group's Leeds branch is decorated and furnished to a high standard after and the brasserie is no exception, with plush leather booths and fireplaces under its elegant ceiling. The cooking is built on quality ingredients, and talented chefs are clearly at work.

Open All Year

Fourth Floor Café

◉ CLASSIC

0113 204 8888 | 107–111 Briggate, LS1 6AZ

www.harveynichols.com/restaurant/leeds-dining

As the name suggests, the restaurant is located on the fourth floor and it has a similarly chic, minimalist style as other in-store restaurants in the Harvey Nichols collection. The dining area is flanked by the bar and an open kitchen.

Chef Lee Heptinstall **Seats** 70 **Closed** 25 December, 1 January, Easter Sunday **Prices from** S £6, M £18, D £6 **Notes** Vegetarian dishes, Children welcome

The Man Behind The Curtain

◉◉◉◉ MODERN EUROPEAN 𝗩

0113 243 2376 | 68–78 Vicar Lane, Lower Ground Floor Flannels, LS1 7JH

www.themanbehindthecurtain.co.uk

The determinedly monochrome basement room of Michael O'Hare's contemporary restaurant is in stark contrast to the culinary approach. While black marble tables and floor tiles offset the grey-veined walls, which are lightened with vertical displays of skateboards, marble surfboards and scrawls of incoherent graffiti, the black-shaded lamps illuminate plates – and many another receptacle – of cutting-edge experimental food that manages to avoid a lot of what have become the modern clichés.

The standard offering is a taster of 10 to 14 'sequences', with a digested version at lunchtime, built around a repertoire of dazzlingly imaginative dishes. A single octopus tentacle in butter emulsion has a strong hit of paprika, while a pâté of perfect crab is balanced on a crisp cracker and topped with a quail egg. Coarsely sliced, eloquently fatted Wagyu beef in olive juice with a sheet of potato paper is extraordinary in its impact, and the delicacy of judgment extends to a hake dumpling covered in hair-fine filaments of chilli for discreet heat. A dish that proved controversial on the BBC *Great British Menu*, O'Hare's fish and chips, is a model of concentrated refinement, expressively flavoured cod in miso broth with salt-and-vinegar straw potatoes, while a new spin on Rossini made with ox cheek is full of savoury, sticky richness. Creativity is unflagging to the end, which might feature milk chocolate mousse with honey and violet ice cream, cardamom and lemongrass soup with chilli sorbet, or potato puffs sprinkled with beetroot powder. It's all served forth to a soundtrack of throbbing rock.

Chef Michael O'Hare Seats 44 Closed 21 December to 13 January Notes No children under 8 years at dinner

Salvo's Restaurant & Salumeria

◉ ITALIAN

0113 275 5017 | 115 Otley Road, Headingley, LS6 3PX
salvos.co.uk
A lively, family-friendly and family-run restaurant, Salvo's has been on the Leeds foodie map since 1976. Looking smart and uncluttered after a refurb, the place will sort you out for some rustic and hearty southern Italian cooking. When only a pizza or a plate of pasta will do, you're spoiled for choice and won't leave disappointed.

Chef Geppino Dammone, Oliver Edwards Seats 88, Private dining 24 Closed 25–26 December and 1 January Prices from S £4, M £11, D £5 Notes Vegetarian dishes, Children welcome

Thorpe Park Hotel & Spa

◉ BRITISH, FRENCH

01132 641000 | Century Way, Thorpe Park, LS15 8ZB
www.thorpeparkhotel.co.uk/food-drink
With quick access into Leeds or the countryside, the modern Thorpe Park Hotel is a handy base for exploring the area. The split-level dining room has a contemporary finish with artwork on the walls, and black leather-type chairs. The populist menu offers feel-good stuff.

Open All Year

LIVERSEDGE

MAP 16, SE12

Healds Hall Hotel & Restaurant

◉ MODERN BRITISH

01924 409112 | Leeds Road, WF15 6JA
www.healdshall.co.uk
This stone-built, family-owned hotel is definitely worth leaving the M62 for, In order to dine in either the open-plan Bistro or its conservatory extension, furnished with wicker-style chairs and tables with tea lights. There's a more formal restaurant, which fills up on busy evenings.

Chef Andrew Ward Seats 46, Private dining 30 Closed 27–29 December, 1 January, bank holidays Prices from S £5.95, M £13.95, D £5.95 Parking 50 Notes Vegetarian dishes, Children welcome

PONTEFRACT

MAP 16, SE42

Wentbridge House Hotel

◉◉ MODERN BRITISH V ▓ NOTABLE WINE LIST

01977 620444 | The Great North Road, Wentbridge, WF8 3JJ
www.wentbridgehouse.co.uk
Set in 20 acres of landscaped grounds in a conservation village, Wentbridge is a stone-built grand manor house. There's a degree of glossy formality, where candy-coloured upholstery creates a light, bright effect, and the cooking reaches out in all directions for its references.

Chef Ian Booth Seats 60, Private dining 36 Open All Year Prices from S £6.95, M £15.95, D £6.95 Parking 100 Notes Children welcome

WAKEFIELD

MAP 16, SE32

Waterton Park Hotel

◉ MODERN, TRADITIONAL BRITISH V

01924 257911 | Walton Hall, The Balk, Walton, WF2 6PW
www.watertonparkhotel.co.uk
This Georgian hotel stands on an island in a 26-acre lake, with a modern extension on the shore accessed via a bridge, which explains how the attractive Bridgewalk restaurant was named. Dishes are admirably understated and flavours are to the fore.

Chef Armstrong Wgabl Seats 50, Private dining 40 Open All Year Parking 200 Notes Children welcome

WETHERBY

MAP 16, SE44

Wood Hall Hotel & Spa

◉◉ MODERN BRITISH

01937 587271 | Trip Lane, Linton, LS22 4JA
www.handpickedhotels.co.uk/woodhall
High on a hill with fine views, the Georgian Wood Hall retains much of its original detailing. Its dining room is an elegant, relaxing space where a rigorous dedication to Yorkshire produce is observed, and the cooking is marked by clear, distinct flavours.

Open All Year

CHANNEL ISLANDS

■ GUERNSEY

ST MARTIN
MAP 24

La Barbarie Hotel
◉ TRADITIONAL BRITISH
01481 235217 | Saints Road, Saints Bay, GY4 6ES
www.labarbariehotel.com
This former priory is now a comfortable hotel
with a soothing vibe and a restaurant using the
peerless fresh produce of Guernsey's coasts and
meadows. The kitchen looks to the French
mainland for inspiration in their repertoire of
simply cooked and presented dishes.

Closed mid November to mid March

Bella Luce Hotel, Restaurant & Spa
◉◉ FRENCH, MEDITERRANEAN *V*
01481 238764 | La Fosse, GY4 6EB
www.bellalucehotel.com
With its 12th-century granite walls, period charm
and luxe boutique finish, Bella Luce is a class act.
The culinary action takes place in the romantic
restaurant, where there's some sharp,
contemporary European cooking built on a good
showing of local produce.

Chef Patricio Felipe **Seats** 70, Private dining 20
Closed 2 January to 31 March **Prices from** S £9, M £15,
D £7 **Parking** 38 **Notes** Children welcome

ST PETER PORT
MAP 24

The Duke of Richmond Hotel
◉ MODERN, BRITISH, FRENCH
01481 726221 | Cambridge Park, GY1 1UY
www.dukeofrichmond.com
The Leopard Bar and Restaurant, with its
distinctive style and excellent quality ingredients,
has developed a unique identity. Guests might
choose to dine alfresco on the large terrace, but
those who dine inside will have a view through to
the open kitchen.

Closed 1st 6 weeks after New Year

The Old Government House Hotel & Spa
◉ MODERN EUROPEAN
01481 724921 | St Ann's Place, GY1 2NU
www.theoghhotel.com
The beautiful white Georgian building was once
the island governor's harbourside residence,
converted into a hotel in 1858. Among several
dining options at the hotel, The Brasserie is the
place to be, offering fresh Guernsey fish as part
of the menu at lunch and dinner.

Chef Robert Newall **Seats** 60, Private dining 12 **Open** All
Year **Prices from** S £11, M £18, D £7 **Notes** Vegetarian
dishes, Children welcome

St Pierre Park Hotel, Spa and Golf Resort
◉ BRITISH
01481 736676 | Rohais, GY1 1FD
www.handpickedhotels.co.uk
One mile from St Peter Port, this peaceful hotel is
surrounded by 35 acres of grounds and a golf
course. Overlooking the garden and with its own
terrace and water feature, the bright and
contemporary Pavilion Restaurant offers a crowd-
pleasing menu with something for everybody.

Open All Year

■ HERM

HERM
MAP 24

White House Hotel
◉◉ EUROPEAN, TRADITIONAL BRITISH
01481 750000 | GY1 3HR
www.herm.com
The island's only hotel is a real time-warp
experience, dispensing with TVs, phones and
clocks. Every table has a sea view in the
Conservatory Restaurant, where pin-sharp
technique and peerless raw materials combine to
impressive effect in the contemporary menu.

Chef Krzysztof Janiak **Seats** 100, Private dining 12
Closed November, January, February **Notes** Vegetarian
dishes, Children welcome

■ JERSEY

GOREY
MAP 24

The Moorings Hotel & Restaurant
◉◉ TRADITIONAL
01534 853633 | Gorey Pier, JE3 6EW
www.themooringshotel.com
Smack on Gorey's picturesque harbour front,
The Moorings has a continental feel with its
pavement terrace overlooking the sea and the
ruins of Mont Orgueil Castle. With the smell of
the sea in the air, it's no surprise to see plenty
of local seafood.

Open All Year

Sumas
◉◉ MODERN BRITISH *V*
01534 853291 | Gorey Hill, JE3 6ET
www.sumasrestaurant.com
Overlooking the harbour, and with fab views of
Mont Orgueil, terrace tables at Sumas are in high
demand when the sun shines. Needless to say,
there's plenty of seafood on the menu, from local

hand-dived scallops to brill or crab ravioli. There's a vegan menu too.

Chef Dany Lancaster **Seats** 40 **Closed** late December to mid January (approximately) **Prices from** S £8, M £17, D £2 **Notes** Children welcome

ROZEL
MAP 24

Château la Chaire

Rosettes suspended CLASSIC, TRADITIONAL *V*

01534 863354 | Rozel Bay, JE3 6AJ

www.chateau-la-chaire.co.uk

The Rosette award for this establishment has been suspended due to a change of chef and reassessment will take place in due course. Snuggled into a wooded valley, and yet only moments from the seashore, La Chaire is an early Victorian edifice with grounds laid out by the Kew Gardens luminary Samuel Curtis, and interiors full of oak panelling and intricate plaster scrollwork. The conservatory dining room capitalises fully on the majestic green views.

Chef Jason Williamson **Seats** 60, Private dining 28 **Open** All Year **Prices from** S £9.95, M £26.95, D £9.95 **Parking** 30 **Notes** Children welcome

ST AUBIN
MAP 24

The Boat House

BRITISH

01534 744226 | 1 North Quay, JE3 8BS

www.randalls-jersey.co.uk/the-boat-house

With its full-drop glass walls overlooking the harbour and town, The Boat House has staked its claim to the best spot in St Aubin. Light and airy with an open kitchen, the first-floor restaurant deals in fresh, modern and traditional food, mixing fine ingredients and confident technique.

ST BRELADE
MAP 24

L'Horizon Beach Hotel and Spa

MODERN BRITISH *V*

01534 743101 | St Brelade's Bay, JE3 8EF

www.instagram.com/lhorizon.hotel/

The view over the bay is a big draw here but the Grill restaurant really puts the place on the map. It's a smart room with neutral colours, and the menu makes excellent use of the island's bounty, in bright, modern dishes.

Chef Andrew Soddy **Seats** 44, Private dining 300 **Closed** 25 December **Prices from** S £7, M £16, D £7 **Parking** 70 **Notes** Vegetarian dishes, Children welcome

Ocean Restaurant at The Atlantic Hotel

MODERN BRITISH *V* NOTABLE WINE LIST

01534 744101 | Le Mont de la Pulente, JE3 8HE

www.theatlantichotel.com

There is a timelessness to a sea view of which it is impossible to tire, and the prospect over the hotel gardens to the blue briny beyond from the louvred windows of the Ocean Restaurant is the jewel in the crown of The Atlantic Hotel. Staff run the place with well-polished pride, doing things properly without pomp or undue circumstance, and chef Will Holland capably maintains the stellar culinary reputation the place enjoys. A taste of the sea is a virtual must, seen to great distinction in an opener of accurately seared scallops with salt cod brandade, carrot remoulade and sweet-and-sour carrot purée, a sensational marriage of sweet and salty savour. That could be followed by tenderly juniper-roasted venison loin with a breaded bonbon of the meat, smoked bacon choucroute, salsify and pickled blueberries, in a glossy, deeply resonant bitter chocolate jus. The showstopping finale is an apple study combining fresh diced fruit, flavoured marshmallow, sorbet and a tuile with praline crémeux and layered almond dacquoise. Chocoholics will gravitate to cacao streusel coated with Guanaja, with 70% chocolate gelée and coffee ice cream.

Chef Will Holland **Seats** 60, Private dining 60 **Closed** January **Prices from** S £15, M £30, D £15 **Parking** 60 **Notes** Children welcome

Oyster Box

MODERN BRITISH

01534 850888 | St Brelade's Bay, JE3 8EF

www.oysterbox.co.uk

The views of St Brelade's Bay are unbeatable from the Oyster Box, whether you're dining on the terrace or in the cool, contemporary dining room. A starter of Jersey rock oysters is hard to beat, followed by brill 'chop' served on the bone with spinach, Jersey Royals and brown shrimp béarnaise.

Chef Tony Dorris **Seats** 100 **Closed** 25-26 December **Prices from** S £7.80, M £15.75, D £6.50 **Notes** Vegetarian dishes, Children welcome

ST CLEMENT

MAP 24

Green Island Restaurant

◉ MEDITERRANEAN, SEAFOOD

01534 857787 | Green Island, JE2 6LS

www.greenisland.je

This laid-back beach café and restaurant claims to the most southerly eatery in the British Isles, so kick back and bask in sun-kissed views over the sandy bay. The emphasis is on fish and shellfish, and the kitchen has the nous to treat them with a light touch to let the freshness and quality do the talking.

Chef Daniel Teesdale **Seats** 40 **Closed** Christmas, New Year, January **Prices from** S £9.25, M £18.95, D £6.95 **Parking** 20 **Notes** Vegetarian dishes, Children welcome

ST HELIER

MAP 24

Best Western Royal Hotel

◉ MODERN EUROPEAN

01534 726521 | David Place, JE2 4TD

www.morvanhotels.com

In the hotel's Seasons restaurant, a predominantly white colour scheme, with lightwood flooring, flowers on the tables and comfortable leather chairs, creates a coolly elegant atmosphere, appropriate surroundings for some polished cooking. A decent choice of bread, all made on the premises, is offered.

Open All Year

Bohemia Restaurant

◉◉◉◉◉ MODERN FRENCH, BRITISH 𝗩 ▲NOTABLE WINE LIST

01534 880588 | The Club Hotel & Spa, Green Street, JE2 4UH

www.bohemiajersey.com

When a road sign in southern England points to The North it could mean a journey of perhaps a couple of hundred miles; not so in Green Street, St Helier, where an identically worded sign means an easy four- or five-mile trip to Jersey's north coast. The road soon passes The Club Hotel & Spa, in the shadow of Fort Regent, the island capital's 19th-century fortifications, and from the hotel's rooftop terrace there's a good view across this essentially low-rise town. A separate entrance leads from the street to the Bohemia Bar & Restaurant, the bar area itself providing an informal setting for lunch, dinner, drinks and afternoon tea, while the restaurant serves high-quality cuisine created by Steve Smith, its much accoladed head chef. Diners are presented with quite a choice of menus, among them a three-course lunch; the Classic; one for fish lovers; two tasting menus, one eight-course, the other a six-course Surprise, with optional wine flights; and the Prestige. A snapshot from the Classic reveals Cartmel Valley venison with cauliflower, almonds, cherry, nasturtium and bitter chocolate, while a quick scan of the seafood- and fish-focused Pescatarian discloses lightly poached Jersey oyster with pickled cucumber, dill and yuzu; and Smith's signature seared scallop with celeriac and truffle purée, apple and smoked eel. Diners taking the Prestige route might opt for a starter of butternut and parmesan velouté with Paris brown mushroom and quail's egg, followed by Brittany turbot with onion, smoked eel, samphire and mustard sauce, and close with Jivara chocolate crémeux and mango sorbet. Which leaves just a tasting menu, maybe offering the opportunity to sample foie gras cream with duck salad, sea buckthorn, orange and pistachio; Cumbrian Saddleback pork with sweetcorn, morels, chard-like monk's beard with cider; and beetroot and pecan cake with blueberry and yogurt.

Chef Steve Smith **Seats** 60, Private dining 24 **Closed** 24–30 December **Notes** Children welcome

Doran's Courtyard Bistro

◉ BRITISH, FRENCH, STEAKS, SEAFOOD

01534 734866 | The Hotel Revere, Kensington Place, JE2 3PA

www.reverehoteljersey.com

It's easy to see why Doran's is popular with the locals as well as with guests staying at The Hotel Revere. Service is relaxed in the cosy restaurant with stone-flagged floors and exposed oak beams, and the menu is simple but well done.

Chef Gary Skipper **Seats** 50 **Closed** Christmas, New Year, bank holidays **Prices from** S £5.50, M £12.50, D £5.50 **Notes** Vegetarian dishes, Children welcome

AWARD-WINNING BRITISH CUISINE

With views out to the marina, Sirocco is the perfect setting for a relaxed meal with friends and family or an informal business dinner. Watch as head chef, Steve Walker and his team prepare contemporary dishes that burst with island flavour.

Choose à la carte or the three course table d'hôte menu; there's an exciting wine list to match. Sirocco is also open for delicious breakfasts, with dining available inside or out on the heated terrace. What's not to enjoy!

FIRST FLOOR
THE ROYAL YACHT

DINNER
7PM - 9.30PM
EVERY DAY

RESTAURANT
Sirocco

Restaurant Sirocco@The Royal Yacht

◎◎◎ **MODERN BRITISH**
01534 720511 | The Weighbridge, JE2 3NF
www.theroyalyacht.com

Bright Jersey cooking with harbour views

Curvaceous, wave-shaped balconies echo the maritime location at this contemporary harbourfront bolt-hole, but it's definitely not an actual yacht. It's a slick, upmarket affair, with a glossy spa centre, plus ample dining and drinking opportunities to keep you refuelled and refreshed, the pick of the bunch being the snazzy Sirocco with its huge terrace opening up sweeping views over the marina through full-drop windows. A cosmopolitan ambience and designer-chic looks conjure a fittingly slick setting for pin-sharp modern British cooking. Steve Walker's menus are big on flavour and technical panache and put together with a keen eye on the seasons. A starter of pan-seared smoked foie gras comes with pear in various textures, plus rosemary and pistachio, or you might get going with the luxury of butter-poached lobster helped along by cocoa butter, parsnip and caviar. As you would hope, the

island's fine produce gets star billing among main courses – witness a triumphant partnership of well-timed Jersey beef fillet and cheek matched with morels, asparagus and deeply flavoured jus, or if you're a sucker for timeless tableside theatre, go for a classic steak Diane, flambéed at the table and partnered with Lyonnaise potatoes and green beans. Locally landed fish is also a strong suit, perhaps halibut with cucumber, sweet potato, oxtail and Roscoff onion, or a modern treatment of Dover sole, simply grilled and served up with kohlrabi, apple, crab and dill.

Desserts are also handled with impressive dexterity, as seen in a lovely looking and technically adept alliance of a chocolate sphere with salted caramel and honeycomb, otherwise you might take a

"menus are big on flavour and technical panache and put together with a keen eye on the seasons"

trip to the tropics via a perfectly risen coconut soufflé served with spicy mango sorbet. The evident balance and thoughtful composition in the food is reflected in a pedigree wine list that takes off in France then spreads its wings around carefully chosen bottles from all around the world.

Chef Steve Walker
Seats 65, Private dining 20
Open All Year
Prices from S £9.50, M £17.50, D £9
Notes Vegetarian dishes, Children welcome

See advertisement on page 433

Hampshire Hotel

@ MEDITERRANEAN

01534 724115 | 53 Val Plaisant, JE2 4TB

www.hampshirehotel.je

The Hampshire Hotel has a contemporary restaurant sporting a colonial look with rattan chairs, ceiling fans and pot plants. There are simple steaks as well as more refined options and a terrific value daily menu, with desserts running to the likes of sticky toffee pudding.

Chef Edwin Ombunah **Seats** 100 **Open** All Year **Prices from** S £7.95, M £25, D £4.75 **Parking** 28 **Notes** Vegetarian dishes, Children welcome

Restaurant Sirocco@The Royal Yacht

@@@ MODERN BRITISH

See pages 434–435

See advertisement on page 433

Samphire

@@@ MODERN EUROPEAN *V*

See pages 438–439

See advertisement opposite

Tassili

@@@@ BRITISH, FRENCH *V*

01534 722301 | Grand Jersey Hotel & Spa, The Esplanade, JE2 3QA

www.handpickedhotels.co.uk/grandjersey

The Grand Jersey is a rather splendid late-Victorian hotel with all the glamour and confidence of the Belle Epoque. There are wonderful views from the terrace, just a stone's throw from the waters of St Aubin's Bay, and a deeply indulgent spa. But that's all a bonus – you're here for the food. The restaurant, Tassili, is a darkly luxurious space that comes into its own in the evenings. Service is excellent, with a great eye for detail, and you can expect high-level French technique from Nicolas Valmagna and his team, taking inspiration from the island's produce and ideas from further afield.

An early spring menu offers a delightfully presented starter of Nantes duck liver terrine, full of flavour and richness, with charred sweetcorn providing sweetness and balance. Main course of Anjou pigeon, with cromesquis

leg and a vibrant candied heritage beetroot sorbet is a great dish, the pigeon perfectly timed and very tender, or you might choose a delicious cut of spring lamb, served with a subtle wild garlic foam, black garlic gel and violet artichoke. A beautifully constructed dessert of Valrhona chocolate with orange cremeux, sweetly peppery piment d'espelette ganache and Jivara chocolate sorbet proves an unexpected yet brilliant combination of flavours.

Chef Nicolas Valmagna **Seats** 24 **Closed** 25 December, 1–30 January **Parking** 32 **Notes** No children under 12 years

---

ST PETER

MAP 24

Greenhills Country Hotel

@ MODERN, MEDITERRANEAN, BRITISH, FRENCH *V*

01534 481042 | Mont de L'Ecole, JE3 7EL

www.greenhillshotel.com

There is much to like about this relaxed country hotel with its riotously colourful gardens, heated outdoor pool and bags of traditional charm. The kitchen team turns out a wide-ranging menu taking in everything from a classic straight-up fillet steak to more ambitious ideas.

Chef Lukasz Pietrasz **Seats** 80, Private dining 40 **Closed** 23 December to 12 February **Prices from** S £11, M £23, D £8 **Parking** 45 **Notes** Vegetarian dishes, Children welcome

Mark Jordan at the Beach

@@ ANGLO-FRENCH

01534 780180 | La Plage, La Route de la Haule, JE3 7YD

www.markjordanatthebeach.com

This white-walled restaurant truly benefits from its south-facing beachside location. Refined modern British cooking – but no fish and chips, they say – celebrates island produce like pan-seared Jersey scallops, and the Jersey Royal potatoes that accompany grilled plaice with prawn and cockle butter. More distant in origin is fillet of Irish beef. A proposed conservatory will replace the terrace.

Chef Mark Jordan **Seats** 50 **Closed** 23 December to 15 January **Prices from** S £8.50, M £16.50, D £8 **Parking** 16 **Notes** Vegetarian dishes, Children welcome

SAMPHIRE

RELAXED YET POLISHED

In the heart of St Helier, Samphire welcomes you to a relaxed atmosphere with all day dining choices. The Michelin starred restaurant boasts a series of contemporary menus using fresh local produce, from casual dishes to gastronomic plates, and a killer cocktail list. Unwind at Samphire in the main dining room, bar or choice of two terraces any time of the day.

All day dining | Open Monday – Saturday

Breakfast: 8.30 – 11.00 (excluding Sat) | Brunch: 10.30 – 14.15 (Sat only) | Lunch: 12.00 – 14.15
Afternoon: 14.15 – 18.30 | Dinner: 18.30 – 22.00 | Drinks: ALL DAY

www.samphire.je | 01534 725100 | book@samphire.je | 7-11 Don Street, St Helier, Jersey JE2 4TQ

Samphire

◉◉◉ **MODERN EUROPEAN** *V*
01534 725100 | 7–11 Don Street, JE2 4TQ
www.samphire.je

Sophisticated dining in a sleek setting

Gorgeously done out with clean art deco-style lines worthy of a 1920s ocean liner, Samphire looks stunning with its wooden floors, plush blue velvet banquettes and mustard yellow leather seating. The place will sort you out all day from breakfast, through brunch and onwards to killer evening cocktails in a lively ground-floor bar, a see-and-be-seen terrace on the street out front and, up on the roof, a garden terrace for those balmy Jersey days. And so to the food: head chef Lee Smith's menus showcase the island's finest materials in modern European dishes that borrow ideas from the global larder and are memorable for their depth of natural flavour and beautiful presentation – tender octopus, deftly accessorised with almond, whipped cod's roe and couscous, and boosted with pepper and lemon could come together in a thrilling starter, or you might open the show with a Japanese-

influenced treatment of tuna tartare, enlivened with miso, radish, soy and dashi.

Impressive, highly-detailed main courses are dedicated to delivering the essence of each ingredient, so monkfish could follow, its sea-fresh flavour accentuated by carrot, lemongrass and the Indian spicing of vadouvan sauce and Bombay mix. Meat, too, is handled with aplomb – pork belly might get an Iberian spin with morcilla sausage, romesco sauce, fennel and apple ketchup, while classic beef fillet Rossini with foie gras and Madeira sauce assuages luxury-seeking traditionalists.

At the opposing ideological end of the culinary spectrum, meat avoiders are not sidelined: a dedicated vegan menu comes up with ideas such as tagliatelle with mushrooms, truffle oil and fresh herbs, while beetroot tartare and sorbet might be boosted by dukkah spices and balsamic. Attention to detail is spot-on, all the way through to masterfully executed desserts such as rhubarb Pavlova with vanilla ice cream, rhubarb sorbet and white chocolate, or a super-indulgent chocolate workout involving millefeuille, dark and white chocolate crémeux and chocolate sorbet.

Chef Lee Smith
Seats 50, Private dining 14
Closed 25 December
Prices from S £10, M £18, D £9.50
Notes Children welcome

See advertisement on page 437

ST SAVIOUR

MAP 24

Longueville Manor Hotel

◎◎◎ MODERN ANGLO-FRENCH V NOTABLE WINE LIST

01534 725501 | JE2 7WF

www.longuevillemanor.com

Set on a lovely 18-acre estate, with woodland walks, restored Victorian kitchen garden, and a lake, Longueville Manor has been the grande dame of the Jersey hotel scene since the 1940s. Andrew Baird's kitchen focuses on local produce – plenty of which comes from that beautiful kitchen garden – and the cooking is a refined, innovative Anglo-French take on classic techniques. The Oak Room is a wonderfully atmospheric panelled dining room, a delightful setting for compelling dishes inspired by wonderful produce. Start with impeccable, perfectly-timed scallops served with caramelised apple, apple, cider butter sauce, crisp pancetta and potato rösti, perhaps, followed by a beautifully cooked piece of turbot with a vibrant Beaufort crust, fricassee of woodland mushrooms and salsify. Bring things to a close with a superbly fresh-tasting garden lemon mousse, accompanied by a ginger sable and gin and tonic sorbet. The state-of-the-art wine cellar, home to some 4,500 bottles, needs to be seen to be believed.

Chef Andrew Baird **Seats** 65, Private dining 40 **Open** All Year **Parking** 45 **Notes** Children welcome

■ SARK

SARK

MAP 24

Stocks Hotel

◎◎◎ MODERN BRITISH

01481 832001 | GY10 1SD

www.stockshotel.com

Tucked away in a tranquil and picturesque valley – but then again just about everywhere on Sark is quiet and picturesque – Stocks is a smart hotel built around a Georgian farmhouse. It's done out in a traditional manner, and that goes for the fine-dining restaurant, too. With its opulent drapes and white tablecloths, the panelled dining room provides a traditional and formal setting for technically adept cooking that pays its dues to modern ideas and is also – thanks to a kitchen that has close links with local fishermen and farms – solidly ingredient driven. Citrus-cured monkfish with gin-infused cucumber, borage and yogurt is a fresh and vivid starter, and the bar stays high for a dish of Guernsey turbot with braised chicken wings, baby gem, Jerusalem artichoke and chicken jus. A perfectly risen coconut soufflé partnered with coconut sorbet and a zippy pineapple and chilli salsa is proof that desserts are a major strength too.

Chef Daniel Wood **Seats** 60, Private dining 12 **Closed** 2 January to 1 March **Prices from** S £12.50, M £25, D £12.50 **Parking** 36 **Notes** Vegetarian dishes, Children welcome

SCOTLAND

■ ABERDEEN

ABERDEEN
MAP 23, NJ90

Chez Mal Brasserie
◉ MODERN FRENCH
01224 327370 | Malmaison Aberdeen,
49-53 Queens Road, AB15 4YP
www.malmaisonaberdeen.com
Built from the solid granite that gives the city its moniker, the Aberdeen Mal is suitably dashing, with boutique allure and a cool industrial-chic finish. The brasserie is at the heart of the operation, with an open-to-view kitchen revealing the Josper grill.

Open All Year

IX Restaurant
◉◉ MODERN SCOTTISH
01244 327777 | The Chester Hotel, 59-63 Queens Road, AB15 4YP
www.chester-hotel.com
The kitchen team behind this glossy contemporary grill are on a mission to be one of Aberdeen's top restaurants, and their switched-on menu is heading straight for that target. Happily, the food here is about great flavours rather than ego.

Chef Kevin Dalgleish Seats 85, Private dining 22
Open All Year Prices from S £8, M £18, D £9 Parking 77
Notes Vegetarian dishes, Children welcome

Moonfish Café
◉ MODERN BRITISH
01224 644166 | 9 Correction Wynd, AB10 1HP
www.moonfishcafe.co.uk
Tucked away in a medieval wynd, or narrow lane, Moonfish Café has that fit-for-purpose, ready-to-go look about it. And go it does, with innovative modern British cooking, perhaps opening with crispy potato, cheese custard and Madras curry, then hake with onion, rice and brown butter, ending with rhubarb millefeuille, mascarpone and vanilla.

Chef Brian McLeish Seats 36 Closed 25-26 December,
1 January, 1st 2 weeks January Notes Vegetarian
dishes, Children welcome

The Silver Darling
◉◉ SEAFOOD
01224 576229 | Pocra Quay, North Pier, AB11 5DQ
www.thesilverdarling.co.uk
A refurbished harbour-mouth restaurant specialising in fish and seafood in the old customs house, whose huge windows provide a ringside view of trawlers off to catch it. Indubitably Scottish are Loch Fyne oysters and Cullen skink starters; although they sound more cosmopolitan, mains such as pan-seared monkfish, sole goujons, chargrilled steak and seasonal game are just as patriotic.

Chef Craig Somers Seats 62, Private dining 12
Closed 25-26 December, 1-2 January Prices from S £7,
M £14, D £7 Notes Vegetarian dishes, Children welcome

■ ABERDEENSHIRE

BALLATER
MAP 23, NO39

Loch Kinord Hotel
◉ TRADITIONAL SCOTTISH
01339 885229 | Ballater Road, Dinnet, AB34 5JY
www.lochkinord.com
Built in granite in Victorian times, Loch Kinord has homely lounges with real fires, a small bar and a dining room done out with tartan wallpaper and plush red and gold carpets. There's a classical leaning to the kitchen's output.

Open All Year

BALMEDIE
MAP 23, NJ91

The Cock and Bull
◉ MODERN SCOTTISH, BRITISH
01358 743249 | Ellon Road, Blairton, AB23 8XY
www.thecockandbull.co.uk
Open fires and modern artworks bring cossetting warmth to this creeper-clad, stone-built coaching inn standing in open farmland north of Aberdeen. You can be sure of a well-kept pint and no-nonsense food ranging from pub classics to more accomplished dishes based on Peterhead-landed fish and shellfish, or regionally sourced meats.

Chef Ric Broadwith Seats 80, Private dining 30
Closed 26 December, 2 January Prices from S £5,
M £10.95, D £6.95 Parking 50 Notes Vegetarian
dishes, Children welcome

BANCHORY
MAP 23, NO69

The Falls of Feugh Restaurant
◉ MODERN BRITISH
01330 822123 | Bridge of Feugh, AB31 6NL
www.thefallsoffeugh.com
In a bucolic spot by the river, surrounded by trees, the sound of running water is particularly evocative if you're sitting on the small terrace. There's a charming café, but the main draw is the

modern French- and Scottish-inflected food on offer in the restaurant.

Chef John Chomba **Seats** 96, Private dining 40 **Closed** 1 January **Prices from** S £5, M £14.95, D £6 **Parking** 20 **Notes** Vegetarian dishes, Children welcome

The Tornacoille Restaurant

◉◉ MODERN BRITISH

01330 822242 | Tor Na Coille Hotel & Restaurant, Inchmarlo Road, AB31 4AB

www.tornacoille.com

Peeping out from the trees in acres of wooded grounds, the Victorian granite mansion has become a smart country-house hotel, with a classy but relaxed restaurant providing appetising views of the surrounding countryside. It's a glorious setting for seasonally astute menus of modern food with sound classical roots.

Open All Year

ELLON *MAP 23, NJ93*

Eat on the Green

◉◉ BRITISH, SCOTTISH, EUROPEAN

01651 842337 | Udny Green, AB41 7RS

www.eatonthegreen.co.uk

In a picture-perfect Scottish stone house with a gloriously inviting interior of rich colours, Eat on the Green is going from strength to strength. Attention to detail is everything for the 'kilted chef' here, with vegetables and herbs picked from their own gardens and meat and game arriving from local farms. They have a 'Gin Garden' too.

Chef Craig Wilson **Seats** 48, Private dining 16 **Closed** 1 week January **Parking** 7 **Notes** Vegetarian dishes, Children welcome

---

KILDRUMMY *MAP 23, NJ41*

Kildrummy Inn

◉◉ MODERN SCOTTISH

01975 571227 | AB33 8QS

www.kildrummyinn.co.uk

Kildrummy Inn has an authenticity that appeals to tourists and locals, while the output from its dynamic kitchen has put it on the foodie map. Menus reveal classical sensibilities and a contemporary touch and flavours hit the mark when it comes to desserts, too.

Closed January

OLDMELDRUM *MAP 23, NJ82*

Meldrum House Country Hotel & Golf Course

◉◉ MODERN SCOTTISH

01651 872294 | AB51 0AE

www.meldrumhouse.com

Even if you're not nifty with a niblick, Meldrum House is a good place to marinate in the luxury of a turreted baronial pile. The traditional country-house hotel has 350 acres of wooded parkland and is a lovely setting for the Scottish country-house cooking.

Chef Paul Grant **Seats** 70, Private dining 30 **Open** All Year **Prices from** S £7, M £20, D £9 **Parking** 70 **Notes** Vegetarian dishes, Children welcome

---

PETERHEAD *MAP 23, NK14*

Buchan Braes Hotel

◉ MODERN SCOTTISH, EUROPEAN

01779 871471 | Boddam, AB42 3AR

www.buchanbraes.co.uk

The low-slung Buchan Braes won't win any architectural prizes, but it's a splendid contemporary hotel with a rural aspect and up-to-date wedding and conference facilities to boot. There's also the Grill Room restaurant, with its open kitchen and warmly colourful decor.

Chef Paul McLean **Seats** 70, Private dining 80 **Open** All Year **Prices from** S £6.50, M £14.95, D £7 **Parking** 100 **Notes** Vegetarian dishes, Children welcome

---

STONEHAVEN *MAP 23, NO88*

The Tolbooth Seafood Restaurant

◉ MODERN BRITISH, SEAFOOD

01569 762287 | Old Pier, Stonehaven Harbour, AB39 2JU

www.tolbooth-restaurant.co.uk

There can't be many better spots than this for tucking into seafood: it's right on the harbour wall, with a museum on the ground floor and the upstairs restaurant giving sea views. What you eat depends on what's been landed that day.

Chef Tyron Ellul **Seats** 46 **Closed** 1st 3 weeks in January **Prices from** S £7.50, M £16.50, D £6.50 **Notes** Vegetarian dishes, Children welcome

TARLAND
MAP 23, NJ40

Douneside House

⊚⊚⊚ CLASSIC

013398 81230 | AB34 4UL

www.dounesidehouse.co.uk

Initially bought as a holiday home by the MacRobert family in the 1880s, Douneside was creatively enhanced with a crenellated tower and extra rooms, and presents a pleasingly asymmetrical façade to the world. The family trust still oversees the running of the place, from its excellent gardens to the fully equipped spa hotel. Completing the picture is a dynamic kitchen supplied by an industrious kitchen garden, fish from the Peterhead boats, and meat from a local butcher with a royal warrant. David Butters combines forward-looking culinary thinking with plenty of old-school opulence on menus that might open with new season asparagus and truffle mousse, with a salad of raw and pickled vegetables and aged parmesan. Move on to loin and belly of Fife pork, or seared fillet of halibut, before finishing triumphantly with rhubarb bavarois with vanilla custard, ginger ale and rhubarb sorbet. There's a five-course tasting menu too, available Thursday to Saturday.

Chef David Butters **Seats** 40, Private dining 12 **Open** All Year **Parking** 40 **Notes** Vegetarian dishes, Children welcome

◼ ANGUS

CARNOUSTIE
MAP 21, NO53

Carnoustie Golf Hotel & Spa

⊚ BISTRO, SCOTTISH, EUROPEAN

01241 411999 | The Links, DD7 7JE

www.bespokehotels.com/carnoustiegolfhotel

Calder's Bistro enjoys a stunning location overlooking the 1st tee and 18th green of the world-famous Carnoustie Links golf course. With floor-to-ceiling windows providing impressive views of the golf course, this makes a pleasant place to sample an eclectic range of dishes.

Open All Year

FORFAR
MAP 23, NO45

Drovers

⊚ MODERN SCOTTISH

01307 860322 | Memus By Forfar, DD8 3TY

www.the-drovers.com

Surrounded by beautiful glens, Drovers is the kind of wild place you want to be stranded when the weather closes in. Although a modern pub in many ways, the walls of antlers remind you this rustic bolt-hole has been around for many years.

Open All Year

INVERKEILOR
MAP 23, NO64

Gordon's

⊚⊚⊚ MODERN SCOTTISH

01241 830364 | Main Street, DD11 5RN

www.gordonsrestaurant.co.uk

Blink, and you'd miss the tiny coastal hamlet of Inverkeilor, were it not for for the discreet restaurant with rooms along the high street that's put the village on the map of gastronomic destinations. Thanks to the Watson family's efforts over 30-odd years, the place ticks all the boxes for a food-and-sea-themed getaway, with boutique rooms and a beamed and stone-walled dining room. These days, Gordon's son Garry heads up the kitchen side of things, keeping all-comers on side with his precise modern Scottish cooking. The drill is a fixed-price menu of five courses at dinner, opening with roe deer tartare, perhaps, enriched with quail's egg yolk and served with pickled shimeji, hazelnut aïoli and apple salad. A fish main might be a beautiful piece of turbot, served with brown shrimps, couscous, squash, and curry dressing; a very thoughtfully-constructed, well-balanced dish with precise flavours. Finish with pistachio crème brûlée, raspberries and chocolate.

Chef Garry Watson **Seats** 24, Private dining 8 **Closed** January **Parking** 6 **Notes** Vegetarian dishes, No children under 12 years

◼ ARGYLL & BUTE

COVE
MAP 20, NS28

Knockderry House

⊚⊚ MODERN SCOTTISH

01436 842283 | Shore Road, G84 0NX

www.knockderryhouse.co.uk

Standing on the shore of Loch Long, this much-altered Victorian house is a period treat inside, with a billiard room, intricate wood panelling and magnificent stained windows in the dining room. Gloved staff serve Scottish food that embraces modern techniques.

Chef Stuart Black **Seats** 30, Private dining 50 **Closed** 12–28 December **Parking** 15 **Notes** Vegetarian dishes, Children welcome

ERISKA

MAP 20, NM94

Restaurant at Isle of Eriska NEW

◉◉◉ CLASSIC

01631 720371 | PA37 1SD

www.eriska-hotel.co.uk

It may be just a short drive north of Oban, but this Victorian baronial-style country house on its own 300-acre private island exudes an exclusivity factor that makes you feel you should arrive by helicopter. Add in a nine-hole golf course, a serious spa and leisure package, and the undeniable magic in the gorgeous views overlooking Loch Linnhe and the dramatic Morvern mountains beyond, and you're in for a truly unique and memorable experience. Seriously good food is, of course, a major part of the deal, and Graeme Cheevers delivers that in spades with refined, classically based cooking grounded firmly in the abundant regional larder. A well-balanced starter brings superb scallops offset by grapefruit-glazed sea kale and citrus butter sauce, while main-course saddle of roe deer is supported by baked celeriac, morels, spelt and green pepper sauce. Presentation, right through to a dessert of poached Yorkshire rhubarb with white chocolate mousse and rhubarb and ginger sorbet, is impeccable.

Chef Graeme Cheevers

HELENSBURGH

MAP 20, NS28

AA Restaurant of the Year for Scotland 2019-20

Sugar Boat

◉◉ MODERN SCOTTISH

01436 647522 | 30 Colquhoun Square, G84 8AQ

www.sugarboat.co.uk

On a square in the heart of town, with tables out front and back, Sugar Boat is an all-day bistro with real foodie credentials. The design is done out in natural colours of earth and sea, with a marble-topped bar and viewable kitchen. The hearty modern bistro cooking features big flavours and an essentially simple approach to treating Scottish produce with care and attention and not a little European flare.

Chef Scott Smith Seats 65 Closed 1 January
Prices from S £5.50, M £10.50, D £5.50
Notes Vegetarian dishes, Children welcome

INVERARAY

MAP 20, NN00

Clansman Restaurant

◉ CLASSIC, TRADITIONAL V

01499 302980 | Loch Fyne Hotel & Spa, Shore Street, PA32 8XT

www.crerarhotels.com/loch-fyne-hotel-spa

On the bonny banks of Loch Fyne, the restaurant of the titular hotel goes for the time-honoured stone-walls-and-tartan-carpet school of cosiness, with slate mats on burnished mahogany tables to boost the sense of well-being. In such a location you'd hope for seafood, and the menu duly obliges with bounteous seafood from the loch.

Chef James Sharp Seats 150, Private dining 20 Open All Year Prices from S £7, M £15, D £7 Parking 60
Notes Children welcome

KILCHRENAN

MAP 20, NN02

Taychreggan Hotel

◉◉ CLASSIC FRENCH, SEAFOOD

01866 833211 | PA35 1HQ

www.taychregganhotel.co.uk

The whitewashed 17th-century hotel lies a short drive from Oban on a peninsula jutting into Loch Awe, framed by timeless Highland landscapes. The kitchen delivers five-course set dinner menus beginning with a soup such as courgette, with perch and tarragon oil.

Closed 3-21 January

LOCHGOILHEAD

MAP 20, NN10

The Lodge on Loch Goil

◉◉ MODERN SCOTTISH

01301 703193 | Loch Goil, PA24 8AE

www.thelodge-scotland.com

At the head of a sea loch, the beautifully restored Lodge offers three dining spaces: the Orangery, the Treehouse and the lochside Arts & Crafts restaurant. Scottish produce leads the menu; indeed, many ingredients are grown in the Lodge's gardens or at least locally foraged. With the sea so close, expect seafood too.

Open All Year

LUSS

MAP 20, NS39

The Lodge on Loch Lomond

◉◉ MODERN INTERNATIONAL *V*

01436 860201 | G83 8PA

www.loch-lomond.co.uk

Situated on the edge of Loch Lomond, The Lodge occupies a peaceful woodland setting. The unbeatable loch views and sense of tranquillity in the balcony restaurant give the impression that you are floating on water. The modern food is underpinned by classic technique.

Chef Graham Harrower **Seats** 100, Private dining 100 **Open** All Year **Prices from** S £4.95, M £12, D £6 **Parking** 70 **Notes** Children welcome

OBAN

MAP 20, NM82

Coast

◉ MODERN BRITISH

01631 569900 | 104 George Street, PA34 5NT

www.coastoban.co.uk

Next door to the art gallery, Coast is the very image of a modern brasserie, with a seasonally changing menu of vivacious dishes. Start with home-made chicken liver parfait with apple chutney, and move on to haunch of Argyll venison with spiced red cabbage, pickled walnuts and a mash fired up with truffle and chives.

Chef Richard Fowler **Seats** 46 **Closed** 25 December, 2 weeks January **Prices from** S £7.45, M £28, D £6.95 **Notes** Vegetarian dishes, No children under 10 years after 8pm

Manor House Hotel

◉◉ SCOTTISH, EUROPEAN

01631 562087 | Gallanach Road, PA34 4LS

www.manorhouseoban.com

Built for the Duke of Argyll in 1780, the Manor House sits in a commanding position overlooking the harbour at Oban. Half-panelled walls and original oils set a heightened tone. Fine regional Scottish produce is celebrated in menus that aim for a soft-focus, country-hotel approach.

Chef Gerard McCluskie **Seats** 34 **Closed** 25-26 December **Prices from** S £12, M £26, D £10 **Parking** 20 **Notes** Vegetarian dishes, No children under 12 years

PORT APPIN

MAP 20, NM94

Airds Hotel and Restaurant

◉◉◉ MODERN SCOTTISH *V* ⚑ NOTABLE WINE LIST

01631 730236 | PA38 4DF

www.airds-hotel.com

The short drive from Fort William to Port Appin is a tonic in itself, but the location of the Airds Hotel, on the shore of Loch Linnhe, looking over to the Isle of Lismore, is guaranteed to unwind the troubled mind. In a long, low-ceilinged dining room, an atmosphere of considerate civility reigns, and the cooking is characterised by classical techniques delivered with polish and the kind of simplicity that allows quality to shine through. Roulade of Mull crab presents you with sweetly flavoured fresh meat, watercress gel and a grain mustard sabayon, a satisfying introduction before moving on to roast breast of Gressingham duck with pommes Anna, creamed cabbage, and carrot and anise purée. Rhubarb soufflé comes with walnut crumble ice cream and a vanilla doughnut. Breads are excellent – look out for the pumpkin seed loaf and the sourdough in particular.

Chef Chris Stanley **Seats** 30 **Notes** No children under 8 years

The Seafood Restaurant

◉ SEAFOOD

01631 730302 | The Pierhouse Hotel, PA38 4DE

www.pierhousehotel.co.uk

Tucked away on a quiet arm of Loch Linnhe, this waterside restaurant is a simple, magnolia-painted space – there's no point fretting over interior design when all eyes are turned towards the mountains stretching across the skyline above the loch.

Closed 25-26 December

PORTAVADIE

MAP 20, NR96

Portavadie Marina Restaurant

◉◉ SCOTTISH

01700 811075 | PA21 2DA

www.portavadie.com

Floor-to-ceiling glass awaits you here, with a view of the marina and beyond from every table. There's local produce in abundance, of course, to wit hand-dived Tarbert-landed scallops with crispy pork belly; Isle of Gigha halibut with dulse (seaweed) butter sauce; and lavender crème brûlée with Scottish strawberries and shortbread.

Chef Liam Murphy **Seats** 120 **Open** All Year **Prices from** S £7, M £13, D £6 **Parking** 200 **Notes** Vegetarian dishes, Children welcome

See advertisement opposite

STRACHUR

MAP 20, NN00

Inver Restaurant

◉◉◉ MODERN SCOTTISH

01369 860537 | Strathlachlan, PA27 8BU

www.inverrestaurant.co.uk

The uplifting setting on the shores of Loch Fyne is in itself worth the trip out to this unassuming little restaurant in a whitewashed cottage done out with cool Scandi minimalism. The Nordic inspiration is plain to see in its simple wood tables and bench seating, while chef Pam Brunton's stint at Copenhagen's Noma informs trend-conscious cooking showcasing wild and regional produce in an imaginative carte, and a dinner-only, four-course taster that opens with a quartet of appetiser mouthfuls. A faultlessly simple opener of potted pork topped with marinated shallots, green peppercorns, seeds and edible flowers is full of pin-sharp, invigorating flavours, while main-course Gigha halibut is timed to perfection, its skin crisped and added to an umami-laden medley of seaweed greens and succulent mussels in a smoky butter sauce. An unpretentious apricot and bitter almond sponge cake with marinated almonds and cream showcases the kitchen's baking skills, as does the divine sourdough bread and home-cultured butter.

Chef Pamela Brunton **Seats** 40 **Closed** Christmas and January to February **Prices from** S £6.50, M £14.50, D £7.50 **Parking** 20 **Notes** Vegetarian dishes, Children welcome

TARBERT

MAP 20, NR86

Stonefield Castle Hotel

◉ SCOTTISH

01880 820836 | PA29 6YJ

www.bespokehotels.com/stonefieldcastle

This fine example of 19th-century Scottish baronial architecture sits proudly on the Kintyre peninsula overlooking Lock Fyne. Richly decorated public spaces speak of the long history here, while open fires and stunning views set the scene for simple cooking with a country-house feel.

Open All Year

■ SOUTH AYRSHIRE

AYR

MAP 20, NS32

Fairfield House Hotel

◉ MODERN, TRADITIONAL

01292 267461 | 12 Fairfield Road, KA7 2AS

www.fairfieldhotel.co.uk

With its views across to the Isle of Arran, this seafront hotel puts contemporary cooking at the forefront of menus in Martin's Bar & Grill with its walls displaying modern Scottish artwork. Pedigree local produce is the cornerstone of big-flavoured dishes like breast of duck, black cabbage, plum, potatoes and redcurrant jus.

Chef Robert Jackson **Seats** 80, Private dining 12 **Open** All Year **Prices from** S £4.50, M £11, D £5 **Parking** 50 **Notes** Vegetarian dishes, Children welcome

BALLANTRAE

MAP 20, NX08

Glenapp Castle

◉◉◉ MODERN BRITISH V ⚑ NOTABLE WINE LIST

01465 831212 | KA26 0NZ

www.glenappcastle.com

Glenapp is a Victorian creation in the Scottish baronial style, of the same vintage as Balmoral and almost as turrety. On a fine day you can see the curiously-shaped island of Ailsa Craig from the oak-panelled dining room. The principal business of the kitchen is a six-course dinner menu, including a pre-dessert, with a choice at main and another for either cheese or dessert. A mouthful of breaded John Dory comes with tartare sauce, before you move on, perhaps to pea risotto with mint, feta and parmesan. A fish course of west coast cod is accompanied by parsley sauce, and then you have to choose – roast Goosnargh duck breast with butternut squash purée and a haggis bonbon, or fillet of salmon with Jersey Royals, new season asparagus and chive hollandaise. Dessert brings buttermilk and rosewater pannacotta, with Scottish strawberries, raspberry coulis and pink peppercorn honeycomb. Cheese comes with wholemeal crackers, oatcakes and walnut bread.

Chef David Alexander **Seats** 34, Private dining 20 **Open** All Year **Parking** 20 **Notes** Children welcome

TROON
MAP 20, NS33

Lochgreen House Hotel
◉◉◉ MODERN FRENCH

01292 313343 | Monktonhill Road, Southwood, KA10 7EN

www.lochgreenhouse.com

Dating back to 1905, this splendid white-painted house enjoys a stunning setting, overlooking the Ayrshire coast and the fairways of Royal Troon. With beautiful gardens and 30 acres of woodland, it's a gloriously quiet and comfortable place to escape the rat race. Service is very efficient and friendly in the newly-refurbished Bisque Restaurant, a high-ceilinged, airy room, with elegant table settings and crystal chandeliers. The modern cooking has a firm basis in classic French technique, and presentation is very stylish. You might begin with chilled pineapple carpaccio with passionfruit and chilli salsa and a minted lime sorbet, or, if you're feeling extravagant, what about a half or whole grilled lobster with Café de Paris butter? Mains might include monkfish and king scallop Goan-style curry with coconut, tamarind, cumin scented rice and cashew nuts, while dessert brings salted caramel tart with walnut ice cream, or Valrhona chocolate fondant with cappuccino ice cream

Chef Andrew Costley, Iain Conway Seats 80, Private dining 40 Open All Year Prices from S £9, M £18, D £6 Parking 90 Notes Vegetarian dishes, Children welcome

MacCallums of Troon
◉ INTERNATIONAL, SEAFOOD

01292 319339 | The Harbour, KA10 6DH

www.maccallumsoftroon.co.uk

There should really only be one thing on your mind when dining at the Oyster Bar. It's all about the bass, the turbot, the sole... for this is a seafood restaurant in a glorious harbourside setting within a converted pump house.

Closed Christmas, New Year

TURNBERRY
MAP 20, NS20

1906
◉ TRADITIONAL FRENCH

01655 331000 | Trump Turnberry, Maidens Road, KA26 9LT

www.turnberry.co.uk

The 1906 restaurant at this luxurious golf-centric hotel, with sweeping views across greens and fairways to the hump of Ailsa Craig, is named after the year it opened. The setting resembles a giant wedding cake, and the kitchen puts a luxury modern spin on Escoffier's classics.

Open All Year

■ DUMFRIES & GALLOWAY

AUCHENCAIRN
MAP 21, NX75

Balcary Bay Hotel
◉◉ MODERN EUROPEAN

01556 640217 | Shore Road, DG7 1QZ

www.balcary-bay-hotel.co.uk

The solid-looking white hotel stands on the shore of the Solway Firth with views across the water to Heston Isle and the Lake District beyond. The hotel might be in a secluded spot, but the kitchen team proves to be a forward-looking lot.

Chef Craig McWilliam Seats 55 Closed December to January Parking 50 Notes Vegetarian dishes, Children welcome

DUMFRIES
MAP 21, NX97

The Auldgirth Inn NEW
◉◉ MODERN SCOTTISH

01387 740250 | Auldgirth, DG2 0XG

auldgirthinn.co.uk

Discover a relaxing dining experience at this 500-year-old inn where the locally sourced produce is transformed into contemporary British cuisine with a classical basis, finished with more modern techniques and innovative touches. The menu features a collection of bold and ambitious dishes, all with good balance of flavour and clarity, which is evident in the taste.

Chef Arran Seymour, Robert McAlesse Seats 70 Open All Year Prices from S £5.50, M £14.50, D £6.95 Parking 20 Notes Vegetarian dishes, Children welcome

GRETNA
MAP 21, NY36

Smiths at Gretna Green
◉◉ MODERN BRITISH, INTERNATIONAL

01461 337007 | Gretna Green, DG16 5EA

www.smithsgretnagreen.com

Smiths certainly extends the options for those fleeing here with marriage on their minds, and makes a stylish stay to celebrate a landmark anniversary. The imaginative menus are especially good at game. Don't miss the excellent bread, which comes in a plant-pot.

Closed 25 December

MOFFAT
MAP 21, NT00

Brodies
◉ MODERN BRITISH

01683 222870 | Holm Street, DG10 9EB

www.brodiesofmoffat.co.uk

Just off the high street, there's a contemporary sheen to Brodies that really pays off in the evening when it becomes quite a smart dining spot. The bistro-style menu offers some interesting stuff made with high-quality ingredients. Sunday lunch is a classic affair.

Chef Russell Pearce **Seats** 40 **Closed** 25–27 December **Prices from** S £4.95, M £12.95, D £6 **Notes** Vegetarian dishes, Children welcome

PORTPATRICK
MAP 20, NW95

Knockinaam Lodge
◉◉◉ MODERN SCOTTISH ⬥ NOTABLE WINE LIST

01776 810471 | DG9 9AD

www.knockinaamlodge.com

For a small country hotel, Knockinaam is something of a knockout. About three miles out of Portpatrick, it stands in 30 acres, with access to a private shingle beach. It's decorated in elegant but homely style, with panoramic views of the Irish Sea from the dining room. Tony Pierce's career began with waitering gigs in Manchester while he trained, and after compiling a star-studded CV, he has brought distinction to the kitchens here. The evening agenda is a fixed-price, four-course affair, beginning on summer's night with a perfectly balanced dish of pan-seared Skye scallops, simply paired with caviar and a chive beurre blanc. Main course is a vibrantly presented roast breast of St Brides chicken, served with a chicken and truffle ravioli, courgette, charred baby leek and a Madeira emulsion. The final course requires a choice between British and French cheeses with walnut bread, or a Knockinaam marmalade soufflé with double vanilla bean ice cream.

Chef Anthony Pierce **Seats** 32, Private dining 18 **Open** All Year **Parking** 20 **Notes** No children

SANQUHAR
MAP 21, NS70

Blackaddie House
◉◉ MODERN BRITISH

01659 50270 | Blackaddie Road, DG4 6JJ

www.blackaddiehotel.co.uk

This stone-built house on the east bank of the River Nith is in the perfect location for sourcing top-drawer produce. Firm classical underpinnings produce a Scotch beef study that combines sautéed fillet, a sticky ragoût and beef terrine with accompanying greens.

Chef Ian McAndrew **Seats** 20, Private dining 20 **Open** All Year **Parking** 20 **Notes** Vegetarian dishes, Children welcome

THORNHILL
MAP 21, NX89

The Buccleuch and Queensberry Arms Hotel
◉ MODERN SCOTTISH

01848 323101 | 112 Drumlanrig Street, DG3 5LU

www.bqahotel.com

The BQA to its friends, this family-run hotel is looking very smart these days, with a satisfying Scottish-ness to the place which extends to the culinary output. The region's produce figures large on menus that show pan-European leanings and no lack of ambition.

Open All Year

◼ WEST DUNBARTONSHIRE

CLYDEBANK
MAP 20, NS47

Golden Jubilee Conference Hotel
◉ MODERN BRITISH

0141 951 6000 | Beardmore Street, G81 4SA

www.goldenjubileehotel.com

A hotel and conference centre next to the Jubilee hospital, the Golden Jubilee Conference Hotel is a multi-purpose hub for business meetings, fitness workouts and aspirational dining with a new spin on some classics. Ecclefechan tart with toffee ice cream is a fine regional speciality.

Chef Iain Ramsay **Seats** 70, Private dining 200 **Open** All Year **Prices from** S £6, M £12, D £7 **Parking** 300 **Notes** Vegetarian dishes, Children welcome

■ DUNDEE

DUNDEE

Castlehill Restaurant

◉◉ MODERN SCOTTISH

01382 220008 | 22–26 Exchange Street, DD1 3DL

www.castlehillrestaurant.co.uk

Close to the city's booming waterfront, Castlehill is a sophisticated spot with a decorative style evoking the colours and textures of Scotland. There's a real sense of place to the menu, too, with Scottish ingredients to the fore, while the cooking is thoroughly modern and creative.

Closed 25–26 December, 1 January

Chez Mal Brasserie

◉ BRITISH, FRENCH

01382 339715 | Malmaison Dundee, 44 Whitehall Crescent, DD1 4AY

www.malmaison.com

The Dundee branch of the Malmaison chain is a majestic old hotel with a domed ceiling above a central wrought-iron staircase, with the trademark sexy looks, which run through to the candlelit brasserie's darkly atmospheric colour scheme. The menu plays the modern brasserie game.

Chef Paul Duncan Seats 110, Private dining 12 Open All Year Prices from S £5, M £12, D £5 Notes Vegetarian dishes, Children welcome

Daisy Tasker NEW

◉◉ MODERN SCOTTISH

01382 472110 | Hotel Indigo Dundee, Lower Dens Mill, Constable Street, DD4 6AD

hindundee.co.uk

Exposed ducting, subway-tiled walls and hardwood floors are a nod to the industrial past of this stylishly minimalist restaurant in a former jute mill-turned-hotel. Friendly service is in tune with the 21st-century mood, and the modern British food is robust, comfort oriented and offers plenty to keep fans of local, seasonal ingredients happy.

Chef Stewart Macaulay Seats 100, Private dining 18 Open All Year Prices from S £3.50, M £12.50, D £4 Parking 18 Notes Vegetarian dishes, Children welcome

The Tayberry

◉◉ SCOTTISH *V*

01382 698280 | 594 Brook Street, Broughty Ferry, DD5 2EA

www.tayberryrestaurant.com

This relaxed, contemporary operation has made quite a splash on the local culinary scene. Spread over two floors, its purple-toned decor is a nod to the namesake berry, and views across the River Tay from the first-floor tables are a real bonus. Focused, modern dishes allow local produce to shine.

Chef Adam Newth Seats 36, Private dining 16
Closed 25–27 December Prices from S £11, M £23, D £11
Notes No children after 8pm

■ EDINBURGH

EDINBURGH

Bia Bistrot

◉ BRITISH, FRENCH

0131 452 8453 | 19 Colinton Road, EH10 5DP

www.biabistrot.co.uk

The 'Bia' element of the name is the Gaelic for food, the 'Bistrot' part more self-evident, and it's the winning setting for the cooking of husband-and-wife team Roisin and Matthias Llorente. Their Irish/Scottish and French/Spanish backgrounds are apparent in well-crafted and satisfying food in a charming and easy-going environment with wooden tables and smart leather seats.

Chef Roisin and Matthias Llorente Seats 60, Private dining 24 Closed 1 January, 1 week at Easter, 2nd week in July, 1 week in October Prices from S £4, M £13.85, D £2.50 Notes Vegetarian dishes, Children welcome

Bistro Deluxe

◉◉ MODERN SCOTTISH

0131 550 4500 | Macdonald Holyrood Hotel,
Holyrood Road, EH8 8AU

www.macdonaldhotels.co.uk/our-hotels/
macdonald-holyrood-hotel/eat-drink/

In Edinburgh's historic old town, just a couple of
minutes from Royal Mile, this modern hotel is well
positioned and the elegant, brasserie-style Bistro
Deluxe restaurant is a destination in itself. The
kitchen makes good use of prime Scottish
ingredients in the contemporary European dishes.

Open All Year

The Brasserie – Norton House Hotel & Spa

◉ MODERN BRITISH

0131 333 1275 | Ingliston, EH28 8LX

www.handpickedhotels.co.uk/nortonhouse

Buffered by 50-odd acres of well-tended
grounds, you'd hardly know that this Victorian
country house is handy for motorways and the
airport. After you've worked up an appetite in the
spa's swimming pool, the brasserie offers an
unbuttoned, contemporary setting and modern
Scottish food to match.

Open All Year

The Café Royal

◉ MODERN SCOTTISH

0131 556 1884 | 19 West Register Street, EH2 2AA

www.caferoyaledinburgh.co.uk

The Café Royal's Victorian-baroque interiors
simply cry out to be the scene of grand dining
with their gilt pillars, panelled ceilings and
stained windows. These days, traditional Scots
fare mingles with modern thinking on menus that
open with oysters on mounds of crushed ice.

Open All Year

Castle Terrace Restaurant

◉◉◉ SCOTTISH, FRENCH 𝒱 NOTABLE WINE LIST

0131 229 1222 | 33–35 Castle Terrace, EH1 2EL

www.castleterracerestaurant.com

A venue in the environs of a castle has got to
have a head start anywhere, perhaps particularly
in Edinburgh, and the sibling restaurant to the
much-lauded Kitchin at Leith steps up to the
challenge. In a dark blue room with a spacious
modern feel and an outline image of the castle
picked out on the wall, Dominic Jack plies a
contemporary Scottish nature-to-plate style,
with enough brio to offer a Land and Sea surprise
menu with optional wine pairings, opening with a
glass of champagne. The carte itself furnishes a
heartening spread of choice, with main courses
along the lines of fillet, belly and cheek of
Ayrshire pork with black pudding, fondant potato
and creamed cabbage, or the house take on
paella, served on spelt risotto. A signature
dessert of apple mascarpone cheesecake with
caramelised sesame seeds and apple sorbet
competes for attention with dark chocolate and
orange délice.

Chef Dominic Jack **Seats** 75, Private dining 16
Closed 9–13 April, 24 December to 13 January
Notes No children under 5 years

Chaophraya

◉ THAI

0131 226 7614 | 4th Floor, 33 Castle Street, EH2 3DN

www.chaophraya.co.uk/edinburgh/

Located on the 4th floor, this panoramic
restaurant offers magnificent rooftop views of
Edinburgh all the way to the Forth. Helpful,
courteous staff offer a traditional welcome and
explain the lengthy menu, which combines
traditional Thai dishes with more modern
interpretations. Great cocktails, too.

Open All Year

Chez Mal Brasserie

🍴 BRITISH, FRENCH

0131 468 5000 | Malmaison Edinburgh,
One Tower Place, Leith, EH6 7BZ
www.malmaison.com

This was the first opening for the Malmaison chain, housed in a renovated seamen's mission on the waterfront in the old part of Leith, and is nowadays the grande dame of the boutique chain. The restaurant overlooks the docks with a terrace for alfresco dining.

Open All Year

The Dining Room

🍴🍴 MODERN FRENCH, SCOTTISH *V*

0131 220 2044 | 28 Queen Street, EH2 1JX
www.thediningroomedinburgh.co.uk

Climb the spiral staircase to the restaurant of the Scotch Malt Whisky Society, where a light, smart room is furnished with linened tables, primrose-hued walls and colourful food and drink-themed pictures. The cooking has more than a hint of French classicism to it.

Chef James Freeman **Seats** 66, Private dining 20
Prices from S £10, M £25, D £10 **Notes** No children

Divino Enoteca

🍴 MODERN ITALIAN, INTERNATIONAL ▮ NOTABLE WINE LIST

0131 225 1770 | 5 Merchant Street, EH1 2QD
www.divinoedinburgh.com

A hip venue with contemporary artworks on the walls, exposed brickwork and displays of wine bottles wherever you look: it's dark, moody, and a lot of fun. The kitchen's Italian output includes an excellent range of antipasti plus some more modern interpretations of the classics.

Chef Francesco Ascrizzi **Seats** 50, Private dining 14
Open All Year **Notes** Vegetarian dishes, Children welcome

The Dungeon Restaurant at Dalhousie Castle

🍴🍴 TRADITIONAL EUROPEAN

01875 820153 | Bonnyrigg, EH19 3JB
www.dalhousiecastle.co.uk

Dalhousie Castle is a 13th-century fortress in wooded parkland on the banks of the River Esk, so you know you're in for something special at The Dungeon Restaurant. The cooking here has its roots in French classicism and a bedrock of top-class Scottish ingredients.

Open All Year

l'escargot blanc

🍴 FRENCH

0131 226 1890 | 17 Queensferry Street, EH2 4QW
www.lescargotblanc.co.uk

A West End fixture for more than 20 years, the first floor l'escargot blanc is accessed via the restaurant's own standalone wine bar. The intimate restaurant is classic bistro through and through, from the stripped wooden floors and distressed furniture to the Gallic objets d'art.

Closed 1st week January, 2nd week July

l'escargot bleu

🍴 FRENCH, SCOTTISH

0131 557 1600 | 56 Broughton Street, EH1 3SA
www.lescargotbleu.co.uk

L'escargot bleu is indeed blue – on the outside at least, and snails are present and correct among les entrées. The bilingual menu deals in classic bistro dishes such as those snails, which come from Barra in the Outer Hebrides, and there's a Scottish flavour throughout.

Chef Fred Berkmiller **Seats** 55, Private dining 18
Closed 1 week January, 1 week July **Notes** Vegetarian dishes No children after 9pm

La Favorita

🍴 MODERN ITALIAN, MEDITERRANEAN

0131 554 2430 | 325–331 Leith Walk, EH6 8SA
www.la-favorita.com

Well-sourced Italian ingredients supply the wherewithal for the Vittoria group's Leith pizzeria. From its wood-fired ovens comes a compendious list of pizzas, as well as cured meat platters and an imaginative diversity of pasta dishes and risottos. The ambience is upbeat and casual, and there's a bargain weekday set-price lunch worth considering.

Chef Jarek Splawski **Seats** 120, Private dining 30
Closed 25 December **Prices from** S £4.50, M £25.50, D £6.50 **Notes** Vegetarian dishes, Children welcome

The Gardener's Cottage

◉ BRITISH

0131 677 0244 | 1 Royal Terrace Gardens, London Road, EH7 5DX

www.thegardenerscottage.co

With its blackboard menu in the gravel outside, this restaurant with full-on royal connections is an oasis of pastoral calm in the bustling city. Cosy up in wicker chairs at big communal tables for Scottish cooking that takes pride in its carefully sourced prime materials. That's clear from a starter of mutton and roe-deer meatballs in maltagliati pasta.

Chef Edward Murray, Dale Mailley **Seats** 30, Private dining 10 **Closed** Christmas and New Year **Notes** Vegetarian dishes, Children welcome

La Garrigue

◉ FRENCH, MEDITERRANEAN 🍷 NOTABLE WINE LIST

0131 557 3032 | 31 Jeffrey Street, EH1 1DH

www.lagarrigue.co.uk

Named for the wild, herb-scented scrubland in Provence and Languedoc in the south of France. Chef-patron Jean-Michel Gauffre has brought the region's honest rustic cooking to his smart neighbourhood restaurant in Edinburgh's old town. Born in the heartlands of cassoulet, his take on the hearty stew of belly pork, duck confit, Toulouse sausage and white beans is the real deal.

Chef Jean-Michel Gauffre, Peter Duck **Seats** 48, Private dining 11 **Closed** 26–27 December, 1–2 January **Prices from** S £5.25, M £16.50, D £6.50 **Notes** Vegetarian dishes, Children welcome

Harajuku Kitchen

◉ JAPANESE *V*

0131 281 0526 | 10 Gillespie Place, EH10 4HS

harajukukitchen.co.uk

Named after an area of Tokyo, this bistro offers authentic Japanese dishes with a touch of panache in an informal café-like atmosphere of exposed stone, vibrant artworks and chunky wood tables and low-back chairs. Family run, the kitchen sends out exciting and authentic cooking, with some dishes passed down through three generations.

Chef Nobuo Sasaki, Kaori Simpson **Seats** 30 **Closed** 25 December, 1 January **Prices from** S £3.95, M £9.85, D £4.80 **Notes** Children welcome

Harvey Nichols Forth Floor Restaurant

◉ MODERN EUROPEAN *V* 🍷 NOTABLE WINE LIST

0131 524 8350 | 30–34 St Andrew Square, EH2 2AD

www.harveynichols.com/restaurants

With views of the castle and the Forth Bridge, the top floor of Harvey Nic's Edinburgh restaurant serves up the city on a plate. The restaurant is a slick contemporary space with white linen on the tables, burgundy-coloured leather seats and a smart line in seasonal dishes combining contemporary finesse with Scottish ingredients.

Chef Robert Meldrum **Seats** 47, Private dining 14 **Closed** 25 December, 1 January **Notes** Vegetarian dishes, Children welcome

The Honours

◉◉ MODERN FRENCH

0131 220 2513 | 58a North Castle Street, EH2 3LU

www.thehonours.co.uk

Martin Wishart is a shining star of the Scottish restaurant firmament, his self-named restaurant in Leith, his flagship. Here, he's brought his dedication to high quality and his attention to detail to French brasserie classicism. There's a contemporary sheen to the place.

Chef Rikki Preston **Seats** 65 **Closed** Christmas and 1–3 January **Prices from** S £8.95, M £18.50, D £9.50 **Notes** Vegetarian dishes, Children welcome

Hotel du Vin Edinburgh

◉ CLASSIC FRENCH

0131 247 4900 | 11 Bristo Place, EH1 1EZ

www.hotelduvin.com

The former city asylum is the setting for HdV's Edinburgh outpost. The setting is considerably more cheerful thanks to the group's trademark gentleman's-club look of well-worn leather seats and woody textures. There's a splendid tartan-clad whisky snug, plus a buzzy mezzanine bar overlooking the bistro.

Open All Year

Kanpai Sushi

🏵 JAPANESE

0131 228 1602 | 8-10 Grindlay Street, EH3 9AS

www.kanpaisushiedinburgh.co.uk

Just around the corner from the Usher Hall and the Traverse Theatre, Kanpai is a diminutive but elegant sushi place with an open kitchen counter where you can watch its well-drilled artistry take place. Attention to fine detail, and exemplary freshness are the hallmarks. Make sure to check out the list of sake and shochu spirits.

Chef Max Wang **Seats** 45, Private dining 8 **Closed** Christmas, New Year **Prices from** S £2.50, M £9.90, D £4.90 **Notes** Vegetarian dishes, No children under 5 years

The Kitchin

🏵🏵🏵🏵🏵 SCOTTISH, FRENCH *V* ♦ NOTABLE WINE LIST

0131 555 1755 | 78 Commercial Quay, Leith, EH6 6LX

www.thekitchin.com

A former whisky warehouse in the regenerated Leith docklands has been Tom Kitchin's address since 2006, and immediately shot into the premier league of the top foodie destinations in the country. The interior looks sharp in hues of teal blue and grey, with exposed stone walls, painted brick pillars and industrial girders, while Kitchin's 'From Nature to Plate' mantra is articulated through cooking that applies top-level refinement and technical skills to Scotland's finest materials.

The three-course set lunch menu offers remarkable value, delivering a starter of crispy veal sweetbreads atop Jerusalem artichoke risotto, hen of the woods mushrooms and hazelnuts. Next comes sea-fresh Scrabster monkfish wrapped in salty pancetta, alongside fondant new potatoes, sea vegetables, plump mussels, chanterelles, confit garlic and an outstanding chicken gravy with lemon and thyme. Desserts are also handled with awe-inspiring dexterity, as in the masterclass blueberry crumble soufflé served with the balancing sharpness of yogurt ice cream.

Chef Tom Kitchin **Seats** 75, Private dining 20 **Closed** 2-6 April, 16-20 July, 15-19 October, 24 December to 11 January **Parking** 30 **Notes** No children under 5 years

Locanda De Gusti

🏵🏵 ITALIAN, MEDITERRANEAN, SEAFOOD

0131 346 8800 | 102 Dalry Road, EH11 2DW

www.locandadegusti.com

With its painted brickwork and all-round rustic appeal, this inviting restaurant has more than a hint of an Italian domestic kitchen about it. Translating loosely as 'inn of taste', you'll certainly find heaps of flavour in the kitchen's big-hearted cooking; top-drawer local produce is boosted by ingredients shipped in from Italy to keep it all authentic.

Chef Rosario Sartore **Seats** 30 **Closed** 1 week in January, 1 week at Easter, 2 weeks in July, 1 week in October **Prices from** S £5.95, M £9.95, D £4.95 **Notes** Vegetarian dishes, Children welcome

Mother India's Cafe

🏵 INDIAN TAPAS

0131 524 9801 | 3-5 Infirmary Street, EH1 1LT

www.motherindia.co.uk

Open since 2008 and a boisterous Edinburgh sibling to the Glasgow mothership, this bustling Indian café is tucked away behind the university buildings but it's well worth going off the beaten track for. With its mismatched furniture, unclothed tables and disposable napkins, it's chaotic and unpretentious.

Closed 25-26 December and 1 January

Mumbai Diners' Club

🏵🏵 MODERN INDIAN *V*

0131 229 8291 | 3 Atholl Place, EH3 8HP

www.mumbaidinersclub.co.uk

An Indian restaurant where both the interior design and menu take a glamorous and contemporary approach. A statement chandelier, plum-coloured columns and chairs, and chunky wooden designer tables make for an appealing space, watched over by a smartly turned-out service team.

Chef Pramod Kumar Nawani **Seats** 85 **Open** All Year **Prices from** S £4.50, M £12.95, D £5.95 **Notes** Children welcome

NAVADHANYA

◎ MODERN INDIAN *V*

0131 269 7868 | 32–34 Grindlay Street, EH3 9AP

www.navadhanya-scotland.co.uk

Navadhanya's Haymarket venue was always a popular spot and this continues in their newer, larger and more central premises on Grindlay Street. The modern Indian food steers clear of the usual high street curry and offers an inventive menu of regional dishes. Sunhari Jhingha (chargrilled king prawns, mustard, cumin and coriander chutney) is a strong way to start, perhaps followed by slow-cooked Hyderabadi lamb shank.

Chef I Tharveskhan **Seats** 66 **Closed** Christmas and New Year **Prices from** S £6.75, M £13.95, D £4 **Notes** Children welcome

New Chapter

◎◎ SCOTTISH, EUROPEAN

0131 556 0006 | 18 Eyre Place, EH3 5EP

www.newchapterrestaurant.co.uk

A godsend for the neighbourhood, this cheery venue combines a laid-back demeanour with clean-cut, contemporary looks, breezy service, and a kitchen that produces unfussy, full-flavoured dishes with European leanings. If you're after top value, the lunch menu is a steal.

Chef Maciej Szymik **Seats** 96, Private dining 30 **Closed** 25 December **Prices from** S £8.50, M £16.50, D £5.50 **Notes** Vegetarian dishes, Children welcome

Number One, The Balmoral

◎◎◎◎ MODERN SCOTTISH *V*

0131 557 6727 | 1 Princes Street, EH2 2EQ

www.roccofortehotels.com

Red-jacketed porters no longer meet The Balmoral's guests off the trains in Waverley Station, but modern guests can't really find fault with the luxury on offer at this magnificent Edinburgh landmark. Lavish public areas have as much marble and fancy plasterwork as anyone could wish for, and the Number One dining room looks classy with its oak flooring offset by dove-grey banquettes, and striking artworks on loan from the Royal College of Art adding interest to its red lacquered walls. Executive chef Jeff Bland and head chef Mark Donald send out reliably sophisticated food full of creative modern panache, delivered via a carte or seven- and 10-course tasting workouts.

Seasonal Scottish ingredients are given star billing, as in the Highland Wagyu beef main course that comes with beetroot, smoked marrow and bitter leaves. Before you get to that point, though, there's a starter of hand-dived scallop with Ibérico pork, redcurrants, and black garlic ketchup, or smoked potato with egg yolk, onion broth, pickled leeks and aged Comté. Another main course might be North Sea cod with pickled clams, and then it's time for dessert, perhaps roast pineapple soufflé with coconut and liquorice root. It's all backed by a heavyweight wine list and a knowledgeable, pitch-perfect service team.

Chef Mark Donald, Jeff Bland **Seats** 60 **Closed** 2 weeks in January **Notes** No children under 5 years

Ondine Restaurant

◎◎ SEAFOOD

0131 226 1888 | 2 George IV Bridge, EH1 1AD

www.ondinerestaurant.co.uk

Ondine has earned a loyal following on the city's culinary scene, and it's not hard to see why: just off the Royal Mile, on George IV Bridge, it's a contemporary space with an upbeat bustle and great views out over the old town. Sustainable seafood, prepared simply and with an eye on exciting global flavours, is the main draw.

Chef Roy Brett **Seats** 82, Private dining 10 **Open** All Year **Prices from** S £9, M £18, D £8 **Notes** Vegetarian dishes, Children welcome

One Square

◎ MODERN SCOTTISH

0131 221 6422 | Sheraton Grand Hotel & Spa, 1 Festival Square, EH3 9SR

www.onesquareedinburgh.co.uk

The views of Edinburgh Castle give a sense of place to this slick, modern dining option. The floor-to-ceiling windows add a cool, classy finish. The lunch and dinner menus have a sharp focus on Scotland's fine produce in their crowd-pleasing medley of modern ideas.

Open All Year

The Pompadour

◉◉◉ MODERN BRITISH *V*

0131 222 8945 | Waldorf Astoria Edinburgh – The Caledonian, Princes Street, EH1 2AB

www.thepompadour.com

The name gives a little clue as to the other-worldly grandeur of the setting, a lavishly appointed dining room at the Waldorf Astoria with hand-blocked floral wall designs, a gigantic oval mirror, and views through half-moon windows towards the castle. The menus embrace multi-course specials with vegetarian counterparts, as well as a shorter seasonal offering and the standard carte, deal in modern British dishes of impact and finesse. A main course might see roast veal sweetbreads, pearl barley and pea risotto and morels, strongly accented with wild garlic, or turbot poached in dashi and partnered with an oyster and slivered radish. Incomparable technique distinguishes a salt caramel soufflé with a scoop of bourbon vanilla ice cream dropped into it, or there could be a bang-up-to-date mousse of Manjari chocolate and praline with toasted hay ice cream and almond gel.

Chef Daniel Ashmore **Seats** 60, Private dining 20 **Closed** 2 weeks in January **Parking** 48 **Notes** Children welcome

Restaurant Martin Wishart

◉◉◉◉ MODERN FRENCH *V* 🍷 NOTABLE WINE LIST

0131 553 3557 | 54 The Shore, Leith, EH6 6RA

www.restaurantmartinwishart.co.uk

Leith's port is rich with bars and restaurants these days, and Martin Wishart was one of the trailblazers who breathed life back into this neglected area. It was a brave move, and the restaurant is now one of the top dining addresses in the UK. The chef hasn't let the grass grow under his feet either, opening a number of other dining destinations, developing a media profile, and working as a consultant. An empire built on a passion for French cuisine, where experience working with the Roux brothers and Marco Pierre White was a grounding that has taken him to the very top. The dining room is elegant and stylish, but understated, and the attention to detail in everything that arrives on the plate is breathtaking at times.

Scottish produce leads the line on menus that combine French classical ways with contemporary creativity; choose from a fixed-price four-course carte or six- or eight-course tasting menus, including outstanding vegetarian versions. Begin with céviche of Gigha halibut, with mango and passionfruit, followed by roast breast and pastilla of Goosnargh duck with red cabbage, beetroot, macadamia and redcurrant. The wine list is out of the top drawer, covering the globe and truly excelling itself in the French regions.

Chef Martin Wishart, Joe Taggart **Seats** 50, Private dining 10 **Closed** 25-26 December, 1 January, 2 weeks in January **Notes** No children under 7 years

Rhubarb at Prestonfield

◉◉ TRADITIONAL BRITISH 🍷 NOTABLE WINE LIST

0131 225 1333 | Priestfield Road, EH16 5UT

www.rhubarb-edinburgh.com

One of the city's most visually impressive dining rooms, Rhubarb at Prestonfield is a real stunner. Classical preparations mix with contemporary ideas in a menu with broad appeal. Have a classic Scottish steak followed by tarte Tatin for two.

Chef John McMahon **Seats** 90, Private dining 500 **Open** All Year **Prices from** S £9.50, M £19, D £6.50 **Parking** 200 **Notes** Vegetarian dishes, No children under 12 years

The Scran & Scallie

◉ TRADITIONAL SCOTTISH *V* 🍷 NOTABLE WINE LIST

0131 332 6281 | 1 Comely Bank Road, EH4 1DR

www.scranandscallie.com

The focus is firmly on food in top chefs Tom Kitchin and Dominic Jack's pub. The place goes for a fashionable shabby-chic look – just the right sort of setting for a menu of pub fodder classics running in tandem with some more on-trend combos, all chiming with the 'from nature to plate' house ethos.

Chef Jamie Knox, Tom Kitchin, Dominic Jack **Seats** 75, Private dining 14 **Closed** 25 December **Prices from** S £7.50, M £12.50, D £8 **Notes** Children welcome

Timberyard

🏅🏅🏅 **MODERN BRITISH** *V* 🍷 NOTABLE WINE LIST

0131 221 1222 | 10 Lady Lawson Street, EH3 9DS

www.timberyard.co

Understated menus belie the delights to come

Located in a former warehouse just to the south of Edinburgh Castle, the premises are as dressed-down as it gets, with oversize red garage doors leading into a brick-walled space with bare wood floors and a south-facing, sun-trap yard. Herbs and edible flowers grow outside, while Scottish artisan breeders and foragers help to furnish a menu that deals in modern food that delivers strikingly on the palate. Menu descriptions are economically worded, but there's no doubt about the delights they signpost, whether you choose the three- or five-course lunch version, the pre-theatre, the four-course dinner, the pescatarian for vegetarians who eat fish, or the full vegetarian option.

For a starter, torched fillet of mackerel comes with freshly grated horseradish, pickled daikon and parsley mayonnaise, followed perhaps by barbecued pork with swede, cabbage and kale, or sole roasted

golden on the bone and napped with beurre blanc, alongside a bowl of creamed smoked potatoes with raisin purée and capers. Making an appearance on the fish menu might well be mackerel again, this tIme wIth cucumber and dill, and cod with courgette and coastal herbs, the two dishes separated by a plate of hen's egg with asparagus, hen of the woods and hemp. Committed vegetarians could head for the eight-courser, among which might be heritage tomato with lovage, sorrel and yoghurt; and barbecued leeks with ramsons, potato and smoked curd. Intriguing textural counterpoints distinguish a dessert of caramelised poached pear on fig-leaf ice cream with fig jam and crumbled hazelnuts.

Expertly categorised not just by country, but by region, are artisanal wines from a wide slice of continental Europe, Including all the obvious candidates, as well as varieties from Hungary, Slovenia, Switzerland and even Wales. All in all, it's not surprising that the knowledgeable staff give off a happy vibe and it's clear that they are proud to work here.

Chef Ben Radford
Seats 65, Private dining 10
Closed 24–26 December, 1st week in January, 1 week in April, October
Prices from S £7, M £13, D £5
Notes No children under 12 years at dinner

EDINBURGH continued

Southside Scran NEW

◉ FRENCH, SCOTTISH *V*

0131 342 3333 | 14–17 Bruntsfield Place, EH10 4HN

www.southsidescran.com

In the Bruntsfield area of Edinburgh, this latest addition to the Tom Kitchin empire is styled as a French bistro and it's all very informal with many dishes cooked on the rotisserie grill in the open kitchen. Try Borders roe deer pithiver and rhubarb followed by North Sea plaice, pancetta, gnocchi, mussels and wild garlic.

Chef Craig McKenzie **Seats** 65 **Closed** 25 December
Prices from S £8.50, M £10.50, D £7.50
Notes Vegetarian dishes, Children welcome

The Stockbridge Restaurant

◉◉ MODERN, CLASSIC BRITISH

0131 226 6766 | 54 St Stephen Street, EH3 5AL

www.thestockbridgerestaurant.com

What you see in this Georgian-terrace restaurant are quality linen, fresh flowers and fairy lights; what you get are impeccable service and modern, classic British food. Start perhaps with seared hake, crab spring roll, shellfish risotto with avocado ice cream; and, for a main, Aberdeen Angus sirloin steak with braised ox-tail tortellini is a good choice.

Chef Jason Gallagher **Seats** 40 **Closed** 24–25 December, 1st 2 weeks January **Prices from** S £8.95, M £20.95, D £5.50 **Notes** Vegetarian dishes, No children after 8pm

Ten Hill Place Hotel

◉ MODERN, TRADITIONAL BRITISH

0131 662 2080 | 10 Hill Place, EH8 9DS

www.tenhillplace.com

Can there be another hotel that uses its profits to help train the world's would-be surgeons? That is what this part-Georgian, part-new hotel owned by The Royal College of Surgeons of Edinburgh does. If you're thinking of trying Scotland's classic dishes for the first time, then there's no better place than this elegantly decorated and furnished restaurant.

Chef Alan Dickson **Seats** 80 **Open** All Year
Prices from S £6, M £14, D £7 **Notes** Vegetarian dishes, Children welcome

Timberyard

◉◉◉ MODERN BRITISH *V* ♦ NOTABLE WINE LIST

See pages 458–459

21212

◉◉◉◉ MODERN FRENCH ♦ NOTABLE WINE LIST

0131 523 1030 | 3 Royal Terrace, EH7 5AB

www.21212restaurant.co.uk

Paul Kitching and Katie O'Brien's sumptuous restaurant with rooms is not one to follow the herd. The sandstone Georgian townhouse on Royal Terrace seems par for the course for a high-end joint, while inside there's contemporary design and classic elegance combining in a true one-off operation. The four bedrooms have a glossy finish, and the swish restaurant works a dramatic look, mingling ornate plasterwork, curvaceous banquettes and quirky design; a glass partition lets you eyeball the open-to-view kitchen where Paul gives full rein to his off-the-wall culinary artistry.

The place's name derives from the weekly-changing five-course menu format: a choice of two starters, two mains and two desserts, punctuated by one soup course and a cheese course – that's if you're doing lunch – the line-up jumps to 31313 at dinner. Cryptic menu descriptions will need some elucidation from Katie, who orchestrates front-of-house with charm and efficiency, but you can expect creative and dynamic modern cooking in dishes that are unconventional and thought provoking. Main course 'Silk Road' is a fantastically complex yet subtle and harmonious dish based around confit trout. A reworking of the classic custard tart is a real 'wow' finale, with gravity-defying crisply-bruléed custard on lemon-infused barley and a mango purée – light, fresh, and perfectly-balanced.

Chef Paul Kitching **Seats** 36, Private dining 10
Closed 2 weeks in January, 2 weeks in summer
Notes Vegetarian dishes, No children under 5 years

The Witchery by the Castle

◉ TRADITIONAL SCOTTISH ♦ NOTABLE WINE LIST

0131 225 5613 | Castlehill, The Royal Mile, EH1 2NF

www.thewitchery.com

One of several historic buildings at the gates of Edinburgh Castle, the baroque, oak-panelled restaurant within this 16th-century merchant's house makes for an atmospheric dining experience. Built around traditional dishes and native produce, the assured cooking follows a contemporary and seasonal route with Scottish seafood getting a strong showing.

Chef Douglas Roberts **Seats** 110, Private dining 60
Closed 25–26 December **Prices from** S £9.50, M £19, D £7 **Notes** Vegetarian dishes, No children after 7pm

RATHO

MAP 21, NT17

The Bridge Inn at Ratho

◉ MODERN BRITISH

0131 333 1320 | 27 Baird Road, EH28 8RA

www.bridgeinn.com

Right by the Union Canal, with views over the water from both garden and restaurant, The Bridge Inn is the perfect spot for watching the passing boats. If the canal-side action doesn't float your boat, there are cask ales, regional whiskies, and an appealing menu.

Closed 25 December

■ FALKIRK

BANKNOCK

MAP 21, NS77

Glenskirlie House & Castle

◉◉ MODERN BRITISH *V*

01324 840201 | Kilsyth Road, FK4 1UF

www.glenskirliehouse.com

A castle for the 21st century, Glenskirlie is a bright white pile, kitted out with a conical-roofed turret here, a little step-gabling there. The restaurant has a good ambience and a friendly and brisk service from staff.

Chef Richard M Leafe **Seats** 54, Private dining 150
Closed 26–27 December, 1–4 January
Prices from S £5.90, M £16.90, D £6.50 **Parking** 100
Notes Children welcome

POLMONT

MAP 21, NS97

Macdonald Inchyra Hotel and Spa

◉ SCOTTISH

01324 711911 | Grange Road, FK2 0YB

www.macdonaldhotels.co.uk

The solid-stone Inchyra is a smart hotel with a plush spa and all mod cons. It's home to The Scottish Steak Club, a brasserie-style dining option done out in swathes of rich leather, animal prints and dark wood. The menu is a foray into brasserie-land.

Chef Richard Dickson **Seats** 90, Private dining 35
Open All Year **Prices from** S £6, M £10, D £5 **Parking** 100
Notes Vegetarian dishes, Children welcome

■ FIFE

ANSTRUTHER

MAP 21, NO50

The Cellar

◉◉◉ MODERN BRITISH

01333 310378 | 24 East Green, KY10 3AA

www.thecellaranstruther.co.uk

Squirrelled away just off the harbourfront, this 17th-century house has food and drink in the very bones of its history. A one-time cooperage and smokehouse, it now houses a destination restaurant where chef-patron Billy Boyter continues the traditions by drying, fermenting, salting and smoking his ingredients. The ambience is captivatingly rustic-chic, with beamed ceilings, rough stone walls and wood-burning stoves, and friendly staff playing their part in its appeal. Boyter's intelligent modernist cooking draws the faithful for eight-course tasting menus at dinner (six if you're in for lunch). An inventive workout opens with an intense pairing of ox tongue with 36-month-aged parmesan cream and cherry tomatoes, then introduces an Eastern note via the pork fat dashi that intensifies a plate of halibut, razor clams and wild garlic. Meaty mains match local beef rump and shin with yellow carrots, and the finale arrives in the form of a creative composition of koji rice, black banana, finger lime and chocolate.

Chef Billy Boyter **Seats** 28 **Closed** 25–26 December, 1 January, 3 weeks January, 1 week May, 10 days September **Notes** Vegetarian dishes, No children under 5 years at lunch, 12 years at dinner

CAIRNEYHILL

MAP 21, NT08

The Restaurant and Acanthus

◉◉ MODERN BRITISH

01383 880505 | Forrester Park, Pitdinnie Road, KY12 8RF

www.forresterparkresort.com

Forrester Park is a chic, contemporary take on a traditional Scottish mansion. There are two dining rooms, The Restaurant is smaller and more modern in style, while the much larger Acanthus is all starched white linen and chandeliers. The same set-price dinner menu is served in both.

Chef Alistair Clark **Seats** 240, Private dining 30
Closed Christmas and New Year **Prices from** S £6, M £12.50, D £7 **Parking** 120 **Notes** Vegetarian dishes, Children welcome

CUPAR
MAP 21, N031

Ostlers Close Restaurant
◉◉ MODERN SCOTTISH V
01334 655574 | Bonnygate, KY15 4BU
www.ostlersclose.co.uk

This one-time scullery of a 17th-century temperance hotel has been a popular destination since 1981. With red-painted walls and linen-clad tables, it's an intimate space run with charm and enthusiasm. Concise handwritten menus showcase produce from the garden and wild mushrooms from local woods.

Chef James Graham **Seats** 26 **Closed** 25–26 December, 1–2 January, 2 weeks January, 2 weeks April **Notes** No children under 6 years at dinner

ELIE
MAP 21, N040

The Ship Inn NEW
◉ MODERN, SEAFOOD
01333 330246 | The Toft, KY9 1DT
www.shipinn.scot

Not many pubs can boast a beachside beer garden and cricket matches played on the sand, but The Ship Inn is no ordinary tavern. Overlooking the briny, the first-floor restaurant sports a jaunty modern look involving bare tables and duck-egg-blue panelling and serves an unfussy roll-call of eclectic modern dishes, including splendid local seafood.

Open All Year

NEWPORT-ON-TAY
MAP 21, N042

The Newport Restaurant
◉◉ MODERN SCOTTISH V
01382 541449 | 1 High Street, DD6 8AB
www.thenewportrestaurant.co.uk

There's not much better publicity than winning *MasterChef: The Professionals*, so 2014 winner Jamie Scott got off to a flyer when he opened his own restaurant. Cheerful and enthusiastic service and a breezy contemporary decor make for a relaxed dining experience, while pin-sharp contemporary cooking from Scott and his team make it a hot ticket.

Chef Jamie Scott **Seats** 52, Private dining 30 **Closed** 24–26 December, 1–8 January **Parking** 10 **Notes** Children welcome

ST ANDREWS
MAP 21, N051

The Adamson
◉◉ MODERN BRITISH
01334 479191 | 127 South Street, KY16 9UH
theadamson.com

Once home to photographer and physician Dr John Adamson (hence the name), the handsome building now houses a cool restaurant with exposed bricks, darkwood tables, an open kitchen, and a bar serving up creative cocktails. The menu brings up-to-date oomph to the brasserie format with oodles of contemporary style and high-quality ingredients.

Chef David Lilley **Seats** 75 **Closed** 25–26 December, 1 January **Prices from** S £5.50, M £14.95, D £5.25 **Notes** Vegetarian dishes, Children welcome

The Grange Inn NEW
◉◉ MODERN SCOTTISH
01334 472670 | Grange Road, KY16 8LJ
thegrangeinn.com

A lovely 17th-century converted farmhouse is the setting for this delightful restaurant with panoramic views looking out over St Andrews and St Andrews Bay. Chef-proprietor John Kelly has created a superb menu finished with modern techniques and innovative touches using the freshest of local produce available. There's a warm and welcoming ambience throughout.

Chef John Kelly **Seats** 26, Private dining 10 **Closed** January **Parking** **Notes** Vegetarian dishes, No children under 12 years at dinner

The Peat Inn
◉◉◉ MODERN BRITISH
01334 840206 | KY15 5LH
www.thepeatinn.co.uk

This inn has been enough of a local landmark since the mid-18th century that the village in which it stands was named after it, rather than the other way round. It's a handsomely white-fronted, stone-built former coach-stop, the dining room decorated in sleek contemporary fashion with light woods, thick cloths and smart tableware. Geoffrey Smeddle has maintained the place in the upper ranks of Scottish gastronomy over an impressive stretch, and the modernist flourishes and precise presentations confer real character on the cooking. Begin with warm St Andrews Bay lobster with romesco sauce, cauliflower pannacotta (with perfect 'wobble') and sea herbs. For main, roast crown and smoked legs of Scottish partridge come with young parsnips, spiced Puy lentils and a thyme and cider velouté. A mille feuille of lemon posset and blackberries with an intense lemongrass, chilli and ginger sorbet is beautifully made, with delicate pastry and great flavour.

Chef Geoffrey Smeddle **Seats** 50, Private dining 12
Closed 25–26 December, 1–10 January
Prices from S £9, M £18, D £9 **Parking** 24
Notes Vegetarian dishes, No children under 7 years at dinner

Playfair's Restaurant and Steakhouse
@ STEAKHOUSE, SCOTTISH
01334 472970 | Ardgowan Hotel, 2 Playfair Terrace, North Street, KY16 9HX
www.playfairsrestaurant.co.uk
The Playfair's Restaurant and Steakhouse is located under the reception, and the configuration means that diners can often find themselves eating close to drinkers using the bar. It all makes for a relaxed atmosphere, while linen-clothed tables in the restaurant add a touch of formality.

Chef Duncan McLachlan **Seats** 45 **Closed** Christmas, New Year **Prices from** S £4.50, M £12.95, D £4.95
Notes Vegetarian dishes, Children welcome

Road Hole Restaurant
@@@ MODERN, STEAK, SEAFOOD
See pages 464–465

Rocca Restaurant
@@@ MODERN BRITISH
01334 474321 | Macdonald Rusacks Hotel, Pilmour Links, KY16 9JQ
www.macdonaldhotels.co.uk/our-hotels/scotland/ st-andrews/macdonald-rusacks-hotel/eat-drink
For many people, particularly the legions of international pilgrims who jet in from the States and Asia, St Andrews is all about golf. If you happen to be a golf-mad foodie, both passions are catered for simultaneously in the Macdonald Rusacks Hotel, where front-row balcony seats for the golfing action at the 18th hole of the Old Course are available for the price of a meal in the Rocca Restaurant amid a chic contemporary decor of richly-coloured fabrics and darkwood tables. The kitchen's food is modern, ingredients-led from the best local supply lines, and provides deep satisfaction. The six-course taster opens, perhaps, with cured salmon supported by pressed cucumber, lemon, hazelnuts and fennel, followed by trompette mushroom risotto with parmesan crisp and cep foam. Classy fish dishes may include halibut served with clams, seafood chowder and chorizo, while meatier ideas take in braised beef cheek with Savoy cabbage, potato mash, Puy lentils and confit shallot. Desserts aim for the same level with the likes of lemon curd sponge with raspberry ice cream.

Chef Glen Roach **Seats** 70, Private dining 35 **Open** All Year **Parking** 23 **Notes** Vegetarian dishes, Children welcome

St Andrews Bar & Grill
@ SCOTTISH, SEAFOOD
01334 837000 | Fairmont St Andrews, Scotland, KY16 8PN
www.fairmont.com/standrews
A free shuttle bus takes you from the Fairmont to this dining option in the clubhouse, but it is a lovely walk. Spectacularly situated on a promontory overlooking St Andrews Bay, the evening sees the seafood bar and grill come into their own.

Chef Christopher Niven **Seats** 80 **Open** All Year
Prices from S £8, M £14, D £6 **Parking** 40
Notes Vegetarian dishes, Children welcome

Sands Grill
@ MODERN SCOTTISH
01334 474371 | Old Course Hotel, Golf Resort & Spa, KY16 9SP
www.oldcoursehotel.co.uk
Overlooking the world-famous golf course and the coast beyond, the Old Course Hotel occupies a desirable position and offers a wide range of dining options. The Sands Grill is the more informal option, a contemporary brasserie run by slick, unstuffy staff.

Open All Year

Seasons at Rufflets St Andrews
@@ MODERN BRITISH, EUROPEAN ⬥ NOTABLE WINE LIST
01334 460890 | Strathkinness Low Road, KY16 9TX
www.rufflets.co.uk/wine-dine/seasons-restaurant/
The creeper-covered turreted mansion has been in the same family since 1952, sitting in 10 acres of exquisite gardens. Its name refers to the 'rough flat lands' that once comprised the local landscape. The cooking is as modern as can be.

Chef David Kinnes **Seats** 60, Private dining 130 **Open** All Year **Parking** 50 **Notes** Vegetarian dishes, Children welcome

Road Hole Restaurant

◉◉◉ **MODERN, STEAK, SEAFOOD**
01334 474371 | Old Course Hotel, Golf Resort & Spa, KY16 9SP
www.oldcoursehotel.co.uk

Steaks, seafood and modern dishes with views of the golf

There is no shortage of five-star hotels on the Scottish golfing circuit, but for golf-mad gourmets only one do: the Old Course overlooks the cradle of the game at the world-famous links at St Andrews and will certainly keep you fed and watered in grand style while basking in a spectacular location with views of West Sands beach and the majestic coastline. The grand old pile towers above the 17th hole, the 'Road Hole', so it seems only right that the main dining room here has been named after it. It's a civilized, upmarket spot with highly professional, genuinely engaged staff delivering perfectly pitched service, and an open kitchen providing an alternative theatre for those who have no interest in the stick-swinging action outside.

Given the setting, luxurious items come as no surprise – Martin Hollis's modern Scottish menus are built on the finest produce from Scotland's larder, including

> "It's a civilized, upmarket spot with highly professional, genuinely engaged staff delivering perfectly pitched service"

some classic local seafood and steak options, so why not open with some thoroughbred shellfish? Keep it simple with Kyle of Tongue oysters brought to life with the acidic kiss of shallot vinegar and lemon, or if you'd prefer the chefs to do more than merely open shells, langoustines paired with pork belly come with the textural interest of crisp pancetta and crackling, all enhanced with liquorice sauce. As for main courses, Dover sole fillet comes with crab, crushed Jersey Royals, sauce Grenoble and lemon gel,

while red meat aficionados can expect prime cuts of pedigree Black Isle rib-eye or fillet, or perhaps a modernist idea serving venison loin with vanilla mash, ginger and lime swede, rhubarb, and ginger sauce.

Waiting at the end, the grown-up bitterness of an ultra-rich Guanaja chocolate marquise is offset by salted toffee, honeycomb and white chocolate ice cream. If you prefer a savoury finish, superb artisanal cheeses come with truffle honey and black grapes.

Chef Martin Hollis
Seats 70, Private dining 16
Open All Year
Parking 150
Notes Vegetarian dishes, Children welcome

ST MONANS

MAP 21, NO50

Craig Millar@16 West End

◉◉ MODERN SCOTTISH 🍷 NOTABLE WINE LIST

01333 730327 | 16 West End, KY10 2BX

www.16westend.com

Sweeping views of the Firth of Forth and St Monans harbour can get dramatic when winter waves surge over the sea wall, but the proximity of the sea is a reminder of the business here: serving seafood with an exciting modern spin.

Chef Craig Millar **Seats** 40, Private dining 24 **Closed** 25-26 December, 1-2 January, 2 weeks January **Parking** 6 **Notes** Vegetarian dishes, No children under 5 years at lunch, 12 years at dinner

■ GLASGOW

GLASGOW

MAP 20, NS56

La Bonne Auberge

◉ FRENCH, MEDITERRANEAN

0141 352 8310 | Holiday Inn Glasgow City Centre - Theatreland, 161 West Nile Street, G1 2RL

www.labonneauberge.co.uk

This ever-popular venue is kitted out in contemporary style with exposed brickwork, tiled and wooden flooring and lamps on wooden tables, and has attentive and friendly staff. Meats, including BBQ pork loin and rib-eye steaks, are cooked on the grill.

Open All Year

Cail Bruich

◉◉◉ MODERN SCOTTISH 𝒱 🍷 NOTABLE WINE LIST

0141 334 6265 | 752 Great Western Road, G12 8QX

www.cailbruich.co.uk

It isn't always necessary to head out into the Highlands in search of country cuisine. Here in Glasgow's swinging West End, the Charalambous brothers bring it to the city doorstep, in a modern bistro setting where hanging baskets flank the door, and rows of tables at crimson banquettes form a long, informal space. The vegetarian dishes alone are inspired, offering spelt with Jerusalem artichoke, lettuce and Brinkburn goats' cheese, for mains. Elsewhere, stimulating combinations distinguish the seasonally-changing menus, perhaps Loch Fyne scallop with smoked eel, sour cabbage and apple, and then lamb with sprouting broccoli, anchovies and

black olives, or stone bass with langoustine, clementine and pumpkin. For the seven-course taster, there are fish or meat alternatives at two stages, and caramelised whey with sea buckthorn, apple and fennel pollen makes for a thoroughly modern finale. Speciality beers and a tempting list of imaginative cocktails supplement the commendable wine list.

Chef Chris Charalambous **Seats** 48 **Closed** 25-26 December, 1 January, 1 week January **Notes** No children under 8 years

Chez Mal Brasserie

◉ MODERN FRENCH

0141 572 1001 | Malmaison Glasgow, 278 West George Street, G2 4LL

www.malmaison.com

The Glasgow Mal has made its home in a deconsecrated Greek Orthodox church. A mix of traditional and modern French brasserie cooking is the draw, with select breeds and cuts of thoroughbred beef the backbone. Soufflé du jour is worth a look at for dessert.

Open All Year

The Fish People Café

◉ MODERN SEAFOOD

0141 429 8787 | 350a Scotland Street, G5 8QF

www.thefishpeoplecafe.co.uk

This lively little fish restaurant run by the fishmonger next door is done out with a French bistro-inspired look, a marble-topped bar and blackboards touting the day's specials. It sounds an irresistible proposition, and the skilled team in the kitchen know how to handle the peerless piscine produce, turning out uncomplicated dishes with pin-sharp technique and timings.

Chef John Gillespie **Seats** 32 **Closed** 25-26 December, 1st week January (including 1 January) **Prices from** S £5.50, M £17.50, D £6.50 **Notes** Vegetarian dishes, Children welcome

The Gannet
⊛⊛⊛ MODERN SCOTTISH *V*
0141 204 2081 | 1155 Argyle Street, G3 8TB
www.thegannetgla.com
Conceived on a research trip to the Hebridean
west of Scotland, the Reid brothers' venue in the
Finnieston district of the city is a tribute to the
produce of the growers, breeders and gatherers
of the islands and coasts. Transposed into the
urban setting of a modern bistro with walls of
bare brick and stone, It takes on a new identity in
the form of lively tasting menus (including four-
and six-course vegetarian offerings) of European
dishes that mobilise up-to-date technique
without undue complication. A spring example of
the six-course seasonal menu takes in Gigha
halibut with horseradish and kombucha, and
Hereford beef followed by monkfish from
Scrabster. Next up is hogget from the Borders,
accompanied by aubergine, miso, orache and
kidney fat sauce. Then there's cheese if you want
it, then rhubarb with yogurt, and salted caramel
with gorse. A wine list of true discernment
includes Coravin selections by the glass.

Chef Peter McKenna, Ivan Stein **Seats** 45, Private
dining 14 **Closed** 25-26 December, 1-2 January
Notes Children welcome

The Hanoi Bike Shop
⊛ VIETNAMESE
0141 334 7165 | 8 Ruthven Lane, G12 9BG
www.hanoibikeshop.co.uk
Sister restaurant to the Ubiquitous Chip and
Stravaigin, this colourful West End venture is set
across two buzzing floors. The canteen-style
vibe suits the authentic street food menu of
dazzling Vietnamese flavours. The menu gives
the Vietnamese names of dishes followed by an
English translation.

Closed 25 December, 1 January

Mother India
⊛ INDIAN
0141 221 1663 | 28 Westminster Terrace,
Sauchiehall Street, G3 7RU
www.motherindia.co.uk
This landmark restaurant, launched in 1990,
continues to draw the crowds with its inventive,
flavour-packed Indian food. Spread over three
floors, Mother India avoids cliché in its decor.
The menu takes a step away from curry-house
standards to deliver broadly appealing dishes.

Closed Christmas, New Year

Number Sixteen
⊛⊛ MODERN INTERNATIONAL
0141 339 2544 | 16 Byres Road, G11 5JY
www.number16.co.uk
This dinky neighbourhood restaurant has a
strong local following. It's an elbow-to-elbow
sort of place with a pocket-sized downstairs
area, and a mini-mezzanine above, all decorated
with colourful artwork, and kept ticking over by
casually dressed, on-the-ball staff. The chefs in
the open-to-view kitchen aren't scared to
experiment with a vibrant barrage of flavours,
without losing sight of the seasons.

Chef Sean Currie **Seats** 36, Private dining 17
Closed 25-26 December, 1-2 January
Prices from S £5.95, M £15.95, D £7.95
Notes Vegetarian dishes, Children welcome

One Devonshire Gardens by Hotel du Vin
⊛⊛ MODERN FRENCH *V* NOTABLE WINE LIST
0141 339 2001 | 1 Devonshire Gardens, G12 0UX
www.hotelduvin.com
This supremely elegant Victorian terrace in the
heart of Glasgow – with a long-standing foodie
reputation to maintain – is the jewel in the crown
of the Hotel du Vin group. The restaurant is an
elegant setting for lunch and dinner where chef
Gary Townsend has put his own contemporary
European stamp on the kitchen's output bringing
fresh, seasonal and locally sourced produce to
the fore.

Chef Gary Townsend **Seats** 78, Private dining 80
Open All Year **Prices from** S £9.75, M £25.95, D £9
Notes Children welcome

111 by Nico

⊛ MODERN EUROPEAN

0141 334 0111 | 111 Cleveden Road, Kelvinside, G12 0JU

www.111bynico.co.uk

Nico Simeone's altruism in employing youngsters who didn't get the best start in life is thoroughly commendable. Together, they produce contemporary cooking for a city-smart audience, the kind that appreciates Ingenious duck leg croustillants with textures of parsnip including an Indian-spiced purée.

Opium

⊛ CHINESE, ORIENTAL FUSION

0141 332 6668 | 191 Hope Street, G2 2UL

www.opiumrestaurant.co.uk

A pin-sharp, contemporary-styled Asian-fusion restaurant in the heart of Glasgow. Big picture windows allow light to flood into a slick space where communal tables share the space with conventional seating. Kwan Yu Lee has honed an on-trend mix of classical and modern Asian fusion dishes.

Open All Year

Ox and Finch

⊛⊛ MODERN BRITISH *V*

0141 339 8627 | 920 Sauchiehall Street, G3 7TF

www.oxandfinch.com

Tapas-size portions are the deal at this buzzing venue. Bare brick walls, roughly painted wooden floors, banquette and booth seating and unbuttoned service create a casual, laid-back atmosphere. The menu is divided into such headings as 'snacks' and 'raw, cured and cold'.

Chef Daniel Spurr, Aurelien Mourez **Seats** 70, Private dining 14 **Closed** 25 December and 1 January **Notes** Children welcome

Shish Mahal

⊛ INDIAN, PAKISTANI *V*

0141 339 8256 | 60-68 Park Road, G4 9JF

www.shishmahal.co.uk

Opened in the 1960s by the charismatic 'Mr Ali', Shish Mahal is a Glaswegian institution which has moved with the times. There's a smart modern feel to the restaurant, while the menu takes in old favourites as well as exploring plenty of intriguing new ideas.

Chef I Humayun **Seats** 84, Private dining 14 **Closed** 25 December **Prices from** S £3.25, M £9.95, D £3.95 **Notes** Children welcome

Stravaigin

⊛ MODERN INTERNATIONAL, SCOTTISH *V*

0141 334 2665 | 28 Gibson Street, Kelvinbridge, G12 8NX

www.stravaigin.co.uk

In a busy West End street, this popular all-day bar/restaurant abides by its maxim "Think global, eat local". So, expect the unexpected, such as Peterhead monkfish cheek with red lentil dhal; sticky pork belly with rice noodles; and bay leaf and cardamom custard tart, as well as others from India, Korea, Mexico and elsewhere.

Chef James MacRae **Seats** 62 **Closed** 25 December, 1 January **Prices from** S £6.50, M £12.50, D £7 **Notes** Children welcome

See advertisement opposite

Ubiquitous Chip Restaurant

⊛⊛ SCOTTISH *V* NOTABLE WINE LIST

0141 334 5007 | 12 Ashton Lane, G12 8SJ

www.ubiquitouschip.co.uk

Affectionately known by Glaswegians as The Chip, its long-held inspiration owes much to Scottish regional dishes. At least one – venison haggis – has been served here since opening day in 1971, but regardless of time served, there's Eyemouth crab, Barra scallops, Ayrshire chicken breast or Aberdeen Angus beef.

Chef Andrew Mitchell **Seats** 120, Private dining 45 **Closed** 25 December and 1 January **Prices from** S £9.95, M £19.95, D £7.45 **Notes** Children welcome

See advertisement on page 470

Wee Lochan

⊛ MODERN SCOTTISH

0141 338 6606 | 340 Crow Road, Broomhill, G11 7HT

www.an-lochan.com

The black frontage gives a distinguished look to a neighbourhood restaurant in the quiet, leafy reaches of the West End, its wide terrace allowing pleasant outdoor dining in summer. The contemporary Scottish cooking scores a hit with precise, defined flavours.

Chef Chris Bryers **Seats** 50 **Closed** 25-26 December, 1-2 January **Prices from** S £6.50, M £14.50, D £6 **Notes** Vegetarian dishes, Children welcome

Stravaigin

- WANDERING SINCE 1994 -

28 Gibson Street, Glasgow G12 8NX
Stravaigin.co.uk
0141 334 2665

Ubiquitous Chip

■ HIGHLAND

ACHARACLE
MAP 22, NM66

Mingarry Park
◉◉ MODERN BRITISH
01967 431202 | Mingarry, PH36 4JX
www.mingarryparkhouse.co.uk
The relaxing dining room at Mingarry Park enjoys spectacular views, setting the scene for a bold menu. Creativity is shown in dishes such as sous-vide Moidart venison loin accompanied by carrot purée, maple-glazed Chantenay carrots, a summer greens sponge and an intense red wine jus.

Chef David Punter **Closed** November to April **Parking** 20 **Notes** Vegetarian dishes, Children welcome

ARISAIG
MAP 22, NM68

Arisaig House *NEW*
◉◉ MODERN SCOTTISH *V*
01687 450730 | Beasdale, PH39 4NR
www.arisaighouse.co.uk
Enjoy freshly prepared meals at this country house hotel where the daily-changing menus make good use of local produce and the kitchen garden dictates the menu content, when In season. Look out for the Arisaig House Cranachan showcasing a skilful display of patisserie techniques.

Chef Colin Nicholson **Seats** 30, Private dining 10 **Closed** November to March **Parking** 20 **Notes** Children welcome

CROMARTY
MAP 23, NH76

The Factor's House
◉ MODERN BRITISH
01381 600394 | Denny Road, IV11 8YT
www.thefactorshouse.com
This attractive red sandstone house on a coastal inlet features a wood-floored dining room with walls in burgundy and grey. A daily-changing four-course dinner menu, including Scottish cheeses, is the offering, and there is a real personality to the dishes.

Closed 15 December to 5 January

DORNOCH
MAP 23, NH78

Links House at Royal Dornoch
◉◉ CLASSIC SCOTTISH
01862 810279 | Links House, Golf Road, IV25 3LW
www.linkshousedornoch.com
Links House is single-mindedly devoted to the pursuit of golf and pictures of fairways and bunkers adorn the dining room, where a peat-burning fireplace is a feature. The head chef brings his classical French training to the Orangery restaurant here.

Chef Javier Santos **Seats** 33 **Closed** Christmas, 3 January to 25 March **Parking** 6 **Notes** Children welcome

FORT AUGUSTUS
MAP 23, NH30

The Inch
◉◉ TRADITIONAL SCOTTISH
01456 450900 | Inchnacardoch Bay, PH32 4BL
www.inchhotel.com
The Inch occupies an old hunting lodge above Inchnacardoch Bay and the hotel's restaurant boasts one of the best views over the iconic and dramatic Loch Ness. The food has a strong sense of place, with Scottish produce dominating the impressive menu.

Chef Philip Carnegie **Seats** 36 **Closed** 31 October to 31 March **Prices from** S £5.95, M £13.50, D £5.95 **Parking** 18 **Notes** Vegetarian dishes, Children welcome

FORT WILLIAM
MAP 22, NN17

Inverlochy Castle Hotel
Rosettes suspended MODERN FRENCH *V* NOTABLE WINE LIST
01397 702177 | Torlundy, PH33 6SN
www.inverlochycastlehotel.com
The Rosette award for this establishment has been suspended due to a change of chef and reassessment will take place in due course. This very grand baronial castle is set in a wonderfully verdant valley at the foot of Ben Nevis. Views are spectacular, and there's a real sense of history and opulence in the richly decorated public spaces, with all the high ceilings, antiques and crystal chandeliers you could wish for. The restaurant is more intimate and extremely formal in approach – white gloves are worn by smartly attired staff and gentlemen guests will need their jackets. Don't be intimidated, though – the team are wonderfully hospitable.

Chef Mark Rossi **Seats** 40, Private dining 20 **Open** All Year **Prices from** S £19, M £40, D £16 **Parking** 20 **Notes** No children under 8 years

GLENFINNAN
MAP 22, NM98

The Prince's House
🏵🏵 MODERN BRITISH

01397 722246 | PH37 4LT

www.glenfinnan.co.uk

Kieron and Ina Kelly's white-fronted house has charm in bucket loads. The dining room is hung with a fine art collection and the small conservatory has ravishing views over the glen. Kieron Kelly's cooking steps up to the regional plate in four-course set menus.

Chef Kieron Kelly **Seats** 30 **Closed** Christmas, October to March **Parking** 18 **Notes** Vegetarian dishes, Children welcome

GRANTOWN-ON-SPEY
MAP 23, NJ02

Garden Restaurant NEW
🏵 MODERN SCOTTISH

01479 872526 | Grant Arms Hotel, 25–27 The Square, PH26 3HF

www.grantarmshotel.com

When you've sharpened your appetite with a day's wildlife watching and outdoor activities in the magnificent Cairngorms, the restaurant of this handsome Victorian hotel makes a fitting spot for a seasonal menu of impeccable local produce. The cooking is hearty, traditional and straightforward with no frills or frippery.

Open All Year

INVERGARRY
MAP 22, NH30

Glengarry Castle Hotel
🏵 SCOTTISH, INTERNATIONAL

01809 501254 | PH35 4HW

www.glengarry.net

The Glengarry, overlooking Loch Oich, is a slice of Victorian Scottish baronial, built in the 1860s. Spotless white linen and quality glassware glow beneath the chandelier in the opulent dining room, where lightly modernised traditional fare is the order of the day.

Chef Romuald Denesle **Seats** 40 **Closed** mid November to mid March **Parking** 30 **Notes** Vegetarian dishes, Children welcome

INVERGORDON
MAP 23, NH77

Kincraig Castle Hotel
🏵 MODERN SCOTTISH

01349 852587 | IV18 0LF

www.kincraig-castle-hotel.co.uk

Pretty gables and wee turrets give this former ancestral seat of Clan MacKenzie a bit of gravitas, while its lush lawn sweeps down towards the Cromarty Firth. The house is decorated to suit the grand baronial setting, and the traditional Alexander Restaurant matches the mood.

Open All Year

INVERNESS
MAP 23, NH64

Bunchrew House Hotel
🏵🏵 MODERN BRITISH

01463 234917 | Bunchrew, IV3 8TA

www.bunchrewhousehotel.com

Bunchrew House is a magnificent 17th-century mansion, complete with turrets and a pink façade, on the water's edge of the Beauly Firth. Modern British with a basis of classical influence is the kitchen's view of its culinary world. There is a daily changing menu.

Closed 23–26 December

Contrast Brasserie
🏵 SCOTTISH V

01463 223777 | Glenmoriston Town House Hotel, 20 Ness Bank, IV2 4SF

www.glenmoristontownhouse.com

As Glenmoriston Town House Hotel's main restaurant, Contrast has a rather romantic air, thanks to low lighting and an evening pianist. Unsurprisingly, Scottish produce makes appearances, as in spiced North Uist scallops, and West Coast sea trout. Overall, though, the cooking is modern and international, so dishes of pan-seared Gressingham duck breast; and mugi miso monkfish also star.

Chef Andrea Calistro **Seats** 56, Private dining 90 **Open** All Year **Prices from** S £4.95, M £12, D £5.95 **Parking** 45 **Notes** Children welcome

Loch Ness Country House Hotel
MODERN BRITISH
01463 230512 | Loch Ness Road, IV3 8JN
www.lochnesscountryhousehotel.co.uk
This creeper-covered Georgian house in lovely grounds is not actually on Loch Ness, but is three miles outside Inverness. The classy interiors are all stripes and tartan, with three dining rooms, each with only a few tables, decorated in restrained greys and browns.

Open All Year

Rocpool
MODERN EUROPEAN
01463 717274 | 1 Ness Walk, IV3 5NE
www.rocpoolrestaurant.com
A sweeping glass frontage reveals floodlit views of the river and castle at night from this buzzy brasserie on the banks of the River Ness. The interior is no slouch either, its sharp contemporary design featuring lots of wood and natural tones as a backdrop to an appealing cast of modern European dishes built on top-class Scottish produce.

Chef Steven Devlin Seats 55 Closed 25–26 December, 1–3 January Prices from S £5.95, M £13.95, D £7.95 Notes Vegetarian dishes, Children welcome

Rocpool Reserve and Chez Roux
FRENCH, SCOTTISH V
01463 240089 | 14 Culduthel Road, IV2 4AG
rocpool.com
With the hallowed Roux name above the door (Monsieur Albert in this case), the auld alliance is alive and well at this contemporary restaurant close to the castle. A vein of French classicism runs through the cooking, while the impeccable Scottish credentials of the produce is trumpeted too.

Chef Lee Pattie Seats 60, Private dining 14 Open All Year Prices from S £10.50, M £18.50, D £8.50 Parking 14 Notes Children welcome

Table Manors Restaurant
TRADITIONAL SCOTTISH
01463 831878 | Achnagairn Estate, Kirkhill, IV5 7PD
www.perfect-manors.com
Table Manors is part of the Achnagairn Estate, whose luxury lodges are nicknamed the 'perfect manors'. Designed in contemporary style, the restaurant demonstrates the importance of space and light. Wordplay continues on the compact menu includes 'Crabbing the Nettle' – sweetcorn pannacotta, white crab, hazelnut, avocado and nettle.

Closed Monday to Tuesday (winter and spring)

KINGUSSIE
MAP 23, NH70

The Cross
MODERN SCOTTISH V NOTABLE WINE LIST
01540 661166 | Tweed Mill Brae, Ardbroilach Road, PH21 1LB
www.thecross.co.uk
A converted 19th-century tweed mill standing in four acres of riverside grounds in the Cairngorms National Park, The Cross is a country restaurant with rooms on the human scale, with eight brightly designed bedrooms and a beamed restaurant where a mood of informal tranquillity reigns. The cooking is modern, ingredients-led and matches the pastoral surroundings with locally reared meats a speciality – witness lamb served two ways, roast loin, and cannelloni of the shoulder, together with artichoke, broccoli purée and glazed shallots in jus gras, or roast quail breast with leg meat bonbons, parsnip purée, apple and richly truffled jus. Elsewhere, seared John Dory is nicely matched with roast langoustine, confit sun-blushed tomato, onion purée and shellfish foam, while dessert is a dark chocolate shell filled with an irresistible cinnamon brulée mousse. A six-course taster picks out some of the main menu's highlights, while the three-course lunch deal, with three choices at each stage, delivers stonking value.

Chef David Skiggs Seats 26 Closed Christmas and January (excluding New Year) Parking 12 Notes Children welcome

STRONTIAN

Kilcamb Lodge Hotel

◉◉◉ **MODERN SCOTTISH, SEAFOOD** *V* 🍷 NOTABLE WINE LIST
01967 402257 | PH36 4HY
www.kilcamblodge.co.uk

Standing on the shore of Loch Sunart in 22 acres of sumptuous grounds, Kilcamb offers unruffled tranquillity and seclusion, the journey alone providing a delightful taste of the wild Ardnamurchan Peninsula. With just 12 rooms, the Georgian house is an intimate hideaway that delivers old-school country-house comforts all the way to the elegant dining room, where linen is crisp, cutlery and glassware sparkle, and the loch views paint an unforgettable backdrop to modern Scottish cooking. Gary Phillips provisions the larder from local crofts, estates and fishing boats, the latter's catch showcased in daily-changing seafood specials. Hand-dived scallops might open the show in the vibrant company of ham hock terrine and pickled cauliflower. Next up, perhaps braised featherblade of superb Highland beef with herb mashed potato, crispy haggis cannelloni and bourguignon sauce.

Chef Gary Phillips **Seats** 40, Private dining 14
Closed 1 January to 1 February
Prices from S £6.50, M £17.50, D £8 **Parking** 28
Notes Children welcome

LOCHALINE
MAP 20, NM64

The Whitehouse Restaurant
◉◉ MODERN SCOTTISH *V*
01967 421777 | PA80 5XT
www.thewhitehouserestaurant.co.uk

A five-minute uphill walk from the CalMac ferry on the remote Morvern shores, this intimate little restaurant overlooks the Sound of Mull from a light-flooded, nautical-themed dining room. The kitchen cooks whatever its suppliers have provided on the day – this splendid local bounty appears in dishes that maintain integrity through simplicity.

Chef Michael Burgoyne, Lee Myers **Seats** 26
Closed November to March, 25 June to 1 July **Parking** 10
Notes Children welcome

NAIRN
MAP 23, NH85

Hickory
◉ TRADITIONAL, INTERNATIONAL
01667 452301 | Golf View Hotel & Spa, Seabank Road, IV12 4HD
www.crerarhotels.com/golf-view-hotel-spa

In case you get the impression there's only golf to look at, this hotel's seaside location looks out over the Moray Firth. Expect locally-sourced produce at Hickory with meat from the Crerar Home Farm pedigree herd.

Chef Jon Wood **Seats** 70 **Open** All Year **Parking** 30
Notes Vegetarian dishes, Children welcome

SPEAN BRIDGE
MAP 22, NN28

Russell's at Smiddy House
◉◉ MODERN SCOTTISH
01397 712335 | Roy Bridge Road, PH34 4EU
www.smiddyhouse.com

The AA has long recognised the well-presented Scottish cuisine served in this intimate, candlelit restaurant, once the village blacksmith's. Scottish produce is key. Menu highlights include Wester Ross salmon, Arisaig prawns, scallops from the Isle of Mull, Perthshire wood pigeon, Highland game, lamb and beef, pine nut-crusted monkfish and, of course, Scottish cheeses.

Chef Glen Russell **Seats** 38 **Parking** 15
Notes Vegetarian dishes, No children under 12 years

STRONTIAN
MAP 22, NM86

Kilcamb Lodge Hotel
◉◉◉ MODERN SCOTTISH, SEAFOOD *V* ⚑ NOTABLE WINE LIST
See opposite

TAIN
MAP 23, NH78

Dining Room NEW
◉◉ FRENCH, SCOTTISH
01862 871671 | Glenmorangie House, Cadboll, By Fearn, IV20 1XP
www.theglenmorangiehouse.com

Glenmorangie House is an intimate country bolthole and a pilgrimage spot for fans of its eponymous single malt whisky. The cooking here is on song, its modern approach teaming up prime local ingredients with a resourceful range of ideas and techniques. And yes, the odd shot of that malt may well find its way into the dishes.

Chef John Wilson **Seats** 38, Private dining 12
Closed January **Parking** 20 **Notes** Vegetarian dishes, No children

THURSO

Forss House Hotel

◉◉ MODERN SCOTTISH

01847 861201 | Forss, KW14 7XY

www.forsshousehotel.co.uk

You can't get much further away from urban bustle in the mainland British Isles than the northern Highlands, where this Georgian country-house hotel luxuriates in tranquillity below a waterfall on the River Forss, amid acres of woodland. Plenty of pedigree Highland produce is on parade.

Chef Andrew Smith **Seats** 26, Private dining 14 **Closed** 23 December to 4 January **Prices from** S £6, M £15, D £6.50 **Parking** 14 **Notes** Vegetarian dishes, Children welcome

TORRIDON

The Torridon

◉◉◉ MODERN SCOTTISH *V*

01445 791242 | By Achnasheen, Wester Ross, IV22 2EY

www.thetorridon.com

You have to be pretty determined to track down The Torridon, but the reward for the hunt is a turreted Victorian lochside lodge that still offers plenty of sporting activity, a copiously stocked whisky bar, and a panelled and leathered ambience for sinking into while you forget the rigorous journey. Ross Stovold has the produce of a two-acre kitchen garden at his disposal in the 1887 Restaurant, where he offers contemporary Scottish cuisine in dishes that are presented with artful simplicity. Textures and flavours work in harmony in a fantastically simple yet refined starter of charred Arbroath asparagus with confit egg yolk and crowdie curd cheese, hen of the woods adding a subtle earthiness. Main course halibut from Scrabster is accompanied by three versions of cauliflower – puréed with miso, pickled and charred – Shetland mussels and cured trout. For dessert, try the hazelnut praline sponge with cocoa nibs, malt and smoked butterscotch.

Chef Ross Stovold **Seats** 38, Private dining 16 **Closed** 2 January for 5 weeks **Parking** 20 **Notes** No children under 10 years

WICK

Mackay's Hotel

◉ MODERN SCOTTISH *V*

01955 602323 | Union Street, KW1 5ED

www.mackayshotel.co.uk

Mackay's is home to the No. 1 Bistro, a contemporary restaurant with a relaxed vibe. The kitchen makes good use of quality local ingredients, and there's a modernity to the output. There's a buzzy bar for real ales, cocktails and a terrific range of whiskies.

Chef Ray McRitchie **Seats** 40, Private dining 30 **Closed** 24-25 December and 1-2 January **Prices from** S £5, M £11, D £6 **Notes** Children welcome

◼ SOUTH LANARKSHIRE

BLANTYRE

Crossbasket Castle

◉◉◉ CLASSICAL FRENCH *V*

01698 829461 | Crossbasket Estate, Stoneymeadow Road, G72 9UE

www.crossbasketcastle.com

Not far from Glasgow, Crossbasket was conjured out of a much older castle in the 17th century, complete with crenellated façade and spiral turret staircases. An elegant dining room of pale yellow wallpaper, a winter fire and linened tables under an ornate gold-leafed plasterwork ceiling, offering superb views over the gardens, is a refined backdrop for a Roux operation, père et fils, in which the classical French dishes are finished with some innovative touches. Jerusalem artichoke velouté comes with chestnut cream and artichoke crisps, while torchon of duck liver and braised pig's head is accompanied by Sauternes jelly and truffled brioche. At main course there might be roast fillet of Orkney beef, short rib and cheek with heritage carrots and bone marrow jus, or fillet of wild Scottish halibut with crisp confit chicken thigh. Desserts range from Yorkshire rhubarb with sour cream vacherin to carrot cake with praline cream, blood orange and carrot sorbet.

Chef Albert and Michel Roux Jnr, Aaron Sobey **Seats** 30, Private dining 250 **Open** All Year **Prices from** S £11, M £19, D £9 **Parking** 120 **Notes** Vegetarian dishes, Children welcome

EAST KILBRIDE
MAP 20, NS65

Macdonald Crutherland House
BRITISH

01355 577000 | Strathaven Road, G75 0QZ

www.macdonald-hotels.co.uk

Dating from the early 1700s, Crutherland House stands in nearly 40 acres of peaceful grounds. The restaurant keeps things traditional, with its panelled walls, paintings and burnished darkwood tables. The menu takes a classical approach to things, with plenty of Scottish ingredients on show.

Open All Year

■ EAST LOTHIAN

ABERLADY
MAP 21, NT47

Ducks Inn
MODERN BRITISH

01875 870682 | Main Street, EH32 0RE

www.ducks.co.uk

Located in the heart of a small village, Ducks Inn covers all the bases with its bar-bistro, restaurant and smart accommodation. The good-looking dining area is matched by the attractiveness of what arrives on the plate. The kitchen turns out appealing flavour combinations.

Closed 25 December

GULLANE
MAP 21, NT48

Greywalls and Chez Roux
MODERN FRENCH COUNTRY V

01620 842144 | Muirfield, EH31 2EG

www.greywalls.co.uk

Golfers enjoy views of Muirfield's 9th and 18th holes from Albert Roux's elegant, Lutyens-designed country house hotel. Spread through four rooms, Chez Roux restaurant impresses and delights with Isle of Mull scallops and chicory; roast veal with sweetbreads; roast Loch Fyne salmon with fennel ravioli; and classic lemon tart with raspberry sorbet originally created by the figurehead himself.

Chef Ryan McCutcheon **Seats** 80, Private dining 20
Open All Year **Prices from** S £9.50, M £25.50, D £9
Parking 40 **Notes** Children welcome

The Stables at The Bonnie Badger NEW
SCOTTISH V

01620 621111 | Main Street, EH31 2AB

bonniebadger.com

Handy for Gullane's golfing and beaches, Tom Kitchin's restaurant with rooms is a sure-fire hit with its stylish Highlands-meet-Scandi makeover and some seriously good food driven by the 'from nature to plate' philosophy of its founders. Soaring rafters and original sandstone walls create the setting for a roster of updated comfort-food classics.

Chef Matthew Budge **Seats** 106, Private dining 32
Open All Year **Prices from** S £6, M £12.50, D £8
Notes Children welcome

NORTH BERWICK
MAP 21, NT58

Macdonald Marine Hotel & Spa
EUROPEAN

01620 897300 | Cromwell Road, EH39 4LZ

www.macdonaldhotels.co.uk/marine

The Marine Hotel is an upscale Grade II listed Victorian manor overlooking the East Lothian golf course. The Craigleith Restaurant surveys the action through the sweeping bay windows. The kitchen follows contemporary culinary style, while showing respect for classical thinking.

Open All Year

■ WEST LOTHIAN

UPHALL
MAP 21, NT07

Macdonald Houstoun House
TRADITIONAL BRITISH, MODERN SCOTTISH

01506 853831 | EH52 6JS

www.macdonaldhotels.co.uk/our-hotels/
macdonald-houstoun-house

The white-painted house, surrounded by 22 acres of woodlands, dates from the 16th century. The restaurant sports deep burgundy walls, chandeliers and elegant unclothed tables. The kitchen relies heavily on quality Scottish ingredients and presents them in a modern, unfussy style.

Open All Year

■ MORAY

FORRES
MAP 23, NJ05

Cluny Bank
◉ TRADITIONAL EUROPEAN
01309 674304 | 69 St Leonards Road, IV36 1DW
clunybankhotel.co.uk
A substantial Victorian mansion in lush gardens, Cluny Bank has traditionally styled decor and a small, smart restaurant called Franklin's. There is a lot of period charm to the restaurant and a definite air of sophistication, while the menu name-checks the local Moray suppliers.

Chef Lloyd Kenny **Seats** 24 **Open** All Year
Prices from S £5.25, M £22.55, D £6.50 **Parking** 10
Notes Vegetarian dishes, No children under 8 years

■ PERTH & KINROSS

ABERFELDY
MAP 23, NN84

Thyme Restaurant
◉◉ SCOTTISH, INTERNATIONAL
01887 820850 | Errichel House, Errichel, Crieff Road, PH15 2EL
www.errichel.co.uk
Thyme is located within the Roundhouse at Errichel, a very impressive contemporary building. The weekly-changing menu features lamb, beef and pork from the surrounding working farm itself, along with many other ingredients – real 'farm to fork' in action.

Chef Paul Newman **Seats** 40 **Closed** 25-26 December
Parking 10 **Notes** Vegetarian dishes, No children under 12 years

AUCHTERARDER
MAP 21, NN91

Andrew Fairlie at Gleneagles
◉◉◉◉ FRENCH, SCOTTISH V ▲NOTABLE WINE LIST
01764 694267 | The Gleneagles Hotel, PH3 1NF
www.andrewfairlie.co.uk
A shining beacon of the Scottish culinary scene until his untimely death in January 2019, Andrew Fairlie's legacy lives on in his namesake restaurant's cooking today. Fairlie was the winner of the first Roux Scholarship back in 1984 and received the accolade of AA Chefs' Chef of the Year in 2006. His success continues to inspire and set many young chefs on the road to success, and that ethos is carried forward here by head chef Stephen McLaughlin, whose passion

for French cuisine runs deep. What is particularly striking is the pursuit of excellence that shines through in a team that delivers finely crafted, dazzlingly creative, contemporary French cuisine. The five-star hotel and its three championship golf courses need little introduction and, after so many years at the top of the Scottish dining scene, neither does the restaurant. An independent business in the heart of the hotel, the lavish windowless dining room is a deeply cossetting space, a shimmering haven with atmospheric lighting and original artworks, watched over by a passionate team who make you feel at ease.

Choose between the à la carte or eight-course dégustation menus, and be prepared for high-intensity food from a team that puts in the hard graft to max out flavours, so Scottish lobster shells are oak-smoked for hours, before the sweet meat is returned to the shell and dressed with warm lime butter sauce and fresh green herbs. Next, comes rose veal, the deeply caramelised fillet and crisp sweetbread matched with braised oxtail, celeriac purée, asparagus and truffle – another winning combination of precisely engineered flavours and textures. To finish, a superb millefeuille of exemplary flakiness, layered with vanilla custard and poached Yorkshire rhubarb, is served with a trenchant rhubarb sorbet. Go for broke with wine flight options from a list that is big on Burgundy, Bordeaux and Champagne.

Chef Stephen McLaughlin **Seats** 54 **Closed** 25-26 December, 3 weeks in January **Prices from** S £38, M £54, D £18 **Parking** 300 **Notes** No children under 5 years

The Strathearn
◉◉ FRENCH, SCOTTISH V
01764 694270 | The Gleneagles Hotel, PH3 1NF
www.gleneagles.com
The Strathearn is a splendid art deco room with columns and moulded ceilings. The number of trolleys wheeled to the tables may create the impression that the restaurant is in some time warp, but the kitchen embraces the contemporary as well as the classics.

Chef Jason Hardcastle **Seats** 250 **Open** All Year
Parking 300 **Notes** Vegetarian dishes, Children welcome

COMRIE
Royal Hotel
⊛ TRADITIONAL SCOTTISH
01764 679200 | Melville Square, PH6 2DN
www.royalhotel.co.uk
The 18th-century stone building on the main street of this riverside village is now a plush small-scale luxury hotel, with a restaurant split into two areas linked by double doors. Trustworthy sourcing for the seasonally-changing menu is clear in pink slices of excellent quality venison.

Closed 24-26 December

FORTINGALL
Fortingall Hotel
⊛ MODERN SCOTTISH
01887 830367 | PH15 2NQ
www.fortingall.com
Fortingall, though tiny, is very much a tourist destination, and many end up at this Victorian country-house hotel. Dining takes place in two rooms, the main one done out in Arts and Crafts style, with a red carpet, open fire, paintings on the walls and tartan-effect curtains.

Closed January

KILLIECRANKIE
Killiecrankie Hotel
⊛⊛ MODERN BRITISH *V* ❧ NOTABLE WINE LIST
01796 473220 | PH16 5LG
www.killiecrankiehotel.co.uk
Three miles north of Pitlochry in tranquil countryside, the views across the Pass of Killiecrankie and the River Garry from this Victorian hotel are breathtaking. The kitchen delivers interesting menus that might open with wild mushroom ravioli, chorizo and parsley cream sauce and continue with sea bream with lemon and herb couscous.

Chef Mark Easton Seats 36, Private dining 12
Closed January to February Parking 20 Notes Children welcome

KINCLAVEN
Ballathie House Hotel
⊛⊛ MODERN BRITISH *V*
01250 883268 | PH1 4QN
www.ballathiehousehotel.com
This turreted mansion overlooking the River Tay hosts a restaurant that impresses with its dedication to local ingredients. The dining room has a classical elegance. Traditional flavours combine with a moderated degree of invention to create dishes that seem entirely in keeping with the setting.

Chef Scott Scorer Seats 60, Private dining 35 Open All Year Parking 100 Notes No children

PERTH
Deans Restaurant
⊛⊛ MODERN SCOTTISH
01738 643377 | 77-79 Kinnoull Street, PH1 5EZ
www.letseatperth.co.uk
In the city centre, buzzy Deans and its Rose Lounge are ever popular. Here the kitchen turns out modern Scottish and other dishes, some declaring their origin up front, such as Shetland oysters with black pudding; Thai fragrant rice with pak choi and Marsala cream sauce; and Perthshire strawberries, elderflower liquor mousse and shortbread crumble.

Chef Willie and Jamie Deans Seats 70 Closed 1st 2 weeks in January, 1 week in November
Prices from S £5.50, M £16, D £6.50 Notes Vegetarian dishes, Children welcome

Murrayshall Country House Hotel & Golf Club
⊛ MODERN BRITISH
01738 551171 | New Scone, PH2 7PH
www.murrayshall.co.uk
With two golf courses, Murrayshall doesn't do anything by halves. The main dining option is the Old Masters restaurant, a series of elegant spaces with views over the Perthshire landscape. The menu is rich with Scottish ingredients, while cooking techniques combine contemporary and traditional elements.

Chef Craig Jackson Seats 72, Private dining 40 Open All Year Prices from S £4.50, M £14, D £6 Parking 120 Notes Vegetarian dishes, Children welcome

The North Port Restaurant
⊛⊛ SCOTTISH *V*
01738 580867 | 8 North Port, PH1 5LU
www.thenorthport.co.uk
This charming restaurant is full of Jacobean charm, with dark oak panels, a spiral staircase, wooden floors and a candle-filled fireplace. Staff are friendly, and the menus focus on fresh Scottish produce from local suppliers, with a slightly more sophisticated choice of dishes available at dinner.

Chef Andrew Moss Seats 32, Private dining 16 Closed 24 December to 3 January Prices from S £4.95, M £13.95, D £6.95 Notes Children welcome

The Roost Restaurant

◉◉ MODERN SCOTTISH

01738 812111 | Forgandenny Road, Bridge of Earn, PH2 9AZ

www.theroostrestaurant.co.uk

Resembling a farmyard building, The Roost is smart as can be inside, with crisply clad tables and a plethora of pictures and mirrors. Thoroughbred Scottish ingredients include some from the Roost's own kitchen gardens and starters of seared Rougié foie gras set the scene.

Chef Tim Dover **Seats** 24 **Closed** 25 December, 1-18 January **Prices from** S £7.50, M £14.50, D £7.50 **Parking** 6 **Notes** Vegetarian dishes, Children welcome

63@Parklands

◉◉ MODERN EUROPEAN *V*

01738 622451 | Parklands Hotel, 2 St Leonards Bank, PH2 8EB

www.63atparklands.com

Overlooking South Inch Park, this spacious hotel restaurant offers a good degree of dining comfort. A strong emphasis on seasonality and local produce steers the menu, which might present pigeon espice, burnt onion, honey and truffle ricotta followed by Highland red deer saddle and shoulder casserole with fermented barley and baked neeps purée.

Chef Graeme Pallister, John Taylor **Seats** 32, Private dining 22 **Closed** 25 December to 8 January **Parking** 25 **Notes** Children welcome

63 Tay Street Restaurant

◉◉ MODERN SCOTTISH 🍷 NOTABLE WINE LIST

01738 441451 | 63 Tay Street, PH2 8NN

www.63taystreet.com

Graeme Pallister's restaurant occupies part of the ground floor of an imposing stone building; there's a red and grey modern colour scheme with tartan carpet adding a touch of luxury. 'Local, honest, simple' is the aim, although the kitchen adds a degree of complexity.

Chef Graeme Pallister **Seats** 38 **Closed** Christmas, New Year, 1st week in July **Prices from** S £7, M £13.50, D £6 **Notes** Vegetarian dishes, Children welcome

Tabla

◉ INDIAN *V*

01738 444630 | 173 South Street, PH2 8NY

www.tablarestaurant.co.uk

At the Kumar family's central Perth eaterie the ambience has more personality than many a formula Indian restaurant, with exposed stone walls, full-drop windows and a glass panel looking into the kitchen. Indian music featuring the eponymous tabla drums plays softly. A full listing of vegetarian dishes is prominent on the menu.

Chef Praveen Kumar **Seats** 42 **Open** All Year **Prices from** S £4.95, M £10.95, D £4.95 **Notes** Children welcome

PITLOCHRY *MAP 23, NN95*

Fonab Castle Hotel & Spa

◉◉◉ MODERN SCOTTISH *V*

01796 470140 | Foss Road, PH16 5ND

www.fonabcastlehotel.com

Built of red sandstone in 1892 in the Scots baronial style for a scion of the Sandeman port-shipping family, Fonab Castle stands on a wooded hillside overlooking Loch Faskally. It embarked on its career as a top-end hotel only in 2013, and its surviving panelled hall, exquisite plasterwork and magnificent stone fireplaces make an appealing contrast to the spa facilities and contemporary Scottish cooking also on offer. That latter is enjoyed at its best in the Sandeman Fine Dining restaurant, where the six-course taster offers an exciting programme of cutting-edge dishes, with appetisers and a pre-dessert filling in the gaps between main items. These could take in braised shin of Highland beef with pumpkin espuma, before moving on to venison with salsify purée, baked and raw beetroot and a rich, glossy sauce with clear notes of bitter chocolate. An excellent slate of wines by the glass is an asset.

Chef Paul Tyrrell, David Barnett **Seats** 60, Private dining 40 **Open** All Year **Prices from** S £8.95, M £18.95, D £6.50 **Parking** 50 **Notes** Children welcome

Knockendarroch

⊚⊚ MODERN SCOTTISH

01796 473473 | Higher Oakfield, PH16 5HT

www.knockendarroch.co.uk

A handsome sandstone house in a wooded setting, Knockendarroch has country-house comforts and a diminutive restaurant delivering daily-changing menus of classy modern Scottish food. It's very traditional within, with warming fires in the cooler months, ornate cornicing, chandeliers and the like, while hospitality is friendly and genuine.

Chef Graeme Stewart **Seats** 24 **Closed** mid December to mid February **Parking** 12 **Notes** Vegetarian dishes, No children under 10 years

RANNOCH STATION
MAP 23, NN45

Moor of Rannoch Restaurant & Rooms NEW

⊚⊚ SCOTTISH

01882 633238 | PH17 2QA

www.moorofrannoch.co.uk

If you're serious about getting away from it all, this remote restaurant with rooms should do the job. Lost among a vast moorland wilderness, you might be lucky to spot wildlife wandering and flying past as you tackle a daily-changing menu of skilfully-cooked food that puts a modern twist on classical ideas.

Chef Stephanie Meikle **Seats** 20 **Closed** November to mid February **Parking** 10 **Notes** Children welcome

ST FILLANS
MAP 20, NN62

The Four Seasons Hotel

⊚ MODERN INTERNATIONAL

01764 685333 | Loch Earn, PH6 2NF

www.thefourseasonshotel.co.uk

Perched right on the edge of Loch Earn, The Four Seasons Hotel has breathtaking views over the water and the wooded hills. In the waterside restaurant, those stunning views complement the modern menu which is built on spectacular Scottish ingredients.

Chef Chris Temple **Seats** 40, Private dining 20 **Closed** October to December, February to Easter **Prices from** S £8, M £16, D £8 **Parking** 30 **Notes** Vegetarian dishes, Children welcome

■ SCOTTISH BORDERS

KELSO
MAP 21, NT73

The Cobbles Freehouse & Dining

⊚ MODERN BRITISH

01573 223548 | 7 Bowmont Street, TD5 7JH

www.thecobbleskelso.co.uk

Tucked just off the town's main square, this old Inn has successfully negotiated the pub/restaurant dynamic. There are bar snacks such as wraps and burgers on offer, but in the dapper restaurant you'll find Scottish-inspired dishes that really impress. Steaks are sourced from Scottish herds.

Closed 25 December

Ednam House Hotel

⊚ MODERN EUROPEAN

01573 224168 | Bridge Street, TD5 7HT

www.ednamhouse.com

Located just off the town square and enjoying idyllic views of the Tweed, this lovely Georgian hotel is full of character. The triple-aspect restaurant looks over the gardens and across the river to Floors Castle. Main courses could be roast loin of venison with pomme purée, red cabbage, baby beetroot and bitter chocolate sauce.

Chef Peter Carr **Seats** 60, Private dining 20 **Parking** 40 **Notes** Vegetarian dishes, Children welcome

WALKERBURN
MAP 21, NT33

Windlestraw

⊚⊚ MODERN SCOTTISH, BRITISH *V*

01896 870636 | Galashiels Road, EH43 6AA

www.windlestraw.co.uk

Located only 40 minutes from Edinburgh, in the rolling hills of the Scottish Border country, Windlestraw is a beautiful venue set in two acres of grounds and lovingly restored by its present owners. Service is both personal and attentive in the oak panelled restaurant where well-balanced modern Scottish fare makes its way onto the menus.

Chef Stu Waterston **Seats** 20, Private dining 20 **Closed** mid December to mid February **Parking** 10 **Notes** No children under 11 years

■ STIRLING

ABERFOYLE
MAP 20, NN50

Macdonald Forest Hills Hotel & Resort
◉ MODERN SCOTTISH

01877 389500 | Kinlochard, FK8 3TL
www.macdonald-hotels.co.uk/foresthills
Twenty-five acres of mature gardens run down to
Loch Ard at this white-painted mansion, where
'keep it simple' might be the kitchen's mantra and
flavours are undiluted by an over-abundance of
ingredients. You might finish an enjoyable meal
with satsuma crème brûlée with decadent
chocolate chip cookies.

Chef Paul Whitecross **Seats** 78, Private dining 20
Open All Year **Prices from** S £7.50, M £15, D £6.50
Parking 50 **Notes** Vegetarian dishes, Children welcome

CALLANDER
MAP 20, NN60

Roman Camp Country House Hotel
◉◉◉ MODERN FRENCH V

01877 330003 | FK17 8BG
www.romancamphotel.co.uk
Dating back to the 17th century, this stately old
house with its pale pink walls is wonderfully
located in the Loch Lomond and the Trossachs
National Park. A hotel since the 1930s, it has 20
acres of gardens and a truly beautiful interior,
with fine period details, from the secret chapel
to the panelled library, and an antique grand
piano and more than 40 malt whiskies in the bar.
The two dining rooms are sumptuous and
splendid, with attentive, well-trained staff, and
the food is focused and contemporary. The short
carte and set-price menus are attentive to the
seasons, so caramelised sweetbreads might
appear with Toulouse sausage, sweet and sour
apricots and roasted garlic purée, before a main
course of perfectly-timed hazelnut-crusted
halibut with potato dumplings and crab and
lemongrass mousse. A milk chocolate and salted
caramel delice is a beautiful dish, with a
deliciously refreshing blood orange sorbet.

Chef Ian McNaught **Seats** 120, Private dining 36 **Open** All
Year **Prices from** S £14.80, M £29.50, D £11.50
Parking 80 **Notes** Children welcome

DUNBLANE
MAP 21, NN70

Cromlix and Chez Roux
◉◉◉ MODERN SCOTTISH V

01786 822125 | Kinbuck, FK15 9JT
www.cromlix.com
Built for one Captain Arthur Drummond in the
1870s, when it was known with becoming
modesty as Cromlix Cottage, then promptly
rebuilt the same decade when it burned down,
the turreted manor house is now owned by local
boy Sir Andy Murray. Public rooms are the height
of country-house elegance, the dining room a
glassed-in conservatory that looks over the
sumptuous grounds. Named in honour of its
executive presence, the much-garlanded Albert
Roux, Darin Campbell's kitchen aims high,
blending elements of French gastronomic
classicism with vivacious cooking in the modern
global style. Orkney hand-dived scallops come
with a salad of Cromlix garden rainbow chard and
edamame beans, making a fine beginning,
followed perhaps with mallard from the Braco
Estate. Spiced French pumpkin soufflé with
chocolate orange ice cream is an unusual
dessert with great depth of flavour. The French-
leaning wine list offers an impressive selection
of half bottles and wines by the glass.

Chef Darin Campbell **Seats** 60, Private dining 50
Open All Year **Prices from** S £9, M £24, D £8 **Parking** 30
Notes Children welcome

FINTRY
MAP 20, NS68

Culcreuch Castle Hotel & Estate
◉ TRADITIONAL SCOTTISH V

01360 860555 | Kippen Road, G63 0LW
www.culcreuch.com
Standing in 1,600 acres of grounds, including a
picturesque loch, Culcreuch Castle has all the
medieval accoutrements that could be desired.
Country-house cooking with some imaginative
touches is the approach. A deceptively complex
Culcreuch lamb dish with peas, mint and sheeps'
milk showcases the estate's produce.

Chef James Reynolds **Seats** 22, Private dining 30
Closed 25–26 December, 1st 2 weeks January
Prices from S £5, M £11, D £5.50 **Parking** 60
Notes Children welcome

SCOTTISH ISLANDS

COLBOST   MAP 22, NG24

The Three Chimneys & The House Over-By

◉◉◉ SCOTTISH, NORDIC INFLUENCE ▮ NOTABLE WINE LIST

01470 511258 | IV55 8ZT

www.threechimneys.co.uk

Exceptional cooking in a wild, romantic location

After 34 years as custodians of The Three Chimneys, Eddie and Shirley Spear handed over the reins to a new owner in April 2019. During this time, the remote restaurant with rooms has made its mark, on both the local economy and on the island's culinary reputation – and, fear not if you're making the long trek to this site of gastronomic pilgrimage, head chef Scott Davies and the kitchen team will continue to uphold their foodie-destination status under the new regime, which plans to take a 'leave well alone' approach. Inside the whitewashed cottage, next door to which ('over by') is the accommodation building (staying over is a good option – let's face it: you're hardly likely to be just passing by this remote spot), a number of small, low-ceilinged interconnected rooms reflect a sense of place with exposed stone walls, polished dark wood floors and tables simply set with black slate place mats.

> "… with Loch Dunvegan filling the view, the mind understandably turns to seafood"

As the years have passed, the cooking has become noticeably more complex, still firmly rooted in its island environment naturally, and with Loch Dunvegan filling the view, the mind understandably turns to seafood, particularly since that's the source of the scorched langoustine tails that open proceedings, paired with crispy rose veal sweetbreads, pickled mussels and Jerusalem artichoke purée and crisps. Main courses deliver impeccably sourced meats – wood-roasted Skye venison arrives atop a cabbage-wrapped ball of shredded venison, offset with a medley of turnip, charred Brussels sprouts, quince, and chocolate-enriched sauce.

Fish-wise, there may be roasted monkfish in a thoughtfully composed dish involving cauliflower, kimchi and crispy chicken wings. A pitch-perfect dessert brings a technically masterful riff on bitter chocolate textures matched with the subtle flavours of smoked praline, whisky and maple syrup, or you might opt for the seasonal delight of forced rhubarb, its tart lash perfectly complemented by miso biscuit, crowdie mousse and ginger cream.

Chef Scott Davies
Seats 40
Closed 16 December to 16 January
Parking 12
Notes Vegetarian dishes, No children under 5 years at lunch and 8 years at dinner

----

Kinloch Lodge

◉◉◉ **FRENCH, SCOTTISH** 𝐕 | NOTABLE WINE LIST

01471 833214 | Sleat, IV43 8QY

www.kinloch-lodge.co.uk

Finest Skye produce in a glorious setting

A contender for a 'remotest country hotel' award, the handsome whitewashed house sits in a wild and elemental location, making a memorable sight when it comes into view as you follow the single-track lane along Loch na Dal, with the Sound of Sleat as a glorious backdrop. And so it should, since this is the ancestral home of the high chief of the Clan Donald, and was turned into a hotel and restaurant by the current incumbents, Godfrey (the 34th hereditary Lord MacDonald) and Lady Claire, a renowned cookery writer, although the mantle has now been passed to daughter Isabella who continues the same ethos of elegant dining in a seriously comfortable retreat.

Kinloch maintains a wonderfully relaxing atmosphere in its modestly elegant public rooms, while dark grey walls and antique paintings make for a refined, traditional setting in the dining room. And if all this is

not reason enough to make the long trek, then Marcello Tully's fine-tuned cooking certainly is. The food, which showcases a remarkable cornucopia of top-quality ingredients, takes a classically French approach – Tully honed his craft in the kitchens of the illustrious Roux brothers, after all – broadening out to take in influences from Scotland and beyond. The five- and seven-course dinner menus kick off with a 'soupçon' incorporating celeriac and Strathdon blue cheese, followed by the first course proper of seared pigeon breast with Stornoway black pudding, textures of sweetcorn and beetroot, and citrus jus.

Next up, Portree Bay monkfish is wrapped in Parma ham and pointed up with umami-laden miso, followed by a meat course starring Black Isle lamb fillet

"The food, which showcases a remarkable cornucopia of top-quality ingredients, takes a classically French approach"

matched with mint, cashew nut, black olive and dauphinoise potato. A crossover dish of chargrilled goats' cheese with sweet balsamic and fig relish paves the way for a very fine dessert of dark chocolate and hazelnut cheesecake served with excellent yogurt ice cream.

Chef Marcello Tully
Seats 55, Private dining 12
Open All Year
Parking 40
Notes Children welcome

WALES

■ ISLE OF ANGLESEY

BEAUMARIS MAP 14, SH67

Bishopsgate House Hotel
◉ TRADITIONAL WELSH
01248 810302 | 54 Castle Street, LL58 8BB
www.bishopsgatehotel.co.uk
The mint-green façade of Bishopsgate House stands out on its Georgian terrace overlooking Beaumaris Green and Snowdonia across the Menai waterfront, while the intimate, low-ceilinged restaurant is full of old-world charm. Straightforward menus might finish with pecan tart and honeycomb ice cream.

Open All Year

Château Rhianfa
◉ MODERN FRENCH
01248 713656 | LL59 5NS
www.chateaurhianfa.com
Oak panels and a grand fireplace certainly make for an impressive dining room, but one would expect nothing less in this swanky 19th-century French chateau-style hotel surveying Snowdonia's peaks across the Menai Strait. The kitchen doesn't pull any left-field tricks, sticking to hearty country-house dishes.

Open All Year

MENAI BRIDGE MAP 14, SH57

Sosban & The Old Butcher's Restaurant
◉◉◉◉ MODERN
01248 208131 | Trinity House, 1 High Street, LL59 5EE
www.sosbanandtheoldbutchers.com
Dining at Sosban is a hot ticket, and definitely not your everyday restaurant experience. There is only room for 16 souls at any one time and it only happens three evenings and one lunch a week. But once you're inside you don't have to do

much but give yourself over to the prodigiously talented Stephen Stevens, who will serve up his no-choice menu at a fixed time. Allow four hours from start to finish.

The one-time butcher's shop on the high street has a rustic simplicity reflecting its former life, and it perfectly suits the modern mood. The procession of dishes displays amazing creativity, compelling visuals, and mightily impressive flavours. Reindeer moss is a stellar opening mouthful, rich with mushroom and fermented egg yolk, and your off, on to raw hand-dived scallop with ox heart, smoked broccoli and turnip. Next up, kale and chicken caesar, before you're moving on to lamb's tail with artichoke, leek and shrimp. Duck with beetroot, anise, yogurt and mustard leaf follows. Rhubarb and custard gets a reappraisal when a crisp rhubarb sphere is filled with duck egg custard and hits of rhubarb from poached and freeze-dried fruit. Complex, creative cuisine and at its best well worth the wait.

Chef Stephen Stevens **Seats** 12 **Closed** Christmas, New Year, January **Notes** No children

NEWBOROUGH MAP 14, SH46

Marram Grass
◉◉ MODERN BRITISH
01248 440077 | White Lodge, LL61 6RS
www.themarramgrass.com
There's no escaping it, this restaurant is actually a shed on a campsite. But make no mistake, it's a pretty smart shed; it even has a slate-topped bar. Anglesey's island status provides the ingredients - crab risotto with roast celeriac, local apple, garlic and sea truffle, for example.

Open All Year

■ BRIDGEND

BRIDGEND

MAP 9, SS97

Leicesters Restaurant NEW

◎◎ MODERN CLASSIC

01656 657644 | The Great House, 8 High Street, Laleston, CF32 0HP

www.great-house-laleston.co.uk

The 15th-century Great House, a Grade II listed building, is home to this restaurant that aims to provide an exquisite dining experience in welcoming and relaxed surroundings. Reflecting excellent Welsh cooking, expect bold, inventive food that's underpinned by a sense of quality and local sourcing.

Chef Gareth Denyer **Seats** 60, Private dining 40 **Closed** 26 December **Prices from** S £6, M £14, D £7 **Parking** 25 **Notes** Vegetarian dishes, Children welcome

■ CARDIFF

CARDIFF

MAP 9, ST17

Bully's

◎◎ FRENCH

029 2022 1905 | 5 Romilly Crescent, CF11 9NP

www.bullysrestaurant.co.uk

Bully's restaurant fills virtually every inch of its walls with a quirky pot pourri of pictures, mirrors and other retro paraphernalia. The kitchen may well rely on Welsh providers for its materials but wears its Gallic culinary allegiance on its sleeve in menus grounded in the French repertoire, spiced with the odd foray into global ideas.

Chef Christie Matthews **Seats** 40 **Closed** 24-26 December, 1 January **Prices from** S £7.50, M £16.95, D £7.95 **Notes** Vegetarian dishes, Children welcome

Park House Restaurant

◎◎ MODERN FRENCH

029 2022 4343 | 20 Park Place, CF10 3DQ

www.parkhouserestaurant.co.uk

Housed in a Gothic architectural extravagance, the splendid panelled restaurant overlooks the gardens of the National Museum of Wales. Do try the chocolate platter involving a rich pavé and 'pulled' chocolate with a peppermint macaroon and spearmint sorbet.

Chef Matthew Waldron **Closed** 26-28 December, 1-4 January

■ CARMARTHENSHIRE

LLANSTEFFAN

MAP 8, SN31

Mansion House Llansteffan

◎◎ MODERN BRITISH

01267 241515 | Pantyrathro, SA33 5AJ

www.mansionhousellansteffan.co.uk

The Mansion has five acres of windswept hilltop to itself, and a commanding position overlooking Carmarthen Bay, with the remains of a Norman castle for a near neighbour. In the Moryd Restaurant, which enjoys those views to the full, a straightforward but conscientiously rendered menu of modern brasserie food is offered.

Chef Paul Owen **Seats** 32, Private dining 24 **Prices from** S £4.95, M £16, D £4.95 **Parking** 50 **Notes** Vegetarian dishes, Children welcome

See advertisement on page 494

NANTGAREDIG

MAP 8, SN42

Y Polyn

◉◉ CLASSIC EUROPEAN ⚑ NOTABLE WINE LIST

01267 290000 | SA32 7LH

www.ypolyn.co.uk

This hospitable country pub is certainly more about dining than propping up the bar with a pint. Its owners win praise for hauling in the finest produce they can lay their hands on – salt marsh lamb and Welsh beef, for example – and transforming it into satisfyingly rustic lip-smacking dishes. The home-baked breads are fab too.

Chef Susan Manson **Seats** 100, Private dining 40 **Prices from** S £7.50, M £16.50, D £8.50 **Parking** 35 **Notes** Vegetarian dishes, Children welcome

■ CEREDIGION

CARDIGAN

MAP 8, SN14

Caemorgan Mansion

◉ MODERN EUROPEAN

01239 613297 | Caemorgan Road, SA43 1QU

www.caemorgan.com

Close to the beautiful Bay, Caemorgan Mansion occupies a peaceful location on the outskirts of Cardigan itself. Red walls dotted with local photographs and artwork gives the restaurant a contemporary look and it's an intimate platform to showcase carefully prepared Welsh produce.

Open All Year

EGLWYS FACH
MAP 14, SN69

Ynyshir
◉◉◉◉◉ MODERN BRITISH ⬥ NOTABLE WINE LIST
01654 781209 | SY20 8TA
www.ynyshir.co.uk
On the south bank of the River Dovey, deep within a 2,000-acre RSPB reserve, this white-fronted country manor is one of the Principality's most treasured restaurants. Once owned by Queen Victoria, the house and its lush green gardens are framed by the imposing Cambrian Mountains, which separate two National Parks, Snowdonia to the north and Brecon Beacons to the south. With chef-patron Gareth Ward at the helm, Ynyshir has been on the foodie trail for some time. At the heart of the operation, as you would expect, are the dining room and a no-shouting-zone kitchen opening off it. While cooking is clearly the kitchen team's priority, they also do their fair share of pickling, salting, fermenting, plus preserving fruits, leaves and berries. Guests here to enjoy a 17-or 20-course tasting menu are invited to assemble in the bar at a given time before taking their seats half an hour later. Neither lunch nor dinner is a hurried affair - with so many courses, how could they be? - so expect at least a four-hour sitting. Each of the five small tables is served by the chefs, who happily explain the genesis of the dishes, or what Ward calls Alternative British Snap. Using only brief descriptions, the menus signpost what's to come, such as one that began with the enigmatic Not French Onion Soup and ended with Welsh Wagyu fudge, having travelled via Goosnargh chicken katsu, aged mackerel with wasabi, pork belly char siu, garlic prawn, yuzu slushy, rhubarb and custard and tiramisù. During the hunting season expect to see local venison, duck, grouse and partridge, and Welsh lamb in summer. The distinguished Old and New World varietals and vineyards on the detailed wine list substantiate its Notable Wine List award. With dinner lasting four hours, it's a good idea to book an overnight room too.

Chef Gareth Ward **Seats** 18, Private dining 6 **Closed** 6 weeks during the year **Parking** 15 **Notes** Children welcome – must eat from tasting menu

LAMPETER
MAP 8, SN54

The Falcondale Hotel & Restaurant
◉◉ MODERN BRITISH
01570 422910 | Falcondale Drive, SA48 7RX
www.thefalcondale.co.uk
An Italianate mansion built in beautiful countryside, Falcondale has 14 acres all to itself. It's the kind of country-house hotel that delivers peace and that getting-away-from-it-all vibe. Cooking reveals classical roots, but this is gently modernised stuff, and good use is made of the regional bounty.

Chef Tony Shum **Seats** 36, Private dining 20 **Open** All Year **Prices from** S £7, M £18, D £6 **Parking** 60 **Notes** Vegetarian dishes, Children welcome

LLECHRYD
MAP 8, SN24

Hammet @ Castell Malgwyn
◉◉ MODERN BRITISH
01239 682382 | SA43 2QA
castellmalgwyn.wales
The prim, creeper-swathed Georgian house opens into a designer-led contemporary space, blending period plasterwork and high ceilings with an up-to-date palette of neutral greys and striking artworks. Darkwood floors, perspex dining chairs and neatly clothed tables continue the theme in the restaurant, where the cooking is as up-to-date as the surroundings.

Open All Year

TREGARON
MAP 9, SN65

Y Talbot
◉◉ MODERN BRITISH
01974 298208 | The Square, SY25 6JL
www.ytalbot.com
Drovers of old began their long treks to the markets of the Midlands and London from Tregaron, no doubt first fortifying themselves in this part-17th-century inn. Through the pillared front doorway there's a bar one side and a restaurant on the other, with bilingual, wide-choice menus on offer.

Chef Dafydd Watkin **Seats** 40, Private dining 8 **Open** All Year **Prices from** S £6, M £12, D £7 **Parking** 8 **Notes** Vegetarian dishes, Children welcome

■ CONWY

ABERGELE
MAP 14, SH97

Brasserie 1786
◉◉ MODERN BRITISH
01745 832014 | The Kinmel, St George's Road, LL22 9AS
www.thekinmel.co.uk
After a day in the Kinmel's spa, the hotel's bright, contemporary Brasserie 1786 is the place to head for some plain-speaking, seasonal food. Despite the chic, minimalist looks, the place has been in the hands of the same family since, well, the clue's in the name.

Open All Year

BETWS-Y-COED
MAP 14, SH75

Craig-y-Dderwen Riverside Hotel
◉ TRADITIONAL, INTERNATIONAL
01690 710293 | LL24 0AS
www.snowdoniahotel.com
Built in the 1890s for an industrialist, the partly timbered house became a favourite bolt-hole for Sir Edward Elgar. A hotel since the 20s, it offers the full country-house package, complete with views of a riverside teeming with wildlife (do look out for the otters).

Chef Paul Goosey Seats 60, Private dining 40 Closed 2 January to 1 February Prices from S £7.25, M £14.95, D £7.45 Parking 50 Notes Vegetarian dishes, Children welcome

Llugwy River Restaurant@Royal Oak Hotel
◉ MODERN BRITISH, WELSH
01690 710219 | Holyhead Road, LL24 0AY
royaloakhotel.net
Cappuccino-coloured walls with yellow sconces and ceiling chandeliers characterise the restaurant at this Victorian coaching inn. The kitchen supports local suppliers and the menu buzzes with interest. Game shows up in season, perhaps wild mallard with root vegetable gâteau, sticky red cabbage and damson jus.

Chef Samantha Plester Seats 40, Private dining 20 Closed 25-26 December Prices from S £4, M £13, D £5.25 Parking 100 Notes Vegetarian dishes, Children welcome

CAPEL CURIG
MAP 14, SH75

Bryn Tyrch Inn
◉ MODERN WELSH
01690 720223 | LL24 0EL
www.bryntyrchinn.co.uk
The old whitewashed roadside inn with a stunning Snowdonia backdrop offers sanctuary to walkers, climbers and families. The interior has plenty of charm and you can eat in the bar or the terrace dining room and expect simple, homely stuff based on regional produce.

Closed 15-27 December

COLWYN BAY
MAP 14, SH87

**AA Restaurant of the Year for Wales
2019–2020**

Bryn Williams at Porth Eirias
◉◉ BRITISH, SEAFOOD
01492 577525 | The Promenade, LL29 8HH
www.portheirias.com
Floor-to-ceiling windows offer sweeping views of Colwyn Bay, and exposed steelwork, pendant lights and industrial-chic create the feeling of a hip, big-city eatery. Bryn Williams made his name alongside celebrated chefs and has been chef-patron of Odette's in London's Primrose Hill since 2008, so you can expect sharp, modern British bistro ideas.

Chef Bryn Williams, John Wynne Seats 66 Open All Year Prices from S £6, M £14, D £6 Parking 25 Notes Vegetarian dishes, Children welcome

CONWY
MAP 14, SH77

Castle Hotel Conwy
◉ MODERN BRITISH
01492 582800 | High Street, LL32 8DB
www.castlewales.co.uk
With its courtyard garden and stylish decor, Dawsons Restaurant & Bar offers modern British menus that deliver brasserie-style dishes and classic comfort options. Start with pan-seared king scallops, celeriac purèe, black pudding and chorizo jam and follow it with fillet of sea bass, sweet potato fondant, buttered tenderstem broccoli and tomato pickle.

Chef Leigh Marshall Seats 50, Private dining 18 Closed 25 December, 31 December Prices from S £6, M £15, D £6 Parking 36 Notes Vegetarian dishes, Children welcome

Signatures Restaurant

◉◉ MODERN BRITISH *V*

01492 583513 | Aberconwy Resort & Spa, Aberconwy Park, LL32 8GA

www.darwinescapes.co.uk/parks/aberconwy-resort-spa/signatures-restaurant

The seaside holiday park location is a little left-field, but Signatures is well worth tracking down for its inspired modern cooking. An open kitchen adds to the buzz, and menus are full of modern accents, so prepare yourself for the likes of home-made black pudding and smoked bacon and leek rösti enriched with a runny egg, and mustard dressing. There's plenty of craft and attention to detail throughout.

Chef Jimmy Williams, Alan Rees, Ben Jones **Seats** 58 **Open** All Year **Prices from** S £7.25, M £17.95, D £6.95 **Parking** 40 **Notes** Children welcome in restaurant only

DEGANWY
MAP 14, SH77

Quay Hotel & Spa

◉ MODERN EUROPEAN

01492 564100 | Deganwy Quay, LL31 9DJ

www.quayhotel.co.uk

Beautifully located on the Conwy estuary, with views across the marina to the castle, this is a stylish, modern boutique hotel. The smart Grill Room offers a relatively informal setting for straightforward European cooking. Locally-landed fish and seafood feature on the menu.

Open All Year

LLANDUDNO
MAP 14, SH78

Bodysgallen Hall and Spa

◉◉◉ MODERN, TRADITIONAL *V*

01492 584466 | The Royal Welsh Way, LL30 1RS

www.bodysgallen.com

A couple of miles south of Llandudno, Bodysgallen is a supremely elegant, stone-built Stuart mansion in 200 acres of parkland. In the immediate environs of the house, a box-hedged parterre laid out in the 17th century is redolent of herbs to this day. Inside, the sober oak panelling is softened by garden views through mullioned windows framed by gathered drapes, and by sympathetic, personable service. Balancing traditional and modern British modes has become an essential skill of today's aspirant chefs, and John Williams possesses it in abundance, garnishing barbecued ox tongue to start with deconstructed piccalilli and a cauliflower cheese fritter. A main of slow-cooked

saddle of Welsh lamb is accompanied by glazed Bodysgallen root vegetables and tenderstem broccoli, and you might draw things to a conclusion with a soft and yielding cereal milk pannacotta with apricot sorbet and Mirabelle plum compôte. Excellent coffee and petits fours finish things off nicely.

Chef John Williams **Seats** 60, Private dining 40 **Closed** 24–26 December **Parking** 40 **Notes** No children under 6 years

Dunoon Hotel

◉◉ MODERN BRITISH

01492 860787 | Gloddaeth Street, LL30 2DW

www.dunoonhotel.co.uk

The restaurant here is full of old-world charm, with oak-panelled walls, brass fittings and chandeliers, flowers and linen napery on the tables and a cooking style that's more likely to reassure than to startle, the kitchen quite rightly keeping its customers happy.

Chef Rob Kennish **Seats** 80, Private dining 16 **Closed** mid December to 1 March **Parking** 20 **Notes** Vegetarian dishes, Children welcome

Imperial Hotel

◉◉ MODERN, TRADITIONAL BRITISH

01492 877466 | The Promenade, Vaughan Street, LL30 1AP

www.theimperial.co.uk

The wedding-cake stucco façade of the Imperial is a landmark on Llandudno's seafront. On a balmy day, alfresco dining on the terrace with a splendid backdrop of the bay is on the cards. The kitchen turns out menus of classically-inflected modern cooking featuring a sound showing of fine Welsh produce.

Chef Leighton Thomas **Seats** 150, Private dining 30 **Open** All Year **Prices from** S £7.75, M £19.50, D £7.75 **Parking** 20 **Notes** Vegetarian dishes, Children welcome

The Lilly Restaurant with Rooms

◉ MODERN WELSH

01492 876513 | West Parade, West Shore, LL30 2BD

www.thelillyllandudno.co.uk

Located in the sedate West Shore part of the town, and with unrestricted views over the coastline and restless sea, The Lilly can offer snacks and grills in its Madhatters Brasserie, or the Full Monty in the flamboyantly decorated restaurant.

Open All Year

St George's Hotel
@ MODERN, TRADITIONAL, WELSH
01492 877544 | The Promenade, LL30 2LG
www.stgeorgeswales.co.uk
Llandudno's prom is the place to be for splendid
sunsets and sweeping views across the bay, and
St George's Hotel sits centre stage. The place is a
timeless slice of Victorian wedding-cake
grandeur, with an irresistible terrace and floor-
to-ceiling windows in the restaurant.

Open All Year

■ GWYNEDD

ABERDYFI
MAP 14, SN69
Penhelig Arms
@ BRITISH
01654 767215 | Terrace Road, LL35 0LT
www.sabrain.com/pubs-and-hotels/north-wales/
gwynedd/penhelig-arms-hotel
Originally a collection of fishermen's cottages on
the Dyfi estuary, the Penhelig Arms overlooks
what centuries ago was a shipbuilding harbour.
Its two blue-themed dining areas – the
Fisherman's Bar and the restaurant – share a
menu, backed up by specials.

Chef Gabriel Badescu **Open** All Year **Parking** 5
Notes Vegetarian dishes, Children welcome

ABERSOCH
MAP 14, SH32
The Dining Room
@ WELSH BISTRO
01758 740709 | 4 High Street, LL53 7DY
www.thediningroomabersoch.co.uk
In pole position among the buzzy bars and hip
surfie shops of trendy Abersoch's main drag, this
low-key bistro with a tea-shop frontage and
mismatched chairs and tables is building a loyal
fan base for its warm hospitality and confidently
executed food.

Chef Si Toft **Seats** 24 **Open** All Year **Notes** Vegetarian
dishes, No children under 12 years

Porth Tocyn Hotel
@@ MODERN BRITISH ❶ NOTABLE WINE LIST
01758 713303 | Bwlchtocyn, LL53 7BU
www.porthtocynhotel.co.uk
The Fletcher-Brewer family converted a terrace
of lead miners' cottages into the comfortable,
relaxed and unstuffy place we see today. Inside
are antique-filled lounges and a smart
restaurant, with spectacular views over Cardigan

Bay to Snowdonia. Louise's repertoire combines
traditional values and more modern sensibilities.

Chef Louise Fletcher-Brewer, Darren Shenton Morris
Seats 50 **Closed** November, 2 weeks before Easter
Parking 50 **Notes** Vegetarian dishes, No children
under 6 years at dinner

BALA
MAP 14, SH93
Palé Hall Hotel & Restaurant
@@@ BRITISH, EUROPEAN **V**
01678 530285 | Llandderfel, LL23 7PS
www.palehall.co.uk
In the lush Dee Valley, with all Snowdonia laid out
before it, Palé Hall (note the accent – there is
nothing pale about Palé) is a plutocratic Victorian
industrialist's idea of a bijou residence, built to
the dimensions of a medieval castle. Its interiors
are beautifully decorated in pastel tones and
light wood panelling, with a bolder amber hue in
the dining room, where still-lifes of fruit crowd
the walls. Gareth Stevenson's menus are
informed by the grandeur of the surroundings,
but with today's ingenuity of approach adding
interest throughout. As well as two tasting
menus, there's the Classics Menu, with things like
scallops with pea purée and fillet of Welsh Black
beef. The six-course tasting menu might feature
grilled mackerel with Jersey Royals,
Denbighshire wood pigeon with blueberries and
Savoy cabbage, and desserts of rhubarb compôte
with custard and a sorrel granita, and wild
strawberry mousse with yuzu, and yogurt sorbet.
It's worth considering the wine flights too.

Chef Gareth Stevenson **Seats** 40, Private dining 40
Open All Year **Parking** 40 **Notes** Children welcome

CAERNARFON
MAP 14, SH46
The Gun Room *NEW*
@ MODERN BRITISH
01286 830214 | Plas Dinas Country House,
Bontnewydd, LL54 7YF
www.plasdinas.co.uk/dining
Plas Dinas was once home to the Armstrong-
Jones family and retains a comforting sense of
small-scale intimacy in The Gun Room. Done out
with classy restraint – dark oak floors,
high-backed leather seats, white linen, and
ancestral oils on the walls – it's a serene setting
for modern British cooking founded on a bedrock
of splendid local ingredients.

Chef Daniel ap Geraint **Open** All Year **Notes** No children
under 6 years

Tŷ Castell NEW

◉◉ WELSH TAPAS V

01286 674937 | 18 Stryd Fawr, LL55 1RN

www.tycastell.cymru

Close to Caernarfon Castle and occupying a notable 18th-century building, this contemporary restaurant looks far beyond Wales for its culinary inspiration. The interesting tapas-style menu has a global influence, from dishes like cured salmon, pink grapefruit, white radish and ponzu dressing to the teriyaki beef, braised onion and sautéed mushrooms.

Chef Robbie Worgan **Seats** 45, Private dining 19 **Open** All Year **Notes** No children under 11 years at dinner

CRICCIETH
MAP 14, SH53

Bron Eifion Country House Hotel

◉ MODERN BRITISH, WELSH

01766 522385 | LL52 0SA

www.broneifion.co.uk

Built in 1883, the creeper-clad house has the dual charm of ravishing gardens and stone's-throw proximity to Criccieth's beach. A majestic staircase, oak panelling and comfortable country-house furniture give the right impression, though the Garden Room restaurant offers a more contemporary experience.

Chef Marius Curelea **Seats** 150, Private dining 24 **Open** All Year **Parking** 50 **Notes** Vegetarian dishes, Children welcome

DOLGELLAU
MAP 14, SH71

Bwyty Mawddach Restaurant

◉ EUROPEAN

01341 421752 | Pen-y-Garnedd, Llanelltyd, LL40 2TA

www.mawddach.com

As barn conversions go, this one is rather impressive. Ifan Dunn turned the old granite building on the family farm into a snazzy modern restaurant with views over the Mawddach Estuary and the slopes of Cader Idris through its glass wall.

Chef Ifan Dunn **Seats** 40 **Closed** 26 December, 1 week January and April, 2 weeks November **Prices from** S £7.50, M £15, D £7 **Parking** 20 **Notes** Vegetarian dishes, No children under 5 years

---

Winner of the AA Wine Award for Wales
2019–2020

Penmaenuchaf Hall Hotel

◉◉ MODERN BRITISH ❦ NOTABLE WINE LIST

01341 422129 | Penmaenpool, LL40 1YB

www.penhall.co.uk

The greystone Victorian hall gives spectacular views to Cader Idris and the Mawddach Estuary. Within, oak floors, panels, artwork and fresh flowers give a real sense of age and quality. The menu pays homage to indigenous produce, and there's no lack of contemporary, creative flair.

Chef Daniel Peale, Tim Reeve **Seats** 36, Private dining 20 **Open** All Year **Prices from** S £8, M £20.50, D £8.50 **Parking** 36 **Notes** Vegetarian dishes, No children under 6 years

LLANBERIS
MAP 14, SH56

Padarn Brasserie NEW

◉ MODERN BRITISH V

01286 870253 | The Royal Victoria Hotel Snowdonia, LL55 4TY

www.theroyalvictoria.co.uk

Set within Snowdonia National Park, this Victorian hotel occupies a magnificent spot overlooking the village of Llanberis. Popular with walkers and tourists as much as locals, the modern British menu keeps things simple. Chicken liver parfait and onion marmalade might precede pan-fried sea bream, ratatouille, chorizo, chilli, coriander pesto and straw potatoes.

Chef Aron Davies **Seats** 120, Private dining 40 **Open** All Year **Parking** 200 **Notes** Vegetarian dishes, Children welcome

PORTMEIRION
MAP 14, SH53

The Hotel Portmeirion

◉◉ MODERN WELSH

01766 770000 | Minffordd, LL48 6ET

www.portmeirion-village.com

The fantasy Italianate village, created by Sir Clough Williams-Ellis, was conceived around the ruin of what is now the hotel. When the whole place began to materialise in 1926, the hotel became its focal point. Today, expect the fresh, lively, modern Welsh cooking to enhance the whole experience.

Closed 2 weeks November

■ MONMOUTHSHIRE

ABERGAVENNY
MAP 9, SO21

Angel Hotel
⊛ BRITISH, INTERNATIONAL
01873 857121 | 15 Cross Street, NP7 5EN
www.angelabergavenny.com
This hotel in the heart of the town was a posting inn in the first half of the 19th century, and its Georgian façade and spacious interiors are in fine fettle today. The brasserie-style menu is offered in both the Foxhunter Bar and the Oak Room restaurant.

Chef Wesley Hammond, Paul Brown Seats 80, Private dining 120 Closed 25 December Prices from S £6, M £14, D £6 Parking 30 Notes Vegetarian dishes, Children welcome

The Hardwick
⊛⊛ MODERN BRITISH
01873 854220 | Old Raglan Road, NP7 9AA
www.thehardwick.co.uk
Hard at work in a revamped old inn just outside Abergavenny is Stephen Terry, a chef with a wealth of experience at the sharp end of the restaurant biz. Food is unpretentious, mood-enhancing stuff. Set lunches and Sunday lunch are a cut above the norm.

Closed 25 December

Restaurant 1861
⊛⊛ MODERN BRITISH, EUROPEAN *V*
01873 821297 | Cross Ash, NP7 8PB
www.18-61.co.uk
Built as a pub in 1861, this place much, much later became Simon and Kate King's attractive, slightly isolated restaurant. A starter of ethically produced foie gras or dill-cured mackerel might be followed by a fricassée, either rose veal or woodland mushrooms; or fillet of hake or sea trout. Kate's dad grows most of the vegetables.

Chef Simon King Seats 40 Closed 1st 2 weeks in January Prices from S £8.50, M £22, D £7.50 Parking 20 Notes Children welcome

The Walnut Tree Inn
⊛⊛⊛ TRADITIONAL BRITISH
See pages 502-503

See advertisement opposite

ROCKFIELD
MAP 9, SO41

The Stonemill & Steppes Farm Cottages
⊛⊛ MODERN BRITISH
01600 716273 | NP25 5SW
www.thestonemill.co.uk
A beautifully converted barn in a 16th-century mill complex provides an impressive setting for accomplished cooking. It's a riot of beams and vaulted ceilings, with chunky rustic tables around an ancient stone cider press. The kitchen uses regional produce to deliver simply presented modern dishes.

Chef Ben Mathias Seats 56, Private dining 12 Closed 25-26 December, 2 weeks in January Parking 40 Notes Vegetarian dishes, Children welcome

USK
MAP 9, SO30

Newbridge on Usk
⊛⊛ TRADITIONAL BRITISH
01633 451000 | Tredunnock, NP15 1LY
www.celtic-manor.com
On a bend in the Usk, with river views, this restaurant with rooms is surrounded by well-tended gardens. The property dates back 200 years, so you can expect the usual beams and fireplaces, while the two-level restaurant has a rustic charm.

Chef Adam Whittle Seats 90, Private dining 16 Open All Year Prices from S £6.50, M £16, D £6.95 Parking 60 Notes Vegetarian dishes, Children welcome

The Raglan Arms
⊛ MODERN BRITISH
01291 690800 | Llandenny, NP15 1DL
www.raglanarms.co.uk
This unassuming property looking more like a private house is home to bistro-style cooking and a friendly atmosphere. Log burners and scrubbed tables bring home the inn-like feel, and a decked terrace allows diners to sit and enjoy the rural location.

Chef Peter Hulsmann Seats 64 Prices from S £5.95, M £15.50, D £7 Parking 20 Notes Vegetarian dishes, Children welcome

THE WALNUT TREE

The famous Michelin-starred restaurant located two miles east of Abergavenny offers dishes based on Shaun Hill's personal taste paired with sound cooking techniques and truly exceptional ingredients. Open Tuesday to Saturday.

01873 852797
Llanddewi Skirrid, Abergavenny, NP7 8AW
www.thewalnuttreeinn.com

MAP 9, SO21

The Walnut Tree Inn

◎◎◎ **TRADITIONAL BRITISH**
01873 852797 | Llanddewi Skirrid, NP7 8AW
www.thewalnuttreeinn.com

Blissfully unfussy and focused cooking from a culinary mastermind

The Walnut Tree Inn has been on the gastronomic map one way or another since the 1960s. Ensconced amid rolling fields a couple of miles to the northeast of Abergavenny, the place is today the preserve of Shaun Hill, for many decades one of Britain's principal movers and shakers. With productive stints at Devon's Gidleigh Park and the Merchant House in Ludlow on his CV, Hill has also been one of the country's great culinary thinkers, and

author of some of the more thoughtful chef's cookbooks of recent years. With its whitewashed frontage and potted topiary, the inn looks every inch the rural retreat. The dining area is done in unpretentious country style, with bare tables simply laid up, sprays of foliage, and some striking artworks for sale.

Shaun has always taken an eclectic approach, anticipating the current global tendency in British cooking by a

Shaun has always taken an eclectic approach, anticipating the current global tendency in British cooking by a generation

generation. He cooks what he himself likes to eat, in a resourceful style that is unified by the core of excellent ingredients on which the kitchen calls. A starter of scallops with lentils and coriander will be just that, the flavours all ringing true, while those with an eye for a more visceral opener could go for caramelised calves' brains, the lobes highlighted with brown butter, parsley and capers. A taste of the distant sea might come as a main course of cod with Jerusalem artichoke and hazelnut dressing, while meaty ideas could

take in a robust partnership of beef fillet with beef shin bourguignon. At the close, expect generous and satisfying desserts – ginger loaf with butterscotch sauce and poached pear, say, as well as the signature somloi, a carefully researched Hungarian trifle of apricots, walnuts and rum, not to mention a clutch of pedigree French cheeses.

Chef Shaun Hill
Seats 70, Private dining 26
Closed 1 week at Christmas
Prices from S £11, M £16, D £9
Parking 30
Notes Vegetarian dishes, Children welcome

See advertisement on page 501

WHITEBROOK

MAP 4, SO50

The Whitebrook

◉◉◉◉ MODERN BRITISH, FRENCH V **₤** NOTABLE WINE LIST

01600 860254 | NP25 4TX

www.thewhitebrook.co.uk

The lush Wye Valley that surrounds this whitewashed former drovers' inn is also the source of a good deal of the menu, such is chef-patron Chris Harrod's passion for the food on his doorstep. This restaurant with rooms seems to fit organically into its environment, with stylishly neutral bedrooms and a restaurant decorated in soothingly light and natural shades. It's an unpretentious and relaxing setting for dynamic cooking, offered on the tasting menu (and three-course lunch option). Begin with a visually appealing starter of roast Jerusalem artichoke, local goats' curds and 'forest findings' – a delightfully refined dish, the zesty, creamy curd working beautifully with the artichoke, while foraged pennywort adds a fresh vibrancy. Next up, a well-balanced dish of Cornish crab with charlock, brassica, horseradish and roast chicken skin.

There is real vitality to each course – an excellent plate of Cornish brill is accompanied by sweet and creamy crown prince pumpkin, plump mussels, rainbow chard and garlic chives. Sweet courses like the palate-cleansing blackberry and chamomile with blackcurrant sage are thoughtfully conceived, while 'Tea & Cake' is a *Great British Menu*-winning dish and a stunning end to the meal, every mouthful a different journey. The vegetarian menu is equally creative and compelling, and the wine list includes bottles from organic and biodynamic growers.

Chef Chris Harrod **Seats** 26 **Closed** 2 weeks in January **Parking** 20 **Notes** No children under 12 years at dinner

■ NEWPORT

NEWPORT

MAP 9, ST38

Gemelli Restaurant

◉◉ ITALIAN, INTERNATIONAL V

01633 270210 | G1, Tesco Store, Newport Retail Park, NP19 4TX

www.gemellinewport.co.uk

Located beneath a supermarket in a retail park, this family-run restaurant has recreated their own piece of Italy with a restaurant, deli and ice cream parlour. Banquette seating and white linen add a formal touch. Italian classics with a twist is the motto here.

Chef Sergio Cinotti **Seats** 60, Private dining 15 **Closed** Easter and Christmas **Prices from** S £7.50, M £12.95, D £5.50 **Parking** 80 **Notes** Children welcome

Gem 42 NEW

◉◉ MODERN BRITISH V

01633 287591 | 42 Bridge Street, NP20 4NY

www.gem42.co.uk

The unassuming building is easy to miss, but once inside you're hardly likely to forget the exuberant Botticelli-style ceilings and crisply dressed tables with Murano glass ornaments. The food is a cut above the average trattoria too – the kitchen works a gleeful fusion of classical foundations and contemporary molecular techniques to deliver an entertaining medley of textures and flavours.

Chef Sergio Cinotti **Seats** 32 **Closed** 25–26 December, Easter **Prices from** S £8, M £15.20, D £7.20 **Parking** 7 **Notes** Children welcome

Steak on Six

◉◉ MODERN BRITISH

01633 413000 | The Celtic Manor Resort, Coldra Woods, NP18 1HQ

www.celtic-manor.com/steak-on-six

The 'Six' in question is the sixth floor of the upmarket, golf-centric Celtic Manor Resort, where this stylish, contemporary steakhouse looks out over Coldra Woods. When the culinary proposition is this straightforward, the quality of the raw materials is key, and the pedigree meat here proudly flies the flag for prime British protein.

Chef Michael Bates, Simon Crockford **Seats** 60 **Open** All Year **Prices from** S £8.50, M £28.50, D £6.95 **Notes** Vegetarian dishes, No Children

Rafters

◉ WELSH

01633 413000 | The Celtic Manor Resort, Coldra Woods, NP18 1HQ

www.celtic-manor.com

There are views over the Ryder Cup course from Rafters, a classy grill restaurant within the Twenty Ten Clubhouse at the Celtic Manor Resort. Welsh ingredients take centre stage and there are locally reared, 21-day-aged steaks as the star attraction.

Open All Year

■ PEMBROKESHIRE

HAVERFORDWEST
MAP 8, SM91

Slebech Park Estate
◉◉ MODERN, CLASSIC
01437 752000 | SA62 4AX
www.slebech.co.uk
The castellated, 18th-century Slebech manor house stands in 700 acres of parkland, part-bordered by the Eastern Cleddau River. Overlooking this so-called 'hidden waterway', the naturally lit modern restaurant is a big draw for its Little Haven picked crab and laverbread; roast halibut; 28-day, dry-aged Welsh beef fillet; and butternut squash and sweet potato pithivier.

Chef **Seats** 40, Private dining 20 **Open** All Year
Prices from S £8, M £16, D £7 **Parking** 40
Notes Vegetarian dishes, Children welcome
See advertisement on page 506

NARBERTH
MAP 8, SN11

The Fernery
◉◉◉ MODERN BRITISH *V*
See pages 508–509

See advertisement on page 507

NEWPORT
MAP 8, SN03

Llys Meddyg
◉◉ CLASSIC
01239 820008 | East Street, SA42 0SY
www.llysmeddyg.com
The handsome Georgian townhouse is in the centre of Newport village: converted from a coaching inn, it is a smartly-done-out restaurant with rooms. There's a cosy stone-walled cellar bar, a lovely kitchen garden for pre-dinner drinks, and an elegant restaurant. The kitchen champions local produce, and goes foraging to boost the repertoire.

Chef David Richmond **Seats** 30, Private dining 14
Open All Year **Prices from** S £6, M £14, D £7 **Parking** 8
Notes Vegetarian dishes, Children welcome

PORTHGAIN
MAP 8, SM83

The Shed
◉ FISH, TRADITIONAL BRITISH, MEDITERRANEAN
01348 831518 | SA62 5BN
www.theshedporthgain.co.uk
Seafood is king at this simple beach hut-style 'fish and chip bistro' right on the quayside in this dinky fishing village. The place sells its own-caught and local sustainable fresh fish and seafood from a counter during the warmer months, and sitting outdoors with a glass of wine, you couldn't ask for a more delightfully unaffected venue.

Chef Rob and Caroline Jones **Seats** 70 **Open** All Year
Prices from S £5.95, M £12.95, D £4.95
Notes Vegetarian dishes, Children welcome

ST DAVIDS
MAP 8, SM72

Blas Restaurant
◉◉ MODERN BRITISH
01437 725555 | Twr Y Felin Hotel, Caerfai Road, SA62 6QT
www.twryfelinhotel.com
The low-lit Blas Restaurant (blas meaning 'taste') dining room at Twr Y Felin features striking modern paintings and prints that take centre-stage. The cooking is equally aesthetically conceived, with bold assemblages delighting eye and palate – availability is dependent on what can be locally sourced or foraged.

Chef Sam Owen **Seats** 54 **Open** All Year
Prices from S £9, M £19, D £9 **Parking** 26
Notes Vegetarian dishes, Children welcome

SAUNDERSFOOT
MAP 8, SN10

Coast Restaurant
◉◉ MODERN BRITISH, SEAFOOD
01834 810800 | Coppet Hall Beach, SA69 9AJ
www.coastsaundersfoot.co.uk
On the shoreline of lovely Coppet Hall Beach, this contemporary wooden structure provides diners with unrivalled bay views. Simple furnishings with a sea and sand colour scheme are complemented by a menu with a strong seafood theme. The sticky toffee pudding makes for a good finish.

Closed 7–19 January

St Brides Spa Hotel
◉ MODERN BRITISH
01834 812304 | St Brides Hill, SA69 9NH
www.stbridesspahotel.com
In a prime position overlooking Carmarthen Bay, this newly extended and refurbished contemporary spa hotel has two main dining options, the open-plan Cliff Restaurant and the more informal Gallery and its deck, all with excellent sea views. As the lobster tank implies, fresh local seafood is a speciality – try the Atlantic cod with roasted garlic.

Chef Daniel Retter **Seats** 100, Private dining 50 **Open** All
Year **Prices from** S £8.50, M £28, D £8.50 **Parking** 60
Notes Vegetarian dishes, Children welcome
See advertisement on page 510

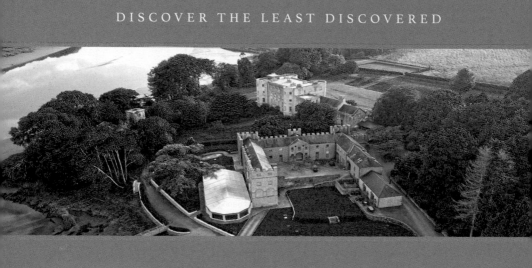

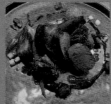

GROVE
NARBERTH

understated luxury, intimate dining and perfect romance

reservations@grovenarberth.co.uk
www.grovenarberth.co.uk
01834 860915

NARBERTH

The Fernery

◉◉◉ **MODERN BRITISH** *V*

01834 860915 | Grove, Molleston, SA67 8BX

www.thegrove-narberth.co.uk

Stunningly restored manor with creative culinary edge

Arriving at the 17th-century manor it is hard to imagine that when Neil and Zoe Kedward got their hands on the place back in 2007 it was derelict, unloved, and long forgotten. Following a stunning restoration of the main house and outbuildings, today's boutique hotel is an idyllic getaway. The setting is also part of its appeal, with the 26-acre estate including four acres of pretty gardens to explore, with soaring trees, colourful rhododendrons and a kitchen garden, the fruits of which you will meet later (70 or so varieties of vegetables, fruits and herbs as it happens) in The Fernery restaurant. The interior of the house feels like no less of a haven, with its elegant blend of traditional comforts and contemporary touches, with bedrooms in the main house and various cottages.

The cocktail bar is the spot to head for before you eat, and maybe after, with four lounges on hand if sinking into a comfy

> The restaurant is an intimate and understated setting for dynamic, contemporary food

settee fits the bill. The restaurant is an intimate and understated setting for dynamic, contemporary food delivered via a fixed-price carte and an eight-course tasting menu. Expect dazzling flavours and high-level technical skills, with starters of scallops with cauliflower, jasmine raisins, brown butter and apple, or cured mackerel with marinated daikon, Exmoor caviar and cucumber butter sauce showing the creative style. Mains might star saddle of Preseli lamb in the company of turnips, rösti, charred leeks, hen of the woods mushrooms and capers, while stone bass is roasted with star anise and matched with saffron onions, tapenade and bouillabaisse. There's no less creativity in desserts; Muscovado set custard, say, with spiced fig jam, candied pecans and coffee ice cream, or peanut butter parfait with raspberry jelly and sorbet and peanut nougatine.

Chef Douglas Balish
Seats 34, Private dining 25
Open All Year
Parking 42
Notes No children under 12 years

See advertisement on page 507

SOLVA

MAP 8, SM82

Crug Glâs Country House

◉◉ MODERN BRITISH

01348 831302 | Abereiddy, SA62 6XX

www.crug-glas.co.uk

Owners Janet and Perkin Evans have renovated 12th-century Crug Glâs using local materials to achieve smart modernity without trampling on the house's history. At the end of the day, kick off the walking boots and settle into the formal Georgian dining room for country-house cooking.

Closed 25–26 December

TENBY

MAP 8, SN10

Penally Abbey Hotel

◉◉ MODERN *V*

01834 843033 | Penally, SA70 7PY

www.penally-abbey.com

Overlooking Carmarthen Bay, with the 12th-century ruins of the original chapel still be seen in the grounds, the fully restored 18th-century Penally Abbey has soothingly elegant interiors, where the pale colour scheme and delightful period details – lend an air of quiet luxury. In the candlelit restaurant you can look forward to relaxed fine dining, with intensely flavoured, well-constructed dishes.

Chef Richard Browning **Seats** 25, Private dining 30
Closed January **Prices from** S £8.95, M £16.50, D £9.50
Parking 15 **Notes** Children welcome

The Salt Cellar

◉◉ MODERN BRITISH *V*

01834 844005 | Atlantic Hotel, The Esplanade, SA70 7DU

www.thesaltcellartenby.co.uk

Occupying an enviable spot in a Victorian seafront hotel, The Salt Cellar is run by an independent team with a passion for prime Pembrokeshire produce. The setting is appropriately modern and the kitchen doesn't try to reinvent the culinary wheel.

Chef Duncan Barham, Matthew Flowers **Seats** 32
Closed 24–26 December, 2–6 January
Prices from S £8.50, M £19, D £8 **Notes** Children welcome

Trefloyne Manor
◎ CLASSIC BRITISH
01834 842165 | Trefloyne Lane, Penally, SA70 7RG
www.trefloyne.com
This elegant manor house provides a relaxed country club setting in the heart of bustling Tenby. Accessed through a cosy bar area, the restaurant occupies a large glass-fronted orangery. The menu is supplemented with blackboard specials and a fish board, with classic British dishes.

Closed 25 December

WOLF'S CASTLE *MAP 8, SM92*
Wolfscastle Country Hotel
◎◎ MODERN, TRADITIONAL
01437 741225 | SA62 5LZ
wolfscastle.com
It's said that Welsh rebel leader Owain Glyndwr may be buried in the field alongside this old stone country hotel. Here, the principal restaurant offers unclothed tables and a menu of modern classics. Save room for chocolate fondant, served with salted caramel ice cream and orange jelly.

Chef Keith Robinson **Seats** 55, Private dining 40 **Closed** 24–26 December **Prices from** S £6.95, M £16.95, D £6.50 **Parking** 75 **Notes** Vegetarian dishes, Children welcome

 POWYS

BRECON *MAP 9, SO02*
Peterstone Court
◎ MODERN BRITISH, EUROPEAN
01874 665387 | Llanhamlach, LD3 7YB
www.peterstone-court.com
Georgian proportions and its position in the Brecon Beacons make Peterstone Court an ideal base for exploring the landscape. There's a contemporary feel and the classy finish includes a swish bar and a spa. Best of all, there's nifty modern food in the Conservatory Restaurant.

Open All Year

Three Horseshoes Inn
◎◎ BRITISH
01874 665672 | Groesffordd, LD3 7SN
www.threehorseshoesgroesffordd.co.uk
Just what you need to fuel a day in the great outdoors, this cosy pub is justifiably popular with hikers and bikers. The interior looks up to snuff with its original slate floors, heritage paint palette and modern sheen, while the food is buttressed by local suppliers – the lamb, for example, comes from the neighbouring farm.

Chef Connor Turner **Seats** 46 **Open** All Year **Prices from** S £6.95, M £14.95, D £6.45 **Notes** Vegetarian dishes, Children welcome

CRICKHOWELL *MAP 9, SO21*
The Bear
◎ MODERN BRITISH, INTERNATIONAL
01873 810408 | High Street, NP8 1BW
www.bearhotel.co.uk
The Bear goes back 500 years, as its ancient oak beams and stones testify. The food, though, is right up-to-date, borne out by a menu offering a duck liver, Armagnac parfait and red onion marmalade starter; a main of Welsh lamb rump, garlic mash and green beans; and apple and frangipane tart with pistachio ice cream.

Chef Padrig Jones **Seats** 60, Private dining 30 **Closed** 25 December **Parking** 40 **Notes** Vegetarian dishes, No children under 7 years

Manor Hotel
◎ BRITISH
01873 810212 | Brecon Road, NP8 1SE
www.manorhotel.co.uk
The sparkling-white hotel stands on an enthralling spot under Table Mountain. The relaxing dining room with tall plants and elegant furniture has views out towards the hills, and its bistro-style menu hauls in most of its prime materials from the family farm seven miles away.

Chef Glyn Bridgeman **Seats** 54, Private dining 26 **Closed** 24–26 December (25 December bookings only) **Prices from** S £5.50, M £13, D £6.50 **Parking** 200 **Notes** Vegetarian dishes, Children welcome

HAY-ON-WYE
MAP 9, SO24

Old Black Lion Inn

🏵 MODERN BRITISH

01497 820841 | 26 Lion Street, HR3 5AD

www.oldblacklion.co.uk

Dating from the 17th century, the whitewashed inn has bags of character, with beams, low ceilings and stone fireplaces. You can eat in the bar or in the dining room. The kitchen proudly sources all their meats from organic farms in the foothills of Hay Bluff.

Chef Mark Turton **Seats** 40, Private dining 24 **Closed** 25 December **Prices from** S £6, M £12.90, D £6 **Parking** 12 **Notes** Vegetarian dishes, Children welcome

LLANFYLLIN
MAP 15, SJ11

Seeds

🏵 MODERN BRITISH

01691 648604 | 5–6 Penybryn Cottages, High Street, SY22 5AP

When you don't require your food to push culinary boundaries or feature froths and gels, head towards Seeds, a little bistro with just 20 seats, run by an amiable husband-and-wife team. Mellow jazz floats around the artworks and curios decorating the low-beamed, slate-floored dining room as chef-patron Mark Seager turns out simple, tasty classic bistro dishes at the stoves of a bijou kitchen.

Chef Mark Seager **Seats** 20 **Closed** 24–26 December, 2 weeks October, 2 weeks June, limited winter opening – phone in advance **Prices from** S £5.50, M £12.95, D £5.95 **Notes** Vegetarian dishes, Children welcome

LLANWDDYN
MAP 15, SJ01

Lake Vyrnwy Hotel & Spa

🏵 MODERN BRITISH

01691 870692 | Lake Vyrnwy, SY10 0LY

www.lakevyrnwy.com

Looking down the length of Lake Vyrnwy, while dining on good food, some grown on the hotel estate itself, is a treat indeed. You might begin with goats' cheese, caramelised onion and crystallised walnut tart, then follow with lamb loin, confit belly and dauphinoise potatoes, finishing with banana, peanut butter, salted caramel and milk chocolate ice cream.

Chef Dan Furnival **Seats** 85, Private dining 220 **Open** All Year **Parking** 80 **Notes** Vegetarian dishes, Children welcome

LLANWRTYD WELLS
MAP 9, SN84

Lasswade Country House

🏵🏵 MODERN BRITISH

01591 610515 | Station Road, LD5 4RW

www.lasswadehotel.co.uk

Run with great charm by owners Roger and Emma Stevens, this Edwardian house offers 360-degree views of the Cambrian Mountains and Brecon Beacons. In the kitchen, Roger keeps combinations straightforward, timings accurate, and interweaves flavours intelligently in daily-changing dinner menus.

Chef Roger Stevens **Seats** 20, Private dining 20 **Closed** 25–26 December **Parking** 6 **Notes** Vegetarian dishes, No children under 8 years

LLYSWEN
MAP 9, SO13

Llangoed Hall

🏵🏵🏵 MODERN BRITISH ***V*** 🍷 NOTABLE WINE LIST

01874 754525 | LD3 0YP

www.llangoedhall.co.uk

An extensive kitchen garden and a smokehouse in the 17-acre grounds of this handsome Edwardian mansion in the Wye Valley attest to the culinary focus at Llangoed. Originally Jacobean, Clough Williams-Ellis (of Portmeirion fame) rebuilt the place in the early 20th century, so expect luxurious lounges full of original features, fine furniture, and original artworks by Whistler and Augustus John. Nick Brodie and his team put organic pickings from the garden into various tersely-worded menus (including vegan/gluten free versions) of polished modern British cooking. What arrives is savvy, sophisticated and complex stuff, including fashionably foraged and fermented ingredients – perhaps langoustine with coffee bisque and foie gras, or beef tartare with oyster, brioche and egg yolk, then a main course matching suckling pork with kimchi, shiitake and bok choi. Presentation is delightful, and there's no lack of invention among desserts either; a dish starring rhubarb, passionfruit and ginger, for example, or mango with mascarpone and ravioli.

Chef Nick Brodie **Seats** 40, Private dining 80 **Open** All Year **Parking** 150 **Notes** Children welcome

MONTGOMERY

The Nags Head Inn
@ MODERN BRITISH
01686 640600 | Garthmyl, SY15 6RS
www.nagsheadgarthmyl.co.uk
The Grade II listed coaching inn on the A483
stands only a few yards from the Severn and the
Montgomery Canal, a pleasant spot for an
intelligently renovated country pub. The dining
area is an expansive space opening on to a patio.

Chef Colin Clark **Seats** 50 **Open** All Year
Prices from S £5.50, M £11.50, D £5.50
Notes Vegetarian dishes, No children after 9pm

MAP 15, SO29

■ RHONDDA CYNON TAF

PONTYCLUN

MAP 9, ST08

La Luna
@ MODERN INTERNATIONAL
01443 239600 | 79–81 Talbot Road, Talbot Green,
CF72 8AE
www.la-lunarestaurant.com
The family-run La Luna has an easy-going
atmosphere and a contemporary finish, which
fits the kitchen's sunny Med-style, brasserie-
inspired output. There's an early evening menu,
too, and some fair-weather outside tables.

Closed 24 December, 1 January and bank holidays

PONTYPRIDD

MAP 9, ST08

Llechwen Hall Hotel
@ MODERN WELSH
01443 742050 | Llanfabon, CF37 4HP
www.llechwen.co.uk
The low-ceilinged, heavily beamed restaurant at
this mid-sized manor house has plenty of
atmosphere with its whitewashed walls, tiled
floor and bare wood tables. The restaurant has
been extended with a garden room-style glazed
extension to the original room. The uniformed
staff serve up well-considered seasonally
changing menus.

Chef Paul Trask **Seats** 50, Private dining 300 **Open** All
Year **Prices from** S £5.50, M £14.95, D £5.50 **Parking** 100
Notes Vegetarian dishes, Children welcome

■ SWANSEA

BISHOPSTON

MAP 8, SS58

The Plough & Harrow
@ MODERN EUROPEAN
01792 234459 | 88 Oldway, Murton, SA3 3DJ
www.ploughandharrow.eu
This unassuming gastro pub is in a quaint village
near to Swansea on the Gower peninsula. Inside
the old building, it's modern with a colour palette
of cream, chalky blue and grey, a wood-burner,
stacked logs and bare stone walls.

Chef Nick Jones **Seats** 40, **Prices from** S £7, M £16,
D £7 **Parking** 16 **Notes** Vegetarian dishes, No children
under 12 years

OXWICH

MAP 8, SS48

Beach House Restaurant at Oxwich Beach
@@@ MODERN WELSH V ■ NOTABLE WINE LIST
01792 390965 | SA3 1LS
www.beachhouseoxwich.co.uk
With its stone walls rising from the sands of
Oxwich Bay on the Gower Peninsula, the views
from the Beach House are hard to beat. The
repurposed coalhouse is now a bright and breezy
contemporary venue done in beachcomber-chic
tones of blue, with exposed rafters, full-length
windows opening onto the bay, and a concise
menu of modern bistro cooking built on pedigree
Welsh produce. Chef Hywel Griffith's cooking
delights with its gleeful fusion of local and global
flavours, starting with a pairing of thyme-
scented veal sweetbreads with Welsh asparagus,
puffed rice, wild garlic flowers and the salty hit of
Morteau sausage. Lobster landed that very
morning from Oxwich Bay provides the filling for
a main course of delicate cannelloni and a rich
bisque served with braised vegetables and
Lyonnaise potatoes lifted with lemon thyme.
Finally, top-class pastrywork distinguishes a
richly eggy, vanilla and nutmeg-scented custard
tart offset by the sharp kiss of poached rhubarb
and blood orange ice cream.

Chef Hywel Griffith **Seats** 46 **Closed** 2nd and 3rd week
January **Prices from** S £11, M £23, D £10 **Notes** Children
welcome

SWANSEA

Hanson at the Chelsea Restaurant
◉ MODERN WELSH, FRENCH

01792 464068 | 17 St Mary Street, SA1 3LH

www.hansonatthechelsearestaurant.co.uk

Andrew Hanson's unassuming-looking restaurant resembles a classic modern bistro inside with clothed tables pressed in cheek by jowl, blackboard menus and small framed pictures against a delicate yellow colour scheme. The cooking is an appealing mix of local produce and French influences, with the emphasis on fish and seafood, but not forgetting fine Welsh lamb.

Chef Andrew Hanson, Nathan Kirby **Seats** 50, Private dining 20 **Closed** 25–26 December **Notes** Vegetarian dishes, Children welcome

■ TORFAEN

CWMBRAN

The Parkway Hotel & Spa
◉◉ MODERN EUROPEAN

01633 871199 | Cwmbran Drive, NP44 3UW

www.parkwayhotelandspa.com

Over seven acres of gardens surround the Parkway, making for a relaxing ambience. Ravellos Restaurant is at the heart of it all, with large geometric modern artworks to break up the white-walled space, and a fountain to distract you. Modern menus reveal sensibly balanced and confident dishes.

Chef Clive Williams **Seats** 85, Private dining 250 **Open** All Year **Prices from** S £6, M £15, D £7 **Parking** 250 **Notes** Vegetarian dishes, Children welcome

See advertisement opposite

PONTYPOOL

The Lion NEW
◉ CLASSIC WELSH

01495 792516 | 41 Broad Street, Blaenavon, NP4 9NH

www.thelionhotelblaenavon.co.uk

At the heart of UNESCO World Heritage-recognised Blaenavon, The Lion has been revamped with a clean-lined modern look. Its relaxed dining room blends bare tables with neutral grey hues and light fittings that reference the bygone mining days. The food fits the bill, deploying excellent local ingredients in hearty, crowd-pleasing dishes.

Chef Jon Wellington **Seats** Private dining 42 **Open** All Year **Prices from** S £4.95, M £12.95, D £3.95 **Parking** 10 **Notes** Vegetarian dishes, Children welcome

■ VALE OF GLAMORGAN

COWBRIDGE

Hare & Hounds NEW
◉◉ BRITISH, WELSH

01446 774892 | CF71 7LG

www.hareandhoundsaberthin.com

If you're looking for elevated country classics where local sourcing is key then look no further than the innovative and interesting food at the Hare & Hounds. This unassuming stone pub sits quietly on the main road in this peaceful Welsh village. Inside, a large inglenook fireplace, open kitchen and relaxed yet attentive service completes the picture.

Chef Tom Watts-Jones **Open** All Year **Prices from** S £5, M £9, D £2.20 **Parking** 6 **Notes** Vegetarian dishes, Children welcome until 7.30pm in pub, no restriction in dining room

HENSOL

Llanerch Vineyard
◉ MODERN WELSH

01443 222716 | CF72 8GG

www.llanerch-vineyard.co.uk

Around 22 acres of south-facing slopes of the Ely Valley have been planted with vines since 1986, and you can raise a glass to the industrious owners while dining in their restaurant or bistro, both of which offer the same menu. To wash it down – what else? ... Welsh wine of course.

Chef Michael Hudson, Andy Aston **Seats** 80, Private dining 80 **Closed** 25–26 December **Prices from** S £7, M £14, D £6.50 **Parking** 400 **Notes** Vegetarian dishes, Children welcome

Vale Grill
◉ MODERN BRITISH

01443 667800 | The Vale Resort, Hensol Park, CF72 8JY

www.vale-hotel.com

The Resort luxuriates in 650 acres of the Vale of Glamorgan, but is only 15 minutes' drive from Cardiff. A bright airy room, the Vale Grill is one dining option, or there's a linen-clad restaurant, La Cucina, as well as a champagne bar.

Chef Dean Milburn **Seats** 140, Private dining 20 **Open** All Year **Prices from** S £6.95, M £13.95, D £6.95 **Parking** 400 **Notes** Vegetarian dishes, Children welcome

Cwmbran Drive
Cwmbran
NP44 3UW
Tel: 01633 871199
www.parkwayhotelandspa.com

PARKWAY
HOTEL AND SPA

★★★★

Food . . . Just the way you like it

Located at the heart of the hotel, Ravellos is popular with both hotel residents and guests who live in the surrounding area.

We have been awarded our second AA Rosette, which reflects the passion that our Kitchen Brigade put into their food. There is an extensive A La Carte menu that reflects the use of Fresh Local Produce.

We pride ourselves on the best Sunday Lunch for miles, using only the best cuts of local meats.

Opening Hours
Breakfast from 7am – 9.30am
Dinner 6.30pm – last orders 9.30pm
Open for Sunday Lunch 12pm – last orders 2.30pm

LLANCARFAN
MAP 9, ST07

The Fox & Hounds
◉ MODERN, CLASSIC, BRITISH

01446 781287 | CF62 3AD

www.fandhllancarfan.co.uk

Next to a stream in the heart of the pretty village of Llancarfan, The Fox & Hounds occupies a peaceful location next to the 15th-century St Cadoc's Church, but it's only 15 minutes from the M4. The restaurant offers pub classics.

Chef Jim Dobson **Seats** 80 **Open** All Year
Prices from S £5, M £10, D £6 **Parking** 15
Notes Vegetarian dishes, Children welcome

PENARTH
MAP 9, ST17

Holm House Hotel *NEW*
◉ MODERN BRITISH

029 2070 6029 | Marine Parade, CF64 3BG

www.holmhousehotel.com

In a tranquil, affluent area of Penarth known as 'Millionaires' Row', the restaurant of this handsome 1920s mansion overlooks pretty gardens and the Bristol Channel beyond. The setting is smart, uncluttered and modern – it's all slate floors, unclothed tables and maritime shades of blue – and the kitchen delivers carefully executed modern British dishes with heaps of local flavour.

Open All Year

Restaurant James Sommerin
◉◉◉◉ MODERN BRITISH V ♦ NOTABLE WINE LIST

029 2070 6559 | The Esplanade, CF64 3AU

www.jamessommerinrestaurant.co.uk

Reach the Severn Estuary and head for Penarth pier and just across the esplanade you'll find Restaurant James Sommerin (RJS) in a handsome Victorian terrace. The view is lovely and if the weather is not always calm and soothing, head indoors where you'll be greeted warmly and seated in the charmingly civilised dining room. It's a smart, contemporary space, with linen tablecloths and velour seats to sink into. RJS also has deliciously designed rooms if you've a mind to stop over, with sea views from the best of them.

The eponymous chef-patron's menus don't give a lot away, with simple descriptions belying the complexity and creativity of each course from the carte or two tasting menus (six or nine courses). The seasons lead the way and a good deal of the produce comes from around these parts, with more than a whiff of European détente. The pea ravioli is a dish that took James all the way to the BBC *Great British Menu* final, an excellent combination of classic ingredients with beautifully fresh silky pasta. Main course delivers a superbly memorable dish of Welsh lamb with cumin, mint, and butternut squash purée. The wine list includes Welsh organic and biodynamic wines.

Chef James Sommerin **Seats** 65, Private dining 12
Closed 26 December, 1 January **Prices from** S £9, M £19.50, D £9 **Notes** Children welcome

■ WREXHAM

LLANARMON DYFFRYN CEIRIOG
MAP 15, SJ13

The Hand at Llanarmon
◉◉ CLASSIC BRITISH

01691 600666 | Ceiriog Valley, LL20 7LD

www.thehandhotel.co.uk

All the usual suspects – beams, open fires, etc – are in this whitewashed country inn; the stuffed fox, however, is decidedly more unusual. The classic and modern pub food menu changes frequently, but old favourites, like slow-braised Welsh lamb shoulder, refuse to budge. Grilled Ceiriog trout is also one to try.

Chef Grant Mulholland **Seats** 40 **Open** All Year
Prices from S £6, M £14.50, D £6.50 **Parking** 15
Notes Vegetarian dishes, Children welcome

NORTHERN IRELAND

■ COUNTY ANTRIM

BALLYMENA
MAP 1, D5

Galgorm Spa & Golf Resort
●●● MODERN IRISH *V* **♨** NOTABLE WINE LIST

See pages 520–521

See advertisement opposite

BUSHMILLS
MAP 1, D1

Bushmills Inn Hotel
● MODERN, TRADITIONAL

028 2073 3000 | 9 Dunluce Road, BT57 8QG
www.bushmillsinn.com

For centuries a coaching inn at the heart of this world-famous whiskey village, this is now an upmarket boutique hotel. The peat fires may remain from the days when guests arrived by horse but modern-day visitors are more likely to arrive via helipad.

Open All Year

NEWTOWNABBEY
MAP 1, D5

Sleepy Hollow
● MODERN IRISH

028 9083 8672 | 15 Kiln Road, BT36 4SU
www.sleepyhollowrestaurant.com

It would take a jaded palate not to be thrilled by the hearty modern Irish cooking in this rustic restaurant. Locally-sourced artisan produce is at the heart of things, with meat and game supplied by neighbouring farms and estates, butchered in-house, and handled without fuss.

Closed 24–26 December

■ BELFAST

BELFAST
MAP 1, D5

Deanes at Queens
●● MODERN BRITISH *V*

028 9038 2111 | 1 College Gardens, BT9 6BQ
www.michaeldeane.co.uk

In a stylish, contemporary space of chrome and glass, the cooking matches the modernity of the setting, delivering a genuine Irish flavour and some creative combinations. Perhaps try a starter of roast cauliflower and aged parmesan risotto, Ryan's Farm black pudding and tarragon, followed by crisp confit duck leg, poached Armagh pear with blue cheese and salted walnuts.

Chef Chris Fearon **Seats** 120, Private dining 44
Closed 25–26 December, 1 January, Easter Monday and Tuesday, 12–13 July **Prices from** S £5, M £14, D £6
Notes Children welcome

Deanes EIPIC
●●● MODERN EUROPEAN *V*

See page 522

Fitzwilliam Hotel Belfast
● MODERN *V*

028 9044 2080 | 1–3 Victoria Street, BT2 7BQ
www.fitzwilliamhotelbelfast.com

Next door to the Grand Opera House, the sleek Fitzwilliam Hotel makes a splendid upscale Belfast base for business or pleasure. The restaurant takes its style cues from Scandi minimalism, using blond wood tables and space-age, cherry-red seating as a setting for some well-conceived modern dishes.

Chef Dean Butler **Open** All Year **Notes** No children

James St
● MODERN, CLASSIC

028 9560 0700 | 21 James Street South, BT2 7GA
www.jamesstandco.com

Now combined with its former sister restaurant, James St offers the best of both. Among modern Irish dishes are classics of fruits de mer, fresh whole fish and chargrills. Start with a tasty crispy garlic squid and pickled shallots, then striploin and shoulder of spring lamb, ending with caramelised white chocolate profiteroles and poached rhubarb.

Chef David Gillmore **Seats** 120, Private dining 40
Closed 1 January, Easter Monday, 12–15 July, 25–26 December **Prices from** S £5, M £12.50, D £5
Notes Vegetarian dishes, Children welcome

A Culinary Destination

- 122 Guestrooms
- Unique Spa Village
- 4 Restaurants
- 4 Bars

Galgorm Spa & Golf Resort
Co. Antrim, Northern Ireland
BT42 1EA

028 2588 1001
reservations@galgorm.com
galgorm.com

Galgorm Spa & Golf Resort

◉◉◉ MODERN IRISH *V* ◗ NOTABLE WINE LIST

028 2588 1001 | 136 Fenaghy Road, Galgorm, BT42 1EA

www.galgorm.com

Ambitious contemporary cooking and river views

This upscale country resort hotel stands in 163 acres of parkland with the River Maine flowing through. Add luxurious bedrooms, a swish spa, posh conference and wedding facilities, and three dining venues, and you have a package to keep most people happy. On the food front, there's a brasserie and grill in former stables and a relaxed Italian venue, but gastronomy here gets serious in the aptly named River Room Restaurant, where the floodlit river creates a seductive atmosphere after dark, and its floor-to-ceiling windows mean everyone gets the watery views. This is chef Chris Rees's domain and he sets out his stall with a five-course tasting menu and a thoughtfully composed à la carte designed to showcase his impressive skills, as well as the splendid produce from trusty local suppliers (and as you'd hope with all those acres out there, a kitchen garden chips in with freshly plucked seasonal goodies).

Things get off the blocks with a well-crafted warm terrine of local rabbit and ham pointed up with crispy potatoes, purées of pea and black garlic, and wilted gem lettuce. Clarity of flavour is key, and while Rees is happy to use clever technical ideas when appropriate, the base of it all is solidly grounded in modern European thought, so main course showcases exquisite Mourne lamb, a cutlet and sliced rump delivered in a pretty-as-a-picture medley with courgette, fennel, tomato and artichoke. Fish cookery, too, shows real skill and confidence – perhaps halibut with cured egg, leeks, bacon and salsify.

Desserts are a high point, especially when baked caramel tart comes with roasted macadamia nuts, dark chocolate sorbet and coffee, or you might bow out on

> "... the base of it all is solidly grounded in modern European thought"

a pungent note with artisan Irish cheeses ripened to prime condition. All the peripherals, from the excellent home-made bread and inventive canapés to the superb petits fours are crafted with impressive attention to detail.

Chefs Israel Robb, Chris Rees
Seats 50
Open All Year
Prices from S £10, M £30, D £10
Parking 200
Notes No children under 12 years

See advertisement on page 519

Deanes EIPIC

◉◉◉ **MODERN EUROPEAN** *V*
028 9033 1134 | 36–40 Howard Street, BT1 6PF
www.deaneseipic.com

It may be a little confusing for first-timers, but Deanes is a tripartite set-up, with dedicated meat and fish restaurants, through which bustly environs you pass to reach the more softly accented EIPIC dining room, a soothingly lit space adorned with a trio of stylised full moons. Alex Greene worked his way from Dundrum to London and back to Belfast, and brings a cosmopolitan modernist sensibility to the kitchen, sending out a four- and six-course menus, plus a cracking value three-course lunch that speaks of confidence and innovative energy at every turn. Highlights might be aged Shorthorn beef with mooli radish, ponzu and quail's egg, followed by a flawlessly timed turbot with shiitake mushrooms, smoked bacon dashi, turnip and wild leek. Dessert might combine Guanaja chocolate, coconut, yuzu and coffee. Accompanying wines are served either by small glass or shot measure, a helpful touch of flexibility.

Chef Michael Deane, Alex Greene **Seats** 30 **Closed** 25–26 December, 1–14 January, 1 week in mid April, 2 weeks in early July **Notes** Children welcome

BELFAST continued

The Merchant Hotel
◉◉ MODERN CLASSIC **V** ⚑ NOTABLE WINE LIST

028 9023 4888 | 16 Skipper Street, Cathedral Quarter, BT1 2DZ

www.themerchanthotel.com

The former headquarters of Ulster Bank is a grand building and these days the beneficiaries are those who rock up for lunch or dinner. The kitchen delivers a classical-meets-modern repertoire where tip-top regional produce, such as lobster and scallops, is treated with respect.

Chef John Paul Leake **Seats** 85, Private dining 18 **Open** All Year **Prices from** S £6.95, M £21.50, D £8.50 **Notes** Children welcome

OX
◉◉◉ MODERN IRISH **V**

028 9031 4121 | 1 Oxford Street, BT1 3LA

www.oxbelfast.com

Right by the famous 'Rings' statue on the Lagan waterfront, OX is a pared-down space with board floor, teal colour scheme and a mezzanine level with extra tables. Friendly staff are ready with explanations of the tasting menus, which deal in first-class regional produce prepared with innovative flair. Lunch might open with spelt risotto adorned with girolles, shaved summer truffle and persillade, before delicately Indian-spiced halibut appears with bergamot-scented fennel and romanesco. Pedigree meats such as Chateaubriand and bone marrow with salsify and wild garlic are the stars of the evening show, perhaps following cured sea trout with pickled mussels in buttermilk. Intriguing, refreshingly light desserts encompass blood orange on caramelised pastry with mascarpone, or blackberry sorbet and lemon verbena on a sablé biscuit and custard. The attention to detail in extras like the onion galette topped with tomato, olive and shiso, or the hand-churned Cuinneog butter with the sourdough, inspires confidence.

Chef Stephen Toman **Seats** 40 **Closed** Christmas, 1 week April, 2 weeks July **Notes** Children welcome

Seahorse Restaurant *NEW*
◉ MODERN **V**

028 9023 1066 | Hastings Grand Central Hotel, Bedford Street, BT2 7FF

www.grandcentralhotelbelfast.com

The hotel's main dining room is built to impress with its high ceilings, soaring walls of glass and sleek art deco-inspired lines. Caramel leather banquettes, plush fabrics and marble-topped tables add further to the allure, while the modern cooking scores a hit for its local ingredients handled with finesse, style and imagination.

Chef Damian Tumilty **Seats** Private dining 40 **Open** All Year **Prices from** S £7, M £19, D £7 **Parking** 10 **Notes** Vegetarian dishes, Children welcome

Shu
◉◉ MODERN IRISH

028 9038 1655 | 253–255 Lisburn Road, BT9 7EN

www.shu-restaurant.com

Situated in a Victorian terrace, Shu is an airy, good-looking space with an open-to-view kitchen, a lively buzz, and service taken care of by a smartly turned-out team. The cooking has its heart in French classics but global influences – particularly Japanese flavours – all make themselves felt in creative dishes.

Chef Brian McCann **Seats** 100, Private dining 24 **Closed** 25–26 December, 1 January, 12–13 July **Prices from** S £5.50, M £12.50, D £6.50 **Parking** 4 **Notes** Vegetarian dishes, Children welcome

■ COUNTY DOWN

DUNDRUM   *MAP 1, D5*

Mourne Seafood Bar
◉ SEAFOOD

028 4375 1377 | 10 Main Street, BT33 0LU

www.mourneseafood.com

With a sister establishment in Belfast, the Dundrum branch of Mourne Seafood Bar is in a refreshingly peaceful location. At the foot of the Mourne mountains, with a nature reserve nearby, it's dedicated to fish and shellfish, much of which comes from their own shellfish beds.

Closed 18–20 and 24–26 December

NEWCASTLE MAP 1, D5

Vanilla Restaurant *NEW*

◉ MODERN IRISH

028 4372 2268 | 67 Main St, BT33 0AE

www.vanillarestaurant.co.uk

The head chef's past travels and experience in fusion cooking contribute towards the modern Irish cooking at Vanilla that transforms the best ingredients that the local markets have to supply. Think Thai beef sin spring rolls to start followed by a well-prepared confit of pork belly, glazed pork cheek, caramelised mooli purée, grilled and pickled radishes, apple purée and crisp onions. It's all very relaxed and sociable.

Closed 25-26 December

NEWTOWNARDS MAP 1, D5

Balloo House

◉ MODERN BRITISH *V*

028 9754 1210 | 1 Comber Road, Killinchy, BT23 6PA

www.balloohouse.com

Balloo House's original historical features remain, while the additions of darkwood panelling and peacock-blue and tan leather booth seating helped to create an intimate atmosphere. When it comes to the menu, dishes like roast Kilmore pigeon, apple and celeriac remoulade, hazelnut and red wine vinegrette set the style.

Chef Grainne Donnelly, Danielle Barry **Seats** 80, Private dining 30 **Closed** 25 December **Prices from** S £5.50, M £14, D £6.50 **Parking** 60 **Notes** Children welcome

■ COUNTY FERMANAGH

ENNISKILLEN MAP 1, C5

Lough Erne Resort

◉◉◉ MODERN, TRADITIONAL *V*

028 6632 3230 | Belleek Road, BT93 7ED

www.lougherneresort.com

Piling on the style with Thai spa treatments, up-to-the-minute golf facilities and restorative views of the Fermanagh Lakelands, Lough Erne is one of the joys of north-west Ireland. Among the dining options, the pick is The Catalina restaurant, named after the seaplanes that were once stationed on the lough. There are views over the 18th hole, but for those with their minds on dining, the charming service approach lends a mood of relaxed civility. Noel McMeel maintains his highly burnished style of locally supplied, traditionally rooted cooking, opening perhaps with a salad of Kilkeel crab, with a Ballycastle scallop, shaved pickled fennel and fresh orange salad with blood orange gel. 'Sperrin Venison' is the signature dish here – dry aged venison loin with crispy shoulder and pickled shallots, quince and apple butter, braised leek and celeriac. Incomparable technique makes a white chocolate parfait with violet meringue, raspberry gel and croquant tuile a real delight.

Chef Noel McMeel **Seats** 72, Private dining 30 **Open** All Year **Parking** 200 **Notes** Children welcome

Manor House Country Hotel

◉ IRISH, EUROPEAN

028 6862 2200 | Killadeas, BT94 1NY

www.manorhousecountryhotel.com

The colonel who rebuilt this old manor in the 1860s brought craftsmen over from Italy to spruce up the interior. The fine-dining action takes place in the Belleek Restaurant, housed in a conservatory extension that gets the very best of the view of the lough.

Open All Year

■ COUNTY LONDONDERRY DERRY

LONDONDERRY DERRY
MAP 1, C5

Browns Bonds Hill
❀ MODERN IRISH **V**
028 7134 5180 | 1 Bonds Hill, Waterside, BT47 6DW
www.brownsrestaurant.com
Situated on the edge of the city centre by Lough Foyle, Browns has built a local following for over 10 years. Get in the mood with some bubbly in the champagne lounge, then head for one of the white linen-swathed tables in the sleek, contemporary dining room. The kitchen turns out an appealing roll call of modern Irish ideas, with fish and seafood strong suits.

Chef Ian Orr, Phelim O' Hagan **Seats** 60 **Closed** 3 days at Christmas **Prices from** S £7, M £22, D £6 **Notes** Children welcome

The Gown Restaurant
❀ MODERN IRISH
028 7114 0300 | Bishop's Gate Hotel, 24 Bishop Street, BT48 6PP
www.bishopsgatehotelderry.com
In the heart of Cathedral Quarter, The Gown is the focal point of the late 19th-century Bishop's Gate Hotel. Original wall panelling and wooden flooring make an attractive setting for dining from the modern Irish menu's signature dishes, among them chargrills and fresh seafood. International influences are evident, too.

Closed 25 December

MAGHERA
MAP 1, C5

Ardtara Country House
❀❀ MODERN IRISH
028 7964 4490 | 8 Gorteade Road, BT46 5SA
www.ardtara.com
Built in the 19th century by a linen magnate, Ardtara is a country-house hotel in glorious grounds. It's an engaging spot for afternoon tea, and the restaurant, with its real fireplaces and oak panels, is a smart setting for the bright, contemporary cooking on offer.

Closed 25–26 December

REPUBLIC OF IRELAND

■ COUNTY CARLOW

LEIGHLINBRIDGE
MAP 1, C3

Lord Bagenal Inn
◉ MODERN IRISH
059 9774000 | Main Street
www.lordbagenal.com
In 1979, the original roadside restaurant was almost killed off by the advent of a new motorway, but the enterprising owners built a hotel on the site. It's distinctly contemporary these days, with its Signature Restaurant and bar revamped to create an open-plan space.

Chef Shein Than, George Kehoe **Seats** 85, Private dining 60 **Closed** 25–26 December **Prices from** S €5.20, M €15, D €6.25 **Parking** 100 **Notes** Vegetarian dishes, Children welcome

TULLOW
MAP 1, C3

Mount Wolseley Hotel, Spa & Golf Resort
◉ MODERN IRISH
059 9180100
www.mountwolseley.ie
The restaurant here encompasses a stylish split-level dining room overlooking a garden courtyard, where smartly attired staff attend at well turned-out tables. Seafood is a forte. There's also the Aaron Lounge for casual all-day dining.

Closed 24–26 December

■ COUNTY CAVAN

CAVAN
MAP 1, C4

Cavan Crystal Hotel
◉ MODERN IRISH
049 4360600 | Dublin Road
www.cavancrystalhotel.com
Sharing the same site as its factory, Ireland's second oldest crystal manufacturer also has a smart contemporary hotel, a leisure club and the clean-lined Opus One restaurant. It's a relaxed spot and food chimes in tune with the setting: confident, modern and uncomplicated.

The Cedar Rooms
◉◉ CLASSIC IRISH 𝐕
049 4377700 | Farnham Estate
www.farnhamestate.ie
Whether you're here for the golf, spa pampering or simply recharging the batteries on Farnham Estate's 1,300 acres, The Cedar Rooms restaurant is the place to end the day in an atmospheric setting of exposed stone walls and sleek modern decor. The kitchen's passion for prime local ingredients underpins the unfussy cooking.

Chef Daniel Willimont **Seats** 110, Private dining 40 **Open** All Year **Parking** 400 **Notes** Children welcome

■ COUNTY CLARE

BALLYVAUGHAN
MAP 1, B3

Gregans Castle
◉◉◉ MODERN IRISH, EUROPEAN
065 7077005
www.gregans.ie
It may not be an actual castle, but the 18th-century manor house is undeniably a luxurious hideaway filled with antiques and period Georgian elegance that is unlikely to disappoint. The location is a dream, set in the photogenic south-western wilderness that is The Burren, with sweeping views towards Galway Bay. The restaurant is a romantic and traditional room where picture windows open on to the views, candlelight flickers in the evening and the family-run hospitality is warm and welcoming. Head chef Robbie McCauley's menus are packed with modern ideas, where flavour, seasonality and ingredients from the local landscape point the way. Dishes are picture perfect, from starters of heritage beetroot with St Tola goats' curd, sorrel and apple, to mains like Kilshanny lamb with wild garlic, violet artichoke and white asparagus, or free-range suckling pig with broad beans, fennel and preserved lemon. For dessert, there could be forced rhubarb with Ivoire white chocolate and crème fraîche.

Chef Robbie McCauley **Seats** 50, Private dining 30 **Closed** December to mid February **Parking** 20 **Notes** Vegetarian dishes, Children under 7 years dine at 6pm

ENNIS
MAP 1, B3

Legends Restaurant
◉ MODERN INTERNATIONAL 𝐕
065 6823300 | Temple Gate Hotel, The Square
www.templegatehotel.com
Set in a former convent, the fine dining restaurant of the Temple Gate Hotel is an impressive space with its soaring hammerbeam roof and striking contemporary decor. There's a capable hand in the kitchen, and daily specials mean that seasonal produce is well represented.

Chef Reinhard Sprengard **Seats** 100, Private dining 60 **Closed** 25–26 December **Parking** 50 **Notes** Children welcome

LAHINCH
MAP 1, B3
Moy House
◉◉ MODERN FRENCH
065 7082800
www.moyhouse.com
Standing proud in 15 acres of grounds overlooking the bay at Lahinch, Moy House is full of period character, though the dining room with its minimalist chandeliers and panoramic views is more contemporary. As is the food, which includes a tasting menu and draws on unimpeachable local supply lines.

Closed November to March

VL Restaurant
◉◉ MODERN FRENCH, IRISH *V*
065 7081111 | Vaughan Lodge Hotel, Ennistymon Road
www.vaughanlodge.ie
Overlooking beautiful Liscannor Bay, this modern townhouse hotel is located right next to the world-famous Lahinch Golf Course. Vaughan Lodge's stunning coastal position means the kitchen is blessed with a bountiful supply of excellent fish and seafood including daily landings of langoustine, lobster and scallops.

Chef Pawel Gasiorowski **Seats** 50 **Closed** November to April **Notes** Children welcome

LISDOONVARNA
MAP 1, B3
Sheedy's Country House Hotel
◉◉ CLASSIC IRISH
065 7074026
www.sheedys.com
This small-scale country-house hotel exudes the sort of family-run, unpretentious tradition that keeps fans returning. John Sheedy has long-established local supply lines, and the kitchen garden provides fresh herbs and vegetables to supplement local organic meat and fish landed at nearby Doolin.

Chef John Sheedy **Seats** 28 **Closed** mid October to end March **Prices from** S €10, M €22 **Parking** 25 **Notes** Vegetarian dishes, No children under 12 years

NEWMARKET-ON-FERGUS
MAP 1, B3
Dromoland Castle Hotel
◉◉ TRADITIONAL IRISH, EUROPEAN *V*
061 368144
www.dromoland.ie
As well as a golf course and spa, you'll find turrets and ramparts at this fabulous country-house hotel. Formal dining takes place in the Earl of Thomond restaurant, a spectacular room filled with antiques, oak-panelled period character and a resident harpist.

Chef David McCann **Seats** 80, Private dining 70 **Open** All Year **Prices from** S €16, M €28, D €12 **Parking** 140 **Notes** Children welcome

SHANNON
MAP 1, B3
The Old Lodge Gastro Pub
◉ MODERN IRISH
061 364047 | Shannon Springs Hotel, Ballycasey, V14 A336
www.shannonspringshotel.com
Part of Shannon Springs Hotel, the refurbished Old Lodge features a covered, themed beer garden that includes some old shop-fronts. Specialising in Irish-style food with modern variations, the new gastro menu offers Irish tapas, such as hot 'n' spicy chicken wings; tempura of battered cod; and buffalo mozzarella, with beef tomato tart.

Chef Anthony Walsh **Seats** 60, Private dining 45 **Closed** 25 December **Prices from** S €4.75, M €12.55, D €6.25 **Parking** 105 **Notes** Vegetarian dishes, Children welcome

See advertisement on page 529

■ COUNTY CORK

BALLINGEARY
MAP 1, B2
Gougane Barra Hotel
◉ CLASSIC, TRADITIONAL
026 47069 | Gougane Barra
www.gouganebarrahotel.com
The Cronin family has owned property in hauntingly beautiful Gougane Barra since Victorian times, when its potential as an idyllic retreat was first fully realised. Views over the lake towards the mountains of Cork look especially magnificent from the ample windows of the dining room.

Chef Katy Lucey **Seats** 70 **Closed** Winter **Prices from** S €7, M €19.50, D €7 **Parking** 40 **Notes** Vegetarian dishes, Children welcome

nnovative, Modern, & Devoted to Place

yan McCarthy heads up the kitchen team at the ard-winning Greenes Restaurant and recognises he uniqueness and quality of the outstanding gredients that are available in Cork. His talented eam works in tandem with the best Irish food oducers to create a menu that's devoted to local, seasonal, foraged and organic ingredients.

th a secluded waterfall in its courtyard, Greenes boasts one of the most stunning outdoor areas n the country and its sister venue, multi-award-nning Cask cocktail bar, is the perfect spot for a pre or post-dinner drink.

Greenes
RESTAURANT

Greenes Restaurant, 48 MacCurtain Street, Victorian Quarter, Cork
021 455 2279 | www.greenesrestaurant.com | info@greenesrestaurant.com

BALLYLICKEY *MAP 1, B2*

Seaview House Hotel
◉◉ TRADITIONAL IRISH
027 50073 |
www.seaviewhousehotel.com
The grand white-painted Seaview has the promised vista over Bantry Bay, glimpsed through the trees in the pretty gardens, while the restaurant comprises three rooms including a conservatory. There's much local produce on the menu and everything is handled with care.

Closed November to March

BALTIMORE *MAP 1, B1*

Rolfs Country House
◉ FRENCH, EUROPEAN
028 20289 |
www.rolfscountryhouse.com
Set in beautiful sub-tropical gardens overlooking Baltimore Harbour to Roaringwater Bay and Carbery's 100 islands, it is hardly surprising that the Haffner family have put down roots here since 1979. The kitchen uses produce that is locally grown, reared and caught, organic whenever possible.

Chef Johannes Haffner **Seats** 50, Private dining 14
Closed Christmas **Prices from** S €8.50, M €19, D €7.50
Parking 45 **Notes** Vegetarian dishes, Children welcome

CASTLETOWNBERE *MAP 1, A2*

The Coastal Restaurant *NEW*
◉ MODERN, SEAFOOD
027 71446 | The Beara Coast Hotel, Cametringane
www.bearacoast.com
The Beara Coast Hotel's principal dining space, this restaurant has a very loyal local custom. Given its location at one of Ireland's main fishing ports, seafood is a feature, simply cooked and paired, for example, with crusts and risottos. Expect polished timber tables, banquette seating and comfy tartan upholstered dining chairs. All bakery is done in-house.

CORK *MAP 1, B2*

Bellini's Restaurant
◉◉ MODERN INTERNATIONAL
021 4365555 | Maryborough Hotel & Spa, Maryborough Hill, Douglas
www.maryborough.com
There's a whiff of glamour at this Georgian country-house hotel, with later additions tacked on, surrounded by 14 acres of well-maintained gardens and woodland. The bar and restaurant,

Bellini's, provide a modern glossy sheen. Fresh, locally-sourced produce is the kitchen's stock in trade for their up-to-date menus.

Closed 24–26 December

Greenes *NEW*
◉◉ MODERN
021 4500011 | Hotel Isaacs, 48 MacCurtain Street
www.hotelisaacscork.com

Set in a Georgian former warehouse and given the boutique hotel treatment, Greenes is a bright and airy spot that overlooks a terrace with a red granite waterfall feature. The kitchen goes for home ingredients, serving well-conceived, modern dishes cooked with pin-sharp accuracy, and with a fondness for deploying fashionable pickling and fermenting treatments.

See advertisement on page 531

Panorama Bistro & Terrace *NEW*
◉ MODERN
021 4530050 | The Montenotte Hotel, Middle Glanmire Road, Montenotte
www.themontenottehotel.com
Splendid views over the River Lee and the cityscape beyond are guaranteed whatever the weather thanks to the glass wall and covered cantilevered terrace of this smart boutique hotel's restaurant. A cracking grill-style menu peppered with local artisan flavours and supported by kitchen garden produce offers plenty to please all comers.

Perrotts Garden Bistro
◉◉ MODERN IRISH, MEDITERRANEAN
021 4845900 | Hayfield Manor, Perrott Avenue, College Road
www.hayfieldmanor.ie
Early 19th-century iron baron Richard Perrott lived here in what is today's Hayfield Manor, where the bistro occupies the contemporary conservatory. Glass-topped metal or timber tables, sofas and wine cabinets create a relaxing

environment for international-style dining; eat alfresco, if you prefer. Lunch and dinner menus change frequently.

Open All Year

DURRUS
MAP 1, A2

Blairscove House & Restaurant

◉◉ MODERN EUROPEAN

027 61127

www.blairscove.ie

Blairscove brims with charm, on a promontory overlooking peaceful Dunmanus Bay. The main house is Georgian, and the accommodation and restaurant occupy a pretty development facing a pond, in what were the piggery, stables and barn. The dining room is full of character.

Chef Ronald Klotzer **Seats** 75, Private dining 48 **Closed** November to 15 March **Parking** 30 **Notes** Vegetarian dishes, Children welcome

GOLEEN
MAP 1, A1

The Heron's Cove

◉ CLASSIC IRISH, SEAFOOD

028 35225 | The Harbour

www.heronscove.com

This delightful restaurant sits in an idyllic spot on Goleen harbour near to Mizen Head, where the lonely Fastnet Rock lighthouse beams out across the Atlantic. This is an exceptionally easy-going, friendly place, where you can enjoy sublime sea views on the balcony.

Chef Irene Coughlan **Seats** 30 **Closed** mid November to mid March **Prices from** S €7.95, M €20.95, D €7.95 **Parking** 10 **Notes** Vegetarian dishes, Children welcome

KINSALE
MAP 1, B2

The White House

◉ MODERN IRISH

021 4772125 | Pearse Street, The Glen

www.whitehouse-kinsale.ie

The White House occupies a prime site in the centre of a town that holds a Gourmet Festival every autumn, so there's plenty to live up to in the gastronomic stakes. The kitchen team triumphs with a resourceful repertoire of modern Irish dishes.

Closed 25 December

MALLOW
MAP 1, B2

Springfort Hall Country House Hotel

◉ MODERN, IRISH

022 21278

www.springfort-hall.com

This is an immaculately-preserved Georgian country house where the enthusiastic kitchen team don't cut corners – meat and fish is smoked in-house and everything is made from scratch. In the palatial Lime Tree Restaurant a crystal chandelier hangs above pristine white linen-clothed tables.

Chef Viktor Bosz **Seats** 60, Private dining 40 **Closed** 24–26 December **Prices from** S €8.50, M €17.50, D €8.50 **Parking** 250 **Notes** Vegetarian dishes, Children welcome

ROSSCARBERY
MAP 1, B2

Kingfisher Bistro

◉ SEAFOOD *V*

023 8848722 | The Celtic Ross Hotel

www.celticrosshotel.com

Part of the wonderfully-situated Celtic Ross Hotel, a contemporary building right on the waterfront, with fabulous views, the Kingfisher Bistro is ideally placed to take advantage of the great local produce available in the region. Signature dishes include 'the finest seafood chowder in West Cork', so definitely worth trying.

Chef Alex Petit **Seats** Private dining 250 **Closed** 24–26 December **Prices from** S €5.75, M €16.50, D €6.75 **Parking** 150 **Notes** Vegetarian dishes, Children welcome

SHANAGARRY
MAP 1, C2

Ballymaloe House

◉◉ IRISH, EUROPEAN

021 4652531

www.ballymaloe.com

The Allens were ahead of the curve 50 years ago when they opened a restaurant in their farmhouse. Now there's a cookery school and hotel too, and the idea of fresh produce brought to the table in double-quick time seems the happy norm.

Chef JR Ryall, Dervilla O'Flynn **Seats** 110, Private dining 50 **Closed** Christmas, 6 January to 6 February **Parking** 100 **Notes** Vegetarian dishes, No children under 7 years at dinner

SKIBBEREEN
MAP 1, B1
Kennedy Restaurant
CLASSIC, TRADITIONAL
028 21277 | West Cork Hotel, Ilen Street
www.westcorkhotel.com
This riverside hotel's restaurant offers a carvery at lunchtime with a dessert buffet, while in the evening the à la carte focuses on locally sourced ingredients to ensure a sense of place. It all takes place in a modest yet stylish room with a buzzy atmosphere.

Chef Linda O'Brien **Seats** 60, Private dining 300
Closed 25-27 December **Parking** 50 **Notes** Vegetarian dishes, Children welcome

The Restaurant at Liss Ard NEW
CLASSIC, MODERN
028 40000 | Castletownsend Road, Russagh, P81 NP44
www.lissardestate.com
The Liss Ard Estate offers 163 acres of secluded grounds in which to work up an appetite for some taste-packed food served in the vaulted restaurant. It's all made using the area's finest produce, as well as goodies from their own kitchen garden. Based on sound classical ideas, dishes are given a modern country-house tweak here and there.

Chef Danny Barter **Seats** 60, Private dining 30
Closed Winter **Prices from** S €6.50, M €18, D €4.50
Parking 100 **Notes** Vegetarian dishes, Children welcome

■ COUNTY DONEGAL

BALLYLIFFIN
MAP 1, C6
Jacks Restaurant
MODERN EUROPEAN
074 9378146 | Ballyliffin Lodge & Spa, Shore Road
www.ballyliffinlodge.com
Brown leather seats and banquettes, bare tables and dark wood floors – backed by a pubby bar and an unbuttoned menu are a hit with the guests at Ballyliffin Lodge. There's a clear penchant for oriental accents in starters such as Thai salmon fishcakes, but there's a strong showing of regional flavours too.

Closed 24-25 December

DONEGAL
MAP 1, B5
Harvey's Point Hotel
EUROPEAN, SEAFOOD
074 9722208 | Lough Eske
www.harveyspoint.com
It was the glorious setting that brought the Gysling family from Switzerland to the shores of Lough Eske in order to build their luxurious hotel complex. The kitchen of the Lakeside Restaurant uses top-notch produce in imaginative, contemporary dishes like a main of pan-roasted fillet of turbot, brown shrimp, leek, parsley, gnocchi and verjus.

Chef Chris McMenamin **Seats** 120 **Parking** 200
Notes Vegetarian dishes, Children welcome

The Red Door Country House
MODERN, TRADITIONAL EUROPEAN
074 9360289 | Fahan, Inishowen
www.thereddoor.ie
With views over Lough Swilly, this country house has a restaurant run by a hands-on team. The series of dining rooms – including a sun room – have polished teak tables and smart linen napery. The menu shows a passion for local produce, along with sound classical training and bright modern thinking.

DUNGLOE
MAP 1, B5
The Waterfront Bistro NEW
MODERN IRISH
074 9522444 | Waterfront Hotel Dungloe, Mill Road
www.waterfronthoteldungloe.ie
This bright, busy and buzzy all-day bistro has views of the tide ebbing and flowing into Dungloe Bay. Polished timber tables with comfy leather upholstery provide customers with comfortable seating while they await a daily special from the semi-open kitchen. Primarily a grill, but lots of seafood too.

Chef Brendan Conmey **Seats** 60, Private dining 280
Closed Winter **Prices from** S €4.90, M €13.50, D €4.50
Parking 300 **Notes** Vegetarian dishes, Children welcome

LETTERKENNY
MAP 1, C5
Port Bar & Grill
MODERN IRISH
074 9194444 | Radisson Blu Hotel Letterkenny, Paddy Harte Road
www.radissonblu.com/en/hotel-letterkenny
A modern hotel of glass and steel, this outpost of the Radisson Blu group features the Port Bar & Grill when you can enjoy pub-style food in a casual and relaxed dining environment. Plasma-screen TVs mean you won't miss the latest sports action.

Chef Collette Langan **Seats** 120, Private dining 320
Open All Year **Parking** 150 **Notes** Vegetarian dishes, Children welcome

MOVILLE
MAP 1, C6

Redcastle Hotel, Golf & Spa Resort

◉◉ MODERN, INTERNATIONAL

074 9385555 | Inishowen Peninsula

www.redcastlehotel.com

The Redcastle Estate can trace its lineage all the way back to a 16th-century proprietor called Cathal O'Doherty. At one point, it was owned by a Pennsylvania farming family, but today it makes a superbly located north-western seafront hotel in the modern boutique style.

Chef Gordon Smyth **Seats** 140 **Open** All Year
Prices from S €8.50, M €17, D €8.50 **Parking** 232
Notes Vegetarian dishes, Children welcome

■ DUBLIN

DUBLIN
MAP 1, D4

Balfes at The Westbury

◉ CONTEMPORARY IRISH

01 6463353 | Grafton Street

www.balfes.ie

With its own street entrance, and pavement tables, Balfes is an affable place with white walls, dark leather seats and a long bar-counter down one end. Kick off in the morning with an omelette or blueberry pancakes or come for lunch of roast sea trout.

Closed 25 December

Castleknock Hotel

◉ TRADITIONAL IRISH

01 6406300 | Porterstown Road, Castleknock

www.castleknockhotel.com

Just 15 minutes from Dublin, Castleknock has plenty of pizazz. The pick of its eating and drinking choices is the elegantly finished Earth and Vine Restaurant. There are floor-to-ceiling windows with swagged curtains, richly-coloured walls and large artworks. Steak is the mainstay of the kitchen's output.

Closed 24–26 December

Cliff Townhouse

◉◉ SEAFOOD

01 6383939 | 22 St Stephens Green

clifftownhouse.ie

Dubliners love this intimate seafood-focused restaurant, whether it's for lunch after shopping in classy Grafton Street, or for a pre-theatre dinner in the Oyster & Champagne Bar. Afternoon tea features Yawl Bay crabs and Irish smoked salmon open sandwiches. Thoughtful sourcing of ingredients is, naturally, behind everything.

Chef Sean Smith **Seats** 100, Private dining 44 **Closed** 24 December evening, 25–27 December
Prices from S €7.50, M €19, D €9.50 **Notes** Vegetarian dishes, Children welcome

Fahrenheit Restaurant

◉◉ MODERN IRISH

01 8332321 | Clontarf Castle Hotel, Castle Avenue, Clontarf

www.clontarfcastle.ie

Fahrenheit is the destination restaurant of Dublin's Clontarf Castle Hotel, a beguiling mix of the ancient (12th-century roots) and a modern boutique, and it's a dramatic showcase for some striking modern Irish cooking. Try beetroot-cured wild salmon with smoked salmon mousse, beetroot gel and horseradish.

Open All Year

The Italian Kitchen *NEW*

◉ ITALIAN

018711255 | Clayton Hotel Dublin Airport, Stockhole Lane, Swords

www.theitaliankitchen.ie

This is a smart, contemporary addition to the dining options at the Clayton Hotel Dublin Airport. They have gone to great lengths to create an authentic Italian experience by importing ingredients directly, together with an interesting wine selection. There is always a good selection of seasonal fish on offer, with high quality meats also a feature.

Chef Jonathan Bone **Seats** Private dining 120
Prices from S €4.95, M €13.95, D €5.50
Notes Vegetarian dishes, Children welcome

The Iveagh Bar

◉ IRISH, EUROPEAN

01 6772324 | Ashling Hotel, Dublin, Parkgate Street

www.ashlinghotel.ie

The Ashling is a large, modern and glitzy hotel near Phoenix Park and Dublin Zoo, where the restaurant occupies a spacious, softly lit room with plushly upholstered, comfortable dining chairs. The kitchen takes a modern tack with its combinations of flavours.

Closed 24–26 December

DUBLIN   MAP 1, D4

Restaurant Patrick Guilbaud

◉◉◉◉ **MODERN FRENCH** 🍷 NOTABLE WINE LIST
01 6764192 | The Merrion Hotel, 21 Upper Merrion Street
www.restaurantpatrickguilbaud.ie

Bold contemporary cooking with a French soul and an Irish heart

The setting amid the elegant Georgian splendour of the five-star Merrion Hotel hints at the supremely civilised experience that is dining chez Guilbaud, a name that has been the touchstone of fine dining in Ireland since first opening its doors back in 1981. Remarkably, the Paris-born patron has kept the same chef, Guillaume Lebrun (now executive chef), running the kitchen since opening its doors all those decades ago, and the same manager, Stéphane Robin for nearly as long. This remarkable level of consistency has provided a steadfast platform for head chef Kieran Glennon to build upon.

The dining room, with its barrel-vaulted ceiling, is a soothing contemporary space, with warm tones and striking artworks from Irish artists on the walls, the room watched over by a professional and knowledgeable service team. Outstanding produce sourced with passion and care

> Brimful of luxuries, the cooking shows genuine ambition and creativity

from the local area underpins the kitchen's output, from the à la carte, through a four-course dégustation menu (Tuesday to Thursday) and a full-works eight-course taster. Brimful of luxuries, the cooking shows genuine ambition and creativity.

Dinner might open with pan-roast duck foie gras lifted with pineapple, dark rum caramel and tonka bean, or the fresh simplicity of Flaggy Shore Dainty oysters with lovage, horseradish and sour apple. A combination of French classical thinking and global flavours characterises main courses too, perhaps piquillo pepper, wet

garlic and black oil to intensify superb Wicklow Hills lamb fillet, or squab pigeon pointed up with sweet onion, and cumin and yuzu jus. Dessert might be a masterclass Grand Marnier soufflé. The wine list is a tour de force especially when dealing with the best French producers, but the rest of the world is far from excluded; the cellar contains some 30,000 bottles in total, so it is worth making use of the passionate and knowledgeable sommelier to guide the way.

Chef Guillaume Lebrun, Kieran Glennon
Seats 80, Private dining 30
Closed 25–31 December, 1st week in January
Notes Vegetarian dishes, Children welcome

The Marker

◉◉ MODERN INTERNATIONAL

01 6875100 | Grand Canal Square

www.themarkerhoteldublin.com

Set in a cool, contemporary canalside hotel in the rejuvenated Docklands zone, this sleek brasserie is making quite a splash on the local dining scene, and celebrates the pick of Irish produce in its ambitious modernist food. Global accents abound.

Chef Gareth Mullins **Seats** 130, Private dining 250 **Closed** 24–25 December and January **Prices from** S €9, M €38, D €9 **Parking** 40 **Notes** Vegetarian dishes, Children welcome

McLoughlins Restaurant

◉ TRADITIONAL EUROPEAN

01 8433118 | Roganstown Hotel and Country Club, Naul Road, Sword

www.roganstown.com

Golf, spa and conference facilities all feature at this large resort, but for dinner you'll be wanting the impressive, wood-panelled McLoughlins Restaurant. There's plenty of room between the well-dressed tables, and the kitchen seeks out first-class ingredients and delivers an ambitious, contemporary menu.

Chef Thomas Molnare **Seats** 100, Private dining 30 **Closed** 24–25 December and St Stephen's Day **Notes** Vegetarian dishes, Children welcome

No. 10 Fleet Street Restaurant NEW

◉ MODERN, SEAFOOD

01 6437000 | The Morgan Hotel, 10–12 Fleet Street

www.themorgan.com

Occupying the lion's share of the ground floor of the über-stylish Morgan Hotel, this buzzy restaurant and bar sports a sleek big-city aesthetic with its mirrored walls, caramel leather banquettes and pale wood floors. This is a kitchen that focuses on local ingredients, particularly fish and seafood, and knows how to create big-hearted, feel-good flavours.

The Purple Sage Restaurant

◉ MODERN, FUSION

01 2001800 | Talbot Hotel Stillorgan, Stillorgan Road

www.talbothotelstillorgan.com

A hotel with wedding packages among its attractions, the Talbot Hotel Stillorgan is also home to The Purple Sage Restaurant, with its breezy air and contemporary finish. The menu has a gently conceived, modern fusion tack. For dessert, expect bread-and-butter pudding made with croissants.

Closed 25 December

Radisson Blu St Helens Hotel

◉ ITALIAN

01 2186000 | Stillorgan Road

www.radissonblu.ie/sthelenshotel-dublin

This grand old house dates from the mid-17th century but has all the expected mod cons. The Talavera restaurant serves up smart Italian food – especially from Lombardy – in a series of rooms with either traditional country-house decor or more contemporary chic.

Open All Year

Restaurant Patrick Guilbaud

◉◉◉◉ MODERN FRENCH 🍷 NOTABLE WINE LIST

See pages 536–537

Seasons Restaurant NEW

◉◉ CONTEMPORARY IRISH

01 6654000 | Intercontinental Dublin

www.intercontinentaldublin.ie

Set in the des-res area of Ballsbridge, the Intercontinental Dublin's posh Seasons Restaurant proves a comfy fit for the upmarket neighbourhood. It's an elegant high-ceilinged room with picture windows looking into the courtyard garden. The kitchen deals in classic ideas executed with precision and made with as much local produce as can be hauled in.

Chef Alberto Rossi **Seats** 114, Private dining 14 **Open** All Year **Prices from** S €13, M €23, D €12 **Parking** 15 **Notes** Vegetarian dishes, Children welcome

The Shelbourne Dublin

◉◉ CLASSIC, TRADITIONAL **V**

01 6634500 | 27 St Stephen's Green

www.theshelbourne.ie

This grand modern hotel is in a prime location on St Stephen's Green, and offers a range of eating and drinking options culminating in the tip-top Saddle Room. Here a menu of modern brasserie dishes specialises in seafood (including generously loaded platters).

Chef Garry Hughes **Seats** 120, Private dining 20 **Open** All Year **Prices from** S €9, M €25, D €9 **Notes** Children welcome

Tom's Table

◉ IRISH

01 4593650 | Red Cow Moran Hotel, Red Cow Complex, Naas Road

www.redcowmoranhotel.com

The modern Red Cow Moran Hotel is amply equipped with drinking and dining opportunities, the top choice being Tom's Table, an expansive space done out in contemporary city-slicker style. Lit by soaring floor-to-ceiling windows, its toffee-brown banquettes and clean-lined brasserie-style looks make a suitable setting for uncomplicated, modern cooking.

Open All Year

Wilde

◉◉ MODERN IRISH ♦ NOTABLE WINE LIST

01 6463311 | The Westbury, Grafton Street

www.wilde.ie

This prestigious city-centre hotel has a fine-dining restaurant dedicated to Oscar Wilde. The kitchen showcases the cream of Ireland's produce. Puddings are a strong suit especially when they include an authentic rendition of classic crema Catalana, or vanilla pannacotta with poached rhubarb.

Open All Year

■ COUNTY DUBLIN

KILLINEY   *MAP 1, D3*

Fitzpatrick Castle Hotel

◉ MODERN EUROPEAN

01 2305400

www.fitzpatrickcastle.com

The castellated house was built in the 18th century, and now offers a range of hospitable dining venues including the bar, housed in the former dungeon, and the Mapas Restaurant where you'll find a menu of well-wrought modern brasserie cooking.

Closed 25 December

PORTMARNOCK   *MAP 1, D4*

The Seaview

◉◉ MODERN IRISH

01 8460611 | Portmarnock Hotel and Golf Links

www.portmarnock.com

The Portmarnock Hotel and Golf Links stands on the estate that was once home to the Jameson Irish Whiskey family and a bar named after the dynasty is a fitting venue for a pint or a dram before a meal at the stylish Seaview restaurant. The coastal location means there are close links between the kitchen and local fishermen and seafood is handled with respect. Local meat is also well represented.

Chef Thomas Haughton **Seats** 40 **Open** All Year **Parking** 100 **Notes** Vegetarian dishes, Children welcome

SAGGART   *MAP 1, D3*

Woodlock Brasserie *NEW*

◉ MODERN

01 4010500 | Citywest Hotel

www.citywesthotel.com

Ireland's largest hotel not only boasts 240 acres of parkland with its own golf course, but also this relaxed modern brasserie. Spread over a series of connecting spaces, you can take in the action on the fairways through large windows while the kitchen delivers a please-all roster of straightforward grilled meats and seafood.

■ COUNTY GALWAY

BARNA   *MAP 1, B3*

The Pins Gastro Bar

◉ INTERNATIONAL, MODERN IRISH

091 597000 | The Twelve, Barna Village

www.thetwelvehotel.ie

Part of the boutique-style The Twelve, The Pins is an unusual amalgam of bar, bakery, bistro and pizzeria, the latter being authentic Neapolitan-style thin and crispy pizzas made in a Vesuvian stone oven. There's also a modern gastro-pub menu of championing regional suppliers.

Chef Martin O'Donnell **Seats** 140, Private dining 20 **Open** All Year **Parking** 120 **Notes** Vegetarian dishes, Children welcome

West Restaurant

◉◉ MODERN IRISH ♦ NOTABLE WINE LIST

091 597000 | The Twelve, Barna Village,

www.westrestaurant.ie

A boutique hotel with bags of swagger, The Twelve is in a coastal area a short distance from the town centre. There's a lot going on: a cool bar, a bakery, and a pizza place, but the main action takes place in the upstairs restaurant.

Chef Martin O'Donnell **Seats** 94, Private dining 100 **Open** All Year **Parking** 120 **Notes** Vegetarian dishes, Children welcome

CASHEL
MAP 1, A4

Cashel House Hotel
◉◉ TRADITIONAL IRISH
095 31001
cashelhouse.ie

Standing at the head of Cashel Bay, Cashel House is a gracious 19th-century country pile that has belonged to the McEvilly family since 1968. The restaurant offers French-accented classics, served in either an airy conservatory extension, or a polished traditional setting amid antiques and artworks.

Chef Arturo Tillo **Seats** 70, Private dining 20 **Closed** 2 January to 1 March **Parking** 30 **Notes** Vegetarian dishes, Children welcome

GALWAY
MAP 1, B3

The Ardilaun Hotel
◉ MODERN IRISH
091 521433 | Taylor's Hill
www.theardilaunhotel.ie

Formerly Glenarde House, The Ardilaun was built in 1840 for the Persse family, Galway landowners of some grandeur. It was launched as a modern hotel in 1962, and the Bistro is its venue for dynamic modern Irish cooking that is ambitious in its endeavours.

Chef Ultan Cooke **Seats** 140, Private dining 360 **Closed** 25–26 December **Prices from** S €8, M €19, D €7 **Parking** 250 **Notes** Vegetarian dishes, Children welcome

Dillisk on the Docks
◉ MODERN, TRADITIONAL
091 894800 | The Harbour Hotel, New Dock Road
www.harbour.ie/en/dillisk-on-the-docks-galway

The main restaurant of the waterfront Harbour Hotel sports a sharp contemporary brasserie-style look. It's a buzzy spot with royal blue seats, banquettes and high-level tables providing a variety of settings to suit the mood. Food-wise, the kitchen takes an uncomplicated, please-all approach.

Chef Patrick Anslow **Seats** 96 **Open** All Year **Prices from** S €6.25, M €16.50, D €6.95 **Parking** 70 **Notes** Vegetarian dishes, Children welcome

Gaslight Brasserie
◉ MODERN IRISH
091 564041 | Hotel Meyrick, Eyre Square
www.hotelmeyrick.ie

One of several dining options in the Meyrick, the Gaslight looks out over Eyre Square. Lofty and bright, its seasonal daytime and evening menus usually feature international dishes, including

Malaysian and Vietnamese. End on a high with spiced apple and rhubarb crumble with vanilla ice cream and crème anglaise.

Open All Year

Marinas Grill
◉ MODERN IRISH, SEAFOOD
091 538300 | The Galmont Hotel & Spa, Lough Atalia Road
www.thegalmont.com

Part of The Galmont Hotel & Spa on the banks of Lough Atalia, Marinas Grill overlooks Galway Bay which supplies much of the seafood on the menu. The kitchen lets the raw materials do the talking and the stylish modern dishes are unpretentious and produce-driven.

Open All year **Notes** Children welcome

Park House Hotel & Restaurant
◉ MODERN IRISH, INTERNATIONAL
091 564924 | Forster Street, Eyre Square
www.parkhousehotel.ie

Standing just off Eyre Square and built of striking pink granite, Park House has offered high standards of food and accommodation for over 35 years. Park Restaurant, where paintings of old Galway help keep the past alive, bustles at lunchtime and mellows in the evening.

Chef Robert O'Keefe, Martin Keane **Seats** 145, Private dining 45 **Closed** 24–26 December **Prices from** S €5.95, M €17, D €7.50 **Parking** 40 **Notes** Vegetarian dishes, Children welcome

Pullman Restaurant
◉◉ MODERN FRENCH
091 519600 | Glenlo Abbey Hotel, Kentfield, Bushypark
www.glenloabbeyhotel.ie

As if this grandiose country house built in the early Georgian era didn't have architectural diversion enough, its dining room has been fashioned from a pair of Orient Express railway carriages. It's a splendid design concept, and makes an elegant setting.

Open All Year

Restaurant gigi's at the g Hotel & Spa
◉◉ MODERN IRISH
091 865200 | Wellpark, Dublin Road
www.theghotel.ie

Looking a little like a modern office building, the g is a fashionista's magnet, with an eye-popping dining room in pulsating violet and many another hue. Artful presentations of dishes are the norm, but the food itself is more intuitive than you might expect.

Closed 23–26 December

Screebe House

◎◎ IRISH, SEAFOOD
091 574110 | Rosmuc
www.screebe.com/
This house was a hunting and fishing lodge in the 19th century and is situated right on the edge of Camus Bay – it cannot get any closer to the Atlantic. Dinner is a particular highlight; the daily-changing, seven-course set menu is driven by the season and the market.

Chef Olivier Jasko, Pascal Marinot **Seats** 20
Closed December to 1 March **Parking** 20
Notes Vegetarian dishes, No children

ORANMORE   MAP 1, B3
Basilico Restaurant

◎ ITALIAN
091 788367 | The Coach House Hotel, Main Street
www.basilicorestaurant.ie
Now over 10 years old, Basilico brings an authentic slice of Italy to the heart of Oranmore, just 20 minutes from Galway. A contemporary restaurant decorated with artwork by owner Fabiano Mulas, there is a genuine buzz at each sitting. Crowd-pleasing pizzas are made in a partly-open kitchen.

Closed 25 December

RECESS   MAP 1, A4
Lough Inagh Lodge Hotel

◎◎ IRISH, FRENCH
095 34706 | Inagh Valley
www.loughinaghlodgehotel.ie
This boutique hotel, in a lovely spot on the lough shore, has an oak-panelled bar, a library with a log fire, and a restaurant where silver and glassware reflect candlelight and an oval window gives wonderful views. Chatty and attentive staff are happy to help you choose.

Closed mid December to mid March

The Owenmore Restaurant

◎◎ MODERN IRISH
095 31006 | Ballynahinch Castle Hotel
www.ballynahinch-castle.com
Set in 700 acres of woodland, rivers and walks in the heart of Connemara, Ballynahinch is one of Ireland's most celebrated castle hotels. The work of many great Irish painters hangs on the walls of the elegant Owenmore Restaurant, which overlooks a salmon river. Its position reflects the kitchen's commitment to local provenance.

Chef Pete Durkan **Seats** 80, Private dining 16 **Open** All Year **Parking** 60 **Notes** Vegetarian dishes, Children welcome

■ COUNTY KERRY

DINGLE (AN DAINGEAN)   MAP 1, A2
Coastguard Restaurant

◎ MODERN IRISH
066 9150200 | Dingle Skellig Hotel
www.dingleskellig.com/restaurant
It isn't possible to get much further west on the European continent than here. The Dingle Skellig is a sprawling establishment right on the coast with glorious views all round, best enjoyed from the Coastguard restaurant with its capacious picture windows.

Closed January

KENMARE   MAP 1, A2
Park Hotel Kenmare

◎◎ CLASSIC IRISH *V*
064 6641200 |
www.parkkenmare.com
Set against a backdrop of the Cork and Kerry Mountains, with stunning views over Kenmare Bay, this landmark Victorian hotel dates from 1897. Top-notch ingredients sourced from the surrounding area dominate the menu. A carefully chosen and comprehensive wine list offers some notable bottles.

Chef James Coffey **Seats** 70 **Closed** 10–22 December, 2 January to 16 February **Parking** 60 **Notes** Children welcome

Sheen Falls Lodge

◎◎ MODERN EUROPEAN, FRENCH *V*
064 6641600
www.sheenfallslodge.ie
The cascading, floodlit Sheen Falls make for a memorable backdrop to a meal at this former fishing lodge. The refined La Cascade restaurant offers classical French dishes served by informed staff. An opener of pan-fried foie gras, pistachio, fig and port might precede fillet of halibut, mussels, cauliflower and leek.

Chef Cormac McCreary **Seats** 120, Private dining 100
Closed 2 January to 9 February **Parking** 75
Notes Children welcome

KILLARNEY

MAP 1, A2

Bacchus Restaurant
⊛ TRADITIONAL, FRENCH
064 6639200 | Killarney Riverside Hotel,
Muckross Road
www.riversidehotelkillarney.com
Next to the Flesk River, the Killarney Riverside
Hotel is just a 10-minute stroll from the bustling
town centre in Killarney. Irish ingredients are
given a modern European spin, with first-rate
fish and game getting a strong showing on the
menu.

Closed 22–28 December

Cahernane House Hotel
⊛⊛ CLASSIC, TRADITIONAL
064 6631895 | Muckross Road
www.cahernane.com
Guests can take a meal in the original dining
room of this 19th-century manor house while
enjoying views across parkland which dips down
to the lake. Interesting desserts on the menu
might include choux pastry with blackberry curd,
wild berry crème fraîche.

Chef Eric Kavanagh **Seats** 60 **Closed** November to
December midweek, January to February
Prices from S €10, M €28, D €12 **Notes** Vegetarian
dishes, Children welcome

Danu at The Brehon
⊛⊛ MODERN EUROPEAN
064 6630700 | The Brehon Killarney, Muckross Road
www.thebrehon.com
Brehon was the name for the ancient body of law
that governed Ireland. It gave its subjects an
obligation of hospitality, so is a logical name for
a hotel. The kitchen fast-forwards us to the
present day with contemporary Irish cooking of
impressive depth.

Open All Year

The Lake Hotel
⊛⊛ MODERN IRISH *V*
064 6631035 | On the Shore, Muckross Road
www.lakehotelkillarney.com

On the shore of Killarney's lower lake, Lough Lein,
the hotel has been in the Huggard family for over
a century. The windows reveal one of those
splendid views in which Ireland specialises.
Expect local place names on the menu, as in
Dingle Bay crab.

Chef Noel Enright **Seats** 100, Private dining 65
Closed December to January **Parking** 150
Notes Children welcome

The Lake Room
⊛⊛ MODERN *V*
064 6631766 | Aghadoe Heights Hotel,
Lakes of Killarney
www.aghadoeheights.com
In a perfect setting on the shore of the lake,
amidst some of Kerry's most beautiful
landscapes, the restaurant is part of the
impossibly luxurious Aghadoe Heights Hotel. You
can expect a fine wine list, a cosmopolitan
atmosphere and stunning views – the sunsets
are amazing. On the menu, you'll find precisely
constructed dishes.

Chef David Lee **Seats** 150, Private dining 22 **Open** All
Year **Prices from** S €7.50, M €26, D €12.50 **Parking** 65
Notes Children welcome

The Park Restaurant

◉◉ IRISH

064 6635555 | The Killarney Park Hotel,
Kenmare Place

www.killarneyparkhotel.ie

Dining at The Park Restaurant is a luxurious experience. The linen-clad tables overlooking gardens, the red upholstery, decorative plasterwork ceiling and grand piano make a fine setting. Passionfruit crémaux with a champagne and yogurt sorbet is a real winner.

Closed 23-26 December

The Yew Tree Restaurant

◉◉ IRISH, INTERNATIONAL *V*

064 6623400 | Muckross Park Hotel, Killegy Lower

www.muckrosspark.com

Set in the Victorian lounge of the Muckross Park Hotel, a former coaching inn, The Yew Tree Restaurant enjoys an ornate setting with linen-clad tables, high ceilings and luxurious drapes. A wine trolley holds recommended wines to accompany the dishes, which are seasonal and uncomplicated.

Chef Christian Baer Seats 45, Private dining 30
Closed 25-25 December Prices from S €11, M €25,
D €11.60 Parking 144 Notes Children welcome

KILLORGLIN
MAP 1, A2

Carrig House Country House & Restaurant

◉◉ MODERN IRISH, EUROPEAN

066 9769100 | Caragh Lake

www.carrighouse.com

Carrig is a lovingly restored Victorian country manor in acres of colourful woodland gardens with views across Caragh Lake to the Kerry Mountains. Inside, the dining room is the image of 19th-century chic, with William Morris wallpapers, swagged curtains, polished floorboards, and formally laid tables.

Chef Patricia Teahan Closed November to February
Parking 20 Notes Vegetarian dishes, No children under 8 years

■ COUNTY KILDARE

STRAFFAN
MAP 1, C/D4

The K Club

◉◉ TRADITIONAL FRENCH

01 6017200 | W23 YX53

www.kclub.ie

Once home to the Barton wine family, this luxurious hotel has the look of a French château and there are dining options aplenty, not least of which is the River Restaurant, with its impressive views of the Liffey. The cooking is built around classic technique.

Open All Year

■ COUNTY KILKENNY

KILKENNY
MAP 1, C3

The Yew Restaurant

◉◉ MODERN IRISH, EUROPEAN

056 7760088 | Lyrath Estate, Paulstown Road

www.lyrath.com

The hotel and spa occupies an imposing 17th-century property set in 170 acres of parkland that includes lakes and ornamental gardens. The Yew Restaurant, a large room overlooking the rose garden, is the gem among the dining options. The kitchen works around a modern Irish and European repertoire.

Closed 21-26 December

THOMASTOWN
MAP 1, C3

The Hound NEW

◉◉ IRISH *V*

056 7773000 | Hunters Yard at Mount Juliet, Mount Juliet Estate

www.mountjuliet.ie/restaurant-at-hunters-yard-hotel.html

Sweeping views of the Jack Nicklaus-designed golf course are just one attraction at this easygoing eatery in the Hunters Yard hotel on the Mount Juliet Estate. Factor in a welcoming, family-friendly ambience and a kitchen that deals in crowd-pleasing dishes built on prime Irish produce, and you're onto a winner.

Chef Ken Harker Seats 160, Private dining 45 Open All Year Prices from S €6, M €19.50, D €7 Parking 98 Notes Children welcome

The Lady Helen Restaurant
🏵🏵🏵 MODERN **V**

056 7773000 | The Manor House at Mount Juliet Estate
www.mountjuliet.ie/the-lady-helen.html

It isn't just golfing and spa treatments at the Mount Juliet Estate – archers and falconers are looked after too. It all seems very fitting for a grand Georgian country house, once owned by the late Lady Helen McCalmont, in whose honour the fine dining restaurant has been named. Windows give on to the grounds in a gentle arc in a room done in restrained taupe tones, where produce from the estate finds its way into modern Irish cooking of impressive reach. You might begin with 'crubeens', a rather glamorous interpretation of the traditional Irish dish of crispy pigs' trotters, with two discs of trotter meat enlivened with foie gras mousse. A main course of rabbit roulade and mousse, moist and subtle, comes with grilled fresh langoustines, deliciously sweet carrots and vadouvan spices. Technical wizardry at dessert might produce a pretty walnut praline with pear sorbet and a halo of crisp sugar work.

Chef John Kelly **Seats** 50, Private dining 30
Notes Children welcome

■ COUNTY LAOIS

BALLYFIN
MAP 1, C3

Ballyfin Demesne
🏵🏵 EUROPEAN **V**

057 8755866
www.ballyfin.com

In possibly Ireland's most opulent Regency house, the high-ceilinged dining room gazes out towards a temple where a water feature cascades. A walled garden supplies plenty of produce, as do the resident bees, and lucky humans are regaled with French-inspired contemporary cooking of considerable dazzle.

Chef Sam Moody **Seats** 39, Private dining 39
Closed January to 14 February **Notes** No children under 9 years

■ COUNTY LIMERICK

ADARE
MAP 1, B3

The Oak Room NEW
🏵🏵 MODERN IRISH

061 605200 | Adare Manor
www.adaremanor.com

It's hard not to be impressed when you take a seat in the elegant oak-panelled space that was once the dining room of the Earls of Dunraven. Everything here dazzles, from the opulent decor to the crisp linen, gleaming silver and sparkling glassware. The kitchen rises to the occasion, delivering intricate dishes of refined, contemporary Irish cooking.

LIMERICK
MAP 1, B3

Limerick Strand Hotel
🏵 CONTEMPORARY IRISH

061 421800 | Ennis Street
www.strandlimerick.ie

A new-build riverside hotel with all mod cons, including a bright, airy dining room. Sourcing from within the county supplies a menu of populist brasserie dishes, with an Irish contemporary gloss on international ideas. Good breads come with intensely anchovied tapenade.

Open All Year

■ COUNTY LOUTH

CARLINGFORD
MAP 1, D4

Ghan House
🏵🏵 MODERN IRISH

042 9373682
www.ghanhouse.com

Early 18th-century Ghan House is well placed for walks along the seashore and in the Mourne Mountains, in view across the lough from the restaurant. Several menus are offered; from one, examples include pan-fried Castletownbere scallops; shoulder of Mourne lamb; home-made tagliatelle with wild mushroom fricassée; and hake with langoustine tails.

Chef Stephane Le Sourne **Seats** 50, Private dining 50
Closed 24–26 and 31 December, 1–2 January **Parking** 24
Notes Vegetarian dishes, Children welcome

DROGHEDA
MAP 1, D4

Scholars Townhouse Hotel
◎◎ MODERN IRISH

041 9835410 | King Street
www.scholarshotel.com
Built as a Christian Brothers monastery in 1867,
ceiling frescoes of the Battle of the Boyne in the
interlinked dining rooms furnish a historical note
that's a contrast to the modern Irish cooking.
Praline soufflé with pumpkin ice cream is an
interesting way to finish.

Closed 25-26 December

■ COUNTY MAYO

BALLINA
MAP 1, B4

Belleek Castle
◎◎ MODERN IRISH V

096 22400 | Belleek
www.belleekcastle.com
The multi-award-winning Library Restaurant's
three menus – Early Evening, Market five-course
tasting, and the eight-course Gourmet (all with
vegetarian options) – reflect a change of culinary
focus from international to modern Irish. For
example, West Coast seafood includes Donegal
fresh crab and in-house, hot-smoked gravad lax,
while mountain lamb comes from Achill Island to
the south-west.

Chef David O'Donnell Seats 55, Private dining 30
Closed Christmas, January Prices from S €12.90,
M €27.90 Parking 90 Notes Children welcome
See advertisement on page 546

Mount Falcon Estate
◎◎ TRADITIONAL

096 74472 | Foxford Road
www.mountfalcon.com
The restaurant at this grand baronial-style hotel
on the River Moy is the Kitchen Restaurant, which
occupies the original kitchen and pantry area,
looking good with its linen-clad tables and food-
related prints on the walls. There's a definite
French classicism to the kitchen's output.

Closed 25 December

CONG
MAP 1, B4

The George V Dining Room
◎◎ TRADITIONAL EUROPEAN, INTERNATIONAL V 🍷 NOTABLE WINE LIST

094 9546003 | Ashford Castle
www.ashfordcastle.com
Once home to the Guinness family, Ashford
Castle dates from the 13th century and sits
grandly on the shores of Lough Corrib, amid 350
acres of parkland. The dining room was built to
host a reception for the Prince of Wales in 1906.

Chef Philippe Farineau Seats 120, Private dining 40
Open All Year Parking 115 Notes Children welcome

The Lodge at Ashford Castle
◎◎ CONTEMPORARY IRISH V

094 9545400 | Ashford Estate
www.thelodgeatashfordcastle.com
Wilde's restaurant is named after Sir William
Wilde, a local surgeon who founded the first eye
and ear hospital in Dublin, and, from its first-floor
setting in the original Victorian building, offers
fabulous views over Lough Corrib. The kitchen
impresses with an ambitious, contemporary
range of dishes.

Chef Jonathan Keane Seats 60, Private dining 50
Closed 24-26 December Parking 50 Notes Children
welcome

MULRANY
MAP 1, A4

Mulranny Park Hotel
◎◎ MODERN INTERNATIONAL, CLASSIC

098 36000
www.mulrannyparkhotel.ie
Once the station hotel for Mulranny, opened in
the 1890s, this is now a sumptuous country-
house with sweeping views over the Atlantic. A
duo of Keem Bay smoked salmon and barbecued
fresh salmon with honey-mustard aïoli, pickled
cucumber and red onion dressing might start
proceedings.

Chef Chamila Manawatta Seats 100, Private dining 50
Closed 20 November to 1 February Prices from S €8,
M €28, D €11 Parking 200 Notes Vegetarian
dishes, Children welcome

WESTPORT
MAP 1, B4

Hotel Westport Leisure, Spa & Conference
◎ MODERN IRISH, BRITISH, EUROPEAN

098 25122 | Newport Road
www.hotelwestport.ie
Heavenly scenery frames this expansive family-
run hotel and spa set in seven acres of mature
woodland. Miles of walking and cycling on the
Great Western Greenway close by are more
reasons to bring a keen appetite with you to the
restaurant here.

Chef Fergal Colleran Seats 120, Private dining 45
Open All Year Prices from S €5, M €12, D €6 Parking 220
Notes Vegetarian dishes, Children welcome

Belleek Castle

Weddings. Hotel. Restaurant. Museum. Cafe

JOIN US FOR AN AWARD-WINNING FINE DINING EXPERIENCE on the Wild Atlantic Way. The elegance and splendour of the Library Restaurant is the perfect place to enjoy our elaborate 2AA Rosette cuisine. Relax beside open log fires in the lounge & enjoy a drink in the Spanish Armada Bar before dining in the Library Restaurant. Winner of the "Best Fine Dining Restaurant in Connaught 2019" at the YesChef Ireland Awards. The Library Restaurant is open daily from 5.30pm.

JACK FENN'S COURTYARD CAFE! serves brunch & lunch and is situated in the restored stables & coach house. Winner of the "Cafe of the Year 2019" award in Georgina Campbell's Ireland Guide, it is perfect nourishment before or after the Castle tour & visit to it's Medieval Armoury. The cafe is open daily from Wednesday to Sunday, 11am - 5pm.

Please call in advance to book a table.

We look forward to welcoming you through our doors.

Ballina, Co. Mayo, Ireland Tel: +353 96 22400 **belleekcastle.com**

WESTPORT continued

Knockranny House Hotel
◉◉ MODERN IRISH
098 28600
www.knockrannyhousehotel.ie
This tranquil spa hotel makes the most of its
Mayo situation, with stunning views every which
way. Inside comes with all the accoutrements of
an upscale hotel, including a full-dress dining
room, La Fougère, which eschews modern
minimalism in favour of immaculate linen,
glassware and table settings.

Chef Seamus Commons **Seats** 90, Private dining 120
Closed 23-26 December **Prices from** S €7.50, M €24.50,
D €10 **Parking** 150 **Notes** Vegetarian dishes, Children
welcome

■ COUNTY MEATH

DUNBOYNE
MAP 1, D4
Dunboyne Castle Hotel & Spa
◉◉ MODERN EUROPEAN
01 8013500
www.dunboynecastlehotel.com
A Georgian rebuild following Cromwell's
calamitous intervention in Ireland, Dunboyne,
ancestral home of the Butler family, has fine
plasterwork and ceiling frescoes to look out for
as you head for the Ivy Restaurant, a
contemporary space with smart linen and
enticing, up-to-date country-house cooking.

Chef Ian Daly **Seats** 120 **Open** All Year **Prices from** S €7,
M €19, D €8 **Parking** 360 **Notes** Vegetarian
dishes, Children welcome
See advertisement on page 548

ENFIELD
MAP 1, C4
Fire & Salt
◉ MODERN IRISH
046 9540000 | The Johnstown Estate
www.thejohnstownestate.com
The main restaurant at the sporty Johnstown
Estate in this bright and airy steakhouse offers a
variety of seating options. Although grass-fed,
Irish-bred beef steaks cooked over charcoal on
the grill are the main draw here, there are plenty
of other options on the à la carte including local
seafood.

Open All Year

KILMESSAN
MAP 1, C4
The Signal Restaurant
◉ MODERN IRISH
046 9025239 | The Station House Hotel
www.stationhousehotel.ie
In the heart of the stunning Boyne Valley Drive in
County Meath, The Station House Hotel is set in
its own attractive gardens and surrounded by
beautiful countryside. Its rural location is
reflected in the accomplished food served in
the charming and elegant Signal Restaurant.
A starter of poached hen's egg crostini could
be followed by four-hour braised Boyne Valley
lamb shank.

Chef Thelma Slattery **Seats** 90, Private dining 200
Open All Year **Prices from** S €6.50, M €17.95, D €7.50
Parking 200 **Notes** Vegetarian dishes, Children
welcome

NAVAN
MAP 1, C4
Bellinter House
◉◉ MODERN EUROPEAN
046 9030900
www.bellinterhouse.com
A country-house hotel that is popular on the
wedding scene, its interior combining period
charm with 21st-century boutique glamour. Down
in the vaulted basement there's a slick
contemporary finish to the space and a menu to
match. The kitchen's output is focused on
regional produce.

Closed 24-25 December

SLANE
MAP 1, D4
Conyngham Arms Hotel
◉ TRADITIONAL, INTERNATIONAL
041 9884444 | Main Street
www.conynghamarms.ie
This 18th-century coaching inn is home to a
smart brasserie-style restaurant offering
straightforward food from breakfast through to
dinner. There's a decent amount of Irish produce
on the menu, including goods from the owners'
bakery and coffee shop in the village.

Chef David Doyle **Seats** 35, Private dining 30 **Open** All
Year **Prices from** S €5.50, M €14.50, D €6 **Parking** 8
Notes Vegetarian dishes, Children welcome

THE IVY RESTAURANT
AT DUNBOYNE CASTLE HOTEL & SPA
2 AA ROSETTE AWARD WINNING RESTAURANT

The IVY is about showcasing the best of modern cuisine through innovation and creativity. Our menus only feature ingredients from the finest local suppliers and are strongly influenced by our culinary team's shared passion for using first class produce. The IVY team dedicate their deep felt passion to ensure that you take away the best possible memories of your visit from start to finish, thanks to a perfect dining experience and the exquisite ritual of the service that goes with it. The IVY never fails to impress.

To make a reservation, contact +353 1 801 3500

SLANE continued

Tankardstown – Brabazon Restaurant
◉◉ CLASSIC INTERNATIONAL
041 9824621
www.tankardstown.ie
In the restaurant situated in the one-time cow shed, expect a smart rustic finish with exposed stonework, a central fireplace and pretty terrace. The kitchen calls on the walled organic garden for supplies, and a smoker brings a potent aroma to proceedings.

Chef Jonas Sarkozy, Eoin Gilchrist **Seats** 70 **Closed** 3 days at Christmas **Prices from** S €7.50, M €19.50, D €7.50 **Notes** Vegetarian dishes, Children welcome

TRIM   *MAP 1, C4*

Rococo Restaurant *NEW*
◉ IRISH, INTERNATIONAL
046 9482100 | Knightsbrook Hotel, Spa & Golf Resort, Iffernock, Dublin Road
www.knightsbrook.com
Part of the Knightsbrook Hotel, Spa & Golf Resort, there is a pronounced Irish accent to the international food served in the restaurant.

Typical main courses include pork belly with root vegetable purée, tenderstem broccoli, cherry apple and cider jus. If the warm apple crumble doesn't tempt, there's always the board of Irish cheeses.

Chef Shane O'Neill **Notes** Vegetarian dishes, No children

■ COUNTY MONAGHAN

CARRICKMACROSS   *MAP 1, C4*

Shirley Arms Hotel
◉ MODERN IRISH *V*
042 9673100 | Main Street
www.shirleyarmshotel.ie
The market town of Carrickmacross is home to this handsome stone-built hotel, once called White's, a name that lives on in its principal dining room, which is kitted out in checkered upholstery with wood dividers and big floral pictures. The style is modern Irish brasserie.

Chef Micheál Muldoon **Seats** 90, Private dining 150 **Closed** 25–26 December **Prices from** S €5.50, M €17, D €6.50 **Parking** 150 **Notes** Children welcome

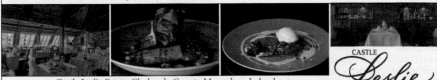

At *Snaffles*, the 2 AA Rosette award-winning restaurant located in The Lodge at Castle Leslie Estate, you can enjoy delicious meals in a relaxed setting. Situated on the first floor in the Lodge, *Snaffles* welcomes both residents and local guests. *Snaffles* is a beautiful open-plan restaurant and is light and spacious with a striking wall of contemporary glass.

Signature dishes are cooked with superb locally sourced food which is prepared and presented with imagination and flair. Full of flavour, the diverse courses and extensive gin menu, with over 100 gins from around the world make Snaffles Restaurant one of Monaghan's top restaurants.

Castle Leslie Estate, Glasslough, County Monaghan, Ireland
Tel: + 353 47 88100 • **Email:** info@castleleslie.com • **Web:** www.castleleslie.com

CASTLE
Leslie
ESTATE

GLASLOUGH
MAP 1, C5

Snaffles Restaurant

⊛⊛ TRADITIONAL IRISH, INTERNATIONAL

047 88100 | The Lodge, Castle Leslie Estate

www.castleleslie.com

Castle Leslie occupies a thousand acres of undulating countryside and is one of the last estates still owned by its founding family. Dinner in Snaffles, on the first floor of The Lodge, might comprise wild rabbit terrine with wild mushrooms; chargrilled fillet of Irish beef with lentil and vegetable cassoulet; and warm poached fruit gratin.

Chef Philip Brazil **Seats** 110, Private dining 50
Closed 24–27 December **Parking** 200 **Notes** Vegetarian dishes, Children welcome

See advertisement on page 549

■ COUNTY ROSCOMMON

ROSCOMMON
MAP 1, B4

The Douglas Hyde Restaurant

⊛⊛ MODERN EUROPEAN *V*

071 9618000 | Kilronan Castle Estate & Spa, Ballyfarnon

www.kilronancastle.ie

Through magnificent gates, overlooking a lough, is the Douglas Hyde, named after the Roscommon-born first President of Ireland (1938–40). Put aside chef David Porter's Aussie origins, it's Irish locations that stand out on the menu: Lough Neagh rainbow trout; Kilmore king scallops; breast of Wicklow pigeon; Thornhill duck breast, for example. For vegetarians, truffle tortellini is a winner.

Chef David Porter **Seats** 80, Private dining 80 **Open** All Year **Prices from** S €8.95, M €25.50, D €8.75
Parking 200 **Notes** Children welcome

See advertisement opposite

■ COUNTY SLIGO

SLIGO
MAP 1, B5

Radisson Blu Hotel & Spa Sligo

⊛ MODERN IRISH

071 9140008 | Rosses Point Road, Ballincar

www.radissonblu.ie/sligo

A classy modern hotel designed with plenty of vivid colour, notably reds and purples in the Classiebawn dining room. Here, the bill of fare is contemporary Irish cooking of notable technical ambition. Why not try a deconstructed egg for your starter?

Open All Year

Sligo Park Hotel & Leisure Club

⊛ MODERN IRISH

071 9190400 | Pearse Road

www.sligopark.com

Covering all the bases, Sligo Park's full-on leisure facilities and surrounding verdant countryside means there's plenty of opportunity to build up an appetite. The dining option is the Hazelwood Restaurant, which has a warm contemporary finish. The kitchen stays true to Irish produce.

Open All Year

■ COUNTY TIPPERARY

CLONMEL
MAP 1, C3

Hotel Minella

⊛ TRADITIONAL

052 6122388

www.hotelminella.com

The hotel's garden runs down to the banks of the River Suir and the Comeragh Mountains loom in the background – it's a charming spot. The restaurant is in the original Georgian house, so has plenty of character and a traditional, period feel. An all-day menu is available.

Open All Year

■ COUNTY WATERFORD

ARDMORE
MAP 1, C2

The House Restaurant

⊛⊛⊛⊛ MODERN IRISH *V* ▲ NOTABLE WINE LIST

See page 552

WATERFORD
MAP 1, C2

Bianconi Restaurant

⊛ TRADITIONAL IRISH

051 305555 | Granville Hotel, The Quay

www.granvillehotel.ie

Occupying pole position on Waterford's river quay, the Georgian Granville Hotel's genteel and elegant Bianconi Restaurant makes the most of those views over the River Suir and the marina from linen-clad tables beneath a coffered ceiling. The kitchen displays a feel for what's right on the plate.

Closed 25–26 December

The Douglas Hyde Restaurant
KILRONAN CASTLE ESTATE & SPA

ROSCOMMON'S ONLY 2 AA ROSETTE WINNING CASTLE RESTAURANT

MALO MORI QUAM FOEDARI

ARDMORE

The House Restaurant

@@@@ MODERN IRISH 𝒱 NOTABLE WINE LIST

024 87800 | Cliff House Hotel

cliffhousehotel.ie

Full-drop picture windows and a marine blue carpet are intuitive features of The House Restaurant, where executive chef Martijn Kajuiter uses Irish produce with a comprehensive range of modern technique, backed up the kitchen garden. A five-course tasting menu, drawn from the carte, is bookended by trios of canapés and desserts for the complete performance. Textural counterpoints are the hallmark of a contemporary classic starter of west Cork scallop with ham, black garlic, Avruga caviar, and spiky, briny codium seaweed. Equally impressive is a main course of crisp-skinned guinea fowl with three-cornered leek and its flowers, earthy morels, and a smoky barbecue jus. Fish could be sea bass with brown shrimp ravioli in a vivid saffron butter sauce, and the tripartite sweet finale comprises glossy organic chocolate with apricot and olive oil, sea buckthorn cream and rice with meringue shards, and a popcorn-garnished nougatine parfait with rhubarb.

Chef Martijn Kajuiter Seats 64, Private dining 20 Closed 23–26 December Parking 30 Notes Children welcome

WATERFORD continued

Faithlegg House Hotel & Golf Resort

◉◉ MODERN IRISH, FRENCH

051 382000 | Faithlegg,

www.faithlegg.com

The original mansion was built in the 1780s and is immaculately restored, while the high-ceilinged restaurant overlooks the garden from what was a pair of drawing rooms. The cooking is based on native produce and a range of neat ideas really make an impact.

Chef Jenny Flynn **Seats** 86, Private dining 50 **Closed** 25 December **Parking** 120 **Notes** Vegetarian dishes, Children welcome

The Munster Room Restaurant

◉◉ IRISH, INTERNATIONAL *V*

051 878203 | Waterford Castle Hotel and Golf Club, The Island

www.waterfordcastleresort.com

With its dark oak panelling, intricate plasterwork ceiling and ancestral portraits, The Munster Room is exactly what you'd expect from the dining room of a luxe hotel set on its own private 300-acre Island. It's a jacket-and-tie affair with a pianist adding to the ambience.

Chef Tom Spruce **Seats** 80, Private dining 24 **Closed** some days in winter **Prices from** S €12, M €29, D €12.95 **Notes** No children after 9pm

■ COUNTY WEXFORD

GOREY *MAP 1, D3*

Amber Springs Hotel

◉◉ MODERN EUROPEAN

053 9484000 | Wexford Road

www.amberspringshotel.ie

A modern hotel with a spa and host of dining opportunities, the Farm Steakhouse makes perfect sense given that the owners keep several hundred head of Angus cattle on their nearby farm. It's a smart dining room done out in dark, moody shades.

Chef William Miller **Seats** 130, Private dining 80 **Open** All Year **Prices from** S €7.95, M €14, D €6.50 **Notes** Vegetarian dishes, Children welcome

Ashdown Park Hotel

◉ IRISH, INTERNATIONAL

053 9480500 | Station Road

www.ashdownparkhotel.com

This modern hotel on a grand scale, within walking distance of Gorey, has 22 acres of grounds to explore before a trip to its Rowan Tree Restaurant. Here, tables are dressed up in crisp white linen, and the kitchen turns out pleasingly straightforward dishes.

Chef, Val Murphy **Seats** 120, Private dining 120 **Closed** 24-26 December, winter and spring open weekends only **Parking** 150 **Notes** Vegetarian dishes, Children welcome

Clonganny House

◉◉ CONTEMPORARY IRISH, FRENCH

053 9482111 | Ballygarrett

www.clonganny.com

A handsome creeper-covered Georgian house at the end of a tree-lined drive, Cloganny has a refined, traditional interior. The highly experienced French chef-patron cooks with confidence and delivers a classically-inspired repertoire via a bilingual carte. Kick off with drinks and canapés in the drawing room.

Chef Phillipe Brillant **Seats** 20 **Open** All Year **Parking** 12 **Notes** Vegetarian dishes, No children

Greenroom Restaurant

◉◉ MODERN IRISH, MEDITERRANEAN

053 9424000 | Seafield Hotel & Spa Resort, Ballymoney

www.seafieldhotel.com

We've Italian designers to thank for the super-cool finish within this luxe spa hotel on the cliffs. The high-end finish extends to the restaurant, where a huge bronze female centaur keeps watch, lighting and music are soft, and the decor is cool black.

Chef Raman Kumar **Seats** 120, Private dining 40 **Closed** Christmas **Prices from** S €12, M €20, D €9.50 **Parking** 100 **Notes** Vegetarian dishes, Children welcome

Marlfield House Hotel

◎◎ CLASSIC

053 9421124 | Courtown Road
www.marlfieldhouse.com

This opulent Regency home is now a smart and luxurious hotel whose dining room consists of several handsomely decorated spaces, leading into an impressive conservatory. Murals and mirrors are interspersed with huge windows opening onto the immaculate garden. The hotel's own kitchen garden delivers first-rate seasonal produce.

Closed Christmas

ROSSLARE

MAP 1, D2

Beaches Restaurant at Kelly's Resort Hotel

◎◎ TRADITIONAL EUROPEAN

053 9132114
www.kellys.ie

Beaches restaurant sits on the golden sands in Rosslare, and is set up to capitalise on the views. The space is bathed in light through good-sized windows, and has restful pastel hues, white linen on the tables, and a mini gallery of original artworks on the walls. The kitchen lets the quality of local produce do the talking in simple contemporary dishes.

Closed mid December to mid February

La Marine Bistro

◎ TRADITIONAL ITALIAN

053 9132114 | Kelly's Resort Hotel & Spa
www.kellys.ie

The more casual stand-alone restaurant of Kelly's Resort Hotel is an easy-going venue with an open kitchen. The shipshape bistro theme suits the beachside setting, as does its menu. Top-class fish and seafood comes a short way from Kilmore Quay.

Closed mid December to February

WEXFORD

MAP 1, D2

Aldridge Lodge Restaurant and Guest Accommodation

◎◎ MODERN IRISH *V*

051 389116 | Duncannon
www.aldridgelodge.com

With its fashionably pared-back looks – wood floors, bare tables and black high-backed seats – chef-patron Billy Whitty's restaurant with

rooms achieves a stylish informality. It has also become something of a hot spot on the local foodie scene thanks to its sharply-executed dishes on the daily-changing menus.

Chef Billy Whitty **Seats** 37 **Closed** 1st week January and 1st week June **Parking** 30 **Notes** Children welcome

Reeds Restaurant at Ferrycarrig Hotel

◎◎ MODERN IRISH *V*

053 9120999 | Ferrycarrig
www.ferrycarrighotel.ie

In an absolutely stunning location overlooking the River Slaney as it meanders towards Wexford town, Reeds Restaurant makes the most of the views from its huge picture windows. The atmosphere in the stylish, contemporary dining room is laid back and relaxed.

Chef Tony Carty **Seats** 100 **Open** All Year **Parking** 200 **Notes** Children welcome

■ COUNTY WICKLOW

BLESSINGTON

MAP 1, D3

Lime Tree Restaurant

◎ MODERN IRISH

045 867600 | Tulfarris Hotel & Golf Resort
www.tulfarrishotel.com

Part of the Tulfarris Hotel & Golf Resort, the first-floor restaurant offers panoramic views towards the Blessington Lakes. The cooking uses intelligent combinations of quality ingredients, whether it's delicious pork belly from Tipperary or fresh fish off the boats in Howth.

Chef Eddie McDermott **Seats** 80, Private dining 50 **Open** All Year **Parking** 150 **Notes** Vegetarian dishes, Children welcome

DELGANY
MAP 1, D3

The Woodlands Restaurant
◎◎ MODERN IRISH, EUROPEAN
01 2873399 | Glenview Hotel, Glen o' the Downs
www.glenviewhotel.ie
The Woodlands Restaurant at this hotel is on the first floor to maximise the view over the Glen o' the Downs, with arched windows looking down the valley. Inside, all is soothing pastels and sparkling glassware. The style is what is loosely termed modern Irish.

Open All Year

ENNISKERRY
MAP 1, D3

Powerscourt Hotel
◎◎ MODERN EUROPEAN
01 2748888 | Powerscourt Estate
www.powerscourthotel.com
With a sweeping Palladian mansion at its heart, the Powerscourt resort has two golf courses, a luxurious spa and an Irish pub, but the main event food-wise is the glamorous Sika Restaurant. There are glorious mountain views from its third-floor dining room.

Open All Year

MACREDDIN
MAP 1, D3

BrookLodge & Macreddin Village
◎◎ MODERN IRISH, ORGANIC
0402 36444 | Y14 A362
www.brooklodge.com
Deep in the countryside, just an hour from Dublin, is this complex of restaurant, bistro, pub and smokehouse. Featuring the freshest free-range, organic and wild foods, some from its full-time forager, The Strawberry Tree Restaurant's daily-changing menu offers mallard, 30-day-aged Irish beef fillet, sika deer from the Wicklow Mountains, and Kilmore Quay-landed sole.

Chef Evan Doyle, James Kavanagh **Seats** 120, Private dining 50 **Closed** 24–26 December **Prices from** S €16, M €37, D €13 **Parking** 200 **Notes** Vegetarian dishes, Children welcome

See advertisement below

Druids Glen Hotel & Golf Resort
◉◉ MODERN EUROPEAN *V*
01 2870800
www.druidsglenresort.com
Druids Glen boasts the full package of spa, golf and leisure facilities with the Wicklow hills thrown in as a backdrop. Stylishly decorated in muted hues, with a feature fire set in a huge granite hearth, the main dining room hotel is Hugo's Restaurant.

Chef Anthony Duggan **Seats** 170, Private dining 22
Open All Year **Prices from** S €14, M €29, D €9
Parking 400 **Notes** Children welcome

Garden Rooms *NEW*
◉ MODERN
01 2870877 | Druids Glen Hotel & Golf Resort
www.druidsglenresort.com
The second dining option at the wonderful Druids Glen Resort, the Garden Rooms is a bright and airy new addition, overlooking the renowned 13th green. The wide-ranging menu is sure to please the most discerning diner, and includes a number of vegan options in collaboration with a nearby specialist vegan restaurant. Dishes are quite light, with an emphasis in salads and dressings rather than heavy sauces.

Open All Year **Notes** Vegetarian dishes, No children after 9pm

Hunter's Hotel
◉ TRADITIONAL IRISH, FRENCH
0404 40106 | Newrath Bridge
www.hunters.ie
Barely half an hour from the Dun Laoghaire ferry, Ireland's oldest coaching inn sits in riotously colourful gardens, its dining room a vision of crisp linen, mahogany and fine living. Expect daily-changing menus; you might be tempted by a selection of Ireland's latest artisan cheeses.

Closed 3 days at Christmas

Tinakilly Country House
◉◉ MODERN IRISH
0404 69274
www.tinakilly.ie
A distinguished Italianate Victorian mansion is the diverting setting for the modernised country-house cooking. The timing and seasoning of dishes does them justice, as does an opening pairing of scallops and the famous Clonakilty black pudding from County Cork, with butternut purée and pea shoots.

GIBRALTAR

■ GIBRALTAR

GIBRALTAR

Nunos
◎◎ ITALIAN, MEDITERRANEAN
00 350 200 76501 | Caleta Hotel,
Slr Herbert Miles Road, GX11 1AA
www.caletahotel.com
Nunos restaurant at the Caleta has a fine-dining air and a stand-alone restaurant vibe, thanks to slick London-style service and Italian cooking. An open-to-view kitchen offers all the theatre of chefs on show. The menu is typically extensive, the colourful, modern-European approach intelligently uncomplicated.

Open All Year

The Rock
◎ MODERN MEDITERRANEAN
00 350 200 73000 | Europa Road, GX11 1AA
www.rockhotelgibraltar.com
Since it opened in 1932, this iconic hotel has attracted notable guests, including Winston Churchill, and John Lennon and Yoko Ono who stayed here when they married in Gibraltar. The restaurant's wisteria-clad terrace is a draw in itself, while the modern Mediterranean food is classy and interesting.

Open All Year

Sunborn Yacht Hotel
◎◎ MEDITERRANEAN
00 350 2001 6000 | Ocean Village, GX11 1AA
www.sunbornyacht.com/gibraltar
Located on a luxurious floating hotel moored in Gibraltar's Ocean Village Marina, this is a rooftop restaurant that offers a contemporary dining experience with views out to sea or overlooking Gibraltar itself. A wrap-around deck offers pleasant alfresco dining.

Open All Year

COUNTY MAPS

England

1 Bedfordshire
2 Berkshire
3 Bristol
4 Buckinghamshire
5 Cambridgeshire
6 Greater Manchester
7 Herefordshire
8 Hertfordshire
9 Leicestershire
10 Northamptonshire
11 Nottinghamshire
12 Rutland
13 Staffordshire
14 Warwickshire
15 West Midlands
16 Worcestershire

Scotland

17 City of Glasgow
18 Clackmannanshire
19 East Ayrshire
20 East Dunbartonshire
21 East Renfrewshire
22 Perth & Kinross
23 Renfrewshire
24 South Lanarkshire
25 West Dunbartonshire

Wales

26 Blaenau Gwent
27 Bridgend
28 Caerphilly
29 Denbighshire
30 Flintshire
31 Merthyr Tydfil
32 Monmouthshire
33 Neath Port Talbot
34 Newport
35 Rhondda Cynon Taf
36 Torfaen
37 Vale of Glamorgan
38 Wrexham

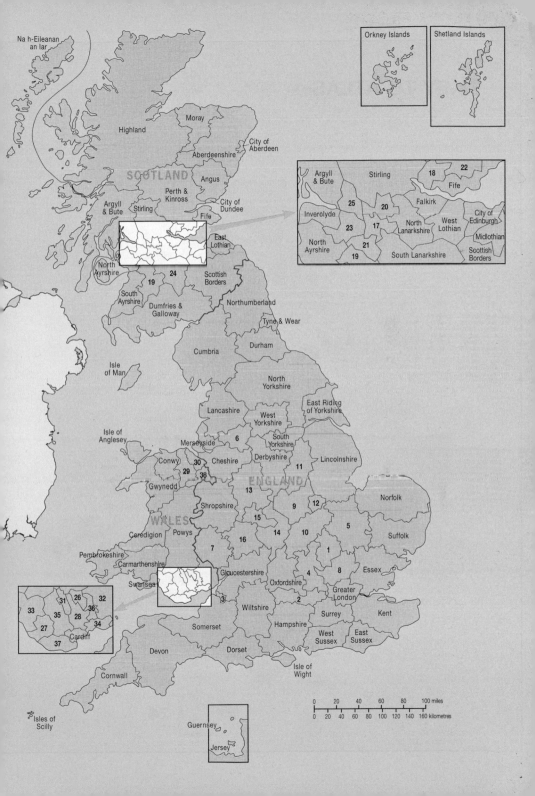

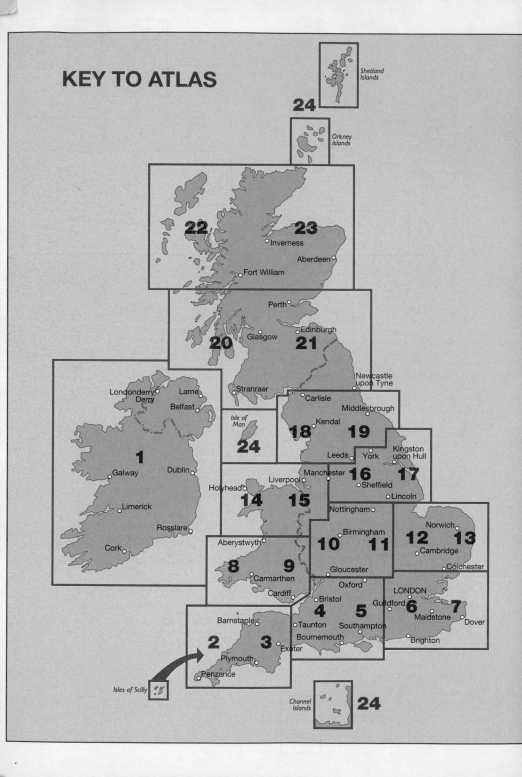

KEY TO ATLAS

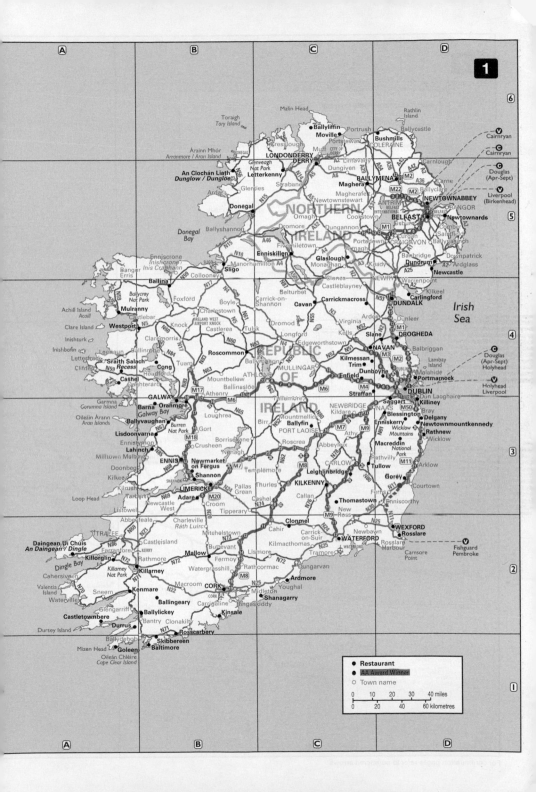

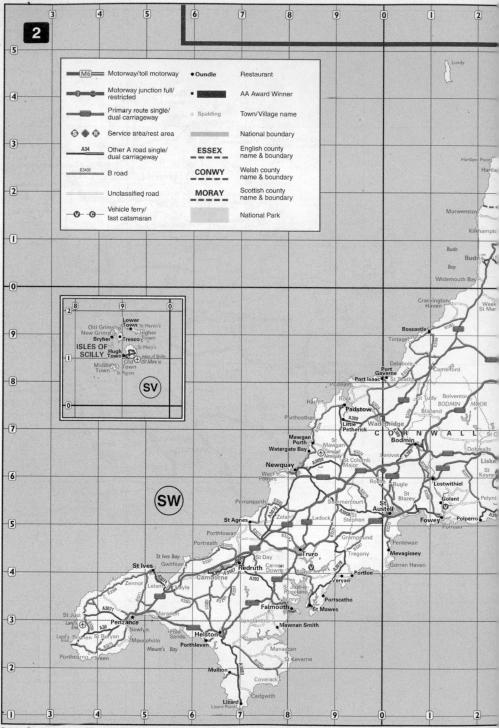

Key / Legend:

- M6 — Motorway/toll motorway
- Motorway junction full/restricted
- Primary route single/dual carriageway
- S ◆ R — Service area/rest area
- A34 — Other A road single/dual carriageway
- B3400 — B road
- Unclassified road
- V — C — Vehicle ferry/fast catamaran
- ● Oundle — Restaurant
- AA Award Winner
- ○ Spalding — Town/Village name
- National boundary
- **ESSEX** — English county name & boundary
- **CONWY** — Welsh county name & boundary
- **MORAY** — Scottish county name & boundary
- National Park

ISLES OF SCILLY

SV

SW

CORNWALL

BODMIN MOOR

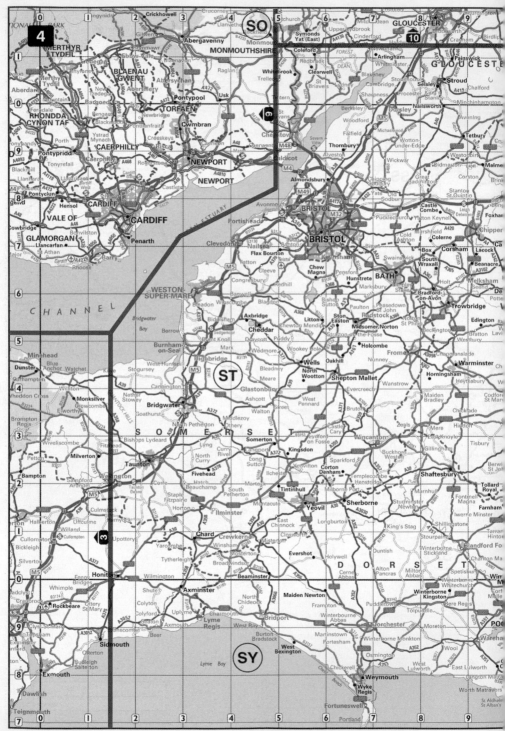

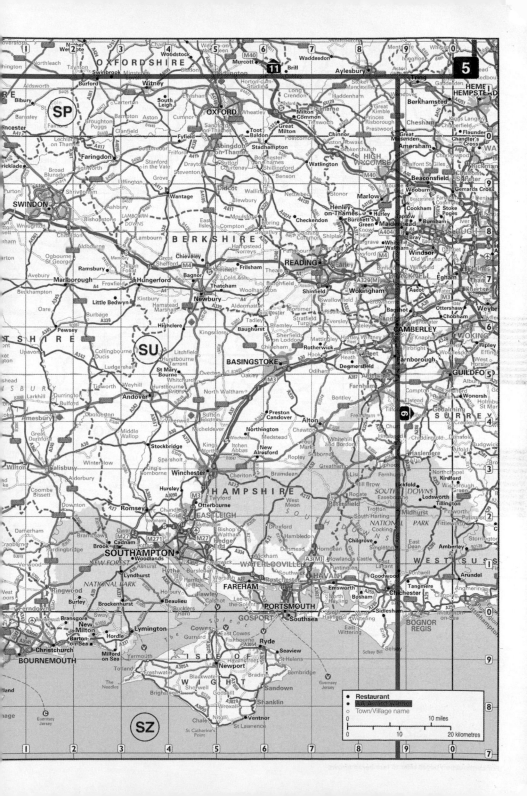

For continuation pages refer to numbered arrows

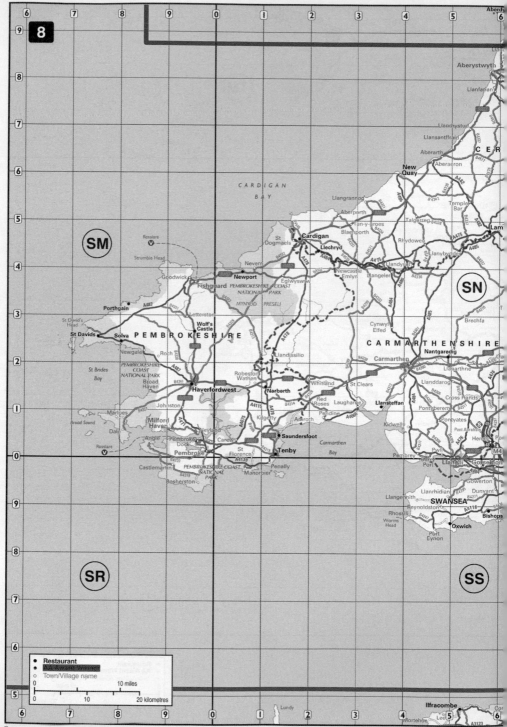

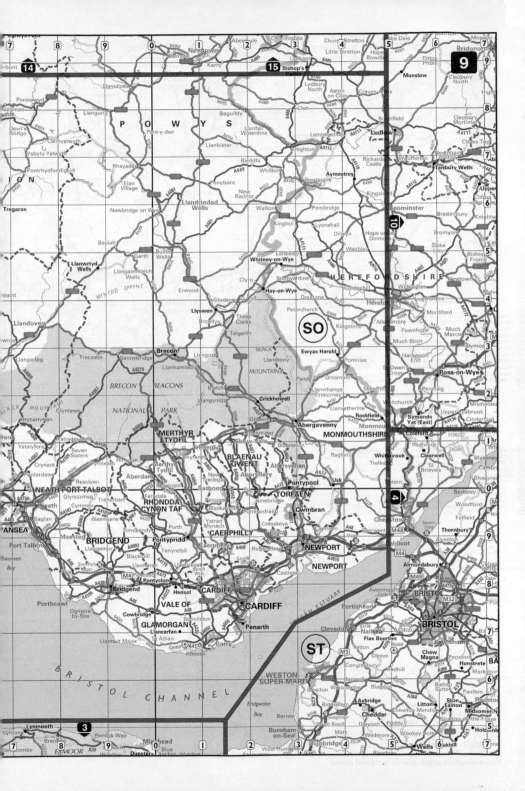

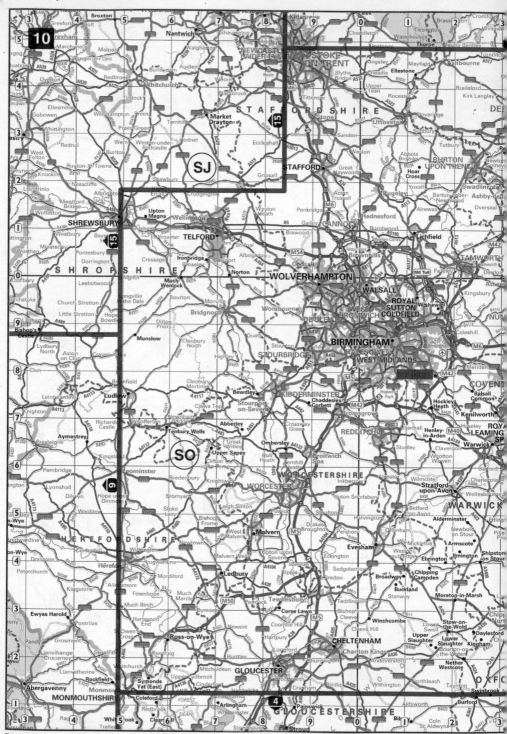

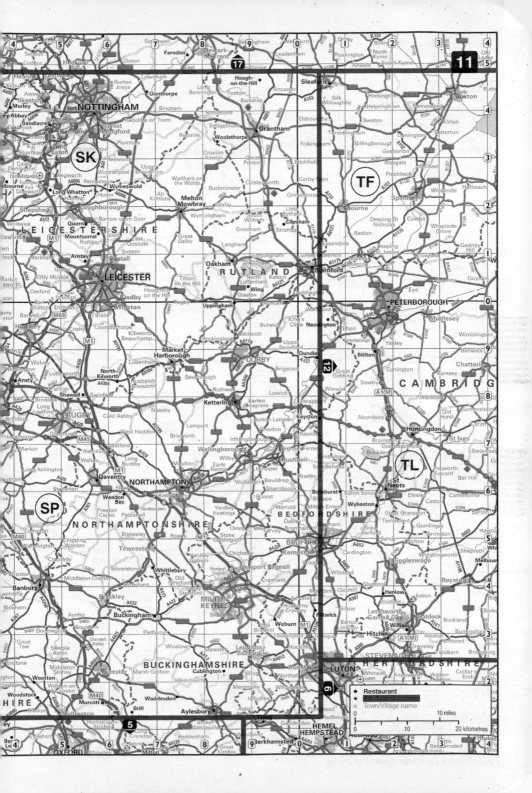

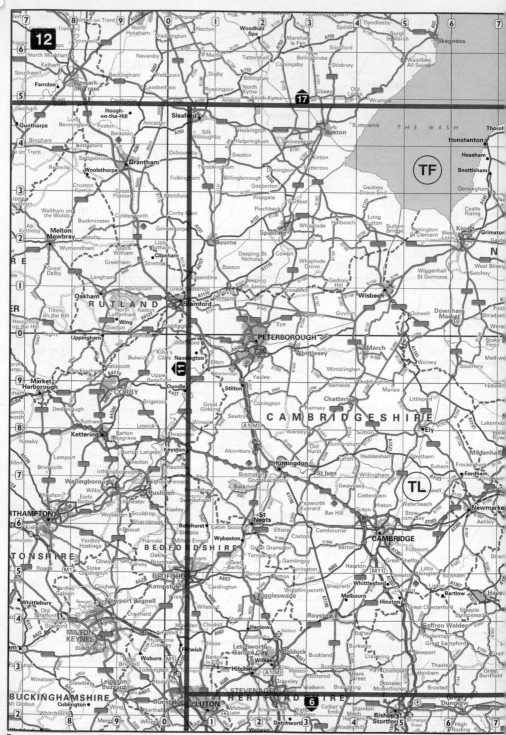

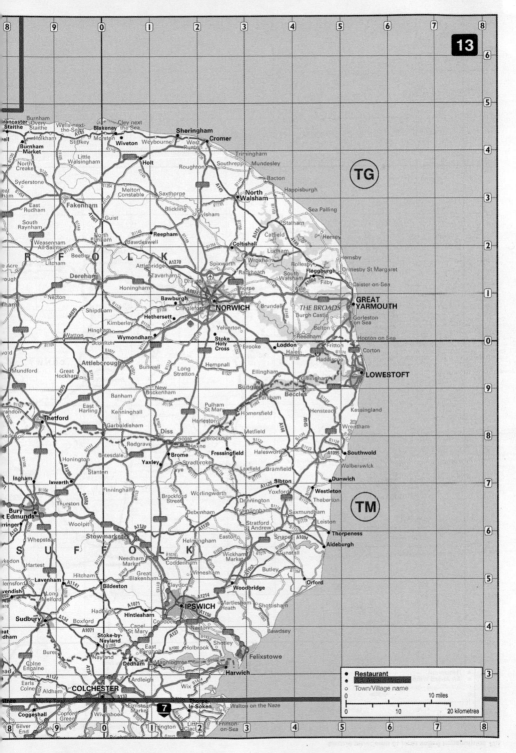

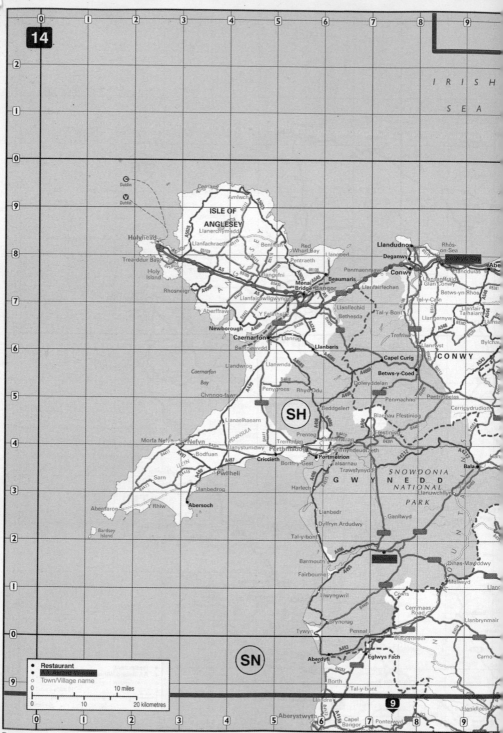

I R I S H

S E A

Dublin

Dublin

ISLE OF ANGLESEY

Cemaes

Amlwch

Llanerchymedd

Holyhead

Llanfachraeth

Benllech

Red Wharf Bay

Llangoed

Trearddur Bay

Holy Island

Llangefni

Pentraeth

Rhosneigr

Aberffraw

Llanfairpwllgwyngyll

Y Felinheli

Menai Bridge Bangor

Beaumaris

Llanfairfechan

Penmaenmawr

Llandudno

Deganwy

Conwy

Rhôs-on-Sea

Abe

Llanddulas

Llansanffraid Glan Conwy

Newborough

Caernarfon

Bethel

Llanrug

Llanberis

Llanllechid

Bethesda

Tal-y-Bont

Betws-yn-Rhos

Tal-y-Cafn

Llangernyw

Llanfair Talhaiarn

Llansa

Caernarfon Bay

Llandwrog

Llanwnda

Capel Curig

Trefriw

Llanrwst

CONWY

Bylchau

Clynnog-fawr

Penygroes

Rhyd-Ddu

Betws-y-Coed

Dolwyddelan

Penmachno

Pentrefoelas

Cerrigydrudion

SH

Beddgelert

Blaenau Ffestiniog

Morfa Nefyn

Nefyn

Llanaelhaearn

PENINSULA

Bodfuan

Llanystumdwy

Tremadog

Prenteg

Minffordd

Penrhyndeudraeth

Ffestiniog

Portmeirion

Porthmadog

Criccieth

Borth-y-Gest

Talsarnau

Trawsfynydd

Pwllheli

LLEYN

Sarn

Harlech

G W Y N E D D

SNOWDONIA

NATIONAL

PARK

Llanuwchllyn

Bala

Aberdaron

Y Rhiw

Llanbedrog

Abersoch

Llanbedr

Dyffryn Ardudwy

Ganllwyd

Dinas-Mawddwy

Mallwyd

Bardsey Island

Tal-y-bont

Barmouth

Fairbourne

Llwyngwril

Corris

Cemmaes Road

Llanbrynmair

Bryncrug

Pennal

Tywyn

Machynlleth

Carno

SN

Aberdyfi

Eglwys Fach

Borth

Tal-y-bont

Llandre

Aberystwyth

Capel Bangor

Ponterwyd

Llanidloes

9

● Restaurant
▬ AA Advised Whatnot
○ Town/Village name

0 ——— 10 miles
0 ——— 10 ——— 20 kilometres

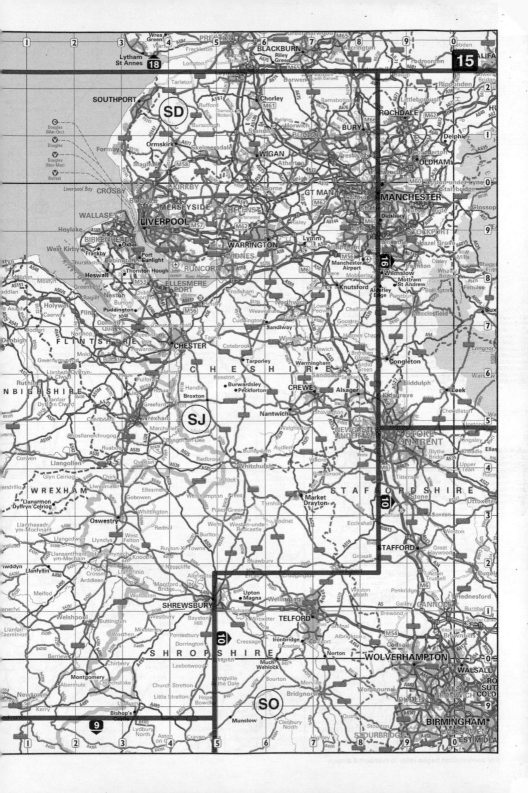

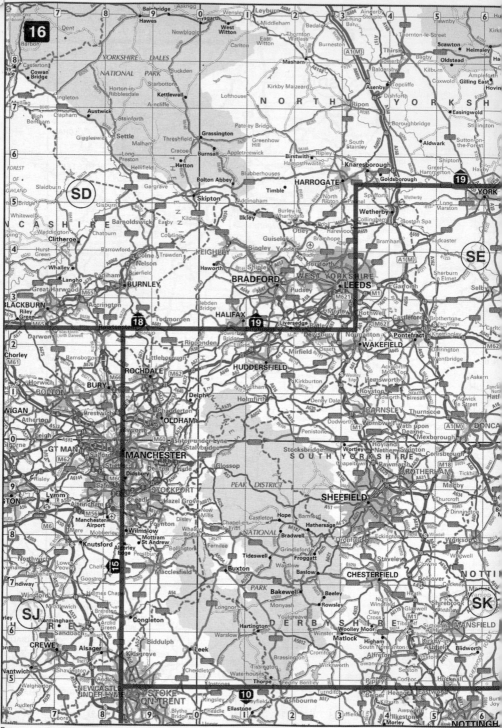

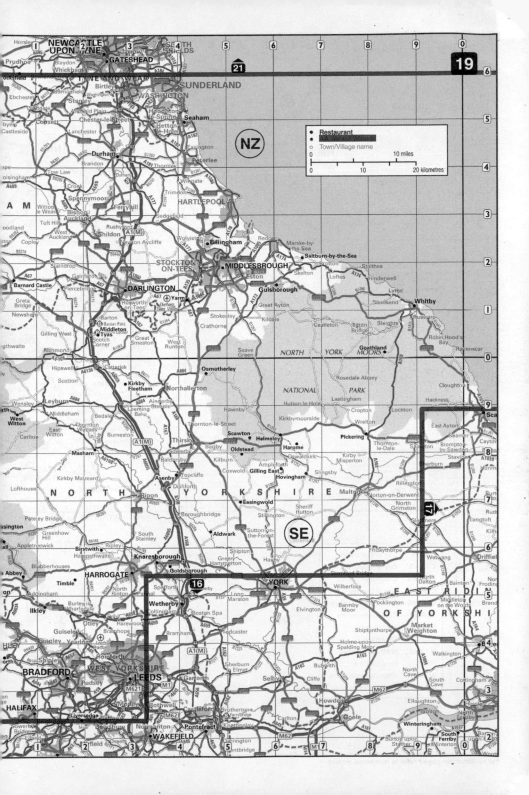

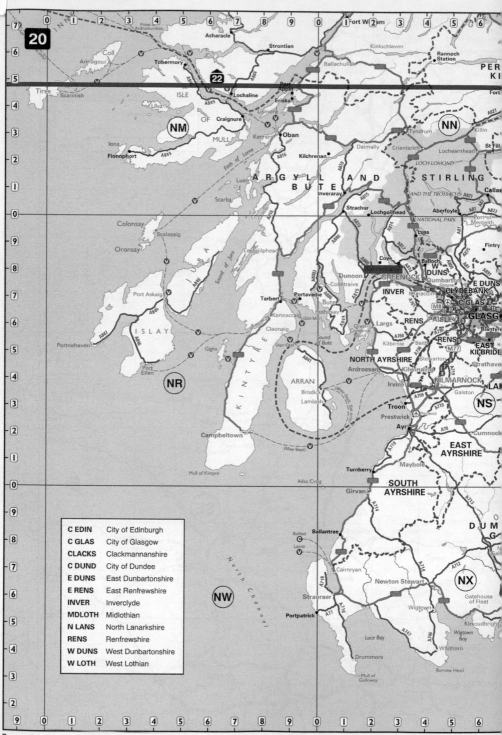

20

22

NM

NN

NR

NS

NW

NX

PER
KI

ARGYLL AND BUTE

STIRLING
AND THE TROSSACHS
NATIONAL PARK

ISLE OF MULL

ISLAY

KINTYRE

ARRAN

NORTH AYRSHIRE

EAST AYRSHIRE

SOUTH AYRSHIRE

DUM
G

LOCH LOMOND

North Channel

C EDIN	City of Edinburgh
C GLAS	City of Glasgow
CLACKS	Clackmannanshire
C DUND	City of Dundee
E DUNS	East Dunbartonshire
E RENS	East Renfrewshire
INVER	Inverclyde
MDLOTH	Midlothian
N LANS	North Lanarkshire
RENS	Renfrewshire
W DUNS	West Dunbartonshire
W LOTH	West Lothian

Fort W
am

Kinlochleven

Rannoch
Station

Acharacle

Strontian

Ballachulish

Tobermory

Coll
Arinagour

Tiree
Scarinish

Lochaline

Port
Appin
Eriska

Fort

Craigunre

Lismore

Killin

Tyndrum

NN

Kerrera
Oban

Dalmally

Crianlarich

Lochearnhead

St Fill

Iona
Fionnphort

Kilchrenan

A816

Luing

Firth of Lorne

Scarba

Inveraray

AND THE TROSSACHS

Callar

Colonsay
Scalasaig

Strachur
Lochgoilhead

Aberfoyle

Port of
Menteith

Oronsay

Lochgilphead

Luss

Fintry

Cove

Balloch
W DUNS
Dumbarton

Port Askaig

Dunoon
Colintraive

GREENOCK

E DUNS
CLYDEBANK

Portavadie

INVER

C GLAS
GLASGOW

Portnahaven

Tarbert

Kennacraig

Bute
Rothesay

Largs

RENS
PAISLEY

Blantyre

Port
Ellen

Gigha

Claonaig

Sound
of Bute

Kilbirnie
Beith

E
RENS

EAST
KILBRIDE

Strathave

ISLAY

Sound of Jura

Arran

Brodick
Lamlash

NORTH AYRSHIRE
Ardrossan

Stewarton

Kilwinning

KILMARNOCK

LA

Campbeltown

Irvine

Galston

Mull of Kintyre

Ailsa Craig

Troon
Prestwick
Ayr

EAST
AYRSHIRE

Cumnock

Turnberry

Maybole

SOUTH
AYRSHIRE

Girvan

Ballantrae

Belfast

Larne

Cairnryan

Newton Stewart

NX

Stranraer

Wigtown

Gatehouse
of Fleet

Portpatrick

Luce Bay

Wigtown
Bay

Kirkcudbright

Drummore

Whithorn

Mull of
Galloway

Burrow Head

For continuation pages refer to numbered arrows

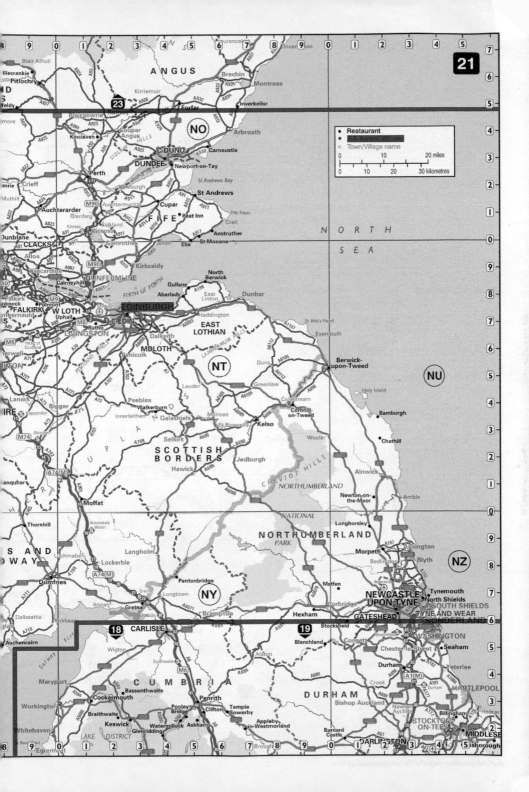

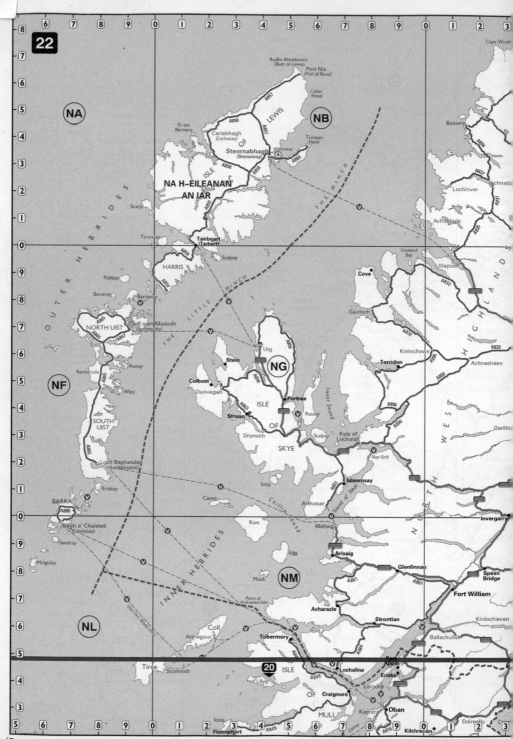

NA

NB

NA H–EILEANAN
AN IAR

OUTER HEBRIDES

Cape Wrath

Rudha Rhobhanais
(Butt of Lewis)
Port Nis
(Port of Ness)

Cellar
Head

A857

LEWIS

A858

Great
Bernera

Carlabhagh
(Carloway)

A858

Tiumpan
Head

Steòrnabhagh
(Stornoway)

A859

A866

Scarp

ISLE

Scaorin

Lochinver

Achiltibuie

THE MINCH

Taransay

Tairbeart
(Tarbert)

A859

HARRIS

Scalpay

Gruinard
Bay

Ullapool

Cove

A832

Gairloch

Pabbay

Boreray

Berneray

Loch nam Madadh
(Lochmaddy)

NORTH UIST

Benbecula

Ronay

A865

A867

A865

Wiay

NF

SOUTH
UIST

A865

Loch Baghasdail
(Lochboisdale)

THE LITTLE MINCH

Uig

A855

Stein

NG

Colbost

Dunvegan

ISLE

A850

A863

A87

Portree

Struan

OF

Drynoch

SKYE

Scalpay

Raasay

Inner Sound

Kinlochewe

Torridon

A832

Achnasheen

A896

Kyle of
Lochalsh

A890

Carinie

(Apr-Oct)

NORTH WEST HIGHLANDS

Soay

Cuillin Sound

Isleornsay

Ardvasar

Sound of Sleat

Invergarry

Barra

A888

Bàgh a' Chaisteil
(Castlebay)

Sandray

Mingulay

Eriskay

Canna

Rùm

INNER HEBRIDES

Point of
Ardnamurchan

Coll

Arinagour

Tiree

Scarinish

Iona

Fionnphort

A849

A849

NL

NM

Muck

Eigg

Mallaig

Arisaig

Glenfinnan

A830

A861

Acharacle

Strontian

Tobermory

A848

ISLE

Ulva

OF

Craignure

MULL

Lochaline

A884

Kerrera

Oban

Lismore

Spean
Bridge

Fort William

Kinlochleven

Ballachulish

Port
Appin

Eriska

A828

A85

Kilchrenan

Dalmally

20

Kyle of
Lochalsh

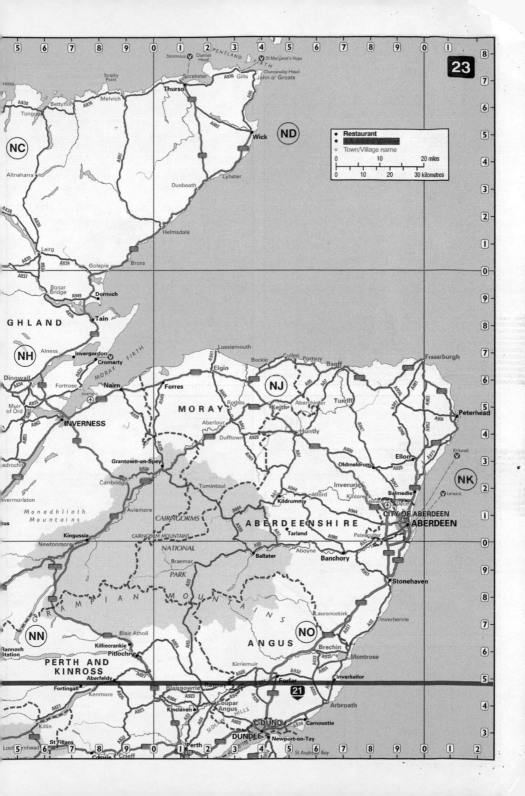

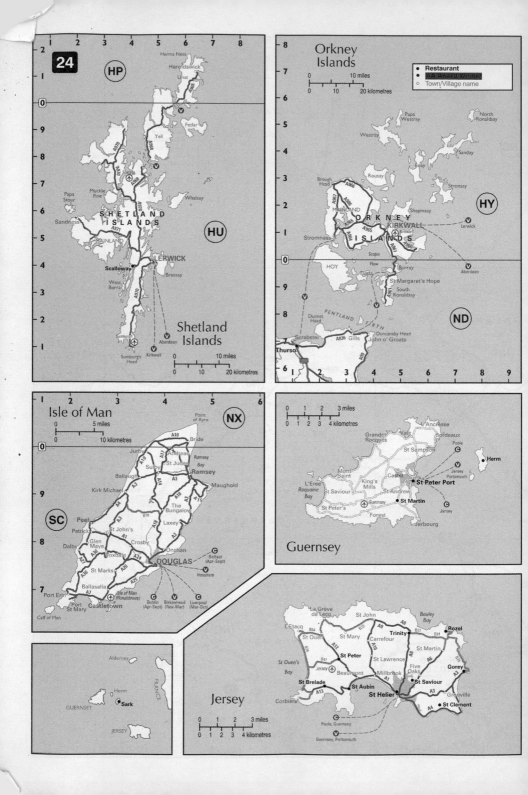

Index

Index

Index

Index

Index

Index